ECONOMICS OF THE FIRM

THEORY AND PRACTICE

ECONOMICS OF THE FIRM

THEORY AND PRACTICE

THIRD EDITION

ARTHUR A. THOMPSON, JR.

The University of Alabama

Prentice-Hall, Inc., Englewood Cliffs, New Jersey 07632

Library of Congress Cataloging in Publication Data

THOMPSON, ARTHUR A
  Economics of the firm.

  Includes bibliographies and index.
  1. Microeconomics. 2. Managerial economics.
I. Title.
HB171.5.T34 1981   338.5   80-23710
ISBN 0-13-231423-1

Editorial/production supervision by Alice Erdman
Cover design by Walter Behnke
Manufacturing buyer: Gordon Osbourne

© 1981, 1977, 1973 by Prentice-Hall, Inc.
Englewood Cliffs, N.J. 07632

Printed in the United States of America

10 9 8 7 6 5 4 3 2 1

Prentice-Hall International, Inc., *London*
Prentice-Hall of Australia Pty. Limited, *Sydney*
Prentice-Hall of Canada, Ltd., *Toronto*
Prentice-Hall of India Private Limited, *New Delhi*
Prentice-Hall of Japan, Inc., *Tokyo*
Prentice-Hall of Southeast Asia Pte. Ltd., *Singapore*
Whitehall Books Limited, *Wellington, New Zealand*

To Hasseline, Polly Beth, and Laura Leigh

CONTENTS

PREFACE

As with its predecessors, this edition has two noteworthy pedagogical features. First and foremost, the text offers a solid treatment of microeconomic theory in which the topical emphasis is on the economics of the firm and how markets function. Second, special pains have been taken to demonstrate the practical value of theoretical analysis and its power to explain real-world microeconomics.

The hoped-for outcome is a text which not only zeros in on the needs of economics majors but which is also broadly suitable for the increasing numbers of MBA and undergraduate business majors being required to take a microtheory course. Non-economics faculty have long been heard to urge that the content of intermediate microeconomics courses should stress what business majors need to know about microtheory rather than being slanted solely toward economics majors. Their point is well taken. Consequently, in agonizing over what to include and what to emphasize, I have tried to follow the rule of including concepts especially pertinent to analyzing the behavior of firms and markets and de-emphasizing topics which either have a "purist" flavor or else relate more directly to nonmarket sectors of the economy. The sought-after compromise is a micro-text (1) that is strong on theory and analysis, (2) that takes as its focal point the economics of the firm in a competitive market environment, and (3) that is in close touch with the reality of applications. In the overall scheme of approaches to microeconomics, the aim has been to place the text more or less mid-way between "pure theory" texts and "managerial economics" texts.

All major aspects of microeconomic theory are covered. The standard models of utility theory, indifference analysis, basic supply and demand, elasticity, production and cost functions, monopoly and perfect competition, resource pricing, and general equilibrium are given thorough exposure. But you will quickly note the inclusion of a number of textual treatments that are intended as improvements in coverage:

> **An introductory chapter on the methodology of economic analysis and the relevance of theory to explaining real-world economic phenomena.
>
> **A birdseye description of what a market is and how the sizes of firms and their respective corporate strategies relate to actual behavior in the marketplace (Chapter 2).
>
> **A survey of the economic aspects of technology and the impetus for R&D and innovation (Chapter 6).
>
> **An in-depth look at profit concepts, profit theories, the debate over profit maximization, and non-profit goals of the firm (Chapter 9).
>
> **An extensive treatment of oligopoly theory which focuses on competitive rivalry among large corporations (Chapter 12).
>
> **A major new chapter on the strategic aspects of competition and on how economic forces combine to shape the nature and strength of competition (Chapter 14).
>
> **A survey of multiple-goal models of the firm (Chapter 15).
>
> **An assessment of overall market performance and the social benefits of competition under conditions of market capitalism and corporate capitalism, using the tools of welfare economics and industrial organization (Chapter 16).
>
> **Sections dealing with multiproduct pricing, price signaling through the public media, the use and abuse of corporate power, taxing excess profits, the competitive roles of advertising and product differentiation, the relevance of corporate strategy to competition analysis, the wage-employment effects of unions and minimum wage legislation, and the economics of productivity changes.

The use of in-depth "applications capsules" to highlight actual applications of microtheory was well-received in the previous edition and has been expanded. The number of capsules has been increased from 24 to 32 and 18 are brand new. As before, these aim at keeping the integration of theory and practice always, before the student without disjointing the theoretical discussion. The applications capsules have been "boxed off" from the text narrative to permit meaningful and detailed discussion, rather than trying to make do with simple examples which can be cited in a passing sentence, footnote, or brief paragraph. Once again, the selection of the capsule topics aims at the mainstream of how a competitive enterprise economy works in actual practice; their pragmatic nature can be easily seen by glancing through the *Table*

short cases for class discussion. In addition to the applications capsules,
summaries of empirical findings and dozens of brief examples are scattered
throughout each chapter.

The attention paid to application and examples has several justifica-
tions. Students are more likely to buckle down and master theoretical material when they are convinced it has a payoff and is not just something that
must be tolerated to get a degree. More fundamentally, though, the worth of
microecomic theory is best proven by its power of application. Indeed, unless
theory truly explains, predicts, and otherwise illuminates the economic
behavior of consumers, firms, and markets, it is of little use and interest.

As has now become customary and proper, the theoretical concepts
are presented in a modestly mathematical vein in belief that most students,
given that they are required to take introductory calculus, are well-equipped
to handle nothing more mathematically complex than first derivatives. All
mathematical concepts requiring more than basic algebra are explained fully
and in terms which can be grasped by the mathematically unsophisticated.
The more advanced mathematical treatments of microeconomics have been
placed in self-contained "capsules" at appropriate places in the book and
can be omitted without a loss of continuity.

Like any new edition, this one too has undergone important revision
and updating. Chapters 1 and 2 reflect a streamlined treatment of what
formerly was organized into three chapters. More attention has been given
to measuring price elasticity and to assessing the conditions which cause
buyers and sellers to be price sensitive. Coverage of the market models of
perfect competition, monopolistic competition, oligopoly, and monopoly is
now divided into four separate chapters, and the discussion of monopoly has
been accorded considerably more emphasis. A brand new chapter on assessing
the nature and strength of competitive market forces has been added to give
more attention to the non-structural aspects of the market interplay among
rival firms; this chapter focuses on competition as a strategic process and the
extent to which competition is influenced by potential entrants, the presence
of substitutes, and the market influences of both suppliers and buyers. The
usual efforts have been made to improve further the clarity of the exposition;
the coverage of some ideas and concepts has been condensed to make room
for the added topics and applications capsules.

All in all, the third edition strives for effective and comfortable balances
between "bare bones" coverage versus in-depth analysis, theory versus application, classical versus contemporary models, mathematical versus ver-
bal/graphical exposition, and conceptual simplicity versus the need of the
student to acquire *some* technical proficiency and analytical skill.

The result, I trust, is (1) a book which is as well-suited for intermediate
microtheory courses required of business school undergraduates and first-
year MBA students as for economics majors and (2) a book which is a
coherent and teachable synthesis of the best of all that is old and new in

microeconomics. Whether I have succeeded is, quite fittingly, for "the market" to decide. Your comments regarding coverage and emphasis will be most welcome, as will your calling my attention to specific errors.

ACKNOWLEDGMENTS

My intellectual debt to both the classical and contemporary economists whose fertile concepts and ideas appear herein will be obvious to any reader familiar with the literature of microeconomics. I have endeavored to acknowledge the scholarly materials and sources relied upon in the many footnotes and bibliographical references. I trust that no violence has been done to their ideas in my attempts to synthesize them into the body of microeconomic analysis.

Both this edition and previous editions have benefited greatly from the comments of students, reviewers, and adopters. Special thanks are due to David Hildebrand and Alice Erdman at Prentice-Hall and to Professor Keith Lumsden (Stanford), Robert Clower (UCLA), Howard Dye (University of South Florida), Lloyd Valentine (University of Cincinnati), Richard Hoffman (formerly of University of Buffalo), Frank Falero (California State at Bakersfield), Dwight Anderson (Arizona State University), Ralph Gray (DePauw University), Thomas C. Anderson (Eastern Michigan University), Jay G. Chambers (University of Rochester), Larry G. Beall (Virginia Commonwealth University) Melvin C. Fredlund (California State at Hayward), Wesley Magat (Duke University), Donald J. Roberts (Northwestern University), Ernest Koenigsberg (University of California), Stephen L. Shapiro (University of North Florida), Stephen Buckles (University of Missouri), John Stevens (Babson College), William A. Hayes (Depaul University), Sharon G. Levin (University of Missouri, St. Louis), and Walter Rice (California Polytechnic State University)—all of whom reviewed portions of this text at various stages. Naturally, however, none of them is responsible for any of the blunders or inadequacies which remain; for those I bow to tradition and accept full responsibility.

Arthur A. Thompson, Jr.
Tuscaloosa, Alabama

NOTE TO THE STUDENT

Courses in intermediate microeconomics typically have the reputation of being among the most challenging in any college curriculum. The reputation is well deserved—this might as well be admitted at the outset. But despite the analytical rigor which characterizes the course, the road ahead is worth exploring, and I have tried to clear the way of unnecessary obstacles. Pains have been taken to make the text readable and interesting, to provide step-by-step explanations of each concept, to keep the graphs uncluttered and the mathematics simplified. Examples and applications of the theory are consistently indicated in enough detail to make them meaningful. Chapter-end problems and questions have been included as a self-test of your command of the material and to increase your mechanical proficiency with important concepts.

Because students begin the course with widely-varying backgrounds and degrees of preparation, the treatment of each new topic is begun at the lowest level of analysis. No prior knowledge of economics is assumed. Thus, while this course is probably not your first exposure to economics, those of you who remember little about previous courses or who feel poorly prepared in economics will find yourselves at no serious disadvantage.

All of this has resulted in a book with more pages to cover. But longer may still be quicker and easier. The intended effect is a more comprehensible presentation that will not only help you to hurdle the more difficult theory in less time but that will also convince you of the value and power of economic analysis.

A textbook is, after all, primarily for the student, not the professor and, in the final analysis, you the student are an excellent judge of how well the teaching/learning objectives of this book are being met. I will be pleased to receive your comments at P. O. Box J, University, AL 35486.

ONE INTRODUCTION TO MICROECONOMICS: SCOPE AND METHODS OF ANALYSIS

George Bernard Shaw is credited with the observation that any reasonably intelligent parrot, provided that he was not tongue-tied, could be instructed in economics; he need only be taught to say "demand" and "supply." This simplification strikes at a central truth in economics: The aggregate of society's material wants far exceeds the available economic resources needed to satisfy them. Indeed, the fundamental economic issue around which economic analysis revolves is how best to employ scarce economic resources (land, labor, capital goods, managerial talents) in supplying goods and services, so as to achieve the greatest fulfillment of society's unlimited wants.

But in exploring the economic ins and outs of how society can do its economic best with what it has to work with, the picture becomes quite muddied and complex. For example, there are millions of individuals and households deciding how to budget a limited income for food, apparel, housing, medical care, transportation, and other goods and services. There are also millions of business firms making decisions about how much time, money, and human effort to devote to manufacturing operations, new product research and development, investment in cleaner and cheaper production technologies, sales promotion, a search for new market opportunities, improving their market standing, and so on. There are hundreds of thousands of government agencies and not-for-profit organizations involved in furnishing public goods and services to persons who need or can take good advantage of them. All are drawing in one way or another upon society's available pool of resources.

Moreover, the actions of each individual, household, business, or public agent are largely autonomous of one another and are based upon different values, preferences, and priorities. An urban household tends to have a life-style and an expenditure pattern different from those of a rural family. The business and product-market situation of a food processor varies significantly from that of an electric utility. The state government of New York confronts different economic problems from those of Texas and is likely to adopt different kinds of economic policies to solve them. In short, each economic unit makes its own economic decisions on the basis of more or less different situations, preferences, values, and objectives. In the process, no reference is made to a grand economic plan for guidance, nor does such an overall plan even exist. The result is a complex network of economic actions and patterns which require systematic analysis to produce intelligent understanding.

WHAT IS MICROECONOMICS?

There are two essentially different levels at which the study of economics takes place. *Microeconomics* deals with the economic behavior and economic activities of specific economic units—individuals, households, firms, and industries. Microeconomics zeros in on such economic variables as the prices and outputs of specific firms and industries, the expenditures of consumers and households, wage rates, competition, and markets. The focus is on the trees, not the forest. In *macroeconomics*, concern centers upon the economy as a whole and the major economic sectors that make up the whole. Macroeconomic analysis tends to view all households as a unit (the household sector), all businesses as an aggregate unit (the business sector), and all state, local, and federal agencies as a unit (the governmental sector) in an effort to obtain an overview of the structure and functioning of the whole economy. The key macroeconomic variables include *total* output, *total* employment, *total* income, *total* spending, and the *overall* price level.

In this book we shall focus almost exclusively on microeconomics, or "the theory of the firm" as it is sometimes described. Our agenda will cover a broad front: What determines whether the demand for a firm's product will be weak or intense? How will consumers probably react to a price increase or to an increase in their disposable incomes? How can a firm tell if its use of resource inputs is efficient? What are economies of scale and what causes them? Are unit costs lowest at a capacity level of output? What is a market and how does it function? How do markets differ from one another? What is the meaning of competition and how does it differ from monopoly? Are large corporations monopolistic? Why is profit important in a competitive enterprise economy? Do business firms seek to maximize profits? How do firms determine the prices they will charge for their products? What determines how much persons ought to be paid for their labor services? Do unions cause wages to be higher than they otherwise would be? Do higher minimum wages create unemployment? These questions are a sample of the microeconomics-related issues which in one way or another affect almost everybody. They are posed here to illustrate not only what microeconomics is about but also to indicate its relevance to practical economic events.

THE METHODS OF ECONOMIC ANALYSIS

The economist's approach to making sense out of the mass of everyday economic events involves the formulation of *economic theory* and the building of empirically based *economic models*. Indeed, economists take considerable pride in their "scientific" approach to economic analysis, believing that a theoretically oriented, model-building approach is essential if there is to be any progress in understanding the intricate workings of economic variables and in developing alternative economic policies. As a prelude to beginning our study of microeconomics, let us take a brief look at what models and theories are and how they fit into the analytical picture.

THE PROCESS OF THEORY FORMULATION AND MODEL BUILDING

Although there is no rigid method of economic analysis, economists (in the tradition of other scientists) follow a fairly common procedure in formulating theories and building models. The research method consists of five distinct phases:

1. Defining the scope of the problem or the exact phenomena to be investigated.
2. Formulating a hypothesis about the relationships among the relevant variables.
3. Deducing testable conclusions and/or predictions from the hypothesis.
4. Testing the appropriateness of the conclusions and/or the accuracy of the predictions by reference to empirical data.
5. Accepting or revising the theory or model on the basis of the tests conducted.

Defining the Problem

Defining the problem involves isolating the exact economic phenomena of interest to the analyst and deciding the specific questions to be explored. Usually, research inquiry is directed toward the causes underlying the behavior of the economic phenomena, the circumstances in which they occur, and the impacts they may produce. The analyst may also be concerned with how a specific set of economic variables ties in with the broader body of economic knowledge.

Formulating the Hypothesis

The next phase consists of a search for regularity and order in the economic phenomena under investigation. This, of course, presumes that some sort of economic order in fact exists and that economic events can be arrayed according to degrees of regular and predictable behavior. Such a presumption is entirely reasonable. Systems of knowledge rest upon the notion of a universal order and, in effect, the job of science is one of differentiating among classes of uniform behavior and then relating these to one another. Even in periods of rapid change, there exists a degree of universal order which, together with identifiable currents of change, can be categorized and analyzed.

Consequently, once the research focus has been decided upon, the task is to discover which variables are important and which are not, to learn how the key variables are related, and to pinpoint cause-effect relationships—thereby allowing the analyst to understand, explain, and predict what happens and why it happens. In the course of this search, many economic happenings and factual details are, and should be, ignored because they have no important bearing upon the problem at hand. But even after the relevant has been sifted from the irrelevant, the number and complexity of economic relationships can still make it infeasible to explore all interrelated events at once. Then the processes of abstraction and generalization are relied upon to bring the inquiry down to manageable proportions.

Abstraction involves sifting through, distilling, selecting, and restricting the variables and information considered, endeavoring to condense an otherwise cumbersome number of factors and details into a reduced set that can be handled and understood. Abstraction may consist, for example, of simplifying the study by focusing only on a manageable, but representative, subgroup or sample having the desired attributes. Or, it may mean making some simplifying *assumptions* that specify the essential features of the economic environment which the analyst wishes to zero in on or that indicate basic behavioral traits about the economic units being investigated. Thus, many economic models of business behavior are based upon the assumption that firms behave as if they seek to maximize profits, the rationale being that, of all the factors that motivate business decisions, profit maximization is likely to be the overriding or governing consideration. And, frequently, in specifying the relationships among economic variables, it is customary to assume that all other relevant factors remain constant so that any influence which these other factors may have will not contaminate the study of the variables and relationships of primary concern.

Assumptions need not be in *exact* accord with reality; it is enough that they be *reasonable* representations of real-world conditions. One of the arts of abstraction is to employ assumptions that are (1) easy to handle, (2) sufficiently realistic, and (3) not so restrictive as to impair the scope and value of the research. If the assumptions are too detailed and too numerous, the model becomes unmanageable and/or of limited import. On the other hand, if the assumptions are gross oversimplifications of reality, even though very interesting conclusions may be drawn, the resulting analysis is likely to fail miserably in explaining real-life behavior.

What constitutes a reasonable abstraction may be illustrated in terms of the study of consumer behavior. Here it is customary for economists to assume that consumers behave as if they seek to maximize the satisfaction obtainable from their incomes. In fact, this assumption may not be literally true, at least for all consumers in each and every situation. Nevertheless, if over a reasonably interesting range of circumstances many consumers do behave as if they attempt to maximize satisfaction, then the assumption that "consumers seek to maximize the satisfaction obtainable from their incomes" is a justifiable and reasonable simplification. To restate the link between assumptions and reality in another way, even though the assumptions of a model may not be literally exact and complete descriptions of real-world behavior, as long as they are sufficiently realistic to allow for a valid analysis of the phenomena being investigated, no harm is done to reality.

After the stage has been set—with abstracting, making assumptions, and simplifying—comes the actual formulation of hypotheses. A *hypothesis* consists of a *tentative* identification of key variables and a *tentative* specification of how these variables may be related in terms of cause-effect or interaction. Hypotheses may be suggested to the analyst by the existing body of knowledge, by experience and familiarity with the problem, by clues uncovered in preliminary investigation, or even by intuition and hunch. The hypothesized relationships are often summarized in graphical or mathematical form to allow systematic analysis and ready determination of how changes in some variables will affect others. Verbal logic and deductive reasoning are used as well. However, research standards require that a hypothesis be logical and that it be subject to empirical verification or disproof. Without these qualities there is no way of judging how good it is at advancing the ability to understand real-world behavior, at predicting future events, or in guiding the formulation of economic policies.

The Deduction of Predictions

Hypotheses do more than suggest explanations for behavior and cause-effect relationships. If properly formulated, they serve as the basis for deriving predictions about future economic impacts and changes. These predictions (forecasts) or conclusions stem mainly from logical deductive reasoning. To take a concrete example, we might hypothesize that the quantity purchased of a commodity tends to increase as the level of advertising expenditures on that commodity is increased, other factors remaining constant. To test whether a cause-effect relationship actually exists between advertising and sales volume, we might logically predict that, in the absence of changes in other relevant factors, if RCA increases its promotional expenditures on color television sets, the sales of RCA color TV sets should rise. An even stronger prediction based on the same hypothesis would entail investigating the extent to which higher levels of advertising are associated with higher levels of unit sales for a representative sample of firms and products. The ability to evaluate predictive accuracy is an essential feature of all soundly constructed hypotheses and models. Unless they yield predictions or conclusions which are capable of being tested, there is no appropriate way to judge their analytical validity.

Testing the Accuracy of the Predictions

Once tentative relations among the variables are established and predictions are obtained, a multistage process of testing the theoretical model begins. First, data must be collected for evaluating the accuracy of the predictions derived from the hypothesized relationships. Likely sources include published statistics from governmental and private institutions, the results of previous research studies, or entirely new information generated from questionnaire surveys, interviews, original source documents, or field studies. For example, if the specific economic problem being studied is the nature of consumer demand for frozen orange juice concentrate, one would need to obtain statistics on the recorded quantities of frozen orange juice concentrate purchased, the prices at which these quantities were sold, the prices of substitute breakfast drinks, the income of consumers, advertising expenditures, and the size of the population. Institutional information about the functioning of the market for frozen orange juice concentrate might also be useful. The items to be included in the actual compilation of information would necessarily depend upon the nature of the problem and the researcher's judgment. When the data are of a quantitative character, it may be useful to bring forth the weaponry of *descriptive statistics* and organize the data in the form of charts and tables for systematic presentation and analysis.

After the necessary data have been assembled, the precise nature of the relationships among the variables must be specified. When quantitative relationships are present in the hypothesis, equations may need to be constructed and values estimated for the coefficients and parameters. Since most of the concepts with which economists deal are empirically based (prices, costs, wage rates, revenues, profits, incomes, production rates, and so on, are all quantifiable), the use of quantitative techniques of one form or another is the rule rather than the exception. For this reason, econometric techniques often enter the picture. *Econometrics* involves (1) expressing the relationships among economic variables in mathematical form, (2) using historical data and statistical procedures to measure the hypothesized relationships, and (3) testing the accuracy of predictions derived from the hypothesized relationships. Even when quantitative expressions are not absolutely necessary, economists use them to facilitate the analysis or to render it more precise. Following the estimation of whatever quantitative and nonquantitative relationships are implied comes formal testing and evaluation of predictive accuracy.

If the prediction is confirmed by real-world events—that is, it corresponds to what is observed—the hypothesis is *accepted*. However, it would not be correct to state that the hypothesis has been *proved*; one can only say that events have failed to *disprove* it. According to one eminent authority, hypotheses can never be proved; they can only be tested by seeing whether predictions made from them are in accord with experimental and observational facts.[1] A favorable finding on the accuracy of predictions derived from a hypothesis does not confirm the truth of the hypothesis because there is room for circumstantial evidence to produce correct predictions from a false or flawed hypothesis.

For instance, the truth of the hypothesis that a corporation's profits arise from the hiring of wise managers is not established by correctly predicting that a change in the management of corporation XYZ will be followed by a rise in XYZ's profits; other factors not related to astute management are perfectly capable of generating higher profits. Strictly speaking, then, a hypothesis is never proved and remains on probation indefinitely. But the more it survives attempts at disproof, the more it is accepted in practice, especially when it is compatible with related theoretical systems.[2] Thus, after a hypothesis successfully survives a number of tests, it becomes part of the knowledge of the discipline until evidence appears which shows that it no longer yields an acceptable degree of accuracy in its predictions.

If the observed facts contradict the predictions, the hypothesis is *disproved* or *rejected* and attempts can then be made to revise the hypothesis in accordance with the empirical evidence.[3] The modified hypothesis is retested and again modified if the test results are unsatisfactory. The process is continued until the investigator is satisfied that the model accounts for the observed facts with sufficient accuracy for the purpose at hand.

Figure 1-1 summarizes the facets of the research process, indicating the close interaction between the real world and the theoretical world. Note that the process of economic investigation begins by observing the real world and finishes by observing the real world. This is as it should be since the major purpose of economic research is to improve the ability to understand, explain, and predict real-world economic phenomena.

WHAT IS A THEORY?

We are now in better position to indicate more precisely what is meant by the terms "hypothesis," "theory," "principle," and "model." It should be noted, however, that authorities are not in agreement on the "definitions"

---

[1]W. I. B. Beveridge, *The Art of Scientific Investigation* (New York: Random House, The Modern Library, 1957), p. 118.

[2]*Ibid.*

[3]Academic lore has it that Max Weber was interrupted during a lecture once by a student protesting "The facts are not in accord with your theory." Weber replied, "So much the worse for the facts," and continued his presentation.

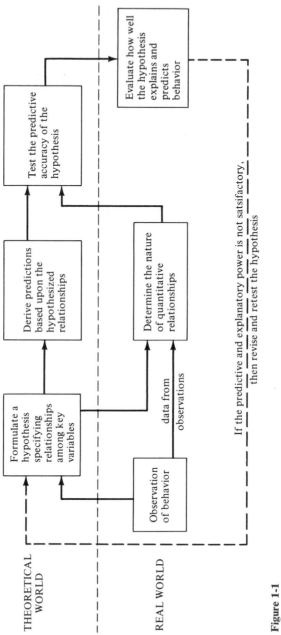

Figure 1-1
Relationship between theory and the real world

of these terms, with the result that their meaning varies somewhat from
discipline to discipline and writer to writer. Nonetheless, what follows represents what is believed to be a general consensus and serves to delineate how the terms will be used in this text.

A *hypothesis* is a tentative explanation of how phenomena are related. It attempts to pinpoint the key variables in a behavior pattern and describe in preliminary fashion how they interact. A hypothesis may originate as an educated speculation, an informed guess, or a mere conjecture. Supporting evidence is lacking or is scanty and unconvincing. The formulation of a hypothesis necessarily involves abstracting the essential features out of the maze of fact and detail surrounding the phenomena being studied.

A *theory* consists of an accepted explanation of and guide to behavior or phenomena in the real world. A theory emerges from the process of formulating a hypothesis, logically deducing predictions from the hypothesis, and testing and retesting the accuracy of the predictions a sufficient number of times to produce a general confidence in its *predictive power*. In other words, a theory has a demonstrated ability to predict how changes in a certain variable will affect other variables. At the same time, though, a theory conveys understanding and insight into real-world behavior; it pinpoints cause-effect relationships and logical connections among the variables. In this sense, a theory has *explanatory power*.

The twin features of explanatory power and predictive power are *equally* important theoretical considerations. Predictive power is essential because it signifies whether a theory has empirical validity and is in accord with the available evidence. But while predictive power is necessary, it is not sufficient. Establishing a level of confidence in the predictions cannot be divorced from whether the theory is logical and consistent with other knowledge about behavior. More confidence resides in a theory whose composition can be defended on logical grounds and on the high degree to which it corresponds with related theory and evidence. One simply cannot have much faith and reliance in a theory that offers no plausible explanation and has little commonsense connection with the event being predicted. Prediction without explanation is sterile. Only when a theory has adequate explanatory and predictive powers should it be used as the basis for formulating policies to improve the functioning of economic processes.

A theory assumes its status when the hypothesis it incorporates has been tested a number of times and the accuracy of its predictions accepted. Should the theory be sufficiently profound and universal it may be termed a *principle* or *law*. A principle implies a very strong degree of empirical regularity; accompanying it is an explanation for its existence and reasons the principle should continue to hold in the future. Thus, in terms of the empirical confidence that can be placed in it, a theory is somewhere between a hypothesis and a principle.

Often one hears the complaint that theory is "unrealistic" and "impractical."[4] Such complaints can be valid only in the case of "bad" theory. "Good"

---

[4]According to one wag, an "ivory tower" economic theorist is said to have remarked upon completing the construction of a new model, "And the beauty of this model, which

theory cannot be unrealistic in an important sense because it *does* explain and predict *real-world behavior*. Nor can good theory be "impractical"; on the contrary, it can serve as a pragmatic guide to decision making and behavior since it has a *demonstrated* ability to explain relationships and to predict phenomena. When a theory truly has appropriate amounts of both explanatory power and predictive power, criticisms of impracticality and lack of realism contain little merit. If a theory is subject to legitimate claims of impracticality and lack of realism, the time has come to reevaluate the theory in light of current empirical evidence and to review its predictive and explanatory powers relative to alternative hypotheses and theories.

Some users of theory find the constant review of existing theory to be a nuisance. Of course, it would be nice if the need for reverification ceased. But in economics it is especially necessary to review the existing body of theory on a regular basis. A moment's reflection is enough to convince one that a nineteenth-century theory of business behavior could easily be lacking in its powers to explain and predict business behavior in the 1980s. The emergence of the giant corporation, the international dimensions of competition, and the imperatives of technological change have made the business environment today significantly different from what it was decades earlier. Thus, emerging economic developments force economic theorists to keep a close check on the explanatory and predictive powers of the existing body of economic theory.

The term *model* is much harder to describe in unambiguous fashion. It is regularly used to refer to such diverse subjects as the women who display the creations of Paris designers and the scaled-down replicas of an architect's proposed building. Even in scientific/theoretical investigations there are physical models, conceptual models, mathematical models, simulation models, input-output models, benefit-cost models, and experimental models, to mention only a few. Although each of these has its own distinguishing features, there is also a common ground. The unifying feature of models, as they have been used in many branches of science, is their attempt to describe the essential features of a system in a way that is simple enough to understand and manipulate, yet close enough to reality to yield meaningful results. Usually, it is neither practical nor possible to represent the system in its original complexity; abstraction must be used, and selecting the appropriate degree of abstraction can greatly enhance the model's value. If the level of abstraction is too low, so that the model has an overabundance of specific detail, the advantages of realism are offset by the unwieldiness of the model and a lack of generalized application. On the other hand, if the model is highly abstract, the advantages gained from its analytic properties

---

will particularly endear it to the hearts of purists, is that under no conceivable circumstances can it be of any possible practical value." Economic theory is not without its actual examples in this regard. According to John Kenneth Galbraith, "Much economic instruction, and notably so in such fields as advanced theory, foreign trade, and monetary policy, depends not on the relevance of the subject matter but on the existence of an intellectually preoccupying theory." J. K. Galbraith, *The New Industrial State* (Boston: Houghton Mifflin Company, 1967), p. 46.

may be more than counterbalanced by its dubious connection with the real world. For example, in analyzing how a market works, if one were to assume complete buyer-seller rationality, full knowledge of economic information, perfect mobility of labor and capital resources, and instantaneous market adjustment to equilibrium, the result could be an economic model which is easily manipulated and which yields intellectually appealing conclusions but which might well lack significant ties to realities of the marketplace.

In the case of a theory-oriented model, the goal is to develop a tool that presents simply and accurately the major variables and relationships of an inadequately understood system—in which case the terms "theory" and "theoretical model" are, for many intents and purposes, synonymous. Both attempt to specify key variables and establish relationships among them. Both provide a logical framework or skeleton in which the complexities of the real world can be understood with greater insight. Both involve predictions or forecasts about phenomena, and both are judged by their accuracy in predicting and explaining the behavior of an actual system. As long as the system that the model is attempting to describe is of sufficient scope and importance, a theory and a model can stand at the same rank. We shall use the terms "model" and "theory" interchangeably.

THE REALISM OF ASSUMPTIONS

One analytical problem remains to be discussed. This concerns the question of the validity of a theory which contains what some investigators consider to be "unrealistic assumptions." Consider, for example, a theory that is based upon the assumption that business firms behave as if they seek to maximize profits. Suppose further that this theory is judged to predict rather well but that there is a serious question as to whether the firms involved actually are trying to maximize profits. Is the theory then "invalid" because it is based upon an assumption that appears to be false? How does one determine whether the assumption of profit-maximizing behavior is, in fact, an accurate description of reality? Does it even make any difference whether the assumption of profit maximization is descriptively accurate or not as long as the predictive power of the theory is judged to be satisfactory for the purpose at hand? Does a theory that predicts behavior also explain behavior? These are very thorny questions, and attempts to answer them have generated a heated debate among some prominent economists.[5]

[5] Milton Friedman, "The Methodology of Positive Economics," *Essays in Positive Economics* (Chicago: University of Chicago Press, 1953), pp. 3–43. Friedman's article has provoked a wealth of comment and rebuttal. See, for example, Eugene Rotwein, "On 'The Methodology of Positive Economics,'" *Quarterly Journal of Economics*, Vol. 73, No. 4 (November 1959), pp. 554–575; R. M. Cyert and E. Grunberg, "Assumption, Prediction, and Explanation in Economics," Appendix A in R. M. Cyert and J. G. March, *A Behavioral Theory of the Firm* (Englewood Cliffs, N.J.: Prentice-Hall, Inc., 1963), pp. 298–311; J. W. McGuire, *Theories of Business Behavior* (Englewood Cliffs, N.J.: Prentice-Hall, Inc., 1964), pp. 7–11; and the papers published in the *American Economic Review, Papers and Proceedings*, Vol. 52, No. 2 (May 1963), pp. 204–236.

One of the principals in this debate is Milton Friedman, who, in an essay on "The Methodology of Positive Economics," maintained that whether the assumptions made in the course of formulating a hypothesis were either "realistic" or "unrealistic" may not really be significant. Friedman argued that the only relevant way to test a hypothesis is to compare its predictions with experience. He stated that there is no meaningful way to test the validity of a hypothesis by comparing its assumptions directly with reality. In support of his position, Friedman said:

> In so far as a theory can be said to have "assumptions" at all, and in so far as their "realism" can be judged independently of the validity of predictions, the relation between the significance of a theory and the "realism" of its "assumptions" is almost the opposite of that suggested by the view under criticism. Truly important and significant hypotheses will be found to have "assumptions" that are wildly inaccurate descriptive representations of reality, and, in general, the more significant the theory, the more unrealistic the assumptions (in this sense). The reason is simple. A hypothesis is important if it "explains" much by little, that is, if it abstracts the common and crucial elements from the mass of complex and detailed circumstances surrounding the phenomena to be explained and permits valid predictions on the basis of them alone. To be important, therefore, a hypothesis must be descriptively false in its assumptions; it takes account of, and accounts for, none of the many other attendant circumstances, since its very success shows them to be irrelevant for the phenomena to be explained. To put this point less paradoxically, the relevant question to ask about the "assumptions" of a theory is not whether they are descriptively "realistic" for they never are, but whether they are sufficiently good approximations for the purpose in hand. And this question can be answered only by seeing whether it yields sufficiently accurate predictions.[6]

Here Friedman is saying that the degree of "realism" in the assumptions is often not apparent in the assumptions themselves but becomes apparent only after the theory is constructed and its predictive power evaluated. In other words, if a theory predicts accurately, then the assumptions are realistic enough despite appearances to the contrary.

Other economists have not found it hard to take issue with Friendman. Naturally, an assumption is "unrealistic" if one is applying the standard that it does not *exhaustively* describe a situation and instead mentions only some of the traits that are present. Yet it is unlikely that any statement of finite length would suffice to identify the totality of the set of characteristics embodied in a real situation. And it tests the imagination to conceive of uses for such a statement were it constructed. It is in this somewhat trivial sense that Friedman seems to be defending the legitimacy of "unrealistic" assumptions.

There are, however, two more worthy instances in which assumptions may be said to be unrealistic. First, an assumption may be unrealistic because it holds only for hypothetical or idealized circumstances. On occasion, models or theories with intentionally unrealistic assumptions are developed: for

---

[6]Friedman, "The Methodology of Positive Economics," pp. 14–15.

example, the frictionless world often posed in physics and the perfectly competitive market model in economics, the latter containing such "ideal" conditions as perfect knowledge on the part of the buyers and sellers, perfect flexibility and mobility in the use of economic resources, and complete freedom of entry and exit of producers into the market. The environmental systems portayed in these models are admittedly hypothetical and serve as intellectual experiments. Their primary purpose is often to highlight the nature of the interaction among key variables, particularly when they are unaffected by numerous other factors whose influence may never be eliminated in the real world but whose effects vary in magnitude with differences in attendant circumstances. They may also be used as a standard of comparison against which the functioning of actual environmental systems can be measured. Models of this type are unique in the sense that when observations do not conform to the predictions given by the model, it is indicative that the conditions upon which the model is predicated are not being met—*not* that the model is invalid.

Second, an assumption can be termed "unrealistic" because it appears false or improbable on the basis of available evidence. Here we find the real bone of contention. Ernest Nagel, an eminent authority on methodological matters, has observed that a theory which contains an unrealistic assumption in the sense that it is false is "patently unsatisfactory, for such a theory entails consequences that are incompatible with observed fact, so that on pain of rejecting elementary logical canons the theory must also be rejected."[7] This view supports the consensus that scientific standards require theories and models to possess logical consistency and to provide explanation as well as prediction. One can scarcely be confident in the explanatory power of a theory which contains false or empirically discredited assumptions—regardless of its ability to predict. Unless the assumptions of a theory or model have been subjected to empirical testing, have not been rejected, and are generally agreed upon as having empirical validity, one has at best *proposed* explanation, not *actual* explanation; moreover, the accuracy of predictions might well be properly ascribed to mere fortuitous circumstances or uncanny chance happenings. Thus, it is imperative that we understand *why* a theory predicts before we give it credence.

Nor, as Friedman's position implies, does it follow that if a theory containing "unrealistic" assumptions has an impressive degree of predictive power, that the theory also possesses satisfactory explanatory power and that the assumptions acquire an acceptable degree of "realism." Cohen and Cyert have adequately demonstrated that Friedman's position can lead to prediction without explanation.[8] A theory or model which seems to predict well enough but which explains poorly should arouse suspicion about whether the true variables are correctly represented. In such a case, any predictive power that

---

[7]Ernest Nagel, "Assumptions in Economic Theory," *American Economic Review, Papers and Proceedings*, Vol. 52, No. 2 (May 1963), pp. 214–215.

[8]K. J. Cohen and R. M. Cyert, *Theory of the Firm: Resource Allocation in a Market Economy*, 2nd ed. (Englewood Cliffs, N.J.: Prentice-Hall, Inc., 1975), pp. 22–24.

the model may have could arise from unknown relationship(s) among variables in the model and/or the influence of unknown variables not included in the model.

It is especially important that a theoretical model possess both predictive power and explanatory power when it is to be used as a guide for control. To properly employ a theory as a basis for formulating control devices, e.g., economic policy, the user must be acutely aware of just how the values of one or more variables must be altered to bring about the desired environmental changes. This clearly requires predictive power, for the user must be able to forecast accurately the consequences of changing the selected control variables. But were the analyst to rely upon a theoretical model which generated accurate predictions without explanation, it is conceivable that the prescribed changes in the control variables could also trigger changes in some of the unspecified variables and/or relationships that had previously led (for reasons unknown) to accurate predictions, thus causing future predictions to be modified in an unpredictable fashion—for the better *or for the worse.*

APPLICATIONS CAPSULE

THE WIZARD WHO OVERSIMPLIFIED: A FABLE

In a certain kingdom, there was a school for the education of princes approaching manhood. Since the king and his court spent much of their time playing chess—indeed, chess was called the sport of kings—it was decided that the subject called "games" should be added to the curriculum of this school. A wizard was engaged to develop the course.

Never having played chess himself, the wizard was a little uncertain about what to teach in this course. (Only a *little* uncertain because his ignorance of chess was outweighed by his strong confidence in his general ability.) He sought the advice of a colleague in another kingdom and from him received the following communication:

"Above all else, a course in games should be rigorous and intellectually challenging. We wizards long ago concluded that chess, as actually played, is so complicated that it is impossible to formulate a body of principles and decision rules; these are essential to the rigorous analysis of any subject. We have therefore introduced a few simplifying assumptions. For example, in chess, the pieces move in a bewildering fashion—some forward, some on the diagonal, and some even at a right angle; we have tidied up this confusion by assuming that all pieces move according to the same rule. With such assumptions, we have been able, albeit with great difficulty, to develop a model, a set of principles, and decision rules which are teachable, and intellectually challenging. A 700-page treatise describing these is enclosed."

The wizard was much impressed by the 700-page treatise, and used it in his course. He found that it was teachable, and that the task of learning this model and solving problems with the decision rules was indeed rigorous and intellectually challenging, as proved by the fact that good students did well on their examinations, while poor students failed them.

The wizard maintained an active correspondence with wizards in other kingdoms about the model and its decision rules. In this correspondence, the game was referred to as "chess" although this was solely for convenience of expression; it was taken for granted that everyone knew that their game was not quite like chess as played in the real world. Eventually, some of this correspondence came to the king's attention. Although he didn't understand the formulas and the jargon, he did notice that the word "chess" was mentioned, so he commanded the wizard to appear before him.

At this audience, the wizard asked, "How can I serve you. O King?"

And the king replied: "I understand that you are teaching the princes how to play chess. I wish to improve my own game. Can you help me?"

"What we call chess may not be exactly like your game, your majesty. So before answering your question, I must analyze the problem. Please describe chess as you play it."

So the king explained the game of chess. As he did so, the wizard noted that it had the same physical layout, the same number of pieces, and apparently the same objective as the game he taught in school. It seemed clear therefore that the solution was simply to apply the decision rules for this game, although he of course did not immediately reveal this fact to the king for he wanted to preserve his reputation for wizardry. Instead, he said thoughtfully: "I will study the problem and return in ninety days."

At the appointed time, the wizard appeared again, carrying a crimson pillow on which lay a spiral-bound report with a Plexiglas cover. It was a paraphrase of the 700-page manuscript. "Follow the rules in this report, your majesty, and you will become the best chess player in the world," he said.

The king avidly studied the report, but soon ran into difficulty. He summoned the wizard again. "I see reference to kings, and men, and squares, which are familiar terms to me; but what is all this about 'jumping,' and 'double jumping,' and 'countervailing force,' 'suboptimization'; and where do you mention queens, rooks, bishops, and knights?"

"But your majesty, as I have clearly explained in the introduction, it was necessary to simplify the environment a trifle. I doubt that these simplifications lessen the practical usefulness of what I have written, however."

"Have you by chance watched some chess players to find out?" asked the king.

"Oh, no, your gracious majesty, but I do carry on an extensive correspondence with other wizards. This is better than observing actual practice because it is generally agreed that wizards are smarter than chess players."

"And your princes. Are they equipped to play chess in the real world because of what they have learned in your course?"

"No offense intended, sir, but we wizards do not believe this to be a proper question. The purpose of our course is to teach princes to think, not to prepare them for a mere vocation."

At this point, the king lost his patience, but since he was a kindly king, he sent the wizard back to his school room rather than to a dungeon.

Moral for economics professors: An education in checkers does not prepare one for a life of chess.

Moral for operations researchers: Half a loaf is not necessarily better than no bread; it may be only chaff.

Moral for businessmen: A consultant who wants to play his own game rather than yours is worthless.

CONCLUDING COMMENTS

The procedures followed by economists in analyzing economic behavior and constructing economic theories consist of five distinct steps:

1. Defining the scope of the problem.
2. Formulating a hypothesis.
3. Deducing predictions from the hypothesis.
4. Testing the accuracy of the predictions.
5. Accepting or revising the hypothesis on the basis of the tests.

These steps delineate the process of theorizing and have as an end result the development of new insights into real-world economic behavior. Economic theory consists of a skeletal framework by which the behavior of economic phenomena can be explained and predicted. Theory attempts to account for what happens and why it happens. On not infrequent occasions, a mathe-

matical formulation of economic theory is especially useful because it allows
analytical maneuvers to be used that are not feasible with verbal or geometric formulations.

The consensus view is that scientific standards require theoretical models to be based upon assumptions that are consistent with observed behavior. Unless the assumptions contained in a theoretical model are reasonable abstractions of reality and have a high degree of empirical validity, the explanatory power of the model is suspect. Moreover, without logical consistency and explanatory power, the usefulness of a theory in assisting to control the environment is also suspect; whatever predictive power it may have demonstrated could be due to circumstance or to undetected cause-effect relationships. Thus, a theory is judged upon (1) its ability to explain cause-effect relations in logical fashion using reasonable assumptions and (2) its powers to predict changes in behavior.

SUGGESTED READINGS

CODDINGTON, A., "The Rationale of General Equilibrium Theory," *Economic Inquiry*, Vol. 13, No. 4 (December 1975), pp. 539–558.

COHEN, K. J., AND R. M. CYERT, *Theory of the Firm: Resource Allocation in a Market Economy*, 2nd ed. (Englewood Cliffs, N.J.: Prentice-Hall, Inc., 1975), Chapter 2.

CYERT, R. M., AND E. GRUNBERG, "Assumption, Prediction, and Explanation in Economics," Appendix A in R. M. Cyert and J. G. March, *A Behavioral Theory of the Firm* (Englewood Cliffs, N.J.: Prentice-Hall, Inc., 1963), pp. 298–311.

FRIEDMAN, M., "The Methodology of Positive Economics," *Essays in Positive Economics* (Chicago: University of Chicago Press, 1953), pp. 3–43.

LEONTIEF, W., "Theoretical Assumptions and Nonobserved Facts," *American Economic Review*, Vol. 61, No. 1 (March 1971), pp. 1–7.

MCGUIRE, J. W., *Theories of Business Behavior* (Englewood Cliffs, N.J.: Prentice-Hall, Inc., 1964), Chapter 2.

MACHLUP, F., *Methodology of Economics and Other Social Sciences* (New York: Academic Press, Inc., 1978).

NAGEL, E., "Assumptions in Economic Theory," *American Economic Review, Papers and Proceedings*, Vol. 52, No. 2 (May 1963), pp. 211–219.

ROTWEIN, E., "On 'The Methodology of Positive Economics,'" *Quarterly Journal of Economics*, Vol. 73, No. 4 (November 1959), pp. 554–575.

QUESTIONS FOR DISCUSSION

1. Characterize each of the steps of economic analysis. How do they compare with "the scientific method?" Which of these steps encompass what might be termed "theorizing?" Explain.
2. What is the difference among the terms "hypothesis," "theory," and "model"?
3. Distinguish carefully between "theory" and a "theoretical model."

4. On what grounds should a theory be evaluated? Which of these are more important, and why?

5. What is the role of assumptions in theory construction?

6. Defend Milton Friedman's position regarding the realism of assumptions. How would one go about measuring or assessing the amount of explanatory power inherent in a theory? Does this have anything to do with Friedman's emphasis on predictive power as the main criterion for judging the worth and merit of a theory?

7. On what grounds, if any, is the presence of explanatory power a desirable feature in a theory?

8. (a) In a recent article, a *Wall Street Journal* columnist raised the economic question of why a pack of cigarettes obtained from a cigarette machine costs more than a pack of cigarettes bought over the counter. Feeling that it should be just the opposite, he observed:[9]

> Everyone knows that a machine is a labor-saving device. It does things faster and easier and, one would expect, cheaper than people can. The cigaret machine at my corner luncheonette can stand there all day, every day without getting fallen arches. It never catches flu or has hangovers or sneaks off for an afternoon at the local ballpark. It doesn't require heating or lighting or air-conditioning or five-minute breaks to go to the restroom. No one has to worry about the cigaret machine getting shortchanged (quite the opposite), or even slipping a couple of packs into its pocket when no one is looking. No, the cigaret machine would seem to be a classic example of an ideal form of people-replacing automation—wageless, undemanding, highly reliable.
>
> So, how come a pack of cigarets from the candy store costs 52 cents and a pack of cigarets from the cigaret machine a couple of doors away costs 65 cents?

Can you identify the variables that might be pertinent in accounting for the puzzlement of the columnist? What hypothesis would you offer as an explanation? How might your hypothesis be tested?

(b) In the same article, the columnist raised the question of why orange soda costs more than gasoline. His analysis ran as follows:[10]

> Gasoline starts with exploration in some God-forsaken part of the world. If oil is found, it has to be drilled for and then pumped out of the ground by pretty expensive equipment. Then it must be sent through a pipeline (a hefty capital investment), loaded into a tanker (ditto), transported over a vast expanse of water, offloaded to another pipeline, and pumped to a refinery (horrendous capital investment). After a complex refining process, what is now gasoline is loaded into railroad tank cars ($$$) and taken to a distributor's tank farm ($$). Now into tank trucks for delivery to gas stations ($). Finally the stuff is pumped into your automobile for about 60 cents a gallon, of which 12 cents is state and federal taxes. Everyone, including the laissez-faire heirs of Adam Smith and John Stuart Mill, agree that this net price of 48 cents a gallon, 12 cents a quart, is a cruel ripoff by greedy oil-producing countries and-or greedy oil companies.

[9]Quoted from John Tracy McGrath, "Ways to Stump an Economist," *The Wall Street Journal*, November 15, 1974, p. 14.
[10]*Ibid.*

Now, orange soda. Like gasoline, soft drinks are produced largely by automated processes. But the equipment is relatively simple and inexpensive. The bottler puts ordinary tap water (sometimes from his own artesian well) into a can or bottle, adds some sugar syrup which also contains flavoring, coloring and a preservative, carbonates the mixture with a shot of carbon dioxide, seals the containers and delivers them by truck to our friend at the candy store. Friend sells soda for 50 cents a quart, $2 a gallon, no tax.

Yes, I know. The price of sugar has risen sharply. But when sugar (and soda) were cheaper, so was gasoline. In just about the same ratio. And bottlers are now using corn syrup along with sugar to sweeten their soft drinks. But most tantalizing is the fact that quinine water and club soda and artifically sweetened diet drinks, none of which contains any sugar at all, also sell for $2 a gallon.

Identify the economic variables that could help explain why orange soda is more expensive than gasoline. What hypothesis would you offer as a possible explanation to the columnist? How would you test the validity of your hypothesis?

TWO THE ROLE OF FIRMS AND MARKETS IN THE MICROECONOMY

To develop some perspective for a study of microeconomics, it helps to begin with a feeling for what an economic system is and how it works. The basic economic activities that take place in a modern economy are summarized in Fig. 2-1. The public, as owners of economic resources, sell their resources to producers in resource markets. From the viewpoint of the public, the sale of these resources generates money income; from the viewpoint of producers, the purchase of economic resources represents costs of production. Producers utilize the resources they purchase to make goods and services, which, in turn, are sold to the public through product markets. The public's source of income to make these purchases is, of course, the money income obtained as resource suppliers. From the public's veiwpoint, the purchases of goods and services are expenditures; from the producer's viewpoint these same dollar flows are revenues. Both the clockwise flow of economic resources and final goods and services and the counterclockwise flow of money incomes and dollar expenditures for final goods and services are simultaneous and repetitive.

Various countries have elected to use different methods both in organizing resources in the production process and in distributing the resultant goods and services. Three basic types of economic systems stand out. A *traditional economic system* relies upon custom, habit, social mores, and tried-and-true methods for achieving economic goals; technology is primitive;

changes are slow and production is undertaken in the same way as last year and the year before. Tradition and the status quo are perpetuated. Examples include the feudal system of the Middle Ages and today's underdeveloped countries. A *command economic system* relies on public ownership and centralized control of the basic means of production; severe limitations are placed upon individual choice when such choices conflict with government-determined economic priorities. Economic plans and activities are under the control of an economic commander-in-chief (a king, czar, prime minister, chairperson, or central planning authority). Heavy use is made of governmental directives, the assumption being that the government is in the best position to decide what economic choices and policies are most beneficial for the economy and its component parts. Both socialistic and communistic nations are examples of command economies. A *capitalistic* or *market economic system* emphasizes private ownership, individual economic freedom, competition, the profit motive, and the price system in the achievement of economic goals. Each economic unit decides what choices and policies are best for it, the thesis being that in encouraging the drive for individual economic self-interest, the outcome proves also to be in the overall best interests of society because of the strong incentives for efficiency, productivity, and satisfaction of consumers. The U.S. economy has a relatively strong capitalistic orientation (although it also has a moderate dose of command and is therefore properly described as a "mixed capitalistic" economic system).

HOW BUSINESS FIRMS FIT INTO THE MICROECONOMICS PICTURE

Although it is not always well recognized, business firms exist by public consent. When society grants business broad operating privileges (not the least of which is the opportunity to seek profit), firms are obligated to serve the needs and wants of society—to the satisfaction of society. This is of the utmost economic significance, because in a capitalistically oriented type of economy, business firms are directly in the flow of most economic activity—as indicated in Fig. 2-1 and the related discussion.

Under capitalism, individual economic freedom and private enterprise are dominant considerations. Business firms serve as society's principal vehicle for supplying goods and services. They, more than any other form of economic organization, are the hub of economic activity. They build new production facilities, invest in more efficient equipment, implement new technologies, market new and better products, determine what kinds of economic resources will be engaged in what kinds of productive activities, and serve as the main source of jobs and incomes. So crucial is the economic role of business firms that the effectiveness with which they carry out their activities is a key determinant of society's economic well-being. Consequently, by focusing attention upon the *economics of the firm*—its decisions, its behavior, and its impact on society—it is possible to arrive at a basic understanding

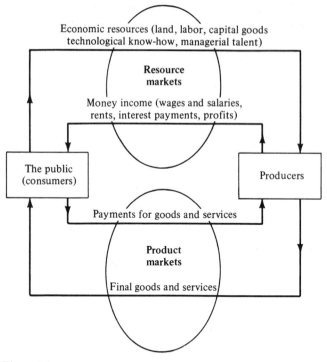

Figure 2-1
Economic activities in a modern economy

and perspective view of the inner workings of a modern capitalistically oriented economy.

THE EMERGENCE OF ENTREPRENEURSHIP

In preindustrial America, firms were typically very small and owner-managers had daily personal contact with their employees, supervising as they worked alongside them. Manufacturing establishments were craft shops in which the owners directly supervised journeymen and apprentices. Gradually, as entrepreneurs increased in number and it became socially acceptable for individuals to pursue their economic self-interest, a social environment evolved in which the energies of individuals were directed by raising or lowering the rewards offered for various tasks.[1] A market-oriented society began to emerge. Competition appeared, making it tougher for any one firm to gain a strategic position for its own advantage. Likewise, buyers were restrained from forcing prices below the costs of production, for other eager

[1]For a more complete discussion of this phase of business history see Robert L. Heilbroner, *The Making of Economic Society* (Englewood Cliffs, N.J.: Prentice-Hall, Inc., 1962), Chapter 3.

buyers would quickly outbid them. The market became a contest wherein buyers sought to pay as little as possible for commodities and sellers sought to extract as high a price as buyers would pay. In the increasingly market-oriented environment of the eighteenth and early nineteenth centuries, consumers catapulted to a new position of prominence. Owner-managers of business firms, prompted by the prospect of profits and a fear of losses, found it advantageous, and even necessary for survival, to synchronize their production decisions with the desires of consumers and the needs of society.

As late as the 1870s, the major business enterprises were engaged in servicing an agrarian economy. Except for a few companies supplying the needs of the rapidly expanding railroad enterprises, the leading firms processed agricultural products and provided farmers with food and clothing. These firms were generally small by today's standards—even though they utilized what then were mass production technologies. They bought their raw materials locally and for the most part they sold their finished goods locally. Where they manufactured for a market more than a few miles away, they distributed their goods through commissioned agents or jobbers who handled the business of several other similar firms.

Then, between 1870 and 1900 a new form of business enterprise appeared, headed by an entirely new breed of entrepreneur—the industrial capitalist. Industrial capitalists, who tended to be very interested in expansion, in growth, and in technological progress, often had a special aptitude for innovation. Factories were their instruments of production. Typically, industrial capitalists did not immerse themselves in day-to-day operational problems inside the factory. These were relegated to salaried production experts—second-echelon plant managers. This left the industrial capitalist free to provide the master touch in overseeing the logistics of the whole enterprise, seeking new ways to increase production efficiencies, devising financial plans, raising capital, implementing new marketing strategies, and outmaneuvering the competition. Above all, the industrial capitalist was an innovator in both production and distribution techniques, a risk-taker, and an opportunist.

A small class of industrial capitalists came to dominate the business environment during the late nineteenth and early twentieth centuries. Edward H. Harriman, William Vanderbilt, and Jay Gould headed an impressive list of railroad entrepreneurs. Until 1900, Andrew Carnegie and Carnegie Steel Company dominated the steel industry. John D. Rockefeller engineered Standard Oil Company to a position of prominence in the oil industry. Most of the meat shipped in interstate commerce came from the packing houses of Philip D. Armour, Gustavus Swift, and Michael Cudahy. The name McCormick was synonymous with farm machinery. J. P. Morgan became the nation's best known and influential banker. Persons such as Henry Ford, the DuPonts, Henry Frick, James J. Hill, Andrew Mellon, Jacob Van Astor, James B. Duke, George Westinghouse, and C. P. Huntington were also counted among the important industrial capitalists.

The regime of the industrial capitalist wrought a profound change in

24

*The Role
of Firms and
Markets in the
Microeconomy*

the form of business enterprise and the structure of markets. Within the span of 30 years, the size and complexity of business enterprise was radically enlarged. Large-scale enterprise spread steadily in the areas of manufacturing and transportation, although less so in trade and service. By 1900 the average manufacturing establishment was doing three times as much business as in 1850.[2] Concomitantly, there was a dramatic concentration of production in these large business units.

> By 1900 the number of textile mills, although still large, had dwindled by a third from the 1880's; the number of manufacturers of agricultural implements had fallen by 60 per cent over the same period, and the number of leather manufacturers by three-quarters. In the locomotive industry, two companies ruled the roost in 1900, contrasted with nineteen in 1860. The biscuit and cracker industry changed from a scatter of small companies to a market in which one producer had 90 per cent of the industry's capacity by the turn of the century. Meanwhile in steel there was the colossal U.S. Steel Corporation, which alone turned out over half the steel production of the nation. In oil, the Standard Oil Company tied up between 80 to 90 per cent of the nation's output. In tobacco, the American Tobacco Company controlled 75 per cent of cigars. Similar control rested with the American Sugar Company, the American Smelting and Refining Company, the United Shoe Machinery Company, and dozens more.[3]

However, large business did not *replace* small business but rather was simply *superimposed* upon it. Wholesale and retail trade, finance, and service activities remained concentrated in small owner-managed firms; almost 1.5 million enterprises were engaged in these functions in 1900 (and in 1976 over 6.3 million enterprises were so engaged).

Initially, the appearance of large enterprises enhanced competition. In the largely agricultural, handcraft, small-factory economy of the early nineteenth century, markets were local, each being insulated from its neighbors by slow, high-cost transportation. Small enterprises lacked the necessary means to invade even adjacent markets, much less regional or national markets. But the industrial capitalists were of a different breed. They aggressively and opportunistically employed the strategies of saturating existing markets, expanding into geographically distant markets, vertical integration, and product diversification. They abandoned purchasing and selling through agents; instead, they created their own multiarea buying and marketing organizations. Increasingly, markets became interconnected and were unified; local monopolies succumbed to outside competition. The outcome was a steady growth in competitive pressures among large-scale firms, replacing the more restricted local competition of the small-business, small-market environment. Price wars repeatedly broke out as rival enterprises sought to capture the new customers requisite for profitable production levels. Bankruptcy on a multimillion-dollar scale came to be a disturbing and omnipresent threat.

---

[2]E. A. J. Johnson and Herman E. Krooss, *The American Economy* (Englewood Cliffs, N.J.: Prentice-Hall, Inc., 1960), p. 239.
[3]Heilbroner, *The Making of Economic Society*, p. 118.

A reaction set in. Predictably, rival firms elected to seek avenues for lessening competitive rigors. Various forms of voluntary cooperation were devised: trade associations, informal pacts to share markets, and gentlemen's agreements to charge mutually satisfactory prices. While these worked modestly well in prosperous times, the temptation to shave prices was powerful when the pressures of depression and shrinking markets periodically appeared. More ingenious and effective devices were needed, and out of this need there developed trusts, holding companies, and mergers.

Yet it would be misleading to presume that the emergence of giant corporations originated solely, or even primarily, from the pyramiding impact of mergers, trusts, and holding companies. The antitrust laws passed in 1890 and 1914 saw in part to that. Equally, perhaps more, important was the process of internal growth. Ford, General Motors, General Electric, DuPont, AT&T, and Carnegie Steel (later U.S. Steel), among others, grew because of rapidly expanding markets for their products and because they were quicker, more able, more efficient, and more aggressive than their rivals. Their gradual ascendency to positions of dominance within their industries is directly attributable to well-executed business strategies and to the significant reduction in unit costs that accompanies mass production and distribution techniques.[4]

THE STRUCTURE OF CONTEMPORARY BUSINESS ENTERPRISE

During the first half of the twentieth century, a third phase in the development of business enterprise began, this one taking the form of an *organizational* revolution. Sustained growth in the size of industrial enterprise made it virtually impossible for one individual to continue to direct operations personally and to amass the financial capital needed to take advantage of continued expansion opportunities. The operation of a successful industrial complex (which the corporation had become) required a growing number of managerial skills. The intricacies of finance, accounting, marketing, labor relations, production, and product research—all of which the entrepreneur-industrial capitalist originally performed personally—became major "departmental" tasks within the firm. Major reorganizations in authority and responsibility produced a parceling out of the entrepreneurial functions to

[4]Several actual examples can be offered to point up the cost reduction associated with mass production and distribution techniques. In increasing its sales of model-T touring cars from 18,664 in 1909–1910 to 730,041 in 1916–1917, Ford realized such large cost reductions that the price of a typical model fell steadily from $950 in 1909–1910 to $360 in 1916–1917. Standard Oil Company found, as early as 1884, that by concentrating 75% of its production in three giant refineries, its average cost of refining a barrel fell to 0.534 cents as compared to 1.5 cents for the rest of the industry. Gustavus Swift discovered that drastic cuts in meat prices could be made possible by constructing large meat-packing houses in the cities on the cattle frontier and then channeling the meat through his own distribution facilities into butcher shops and grocery stores in every major town and city in the East.

26

*The Role
of Firms and
Markets in the
Microeconomy*

managerial specialists. Professional managers replaced the industrial entrepreneur as the directing force of corporate enterprise.

Simultaneously, the ownership of corporations underwent change. As the original founders died, their holdings were fragmented by inheritance; the heirs often preferred to assume the passive role of absentee stockholder. In addition, small investors began to acquire stock in corporations, and by the 1920s, when it was fashionable for the upper and middle classes to dabble in the stock market, the ownership of large corporations had become widely diluted among hundreds or even thousands of stockholders. No longer was it necessary to own a *majority* of the shares of common stock to exercise effective control over the affairs of a large enterprise.[5] As long as the performance of the firm appeared satisfactory to the average stockholder (in terms of dividends and appreciation in the price of the stock), it was easy enough for top management to set corporate policy, subject perhaps only to a perfunctory review by the board of directors.

Most recently, a fourth distinctive feature of major corporations has appeared—diversification into related or unrelated products (or both). By extending its operations to include many different product markets, the fortunes of the diversified firm are not tied to a single commodity group, and it can prosper even though one or several of its products lose consumer favor. Product diversification has freed business firms from the life-and-death cycle of either specific products or industries and provided a strong defense against secular shifts in demand and technology which can be fatal to a single-product enterprise.

The Absolute and Relative Sizes of Firms

Today's population of business enterprises is made up of firms of widely varying sizes—from small shops with annual sales in the thousands to giant corporations with annual sales *and profits* in the billions. Indeed, the sizes of the largest corporations are truly mind-boggling. An examination of corporate operating results in the United States shows that nearly 300 corporations have sales revenues exceeding $1 billion, at least 550 corporations have assets exceeding $1 billion, roughly 150 corporations have after-tax profits exceeding $100 million (6 to 10 firms earn after-tax profits exceeding $1 billion), and over 500 companies have 10,000 or more employees. In 1978 the 1000 largest industrial corporations, together with the 50 largest

[5]By 1963, in *none* of the 200 largest nonfinancial corporations in the United States was as much as 80% or more of the voting stock owned by an individual, family, or group of business associates. In only 9 of the 200 firms was there even majority ownership (where an individual, family, or group owned between 50 and 80%) of the voting stock. Minority control (stock ownership of between 10 and 50%) or joint minority control (two or more minority interests) characterized but 31 of the 200 firms. The remaining 160 firms were classified as "management-controlled" on the belief that no group of stockholders would be able under ordinary circumstances to muster enough votes to challenge management. For more details, see Robert J. Larner, "Ownership and Control in the 200 Largest Nonfinancial Corporations, 1929 and 1963," *American Economic Review*, Vol. 56, No. 4 (September 1966), pp. 777–787.

insurance companies, the 50 largest diversified financial corporations, the 50 largest retailing companies, the 50 largest transportation companies, and the 50 largest utilities, had combined assets of $1.9 trillion, combined sales revenues of almost $1.3 trillion, combined after-tax profits of $63 billion, and combined employment exceeding 23.8 million persons.

Insofar as specific corporations are concerned, the largest U.S. corporation in terms of assets is American Telephone and Telegraph Co.; in 1978 AT&T had assets of $103.3 billion, sales revenues of $41.0 billion, after-tax profits of $5.3 billion, and 999,800 employees. In terms of sales revenues, Exxon ranks as the largest corporation, not just in the United States but in the world as well. In 1979 Exxon had sales revenues of $79.1 billion, after-tax profits of $4.3 billion, assets of $49.5 billion, and 169,000 employees. The gigantic size of the largest corporations is illustrated by the fact that fewer than 25 nations of the world have gross national products greater than the annual sales revenues of Exxon. Comparisons of corporate sales revenue and GNP statistics show that as many as ten of the world's 50 biggest economic entities are U.S. corporations.

The statistics of corporate size suggest that the 1250 or so largest U.S. corporations constitute a massive aggregation of productive capability. Just by themselves these firms would comprise the world's second largest economy—exceeded only by the whole U.S. economy. Moreover, the domain of corporate influence extends into almost every nook and cranny of economic life. The rates at which the largest corporations produce and the aggressiveness with which they expand set the tone of economic activity in general. The prices they charge and the wages they pay affect prices and wages throughout the economy. The pace at which they implement new technologies and introduce new products is a chief determinant of the rate of economic progress and higher standards of living.

All in all, it is fair to say that the mainstream of economic activity runs right through the doors of the nation's largest corporations—a feature that has lead to the U.S. economy being aptly labeled a "corporate economy." We shall use the term *corporate capitalism* to refer to that segment of the economy where:

1. A significant share of the nation's output of goods and services is provided by large corporate firms.
2. The large absolute size of firms gives them substantial economic, social, and political powers.
3. A few, large enterprises dominate the market for a particular product and engage in a personalized sort of rivalry for consumer patronage.

THE FIRM AND THE MARKETPLACE

Conventional economic theory instructs that the firm and its business are governed by forces in the marketplace. The firm is depicted as reacting and responding to market demand and supply conditions—conditions that are

28

*The Role
of Firms and
Markets in the
Microeconomy*

beyond its purview to control. The market, not the firm, is held to be the hub of economic activity and the focus of analytical concern.

Conventional business theory, in sharp contrast, looks upon markets and economic forces as limits to what the firm can do. Present and future market conditions are construed as creating opportunities (and threats) for business action. But market forces are not thought of as decisive in determining what a business is or what it does. A firm's economic mission, its objective, and its strategy for competing in the marketplace are held to be well within the firm's influence; moreover, it is well within the firm's ability to guide and mold market processes with a well-conceived strategy. In short, a particular firm's strategy, if effective, is perceived as having the potential for generating a major impact on markets, buyers, rival firms, and the directions of economic change.

In actuality, there is validity in both views and no need to force a choice between the two. Markets affect firms and firms affect markets.

The Concept of the Market

In a competitive enterprise system "the market" is held to be supreme over all other economic units. Its importance is like that of the sun in solar system—all economic activity revolves around the market. The market is where buyers and sellers conduct their business. The market is, at once, the basic mechanism for organizing an orderly exchange of goods and services and, through competitive interplay, the master over all voluntary transactions. The market is two-sided: it reflects both demand and supply conditions—and does so simultaneously. Through the market consumers make known their decisions to buy or not to buy and on what terms; through the market firms make known their willingness and ability to produce or not to produce and on what terms. According to an old Russian proverb, "once you have gone to market you have told the whole world." The market thus is an elaborate network through which the preferences and freely made decisions of buyers and sellers are communicated, recorded, totaled, and balanced against one another. The market, better than any firm, individual, or governmental agency, is able to signal what the current states of supply and demand are. The market is the first to receive and reflect the winds of economic change. In short, the market's judgment about the balance between supply and demand and its verdict regarding the terms of exchange between buyers and sellers is conclusive and impartial.

How a Market Functions: A Simple Model

The demand side of a market reflects the intensity with which buyers want and are willing to pay for the product in question. This intensity, which can be weak or strong or anywhere in between, can be represented graphically as a line showing the various quantities which buyers are willing to purchase at each of various possible prices, all other things being equal—see line *DD* in Fig. 2-2. Since buyers typically are willing to purchase less at higher prices than at lower prices, the relationship between price and quantity demanded is an inverse one (which makes the demand curve a downsloping line). Events such as rising incomes, changes in the prices of substitute products, and shifts in preferences and life-styles can and do shift the shape and position of the demand curve, thereby creating a revised level of demand intensity.

The supply side of a market concerns the extent to which sellers are willing and able to make supplies of a product available. Although many factors can enter into how much suppliers are willing to offer for sale at any given moment of time, supply conditions are usually such that producers will supply more of a good or service at higher prices than at lower prices. In other words, the economic relationship between price and quantity supplied tends to be a direct one, resulting in an upward-sloping supply curve—line *SS* in Fig. 2-2. The reason for this is that sellers usually find it more profitable and thus more advantageous to increase their production efforts when price rises as compared to when price falls.

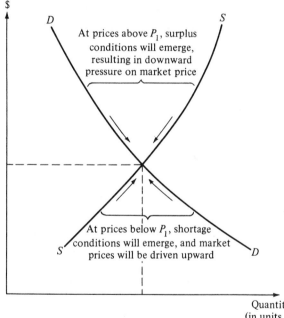

Figure 2-2
The market mechanism: determination of market price and the quantity sold

The interaction of demand and supply determines both the market price and the quantity that changes hands. As depicted in Fig. 2-2, the demand and supply curves intersect at a price of P_1 and a quantity of Q_1. Competition guarantees that any other price-quantity combination will be unstable. If sellers, either deliberately or inadvertently, elect to charge a price above P_1, the surplus conditions that arise will induce competing sellers to shade their prices to work off the excess inventory buildups. As market price drops,

30

*The Role
of Firms and
Markets in the
Microeconomy*

buyers are stimulated to increase their purchases, whereas the quantity supplied (because of reduced profitability) will tend to contract, thereby acting to eliminate surplus conditions.

If the prevailing market price should for some reason be below P_1, the balance between supply and demand is such that shortages will appear. Those buyers who are most anxious to avoid doing without the product will, when confronted with shortage conditions, be inclined to accept a move on the part of sellers to alleviate a shortage through higher prices. Thus, in periods of shortage a competitive scramble among buyers for the available supplies tends to drive price upward—an outcome that automatically acts to eliminate the shortage, owing to the fact that higher prices serve to reduce the overall quantity demanded and to increase the quantity supplied.

In Fig. 2-2, only at price P_1 and quantity Q_1 will the market be cleared. At this price-quantity combination, neither surplus nor shortage conditions exist. A price-quantity *equilibrium* will prevail in the sense that no forces are currently operating to bring about a change in the market result. The tendency of a competitive market to establish a price at which the quantity demanded will equal the quantity supplied is called the *rationing function* of the price system and "the market mechanism" is the vehicle through which it all works.

APPLICATIONS CAPSULE

**WHY THE MARKET IS AN UNFORGIVING TASKMASTER:
A SELLER'S PERSPECTIVE**

In a recent advertising campaign General Motors ran ads which made several statements about how the marketplace affected its car business. The text of the GM ad was as follows:

**Why GM Cars Will Get Better Mileage
than the Government Requires:
the effect of the marketplace
on forward planning**

New marketing reports indicate that public acceptance of smaller, more fuel-efficient cars is growing rapidly, especially for those models that provide the performance, and the passenger and luggage space most customers want. That change in customer acceptance enables us to change both the kind of cars we build and the proportion of small cars to full-size cars.

Long before the recent gas shortage, our shift to smaller cars had been planned to meet what at that time was an evolutionary shift in customer demand. Circumstances and a dramatic change in what you, our customers, are demanding has radically altered the timing of our production plans. Smaller, more fuel-efficient cars will dominate our production much sooner than we expected.

We will continue to build a full line of cars to meet the varied needs of our customers. And we will continue to devote much of our research and engineering effort to finding new ways to make cars with greater carrying capacity more efficient. Customers with large families cannot be left without transportation.

Every advance we make in metallurgy and every breakthrough we make in engineering will make all our cars even more efficient.

Less than a year ago, it did not appear that marketplace demand for smaller cars would allow us to meet fleet-mileage standards set by the government. Stocks of smaller cars—both foreign and American makes—were building up and demand for larger cars was strong. But the picture has changed.

Today we believe the marketplace is demanding cars which, based on a fleet average, will be even more fuel efficient than those required by government. We have always believed that the disciplines of the marketplace are far better than government mandates in achieving fuel economy. It is what the customer wants to buy—and not government rules—that will determine fleet average fuel efficiency.

And the marketplace is an unforgiving taskmaster. Either we build the cars our customers demand, or someone else will. Just meeting government mileage standards for the 1980s won't be enough to keep us in business.

The message from the marketplace is clear. Our response will be equally clear: fuel efficiency. We'll use new electronics, new designs, new engines, new metals and combinations of metals, all the resources of General Motors, to deliver the gas mileage you want. And we'll deliver on demand. That's the way the marketplace works.

Source: Advertisement appearing in *Business Week*, December 3, 1979, p. 120.

Is "the Market" a Place?

Figuratively, the market is where buyers and sellers come together to effect their voluntary, freely made transactions. In this regard, one often hears mention made of "the marketplace," but, strictly speaking, a market is seldom a single, precisely defined geographical place. Some markets are indeed such that buyers and sellers do come face to face at a particular time and place to strike their bargain. A vegetable market or a shopping mall have such attributes. But many, maybe even most, markets range beyond a par-

32

*The Role
of Firms and
Markets in the
Microeconomy*

ticular locale and assume area-wide, regional, national, or worldwide dimensions. A newsprint firm's market may well extend over several states, thereby putting it in direct competition with other newsprint mills in the region. A major oil company such as Exxon does business all over the world and thus competes directly with nearly every other oil company in one place or another. The markets for wheat, coffee, cotton, wool, gold, copper, rubber, aluminum, nickel, iron ore, and cocoa all assume global proportions. And, in the case of these and other highly standardized commodities, the market can function quite effectively without buyers and sellers standing over the goods and haggling over price and other conditions of exchange.

According to Alfred Marshall, the distinguished British economist, the geographical limits of a market are defined by "an area within which buyers and sellers are in such close communication with each other that price tends to be the same throughout the area." However, Marshall's definition of a market is a bit troublesome. Suppose that two groceries located across the street from each other are selling a particular brand of toothpaste at different prices—one for 79 cents and the other for 89 cents. Are we then to infer that the two grocery stores are not in the same market? Or suppose that Avis typically rents cars at prices slightly below Hertz (perhaps because its fleet of cars consists of the less expensive, more economically equipped models); then can we conclude that Avis and Hertz are not head-on rivals competing in the same market? Would it not be more accurate to view Avis and Hertz as operating within the same market but endeavoring to appeal to different *market segments* via price competition? Consequently, whether the size and extent of a market can be delimited solely on the criterion of price uniformity is open to question.

It is agreed, however, that all goods and services and all resources may be regarded as having a market. There is a market for natural gas, a market for pocket calculators, a market for sparkplugs, a market for life insurance, a market for quick copying services, a market for real estate, a market for business school graduates, a market for municipal bonds, a market for pro football players, and a market for the labor services of people skilled in operating bulldozers. It is also possible to describe a market by certain conditions which prevail as well by the product or service being exhanged. Thus, there are "buyers' markets," where conditions of oversupply and excess capacity allow buyers to drive especially good bargains with sellers. There are "sellers' markets," where demand is so strong relative to supply that sellers can command an attractive asking price. There are "perfect markets," where a large number of buyers deal with a large number of sellers, no one of which buys or sells more than an insignificant fraction of the total exchanged, where the commodities being offered by sellers are regarded by buyers as essentially identical, where the only criterion for a transaction is that no better bargain is available (i.e., no buyers have a loyalty or preference for dealing with a particular seller), and where all traders are aware of all offers and deals available. And there are "imperfect markets" where some or all of the foregoing conditions are absent.

Moreover, markets are linked and interconnected with each other.

Markets are linked vertically since some products pass through a series of markets on their way to the final user—farmers sell cotton to ginners, who sell baled cotton fiber to cloth manufacturers, who sell yard goods to garment firms, which sell articles of clothing to department stores, which supply consumers in the retail market. Markets are linked horizontally in the sense that substitute or complementary products create relationships between and among markets for different products. What happens in the market for beef affects the market for pork. Prices in the gasoline market affect the travel and recreation business. Money market conditions affect residential construction activity. Yet each market retains a semblance of uniqueness since its operation is governed by the particular preferences and decisions of the particular buyers and sellers who participate in it as well as by the particular customs and patterns of doing business in that market.

The nature of the markets in which the firm does business is a matter for management to study carefully. The firm's sales, profits, and growth potential are a function of market conditions and the market process. A firm's success hinges upon its ability to analyze the marketplace accurately and position itself as strategically as possible so as to be in the right place, at the right time, with the right products (or services), offered at the right price. The role and function of corporate strategy is to specify how this is to be accomplished.

THE FIRM AND ITS CORPORATE STRATEGY

Any firm has to pose and seek answers to a number of basic questions: What products or services will the firm offer for sale? Who will be the firm's customers? Why will they buy the firm's products (or services)? What should the concept of the firm's business be—now and in the future? What should the firm continue to do, and what should it plan to abandon? How does the firm's economic mission mesh with market and competitive realities? How should the firm try to compete against its market rivals? A firm's answers to these questions comprise what is meant by *corporate strategy* and constitute its directional signals and its master plan.

There are numerous ways for a firm to approach the marketplace and develop viable answers to the questions of "what is our business, what will it be, and what should it be?" It may simply think of its business as being defined by the character of its main product or service; thus, a cement company may view itself as being in the cement business, a loan company as in the loan business, and a pizza villa as in the pizza business. Some firms describe their business by the principal ingredient in their products, as with steel companies, aluminum companies, and paper companies—even though their respective products come in a wide variety of sizes and forms and perform quite different functions. The unifying theme of other enterprises is technology, an example being General Electric, whose thousands of products are related in one way or another to electricity.

Still other firms prefer a concept based upon an expansive view of the

34

*The Role
of Firms and
Markets in the
Microeconomy*

customers or markets they serve. For example, rural electric cooperatives often construe their business as one of supplying electrical service to residents of less-populated rural areas. A sporting goods manufacturer may define its business as supplying sporting equipment to recreation enthusiasts. A home appliance manufacturer may view its business mission as one of offering effort-saving and time-saving devices to households.

In many cases, however, a firm may employ a more explicit and narrowly focused corporate strategy, endeavoring to zero in on a specific *market segment* or distinguishable group of customers having some common (and strategically relevant) characteristic—location, use of the product, timing of purchase, volume bought, service requirements, and so forth. For instance, a book publisher who supplies textbooks to college students is in a business quite distinct from that of publishing potential bestsellers sold to individuals through retail channels. Likewise, the clientele of a major state university is fundamentally different from that of a small private liberal arts college. And the business of a neighborhood convenience food mart is different from that of a large supermarket.

Strictly speaking, most firms are in a variety of lines of business. They sell the same product to different types of customers in distinctly different ways, or they utilize a number of different distribution channels in gaining access to markets and customers, or they have a diversified product line. This can create problems in specifying what the appropriate economic role of the firm is and what its corporate strategy is or should be. For example, a hospital may view its mission and strategy as "providing comprehensive health care to the residents of the surrounding community." But is this to include filling cavities and pulling teeth, making examinations for eyeglasses, nursing the aged, furnishing annual checkups, and rehabilitation services for the handicapped—all of which are often performed by medical professionals outside hospitals? A state university is unquestionably in the business of "higher education," but does this mean it should offer the *full* range of programs in "higher education"—including career-specific training, associate degrees similar to those of junior colleges, adult and continuing education, as well as undergraduate and graduate programs in *all* disciplines and professions? A railroad company may decide to view itself as a "transportation company," but does this mean that it should get into long-haul trucking or airfreight services or fleet car leasing or intercity busing or rapid transit?

THE RELEVANCE AND IMPORTANCE OF CORPORATE STRATEGY

The approach that a firm takes in shaping the nature and direction of its business—as revealed by its corporate strategy—is important from several standpoints. It indicates, first, that the market course a firm charts for itself is a derivative of external economic conditions and internal management preferences and perceptions. A whole host of factors, some related and some not, go into the firm's strategy formulation process. These include consumer buying trends and purchasing habits, market opportunity, competitive pressures and tactics, capital investment requirements, relative profit expectations, the firm's financial condition, an assessment of whether the firm's technical expertise and management know-how qualify it to run a particular business successfully, risk preferences, the personal values and aspirations of management, the firm's obligations to segments of society other than stockholders, government regulations, rates of taxation, and the social, political, and cultural constraints imposed on the firm's scope of action.

Second, in multiproduct, multimarket enterprises, the firm's overall grand strategy, if in fact there is one, is an aggregate of its strategies for the different lines of business, production stages, or geographical areas in which it may operate. There is, however, no overriding necessity for a multiproduct enterprise to have an integrated, consistent, compatible set of strategies for each of its separate product-market activities, as witnessed by the successful performance results achieved by conglomerate companies.

Third, the firm's strategy has a definite bearing on its competitive posture, market behavior, and position in the goods-producing process. For instance, some firms are (or try to be) technological leaders, while others are content with being technological followers. Some firms are self-acknowledged aggressive risk-takers, while others deliberately are more conservative and embrace a strategy of risk avoidance. Some firms emphasize quality and service, while others aim at the low-price, budget-conscious and of the market. Some firms position themselves as *forward satellites* of other companies, specializing in channeling the mass-produced items of these other companies forward to the final user; examples include automobile dealers, wholesale distributorships, and the retail chain stores. Other firms station themselves as *backward satellites* and make their business out of supplying one or more enterprises with raw materials, intermediate goods, or component parts (the apparel firm supplying Sears and the local logging operator whose business is furnishing wood to large paper mills serve as good examples). Some firms base their strategy on carving a niche for themselves on the "competitive fringe" of markets dominated by well-known, brand-name firms; the producers of the so-called "off-brands" exemplify this type of firm.

Last, strategy is the foundation for such fundamental areas of economic decision making within the firm as (1) the choice of product line and/or service mix and whether these adequately create or meet consumer tastes and preferences, (2) selecting the most resource-efficient and cost-efficient technology and production process, (3) determining the optimum production scale and plant location, (4) what price to charge and how much to produce, and (5) how best to respond to competitive pressures and changing demand-supply conditions.

All of this is a way of saying that insights into a firm's strategy help explain its behavior in the marketplace and provide a basis for assessing its chances for competitive survival. Whether a firm is an economic success or

36

*The Role
of Firms and
Markets in the
Microeconomy*

an economic failure is *in part* a function of the caliber of its strategy and not entirely just the economics of the marketplace. In addition, an understanding of the interplay between a firm's strategy and economic forces in the marketplace enters the picture in judging the effectiveness with which a competitive private enterprise system serves the overall economic welfare of consumers.

APPLICATIONS CAPSULE

THE STRATEGIC ASPECTS OF WHY GENERAL ELECTRIC GOT OUT OF THE COMPUTER BUSINESS

In 1970, General Electric unexpectedly sold its computer business to a competitor, Honeywell. The reasons behind GE's divestiture of its computer operations were publicly aired in the trial of the Justice Department's recent civil antitrust suit against International Business Machines (IBM).

In the mid-sixties, GE was considered to be IBM's strongest competitor; however, by 1970, GE's position in the marketplace was weakening and the technical capabilities of its computer products were falling behind those of other firms. From 1957 to 1970, GE sustained net losses from its computer operations of $162.7 million. Meanwhile, having just weathered a costly strike and with the nation in a slight recession, GE was under financial strains. Temporary losses were being incurred in two of its biggest product lines—nuclear power plants and jet aircraft engines; both were deemed vital to GE's overall business and had to be supplied with whatever cash was needed.

It was in this environment that the computer division's management proposed to corporate headquarters to undertake the manufacture of a broad new computer line that would have 20 to 40% better performance than IBM computers and would sell for about the same price. It was estimated that the new computer line would generate revenue of $8.2 billion and profit before taxes of $2.34 billion in the 13 years 1969–1981. However, the program was projected to incur losses through 1973 of $538 million. Profits would begin in 1974, but the cumulative losses would not be offset until 1977. GE's computer heads forecast a net cash drain of $685 million through 1974—a drain which would require GE to borrow at least $500 million to undertake the plan. If the plan succeeded, GE would become a clear second to IBM, with 8% of the market by 1975 and 10% soon thereafter. This compared very favorably with GE's 4 to 5% market share in 1969.

Nonetheless, the plan had some shaky assumptions: (1) that GE could take customers from IBM; (2) that IBM would tolerate a sizable loss in market share without retaliating; (3) that GE could achieve key inventions on schedule and meet developmental deadlines; and (4) a sizable risk that IBM and other computer manufacturers would leapfrog GE by bringing out even better computer products.

Aside from these risks, it was GE's assessment that computer markets were growing fast. The technology and the uses of computers were changing rapidly. IBM would continue to dominate the computer business, owing to its superior sales coverage, low manufacturing costs, and large base of customers—estimated at 72% of the market. IBM had steadily improving profit margins, strength in all aspects of computer technology, and overwhelming programming resources (software) to go with its computers. Although IBM was confronted with antitrust suits, some loss of skilled personnel to other companies, increasing specialization by competitors, and some gradual loss of its position in software and peripheral equipment technology, IBM's competitors still were earning only meager profits.

Whereas some computer companies were managing to compete on the basis of specialization in certain products or uses, GE was a generalist, attempting to compete across the board with IBM. In the view of GE's top executives, GE did not have a strong basis for specializing. Its major computer products were somewhat out-of-date and GE was weak in peripheral, mass-storage, and terminal devices—all of which were viewed as key products of the future. GE had limited technical strength in many areas of computer technology and its customer loyalty was reputed to be the lowest of any firm in the market.

In addition, IBM had 210 sales offices in the U.S. and 17,000 salesmen and systems analysts. GE had 38 offices with a staff of 600. To reach its 1975 objective, GE would have to increase sales force sizes by 60 to 70% per year and, at the same time, develop salesmen who were twice as productive as IBM's. Whereas GE's manufacturing costs were 47 percent of its computer revenue, IBM's were estimated at 20%. GE's assessments of other firms in the computer market included the following:

> Control Data Corporation—4.2% of worldwide computer installations; growing faster than the market; specialists in large computer systems and government applications; technically strong but weak in business applications.
> Burroughs Corporation—2.4% of the market; growing substantially faster than other firms; specialists in banking and some other uses; technically strong.
> National Cash Register Corporation—2.2% of the market; specialists in smaller systems, banking, and first-time users; weak in peripherals and software; unprofitable.
> Sperry Rand (UNIVAC)—6.8% of the market but losing ground; technically strong except for large-system software but had never fully used its strength; a generalist firm with weak marketing organization.

38
*The Role
of Firms and
Markets in the
Microeconomy*

Honeywell—3.9% of the market; growing slower than the market; technically good but with an incomplete and somewhat out-of-date product line; a generalist firm which had seriously delayed product development in order to be profitable.

RCA Corporation—2.9% of the market and losing ground; a generalist firm with no identifitable customer segment; technically poor except in communications; aging and incomplete line; no real strength; unprofitable.

Finally, GE's management viewed the industry as being on the threshold of a major merger movement. No one of the small-share firms was in a position to seriously challenge IBM or make a lasting impact on the market.

Given these considerations, beset with mounting pressures for immediate profit increases, and facing stringent financial demands from is nuclear power and jet engine businesses, General Electric decided to "disengage" from the industry and sell its computer business. Within two months, GE and Honeywell announced an agreement to combine their computer businesses and create a new company controlled and managed by Honeywell.

Questions for Discussion

1. How does GE's decision to get out of the computer business reflect the interplay between the marketplace and a firm's business strategy?
2. Make a list of the factors which appeared to influence GE's decision. Which of these relate to external conditions in the cpmputer market and which relate to internal preferences, perceptions, and influences?

Source: *The Wall Street Journal*, January 12, 1976, p. 26.

THE CONCEPT OF THE FIRM RECONSIDERED

In much of traditional microeconomic theory, the firm is commonly portrayed as directed by an owner-entrepreneur—the risk-taking individual who supplies financial capital, who organizes and supervises the economic resources needed for production, and who has a special genius for new and better ways to run a business.[6] Moreover, the firm is typically viewed as engaging in whatever activities the owner-entrepreneur deems appropriate, with conformity to the chosen goals being purchased by payments (wages, salaries, pres-

---

[6]The late Joseph Schumpeter put it well when he said: "To act with confidence beyond the range of familiar beacons and to overcome that resistance requires aptitudes that are present in only a small fraction of the population and [they] define the entrepreneurial type as well as the entrepreneurial function." Joseph Schumpeter, *Capitalism, Socialism, and Democracy*, 3rd ed. (New York: Harper & Row, Publishers, 1950), p. 132.

tige, power, security) made by the owner-entrepreneur to his or her employees and by a system of internal controls (authority, budgets) that informs employees of management's desires.

This concept of the firm is still appropriate for small businesses, but it is at considerable variance with reality as concerns larger corporations. The policies and behavior of large-scale organizations run by a team of professional managers cannot correctly be viewed as the product of a single-minded individual entrepreneur. In the corporation the patterns of change in prices, output levels, product lines, product mix, resource allocation, and other standard economic variables are the result of a complex (and little understood) decision-making process.

Moreover, the large corporation has a much more sizable constituency than does the small business enterprise. It comes into touch with a far greater number and range of individuals, and its sphere of influence extends to all corners of the economy. As a consequence, it faces different constraints and tends to behave in ways that differ from those of a small entrepreneurial enterprise. These differences are substantive rather than incidental. Indeed, while the small proprietorship with a localized market for its products and its stress upon a single line of technically simple products (which was so characteristic of nineteenth-century business) still remains the most significant form of enterprise in terms of numbers, it is no longer so dominant in terms of economic importance. The hallmark of business development during the twentieth century is the phenomenal rise to positions of productive power of large-scale, multiproduct, transnational corporate enterprises. These enterprises now comprise the core of production activity in modern economies. And it is their central importance that gives rise to such popular labels as "the corporate economy," "the corporate state," and "corporate capitalism."

In the chapters that follow we shall analyze this type of economic environment in greater depth. By zeroing in on the economics of firms operating under various types of situations and conditions, we can indicate the whys and wherefores of microeconomic activity. Our ultimate goal is to identify and explain the economic relationships underlying the demand for a firm's product, the requirements for efficient and low-cost production, the mechanisms of competition and price-output determination in the marketplace, and the functioning of resource markets.

SUGGESTED READINGS

ADELMAN, M. A., "The Two Faces of Economic Concentration," *The Public Interest*, No. 21 (Fall 1970), pp. 117–126.

ANDREWS, K., *The Concept of Corporate Strategy* (Homewood, Ill.: Dow Jones–Irwin, Inc., 1971), Chapters 2, 3, 5.

ANSOFF, H. I., *Corporate Strategy* (New York: McGraw-Hill Book Company, 1965), Chapters 6, 7.

AVERITT, R. T., *The Dual Economy* (New York: W. W. Norton & Company, Inc., 1967), Chapters 2, 5, 6.

40

*The Role
of Firms and
Markets in the
Microeconomy*

BAIN, J. S., *Industrial Organization* (New York: John Wiley & Sons, Inc., 1959), Chapter 3.

BOWER, J. L., "Planning within the Firm," *American Economic Review*, Vol. 60, No. 2 (May 1970), pp. 186–194.

CHANDLER, A., *The Visible Hand: The Managerial Revolution in American Business* (Cambridge, Mass.: Harvard University Press, 1977).

DRUCKER, P. F., "The New Markets and the New Capitalism," *The Public Interest*, No. 21 (Fall 1970), pp. 44–79.

DRUCKER, P. F., *Management: Tasks, Responsibilities, Practices* (New York: Harper & Row, Publishers, 1974), Chapters 6, 7, 55–58, 60, 61.

GALBRAITH, J. K., *Economics and Public Purpose* (Boston: Houghton Mifflin Company, 1973), Chapters 2, 5.

PRESTON, L. E., "Corporation and Society: The Search for a Paradigm," *Journal of Economic Literature*, Vol. 13, No. 2 (June 1975), pp. 434–453.

SCOTT, B. R., "The Industrial State: Old Myths and New Realities," *Harvard Business Review*, Vol. 51, No. 2 (March–April 1973), pp. 133–148.

SOBEL, R., *The Entrepreneurs: Explorations within the American Business Tradition* (New York: Longman, Inc., 1979).

TILLES, S., "Making Strategy Explicit," in *Business Strategy*, H. Igor Ansoff, ed. (New York: Penguin Books, 1970), pp. 180–209.

QUESTIONS FOR DISCUSSION

1. What is a market? What is the difference between a market and a market segment?

2. What criteria determine whether a market should be viewed as essentially being local, regional, national, or international?

3. Try to define and identify the market for each of the following products in terms of (1) market scope (local, regional, national, international), (2) the characteristics of the buyers who make up the demand side of the market, (3) whether the demand side is comprised of several distinctive market segments, and (4) any other relevant and identifiable market characteristics:
   (a) Coca-Cola.
   (b) Textbooks in economics.
   (c) Pro football.
   (d) No-return, throwaway glass containers.
   (e) Compact cars.

4. How would you characterize the strategy of
   (a) McDonald's in the hamburger and fast-food service market?
   (b) *Playboy* in the market for sexy magazines?
   (c) Holiday Inn in the market for hotel and motel accommodations?

5. Many of the major oil companies are beginning to redefine their business from one of "oil" to one of "energy." Why would this make sense from the standpoint of the oil companies? What sort of business activities would an "energy company" be in (or be getting into) that an oil company might shy away from? From a public policy standpoint, do you think it is a good thing for oil companies to become energy companies? Why or why not?

6. What are the qualities of an entrepreneur? How is an entrepreneur different from a manager? From a corporation president? From a chairman of the board of directors?

7. Why does the concept of an entrepreneurial enterprise have questionable validity for large corporations?

THREE FOUNDATIONS OF CONSUMER DEMAND: THE CARDINAL UTILITY MODEL

In modern societies the material wants of the populace tend to be characterized by two important features: (1) diversity and (2) insatiability. Consumer wants are diverse in the sense that satisfying the biological, psychological, and cultural desires of millions of people requires an immense variety of commodities. Individual tastes vary, as do individual circumstances regarding age, education, social status, income, life-style, and so on—all of which give rise to the need for a wide and ever-changing mix of goods to meet consumer preferences. Consumer wants are insatiable in the sense that scarcely anyone is without a "want list." No sooner are some human wants partially fulfilled than additional human wants are activated or created. For instance, once the basic needs for food, shelter, and clothing are somewhat satisfied, people start thinking about acquiring more elaborate creature comforts and conveniences. In addition, new wants are regularly being created by technological advance and new product research efforts aimed at developing goods and services which consumers will find handy or desirable.

The constant gap between the human appetite for goods and services and the resource base available to produce them forces society to establish some sort of allocation system to guide production activity. Plainly enough, when society's demand for goods and services exceeds the capacity to supply them, provisions need to be made for channeling production efforts toward satisfying as many wants as possible and in some order of priority. In a capitalistically oriented society the business firm is squarely in the midst of the process of deciding *what* and *how much* to produce. As a rule, competition and the profit incentive combine to induce each firm to select from among the array of possible goods and services it might offer on the market those which it perceives will be well received in the marketplace by prospective buyers.

The process whereby a firm's product line offering becomes synchronized with consumer demand is simple enough. Each individual consumer can be reliably counted upon to spend a limited income on those goods and services deemed to be most desirable and best suited to his or her situation. Consumer expenditures are, in effect, "dollar votes" whereby priority preferences are registered in the marketplace. If the votes for an item are sufficiently attractive to firms (in terms of price and potential sales volume), some firm can be reliably counted upon to supply the item to any and all who are willing and able to buy it. When the dollar votes are viewed as insufficient (or become so as consumer tastes and preferences change), the resulting slack demand and unattractive profits act as a clear and powerful signal for firms to shift to the production of other items or face the prospect of decline. Through this market process, resources are steered out of the production of goods and services where demand is *relatively* weak and unprofitable and into the production of items where market opportunities are expected to be more rewarding.

In effect, then, how urgently consumers desire various products and services and how able they are to back up their desires with purchasing power governs the process of what and how much to produce. Unless business firms elect to synchronize their production efforts to match the purchasing behavior of consumers (the power of advertising notwithstanding), they face the penalty of unacceptable profits and perhaps even losses and eventual bankruptcy. No firm, no matter how big or how "powerful," can survive producing something consumers do not want or will not buy.[1]

It is of the essence, therefore, that a firm understand consumer behavior and the elements of consumer demand. Indeed, consumer behavior and consumer demand are integral facets of microeconomic analysis. In this chapter we shall explore the hows and whys of consumer purchases, focusing upon how consumers can maximize the satisfaction received from their incomes and upon the derivation of demand curves.

---

[1]The special genius of a capitalistically oriented economic system is its power to furnish consumers with whatever goods and services they want and in whatever amounts they are willing to buy—subject *only* to the constraint that consumers be willing to pay a price high enough to make furnishing the item profitable. Proof for this assertion is readily obtained from an attempt to compile a list of products which are technologically feasible to produce and which consumers truly want and are willing to pay a profitable price for, but which are not available to those who have the money to buy them. It is a safe wager that you (or anyone else) will come up with a *very* short list of such items and even the severest critics of the profit-oriented capitalistic system would have to acknowledge the consumer benefit of this accomplishment.

Economists developed the utility approach to the analysis of consumer demand over a century ago when it was fashionable in psychological circles to assert that much of human behavior could be explained by the desire to achieve pleasure and to avoid pain. This doctrine was quickly borrowed and applied to the sphere of consumer expenditures wherein economists, in their first systematic theory of motivated consumer behavior, held that rational consumers manage their purchases of goods and services so as to realize as much "pleasure" and as little "pain" as possible. The pleasure-pain notion was, however, recast as *utility*.

The concept of utility thus refers to the pleasure or satisfaction associated with having, using, or consuming goods and services. The utility inherent in a good derives from whatever qualities a good has that give it want-satisfying capabilities. The sources and causes of utility are legion: attractive price, esthetic beauty or design, economy of use, efficiency, quality, durability, service, guarantees, convenience of use, convenience of location, luxury, comfort, a sense of individuality, pleasure, prestige, status, pride, security, ego gratification, and power—to mention only the most obvious. Hence, utility has both objective and subjective features and, most particularly, utility is a matter of individual taste, preference, perception, personality makeup, and state of mind.

As a consequence, the utility that a good possesses or is perceived to possess is variable, not absolute. In the first place, no two people necessarily will view a good as having the same degree of want-satisfying power— one individual may derive great utility from smoking cigarettes while someone else finds them distasteful; Cadillacs may be important status symbols to some people (and hence have great utility), yet have little or no appeal to other people. Different people buy the same product for quite different reasons and motivations. Moreover, the utility of a good can vary from time to time or from place to place. Rising gasoline prices quickly modified the utility many people placed on small cars. Wool clothing does not have the same utility or want-satisfying powers for people living in tropical climates as for those living in northern climates. But irrespective of the wide variations that different individuals may place on the utility of a good or service, the utility concept offers a purposeful basis for establishing consumer preferences for what and how much they will purchase because it leads to comparisons of the amounts of satisfaction received from different consumption rates of different goods and services.

It is, of course, doubtful that the intensity of satisfaction one gains from an item can be represented by a *cardinal ranking* pattern whereby numerical values (such as 14, 84.9, or −115) are assigned to represent utility. One may say "broiled lobster is my favorite food" or "I enjoy broiled lobster more than any other seafood or meat"; but if asked "how much do you enjoy broiled lobster?", one can scarcely reply "about seventeen" and expect to convey understanding. The subjective nature of the utility concept is, however, susceptible to *ordinal ranking* measures. In ordinal preference patterns, one only has to be able to rank alternatives—from highest to lowest, best to worst, or most satisfying to least satisfying; no attempt is made to create a basis for comparing the *amount* by which one alternative is better (or worse) than others.

Despite the fact that no way currently exists to quantify utility, it is still analytically useful to assume that utility can be represented by cardinal numbers. By so doing, it is easier to highlight several important aspects of consumer behavior. We shall examine the cardinal utility approach to consumer demand in this chapter and then turn to the ordinal utility approach in Chapter 4.

TOTAL UTILITY FUNCTIONS

For illustrative purposes, assume that we can designate the amount of utility by a unit of measure called a "util." This mythical unit can be viewed as representing some arbitrary amount of satisfaction, and as such it is simply a fictional device for expressing utility in quantitative or cardinal terms.

The *total utility* which a consumer gains from a good or service may be defined as the *entire* amount of satisfaction obtained from a given amount of the item per period of time. A *total utility function* thus reflects the quantitative relationship between the satisfaction yielded by a product and its rate of consumption.[2] Total utility functions may be described in tabular form, with graphs, or with equations. Consider Table 3-1, which uses hypothetical data to illustrate the various amounts of total utility that an individual might obtain from alternative quantities of good X per period of time. As can be seen from columns 1 and 2, the more of good X consumed by the individual per period of time, the greater is his or her total utility (or total satisfaction) measured in utils, up to a consumption rate of 8 units of X. At 8 units, total utility is at its maximum value of 64 utils of satisfaction. This point is called the *saturation rate* because the consumer cannot derive any greater satisfaction from consuming more of good X per period of time. Theoretically, at this juncture, if the consumption rate was increased to 9 or 10 units, total utility would decline, perhaps because such a consumption rate would be a nuisance (having TV sets in each room of a nine-room house) or physically debilitating (eating nine milkshakes a day). The point here is that while a consumer's wants in general may be unlimited or insatiable, his or her wants for specific goods can be totally fulfilled.

A total utility curve corresponding to the information in Table 3-1 is displayed in Fig. 3-1(a). Observe that it rises at a slower and slower rate as

---

[2]The word "function" here is nothing more than a shorthand way of referring to the way in which some factors (the independent variables) affect another factor (the dependent variable). In terms of utility functions, this literally means that the total utility obtained from a commodity varies with the amount of it consumed during some specified period of time, in which case total utility is the dependent variable and the quantity consumed is the independent variable.

**Table 3-1 Relationships among Total Utility,
Marginal Utility, and the Rates of
Consumption of Good X
(hypothetical data for a hypothetical
person)**

Units of Good X Consumed per Period of Time	Total Utility (utils)	Marginal Utility (utils)
0	0	
		15
1	15	
		13
2	28	
		11
3	39	
		9
4	48	
		7
5	55	
		5
6	60	
		3
7	63	
		1
8	64	
		−1
9	63	
		−3
10	60	

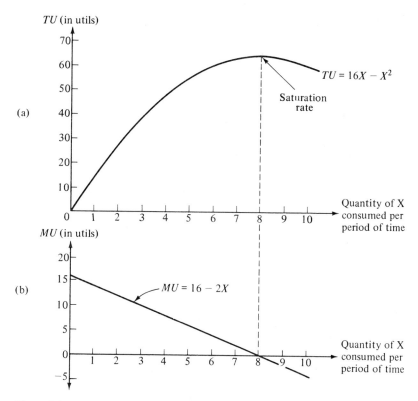

**Figure 3-1
Total and marginal utility functions for a good whose total utility
increases at a decreasing rate**

the consumption rate approaches 8 units of X, reaching a peak at 8 units (the saturation rate) and then declining. The shape of the *TU* curve implies that the more of a specific product a consumer obtains, the less anxious he will be to acquire even more because the additional units yield progressively smaller amounts of *extra* satisfaction. Eventually, the amounts of extra satisfaction diminish to zero, becoming negative thereafter.

Each such total utility function can also be expressed mathematically by an equation relating total utility to the rate of consumption. It so happens that the total utility function shown in Table 3-1 and in Fig. 3-1(a) has the equation

$$TU = 16X - X^2,$$

where *TU* represents total utility in utils and *X* represents the amount of the commodity consumed per unit of time. Hence, if the consumption rate is 5 units of X, then

$$TU = 16(5) - (5)^2 = 80 - 25 = 55 \text{ utils.}$$

Observe that the value of 55 utils corresponds exactly to the value for total utility in Table 3-1 when the rate of consumption is 5 units and, likewise, to the value of total utility in Fig. 3-1(a) at $X = 5$ units. The use of equations to represent total utility functions allows easy calculation of total utility for any consumption rate (X) in which interest may lie.

THE CONCEPT OF MARGINAL UTILITY

Marginal utility may be defined as the change in total utility resulting from a 1-unit change in the consumption of a commodity per period of time. In the case of an increase in consumption, marginal utility refers to the *extra satisfaction* obtained from the *extra* unit of consumption per period of time. In the case of a decline in consumption, marginal utility refers to the amount of the *decline* in total utility associated with the *decline* in the consumption rate. From Table 3-1 it can be seen that when the consumption rate for good X increases from 1 to 2 units, total utility rises from 15 utils to 28 utils. Thus, the marginal utility of the second unit of X is 13 utils. In like manner the remaining values for marginal utility may be computed.

During any relatively short period of time (wherein all other relevant factors can be assumed not to change), if a consumer increases his or her consumption rate of a good or service beyond some point, the marginal utility (or extra satisfaction) which is obtained from successive units becomes smaller and smaller. This phenomenon is known as the *principle of diminishing marginal utility*, and it is held to apply to virtually all individuals for virtually all goods and services. (Can you think of any exceptions?) The values for marginal utility in Table 3-1 begin to diminish at the outset so that, in the example given, the principle of diminishing marginal utility becomes operative

immediately. Each *additional* unit of X consumed per period of time gives less *extra* utility than the previous unit, thereby causing total utility to increase more slowly as the consumption rate rises. The total utility corresponding to any consumption rate can be found from the marginal utility values by calculating the cumulative marginal utility values to that point. Thus, from Table 3-1 the total utility for a consumption rate of 3 units of X equals the marginal utility of the first unit (15 utils) plus the marginal utility of the second unit (13 utils) plus the marginal utility of the third (11 utils) for a total utility of 39 utils.

The marginal utility function corresponding to the previously described total utility function can be illustrated graphically by plotting the marginal utility values given in Table 3-1. The graph of the marginal utility curve is presented in Fig. 3-1(b). In plotting the values for marginal utility from Table 3-1, it is important to note that they are plotted halfway between the two values for total utility from which they were derived. This is as it should be because the marginal utility values determined in this fashion should be representative of the *range* of consumption from which they were derived, and this is at the midpoint of that range. For the example given, the marginal utility function decreases throughout and reaches zero at the same consumption rate at which the total utility function is at its maximum height.

Actually, there is a very precise relationship between total utility functions and marginal utility functions. We shall have so frequent occasion to use these relationships, not only with reference to utility but also with reference to revenue, production, cost, and other magnitudes, that it is both advantageous and efficient to master them at this point.

Consider again the total utility function described earlier:

$$TU = 16X - X^2.$$

Using this expression, we can easily obtain the value of *TU* at any consumption rate of good X by substituting the units consumed of X into the expression and evaluating the right-hand side of the equation.

However, suppose the consumption rate of good X rises from some value X to some value $X + \Delta X$, where ΔX designates an arbitrary increase of any size. We know that total utility must necessarily *change*. Let us symbolize the change that occurs in total utility by ΔTU. Rewriting the total utility function to incorporate the effect of the increase in X to $X + \Delta X$, we have

$$TU + \Delta TU = 16(X + \Delta X) - (X + \Delta X)^2,$$
$$TU + \Delta TU = 16X + 16\Delta X - (X^2 + 2X\Delta X + \Delta X^2),$$
$$TU + \Delta TU = 16X + 16\Delta X - X^2 - 2X\Delta X - \Delta X^2.$$

The last expression above defines the new level of total utility corresponding to a consumption rate of $X + \Delta X$ units. But our major concern is really with the *change* in total utility (ΔTU) associated with the *change* (ΔX) in the consumption rate of good X. We can obtain an expression for determining just the *change* in *TU* by subtracting *TU* from the left-hand side of the equation and its equivalent of $(16X - \Delta X^2)$ from the right-hand side. This operation yields

$$
\begin{aligned}
TU + \Delta TU &= & 16X + 16\Delta X - X^2 - 2X\Delta X - \Delta X^2 \\
-TU &= & -16X \qquad\qquad\quad + X^2 \\
\hline
\Delta TU &= & 16\Delta X \qquad\quad - 2X\Delta X - \Delta X^2.
\end{aligned}
$$

We are now in a position to determine the additional utility per additional unit of good X by dividing both sides of the expression for ΔTU by ΔX:

$$
\frac{\Delta TU}{\Delta X} = \frac{16\Delta X - 2X\Delta X - \Delta X^2}{\Delta X} = 16 - 2X - \Delta X.
$$

The latter equation expresses the change in total utility per unit change in the consumption rate.[3]

Our interest lies yet beyond, however. Up to now all we have done is perform algebraic operations on our original expression of $TU = 16X - X^2$. Something a little different is called for at this point. In particular, we need to know what happens to $\Delta TU/\Delta X$ as the changes in ΔX become smaller and smaller and eventually become very close to zero. The mathematical way of pursuing this question is to determine the "limit" toward which the value of $\Delta TU/\Delta X$ moves as ΔX approaches zero; this limit is symbolized by dTU/dX.[4] Hence, if

$$
\frac{\Delta TU}{\Delta X} = 16 - 2X - \Delta X,
$$

it follows that as ΔX becomes infinitesimally small (approaches zero):

$$
\frac{dTU}{dX} = 16 - 2X.
$$

In terms of economics, the expression $dTU/dX = 16 - 2X$ is the equation for the marginal utility function corresponding to the total utility function $TU = 16X - X^2$. The symbol dTU/dX should be read as the *rate of change in total utility as the consumption rate changes*, which, in turn, is a more rigorous and accurate definition of marginal utility. In terms of differen-

---

[3]More specifically, this equation defines *average marginal utility* or the average change in total utility per unit change in the consumption rate. For example, if total utility increases by 50 utils when the consumption level rises by 10 units, then $\Delta TU/\Delta X = \frac{50}{10} = 5$ utils per unit of consumption. In other words, the average change in total utility (or average marignal utility) is 5 utils for each of the 10 additional units consumed. The concept of average marginal utility is useful whenever the available data do not permit a unit-by-unit calculation of marginal utility.

[4]This is much like asking what happens to the value of y in the expression $y = (x + 1)/x$ as the value of x approaches infinity.

tial calculus, marginal utility is "the first derivative of the total utility function." Consequently, if total utility is given by the expression

$$TU = 16X - X^2,$$

marginal utility (MU) will be given by the function

$$MU = \frac{dTU}{dX} = 16 - 2X,$$

where $16 - 2X$ is the first derivative of the expression $16X - X^2$. Thus, for
each and every total utility function, there is a corresponding marginal utility
function. Fortunately, though, as the examples below show, there is a method
for determining the marginal utility function that shortcuts the preceding
laborious derivation. (The purpose of the lengthy derivation was to illustrate
the logic of determining rates of change in variables for those readers not
familiar with elementary differential calculus.)

The *general* procedure for finding the marginal function for any variable
from the total function for that variable may be illustrated as follows: If the
total function is given by

$$T = aX^n,$$

where a and n are arbitrary constants and X is any variable, then the marginal
function is

$$M = \frac{dT}{dX} = naX^{n-1}.$$

Example 1: If $T = 16X^3$, then

$$M = \frac{dT}{dX} = 3 \cdot 16 \cdot X^{3-1} = 48X^2.$$

Example 2: If $T = 160 + 7X + 4X^2 - 2X^3$, then our general rule is applied to
each term of the expression. Algebraically, the total function may be understood to
be $T = 160X^0 + 7X^1 + 4X^2 - 2X^3$. Hence,

$$M = \frac{dT}{dX} = 0 \cdot 160X^{0-1} + 1 \cdot 7X^{1-1} + 2 \cdot 4X^{2-1} - 3 \cdot 2X^{3-1}$$

$$= \frac{dT}{dX} = 0 \cdot 160X^{-1} + 1 \cdot 7X^0 + 2 \cdot 4X^1 - 3 \cdot 2X^2$$

$$= \frac{dT}{dX} = 0 + 7 + 8X - 6X^2.$$

Note that the derivative (or rate of change) of the constant term in the total function
turns out to be zero; this is as it should be since the rate of change in a value that
is constant is necessarily zero.

Example 3: Suppose that the total function is expressed in the form of a general algebraic equation such as $T = a + bX + cX^2$, where a, b, and c are constants. Since the total function T may be rewritten as $T = aX^0 + bX^1 + cX^2$, the corresponding marginal function M is

$$M = \frac{dT}{dX} = 0 \cdot aX^{-1} + 1 \cdot bX^0 + 2 \cdot cX^1,$$

which simplifies to

$$M = b + 2cX.$$

For readers who feel uncomfortable with the mechanics of derivatives, a number of problems and answers are provided at the end of this chapter to strengthen the ability to use this essential aspect of mathematical economics.

To summarize our brief excursion into the mathematical aspects of economic relationships, the derivative of a function is the rate of change of the dependent variable as the value of the independent variable changes; the derivative of a total function *defines* the marginal function. As applied to utility functions, *marginal utility* is the rate of change in total utility as the rate of consumption of a commodity changes and is calculated mathematically by finding the first derivative of the total utility function.

To return to our original example, we have found that if $TU = 16X - X^2$, then $MU = 16 - 2X$. Knowing the expression for MU allows the value of MU to be calculated easily at any value of X. Moreover, these results may be related to both Table 3-1 and Fig. 3-1. For instance, the equation of the MU function is the exact equation which describes the graph of the marginal utility function in Fig. 3-1(b). Furthermore, we can see from Table 3-1 that the value for MU between 1 and 2 units of X is 13 units (technically, at $X = 1\frac{1}{2}$, $MU = 13$ utils); if we let X assume a value of 1.5 in the equation $MU = 16 - 2X$, we get a value of 13 utils for MU, which corresponds exactly to the value in Table 3-1.

The most significant relationship between the TU and MU functions concerns the shape of the total utility function. Defining MU as the rate of change in total utility as the rate of consumption changes is equivalent to saying that the value for marginal utility at a particular consumption rate equals the *slope of the total utility function* at that consumption rate. In other words, viewed geometrically, the derivative of the total utility function gives us the slope of the total utility function at any X value. When we say that marginal utility is 13 utils at a consumption of 1.5 units of X, we also are saying that at $X = 1.5$ total utility is increasing at a rate of 13 utils per unit of extra consumption, which is, by definition, the slope of the total utility function at the point where $X = 1.5$ units. When total utility is at its highest point, the slope of the TU curve is zero (because the tangent line drawn to the TU function at its highest point is horizontal). Since marginal utility, by definition, has a value equal to the slope of the total utility function, the value of MU corresponding to the peak of the TU function is also zero.

Using these ideas, the total utility function in Fig. 3-1(a) may be said to *increase at a decreasing rate.* Why? Because as the consumption rate increases, the *TU* function rises more slowly [i.e., its slope gets flatter (smaller)]. Consequently, the related values for *MU* must be decreasing since these values, by definition, are equal to the slope of the *TU* function. Fig. 3-1(b) illustrates just such a pattern of change in the values for marginal utility.

Alternative shapes for the *TU* and *MU* functions are shown in Fig. 3-2. In this case, *TU increases at an increasing rate* up to a consumption rate of X_1 units. From X_1 to X_2 units, *TU increases at a decreasing rate.* Point *A* on the *TU* curve is the point of diminishing marginal utility and corresponds to the same consumption rate as point *A'* on the *MU* curve. Point *B* on the *TU* curve defines the saturation rate as does point *B'* on the *MU* graph. Although there are many forms of equations which could represent a total utility function of this shape, the simplest is the general equation for a cubic function:

$$TU = a + bX + cX^2 - dX^3$$

where *X* represents the units consumed; *a*, *b*, and *c* are positive constants; and *d* is a negative constant. Using the mathematical concepts previously developed, the corresponding general equation for marginal utility is

$$MU = \frac{dTU}{dX} = b + 2cX - 3dX^2.$$

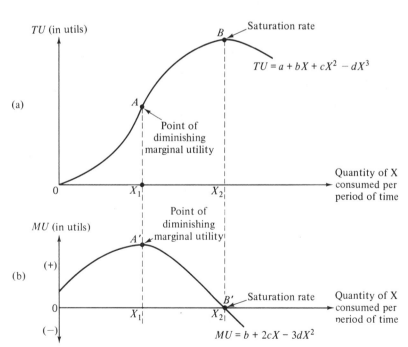

Figure 3-2
Generalized total and marginal utility functions for phases of increasing and decreasing returns as the rate of consumption rises

(Can you think of products or situations in which an individual's *TU* and *MU* functions might assume the shapes shown in Fig. 3-2?)

While the *TU* functions in Figs. 3-1 and 3-2 have shown total utility as being zero when the consumption rate is zero, this need not be the case; in fact, it may not even be typical. Negative amounts of utility (disutility) may arise from having none of an item as it is witnessed by the dismay of individuals who find themselves without aspirin when a headache appears or who run out of gas on a lonely road. In such cases the total utility function may start below the origin and not reach zero utility until the consumption of the item is well above the zero rate. Then, too, total utility functions for a nuisance or unwanted item may originate at a positive value, and *decrease* rapidly as more of the item comes into the possession of the consumer.

MATHEMATICAL CAPSULE 1

DETERMINING THE POINT OF DIMINISHING MARGINAL UTILITY AND THE SATURATION RATE: AN APPLICATION OF THE MATHEMATICAL CONCEPTS OF MAXIMA AND MINIMA

A maximum point on a curve is a point that is higher than its neighboring point to either side such that the curve is concave downward; a minimum point on a curve is a point that is lower than its neighboring points such that the curve is concave upward.

All maximum and minimum values of a function $y = f(x)$ occur where $dy/dx = 0$, since the first derivative of a function is indicative of

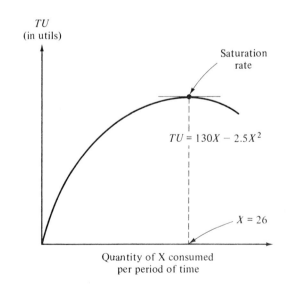

TU
(in utils)

Saturation rate

$TU = 130X - 2.5X^2$

$X = 26$

Quantity of X consumed
per period of time

its rate of change or slope. This characteristic is frequently termed the *first-order* condition.

If, at the value of x at which $dy/dx = 0$, the second derivative is negative, $d^2y/dx^2 < 0$, that value of x defines a maximum value for y, where $y = f(x)$. If at the value of x at which $dy/dx = 0$ the second derivative is positive, $d^2y/dx^2 > 0$, that value of x defines a minimum value for function $y = f(x)$. This requirement for distinguishing between maximum and minimum values is called the *second-order* condition.

Consider the total utility function $TU = 130X - 2.5X^2$, plotted in the accompanying graph. Suppose that we wish to determine the value of X at which TU is maximum—the saturation rate. The saturation rate corresponds exactly to that quantity consumed at which the slope of the total utility function is zero and where $MU = 0$. If $TU = 130X - 2.5X^2$, then $MU = dTU/dx = 130 - 5X$. Setting the marginal utility function equal to zero, we get

$$130 - 5X = 0.$$

Solving for the value of X which satisfies the equation, we find $X = 26$ units. This, then, is the consumption rate where TU is maximum.

Suppose that we wish to find the consumption rate of X at which diminishing MU is encountered for the total utility function presented below:

$$TU = 18X + 7X^2 - \tfrac{1}{3}X^3.$$

Diminishing MU begins at the point where the MU function is at its

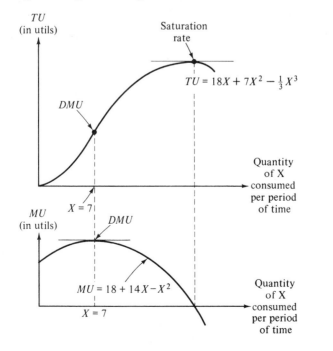

TU
(in utils)

Saturation rate

$TU = 18X + 7X^2 - \frac{1}{3}X^3$

DMU

Quantity of X consumed per period of time

$X = 7$

MU
(in utils)

DMU

$MU = 18 + 14X - X^2$

Quantity of X consumed per period of time

$X = 7$

maximum value. The value of X at which the slope of the MU function is zero $(dMU/dX = d^2TU/dX^2 = 0)$ can be calculated as follows:

$$MU = \frac{dTU}{dX} = 18 + 14X - X^2$$

$$\frac{dMU}{dX} = \frac{d^2TU}{dX^2} = 14 - 2X.$$

Setting dMU/dX equal to zero and solving for X, we obtain $X = 7$, the consumption rate at which diminishing MU sets in.

Exercise

1. Determine the saturation rate and the point of diminishing marginal utility for each of the following TU functions.
   (a) $TU = 36X - X^2$.
   (b) $TU = 10X + 9X^2 - X^3$.

Utility Functions for Related Products

In many instances it is clear that the utility people obtain from one product is related to their consumption of another product. The utility derived from eating cornflakes is partially dependent on the availability of milk or cream; the satisfaction from one's automobile is related to the quantity of gasoline it uses; the enjoyment from one's binoculars is related to the frequency with which one goes to spectator events. Thus, while total utility is a function of the quantities of each product consumed per period of time, it need not be simply the sum of the utilities gained separately from each good or service.

When the satisfaction derived from one item hinges in part upon the amounts consumed of other items, the more appropriate concept of utility is that of a *total utility surface* relating total utility to the *joint rates* of consumption of all goods simultaneously. This notion is illustrated graphically for two products, X and Y, in Fig. 3-3. The consumption rates for X and Y define a horizontal plane with total utility measured as a vertical distance above it. The total utility surface is $OIKB$. If Y_1 units of product Y are consumed per unit of time along with X_1 units of product X, total utility is DD'; if the respective consumption rates are Y_2 and X_1 per period of time, total utility is GG'. The total utility surface pictured in Fig. 3-3 thus indicates how total utility changes as the rate of consumption of one product changes, given the rate of consumption of the other. The shape of the total utility surface depends upon the nature of the interrelationship among the products. In Fig. 3-3, total utility is shown as increasing at an increasing rate for a few units before diminishing marginal utility sets in, thereby making the total utility surface concave upward for this range of consumption; the surface becomes concave downward as diminishing marginal utility is realized. If diminishing marginal utility occurred from the outset for both X and Y, the total utility surface would be concave downward throughout.

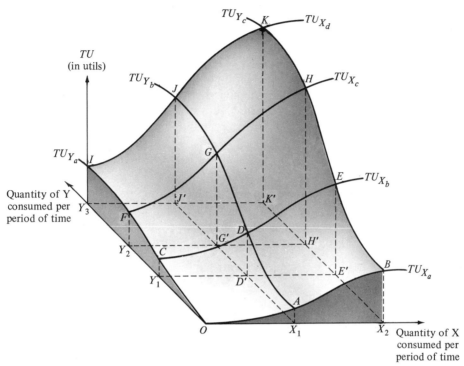

Figure 3-3
Total utility surface for a pair of products characterized by both increasing and decreasing marginal utility

MATHEMATICAL CAPSULE 2

DETERMINING MARGINAL UTILITY FOR MULTIPRODUCT TOTAL UTILITY FUNCTIONS

When the satisfaction derived from one product is related to the amounts consumed of other products, the consumer's total utility function is of the form

$$TU = f(X_a, X_b, \ldots, X_n),$$

where $X_a, X_b, \ldots, X_n$ represent the array of products available. Given such multiproduct *TU* functions, one is often called to examine the effect of a change in the consumption rate of one product upon *TU*, when the consumption rates of other products do not change. The form of the derivative which corresponds to this interest is called the *partial derivative*.

Suppose that the total utility function for two products X and Y is

$$TU = 7X + 4Y - 0.2X^2 - 0.3Y^2 - XY.$$

We can find the impact of a change in the rate of consumption of X upon *TU* when the consumption of Y is kept fixed *by treating Y as a constant* and differentiating the total utility function with respect to X—this gives the partial derivative of *TU* with respect to X and is denoted by $\partial TU/\partial X$. Accordingly, we get

$$\frac{\partial TU}{\partial X} = 7 - 0.4X - Y,$$

which may be interpreted to represent *the rate of change in TU as the rate of consumption of X changes, the rate of consumption of Y being held constant.* This then is the expression for the marginal utility of product X. Similarly, the partial derivative of *TU* with respect to Y is

$$\frac{\partial TU}{\partial Y} = 4 - 0.6Y - X.$$

and it represents the expression for the marginal utility of *Y*.

Exercises

1. Determine the relevant marginal utility functions for each of the following total utility functions.
   (a) $TU = 15X^2Y^2 - X^3Y^2$.
   (b) $TU = 20X + 40Y - 3X^2 - Y^2$.
   (c) $TU = 30XY + 10XZ - 3XYZ - 10Z$.
   (d) $TU = 5.4X^{1/2}Y^{1/3}$.
2. Determine the values for MU_x and MU_y at $X = 5$ and $Y = 3$ in each of the following total utility functions.
   (a) $TU = 16X - X^2 + 10Y - XY$.
   (b) $TU = 33X + 2X^2 - X^3 + 4Y - XY^2$.
   (c) $TU = 16X^2 + 15XY + 17Y^2 - 4X^2Y^2$.

CONSUMER BEHAVIOR IN THE MARKETPLACE

Once a consumer's utility functions are known or ascertainable, it is possible to make judgments about how he or she will act in the marketplace. In approaching the whys and hows of consumer demand, economists assume that rational consumers *attempt* to arrange their purchases so as to *maximize* the total satisfaction that they can get from their money incomes. After all, consumers have no reason to deliberately try to get less than the full obtainable satisfaction from the purchasing power they have available. In reality, of course, the assumption of maximizing utility may not be literally true, at least for all consumers in each and every situation. Imperfect information about alternative purchases and about prices tends to hinder consumer attempts at utility maximization, and an exhaustive search for better information may cost more than it is worth. In addition, impulse buying and force of habit work against consumers actually identifying and purchasing the utility-maximizing combination of goods and services. Nonetheless, the assumption that consumers behave as if they seek to maximize total utility is a justifiable and reasonable abstraction for most consumers most of the time.

Confronted with a limited number of dollars to spend, the price tags on every item, thousands of items to choose among, and imperfect knowledge as to all alternatives, a consumer's task of trying to get the most for his or her money is indeed complex. Obviously, consumers cannot buy everything they want because each purchase exhausts a portion of their available money incomes. They are forced to compromise and decide what and how much of each of the many commodities within their income constraints best suit their needs and tastes. A word about the income constraint facing consumers is in order. As used here, a consumer's money income refers to the total amount of purchasing power available for spending in a given time period; this specifically includes (1) current income from whatever source, (2) any savings the consumer has accumulated from past income periods, (3) any sums the consumer wishes and is able to borrow, and (4) any other wealth the consumer may wish to allocate to current consumption.

Some Simplifying Assumptions

To keep the ensuing analysis of consumer behavior manageable, the following assumptions will be made:

1. Each consumer has full knowledge of all information pertinent to his or her expenditure decision—a definitive set of tastes and preferences, knowledge of the goods and services available, their capacity to satisfy his wants, his money income, and the prices at which specific products can be bought.
2. The consumer's preference pattern for products is one of diminishing marginal utility for each.[5]
3. The utility function for each product is independent of the rate of consumption of other products.

None of these assumptions do violence to the principles of consumer behavior we wish to derive and they make the exposition simpler.

---

[5]Actually, this is a more rigorous assumption than need be made. All we need assume is that the marginal utility of one good decreases *relative* to the marginal utilities of other goods as its consumption rate is increased *relative* to the consumption rate of others. Our analysis will be valid in cases where the marginal utility of a good is increasing, as long as it increases by less than proportionally to the marginal utilities of other goods.

Maximization of Utility

For the time being, suppose that we restrict ourselves to the case of a consumer who is trying to decide what combination of two goods, X and Y, should be purchased with a weekly income of $40. We shall assume that the price of X remains at $3 per unit and the price of Y remains at $5 per unit no matter how much the consumer buys of X and Y. Table 3-2 summarizes the consumer's preference for the two items, along with the consumer's evaluation of the utility obtained from not spending the money, that is, the *marginal utility of saving.*[6]

How should the consumer allocate a $40 weekly income among buying good X, buying good Y, and saving in order to yield maximum satisfaction? To answer this question, let us proceed to ascertain what the consumer should do first. A $40 weekly income allows the consumer to buy some of either X or Y should the consumer decide to do so. If $3 is spent to buy the first unit of X, the consumer receives 54 utils of satisfaction; if $5 is spent to buy the first unit of Y, the consumer receives 75 utils; and if the consumer saves all $40, he or she is well past the saturation rate for money, since the marginal utility for saving a dollar becomes negative when saving exceeds $5. Of these alternatives, the purchase of X is definitely the better bargain, because it gives the consumer 18 utils of satisfaction *per dollar spent*, whereas good Y yields only 15 utils of satisfaction per dollar spent, and saving yields no greater than 9 utils per dollar saved. The proper decision variable in this instance is neither total nor marginal utility, but *marginal utility per dollar of expenditure.* It is the best indicator of value received as it combines the factor of satisfaction with the factor of cost, and both factors are requisite for valid comparisons between goods. Since the consumer receives more satisfaction for the money by buying the first unit of X instead of the first unit of Y or instead of saving, the first act should be to exchange $3 for one unit of good X. By the same reasoning, the consumer's second act can be determined. The second unit of good X will produce 14 units of satisfaction per dollar spent, as will the first of Y; both are superior to saving at this point. Since the consumer has ample funds available for spending ($37 of the original $40), the second and third acts should be to buy the second unit of X and the first unit of Y, leaving the consumer with $29. At each step a consumer must decide whether the marginal utility of a dollar's worth of spending is greater than the marginal utility of a dollar's worth of saving. If it is, the consumer should buy the good yielding the highest marginal utility per dollar of expenditure. If not, the consumer should save the money. In the example

[6]The term "saving" is used here to encompass a variety of acts associated with not spending. Consumers may rationally decide not to spend all of their money income during some period of time because (1) they place a high value on saving a portion of their income in order to provide for emergencies, accumulate an estate, or any one of a hundred other reasons; (2) they are unable to find products precisely suited to their tastes and wish to look further before making a purchase; and (3) they wish to postpone spending until some future period so that they may pay cash for the desired items. In any event, the act of not spending (i.e., saving) may bring the consumer satisfaction or utility just as does the act of consuming goods and services.

given, the consumer will maximize total utility by allocating the $40 income so as to purchase 4 units of X and 5 units of Y and to save $3.

Table 3-2   Utility-Maximizing Combination of Goods X and Y Obtainable from an Income of $40

	GOOD X (Price = $3)				GOOD Y (Price = $5)			SAVING		
Quantity	TU (utils)	MU (utils)	MU/Price (utils/$)	Quantity	TU (utils)	MU (utils)	MU/Price (utils/$)	Number of Dollars Saved	TU (utils)	MU (utils/$1)
0	0			0	0			0	10	
		54	18			75	15			9
1	54			1	75			1	19	
		45	15			60	12			7
2	99			2	135			2	26	
		30	10			40	8			3
3	129			3	175			3	29	
		9	3			25	5			2
4	138			4	200			4	31	
		3	1			15	3			1
5	141			5	215			5	32	
		−3	−1			5	1			0
6	138			6	220			6	32	

No other allocation of the consumer's $40 weekly income will produce as much satisfaction as this one. How do we know? Suppose that our consumer were to buy one less unit of good Y, thereby freeing $5 with which to buy another unit of X and to save an additional $2. This act would reduce total utility. Giving up the fifth unit of Y entails a loss of 15 utils, whereas increasing the purchase rate of X from 4 to 5 units brings 3 utils, and saving two more dollars yields a combined 3 utils, for a total gain of 6 utils from the alternative expenditure of the $5. The consumer would therefore suffer a net loss of 9 utils of satisfaction by transferring dollars out of the purchase of Y and into X and saving. Alternatively, were our consumer to take the $3 saving and apply it to the purchase of the fifth unit of X, he or she would give up 19 utils of satisfaction and acquire only 3 utils of satisfaction, for a net loss in satisfaction of 16 utils. Any act other than buying 4 units of X and 5 units of Y and saving $3 will cause total utility to decline.

Observe carefully the characteristics of the utility-maximizing act. First, the consumer completely utilizes all available purchasing power—all income is allocated either to the purchase of commodities or to saving. There are no idle dollars; the dollars that are saved are constructively deployed every bit as much as are the dollars used for purchasing X and Y—since saving money produces utility. Thus, maximization of utility *does not require* that a consumer spend *all* his or her money—saving has utility and serves to further the motives of the consumer. Second, at the utility-maximizing combination the marginal utilities per dollar spent on the last unit of each item purchased are equal. In other words, the consumer has arranged his or her purchases to get an equivalent amount of satisfaction from the last dollar allocated to each item (including saving) bought.

The Conditions for Utility Maximization

We are now in a position to state the formal conditions for consumer maximization of utility in a multicommodity environment. Two equations will suffice:

$$P_a X_a + P_b X_b + P_c X_c + \cdots + P_n X_n + \text{saving} = \text{income}, \qquad (1)$$

$$\frac{MU_{X_a}}{P_a} = \frac{MU_{X_b}}{P_b} = \frac{MU_{X_c}}{P_c} = \cdots = \frac{MU_{X_n}}{P_n} = MU_{\text{saving}}. \qquad (2)$$

Equation (1) says that the sum of the expenditures on each commodity $(X_a, X_b, X_c, \ldots, X_n)$ plus saving must be equal to the money income (I) that the consumer has available per period of time. Total expenditures cannot *exceed* the available purchasing power; any income that is not used to buy goods and services necessarily is saved. Thus, all the consumer's money income is accounted for by either spending or saving. Equation (2) says that to maximize total utility the consumer must arrange purchases such that the marginal utilities per dollar of expenditure on the last unit of each item purchased are equal to each other and to the marginal utility of saving an additional dollar.

When the various degrees of satisfaction per dollar of marginal outlays are unequal, total satisfaction may be increased by diminishing expenditures for goods where satisfaction is less and enlarging expenditures for goods where satisfaction is greater. To illustrate, suppose that

$$MU_{X_a} = 42 \text{ utils for the last unit purchased,}$$

$$P_a = \$14 \text{ per unit,}$$

$$MU_{X_b} = 60 \text{ utils for the last unit purchased,}$$

$$P_b = \$12 \text{ per unit, and}$$

$$MU_{\text{saving}} = 4 \text{ utils for each additional dollar saved.}$$

Then,

$$MU_{X_a}/\$ \text{ spent on } X_a = MU_{X_a}/P_a = 42 \text{ utils}/\$14 = 3 \text{ utils}/\$, \text{ and}$$

$$MU_{X_b}/\$ \text{ spent on } X_b = MU_{X_a}/P_b = 60 \text{ utils}/\$12 = 5 \text{ utils}/\$.$$

The consumer is realizing more satisfaction per dollar spent on X_b than on X_b. Total utility can be increased by transferring dollars out of the purchase of X_a and into the purchase of X_b until $MU_{X_a}/P_a = MU_{X_b}/P_b = MU_{\text{saving}}$. By reducing the expenditure for X_a, the MU of the last unit purchased of X_a would rise (say to 56 utils), thus raising the ratio MU_{X_a}/P_a (to 4 utils per dollar). By increasing the expenditure for X_b, the MU of the last unit purchased would fall (say to 48 utils), thereby lowering the ratio MU_{X_b}/P_b (to 4 utils per dollar). Since X_a costs \$14 and X_b costs \$12, buying 1 unit less of X_a and 1 unit more of X_b would leave \$2 left over either for the purchase of some other item whose $MU/\$$ of expenditure exceeded 4 utils per dollar or for saving.

Sometimes the indivisibility of units of products can preclude the consumer from *exactly* equating the marginal utilities per dollar spent on the last unit for each and every item. For example, in the case above the consumer might find that there are no other goods which could be bought for \$2 and receive as much as 3.5 utils per dollar; saving the entire \$2 might reduce the MU of the last dollar saved to 3.8 utils. Then Eq. (2) could not be precisely satisfied unless fractional units of X_a and X_b could be bought. Practically speaking, Eq. (2) should be interpreted to mean that a consumer seeking maximum utility from a given money income should spend his or her dollars so as to approach *as nearly as possible* the equality of the marginal utilities per dollar spent on the last unit of each good purchased and further to approach as nearly as possible the point at which the marginal utility of spending a dollar equals the marginal utility of saving a dollar.

It follows from the utility-maximizing condition of

$$\frac{MU_{X_a}}{P_{X_a}} = \frac{MU_{X_b}}{P_{X_b}} = \cdots = \frac{MU_{X_n}}{P_{X_n}}$$

that if the price of a product falls, *other things remaining equal*, a consumer will be induced to buy more of the product. For example, if P_{X_a} declines, the ratio MU_{X_a}/P_{X_a} becomes a larger value than the other ratios ($MU_{X_b}/P_{X_b}, \ldots,$ MU_{X_n}/P_{X_n}). To restore the utility-maximizing condition, the consumer will find it desirable to increase the quantity purchased of item X_a. Conversely, if the price of an item rises (whether it be P_{X_a} or P_{X_b} or $\cdots$ or P_{X_n}), the quantity purchased of that item will tend to fall—all other relevant demand-determining factors remaining equal. This is the basis for the *Law of Demand*, which, simply stated, holds that the price of a product and the quantity purchased of that product vary *inversely* with one another.

MATHEMATICAL CAPSULE 3

DETERMINATION OF THE UTILITY-MAXIMIZING COMBINATION OF PRODUCTS SUBJECT TO AN INCOME CONSTRAINT

Let $P_a, P_b, P_c, \ldots, P_n$ be the prices of products $X_a, X_b, X_c, \ldots,$ X_n, I be a consumer's money income, and $TU = f(X_a, X_b, X_c, \ldots, X_n)$ be the consumer's utility function for n products which the consumer wishes to maximize subject to his or her income constraint

$$I = P_a X_a + P_b X_b + P_c X_c + \cdots + P_n X_n, \tag{1}$$

where saving here is treated as simply one kind of product. To find the utility-maximizing combination of products, a new function is generated which combines the *TU* function to be maximized and the constraint equation. To keep the solution determinate (as many equations as there are unknowns), an artificial unknown, called a *LaGrange multiplier*, is introduced, giving

$$Z = f(X_a, X_b, X_c, \ldots, X_n) \\ + \lambda(I - P_a X_a - P_b X_b - P_c X_c - \cdots - P_n X_n), \tag{2}$$

where λ is the LaGrange multiplier. The partial derivatives of Z are found for each variable and equated to zero to establish the first-order conditions:

$$\frac{\partial Z}{\partial X_a} = \frac{\partial TU}{\partial X_a} - \lambda P_a = 0, \tag{3}$$

$$\frac{\partial Z}{\partial X_b} = \frac{\partial TU}{\partial X_b} - \lambda P_b = 0, \tag{4}$$

$$\frac{\partial Z}{\partial X_c} = \frac{\partial TU}{\partial X_c} - \lambda P_c = 0, \tag{5}$$

$$\vdots$$

$$\frac{\partial Z}{\partial X_n} = \frac{\partial TU}{\partial X_n} - \lambda P_n = 0, \tag{6}$$

$$\frac{\partial Z}{\partial \lambda} = I - P_a X_a - P_b X_b - P_c X_c - \cdots - P_n X_n = 0. \tag{7}$$

These equations may be solved simultaneously to determine the utility-maximizing purchase levels for $X_a, X_b, X_c, \ldots, X_n$. From Eqs. (3) through (6), it is seen that

$$\frac{\partial TU/\partial X_a}{P_a} = \frac{\partial TU/\partial X_b}{P_b} = \frac{\partial TU/\partial X_c}{P_c} = \cdots = \frac{\partial TU/\partial X_n}{P_n}. \tag{8}$$

The terms $\partial TU/\partial X_a, \partial TU/\partial X_b, \partial TU/\partial X_c, \ldots, \partial TU/\partial X_n$ really are $MU_{X_a}, MU_{X_b}, MU_{X_c}, \ldots, MU_{X_n}$, and the value of λ necessarily is equal to the marginal utility of saving. Thus, Eq. (8) translates into

$$MU_{\text{saving}} = \frac{MU_{X_a}}{P_a} = \frac{MU_{X_b}}{P_b} = \frac{MU_{X_c}}{P_c} = \cdots = \frac{MU_{X_n}}{P_n}, \tag{9}$$

which we know to be a necessary condition for consumer maximization of total utility. As an example of the foregoing, suppose that we find the utility-maximizing consumption rate for two products X and Y if the total utility function is

$$TU = 10X + 24Y - 0.5X^2 - 0.5Y^2$$

and if $P_x = \$2$, $P_y = \$6$, and $I = \$44$. Then we have

$$Z = 10X + 24Y - 0.5X^2 - 0.5Y^2 + \lambda(44 - 2X - 6Y),$$

$$\frac{\partial Z}{\partial X} = 10 - X - 2\lambda = 0,$$

$$\frac{\partial Z}{\partial Y} = 24 - Y - 6\lambda = 0,$$

$$\frac{\partial Z}{\partial \lambda} = 44 - 2X - 6Y = 0.$$

Solving $\partial Z/\partial X$, $\partial Z/\partial Y$, and $\partial Z/\partial \lambda$ simultaneously yields $X = 4$, $Y = 6$, and $\lambda = 3$.

Exercise

1. Determine the utility-maximizing combination of X and Y when
   (a) $TU = 15X + 22Y - 4XY$,   (b) $TU = 17X + 20Y - 2X^2 - Y^2$,
       $P_x = \$3$, $P_x = \$3$,
       $P_y = \$6$, $P_y = \$4$,
       $I = \$30$. $I = \$22$.

Evaluation of the Maximizing Rules

Since the foregoing discussion may seem rather formal and abstract, it is fair to ask: How realistic is this description of a consumer's disposition of income, especially considering the fact that most consumers have never heard of the conditions for utility maximization? Does the utility model meet the scientific standards of *explaining* and *predicting* real-world consumer behavior?

Basically, the answers to these two questions are "yes." The conditions for utility maximization are not as far removed from the purchase decisions of consumers as one might think at first glance. Whenever a consumer goes shopping and considers the purchase of a specific item, normally he or she will wonder (consciously or unconsciously) whether the price to be paid is "worth it." If the answer is favorable, he or she can be expected to buy the item, assuming the money is available. If the consumer decides the item is not worth the price, then he or she can be expected not to purchase it and to shop around elsewhere. Translated into the language of utility theory, this mental process is equivalent to deciding whether the $MU/\$$ from consuming the item is greater than the $MU/\$$ of buying some other commodity. If so, the consumer purchases the item; if $MU/\$$ is less, the consumer elects not to buy the item; and if equality between the two prevails, the consumer is indifferent and may rationally decide to buy or not to buy.

Furthermore, it is quite reasonable to expect consumers to continue to spend their income as long as they believe the extra satisfaction that they will get from a commodity exceeds the satisfaction of keeping their money. Only when consumers believe that they will obtain more satisfaction from a dollar's worth of saving than they will from a dollar's worth of spending will saving be induced.

Viewed from this perspective, our model of consumer behavior should be more persuasive, serving at least as a plausible initial approximation. Of course, several factors operate to prevent consumers from realizing the utmost satisfaction from their money incomes. The most important obstacle is a lack of accurate information about the prices charged by various sellers and about product quality.[7] Consumers often pay more for an item at one store than is charged by another store nearby because they are unaware of the price differential. Sometimes they buy products that turn out to be less satisfactory than originally anticipated, perhaps because they mistakenly used price as a surrogate indicator of product quality or because quality was difficult to judge. In these ways they exhaust a larger share of their income than otherwise would have been the case had perfect knowledge existed. On other occasions they buy impulsively, through force of habit, out of brand loyalty, a desire for variety, or just plain curiosity. And on still other occasions, they may be unduly influenced by the appeals and nuances of advertising, brand reputation, and emotion.

One of the most serious objections to the utility model concerns the postulate that the consumer's behavior consists of a steady flow of rational calculations whereby individuals systematically consider all the various conceivable purchase combinations, evaluate the utility attached to each, and then choose the package with the greatest utility. Many observers contend that this view is both oversimplified and inaccurate. Specifically, habit, loyalty, whim, impulse, inertia, and reluctance to change are held to be normal attributes of consumer behavior which invalidate the view of the consumer as a "rational economic person." Consider, for example, the consumer's purchase of groceries, gasoline, cigarettes, and personal-care items. They do not cost much per item; they are purchased frequently; they are available in many stores and locations; they are bought without great forethought and consultation. There is, therefore, recurring opportunity to

[7]However, it must be recognized that there are costs to consumers from searching out more accurate information. The time and expense involved in comparing the many types and features of products and in shopping around for the best buy may outweigh the associated benefits. Thus, to be completely rational, consumers should balance the costs of acquiring better information against the extra satisfaction they gain from having it.

repeat the same behavior often and develop buying habits and brand preferences. Moreover, the small expense involved in each purchase may create the feeling that what is bought and when it is bought is of no great consequence, thus dampening the concern that a significant decision problem exists and that alternatives ought to be carefully evaluated.

And when different brands of the same item are viewed as essentially identical, there is an even greater tendency to make purchase a function of habit and convenience. Information seeking may go no further than scanning newspaper ads for sales and discounts and adjusting one's shopping plans accordingly. Nonetheless, weighing alternatives to buy again what has proved satisfactory in the past may, indeed, represent the simplest way to overcome the anxiety of "did I buy the right thing?" and "did I pay more than I should have?" Consumers would find it neither practical nor rewarding to repeatedly weigh alternatives; discuss and consult with family, friends, and dealers; shop around; seek out information on competing brands and substitutes; and exhibit concern with price every time they repurchase common household items. Hence, reliance upon previous experience with a brand, store loyalty, and advertising may be more "rational" than "irrational," and, as studies have shown, such loyalties and preferences seldom last long when conditions change or dissatisfaction arises.

In addition to the consumers' past experience with particular goods, brands, and stores, such personal factors as the consumers' ego needs, their emotion-colored images of goods, brands, and stores, their desire for conformity and assurance that they are doing the right thing, and their reactions (conscious or subconscious) to on-the-scene factors such as eye appeal, packaging, displays, and store layout all play a role in what they buy and what they do not. Another set of influential factors includes urgent need for an article, the notion that one has a unique opportunity to get an unusually good deal, and satisfaction with other products of the same company.

Granted that these influences exist and that they have a real impact on consumer decision making, does it follow that consumers are often "irrational" and have little interest in or capability for careful, deliberate utility maximization? Or that the consumer's perceptions of utility do not embrace these influences—at least partially? If at the instant of making a purchase decision, the consumer's actions appear to be the best or most satisfying expenditure of his or her income under the circumstances, then the consumer may be said to be rationally endeavoring to maximize utility. Certainly, there is ample reason to presume that if—at the instant of decision—the consumer knew how to spend his or her money to acquire more utility per dollar spent, he or she would do so. This is enough to give the utility model validity, even though the model, admittedly, does not reveal many of the specific factors underlying the consumer's perceptions and motivations. But significantly, there is, to date, no other tested and validated model of consumer decision which is capable of predicting and explaining detailed facets of consumer behavior—despite diligent research efforts to develop more explicit models.

CONSUMER SOVEREIGNTY IN THE MARKETPLACE: FICTION OR REALITY?[8]

The discussion above implies that the worst "enemy" of consumers in attempting to maximize the satisfaction from a limited money income is their own ignorance or irrationality. Even so, consumers are still viewed as possessing the full initiative in buying goods and services. They are assumed to respond only to wants that they originate or needs which are given to them by their environment. They are, above all, independent, and their purchasing behavior in the marketplace instructs producers as to what they want to buy; ultimately, therefore, all power over what and how much is produced is held to lie with consumers—this is what is meant by *consumer sovereignty*.

Obviously, this overstates the situation *somewhat*. Much product differentiation, advertising, and marketing strategy is designed expressly to modify individual preferences and to bend consumer demand toward the product offering of individual firms. To deny that these have any effect is untenable, and any model of consumer behavior that fails to acknowledge the role of the marketer, and, in particular, advertising is sorely lacking in its accounting for real-world purchasing patterns. The attempt to control or manage consumer demand is, in fact, a vast and sophisticated industry in its own right.

Two polar types of advertising and sales promotion strategy may be distinguished: that which is purely informational and that which is purely persuasive. Most advertising strategy incorporates both features and is therefore not pure in either sense. The persuasive type of advertising is of primary concern here.

The significance of persuasive advertising for the study of consumer behavior is that it permits sellers to try to bend consumer tastes and preferences to their own advantage. To the extent that persuasive advertising is successful toward this end, consumer behavior is not purely a response of consumers to their utility schedules. To illustrate: If an individual's satisfaction is less from additional expenditures on soft drinks than on ice cream, this can be just as well "corrected" by a change in the sales strategy of Coca-Cola as by the consumer's increasing his or her expenditures on ice cream. In terms of our utility model, when

$$\frac{MU_{\text{soft drinks}}}{P_{\text{soft drinks}}} < \frac{MU_{\text{ice cream}}}{P_{\text{ice cream}}},$$

either of two acts can restore the equality requisite for consumer equilibrium. The consumer can transfer dollars out of the purchase of soft drinks and into the purchase of ice cream, or the soft drink manufacturers can attempt to revise upward the consumer's marginal utility for soft drinks by means of a more persuasive advertising and sales strategy. Indeed, a major purpose of advertising is to shift the consumer's utility function for the item upward such that he or she will have a more intense desire for it, thereby becoming

[8] The material in this section draws heavily from the ideas expressed by John Kenneth Galbraith in *The New Industrial State* (Boston: Houghton Mifflin Company, 1967), Chapters 18–20.

willing to buy more of it at a given price or else becoming willing to pay a higher price for the same amount currently being purchased.

Consumers, of course, have it well within their powers to reject persuasion. Enough consumers, by their refusal to continue to purchase items they consider unsatisfactory, can force accommodation by producers. Not even cleverly advertised products can survive when consumers find them seriously deficient. The notion of the gullible consumer, naked in the jungle of the marketplace and at the mercy of unscrupulous and misleading advertisements, is greatly exaggerated. Still, it is clear that advertising does influence consumer purchases; it can intensify consumer desire for a commodity to a point where the perceived marginal utility per dollar of expenditure becomes high enough to induce some consumers to buy the item. The public interest and the concept of consumer sovereignty are, therefore, better served by the elimination of deceitful or misleading advertising practices.

APPLICATIONS CAPSULE

HOW ADVERTISING CAN INFLUENCE CONSUMER DEMAND

Mrs. Wilson enjoys drinking freshly perked coffee made from ground coffee beans. She takes more than a normal amount of pride in making a good cup of coffee both for herself and her husband. However, Mrs. Wilson is familiar with both regular grind and instant coffee, although she is much more knowledgeable about regular coffee than instant because of her preferences for freshly ground perked coffee. Nonetheless, Mrs. Wilson does buy instant coffee occasionally because her widowed mother-in-law prefers the convenience of instant to regular coffee.

Over the years Mrs. Wilson has bought three brands of regular coffee: Maxwell House, Folger's, and Yuban. She has a very strong preference for Maxwell House, but she does buy Folger's and Yuban occasionally when they are on sale or if the store where she shops happens to be out of Maxwell House. Mrs. Wilson's strong preference for Maxwell House is based upon Maxwell House's ability to satisfy her criteria of strength, flavor, aroma, and economy. Mrs. Willson is very confident about her preference for Maxwell House because she is quite certain of her evaluations of the other brands she has tried.

One day, while watching television, Mrs. Wilson saw a television commercial from Nestlé introducing Taster's Choice freeze-dried coffee. The commercial described what freeze-dried coffee meant and how it combined the flavor of regular coffee with the convenience of instant coffee. Although she usually ignores most commercials, Mrs. Wilson paid attention to this particular one. In fact, she stopped what she was doing and watched the commercial intensely. Mrs. Wilson was exposed to the following bits of information: (1) Taster's Choice is a totally new kind of coffee, (2) made from a freeze-dry process, (3) that has the flvor and taste of regular coffee, (4) but appears and is used like instant coffee. This information led Mrs. Wilson to conclude that Taster's Choice was a new brand of instant coffee, perhaps better in taste than most other coffees, because it is manufactured by a new process. Nonetheless, Mrs. Wilson viewed what she heard about the freeze-dry concept with some skepticism and ambiguity. She was still convinced that she preferred regular coffee to instant coffee and decided the information about Taster's Choice was not relevant to her.

A few days later Mrs. Wilson was exposed to the same commercial. This time, she did not pay full attention, but she did listen and watch it. At the end, she concluded with greater firmness that Taster's Choice was a new brand of instant coffee, perhaps with improved taste over other instant coffees because of the new process.

The following week, Mrs. Wilson received a sample jar of Taster's Choice in the mail. While she probably would not have bought it, the free sample generated enough motivation and curiosity for her to try a cup. Mrs. Wilson was surprised to find that Taster's Choice was similar to regular coffee in taste, flavor, and aroma. Her mother-in-law, who happened to be visiting, also praised it as being better than her regular brand of instant coffee. With satisfaction, Mrs. Wilson reevaluated her attitude toward Taster's Choice and concluded that it was the most preferred brand of *instant* coffee.

When she went to her Wednesday afternoon bridge club she mentioned Taster's Choice to her friends, trying to find out how they perceived it and whether they had tried it at all. Then, a few days later, she served Taster's Choice to her husband. He, too, liked the taste and praised it. Several of Mrs. Wilson's friends also indicated that they considered it a good product. Mrs. Wilson then began to have such a high opinion of Taster's Choice that she seriously considered it as a replacement for Maxwell House regular coffee. When her sample jar of Taster's Choice was exhausted, she bought another jar to replace it.

Questions for Discussion

1. Do you think Mrs. Wilson was inappropriately influenced by the television commercial to purchase Taster's Choice?
2. How important was advertising in reshaping Mrs. Wilson's preference for Taster's Choice as opposed to Maxwell House coffee?
3. What is there about Taster's Choice that, from Mrs. Wilson's point of view, gave it "utility?" How do you think the utility which Mrs. Wilson associated with Maxwell House compares with the utility she now associates with Taster's Choice?
4. What do you think really caused Mrs. Wilson to think more highly of Taster's Choice?

The utility approach to consumer behavior and the formation of individual consumer demand is grounded upon psychological principles. Rational individuals, it is said, will seek to maximize the degree of "pleasure" and minimize the degree of "pain" in choosing among alternative courses of action. In furtherance of this proposition, the concept of utility has evolved into the economist's major tool for explaining and predicting the consumer's marketplace behavior.

Utility refers to the want-satisfying power of commodities—that is, the amount of satisfaction a consumer receives from consuming various quantities of a good or service per period of time. A consumer's total and marginal utility functions for a product can be represented equally well by tables, graphs, and equations. Marginal utility is defined to be the rate of change in total utility as the rate of consumption of a product changes. For each total utility function, there is a corresponding marginal utility function. Every consumer has his or her own unique set of total and marginal utility functions; these vary according to his or her tastes and preferences for different products. Moreover, the satisfaction a consumer obtains from one products hinges in part upon the amounts consumed of other products.

Consumers maximize the satisfaction they can obtain from their limited money income by meeting two conditions. First, they must fully utilize all their income either by purchasing products or by saving. Second, consumers must arrange their purchases so that the marginal utilities per dollar spent on the last unit of each item purchased are equal. In other words, to maximize satisfaction, consumers must get an equivalent amount of satisfaction from the last dollar allocated to each of the commodities (including saving) that they choose to buy.

Few consumers probably succeed in obtaining the maximum satisfaction from their income. Impulsive buying, habit, imperfect knowledge of product prices and quality, a desire for variety, emotion and personality traits, the pressures of time and circumstances, family roles, and the persuasive powers of advertising, among others, prompt consumers to make purchases with which they may not be fully satisfied.

However, the fact that consumers do not succeed in maximizing utility is not crucial to the validity of utility theory. What is important is whether consumers act consistently on the basis of perceived utility (including both monetary and time considerations) and, accordingly, whether utility theory explains and predicts well.

SUGGESTED READINGS

ALCHIAN, A. A., "The Meaning of Utility Measurement," *American Economic Review*, Vol. 43, No. 1 (March 1953), pp. 26–50.

ELLSBURG, D., "Classic and Current Notions of Measurable Utility," *Economic Journal*, Vol. 64, No. 255 (September 1954), pp. 528–556.

FERBER, R., "Consumer Economics: A Survey," *Journal of Economic Literature,*
Vol. 11, No. 4 (December 1973), pp. 1303–1342.

FRIEDMAN, M., AND L. J. SAVAGE, "The Utility Analysis of Choices Involving Risk,"
Journal of Political Economy, Vol. 56, No. 4 (August 1948), pp. 279–304.

KATONA, G., *Psychological Economics* (New York: American Elsevier Publishing
Co., Inc., 1975).

STIGLER, G. J., "The Development of Utility Theory," *Journal of Political Economy,*
Vol. 58, Nos. 4 and 5 (August and October 1950), pp. 307–327, 373–396.

STROTZ, R. H., "Cardinal Utility," *American Economic Review,* Vol. 43, No. 2
(May 1953), pp. 384–397.

SWALM, R. O., "Utility Theory—Insights into Risk-taking," *Harvard Business
Review,* Vol. 44, No. 6 (November–December 1966), pp. 123–136.

VON NEUMANN, J., AND O. MORGENSTERN, *The Theory of Games and Economic
Behavior,* 3rd ed. (Princeton, N.J.: Princeton University Press, 1953), Chapter
1, Sec. 3, pp. 15–31.

PROBLEMS AND QUESTIONS FOR DISCUSSION

1. Find the first derivatives of each of the following functions.
   (a) $Y = 124 + 6X$.
   (b) $Y = 15X^2 + 2X^3$.
   (c) $TU_x = 17X - 0.5X^2$.
   (d) $TU_a = 16A + 5A^2 - 0.3A^3$.
   (e) $TU_b = -185 + 7B + 1.9B^2 - 0.05B^3$.
   (f) $TU_c = 0.6C^{1/2}$.
   (g) $TU_y = 1.5Y^{.75}$.
   Answers: (a) $dY/dX = 6$.   (b) $dY/dX = 30X + 6X^2$.
         (c) $dTU/dX = 17 - X$.
         (d) $dTU_a/dA = 16 + 10A - 0.9A^2$.
         (e) $dTU_b/dB = 7 + 3.8B - 0.15B^2$.
         (f) $dTU_c/dC = 0.3C^{-1/2}$.   (g) $dTU_y/dY = 1.125Y^{-.25}$.

2. Find the second derivative of each of the following functions (the second
   derivative is the derivative of the first derivative).
   (a) $Y = 124 + 7X^2$.
   (b) $TU_x = 9 + 14X - 0.2X^2$.
   (c) $TU_a = 130 + 14A + 15A^2 - 0.4A^3$.
   (d) $TU_b = 0.6B^{1.5}$.
   Answers: (a) $d^2Y/dX^2 = 14$.   (b) $d^2TU/dX^2 = -0.4$.
         (c) $d^2TU_a/dA^2 = 30 - 2.4A$.   (d) $d^2TU_b/dB^2 = 0.45B^{-.5}$.

3. Explain the nature of the distinguishing features between cardinal and ordinal
   measures of utility.

4. Adam Smith in *The Wealth of Nations* observed: "Nothing is more useful than
   water: but it will purchase scarce anything; scarce anything can be had in
   exchange for it. A diamond, on the contrary, has scarce any value in use; but
   a very great quantity of other goods may frequently be had in exchange for it."
   (a) How do you account for this?
   (b) Is the term *useful* or *usefulness* synonymous with the concept of utility as
   we have defined it?

5. An individual's total utility function for product B is as follows: $TU = 18B - 0.5B^2$.

(a) Graph the TU function, and explain the nature of the individual's utility for the product.

(b) Calculate the equation for marginal utility, and illustrate it graphically.

(c) How much will total utility be at a consumption rate of 10 units? At 15 units?

(d) How much will marginal utility be at a consumption rate of 10 units? At 15 units?

(e) How many units of product B can the individual consume and still gain additional satisfaction?

6. An individual's total utility function for product Q is as follows: $TU = 100Q + 150Q^2 - 2Q^3$.

(a) Determine the expression for marginal utility.

(b) Graph the total and marginal utility functions, and explain the nature of the individual's utility for the product.

(c) How much will total utility be at a consumption level of 5 units? How much will marginal utility be at 5 units?

(d) At what approximate consumption rate does diminishing MU begin?

(e) At what approximate consumption rate does the individual reach his saturation rate?

7. The following table shows the marginal utility, measured in utils of satisfaction, which Mr. Johnson would get by purchasing various amounts of products A, B, C, and D and by saving. The prices of A, B, C, and D are $5, $6, $8, and $20, respectively. Mr. Johnson has a money income of $95 to spend in the current period.

PRODUCT A		PRODUCT B		PRODUCT C		PRODUCT D		SAVING	
Units	MU	Units	MU	Units	MU	Units	MU	No. of $ Saved	MU
1	31	1	20	1	39	1	50	1	6
2	27	2	19	2	36	2	55	2	5
3	23	3	18	3	33	3	50	3	4
4	19	4	17	4	30	4	45	4	3
5	15	5	16	5	27	5	40	5	2
6	11	6	15	6	24	6	35	6	1
7	7	7	14	7	21	7	30	7	$\frac{1}{2}$

(a) How many units of A, B, C, and D must Mr. Johnson purchase in order to maximize total utility?

(b) How many dollars will Mr. Johnson elect to save?

(c) State algebraically the two conditions for utility maximization, and show that your answers to parts (a) and (b) satisfy these conditions.

8. Given the two conditions requisite for utility maximization, is it likely that a consumer would ever reach his saturation rate for any commodity? Why or why not? Under what circumstances *might* it occur?

9. Dr. Holt has $30 per week available to spend as he wishes on commodities A and B. The prices of A and B, the quantities of A and B he is now buying, and his evaluations of the utility provided by these quantities are as follows:

Product	Price	Quantity Bought (units)	Total Utility (utils)	MU of Last Unit Bought (utils)
A	70¢	30	500	30
B	50¢	18	1,000	20

Is Dr. Holt maximizing total utility? If so, *explain why*. If not, what might he do to maximize utility? *Explain* why.

10. Suppose that Mr. Pikard has an income of $60 weekly which he is free to spend or save in any way he sees fit. Mr. Pikard believes that *each* dollar he saves gives him 5 utils of satisfaction. This past week, of the thousands of products available, Mr. Pikard purchased the following list of items and believes he obtained the indicated degrees of utility from them:

Product	Quantity Purchased	Price per Unit	Total Utility (utils)	MU of Last Unit Bought (utils)
A	1	$ 2.50	15	15.0
B	2	.75	16	4.5
C	10	.50	113	3.0
D	3	4.00	248	24.0
E	6	3.00	618	18.0
F	1	15.00	90	90.0

Is it possible, given this information, that Mr. Pikard maximized the total utility he received last week from his $60?

11. The Belmont Company conducted an experiment to see how well its new typewriter would stack up against a typewriter produced by Delta Company, a firm already well established in the market. Belmont utilized three testing conditions: (1) *accurate brand labeling*, whereby both machines were placed in an office use situation with the correct company and brand names indicated; (2) *reverse brand labeling*, whereby both machines were placed in an office use situation with the company and brand names reversed; (3) *blind labeling*, whereby both typewriters were unidentified as to company and brand name. Under test condition (1), Delta's typewriter was rated moderately superior to the Belmont brand, but under test condition (2) Belmont's typewriter was rated far superior to Delta's. In the blind labeling test, the Belmont typewriter was given a slight edge over the Delta machine. (a) How do you account for these results? (b) What criteria do you think were being used to rate the two typewriters? Do you think the user's evaluations were "rational?" (c) Are the results consistent with the utility model of buyer behavior?

12. Louis Harris, the pollster, in a 1975 speech reported that if the American people
were given a choice between seriously trimming their material life-styles or
enduring chronic double-digit inflation and high levels of unemployment, they
would opt for cutting back their material lifestyles by a margin of 77 percent
to 8 percent. He claimed these are significant results, for they signal an enormous change taking place in values. People, he said, no longer aspire to acquire
more and more goods to go with the ones they already have; instead, they are
seeking, yearning, and even crying out for a different kind of existence.

(a) Do you agree?

(b) If Harris is right, what implications does this have for how consumers will
go about maximizing utility? How will a lessening of material values affect
the utility that consumers attach to goods and services?

13. It has been said that "What the customer thinks he is buying, what he considers
value is decisive . . . And what the customer buys and considers value is never
a product. It is always utility, that is, what a product or service does for him."
Comment.

FOUR FOUNDATIONS OF CONSUMER DEMAND: THE INDIFFERENCE CURVE MODEL

While the cardinal utility approach to consumer preference offers useful insights into consumer behavior, the inability to quantify utility in a satisfactory manner caused economists to seek out an alternative mode of individual demand analysis not predicated on numerical measures of satisfaction. The search led to the development of ordinal utility analysis whereby consumer tastes and preferences are indicated by ordering or ranking the utilities of various products.[1] Interestingly enough, this seemingly slight change in approach has produced some versatile analytical tools that stand as an important extension of the cardinal utility concepts of Chapter 3.

[1] Although the concepts of cardinal and ordinal utility are distinct notions, it should be pointed out that there is not a wide gulf between the two. Consumers often experience considerable difficulty in deciding which products they actually prefer. For example, a consumer may have no trouble deciding that he prefers brand X to brand Z and that he prefers brand Y to brand Z, but he may have quite a hard time deciding whether he prefers brand X to brand Y, or vice versa. It can then be reliably hypothesized that the cardinal utility difference between the paired comparisons (X, Z) and (Y, Z) is greater than between (X, Y). To put it another way, a consumer may be able to establish an ordinal ranking among three items, X, Y, and Z, ranking X as first, Y as second, and Z as third. Yet it may be quite clear to him that Z is a poor third, while X barely edged out Y for first; this creates a strong inference that the cardinal utility difference between X and Y is much smaller than between either X and Z or Y and Z. Hence, ordinal utility rankings may permit judgments about the numerical amounts of total utility associated with various items.

The ordinal utility approach to consumer demand is usually called indifference curve analysis because "indifference curves" are its primary analytical tool. To understand the origin and meaning of indifference curves, suppose that we refocus our attention upon the utility interrelationships among goods and services.

Figure 4-1(a) depicts a total utility surface for two desirable goods X and Y. Increasing the rates of consumption of X and Y from zero levels produces the total utility surface $OEFG$. Observe that if the consumption of Y is fixed at Y_1 units, then the consumer's total utility from X and Y increases at a decreasing rate along the path $ECAF$ as the consumption of X per unit

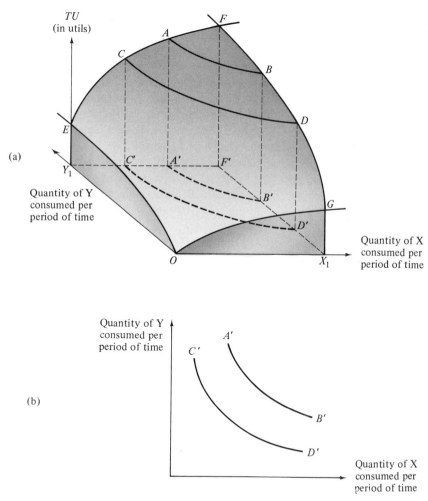

**Figure 4-1
Derivation of indifference curves**

of time rises from zero to X_1 units. In like manner, whenever the consumption of X is fixed, total utility increases at a decreasing rate as the consumption of Y is increased per period of time.

Suppose that we connect all points on the utility surface $OEFG$ which represent a total utility level of CC' (where $CC' = DD'$), thereby obtaining the contour line CD. Thus, all the points along CD are associated with a specific amount of total utility CC' (or DD'). Projecting the curve CD vertically downward onto the XY plane traces out the dashed contour line $C'D'$ and defines all the combinations of products X and Y consumed per unit of time which yield an amount of total utility equal to CC' (or DD'). Logically, a consumer would be *indifferent* as to which one of the combinations of X and Y along $C'D'$ he had since they all are associated with the same amount of total utility.

Following the same procedure, suppose that we move up the utility surface to a higher level of total utility AA' ($= BB'$). Connecting all points on the utility surface $OEFG$ with a total utility of AA' ($= BB'$) gives the contour line AB. Projecting the image of AB perpendicularly onto the XY plane gives the dashed contour line $A'B'$. Any point along AB represents constant total utility of amount $AA' = BB'$, and all combinations of products X and Y lying on $A'B'$ yield this amount of total utility. Again, it is reasonable to conclude that a consumer would be indifferent among the combinations of X and Y along $A'B'$ because they all are equally satisfying.

Predictably enough, the contour lines $C'D'$ and $A'B'$ are called *indifference curves*.[2] An indifference curve is the locus of the various combinations of products that yield an equal amount of satisfaction (total utility) to the consumer, or among which the consumer is indifferent. Figure 4-1(b) illustrates indifference curves $C'D'$ and $A'B'$ in a two-dimensional diagram.

Although a consumer is indifferent as to the various combinations along a particular indifference curve, he is *not* indifferent as to the various combinations between indifference curves. For example, a consumer would prefer *all* combinations of X and Y on $A'B'$ to those combinations on $C'D'$ because the former are associated with a higher total utility ($AA' > CC'$). Greater degrees of total utility are shown by contour lines higher up on the utility surface, while lower degrees of total utility are shown by lower contour lines. Consequently, in a two-dimensional diagram such as Fig. 4-1(b), indifference curves lying farther from the origin represent higher levels of satisfaction than do those lying closer in. Therefore, an indifference curve may additionally be thought of as a boundary between combinations of products which a consumer views as less satisfying and those combinations which he views as more satisfying. To put it another way, a consumer is

---

[2]The total utility surface in Fig. 4-1(a) is mathematically defined by the general expression $TU = f(X, Y)$. The equation for one indifference curve is $TU_1 = f(X, Y)$, where TU_1 is a constant and X and Y represent all the various combinations of two products which yield a utility of TU_1. Other indifference curves on the surface are generated by assigning different values to TU. The family of indifference curves produced by letting TU assume every possible value defines the consumer's indifference map. Significantly, the values for TU need only reflect an ordered preference pattern rather than being expressed as cardinal utility (numerical) values.

indifferent among having any one of the various combinations on a given indifference curve, but he prefers all combinations on higher indifference curves to those on lower indifference curves.

There is an indifference curve associated with each distinct degree of total utility on the total utility surface. In this sense, indifference curves are "everywhere dense," that is, an indifference curve passes through each point in the XY plane. The family of indifference curves which may be derived from the total utility surface comprises an *indifference map*. The indifference map provides a complete description of a consumer's preferences for various combinations of goods and services.

The important point to recognize at this juncture is that the specific degree of utility associated with an indifference curve is in no way crucial. In fact, the information provided by an indifference curve does not specify the *amount* of satisfaction produced by the combinations comprising it. In Fig. 4-1(b), the total utility attached to $C'D'$ and $A'B'$ could be 10 utils and 14 utils, respectively, or 112 utils and 547 utils. The *amount* by which the combinations on a higher indifference curve are preferred to those on a lower indifference curve is unspecified—it could be a little or a lot. All that is necessary for deriving an indifference curve is for the consumer to know his preferences well enough to be able to distinguish whether he prefers one combination of goods to another or whether he views them as equally satisfying.[3] It is in this sense that ordinal utility or indifference curve analysis is free of the need to express utility in numerical terms.

THE SHAPES OF INDIFFERENCE CURVES

Although the height of the total utility surface is immaterial, its *shape* is not. In fact, it is the *shape* of the utility surface which determines the shape of the indifference curves, thereby describing a consumer's taste and preference pattern. Any set of consumer tastes can be portrayed by indifference curves and utility surfaces. Several examples may be given in support of this statement.

First, consider the taste and preference pattern of an individual who enjoys good X immensely (prime ribs) but considers good Y devoid of want-satisfying qualities (parsnips). Figure 4-2(a) depicts a utility surface and indifference map for such a situation. Having more of Y neither raises nor lowers total satisfaction (its marginal utility is zero); only good X has the power to change the level of total utility. The effect is to make each indifference curve in the bottom half of Fig. 4-2(a) a vertical line. As the consumption rate of X is increased per unit of time, utility increases; hence, on the indifference map higher levels of satisfaction are shown by moving rightward along the X-axis.

---

[3]The consumer must be able to avoid being thrust into a position similar to that of Buridan's ass. The ass, it may be recalled, stood midway between two equally sized bundles of hay and finally died of hunger because it could not decide which bundle to eat.

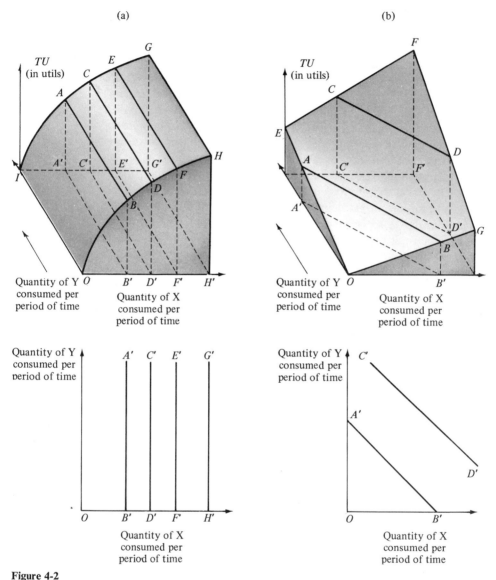

(a)   (b)

Figure 4-2
Total utility surfaces and indifference maps for special types of products

Figure 4-2(b) illustrates a total utility surface and corresponding indifference map for a pair of products that are *perfect substitutes*. Products are said to be perfect substitutes when their qualities are so similar that a consumer would just as soon have more of one as more of the other. Examples could be nickels and dimes (at a constant ratio of two to one), competing brands of pencils, or competing brands of essentially identical food products—

milk, eggs, sugar, and black pepper. The indifference curve for perfect substitutes is a straight line because the consumer considers them as being absolutely equivalent and is willing, therefore, to substitute one for the other at some *constant* ratio, no matter how much he has of either.

In Fig. 4-3 is the indifference map for a pair of products that have a rigid one-to-one complementary relationship in the mind of the consumer (right and left shoes, nuts and bolts). Each indifference curve is a right angle because the consumer is no better off having more of one without the other; this means more units of one complementary item have a marginal utility of zero unless combined with more units of the other complementary item. Therefore, total satisfaction can be increased only by having more of both items. (The shape of the utility surface from which these curves are derived is left as an exercise at the end of this chapter.)

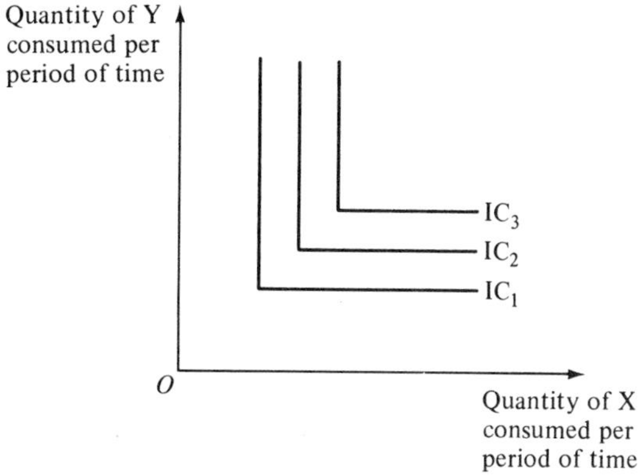

Figure 4-3
Indifference map for perfect complements

THE CHARACTERISTICS OF TYPICAL INDIFFERENCE CURVES

To simplify the exposition of indifference curve analysis it is customary to make three assumptions:

1. All products are continuously divisible into subunits so that a consumer is not constrained by the size of the units in which the item is sold.
2. The consumer's tastes and order of preference among combinations of products is well defined and consistent.
3. The consumer views products as being desirable—having more is always preferred to having less; this means that the marginal utility of additional consumption is positive and, further, that useless and nuisance items are disregarded.[4]

Given these assumptions, indifference curves exhibit four characteristics. From the first assumption it follows that (a) indifference curves are continu-

---

[4]It is easy enough to redefine a nuisance item to make it a desirable item. Instead of garbage, the item can be called garbage removal; instead of polluted water, the item can be defined as clean water.

ous functions rather than collections of discrete points and (b) indifference curves are "everywhere dense"—some indifference curve will pass through every point in the XY-plane (or *commodity space*, as it is sometimes called).

The second assumption, in conjunction with the third, ensures that indifference curves will be nonintersecting. Consider Fig. 4-4, in which two indifference curves, IC_1 and IC_2, are shown intersecting. A moment's reflection should indicate that it is quite illogical for combination A to produce simultaneously two levels of satisfaction—as would be the case were it to lie on two different indifference curves. Thus, intersecting indifference curves deny the condition of consistency (or transitivity).[5] But to say that indifference curves are nonintersecting is *not* to say that indifference curves must be equidistant from one another. Two indifference curves may or may not be the same distance apart throughout. The curves for many, even most, pairs of items may become progressively closer (or farther apart) because of differing MU functions.

The third assumption causes indifference curves to slope downward to the right (i.e., have a negative slope). Negatively sloped indifference curves reflect the general principle that a consumer is willing to give up units of one product if the loss in satisfaction is compensated for by having more of another product. Stated differently, by having more of one good (say X) and by giving up an appropriate amount of another good (say Y), the consumer can be made to feel just as well off as originally (when he had less of X and more of Y). By *substituting* one item for another in such a way that the gain in satisfaction from consuming more of one is exactly offset by the loss of satisfaction from consuming less of another, the consumer's overall satisfaction level can be held constant.

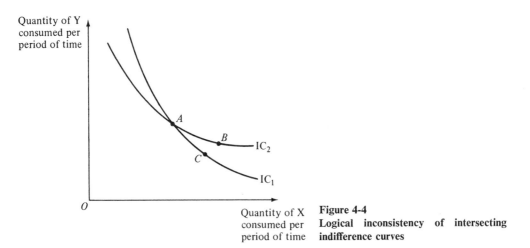

Quantity of Y consumed per period of time

Quantity of X consumed per period of time

Figure 4-4

Logical inconsistency of intersecting indifference curves

[5]Transitivity is a scale of preference such that if A is preferred to B and B is preferred to C, then A must be preferred to C. Clearly, transitivity cannot be present if (1) A and B are viewed as equivalent, (2) A and C are viewed as equivalent, and (3) B is preferred to C (because combination B contains more of both goods X and Y)—this is precisely the illogical condition depicted in Fig. 4-4.

Except in the case of perfect substitutes and perfect complements, indifference curves for desirable products not only slope downward to the right, but they are also *convex* to the origin of the indifference map. The reasons for this convexity derive from the concept of the marginal rate of substitution of one good for another.

The *marginal rate of substitution* (MRS) is the rate at which a consumer is agreeable to trading off some of one good for more of another good while at the same time holding the overall level of satisfaction constant. Consider the indifference curve shown in Fig. 4-5. The consumer is indifferent among

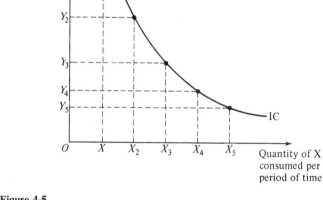

Figure 4-5
Marginal rate of substitution along an indifference curve

combinations $X_1 Y_1$, $X_2 Y_2$, $X_3 Y_3$, $X_4 Y_4$, and $X_5 Y_5$. The horizontal axis is measured so that distances $OX_1 = X_1 X_2 = X_2 X_3 = X_3 X_4 = X_4 X_5 = 1$ unit of X. Starting at combination $X_1 Y_1$ and proceeding down the indifference curve, observe that initially the consumer is willing to give up $Y_1 Y_2$ units of Y to get an additional unit of X and yet have just as much satisfaction as before. But as he or she acquires more and more of X and has less and less of Y left, the amount of Y he or she is willing to give up to get another unit of X becomes progressively smaller. We can express the ratio at which a consumer is willing to exchange one product for another algebraically as

$$\text{MRS}_{xy} = \frac{\Delta Y}{\Delta X},$$

where ΔY represents the number of units of Y the consumer is willing to give up and ΔX represents the number of units of X it will take to compensate the consumer for his or her loss of Y. The expression $\Delta Y/\Delta X$ thus defines the exchange ratio or marginal rate of substitution between Y and X that will precisely maintain the consumer's level of satisfaction. Clearly, the exchange ratio is not constant all along an indifference curve: The ratio becomes smaller going down the curve, and this is what makes the indifference curve convex. Why does the value of MRS_{xy} diminish going down the curve? One explanation for diminishing MRS_{xy} is that as we move down an indifference curve, the remaining units of Y become dearer and the additional units of X yield smaller amounts of extra satisfaction; that is, the marginal utility of the remaining units of Y rises, whereas the marginal utility from additional units of X decreases. This argument, although quite plausible since a state of diminishing marginal utility for X and Y is fairly normal, is not always sufficient. When the utility derived from good Y is partially dependent on the amount consumed of X, increasing the consumption of X may decrease the marginal utility from Y and spoil the argument. Fortunately, more powerful evidence for convexity exists. It can, for example, be demonstrated that if the consumer buys some of each of two products, his or her indifference curves must be convex to the origin; otherwise, only one of the products would be bought.

But there is more to be learned about the marginal rate of substitution. We know that in moving from one point to another on the same indifference curve there is no change in total utility. Consider, for example, the situation in going from point $X_1 Y_1$ to point $X_2 Y_2$ in Fig. 4-5. We can say that the amount of utility "lost" from consuming fewer units of Y (Y_1 to Y_2) is exactly compensated for by the "gain" in utility from consuming more units of X (X_1 to X_2). In more formal terms,

$$\underbrace{-\Delta Y \cdot MU_y}_{\substack{\text{"loss" in utility from} \\ \text{consuming } Y_1 Y_2 \text{ (or} \\ \Delta Y \text{) fewer units of} \\ \text{good Y}}} = \underbrace{\Delta X \cdot MU_x.}_{\substack{\text{"gain" in utility from} \\ \text{consuming } X_1 X_2 \text{ (or} \\ \Delta X \text{) units more of} \\ \text{good X}}}$$

Dividing both terms of this equality by $\Delta X \cdot MU_y$ gives

$$\frac{-\Delta Y \cdot MU_y}{\Delta X \cdot MU_y} = \frac{\Delta X \cdot MU_x}{\Delta X \cdot MU_y},$$

which reduces to

$$-\frac{\Delta Y}{\Delta X} = \frac{MU_x}{MU_y} \quad \text{or} \quad \frac{\Delta Y}{\Delta X} = -\frac{MU_x}{MU_y}.$$

But since $\text{MRS}_{xy} = \Delta Y/\Delta X$, we have

$$\text{MRS}_{xy} = \frac{\Delta Y}{\Delta X} = -\frac{MU_x}{MU_y},$$

which says that the marginal rate of substitution of X for Y is equal to the ratio of MU_x to MU_y. This expression for MRS_{xy} holds true for any two points on an indifference curve. The negative sign in the expression reflects the fact that having more of one good (X) entails having less of the other good (Y). Additionally, it follows that if any two points on a given indifference curve become so close together that they are really one point, then the marginal rate of substitution of X for Y equals the slope of the indifference curve at that point. One final point: The marginal rate of substitution is meaningful only for movements along an indifference curve—never for movements among curves.

THE CONSUMER'S BUDGET CONSTRAINT

A consumer's indifference map indicates his or her subjective attitudes toward various combinations of products. It shows what combinations are preferred to others and the rates at which he or she is willing to substitute one product for another. However, as was seen in Chapter 3, the extent to which the consumer is *able* to satisfy these tastes and preferences hinges upon (1) the available money income and (2) the respective prices of the products the individual is desirous of having. Taken together, these two factors define the individual's *budget constraint*.

For simplicity, suppose that we continue to restrict our analysis to a situation where there are just two goods X and Y with prices of P_x and P_y. As established previously, the consumer's money income (I) is fixed in the short run; he or she has only so much to spend per period of time. The consumer's expenditures for X will be equal to the selling price (P_x) times the amount purchased (X) or $P_x X$; similarly, the expenditure for good Y is $P_y Y$. The sum of the consumer's expenditures for X and Y must be equal to or less than the available income I. Thus, we may write

$$P_x X + P_y Y \leq I.$$

MATHEMATICAL CAPSULE 4

**THE MARGINAL RATE OF SUBSTITUTION,
THE CONVEXITY OF INDIFFERENCE CURVES,
AND DIMINISHING MARGINAL UTILITY**

Suppose that the total utility function for goods X and Y is

$$TU = f(X, Y);$$

then an indifference curve is defined by

$$TU = f(X, Y) = c,$$

where c is a constant. Finding the total differential of $TU = f(X, Y)$ gives

$$dTU = \frac{\partial TU}{\partial X} dX + \frac{\partial TU}{\partial Y} dY = 0,$$

since $TU = c$. Solving the total differential for dY/dX, we have

$$\frac{\partial TU}{\partial Y} dY = - \frac{\partial TU}{\partial X} dX,$$

$$\frac{dY}{dX} = - \frac{\partial TU/\partial X}{\partial TU/\partial Y} \quad \text{or} \quad - \frac{MU_x}{MU_y}.$$

Hence, dY/dX is the slope of the indifference curve or MRS_{xy}. The negative sign reflects the negative slope of the indifference curve. If the TU function is ordinal rather than cardinal, MU_x and MU_y have no meaningful absolute values—only their ratios are relevant and interpretable.

Diminishing MU for X and Y requires that

$$\frac{\partial^2 TU}{\partial X^2} < 0 \quad \text{and} \quad \frac{\partial^2 TU}{\partial Y^2} < 0;$$

however, convexity of the indifference curve requires that $d^2 Y/dX^2 < 0$, which is not the same. Thus, the convexity of indifference curves does not depend on diminishing MU for X and Y.

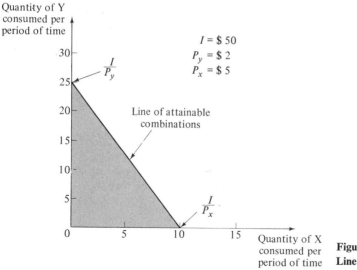

Figure 4-6
Line of attainable combinations

If the consumer elects to spend all of his or her income on X and Y and save nothing, then,

$$P_x X + P_y Y = I.$$

Otherwise, saving accounts for the margin of difference between the consumer's total expenditures on X and Y and income.

Suppose that the available money income is $50, $P_x = \$5$, and $P_y = \$2$. If the entire $50 is spent on good X, a maximum of 10 units (I/P_x) could be bought; if the entire $50 is spent on Y, as much as 25 units (I/P_y) can be purchased. These combinations are illustrated in Fig. 4-6. A straight line joining these two points on the graph shows *all* the other combinations of X and Y that the consumer's income will allow him to purchase at these prices. This line is called the *line of attainable combinations* because it represents the locus of combinations of X and Y that can be purchased when the consumer spends the entire amount of money income available.[6] The consumer can also buy any of the combinations of X and Y inside the line (the shaded area); however, if he or she does so, available purchasing power will not be fully utilized and there will be money left over for saving (or for spending on other products). The equation of the line of attainable combinations in Fig. 4-6 is $\$5X + \$2Y = \$50$, where $5 = the price of product X, $2 = the price of Y, and $50 = the consumer's money income. The set of values for X and Y that satisfy this equation are given by the points comprising the line of attainable combinations.

The general equation for the line of attainable combinations in a two-product economy is $P_x X + P_y Y = I$.[7] The slope of the line of attainable combinations is negative and is numerically equal to the ratio of the prices of X and Y. This is easily verified by considering the slope of the line in Fig. 4-6 between the two extreme points I/P_x and I/P_y:

$$\text{slope of the line of attainable combinations} = \frac{\text{change in the quantity of } Y}{\text{change in the quantity of } X} = \frac{-I/P_y}{I/P_x} = -\frac{P_x}{P_y}.$$

[6]In the literature of indifference curve analysis, the line of attainable combinations is known variously as the budget line, the price line, the budget restraint, the expenditure line, the price-income line, and the consumption possibility line.

In drawing the line as a continuous function, we continue our assumption of the preceding sections that products X and Y are perfectly divisible into subunits and can be purchased in any quantity.

Normally, an individual consumer's purchases of a product are so small relative to the total amount bought that the price of it can reasonably be anticipated to remain constant irrespective of the amount purchased. Thus, a linear line of attainable combinations may be considered typical. However, if by chance the prices of X and Y depend on the amounts the consumer buys, then the line of attainable combinations becomes curvilinear. When product prices fall as the consumer buys more units, the line of attainable combinations is bowed in toward the origin. When product prices rise with increasing purchase levels, the line is bowed out or concave toward the origin.

[7]For *n* number of products and where saving is indicated as a separate activity, the general equation of the line of attainable combinations may be written as

$$P_{x_a} X_a + P_{x_b} X_b + P_{x_c} X_c + \cdots + P_{x_n} X_n + \text{saving} = I,$$

where I = money income and $P_a, P_b, P_c, \ldots, P_{x_n}$ are the prices of products $X_a, X_b, X_c, \ldots, X_n$.

Both changes in money income and changes in product prices have the effect of shifting the position of the line of attainable combinations. Consider first the effect of an increase in money income from I_1 to I_2 when the prices of X and Y remain constant at P_{x_1} and P_{y_1}. The larger money income permits the consumer to purchase more of X, more of Y, or more of both. The maximum amount of X which can be purchased increases from I_1/P_{x_1} to I_2/P_{x_1} as shown in Fig. 4-7(a). The maximum purchase level of Y rises from I_1/P_{y_1} to I_2/P_{y_1}. Since the prices of X and Y are fixed, the slope of the new line of attainable combinations must be identical to the slope at an income of I_1, and it must pass through points I_2/P_{x_1} and I_2/P_{y_1}. Thus, an increase in money income from I_1 to I_2, product prices remaining constant, is shown graphically by a parallel shift in the line of attainable combinations upward and to the right. Likewise, another increase in income (to I_3) will shift the line parallelwise even farther to the right. Conversely, it follows that decreases in money income can be represented by parallel shifts in the line downward and to the left.

Figure 4-7(b) displays the change in the line of attainable combinations when the price of X decreases, the price of Y (P_{y_1}) and money income (I_1) remaining unchanged. Since I_1 and P_{y_1} do not change, the maximum quantity of Y which may be purchased (I_1/P_{y1}) is unaffected by any change in P_x. As

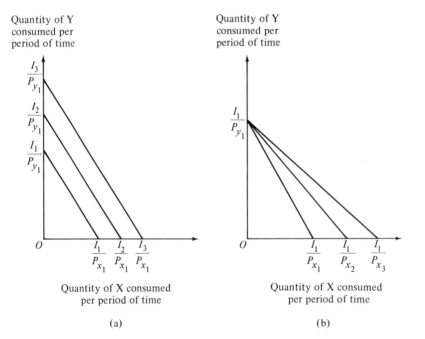

Quantity of Y
consumed per
period of time

Quantity of Y
consumed per
period of time

Quantity of X consumed
per period of time

Quantity of X consumed
per period of time

(a)

(b)

Figure 4-7
Shifts in the line of attainable combinations

the price of X declines from P_{x_1} to P_{x_2} the maximum quantity of X which can
be purchased with I_1 is raised from its original value of I_1/P_{x_1} to I_1/P_{x_2}.
Accordingly, the line of attainable combinations becomes flatter and rotates
to the right about the point I_1/P_{y_1}. Should the price of X decline to P_{x_3} the
line of attainable combinations rotates rightward even more. In contrast, to
represent increases in the price of X the line of attainable combinations is
rotated to the left around the point I_1/P_{y_1}, causing the new line to be more
steeply sloped. These changes in the slope of the line follow directly from our
finding that the slope of the line of attainable combinations is $-(P_x/P_y)$.
Clearly, if P_y is fixed and P_x falls, the slope of the line becomes smaller (or
flatter), and when P_x rises, the slope of the line becomes larger (or steeper).

MAXIMIZATION OF SATISFACTION

The consumer's indifference map provides a diagrammatic representation of
his or her tastes and preferences; that is, it represents a subjective evaluation
of the intensity of desire for different product combinations. The consumer's
purchasing power (and thus ability to satisfy material wants) is reflected by
the line of attainable combinations. Putting the two together provides a way
for showing which of all the product combinations on the indifference map is
the utility-maximizing combination.

In Fig. 4-8, the most satisfying combination among all those which
can be purchased is at point *C*, where the consumer buys X_1 units of X and
Y_1 units of Y. Combinations *A* and *B*, while attainable, are on a lower

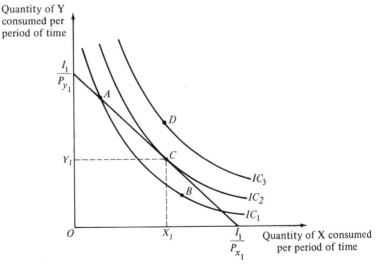

Figure 4-8
Determining the utility-maximizing combination of purchases

indifference curve from C and hence entail lower degrees of satisfaction. Combination D is superior to C, but it costs more than the consumer can afford and therefore is eliminated as an alternative. Indifference curve IC_2 is the highest possible indifference curve that can be reached given the consumer's income constraint, and combination C is the only obtainable combination on that curve. Consequently, C represents the most preferred combination of X and Y and may be said to represent *consumer equilibrium.* In general, the consumer's total utility is maximized *at the point of tangency between the line of attainable combinations and an indifference curve* (provided only that the products are desirable—have positive marginal utilities).

It is relevant at this point to ask: What are the conditions for maximizing satisfaction via indifference curve analysis, and how do these compare with those of cardinal utility analysis? First, we may note that the equilibirum combination of X and Y lies *on* the line of attainable combinations, rather than to the inside. This means that a consumer must *fully utilize* the available income to maximize satisfaction. Such a requirement does not preclude saving since saving may appropriately be considered as a commodity available for "purchase" by the consumer.

Second, at the equilibirum point the slope of the indifference curve is precisely equal to the slope of the line of attainable combinations. This necessarily results from their being tangent at this point. As shown earlier, the respective slopes can be expressed as

$$\text{slope of an indifference curve} = \text{MRS}_{xy} = (-)\frac{MU_x}{MU_y},$$

$$\text{slope of the line of attainable combinations} = (-)\frac{P_x}{P_y}.$$

Consequently, the second condition for maximizing satisfaction requires a consumer to so allocate purchasing power that the marginal rate of substitution of X for Y is equal to the ratio of the price of X to the price of Y. The interpretation of this condition is straightforward. The MRS_{xy} defines the *rate* at which the consumer is *willing to exchange* X for Y. The price ratio (P_x/P_y) shows the *rate* at which the consumer *can exchange* X for Y. Unless the two rates are equivalent, it is possible for the consumer to alter purchases of X and Y and achieve a greater degree of satisfaction. To illustrate: Suppose that at the current purchase combination, $\text{MRS}_{xy} = -4$, meaning that the consumer is willing to exchange 4 units of Y for 1 more unit of X. If $P_x = \$6$ and $P_y = \$2$, then the consumer need only give up 3 units of Y at $2 each to obtain the $6 needed to buy another unit of X. Confronted with these circumstances, the consumer will definitely be induced to make the exchange. Why? Because the preference for X and Y at this point is such that one is willing to trade off 4 units of Y for 1 unit of X, yet one has to give up only 3 units of Y to get 1 more unit of X. In general, then, consumer maximization of satisfaction requires equality between the marginal rate of substitution for any pair of products and the ratio of their prices; otherwise some exchange can be made which will increase the consumer's overall satisfaction. However, the income allocation that will maximize consumer satisfaction can be approached from a more familiar angle. Not only is the slope of the indifference curve equal to the MRS_{xy} at any point, but it is also equal to the ratio of the marginal utilities (ordinally interpreted) of the two goods:

$$MRS_{xy} = (-)\frac{MU_x}{MU_y}.$$

Thus, we may write the second condition for maximizing satisfaction as

$$(-)\frac{MU_x}{MU_y} = (-)\frac{P_x}{P_y}.$$

This equation states that consumers' income should be allocated so as to equate the ratio of the marginal utilities with the ratio of the product prices. Rewriting the last expression, we get

$$MU_x \cdot P_y = MU_y \cdot P_x.$$

Dividing each term by $P_x \cdot P_y$ yields

$$\frac{MU_x \cdot P_y}{P_x \cdot P_y} = \frac{MU_y \cdot P_x}{P_x \cdot P_y},$$

which reduces to

$$\frac{MU_x}{P_x} = \frac{MU_y}{P_y}.$$

In an *n*-commodity economy, the latter expression expands to

$$\frac{MU_{X_a}}{P_a} = \frac{MU_{X_b}}{P_b} = \frac{MU_{X_c}}{P_c} = \cdots = \frac{MU_{X_n}}{P_n} = MU_{saving},$$

which, combined with the requirement for full utilization of the consumer's income, yields exactly the same conditions imposed upon the maximization of consumer satisfaction via the cardinal utility approach. Yet there is one important distinction: We reached these same conditions *without* the necessity for quantifying utility or satisfaction.

THE IMPACT OF INCOME CHANGES UPON CONSUMER PURCHASES

Changes in a consumer's money income often cause alterations in what is purchased. Suppose that we trace the impact of a change in an individual consumer's money income upon purchases of goods and services, assuming that product prices and the consumer's preference pattern remain unchanged.

Given the price of X at P_{x_1}, and the price of Y at P_{y_1}, the utility-maximizing purchase combination at an income of I_1 is shown in Fig. 4-9(a) as

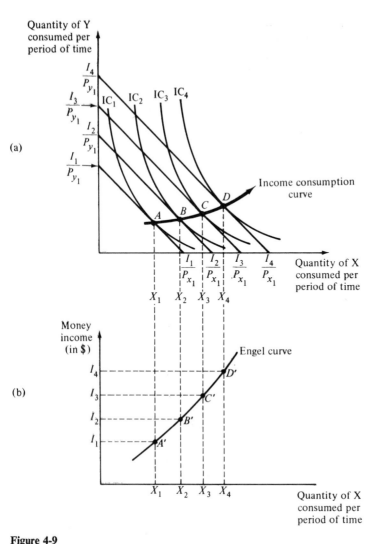

Figure 4-9
The income-consumption curve and derivation of an Engel curve

point A on indifference curve IC_1, where the consumer buys X_1 units of X and Y_1 units of Y. If the consumer's money income rises to I_2, the prices of X and Y remaining unchanged, the line of attainable combinations shifts in parallel fashion upward and to the right. The higher income level allows the consumer to buy more of X, or more of Y, or more of both. According to the preference pattern reflected by the shapes of the indifference curves, an increase in the consumer's money income to I_2 will result in equilibrium purchases of X_2 units of X and Y_2 units of Y at point B on indifference curve IC_2. This is a more satisfying combination of X and Y than was permitted formerly by an income of I_1 because it lies on a higher indifference curve. The consumer would realize a further gain in satisfaction should money income rise to I_3, thereby allowing him or her to reach point C on indifference curve IC_3 and to purchase X_3 units of X and Y_3 units of Y. The line joining the points of consumer equilibrium as income changes is called the *income-consumption curve*. The income-consumption curve is the locus of utility-maximizing combinations of products associated with various levels of money income and constant product prices.

When the resulting income-consumption curve is positively sloped, the products are *normal goods*, meaning that more of the goods are purchased at higher levels of income than at lower levels of income. Such is not always the case. Some items, designated as *inferior goods*, are purchased in smaller amounts when income rises, in which case the income-consumption curve is negatively sloped. Examples of goods that consumers tend to view as inferior include bologna, dried beans, recapped automobile tires, black-and-white camera film, economy or budget-priced durable goods, and reconditioned shock-absorbers.

Derivation of Engel Curves. The information provided by the income-consumption curve may be used to derive *Engel curves* for a product.[8] Engel curves show the equilibrium (utility-maximizing) quantities of a product which a consumer will purchase at various levels of income, other things remaining equal.

An Engel curve for good X is constructed in Fig. 4-9(b). From Fig. 4-9(a), we can see that at an income level of I_1 the consumer's equilibrium purchase level is X_1 units of good X. The values of I_1 and X_1 are plotted as point A' in Fig. 4-9(b). Again from Fig. 4-9(a), we see that when money income is I_2, the consumer will purchase quantity X_2; these values form point B' in Fig. 4-9(b). In like manner, point C' corresponds to a money income of I_3 and the resulting equilibrium purchase of X_3 units of X; and point D' is formed from an income of I_4 and the related purchase of X_4 units of X. Connecting points A', B', C', and D' gives the Engel curve relating purchases of X to changes in money income. An Engel curve of this shape indicates that as the consumer's money increases from very low levels, consumption of product X rises in almost equal proportion.

In other cases, as income rises a consumer's purchases of an item tend to increase less than proportionally to income; additional purchases become less and less sensitive to further gains in income, causing the Engel curve to become more steeply sloped at progressively higher incomes. Examples include newspapers, flour, light bulbs, salt, toothpaste, and most types of basic "necessities." For other normal goods, such as restaurant meals, recreation activities, travel, "luxuries," and saving, a consumer's expenditures tend to expand more rapidly than income. This increasing responsiveness of quantities purchased relative to income changes results in an Engel curve that increases at a decreasing rate. (What is the nature of the Engel curve for an inferior good?)

[8]Engel curves are named for Christian Lorenz Ernest Engel, a nineteenth-century German statistician who was a pioneer in the study of consumer budgets.

Not only do consumers typically adapt their consumption patterns to income changes, but they also react to changes in the price of goods and services. Suppose that we examine what happens to the quantity of X when we vary the price of X and hold constant the consumer's income, the taste and preferences (as reflected by the indifference map), and the price of Y.

Given the price of X at P_{x_1}, the price of Y at P_{y_1}, and money income at I_1, the consumer will maximize satisfaction by purchasing X_1 units of X and Y_1 units of Y, as shown in Fig. 4-10(a). Now suppose the price of X falls to P_{x_2}; the line of attainable combinations will pivot to the right about point

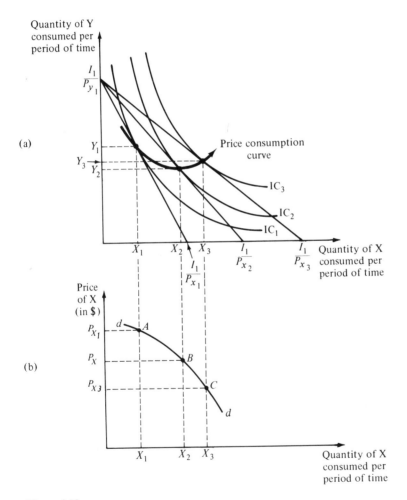

Figure 4-10
Price consumption curve and the consumer's demand curve

I_1/P_{y_1}, allowing the consumer to purchase as much as I_1/P_{x_2} units of X were he or she to spend all income on X. The new line of attainable combinations will necessarily be tangent to a higher indifference curve than previously. Equilibrium will be reestablished by purchasing quantity X_2 of X and quantity Y_2 of Y. In like manner it can be ascertained that a further decline in the price of X to P_{x_3} will permit the consumer to reach an even higher indifference curve, maximizing satisfaction at X_3 and Y_3. The line joining the various points of consumer equilibrium is called the *price-consumption curve*. The price-consumption curve is the locus of the utility-maximizing combinations of products that result from variations in the price of one product, when other product prices, the consumer's tastes and preferences, and his money income are held constant.

Deriving the Demand Curve. The *demand curve* of the individual consumer for product X can be derived directly from the information contained in the price-consumption curve. A consumer's demand curve for a product graphically illustrates the different amounts that the consumer is willing and able to buy at various possible prices during some moment of time wherein all other factors influencing the quantity purchased are held constant. From Fig. 4-10(a) it can be seen that when the price of X is P_{x_1} the consumer's equilibrium purchase is quantity X_1 of X. This establishes one point on his demand curve for product X, shown as point *A* in Fig. 4-10(b). At the lower price P_{x_2} the consumer's purchases rise to X_2 units; this becomes a second point on the demand curve for product X—point B in Fig. 4-10(b). At the still lower price of P_{x_3} the consumer buys X_3 units of X, which gives a third point on his demand curve—point *C* in Fig. 4-10(b). Other points on the demand curve can be derived in analogous fashion, thereby producing line *dd* in Fig. 4-10(b).

Observe that the demand curve slopes downward to the right. This indicates that the price of X and the quantity purchased of X per period of time vary inversely. As P_x rises, the quantity demanded of X falls; or, as P_x falls, the quantity demanded rises. The fundamental principle between selling price and quantity is pure common sense—*other things remaining equal*, a person will be inclined to buy more of a product per period of time at lower prices than at higher prices. Additionally, this principle is reflected by the negative slope of the demand curve.

INCOME AND SUBSTITUTION EFFECTS

When the price of an item changes (and all other relevant factors remain constant), two forces are activated to cause the consumer to alter the quantity purchased. Take the case of a price decline. First, a decrease in price increases the consumer's real income (purchasing power), thus enhancing to some extent the ability to buy more goods and services. Second, a decrease in the price of a product induces some consumers to substitute it for other now relatively higher-priced items. Indifference curve analysis enables us to readily measure the potence of the income and substitution effects.

Consider Fig. 4-11. The consumer's money income is I_1, and the price of Y is P_{y_1}. If the price of X initially is P_{x_1}, then the original equilibrium is at point A on indifference curve IC_1 where the consumer buys X_1 units of X. When the price of X decreases to P_{x_2}, the line of attainable combinations rotates rightward; the consumer moves to a new equilibrium position at B on indifference curve IC_2, purchasing quantity X_2 of X. The overall change in the quantity demanded of X from the first equilibrium point at A to the second equilibrium point at B may be designated as the *total effect* of the price change. The total effect can, in turn, be decomposed into the substitution effect and the income effect.

Let us first isolate the substitution effect and determine its magnitude. The decline in the price of X precipitates an increase in the consumer's real income, as evidenced by the movement to a higher indifference curve even though money income remains fixed. Now imagine that we decrease the consumer's income by an amount *just sufficient* to return to the *same* level of satisfaction enjoyed before the price decline. Graphically, this is accomplished by drawing a fictitious line of attainable combinations with a slope corresponding to the *new* ratio of the product prices (P_{x_2}/P_{y_1}) so that it is just tangent to the *original* indifference curve (IC_1). This produces the line in Fig. 4-11 with extreme points I/P_{y_1} and I/P_{x_2} tangent to IC_1 at point C.

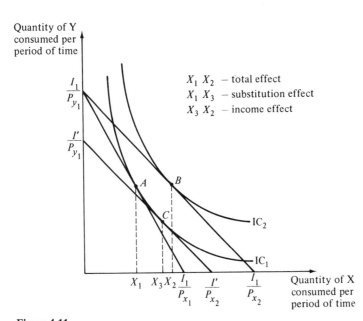

$X_1\ X_2$ — total effect
$X_1\ X_3$ — substitution effect
$X_3\ X_2$ — income effect

Figure 4-11
Income and substitution effects for a normal good in case of a price decline

Combination C is as equally satisfying as combination A because they both lie on the same indifference curve. Yet, given the decline in the price of X from P_{x_1} to P_{x_2} the consumer will be wiser to purchase combination C instead of combination A. Why? Because it is cheaper to buy C rather than A now that the price of X has fallen to P_{x_2}. The effect of the lower price thus is to prompt the consumer to increase consumption of X and cut consumption of Y (i.e., to substitute X for Y). This increase in the consumption of X from X_1 to X_3 is the *substitution effect*; graphically, it is represented by a movement along the original indifference curve IC_1 from point A to the imaginary intermediate equilibrium at point C. More formally, the *substitution effect* refers to the *change in the quantity demanded of a product resulting exclusively from a change in its price when the consumer's real income is held constant, thereby restricting the consumer's reaction to the price change to a movement along the original indifference curve.*

The income effect is determined by observing the change in the quantity demanded of a product that is associated solely with the change in the consumer's *real* income. In Fig. 4-11 letting the consumer's real income rise from its imaginary level (defined by the line of attainable combinations tangent to point C) back to its true level (defined by the line of attainable combinations tangent to point B) gives the income effect. Thus, the income effect is indicated by the movement from the imaginary equilibrium at point C to the actual new equilibrium at point B; the increase in the quantity of X purchased from X_3 to X_2 is the income effect. Formally, the *income effect may be defined as the change in the quantity demanded of a product exclusively associated with a change in real income.*

Comparatively speaking, the magnitude of the substitution effect is ordinarily greater than that of the income effect. Frequently, the change in the consumer's real income resulting from changes in the price of one commodity is so slight that there is little room for the consumer to alter the quantities of goods he purchased.[9] But where items can be readily substituted for one another, price changes are likely to trigger a relatively large substitution effect.

Usually, the income and substitution effects reinforce one another; that is, they operate in the same direction. A *lower* price for a product results in an *increase* in its quantity demanded due to the substitution effect and an *increase* in its quantity demanded due to the income effect. As Fig. 4-12 illustrates, when the price of a product *rises*, the substitution effect will bring about a *decrease* in quantity demanded, and the income effect likewise

[9] For instance, if a consumer with an annual income of $10,000 finds that the price of a good he buys once a month has declined in price from 73 cents to 69 cents, then the consumer's real income has increased—but ever so slightly. The 48 cents saved on the purchase of the good over the period of a year does technically increase the consumer's real income, but it scarcely is sufficient to cause even a minor realignment in the consumer's purchases. Of course, if the item is one that is purchased frequently (cigarettes) and/or is purchased in large quantities (gasoline) and/or has a high price (automobiles), then the effect on real income may be quite significant.

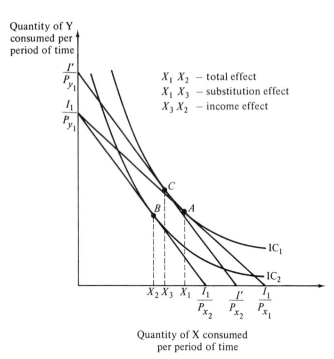

Quantity of Y consumed per period of time

$X_1 X_2$ — total effect
$X_1 X_3$ — substitution effect
$X_3 X_2$ — income effect

$\frac{I'}{P_{y_1}}$

$\frac{I_1}{P_{y_1}}$

C

B A

IC_1

IC_2

$X_2\, X_3\ X_1$ $\frac{I_1}{P_{x_2}}$ $\frac{I'}{P_{x_2}}$ $\frac{I_1}{P_{x_1}}$

Quantity of X consumed
per period of time

Figure 4-12
Income and substitution effects for a normal good in case of a price increase

will bring about a *decrease* in quantity demanded. Note that in the event of either a price decrease or a price increase (Figs. 4-11 and 4-12, respectively), the quantity demanded of a product varies inversely with its price—the law of demand is operative. Second, note that in either event the change in quantity demanded stemming from the income effect moves in the *same* direction as the change in real income—if real income rises, the quantity demanded rises; if real income falls, the quantity demanded falls. These two relationships characterize the class of goods we earlier delineated as *normal goods*.

In the case of *inferior goods*, however, the income and substitution effects work in the *opposite* direction. For an inferior good, a *decrease* in the price of X causes the consumer to buy *more* of it (the substitution effect), but at the same time the higher real income of the consumer tends to cause him to *reduce* consumption of X (the income effect). The income and substitution effects for this situation are diagrammed in Fig. 4-13. Observe that the substitution effect still is the more powerful of the two; even though the income effect works counter to the substitution effect, it does not override it. Furthermore, it follows for an inferior good that in the case of a price *increase* the substitution effect causes *less* of the product to be purchased, whereas the related decline in real income activates a tendency for the consumer to purchase *more* of the good. (The diagrammatics of this situation are left as an exercise for the student.)

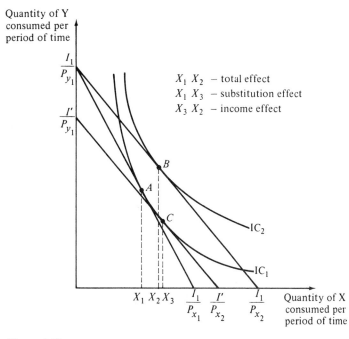

Quantity of Y consumed per period of time

$X_1 \, X_2$ – total effect
$X_1 \, X_3$ – substitution effect
$X_3 \, X_2$ – income effect

$\frac{I_1}{P_{y_1}}$

$\frac{I'}{P_{y_1}}$

B

A

C

IC$_2$

IC$_1$

$X_1 \, X_2 X_3 \quad \frac{I_1}{P_{x_1}} \quad \frac{I'}{P_{x_2}} \qquad \frac{I_1}{P_{x_2}}$ Quantity of X consumed per period of time

Figure 4-13
Income and substitution effects for an inferior good in case of a price decline

On the very rarest of occasions, a good may be so strongly inferior that the income effect actually overrides the substitution effect. Such an occurrence means that a decline in the price of a good will lead to a *decline* in the quantity demanded and that a rise in price will induce an *increase* in the quantity demanded—in other words, price and quantity move in the *same* direction. The name given to such a unique situation is *Giffen's paradox*, and it constitutes the only exception to the law of demand. Figure 4-14 illustrates the income and substitution effects for an inferior good subject to Giffen's paradox. It should be emphasized at this point, however, that the phenomenon of Giffen's paradox is so infrequently observed in the modern world that no current examples can be offered. It does appear that one example of it did appear in the nineteenth century. According to Alfred Marshall, a Sir R. Giffen noted cases where a rise in the price of bread "makes so large a drain on the resources of the poorer labouring families and raises so much the marginal utility of money to them, that they are forced to curtail their consumption of meat and the more expensive farinaceous foods; and, bread being still the cheapest food which they can get and will take, they consume more, and not less of it."[10] But such cases are rare; when they are met with, each must be treated on its own merits. Even in the case of this outdated

[10]Alfred Marshall, *Principles of Economics*, 8th ed. (London: Macmillan and Company, 1920), p. 132.

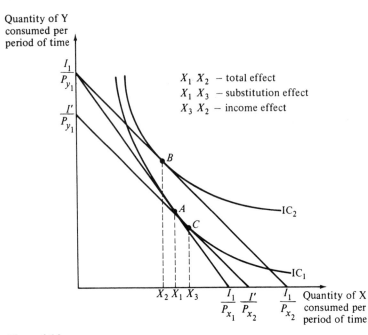

Quantity of Y
consumed per
period of time

$\dfrac{I_1}{P_{y_1}}$

$\dfrac{I'}{P_{y_1}}$

$X_1 \ X_2$ – total effect
$X_1 \ X_3$ – substitution effect
$X_3 \ X_2$ – income effect

B

A

C

IC$_2$

IC$_1$

$X_2 \ X_1 \ X_3$ $\dfrac{I_1}{P_{x_1}}$ $\dfrac{I'}{P_{x_2}}$ $\dfrac{I_1}{P_{x_2}}$ Quantity of X
consumed per
period of time

Figure 4-14
Income and substitution effects for an inferior good subject to Giffen's
paradox

example one may surmise that had the price of bread continued to rise, there quickly would have come a point when the purchases of bread began to decline. Thus, Giffen's paradox is likely to hold only for a fairly narrow range of prices. In our type of society Giffen's paradox is likely to be observed in at most a small minority of consuming units (individuals and households) and then only for precious few types of inferior goods.

MARKET DEMAND CURVES

The *market demand curve* for a product represents the various amounts of a product which consumers as a group are willing and able to purchase at various alternative prices at a specific moment of time wherein other factors influencing consumer behavior are held constant. Thus, the market demand curve isolates the relationship between price and the quantity demanded by all consumers. It is found by summing the quantities of a good that each consumer is willing and able to purchase at each and every alternative price.

Figure 4-15 illustrates this process for a three-person economy with individual demands as indicated. At a price of P_1 dollars, consumer A is willing and able to buy quantity q_A per period of time; consumer B is willing and able to buy quantity q_{B_1} per period of time; and consumer C is willing

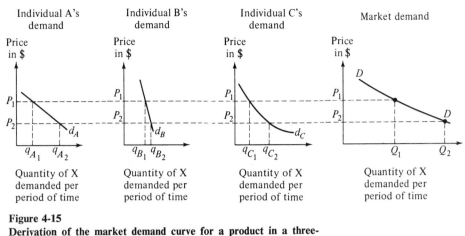

| Individual A's demand | Individual B's demand | Individual C's demand | Market demand |

Figure 4-15
Derivation of the market demand curve for a product in a three-person economy

and able to buy quantity q_{C_1} per period of time. Together they are willing and able to buy $q_{A_1} + q_{B_1} + q_{C_1} = Q_1$ units at a price of P_1 dollars, as indicated by the market demand curve. Likewise, at price P_2, consumer A is willing and able to purchase q_{A_2}; consumer B is willing and able to purchase q_{B_2}; and consumer C is willing and able to purchase q_{C_2}. Taken together, market demand at price P_2 is $Q_2 (= q_{A_2} + q_{B_2} + q_{C_2})$ units. Additional points on the

APPLICATIONS CAPSULE

WHICH IS LESS BURDENSOME—
AN INCOME TAX OR A SALES TAX?

Suppose that a sales tax is levied on cigarettes and that each week Mr. Tanner buys a carton of cigarettes, paying a fixed sum as sales tax on the cigarettes. The payment of the sales tax effectively raises the price of cigarettes and puts him on a lower difference curve, reducing Mr. Tanner's well-being. The graphics are depicted in the accompanying figure.

Assume that Mr. Tanner has an income of OB_1 dollars and, prior to the imposing of the sales tax, that the line of attainable combinations is B_1A_1. If Mr. Tanner spent all his income on cigarettes, he could buy OA_1 units; hence, the pretax price of cigarettes is OB_1/OA_1. The initial equilibrium purchase of cigarettes is at point R on IC_1, where OQ_1 cigarettes are bought and B_1Y_1 dollars are spent to pay for them. The levying of the sales tax shifts the line of attainable combinations to B_1A_2; Mr. Tanner's new equilibrium point is at S on IC_2, with expenditures for cigarettes of B_1Y_2 dollars and consumption of OQ_2 units.

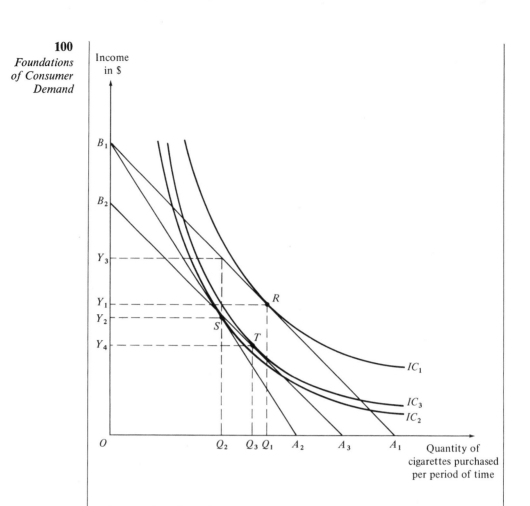

Income
in $

B_1

B_2

Y_3

Y_1

Y_2

S

Y_4

R

T

IC_1

IC_3

IC_2

O

Q_2 Q_3 Q_1 A_2 A_3 A_1 Quantity of
cigarettes purchased
per period of time

Since before the sales tax was imposed, Mr. Tanner could have purchased OQ_2 units for $B_1 Y_3$ dollars, the amount he pays in sales tax is
$Y_2 Y_3$ dollars. (An arithmetic example: Suppose Mr. Tanner formerly
bought 52 cartons per year at $4 per carton but after the sales tax was
imposed buys 40 cartons per year at $5. With the sales tax he is spending
$200 per year for cigarettes. But if there were no sales tax, he would have
had to pay only $160 for 40 cartons. Hence, the sales tax costs Mr.
Tanner $40 per year.)

But how would Mr. Tanner fare if instead of imposing a sales tax
on cigarettes the legislature in his state simply increased his income taxes
by an equivalent amount ($40 per year) to raise the desired tax revenue?
Would Mr. Tanner be better or worse off? Or would it make any difference one way or the other? Graphically, the effect of higher income taxes
is shown by an inward shift of the line of attainable combinations to
$B_2 A_3$, with distance $B_1 B_2$ being exactly equal to the dollar amount of the
income tax (in our example, $40). $B_2 A_3$ is parallel to $B_1 A_1$ because the
income tax need not disturb the price of cigarettes. Mr. Tanner's

equilibrium point, given the income tax, is at point T on IC_3 with purchases of OQ_3 units. Since T is on a higher indifference curve than S, it follows that Mr. Tanner would prefer paying an income tax (of $40) rather than a sales tax of the same dollar amount ($40).

The basic reason for this perhaps surprising result is that while both taxes reduce the consumer's real income, the sales tax also triggers a substitution effect because it alters not just real income but relative prices as well. The imposition of a general income tax brings on only an income effect, and the consumer is free to spend the income he has left without any further impact or adjustment. In contrast, imposing a product-specific (or excise) tax involves both an income and a substitution effect: The sales tax reduces consumer purchasing power and also changes the price attractiveness of the taxed good relative to other goods, thereby producing a greater revision in the consumer's expenditure pattern than an income tax alone.

Problems

1. Suppose that instead of making the dollar amount of the income tax equal to the dollar amount of the sales tax, the size of the income tax is set so as to leave the consumer on the *same* indifference curve as the sales tax. Determine which of the two taxes will raise the most tax revenue.
2. If Congress decided that it was in the public interest to conserve gasoline, would it be more effective to impose a sales tax upon gasoline or to increase personal income taxes? Demonstrate graphically. What reasons can you give for this result?

market demand curve can be similarly determined and the market curve constructed (line DD in Fig. 4-15). Since the individual demand curves are downsloping to the right, the market demand curve must also slope downward to the right. The law of demand holds not only for individual consumer demand but also for market demand.

However, adding together the demand curves of individuals to obtain market demand curves is not entirely valid since it implies that one consumer's purchases are completely independent of another consumer's purchase decisions. It has, for example, been noted that (1) some people buy goods not so much to satisfy inner wants as to impress other consumers with their "conspicuous consumption," (2) the buying habits of some individuals are influenced by the consumption patterns of persons with whom they associate or come into contact (the "demonstration effect"), and (3) some consumers buy goods because of the social status they connote. Consequently, on occasions the amount of an item purchased by one consumer has a bearing upon how other consumers behave. In such cases, individual demand curves, strictly speaking, are not independent, and a more complex adding-up process must be used to obtain the market demand curve.

SUMMARY AND CONCLUSIONS

The ordinal utility approach to consumer demand is both a supplement and an alternative to the cardinal utility approach for describing individual consumer behavior and for establishing the foundations of market demand. Indifference analysis is preferred by some economists in part because it does not require the precise quantification of utility and in part because it does not depend so heavily on the requirement of diminishing marginal utility.

A consumer's taste and preference pattern can be represented by a family of indifference curves. The shapes of the indifference curves are the critical features for displaying a consumer's set of tastes for a pair of commodities. Depending on the consumer's evaluation of the satisfying power of particular commodities, indifference curves can assume a variety of shapes and can be drawn so as to represent any set of tastes and preferences.

A consumer's ability to satisfy his or her tastes and preferences is represented by the line of attainable combinations. This line incorporates into the consumer's choice pattern the restraints imposed by the consumer's money income and by the prices of the goods the consumer may be desirous of purchasing. The point of tangency between the line of attainable combinations and an indifference curve defines the highest level of satisfaction which the consumer is capable of attaining, given his or her income and prevailing prices. The conditions requisite for maximizing satisfaction via the ordinal utility or indifference curve approach are exactly identical to the conditions derived from the cardinal utility approach.

By allowing income to vary, while holding product prices and the consumer's tastes fixed, the consumer's income-consumption curve can be established. The income-consumption curve illustrates the various purchase combinations that will maximize the consumer's satisfaction at different levels of income. From the data provided by the income-consumption curve, an Engel curve showing the relationship between money income and purchases of a good can be derived. Normal goods have positively sloped Engel curves; negatively sloped Engel curves are indicative of inferior goods.

The consumer's price-consumption curve can be found by observing the equilibrium path traced out by changing the price of a product and by holding money income and tastes and preferences constant. Data for plotting the consumer's demand curve are obtained from the price-consumption curve.

When the price of an item rises or falls, other relevant factors remaining unchanged, two factors are activated to prompt consumers to reassess the quantity of the item they are purchasing. The most powerful force, typically, is the substitution effect; it represents the extent to which the consumer is induced to alter what is purchased *solely* because of the change introduced in the relative prices of products. The second, and usually less powerful, force is the income effect; it represents the extent to which the consumer is motivated to buy more or less of a good because of the change in real income brought about by the price change.

In the case of normal goods the income and substitution effects operate in the same direction and reinforce one another. For inferior goods, however, the substitution and income effects work in opposite directions. For most inferior goods, the substitution effect overrides the impact of the income effect and causes the quantity demanded of a good to vary in the opposite direction from the change in the price of the good, thereby validating the law of demand. On the very rarest of occasions, a good may be so strongly inferior that the income effect overpowers the substitution effect and causes the quantity demanded to vary in the *same* direction as the change in price. Such a situation is termed Giffen's paradox and constitutes the only exception to the law of demand.

The market demand curve for a product is obtained by aggregating the quantity demanded by all individual consumers at each alternative market price.

SUGGESTED READINGS

BAILEY, M. J., "The Marshallian Demand Curve," *Journal of Political Economy*, Vol. 62 (June 1954), pp. 255–261.

FRIEDMAN, M., "The Marshallian Demand Curve," *Journal of Political Economy*, Vol. 57 (December 1949), pp. 463–495.

FRIEDMAN, M., "The 'Welfare' Effects of an Income Tax and an Excise Tax," *Journal of Political Economy*, Vol. 60 (February 1952), pp. 25–33.

HENDERSON, J. M., AND R. E. QUANDT, *Microeconomic Theory*, 2nd ed. (New York: McGraw-Hill Book Company, 1971), Chapter 2.

HENDLER, R., "Lancaster's New Approach to Consumer Demand and Its Limitations," *American Economic Review*, Vol. 65, No. 1 (March 1975), pp. 194–199.

HICKS, J. R., *Value and Capital*, 2nd ed. (Oxford: Clarendon Press, 1946), Chapters 1 and 2.

MARSHALL, A., *Principles of Economics*, 8th ed. (London: Macmillan and Company, 1920), Books 3 and 5.

MISHAN, E. J., "Theories of Consumer's Behavior: A Cynical View," *Economica*, New Series, Vol. 28 (February 1961), pp. 1–11.

SAMUELSON, P. A., "Consumption Theory in Terms of Revealed Preference," *Economica*, New Series, Vol. 15 (November 1948), pp. 243–253.

VICKREY, W. S., *Microstatics* (New York: Harcourt Brace Jovanovich, Inc., 1964), Chapter 2.

PROBLEMS AND QUESTIONS FOR DISCUSSION

1. Illustrate by means of indifference curves the taste and preference pattern suggested by the following statements:
   (a) "There is not enough money to make me eat a raw oyster."
   (b) "What good is a cigarette if you don't have a light?"
   (c) "I would just as soon eat broiled lobster as filet mignon."
   (d) "What good is money if you don't spend it? After all, you can't take it with you."

2. Graphically illustrate in three dimensions the nature of the total utility surface for two commodities which are perfect complements.

3. Suppose that a particular consumer has a special dislike for eating turnips but immensely enjoys eating barbecued spareribs. Draw an indifference map for these two commodities. Indicate the direction of higher degrees of satisfaction.

4. Explain the logical inconsistency involved were two indifference curves to intersect.

5. Suppose that the equation of an indifference curve for a consumer is as follows: $XY = 48$, where X = units of good X, Y = units of good Y, 48 = amount of utility or satisfaction expressed in utils.
   (a) Graphically determine the shape and location of this indifference curve. (Use graph paper.)
   (b) Determine the consumer's MRS_{xy} at $X = 4$ and $Y = 12$.
   (c) Suppose that the price of X is $10 per unit and the price of Y is $4 per unit. Determine the equation for the line of attainable combinations if the consumer's income level is $20. What is the slope of the line of attainable combinations at this income? Determine the equation and slope of the line of attainable combinations at an income of $30. Does the change in income from $20 to $30 influence the slope of the line of attainable combinations? Why or why not?
   (d) Illustrate graphically the point of tangency between the indifference curve $XY = 48$ and a line of attainable combinations where $P_x = \$10$ and $P_y = \$4$. How much income will it take for the consumer to attain 48 utils of satisfaction, given these prices?

6. Is a consumer's satisfaction level increased, decreased, or unaffected when the price of a product he or she is purchasing goes down? Illustrate graphically.

7. If indifference curves for perfect substitutes are negatively sloped and linear and if indifference curves for perfect complements are right angles, is it true that the degree of convexity of an indifference curve reflects the degree of substitutability and complementarity among commodities? Explain.

8. Graphically illustrate the combination of goods X and Y that will maximize satisfaction in the following set of circumstances:
   (a) Goods X and Y are perfect substitutes.
   (b) $MRS_{xy} = (-)1$.
   (c) $P_x = \$2, P_y = \$2.25$, and $I = \$18$.

9. Diagrammatically illustrate the income and substitution effects for an inferior good in the case of a price increase.

10. Diagrammatically illustrate the income and substitution effects for an inferior good subject to Giffen's paradox in the case of a price increase.

11. Suppose that two commodities X and Y are judged by consumers to be perfect substitutes for each other. Suppose further that the price of X is higher than the price of Y.
    (a) If consumers behave rationally, what would you predict to happen to sales of the two commodities?
    (b) Where consumers view products which compete against one another as being close or near perfect substitutes, is it surprising to find that their prices are identical or at least nearly so? Explain your answer.

12. Three frequently encountered Engel curves are shown below:

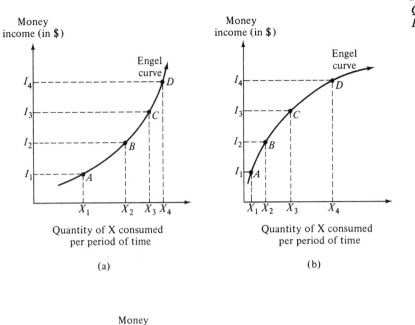

(a)

(b)

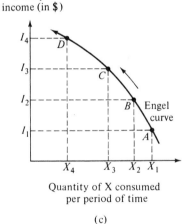

(c)

Describe the nature of the relationship between income and the quantity consumed for each of the three situations. Can you tell from the diagram whether the products in question are normal goods or inferior goods? Why or why not?

FIVE DEMAND FUNCTIONS, REVENUE FUNCTIONS, AND ELASTICITY

Utility analysis provides a good beginning to understanding the foundations of consumer demand. But one must go beyond utility theory to see how the economics of the firm is affected by consumer demand. The role of this chapter is to extend demand analysis to the firm, first by exploring the full complement of determinants of individual demand, second by relating the concept of demand to the firm and examining the demand curves for its products, and third by deriving the revenue functions that correspond to the firm's demand curves. In addition, attention will be focused upon the total and marginal revenue functions associated with demand curves and upon the sensitivity of demand to changes in price and consumer income.

VARIABLES THAT INFLUENCE MARKET DEMAND

Many variables influence the quantity of a good or service that all consumers in the market will purchase at some moment of time. Certainly, price is a primary factor influencing quantity demanded. Just as obviously, other factors are also relevant:

1. Consumer taste and preference patterns (as reflected by the composite of utility functions or indifference maps for individual consumers).

2. Consumers' money income (or purchasing power).
3. The prices of related products (both substitutes and complementary goods).
4. Consumer expectations with respect to future prices, income levels, and product availability.
5. The range of goods and services available for selection by consumers.

A word about each of these is in order.

Consumer Tastes and Preferences. The relevance of consumer tastes for determining demand is easily apparent. When consumer perceptions of a good or service become less favorable, market demand for the item lessens. By the same token, an increase in the intensity of consumer desire for an item tends to increase willingness to pay a higher price or to buy more of it or both. Needless to say, consumer taste and preference patterns undergo continuous review and are subject to change, sometimes gradual and sometimes rapid, over time. The emergence of new and better products, changing values and life-styles, new information about health and safety features of products, the business cycle, rising living standards, higher levels of affluence, and advertising, to mention a few, all exert a pervasive and dynamic influence upon consumer tastes and preferences.

Consumer Income. That income has an impact upon market demand is plain enough. The ability of consumers to buy commodities, as given by their money income and purchasing power, is what permits them to satisfy their material desires. Willingness to buy is in itself insufficient; consumers must be *able to pay* for the commodities they want. Typically, the greater is consumer income the greater will be market demand for goods in general and for some items in particular. Only in the case of inferior goods is rising income accompanied by a weakening of demand.

Prices of Related Items. The prices of related items are an important demand variable because of the interrelationships that exist among goods. In the case of substitute goods, how the price of one compares with the price of competing brands can be a pivotal factor in the consumer's selection process. If Schlitz is cheaper than Budweiser, this fact is sure to influence, at least partially, a consumer's choice of which to buy. In the case of items which have a complementary relationship and are demanded jointly (golf clubs and golf balls, automobiles and gasoline, toothpaste and toothbrushes), it is equally clear that relative prices are pertinent. If the price of popcorn jumps by 50%, the demand for popcorn salt is certain to be weakened; if the price of electricity rises substantially, the demand for air-conditioning is likely to be dampened.

Consumer Expectations. Consumer expectations with respect to future price levels, income levels, and product availability tend to influence current purchase behavior. If consumers believe that the prices of goods they expect to buy shortly are going to rise in price, they will be motivated to buy them

108

*Demand
Functions,
Revenue
Functions,
and Elasticity*

now and escape paying the higher prices. Income expectations work much the same way. Some consumers may purchase goods currently with a view toward paying for them later out of expected increases in income; fears of a recession or impending unemployment make consumers more cautious and thrift conscious. Similarly, if consumers for some reason expect a good to be unavailable or in short supply in the near future (because of a strike, crop failures, production bottlenecks, etc.), they will be induced to increase current purchases.

Range of Available Products. The range of goods and services available for consumers' selection affects the demand for a particular item in the sense that all items compete for consumer dollars. The more alternatives buyers have open to them, the stronger the competition for consumers' attention and the weaker market demand for any one specific item tends to be. Diminishing marginal utility for additional units of a particular good makes consumers more prone to spread their income out over a wider range of commodities when there is more to choose from.

Since the market demand for an item is the summation of individual consumer demands for the item, then it is obvious that the *number of consumers* has a direct bearing on market demand.

SOME ADDED DEMAND DETERMINANTS

While the preceding factors are generally acknowledged as the "major" demand determinants, other variables can assume a significant impact on the nature and intensity of the demand for a product or service. For example, it can make a great difference in the strength of demand whether a product is a "luxury" or a "necessity." Although deciding whether an item should be classed as a luxury or a necessity is largely a function of life-styles and value judgments, the demands for luxuries and necessities are distinctly different in their responses to price changes, recessionary conditions, interest rates and credit availability, and market scope. The necessity-luxury aspect explicitly recognizes the multitude of sociological influences on demand and prompts a more definitive delineation of who buys what and with what degree of urgency.

The demand for an item may be derived from the demand for other goods, thus being known as a *derived demand*. For instance, the demand for steel is derived from the demand for products containing steel or requiring steel somewhere in the course of their production. The demand for newsprint is derived from the demand for newspapers. The demand for typewriters is derived from the demand for secretarial services. When the demand for a good is derived, as in the case of intermediate goods and capital goods, considerable information may be gained from examining the markets for the final goods to which the good in question is ultimately related.

The degree of *market saturation* for a product can be a key factor in the sales volume and sales potential of a product, especially for durable goods. To cite a familiar case, the current market for black-and-white TV sets is largely restricted to a replacement demand with some sales going to newly formed households. Why? Because over 95% of the households today have a TV set. In contrast, the market potential for microwave ovens is far greater. Less than 20% of American households have microwave ovens, thus offering microwave ovens producers a much larger sales potential than would be the case if the household saturation level were higher. The limited demand for items having high saturation levels has prompted some producers of durable goods to adopt a policy of "planned obsolescence," whereby their products are restyled periodically, new features are added, and consumers are in turn induced to increase the frequency with which they replace their "worn-out" and "out-of-date" durable goods.[1]

For those types of consumer goods which are typically purchased with the aid of credit (automobiles, appliances, furniture, houses), the level of consumer debt and prevailing interest rates may be valuable additions to the dimensions of the consumer's buying power and may, in fact, be more closely related to the demand for such items than is current money income. Logic dictates that the higher the ratio of consumer debt to consumer income and the higher the rates of interest on borrowed funds, the less able and less eager will consumers be to make additional commitments toward the purchase of such items until more favorable buying conditions present themselves.

Last, for those items whose purchase is truly discretionary, a superior measure of consumer purchasing power may be derived by considering the consumer's *discretionary income*. This is the residual amount of income remaining after subtracting necessary living expenses and fixed payment charges from disposable personal income. Discretionary income might, for example, be found to be closely related to consumer expenditures for durables, recreation, and travel activities, therefore making it a more valid demand determinant for some goods than other income measures. The National Industrial Conference Board publishes a discretionary income series. Somewhat more refined measures of the discretionary buying power of consumers add to discretionary income such items as cash balances, near-liquid assets, and the availability of new consumer credit, thereby providing a more comprehensive indicator of consumer purchasing power for items which are not in the category of "necessities."

Additional reflection would, no doubt, suggest still other factors which bear upon the demand variables for certain products. It is to be emphasized, however, that each good or service has its own peculiar set of demand determinants and that, in turn, these determinants influence demand in ways that may be unique to each specific item.

[1]For a good discussion of the economics of planned obsolescence, see Ronald J. Dornoff and Esmond T. Adams, "Planned Obsolescence: Stimulus or Crutch," *Mississippi Valley Journal of Business and Economics*, Vol. 6, No. 2 (Winter 1970–1971), pp. 10–19.

The discussion of the circumstances prompting consumers to buy or not to buy a product suggests that the market demand for an item is the result of the complex interaction of a wide variety of forces. In mathematical terms, the demand function for an item can be symbolized as

$$Q_d = f(P, T, I, P_r, E, R, N, O),$$

where Q_d = quantity demanded of the good (or service),
P = market price of the good (or service),
T = consumer tastes and preferences,
I = level of consumer incomes (or purchasing power),
P_r = prices of related items,
E = consumer expectations regarding future prices, incomes, and product availability,
R = range of goods and services available to consumers,
N = number of potential consumers, and
O = all other factors which may influence Q_d.

The major demand determinants (P through N above) are likely to be influential in the case of nearly every product, though their individual impacts certainly will vary in degree and intensity from product to product. The term "all other factors" is composed of those market features specific or unique to the product in question.

Using the functional notation to symbolize the relationship between the quantity demanded of a particular product and specific demand-influencing variables is a more explicit and conceptually accurate way of representing the demand for a product than is the simple graphic portrayal of price-quantity relationships in the form of demand curves.

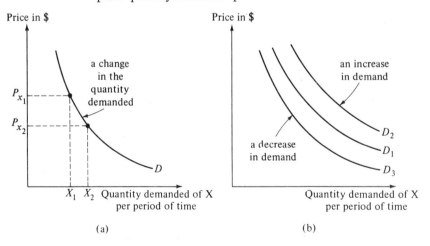

(a) (b)

Figure 5-1
The nature of shifts in consumer purchases and demand intensity

Nevertheless, it is usually convenient to segregate demand determinants into two groups: (1) the selling price of the product and (2) all other demand determinants. Using this dichotomization, variations in the purchases of a product associated solely with changes in product price are customarily termed "changes in the quantity demanded" and are represented graphically by movements *along* a given demand curve. In Fig. 5-1(a), a decrease in the price of X from P_{x_1} to P_{x_2} increases the quantity demanded from X_1 to X_2—all other factors influencing the purchase volume are assumed to remain unchanged. On the other hand, quantity variations which stem from changes in one or more of demand determinants *other than price* are referred to as "changes in demand" and are represented graphically by shifts in the demand curve [Fig. 5-1(b)].[2] For example, such factors as increases in consumer incomes, a larger advertising budget, a more intensive desire for a good, or an increase in the price of substitutes would tend to shift the position of a given demand curve to the right, say from line D_1D_1 to D_2D_2 in Fig. 5-1(b). Such events as a decline in the number of consumers, an increase in the range of goods (especially substitutes) available to consumers, or the expectation of a forthcoming price decrease tend to shift the demand curve to the left, as illustrated by shifting D_1D_1 to position D_3D_3 in Fig. 5-1(b).

The distinction between the two terms "change in quantity demanded" and "change in demand" correctly suggests that graphically representing the price-quantity relationship in the form of a demand curve does *not* mean that the price of an item is the sole, or even the principal, determinant of the amount purchased at some moment of time. All a demand curve purports to show is the impact that different prices will have upon the amounts purchased *when the remaining factors comprising the demand function are fixed in value.*

AVERAGE, TOTAL, AND MARGINAL REVENUE

Now suppose that we focus upon the intensity of consumer demand for a particular firm's product. Figure 5-2 depicts a hypothetical demand curve for a firm. The points along this curve represent the *maximum quantities* per unit

---

[2]The terms "change in the quantity demanded" and "change in demand" can be explained readily in the language of mathematics. Suppose that the equation of the demand curve is given by

$$P = a - bQ,$$

where P represents the selling price of a commodity and Q represents the quantity bought. As long as all the demand determinants other than P remain constant, the parameters a and b also remain constant and the equation $P = a - bQ$ defines a unique demand curve. A change in P will result in a movement along this demand curve to the corresponding value of Q—this is what has been termed a "change in the quantity demanded." However, shifts in demand determinants other than P are reflected by changes in the values of a and b. A change in the value of a shifts the level of the curve, and a change in the value of b alters the slope of the curve—either or both of which represent a "change in demand" and define the equation of a new demand curve.

112

*Demand
Functions,
Revenue
Functions,
and Elasticity*

of time that consumers are willing to buy from this firm at various alternative prices. However, it is equally accurate to view a firm's demand curve as representing the *maximum prices* that buyers are willing to pay a seller to obtain various quantities of his product. In terms of Fig. 5-2, if the firm offered quantity Q_1 for sale, P_1 is the maximum price it would be able to charge and still generate a demand of Q_1 units. (Naturally, consumers would gladly pay less for the item were the opportunity to present itself.) Moreover, it follows that price P_1 represents the *average* amount of revenue the firm will receive *per unit sold* or simply *average revenue* (*AR*). Accordingly, a firm's demand curve can with equal propriety be labeled an average revenue curve.

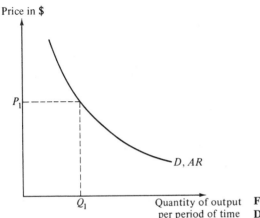

Figure 5-2
Demand or average revenue curve for a firm

As with the firm's demand function, the firm's *AR* function may be expressed as a function of the quantity sold. When a firm sells all its output at the same price, its selling price and its average revenue are the same value, in which case

$$AR = P = f(Q).$$

However, if the firm sells its product at different prices to different customers, average revenue is equal to a weighted average of the selling prices, with the weights being the proportions sold at each price. Then the *AR* function becomes

$$AR = \bar{P} = f(Q),$$

where $\bar{P}$ represents the *average* selling price.

Now let us utilize the demand-*AR* concepts to examine properties of a firm's other revenue functions for each of several possible sets of demand conditions.

Average, Total, and Marginal Revenue
When the Demand Curve Is Horizontal

113

*Average,
Total,
and Marginal
Revenue*

Consider first the simple, but rather unusual, case where the firm confronts a horizontal demand curve for its product, as in Fig. 5-3(a). A horizontal demand curve means that a firm can sell all the units it wishes at the price given by the intersection of the demand curve with the price axis; in Fig. 5-3(a) this is shown as a price of $10.[3] If the firm raises its price above $10,

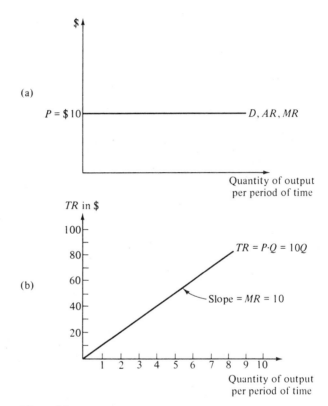

Figure 5-3
Average, total, and marginal revenue functions for a firm whose demand curve is horizontal

[3]Just because a firm's demand curve is horizontal, it does not follow that the law of demand is suspended. Although a firm may be able to sell all it wishes within the limits of its production capacity at a particular price, it still is true that a single consumer will prefer to buy more at lower prices than at higher prices. Likewise, it is still true that consumers as a group will prefer to buy more at lower prices than at higher prices. What may make the demand curve horizontal for a *firm* is the fact that *many* other sellers are offering consumers an *identical* product; thus, all firms may be driven by the market forces of demand and supply to sell at the same price. Because each firm is so small relative to the total market, they are able to sell all they can produce at the prevailing price, and their individual demand curves are, therefore, horizontal.

no units can be sold. Obviously, if the firm can sell all it wishes at a price of $10, it can also sell all it wishes below $10. However, we would logically expect the firm to offer its product for sale at the maximum price of $10, as no advantage can be gained from lowering price. The equation of the firm's average revenue and demand functions in this situation is

$$AR = P = \$10.$$

The firm's *total revenue function* is found by multiplying average revenue (AR) or selling price (P) by the number of units sold (Q) and may be written as

$$TR = AR \cdot Q = P \cdot Q.$$

When the demand curve is horizontal, the corresponding total revenue curve is always a positively sloped linear function starting from the origin and having a slope equal to the product price [see Fig. 5-3(b)]. In this example, the slope of the total revenue function is equal to 10 because every time one more unit is sold, the firm's total revenue rises by $10; the related equation for TR is

$$TR = P \cdot Q = 10Q.$$

Marginal revenue is best defined as the rate of change in total revenue as the rate of output changes. This means, in mathematical terms, that the firm's *marginal revenue function* is the first derivative of the total revenue function. Thus, in our example, if

$$TR = 10Q,$$

then

$$MR = \frac{dTR}{dQ} = 10.$$

The constant value of 10 for MR means that each 1-unit increase in sales will cause total revenue to rise by $10. Geometrically, the value of marginal revenue is always equal to the slope of the total revenue function; hence, given that the firm's TR function is linear whenever the demand curve is horizontal and that linear functions have a constant slope, it follows that the value of MR for a linear TR function is necessarily a constant value no matter what the firm's volume of sales. In other words, if the firm can sell all it wishes at a price of $10, marginal revenue is fixed at $10 and is exactly equal to the firm's selling price and average revenue. The marginal revenue function corresponding to a horizontal demand-AR curve is graphically identical, therefore, to the demand-AR curve, as shown in Fig. 5-3(a).

Sometimes it is helpful to think of marginal revenue as being the change in total revenue associated with a 1-*unit* change in sales ($\Delta TR/\Delta Q$, where $\Delta Q = 1$ unit). This concept of MR is appropriate when one has occasion to calculate the change in total revenue associated with a *discrete* change in output; it will be referred to as *discrete marginal revenue*. But when sales volume can be varied continuously—that is, changes in Q can be infinitesimally small—MR is most appropriately defined and calculated as the derivative of the firm's TR function. We shall refer to the latter concept of MR as *continuous marginal revenue*. Both concepts of MR will have their place in future discussions.

In the example above, the nature of the demand function is such that the values for discrete MR and continuous MR are both $10. This is typical for horizontal demand functions, but it is not true of other types of demand functions, as the next case illustrates.

Average, Total, and Marginal Revenue When the Demand Curve Is Linear and Downsloping

Somewhat more plausible is the product demand circumstance where the firm's demand-AR curve is linear and downsloping. The general equation for linear, downsloping demand-AR functions can be expressed as

$$AR = P = a - bQ.$$

The value of a in the equation is the price at which the demand curve intersects the price axis and, in economic terms, is the price just high enough so that no consumers will be willing to purchase the firm's product. The value of b in the equation is the slope of the demand curve. The minus sign $(-)$ means that the demand curve is negatively sloped and that there exists an inverse relationship between P and Q, all of which is, of course, the usual case. The graph of a linear, downsloping demand-AR curve is shown in Fig. 5-4(a).

Since a firm's total revenue from the sale of a commodity equals average revenue times the quantity sold (or price times the quantity sold), the expression for TR can be obtained by multiplying the demand-AR expression by Q:

$$TR = P \cdot Q \qquad \text{(or } AR \cdot Q)$$
$$= (a - bQ)Q$$
$$= aQ - bQ^2.$$

A total revenue function of this type is graphically portrayed by a parabola of the shape in Fig. 5-4(b).

As before, the corresponding marginal revenue function is the derivative of the total revenue function. Since $TR = aQ - bQ^2$, then

$$MR = \frac{dTR}{dQ} = a - 2bQ.$$

Plotting the MR function on the same diagram as the demand and AR functions [Fig. 5-4(a)] reveals that the MR curve lies below the demand curve. Both curves originate at the same value a, but the slope of the MR function

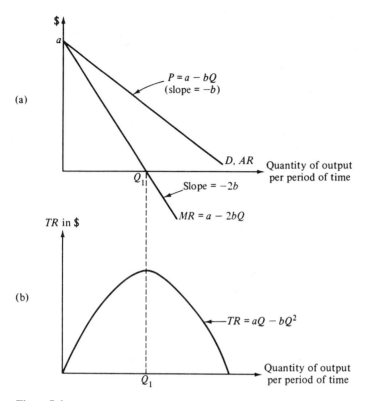

(a)

$P = a - bQ$
(slope = $-b$)

D, AR

Quantity of output per period of time

Q_1

Slope = $-2b$

$MR = a - 2bQ$

TR in $

(b)

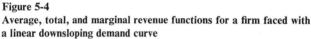

$TR = aQ - bQ^2$

Quantity of output per period of time

Q_1

Figure 5-4
Average, total, and marginal revenue functions for a firm faced with a linear downsloping demand curve

is twice as great as the slope of the demand curve ($-2b$ as compared to $-b$). In geometric terms, the MR curve is located by drawing it so as to bisect the horizontal distance between the demand curve and the vertical axis. However, this procedure is accurate only in the case of a linear demand curve.

Marginal revenue is less than price (average revenue) because with a downsloping demand function the firm must lower its selling price to boost the quantity sold. The lower price applies not only to the additional units sold but also to the units of output which otherwise could have been sold at a higher price. For instance, suppose that a firm can sell 50 units at a price of $1 and realize total revenue of $50. To increase sales by 1 unit to 51 units, the firm must lower its price, say to $0.99 on all units sold. The increase in total revenue is *not* the $0.99 gained from the sale of the 51st unit, because the firm must give up revenue of $0.01 on each of the previous 50 units formerly selling at $1. The net gain in total revenue is $0.99 − $0.50 or $0.49, as can easily be verified by multiplying 51 units times $0.99, which gives a total revenue of $50.49. Hence, the marginal revenue of the 51st unit is $0.49, which is less than its selling price of $0.99.

One further very important relationship remains to be pointed out. This concerns the MR and TR functions. Observe in Fig. 5-4 that the TR function increases at a decreasing rate up to a sales volume of Q_1 units; over this same range, MR is *positive* but decreasing in value. Earlier it was stated that MR at any sales volume Q equals the slope of the TR function at that value of Q. Since the TR function has a positive slope up to an output of Q_1, MR of necessity must be positive; likewise, just as the slope of the TR function diminishes as the sales level approaches Q_1 units, so does the value of MR diminish. Marginal revenue is zero at exactly the same output level (Q_1) at which total revenue is maximum. Past a sales volume of Q_1, TR falls and MR is negative. Consequently, when the slope of the TR function is zero, MR is zero, and when the slope of the TR function is negative, MR is negative.

A numerical example at this point may serve to clarify and illuminate these relationships among AR, TR, and MR. Suppose that a firm's demand-AR function can be represented by the equation

$$P = 12 - Q \qquad (\text{or } AR = 12 - Q).$$

The total revenue and marginal revenue functions can be calculated as follows:

$$TR = AR \cdot Q = P \cdot Q$$
$$= (12 - Q)Q = 12Q - Q^2,$$
$$MR = \frac{dTR}{dQ} = 12 - 2Q.$$

Table 5-1 contains representative values for P, Q, AR, TR, continuous MR, and discrete MR as derived from the preceding equations. Several attributes of the values in Table 5-1 are worth noting. First, when price is \$12 or higher,

Table 5-1 Demand and Revenue Data for a Linear Demand Function

Quantity of Output Demanded	Price ($P =$ $12 - Q$)	Average Revenue ($AR =$ $12 - Q$)	Total Revenue ($TR =$ $12Q - Q^2$)	Continuous Marginal Revenue ($MR =$ $12 - 2Q$)	Discrete Marginal Revenue ($MR =$ $TR_Q - TR_{Q-1}$)
0	\$12	\$12	\$ 0	\$12	
1	11	11	11	10	\$11
2	10	10	20	8	9
3	9	9	27	6	7
4	8	8	32	4	5
5	7	7	35	2	3
6	6	6	36	0	1
7	5	5	35	-2	-1
8	4	4	32	-4	-3
9	3	3	27	-6	-5
10	2	2	20	-8	-7

118

*Demand
Functions,
Revenue
Functions,
and Elasticity*

no consumer is willing to purchase any of the firm's product. Second, selling price and AR are identical; as stated earlier, this is a necessary result of a single-price policy. Third, TR increases rapidly at first, then more slowly, reaches a maximum at 6 units of output, and declines thereafter as sales continue to increase. Fourth, the values for continuous MR are positive but steadily declining for the first 5 units of output; MR is zero where TR is at its maximum value of $36, and MR is ever more negative as the sales volume extends beyond 6 units. Fifth, the discrete MR values (which are computed by subtracting successive values of TR in order to obtain the change in TR associated with a 1-unit change in Q) do not correspond exactly to the values for continuous MR. This is not because the two concepts are inconsistent but because they are really associated with different output or sales levels. For instance, when TR rises from $11 to $20 as a consequence of a rise in sales from 1 to 2 units, it is fair to say that the $9 gain in revenue is not MR when TR is $20 and sales are 2 units but is instead MR *between* 1 and 2 units of output. The values for discrete MR in Table 5-1 are more correctly associated with output rates of $\frac{1}{2}$, $1\frac{1}{2}$, $2\frac{1}{2}$, and so on. This can easily be confirmed by substituting these values of Q into the equation for continuous MR; the resulting values for MR correspond exactly to the values for discrete MR presented in the table. Thus, the discrete and continuous measures of MR are perfectly compatible and define the same MR function and curve. If the TR function is known, it is usually more convenient to use the continuous measure of MR. If MR must be determined from a table of TR values, the discrete measure of MR is the simplest to calculate.

Plotting the values in Table 5-1 will yield curves that possess the relationships alluded to in Fig. 5-4. The reader should verify this.

Average, Total, and Marginal Revenue When the Demand Curve Is Curvilinear

The demand curve for a commodity can assume a wide variety of curvilinear forms. No attempt is made here to catalog the diverse types of demand curves. We shall be content with examining two basic curvilinear demand curves with relatively simple equations.

Suppose that the demand curve for a firm's product is given by the generalized expression

$$P = a - bQ + cQ^2,$$

where a, b, and c are constants. The firm's AR function will likewise be

$$AR = a - bQ + cQ^2.$$

Again, the total revenue function is found by multiplying the demand equation (or *AR* equation) by the quantity sold as follows:

$$TR = P \cdot Q = AR \cdot Q$$
$$= (a - bQ + cQ^2)Q$$
$$= aQ - bQ^2 + cQ^3.$$

The marginal revenue function is the first derivative of the total revenue function, giving

$$MR = \frac{dTR}{dQ} = a - 2bQ + 3cQ^2.$$

The shapes of these functions are pictured in Fig. 5-5. Observe that the *MR* function lies everywhere below the demand function except for their common beginning value. The values for *MR* are declining but greater than zero for the output range where *TR* is rising; *MR* is zero where *TR* is maximum. When the demand curve is convex to the origin, as in this example, the *MR* curve lies to the left of a line bisecting the horizontal distance between the vertical axis and the demand curve.

Another plausible shape for the firm's demand curve to assume is that

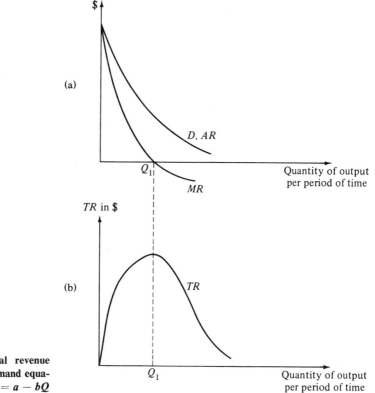

Figure 5-5
**Average, total, and marginal revenue
functions for a firm whose demand equation is of the general form $P = a - bQ$
$+ cQ^2$**

shown in Fig. 5-6 and associated with the general equation

$$P = a + bQ - cQ^2.$$

As before, the AR function has the same equation:

$$AR = a + bQ - cQ^2.$$

The TR function is again derived by multiplying the demand (or AR) equation by Q:

$$\begin{aligned} TR = P \cdot Q &= AR \cdot Q \\ &= (a + bQ - cQ^2)Q \\ &= aQ + bQ^2 - cQ^3. \end{aligned}$$

Taking the derivative of the TR function, we get the MR function:

$$MR = \frac{dTR}{dQ} = a + 2bQ - 3cQ^2.$$

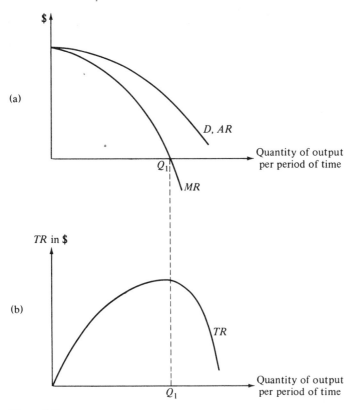

(a)

(b)

Figure 5-6
Average, total, and marginal revenue functions for a firm whose demand equation is of the general form $P = a + bQ - cQ^2$

Note that the graphs of these functions (shown in Fig. 5-6) portray the same basic relations among demand, AR, TR, and MR as stated earlier. Apart from the shapes of the curves, a significant difference between this case and the previous examples is the location of the MR function. Although MR still lies below the demand function, this time it is located to the right of a line bisecting the horizontal distance between the vertical axis and the demand curve.

ELASTICITY OF DEMAND

The concept of *elasticity* is one of the most important aspects of demand analysis. In general terms, elasticity of demand measures the magnitude of the *responsiveness* or *sensitivity* of the quantity demanded of a product to a change in some demand determinant. More specifically, elasticity concerns the extent to which a percentage change in one demand variable causes (or is associated directly with) a percentage change in the quantity demanded. Mathematically, the elasticity of demand ϵ(epsilon) is calculated as

$$\epsilon = \frac{\% \text{ change in quantity demanded}}{\% \text{ change in any demand determinant}}.$$

Elasticity is *always* calculated in relative or percentage terms rather than in absolute or unit terms. This permits comparisons of demand sensitivity for different products, irrespective of the units in which products or product prices are quoted. (A 5% change has the same meaning whether it is measured in tons, dozens, crates, cans, cents, or dollars.) And because elasticity is calculated by dividing a percentage change by a percentage change, the elasticity coefficient (ϵ) is a pure number free of any identification with the units in which the variables are expressed.

There are as many kinds of demand elasticity as there are numbers of demand determinants for a product (price elasticity, income elasticity, and so on).

Price Elasticity of Demand

The relation of product price to sales volume is of major interest to business firms as a basis for pricing policy, sales strategy, and achievement of profit and market share objectives. Consider the case of products X and Y with demand curves as shown in Fig. 5-7. The negative slopes of both curves indicate that as the prices of X and Y fall, the quantities demanded of X and Y rise. From the diagram, when the prices of X and Y are P_{x_1} and P_{y_1} (where $P_{x_1} = P_{y_1}$), the quantities purchased are X_1 units and Y_1 units, respectively. However, if the prices of X and Y decline by an identical amount to P_{x_2} and

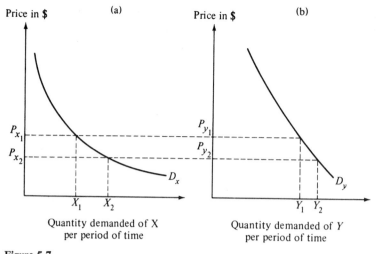

Figure 5-7
Sensitivity of product demand to price changes

P_{y_2}, the change in the quantity demanded of X (X_1 to X_2) is greater than the change in the quantity demanded of Y (Y_1 to Y_2). In other words, the demand for X is more sensitive or responsive to a change in the price of X than the demand for Y is to a change in the price of Y at the indicated prices. Or, in the language of economics, we can say that the price elasticity of demand for X is greater than the price elasticity of demand for Y over the indicated price range.

Price elasticity of demand can be defined more precisely as

$$\epsilon_p = \frac{\% \text{ change in quantity demanded}}{\% \text{ change in price}}.$$

The coefficient of price elasticity is always negative. Why? Because price and quantity demanded are inversely related; when price falls the quantity demanded tends to rise and when price rises the quantity demanded tends to fall. Therefore, with one percentage change being negative and the other being positive, the price elasticity coefficient is necessarily negative.

Two distinct methods for calculating price elasticity exist: the arc elasticity method and the point elasticity method. *Arc elasticity* is a measure of the responsiveness of the quantity demanded between two separate points on a demand curve. *Point elasticity* is a measure of the sensitivity of the quantity demanded at a single point on the curve for an infinitesimal change in price.

Arc Elasticity. To illustrate the arc technique for computing price elasticity, consider a demand curve having two points A and B with price-

	Price	Quantity Demanded
Point A	$12	30 units
Point B	$10	50 units

Now suppose we determine the degree of responsiveness of quantity demanded to a *decrease* in price from $12 to $10—this is equivalent to moving down along the demand curve from point A to point B. It will be recalled that the usual way of computing percentage change is to find the change in a value relative to its original value (designated below by the subscript 1) and multiply by 100 to convert the ratio to a percentage figure. Algebraically, then, our definition of price elasticity is equivalent to

$$\epsilon_p = \frac{\% \text{ change in quantity demanded}}{\% \text{ change in price}} = \frac{[(Q_2 - Q_1)/Q_1] \times 100}{[(P_2 - P_1)/P_1] \times 100},$$

where the pairs (Q_1, P_1) and (Q_2, P_2) represent, respectively, the quantity and price values *before* and *after* their change. Note, however, the multiplication by 100 of both the numerator and denominator is superfluous and can be omitted, as the terms cancel out in dividing. Substituting the appropriate values into the thus simplified formula gives

$$\epsilon_p = \frac{(Q_2 - Q_1)/Q_1}{(P_2 - P_1)/P_1} = \frac{(50 - 30)/30}{(10 - 12)/12} = \frac{20/30}{(-2)/12} = \frac{2}{3} \cdot -\frac{6}{1} = -4.0.$$

Yet, if we compute the sensitivity of the quantity demanded to an *increase* in price from $10 to $12 (equivalent to moving up the demand curve from point B to point A), the coefficient of price elasticity is

$$\epsilon_p = \frac{(Q_2 - Q_1)/Q_1}{(P_2 - P_1)/P_1} = \frac{(30 - 50)/50}{(12 - 10)/10} = \frac{(-20)/50}{2/10} = \frac{-2}{5} \cdot \frac{5}{1} = -2.0.$$

The discrepancy in the two elasticity coefficients arises because the percentage changes going from point A to point B are not the same as those in moving from B to A. Indeed, changing the base values for the percentage calculation from P_1, Q_1 to P_2, Q_2 gives two widely diverging measures of price sensitivity for the very same interval along the demand curve.[4]

[4]This example demonstrates why arc elasticity calculations are only approximations. This is especially true when the shape of the demand curve is not known and data for only a few prices and quantities are given. For example, it may be observed when the price is $8, that 250 units of the item are purchased, and when the price is $7, that 350 units are purchased. However, as the figure on the next page suggests, an infinite number of demand curves can pass through these two points, and these curves in general will possess slightly different elasticities at these prices.

124

*Demand
Functions,
Revenue
Functions,
and Elasticity*

This is a troublesome matter but not one without some remedy. The ambiguity of arbitrarily using one of the two points (*A* or *B*) as the original or base values for calculating the percentage changes can be partially overcome by using the averages of the quantity values as the base for calculating the percentage change in *Q* and the average of the two prices as the base for calculating the percentage change in *P*. Making this adjustment gives the more satisfactory formula

$$\epsilon_p = \frac{\dfrac{Q_2 - Q_1}{\left(\dfrac{Q_1 + Q_2}{2}\right)}}{\dfrac{P_2 - P_1}{\left(\dfrac{P_1 + P_2}{2}\right)}}.$$

With the modified formula it makes no difference which of the two points is point 1 and which is point 2; the same elasticity coefficient is obtained either way. For this reason, the modified formula is the accepted way of computing arc elasticity and is the one we shall use henceforth. Still, for the arc elasticity coefficient to be reliable and susceptible to meaningful interpretation, it should be computed only between points on a demand curve which are reasonably close together. In terms of our previous numerical example, the coefficient of price elasticity for a decline in price from $12 to $10 becomes

$$\epsilon_p = \frac{\dfrac{Q_2 - Q_1}{\left(\dfrac{Q_1 + Q_2}{2}\right)}}{\dfrac{P_2 - P_1}{\left(\dfrac{P_1 + P_2}{2}\right)}} = \frac{\dfrac{50 - 30}{\left(\dfrac{30 + 50}{2}\right)}}{\dfrac{10 - 12}{\left(\dfrac{12 + 10}{2}\right)}}$$

$$= \frac{\dfrac{20}{40}}{\dfrac{-2}{11}} = \frac{1}{2} \cdot -\frac{11}{2} = -\frac{11}{4} = -2.75.$$

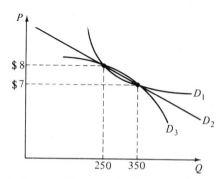

In general, the farther apart the two points between which arc elasticity is computed, the greater is the discrepancy between the price elasticity coefficients obtained from the two-point arc formula.

Returning to our previous numerical example and using the modified formula, -2.75 should be interpreted as meaning that over the indicated range of prices and quantities a 1% change in price will be followed by approximately a 2.75% change in quantity demanded in the *opposite* direction.[5]

Since the sign of the price elasticity coefficient is always negative (in accordance with the law of demand), it is the *size* of the coefficient itself which is most relevant. By convention, economists say that when the coefficient is a number greater than 1, demand is *elastic*, and that when the coefficient is less than 1, demand is *inelastic*. Should the coefficient turn out, by chance, to be exactly 1, demand is said to be *unitary* or of *unitary elasticity*. The rationale for this classification is straightforward. When the coefficient is greater than 1, the percentage change in quantity demanded must necessarily be *larger* than the percentage change in price. It follows, then, that the quantity demanded is relatively responsive or sensitive to price changes— or, in the language of economists, that demand is elastic. On the other hand, when the coefficient is less than 1, the percentage change in quantity demanded is *smaller* than the percentage change in price, clearly implying that the quantity demanded is relatively unresponsive or insensitive (or inelastic) with regard to price changes.

Point Elasticity. Measuring elasticity at a point eliminates the imprecision of the arc elasticity concept. Point elasticity, as the name implies, refers to the responsiveness of quantity demanded to very small price changes from a given point. Algebraically, this translates into the following:

$$\epsilon_p = \frac{\Delta Q/Q}{\Delta P/P} = \frac{\Delta Q}{Q} \cdot \frac{P}{\Delta P} = \frac{\Delta Q}{\Delta P} \cdot \frac{P}{Q}.$$

This expression says that price elasticity at a point equals the ratio of the change in quantity demanded to the change in price multiplied by the ratio of price to quantity demanded at that point. As the changes in price get smaller and smaller and actually approach zero, the ratio of $\Delta Q/\Delta P$ becomes equivalent to the derivative of the demand function with respect to price, or

$$\lim_{\Delta P \to 0} \frac{\Delta Q}{\Delta P} = \frac{dQ}{dP}.$$

[5]The student should verify at this point that exactly the same coefficient is obtained for an increase in price form $10 to $12 as was obtained from a decrease in price from $12 to $10 when the modified arc elasticity formula is used. This will confirm that the modification of averaging the prices and quantities eliminates any difference in the size of the coefficient arising from an arbitrary designation of one of the two points on the demand curve as the reference or base point. The effect of the modified formula is to produce an "average" of sorts of the two results obtained with the initial version of the arc formula. To be more exact, the modified arc elasticity formula yields an estimate of the responsiveness or sensitivity of the quantity demanded at the midpoint of the range defined by the two points on the demand curve.

Hence, the formula for point elasticity becomes

$$\epsilon_p = \frac{dQ}{dP} \cdot \frac{P}{Q}.$$

As illustrations of the point elasticity concept, consider the following two examples.

Example 1: Suppose that the demand function for a commodity is defined by the equation

$$Q = 245 - 3.5P.$$

What, then, is the price elasticity of demand at a price of $10? To determine ϵ_p we need to know P, Q, and dQ/dP. At a price of $10,

$$Q = 245 - 3.5(10) = 245 - 35 = 210.$$

The rate of change in Q as P changes, dQ/dP, is found by calculating the first derivative of the demand function:

$$\frac{dQ}{dP} = -3.5.$$

Hence, we can now substitute directly into the point elasticity formula, obtaining

$$\epsilon_p = \frac{dQ}{dP} \cdot \frac{P}{Q} = -3.5 \cdot \frac{10}{210} = -\frac{1}{6} = -0.167.$$

The ϵ_p value of -0.167 says that if the price of the commodity changes by a small amount (say 1%) from its value of $10, then the quantity demanded will change by approximately 0.167% in the opposite direction. This relatively small response means demand is quite inelastic at a price of $10.

Example 2: On occasion, the demand function may be expressed in terms of quantity rather than price. Consider the demand function

$$P = 940 - 48Q + Q^2.$$

What is the price elasticity of demand at an output of 10 units?
 At $Q = 10$,

$$P = 940 - 48(10) + (10)^2$$
$$= 940 - 480 + 100 = \$560.$$

Now, it remains to find the value of dQ/dP. However, since the equation is expressed in terms of quantity rather than price, we must find dQ/dP by a slightly more circuitous route. We can determine dP/dQ quite easily as follows:

$$\frac{dP}{dQ} = -48 + 2Q.$$

It so happens (the mathematicians have formally proved it) that

$$\frac{dQ}{dP} = \frac{1}{dP/dQ},$$

thereby giving us

$$\frac{dQ}{dP} = \frac{1}{-48 + 2Q}.$$

At $Q = 10$, this becomes

$$\frac{dQ}{dP} = \frac{1}{-48 + 2(10)} = -\frac{1}{28}.$$

Substituting into the point elasticity formula, we have

$$\epsilon_p = \frac{dQ}{dP} \cdot \frac{P}{Q} = -\frac{1}{28} \cdot \frac{560}{10} = -2.$$

Again the proper interpretation of the elasticity coefficient in this case is that for a 1% price change from the current price of $560, the quantity demanded will change by about 2% in the opposite direction. And we would conclude that at a price of $560 demand is elastic.

Price Elasticity and the Slope of the Demand Curve

The concepts of slope and elasticity are frequently confused. It is sometimes fallaciously assumed that the flatter the demand curve, the greater its elasticity, and the steeper the demand curve, the smaller its elasticity. This assumption is categorically false and is so indicated in the definitions of the terms themselves. The slope of a demand curve depends entirely on the size of an absolute change in price as compared to the size of the associated absolute change in the quantity demanded. At any given point on a demand curve the slope equals dP/dQ. Yet, as we have just seen, elasticity is defined mathematically as

$$\epsilon_p = \frac{dQ}{dP} \cdot \frac{P}{Q}.$$

Elasticity is, therefore, equal to the reciprocal of the slope of the demand curve $[dQ/dP = 1/(dP/dQ)]$ multiplied by the ratio of P to Q and is a measure of the relative or *percentage* changes in P and Q. Clearly, then, since the slope (flatness or steepness) of a demand curve is based upon *absolute* changes in P and Q, whereas price elasticity has to do with *percentage* changes in P and Q, the value of the slope of the demand curve can equal the value of the coefficient of price elasticity only by the rarest of arithmetical coincidences. Moreover, in the case of a linear, downward-sloping demand curve, the slope is constant, whereas the price elasticity varies from point to point along the

128

*Demand
Functions,
Revenue
Functions,
and Elasticity*

curve according to the value of P/Q. Thus, any notion that elasticity and slope are the same should be promptly dispelled.

Price Elasticity and Total Revenue

We are now ready to examine some of the practical applications of the price elasticity concept. Of prime interest to business firms is the effect that a price change will have upon sales volume and total revenue. Also, from the viewpoint of consumers it is pertinent to determine the effect of a price change

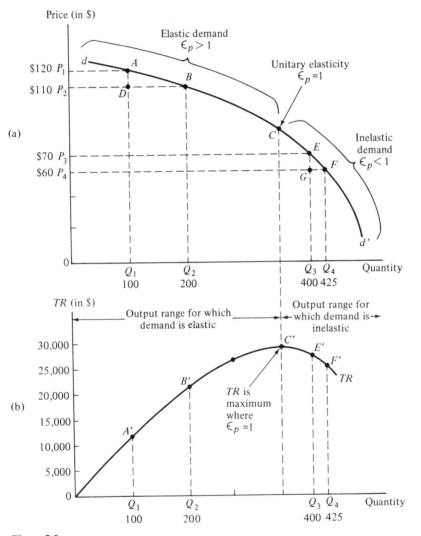

Figure 5-8
Relationships among demand curves, total revenue, and price elasticity

upon the total amount of money consumers are willing and able to spend on   **129**
a given product.   *Elasticity*
                                                                             of Demand

Consider the demand schedule in Table 5-2 and the corresponding demand curve for a firm shown as line dd' in Fig. 5-8(a). At a price of $120 ($P_1$), the firm can sell 100 units (Q_1). If price is lowered to $110 ($P_2$), sales increase to 200 units (Q_2). The *percentage* change in price obviously is small in comparison with the *percentage* change in quantity demanded—the price decline is but a fraction of its original value of P_1, whereas the increase in quantity demanded from Q_1 to Q_2 is double the original volume of 100 units. The information in Table 5-2 verifies that the coefficient of price elasticity over this range is -7.67; thus, demand is *elastic* between points A and B. As shown in Fig. 5-8(b), total revenue increases when price is lowered from $120 to $110. That this is so can also be confirmed indirectly from Fig. 5-8(a). Since total revenue is price times quantity sold, the size of the area shown by rectangle OP_1AQ_1 in Fig. 5-8(a) equals TR at P_1. At price P_2, TR equals the area of rectangle OP_2BQ_2. By inspection, the area of rectangle OP_2BQ_2 exceeds that of rectangle OP_1AQ_1 and, as indicated in Table 5-2, TR at P_2 ($22,000) is larger than TR at P_1 ($12,000). It is larger because the *loss* of revenue due to the lower price per unit (area P_2P_1AD) is *less* than the *gain* in revenue resulting from increased sales (area Q_1DBQ_2). In other words, even though the product is sold at a lower price, the increase in sales at the lower price *more* than makes up for the smaller amount of revenue received per unit sold.

Table 5-2   Elasticity and Total Revenue

Price	Quantity Demanded	Total Revenue	Coefficient of Price Elasticity	Elasticity
$120	100	$12,000	-7.67	Elastic
110	200	22,000	-3.13	Elastic
100	270	27,000	-1.90	Elastic
90	330	29,700	-1.03	Elastic
85	350	29,750	-0.91	Inelastic
80	370	29,600	-0.58	Inelastic
70	400	28,000	-0.39	Inelastic
60	425	25,500		

This behavior of total revenue over elastic portions of the demand curve is not merely coincidental. In fact, we may state, as a general principle, that *whenever demand is elastic, a decline in price will result in an increase in total revenue.* The reasoning is reversible: *When demand is elastic, an increase in price will result in a decline in total revenue,* because should price rise (for example, from P_3 to P_2), the gain in total revenue associated with selling the

130

*Demand
Functions,
Revenue
Functions,
and Elasticity*

commodity at a higher price (area P_3P_2BE) is smaller than the loss in revenue stemming from selling fewer units (area Q_2ECQ_3).

When demand is inelastic with regard to price, a lower price will cause a decline in total revenue. This situation exists for a decrease in price from P_4 ($70) to P_5 ($60), as shown in Fig. 5-8(a). Over this price range, the coefficient of price elasticity is -0.39 (Table 5-2). At a price of $70 and sales of 400 units, *TR* is $28,000, whereas at a price of $60 and sales of 425 units, *TR* is $25,500. Graphically, at a price of P_3, *TR* is equal to the area OP_4EQ_4. Total revenue is lower because the modest increase in sales precipitated by the price decline (Q_3Q_4) is inadequate to offset the adverse impact of the fall in price; consequently, the *loss* in revenue due to the lower price (area P_4P_3EG) *exceeds* the *gain* in revenue associated with selling more units (area Q_3GFQ_4). Table 5-3 summarizes these relationships.

Table 5-3   **Price Changes, Price Elasticity,
and Total Revenue**

	$\epsilon_p > 1$	$\epsilon_p < 1$
$P\downarrow$	$TR\uparrow$	$TR\downarrow$
$P\uparrow$	$TR\downarrow$	$TR\uparrow$

It follows that the positively sloped portion of the *TR* function corresponds to the elastic portion of the demand curve and vice versa (as is illustrated in Fig. 5-8). By the same token, the negatively sloped segment of the *TR* function is associated with inelastic demand. Starting from the top of the demand curve and moving down along it, the coefficient of price elasticity is a decreasing value but remains, nevertheless, larger than 1.0; simultaneously *TR* is increasing. Where *TR* is maximum, the elasticity of demand is unitary ($\epsilon_p = 1$). As we move farther down the demand curve past the point of unitary elasticity, the coefficient of price elasticity is less than 1 and decreasing, and *TR* is declining. These relationships are typical of downsloping demand functions.

There is a tendency, therefore, for most demand curves to be elastic at "high" prices and inelastic at "low" prices. As price falls from high levels, the response of consumers produces strong percentage gains in sales and healthy increases in *TR*. Where $\epsilon_p = 1$ corresponds to the price at which consumers are willing to spend the greatest number of dollars on the commodity; at this price *TR* is maximum and $\epsilon_p = 1$. Further price cuts will not induce consumers to buy enough more units to compensate for the price decline. In other words, they are approaching their saturation level for the commodity, and their marginal utility for additional units is rapidly diminishing; thus, price cuts have less impact upon consumer purchases.

Furthermore, it may be noted that the more elastic demand is, the greater will *TR* rise when price falls. The more inelastic demand is, the greater will *TR* fall when price is lowered. The example in Table 5-2 verifies this.

APPLICATIONS CAPSULE

WHEN A FIRM CAN BE SURE IT'S TIME TO RAISE ITS PRICE

Whenever a firm has good reason to believe that the demand for its product is inelastic at the current selling price, profits can *always* be increased if the firm will raise its price. This outcome stems from the fact that in an inelastic demand situation, a price increase will result in a firm's experiencing (1) rising total revenue and (2) a lower total cost outlay. Whenever the coefficient of price elasticity is less than 1, a price increase will raise total revenues because the revenue gain associated with a higher selling price more than offsets the revenue decline associated with a lower unit sales volume. And a firm's total operating costs ought to fall as a result of a higher price, since the higher price (other things remaining equal) will tend to curtail consumer purchases of the product—thereby prompting the firm to produce fewer units, buy smaller amounts of economic resources, and, consequently, spend fewer dollars in the course of its activities. With *TR* rising and total costs falling, the overall profitability of the enterprise will, of necessity, be improved.

Pursuing the same line of reasoning, a firm contemplating a lowering of its price should beware of an inelastic demand situation. A price decrease in face of an inelastic demand will lead not only to a decline in total revenue, but also to an increase in total costs due to a rising sales volume. The firm's profits will be lowered and under such circumstances a lower selling price would seem ill-advised.

It is fair to state, therefore, that the most profitable volume of sales lies somewhere on the elastic portion of a firm's demand curve.

This relationship between price elasticity and profitability is gaining widespread attention in the business sector. For example, firms in the energy industry have become acutely alert to the inelastic demand situation which they face. Even a casual observer cannot fail to be impressed by the frequency and size of gasoline price increases, yet energy conservation efforts have been modest—a situation highly suggestive that demand is price inelastic and that price increases ought to improve the profitability of the petroleum companies over what it otherwise would be.

132

*Demand
Functions,
Revenue
Functions,
and Elasticity*

Price Elasticity and Linear Demand Curves

Although the law of demand requires only that a demand curve slope downward to the right, we shall find it convenient to represent the demand curve in its simplest form—as a straight line. Thus, it is worthwhile to be familiar with the elasticity characteristics of linear demand curves. Figure 5-9 illustrates a typical linear demand function along with its corresponding total revenue and marginal revenue function. It will be recalled that the general equations for these functions are

$$P = a - bQ,$$

$$TR = P \cdot Q = aQ - bQ^2,$$

$$MR = \frac{dTR}{dQ} = a - 2bQ.$$

Additionally, the slope of the MR function is twice the slope of the demand curve, and MR equals zero where TR is maximum. The geometry of the relationships among the three functions is such that the price and quantity at which $MR = 0$ and TR is maximum is the midpoint of the demand curve; that is, the length of the segment of the demand curve above this point is equal to the length of the segment below it.

From the discussion in the preceding section it should be evident that

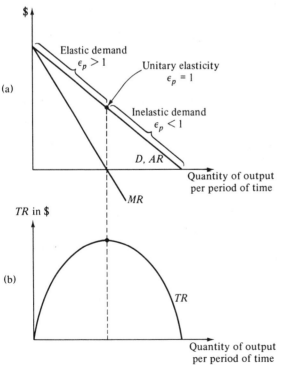

(a)

(b)

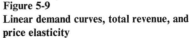

Figure 5-9
**Linear demand curves, total revenue, and
price elasticity**

demand curve and proceeding down along it, the coefficient of price elasticity declines from very large values to a value of one at the midpoint, becomes less than one upon passing the midpoint, and approaches zero as price declines toward zero. As explained previously, this is because at successively lower prices and progressively larger values of Q, the percentage changes in price get larger, while the percentage changes in quantity demanded get smaller. The coefficient of price elasticity, being equal to the ratio of the percentage change in Q to the percentage change in P, thus necessarily declines as one moves down along the demand curve.

It is not accurate, therefore, to describe linear demand curves as being either elastic or inelastic; rather the upper half of the demand curve is elastic and the lower half is inelastic. It is proper to speak of the price elasticity of demand at a given point or between two given points, but it is inappropriate to speak of the price elasticity of the demand curve as a whole.

MATHEMATICAL CAPSULE 5

THE ELASTICITY OF DEMAND AT THE MIDPOINT OF A LINEAR DEMAND FUNCTION

It is relatively simple to show for a linear downsloping demand function that the price elasticity of demand at the midpoint of the demand curve is -1. All we need do is compute the coefficient of price elasticity at the midpoint utilizing the point elasticity formula.

The general equation for a linear demand curve is

$$P = a - bQ.$$

The general equations for the associated TR and MR functions are

$$TR = P \cdot Q = aQ - bQ^2,$$

$$MR = \frac{dTR}{dQ} = a - 2bQ.$$

To compute point elasticity, we must obtain values for dQ/dP, Q, and P at the midpoint of our generalized demand curve. We can find dQ/dP from the demand equation itself as follows:

$$P = a - bQ,$$

$$\frac{dP}{dQ} = -b.$$

134

*Demand
Functions,
Revenue
Functions,
and Elasticity*

Since

$$\frac{dQ}{dP} = \frac{1}{dP/dQ},$$

we have

$$\frac{dQ}{dP} = \frac{1}{-b} = -\frac{1}{b}.$$

The value of Q at the midpoint of the demand can be derived from the fact that at the midpoint of a linear demand curve $MR = 0$ and TR is maximum. Hence, the quantity at which $MR = 0$ can be found by setting the equation for MR equal to zero and solving for the value of Q which will satisfy this condition:

$$MR = a - 2bQ = 0,$$
$$-2bQ = -a,$$
$$Q = \frac{-a}{-2b} = \frac{a}{2b}.$$

When $Q = a/2b$, the corresponding value for P is

$$P = a - bQ$$
$$= a - b\left(\frac{a}{2b}\right)$$
$$= a - \frac{a}{2}.$$
$$= \frac{a}{2}.$$

Substituting the values for $dQ/dP, P,$ and Q into the point elasticity formula, we have

$$\epsilon_p = \frac{dQ}{dP} \cdot \frac{P}{Q}$$
$$= -\frac{1}{b} \cdot \frac{a/2}{a/2b}$$
$$= -\frac{1}{b} \cdot \frac{a}{2} \cdot \frac{2b}{a}$$
$$= -1.$$

Therefore, the coefficient of price elasticity equals -1 at the midpoint of all linear downsloping demand functions, irrespective of the values of a and b in the general equation $P = a - bQ$.

Certain kinds of demand curves have unique price elasticity properties. Three special cases will be noted.

When the firm's demand curve is horizontal (meaning that at the going market price the firm can sell all it is able to produce but that its demand is zero at a higher price), demand is said to be *perfectly elastic* and the coefficient of price elasticity is infinity ($\epsilon_p = -\infty$). Such a demand curve is illustrated in Fig. 5-10(a). The perfectly elastic feature of the horizontal demand curve arises from the fact that should the firm raise its price above P_1, demand would fall to zero—the largest possible response to a price change. In other words, when the firm's demand curve is horizontal, there exists the highest possible degree of sensitivity to price since even if there is a small price increase above P_1, the firm's customers will reduce their purchases from the prevailing amounts to zero.

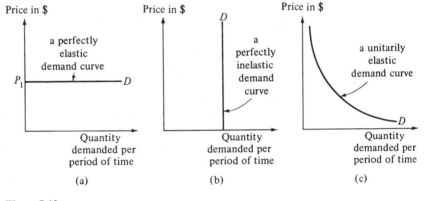

Figure 5-10
Special cases in price elasticity

In the very improbable event that the demand curve for a product is vertical [Fig. 5-10(b)], demand is said to be *perfectly inelastic*. Quantity demanded remains the same despite progressively higher prices. Thus, there is *no response* whatsoever in the quantity demanded to a price change—the least possible degree of price sensitivity. The corresponding coefficient of price elasticity is zero ($\epsilon_p = 0$).

The third special case arises when consumers spend a fixed amount of dollars for a commodity irrespective of the price charged and the quantity bought. Every price-quantity combination results in the same amount of expenditure upon the product. The equation for such a demand curve is

$$P \cdot Q = TR = k,$$

where k is a constant and, graphically, it is illustrated by a rectangular hyperbola, shown in Fig. 5-10(c). At each and every point on the curve price elas-

136 APPLICATIONS CAPSULE

*Demand
Functions,
Revenue
Functions,
and Elasticity*

"NO FRILLS" AIR FARES

As the 1974–1975 recession made inroads into passenger traffic loads of the major airlines, National Airlines persuaded the Civil Aeronautics Board (CAB) to let it try an experiment with a discount of as much as 35% from normal coach fares on certain of its regularly scheduled routes. National, in an effort to build up its load factor, tied its discount fare proposal to the offering of "no-frills" service during the flight, including doing away with complimentary meals, snacks, soft drinks, and coffee so as to reduce costs and partially offset the lower-priced fares. However, passengers using the no-frills plan could selectively purchase these items in-flight if they wished. The no-frills fares were offered only Mondays through Thursdays. The CAB gave the go-ahead to National to experiment with the no-frills fare, with the proviso that National study the plan and report back at a later date. Eastern Airlines and Delta Airlines, both competitors of National on some of the routes where National proposed to implement no-frills fares, were also permitted to use the discount fares for a trial period.

In its report to the CAB on the results of the no-frills approach, National maintained that 56% of the 133,000 passengers who used its no-frills fare from mid-April through June 30, 1975, were enticed to travel by air because of the discount fare plan. According to National, the new passenger traffic generated by discount fares increased its revenues by $4 million during that period. National said that its figures were based upon an on-board survey of 13,500 passengers and represented one of the most exhaustive studies ever conducted for a CAB investigation.

J. Dan Brock, vice president for marketing for National Airlines, was quoted at a news conference as saying that the fare had been an "unqualified success," had created a new air-travel market, and had generated more than twice the volume of new passengers required to offset revenue dilution caused by regular passengers switching to the lower fare. He said the stimulus of the fare gave National a net traffic gain of 74,000 passengers during the initial $2\frac{1}{2}$-month trial. But he also cautioned that the success claims he was making for the no-frills fare did not mean that low fares were the answer to the airline industry's excess capacity problems. Yet Brock did go so far as to state that "what no frills has proved . . . is that a properly conceived discount fare, offered at the right time in the right markets with the right controls, can help airlines hurdle traditionally soft traffic periods."

Eastern Airlines reported a much different experience. Eastern said its studies showed that only 14% of the 55,200 of its passengers who used a no-frills fare between mid-April and May 31 represented newly generated traffic, with the remaining 86% representing passengers diverted from higher fares who would have flown anyway. It said that the effect of the fare in the six major markets it studied was a net loss in revenue to Eastern of $543,000 during the initial $1\frac{1}{2}$ months. At the same time Eastern attacked the credibility of the National Airlines' survey, noting that its own data were based upon an exhaustive and scientific blind telephone survey among persons who did not know the purpose and sponsor of the survey. Eastern claimed that this type of study was more apt to produce unbiased results than National's on-board surveys.

Other airlines joined Eastern in challenging National's survey results in the CAB's hearing to decide whether the no-frills fares should continue to be allowed. Delta Airlines, for example, claimed that the no-frills fare did not even come close to offsetting the dilution it experienced in revenues. Other airline officials observed that while National Airlines might have succeeded through its heavy promotion of the no-frills fares in diverting some business from other carriers, they felt that National's claims of generating many passengers who otherwise would not have flown were "preposterous."

Those airlines in direct competition with National on the routes where the discount fares were tried were vehemently opposed to continuing the discounts. In their view the no-frills approach constituted "economic nonsense." They announced a policy of matching National's discount fare only where forced to for competitive reasons.

Questions for Discussion

1. Did the National Airlines' experiment suggest that the demand for airline service at discount prices is elastic or inelastic? Do Eastern's results indicate that demand is elastic or inelastic?
2. Which of the two studies, the on-board survey of National or the telephone survey of Eastern, do you think would yield the most reliable estimate as to the true elasticity of demand? Is it possible or likely that the elasticity of demand for National is different from the elasticity of demand for Eastern? Why? How would you account for the differences in the experiences of National and Eastern with discount fares?
3. Do you think it would be fair for the CAB to allow National to continue to use the no-frills fare if it wished to do so, even though Eastern Airlines and Delta Airlines and perhaps other airlines were opposed to the no-frills approach? Why?

ticity is unitary ($\epsilon_p = -1$), and total revenue is constant no matter what the values of P and Q.

138

*Demand
Functions,
Revenue
Functions,
and Elasticity*

The Sensitivity of Market Demand to Price Changes

Just what causes the market demand for a good or service to be responsive or unresponsive to price changes? If the firms in an industry reduce prices, will there be a large expansion in market demand for the product, a moderate expansion, or very little expansion at all? The answers depend on a host of market considerations:

1. *The importance of the product to buyers.* When products are very important to consumers from the standpoint of daily living and life-styles (electricity, toothpaste, coffee, haircuts), market demand is often not very sensitive to price; as prices go up, buyers merely dig deeper in their pockets. On the other hand, there are many items which are not viewed as so crucial—going skiing in Colorado, eating T-bone steak twice a week, or buying a microwave oven. Most postponable, less urgent, or "luxury" types of products tend to exhibit higher degrees of price elasticity.

2. *The degree of market saturation for the product.* Market saturation has relevance to price elasticity in the sense that if nearly all households have refrigerators, it is unlikely the appliance manufacturers can stimulate the market demand for refrigerators much by cutting their average selling prices. In contrast, the use of solar water heating is far from widespread and price reductions in installed solar-water-heating equipment would probably trigger a substantial percentage gain in market sales.

3. *The income profile of current consumers of the product.* The demand for truly luxury products (such as 100-foot yachts and diamond necklaces) which are sold more or less exclusively to the very rich may be price inelastic for even fairly large percentage shifts in price. This is because the selling price tends to be a small percentage of the buyer's income—despite the size of the price tag. Yet the market demand for 16-foot Fiberglas outboard runabouts, sold to the "mass market," may be highly sensitive to price changes. When the price of an item is large in relation to income, buyers are more likely to be price-conscious and substitute-conscious; hence a given percentage change in price can be expected to have a significant demand impact, owing to the large difference it makes upon the consumer's pocketbook. From another angle, products such as videotape recorders are often initially priced well above the reach of the mass market, and the first round or so of price cuts may not generate much demand response. But as prices continue to be reduced, successively lower income levels are tapped, and market demand becomes increasingly responsive to lower prices.

4. *The number of good substitutes available at competitive prices.* The market demand for zinc castings for automotive trim may be highly price elastic because of the encroachment of cheaper plastic substitutes as zinc prices climb. On the other hand, there is as yet no good substitute for the use of glass windows and windshields in the manufacture of automobiles, and thus there is little risk of diminished demand through the substitution of other materials, as the price of automotive glass goes up.

5. *The number of uses a product has.* There is a tendency for the demand for a product to be more elastic the wider the range of uses it has. With a larger number of uses, more opportunity exists for variation in the quantity sold when price changes. Increases in price reduce the number of economical uses of a product, whereas price declines expand the range of economically feasible uses. This aspect of demand elasticity is especially pertinent for steel, aluminum, other primary metals, plastics, wool, and paper products.

DO RISING GASOLINE PRICES REDUCE DEMAND?

Public opinion polls have shown that the majority of consumers oppose the decontrol of gasoline prices. Many politicians agree and have taken the position that letting the price per gallon rise to whatever level the market will bear favors the interest of the oil companies over the interests of consumers. Their alternatives, mainly some form of gasoline rationing, seem largely predicated on a belief that the demand for gasoline is highly inelastic and that motorists will continue to pay whatever the asking price is without making any effort to conserve on purchases.

Recent studies of gasoline price elasticity do not bear this out, especially when one takes into account the long-run impact of higher prices rather than just the immediate consumer response. Economists' estimates of the extent to which gasoline demand will lessen as prices rise show that in the immediate short run, the coefficient of price elasticity is -0.10—in which case the quantity of gasoline used can be expected to decline immediately about 1% for each 10% increase in retail prices at the pump. Assuming that this highly inelastic demand estimate is correct, it would take price increases on the order of 30% to bring the rate of growth in gasoline consumption in the United States down from about 3% per year to 0%. However, the elasticity picture changes substantially as the period for examining the response of motorists to higher prices is stretched out. This is because the full impact of a price change on demand does not take place immediately; the longer motorists have to make adjustments in gasoline usage, the greater is their ability to do so in terms of making basic changes in the type of car they own, in their driving habits, and in their dependence on the automobile relative to total miles driven each year.

The price elasticity estimates for periods of 2 to 3 years cluster in the neighborhood of -0.25. Professor Pindyck at MIT projects a 5-year price elasticity figure of -0.49 for the United States. Over a 10-year time frame, his estimate is -0.82 and for 15 years it is -1.03. The sharply increasing degree of price elasticity as the time of response lengthens highlights the fact that the total impact of a change in price may be much more dramatic over the long run than in the short run.

6. *The durability of the product.* Price elasticity can be partly a function of product durability because of the possibility of delaying the purchase of replacements. Postponing the purchase of new durable goods by repairing them may be an effective, albeit temporary, substitute for replacing goods whose prices are rising,

140

*Demand
Functions,
Revenue
Functions,
and Elasticity*

thus making for a more elastic demand in the short run than would otherwise be the case.

7. *The time period under consideration.* In general, the market demand for a product tends to be more elastic in the long run than in the short run. This is primarily due to lags in consumer response to price changes and to increased chances that more good substitutes will appear as the time frame lengthens.

Plainly, more than one of these factors can affect the price elasticity of market demand simultaneously. Moreover, it is important to recognize that different classes of customers within the same market frequently have different price elasticities. For instance, industrial demand for electricity may be much more price sensitive than residential demand for electricity, owing to the greater options of manufacturers to use different fuel sources or to convert to more energy-efficient equipment. Under such circumstances, the total revenues of electric utility firms can be increased by charging higher prices to the market segment where demand is less elastic (residential users) and lower prices to price-sensitive buyers (industrial users).

A final point: when total industry demand is highly elastic at the prevailing price level, firms with access to manufacturing economies of scale are likely to try to expand the total dollar market for the product by initiating lower prices. Since the elastic nature of the market will result in unit volume increasing by greater percentages than the percentage decrease in selling prices, such a move could result in higher industrywide profits, as well as an increased quantity demanded.

Price Elasticity and Demand for the Product of an Individual Firm

The degree to which market demand is price sensitive (elastic) or price insensitive (inelastic) does not completely carry over to the demand for the product of an individual firm. Two factors shape the price elasticity of demand for the products of an individual firm: (1) the elasticity of total *market* demand and the extent to which a firm's *pro rata* market share is affected by a change in the average *market* price, and (2) the ability a firm has to hold onto or increase its market share as it alters its prices above or below the prevailing market level. In other words, price elasticity at the level of a particular firm or brand is affected not only by the factors that govern the price elasticity of total market demand but also by how sensitive the firm's own demand is to the prices being charged by other firms in the marketplace. A couple of illustrations will highlight the reasons for this.

Consider first the case of an industry where the products of different firms are all essentially alike—as is the case with commodity-type markets (wheat, soybeans, gold, copper, steel). The key pricing feature of commodity products is uniformity of price throughout the market, although there may be minor variations depending upon location (New York or London) or time (futures or spot prices). In such markets, an individual firm has very limited pricing discretion. For example, if one coal supplier raised selling price to $30 per ton while the remaining suppliers stayed at $25, the high-priced seller would have difficulty finding buyers and demand for the firm's coal would prove quickly to be highly price elastic. Conversely, if the firm decided to undercut the prices of other coal suppliers by announcing a $20 per ton price, it would be deluged with orders—again a price-elastic condition. But this latter condition may be extremely short-lived, since other firms may be rapidly forced into matching price cuts to prevent losing customers to the low-priced firm. The strong likelihood of matching price cuts transforms what otherwise would be a highly elastic response to a firm's own price cuts into a response where the firm's price elasticity value is equal to the price elasticity of total market demand.

In general, then, when firms sell undifferentiated products using essentially the same marketing mix, any one firm is seldom able to stray much from the prevailing industry average price. When one firm tries to change its price *independent* of other sellers, it quickly learns that the demand for its product is highly elastic above the going market price and much less elastic or even inelastic below the ruling price (depending on how the overall market demand will respond to matching price cuts by all producers).

At the other extreme, there are markets and industries in which the products of competing firms are sufficiently different (and their marketing mixes are sufficiently different in terms of product design, quality, advertising, and so on) that the demand for a particular firm's product becomes somewhat less sensitive to price. Product differentiation allows firms the room to maintain rather diverse prices; indeed, there may no such thing as *the* industry price. In the women's dress market, for instance, there exists a broad range of prices and styles, from the bargain basement to the high-fashion salon, and each merchant is able to establish a differential market image according to the selection of dresses, decor and location of the retail shop, type of sales assistance, credit arrangements, alteration services, advertising, and so forth. High prices may be congruent with one merchant's approach, and low prices with another. In strongly differentiated product markets, the degree of price elasticity confronting the individual seller is influenced by the extent to which that firm's prices are synchronized with (1) the overall character and image of its total product offering, (2) the importance consumers attach to nonprice product features, and (3) the extent to which higher prices can be obtained through increased promotional efforts.

Therefore, in appraising the price elasticity of demand for an individual firm's product, the analyst must take into account the full dimensions along which buyers assess a product's relative attractiveness—consideration of price alone is insufficient. Particularly must one assess how the attributes of a firm's product stack up against the attributes of substitutes. Were all rival firms to have essentially comparable prices and products, one could expect price elasticity among brands to be high, since consumers would be prone to switch readily to lower-priced brands whenever one firm raised its price. But the more strongly differentiated are the products of rival sellers, the less sensitive the demand of any one firm will be to a change in its selling price. Moreover,

142

*Demand
Functions,
Revenue
Functions,
and Elasticity*

if a firm successfully increases the degree of product differentiation between its brand and other brands, it will probably find buyers tolerant of a modest increase in prices—that is, its demand will be less price elastic than before.

Attempting to Calculate Price Elasticity for Particular Products

Attempts to develop meaningful and reliable estimates of price elasticity is a challenging empirical task. To begin with, the coefficient of price elasticity

APPLICATIONS CAPSULE

WHY SOME BUYERS MAY BE LESS PRICE SENSITIVE THAN OTHERS

Buyers of products differ greatly in the degree to which they are sensitive to price changes. The demand curves of some buyers may be very elastic while other buyers may have very inelastic demands. Where buyers are insensitive to price and to price changes, one or more of the following conditions tend to prevail:

1. *The buyer is very concerned about product performance.* Buyer demand tends to be price inelastic whenever a product that "fails" or does not perform up to expectations causes the buyer to incur substantial penalties, costs, or inconvenience. The adverse risks of product failure make it worthwhile for buyers to pay a premium price for high performance characteristics and inclines them to stick with products and brands that have proven reliable in the past. A good example where this happens is in the oil-field-equipment industry. The demand for blowout preventors (a piece of oil field equipment that prevents oil from escaping a well if there is a surge in pressure) tends to be price inelastic; if the blowout preventor fails, the user faces considerable costs in terms of lost oil, lost time of skilled crews, and environmental sanctions, particularly in the case of offshore wells, where the clean up of spills is particularly expensive. As a consequence, buyers of blowout preventors are reluctant to switch from proven brand names even in the face of price increases and even when other companies seeking to penetrate the market offer lower-priced products with allegedly comparable performance features.

2. *The buyer wants a differentiated or custom-designed product and is willing to pay extra for it.* Whenever buyers want a specially designed product to fit their own particular needs, they often become locked into purchasing from a particular supplier who is willing to go to the trouble to satisfy the buyer's special design requests. In such instances, buyers may conclude that extra effort on the part of the supplier merits the compensation of a higher price. Of course, later, the supplier's willingness to accommodate the buyer's wants may provide the leverage needed to impose a price increase without much risk of losing the buyer's business.

3. *The buyer purchases the product because it is perceived to contribute to the high-quality image the buyer is trying to project on behalf of its own product.* Buyers of items that are components of the buyer's own final product often have price-inelastic demands because they perceive that the item's quality will enhance the performance of their product, or because the brand name of the component carries prestige value which reinforces the high-quality image they are trying to project. For example, the manufacturers of expensive pieces of equipment will often use the electric motors of prestige suppliers as a component part because doing so upgrades the image of their machinery and helps enhance its market attractiveness. Manufacturers of the component part, knowing of the benefit their component gives the final product, are then in a position to ask for and get a slightly higher price when other firms cannot.

4. *The buyer obtains major savings from using a particular product or service.* Whenver a product or service can save a buyer time and money because it performs well, the buyer will tend to have an inelastic demand for the product. The same holds true when a buyer can benefit from timely delivery of a product, rapid maintenance and repair in the event of breakdowns, and technical advice. To cite an example, when a firm has high stakes in the outcome of a particular situation (such as an electric utility filing for a \$200 million rate increase), the firm will be willing to pay a premium for the very best advice it can get from lawyers, accountants, consultants, and other experts having specialized knowledge and talents to offer. Another example, drawn again from the oil industry, is where a company such as Schlumberger uses sophisticated electronic techniques to detect the likely presence of oil in substrata rock formations; the information obtained from such instruments has the potential for steering oil-drilling companies away from locations where there is greater probability of a dry hole. Understandably, then, oil-drilling companies are willing to pay substantial fees for Schlumberger's services, particularly when they face difficult and costly drilling expenses because of great depth or offshore location.

5. *The cost of the item is small compared to the buyer's purchasing budget.* Many consumers do not bother to shop around for the best price and to undertake time-consuming product comparisons when the cost of the item is low. This is especially true when the buyer's major motive in purchasing the item is convenience, taste, or some other subjective preference criterion. In the case of industrial buyers, the relevant cost of an item is the firm's total expenditure for the item over some time period (a month or a year), not the cost per unit. Low unit cost is not a sufficient consideration because the number of units purchased may make the dollar costs of the item very important. In industrial purchasing, the purchase of component parts or raw materials that entail a high total dollar cost is usually handled by top executives and/or senior specialist purchasing agents who may well be very price conscious—thereby creating an elastic-demand situation.

6. *The buyer is in a position to absorb a price increase and/or can readily pass on higher costs of component parts and raw materials.* As a rule, the more a firm is in position to pass along rising costs, the less tenacious and aggressive it will be in haggling over prices and price increases. The same can hold true when an industrial buyer has a sufficiently high profit margin that it is willing to absorb a price increase rather than go to the trouble of

144

*Demand
Functions,
Revenue
Functions,
and Elasticity*

seeking out alternative sources of supply. (However, in such instances the item is probably a sufficiently low cost item that the basic reason for price insensitivity is that the buyer falls into category 5.)

7. *The buyer is poorly informed and/or does not adhere to a policy of purchasing according to well-defined specifications.* Buyers tend to be less sensitive to prices and price increases when they are poorly informed about prevailing price conditions, demand-supply conditions, the availability and prices of substitutes, and the performance-quality-service features offered by rival brands and suppliers. More-informed buyers tend to be hard bargainers on price and other conditions of purchase. Indeed, many large purchasers make a special effort to learn the business of their suppliers so well that they know when they are getting a good price and when they are not. A poorly informed buyer is easily swayed by persuasive advertising, a good sales pitch, and efforts to downplay the performance differences among competing products.

8. *The cost to a buyer from switching from one seller to another may be very high.* In some cases, an industrial user of a component part may tie the specifications of its products to that of a particular supplier, or the firm may make heavy investments in installing and using a particular supplier's equipment (as is often the case with a computer). When buyers' switching costs are high, they may well be insensitive to price changes—especially small price changes that would not make it worthwhile to switch.

depends upon which of several prospective prices is currently being charged. Because the price elasticity coefficient varies all along the demand curve, the elasticity estimate may not be the same for a price increase as for a price decrease. Second, it is difficult to hold all other demand determinants constant long enough to isolate the effects of a price change upon quantity demanded. Although there are a variety of econometric techniques available for dealing with situations where several variables are present and undergoing change, these are not always capable of correctly identifying and parceling out how much of the total change in quantity demanded is directly attributable to a price change and how much is attributable to changes in other demand determinants. Finally, the full impact of a price change upon demand frequently occurs after a time lag, owing to the resistance of custom, habit, life-styles, and preferences. The fact that time itself may be a real factor (in the sense that demand can be more elastic in the long run than in the short run) further confounds the calculation problem.

Nevertheless, it should be clear that firms have a definite interest in knowing how sensitive demand is to changes in selling price.

Income Elasticity of Demand

As stated in earlier chapters, the purchase levels of many items are quite sensitive to variations in consumer incomes. The responsiveness of the

quantity demanded to a change in consumer income (other demand determinants being held fixed) is called *income elasticity of demand.*

Just as price elasticity was found by determining the ratio of the percentage change in the quantity demanded to some percentage change in price, so
income elasticity is calculated by finding the ratio of the percentage change
in quantity demanded to a percentage change in income. Hence, we may write

$$\epsilon_I = \frac{\% \text{ change in quantity demanded}}{\% \text{ change in income.}}.$$

As with price elasticity, there are also two measures of income elasticity:
arc elasticity and point elasticity. The arc formula for computing income
elasticity is

$$\epsilon_I = \frac{\dfrac{Q_2 - Q_1}{\left(\dfrac{Q_1 + Q_2}{2}\right)}}{\dfrac{I_2 - I_1}{\left(\dfrac{I_1 + I_2}{2}\right)}},$$

where ϵ_I represents the coefficient of income elasticity and I is income. The
point formula for income elasticity is

$$\epsilon_I = \frac{dQ}{dI} \cdot \frac{I}{Q},$$

where dQ/dI symbolizes the rate of change in the quantity demanded as
income changes.

For all items except inferior goods, the sign of the coefficient of income
elasticity is positive because for normal goods income and quantity purchased
vary in the same direction. If the value of the income elasticity coefficient is
greater than $+1$, the demand for the item is said to be income elastic; if it is
less than $+1$, then demand is said to be income inelastic. The coefficient of
income elasticity is negative for inferior goods. The greater the size of the
coefficient, the greater the degree of responsiveness of the quantity demanded
to a change in income.

Income elasticity varies widely from item to item. Light bulbs, dairy
products, aspirin, and cigarettes are examples of products whose income
elasticities are typically low. In contrast, jewelry, T-bone steak, Cadillacs,
art objects, education, foreign travel, and scotch have high income elasticities.
Generally, products that consumers regard as necessities have low income
elasticities, while luxuries tend to have high income elasticities. Indeed, one
way of designating items as either luxuries or necessities is by the size of their
income elasticities.

The results of some actual studies of price and income elasticity of
demand are shown in Table 5-4.

146

*Demand
Functions,
Revenue
Functions,
and Elasticity*

Table 5-4   Results of Studies of Elasticity of Demand

Product	Elasticity Finding
Air travel	
Short business-oriented routes	Price inelastic
Vacation routes	Highly income elastic
Residential electricity	
Short run (1 year)	−0.06 (price); +0.06 (income)
Long run	−0.52 (price); +0.88 (income)
Cigarettes	−0.3 to −0.4 (price); +0.5 (income)
Coffee	−0.15 (price); +0.29 (income)
China, glassware, tableware, utensils	
Short run	−1.2 (price)
Long run	−1.3 (price)
Kitchen appliances	−0.6 (price)
Tires	
Short run	−0.6 (price)
Long run	−0.4 (price)
Radio and television receivers (short run)	−1.2 (price)
Automobiles (long run)	−0.2 (price)
Legal services	−0.5 (price)
Physicians' services	−0.6 (price)

Sources: H. S. Houthakker and Lester D. Taylor, *Consumer Demand in the United States, 1929–1970* (Cambridge: Harvard University Press, 1966); Philip K. Verleger, Jr., "Models of the Demand for Air Transportation," *Bell Journal of Economics and Management Science*, Vol. 3, No. 2 (Autumn 1972), pp. 437–457; James M. Griffin, "The Effects of Higher Prices on Electricity Consumption," *Bell Journal of Economics and Management Science*, Vol. 5, No. 2 (Autumn 1974), pp. 515–539; S. M. Sackrin, "Factors Affecting the Demand for Cigarettes," *Agricultural Economics Research*, Vol. 14, No. 3 (July 1962), pp. 81–88; and John J. Hughes, "Note on the U.S. Demand for Coffee," *American Journal of Agricultural Economics*, Vol. 51, No. 4 (November 1969).

Cross Elasticity of Demand

Insofar as their demand is concerned, goods can be related in any one of three ways:

1. They may be *competing* products or *substitutes*, in which case an increase in the purchase of one is at the expense of another. So it is with various *brands* of margarine, soap, razor blades, and gasoline; likewise, hamburgers may be a substitute for hot dogs, a trip to Florida may be a substitute for a trip to the Great Smoky Mountains, and a Honda may be a substitute for a Chevette.
2. They may be *complementary* products, in which case an increase in the purchase of one causes a rise in the purchase of another. Complementary implies that goods are consumed *together*. Examples include electric appliances and electric power, shoes and socks, notebook paper and ballpoint pens, and carpets and vacuum cleaners.
3. They may be *independent*, such that the purchase of one has no direct bearing upon the demand of another. Independence implies that goods are neither consumed together nor in place of each other. Pairs of items whose purchases are for all intents and purposes independent include shrimp and pillows, football tickets and a spool of thread, and fishing tackle and lingerie.

Cross elasticity of demand is a measure for interpreting the relationship between products. As between two products X and Y, cross elasticity measures the percentage change in the quantity demanded of product Y in response to a percentage change in the price of product X. In mathematical terms,

$$\epsilon_{yx} = \frac{\% \text{ change in quantity of Y}}{\% \text{ change in price of X}},$$

where ϵ_{yx} symbolizes the coefficient of cross elasticity between X and Y. Again, there are two ways of actually computing cross elasticity. The arc formula for calculating the coefficient of cross elasticity is

$$\epsilon_{yx} = \frac{\dfrac{Q_{y_2} - Q_{y_1}}{\left(\dfrac{Q_{y_1} + Q_{y_2}}{2}\right)}}{\dfrac{P_{x_2} - P_{x_1}}{\left(\dfrac{P_{x_1} + P_{x_2}}{2}\right)}}.$$

The point elasticity formula is

$$\epsilon_{yx} = \frac{dQ_y}{dP_x} \cdot \frac{P_x}{P_y}.$$

The cross elasticity coefficient may be either positive or negative. When ϵ_{yx} is positive, products X and Y are substitutes for each other. This is illustrated by a simple example. Other factors remaining constant, if the price of shipping goods by rail increases, the freight traffic via motor carrier should rise. Conversely, if the price of shipping goods by rail declines, the freight traffic via motor carrier should decrease. In either case, the percentage changes in rail rates and the volume of motor freight are in the same direction. Thus, whether the price changes are up or down, the cross elasticity coefficient is positive.

Complementary goods have negative cross elasticity coefficients. Automobiles and automobile insurance serve as a case in point. An increase in the price of automobiles tends to reduce purchases of automobiles and cuts back on the sales of automobile insurance. In contrast, lower automobile prices tend to stimulate car sales, thereby boosting sales of auto insurance. Hence, a change in the price of automobiles is followed by a change in sales of auto insurance in the opposite direction. As a consequence, the coefficient of cross elasticity is negative.

The strength of the relationship between substitute and complementary products is reflected by the absolute size of the cross elasticity coefficient. The larger the coefficient, the stronger the relationship. Furthermore, it follows that the closer the coefficient is to zero (approached from either the positive or negative side), the weaker is any substitute or complementary relationship between two products and the more independent the two products are. This is so because as ϵ_{yx} approaches zero, variations in the price of one good induce no appreciable change in the quantity demanded of the other; hence, purchases of the products would seem unrelated or independent.

Measures of the cross elasticity of demand may be indicative of the boundaries of an industry. High cross elasticities indicate close relationships and suggest that the goods are part of the same industry, whereas low cross elasticities imply weak relationships and that the goods may be in different industries. If a good has a low cross elasticity with respect to all other goods, then it may be considered to consititute an industry by itself. Similarly, if several products have high cross elasticities among themselves but low cross elasticities with respect to other goods, then the product group may define an industry. For instance, various brands of TV sets have high cross elasticities among each other but low cross elasticities with other household appliances and fixtures.

However, using the cross elasticity concept as a means of delimiting an industry is not without difficulty. In the first place, it is arbitrary as to how high cross elasticities must be to be considered in the same industry. Cross elasticities among canned vegetables may be quite high, yet the cross elasticity between canned vegetables and canned meats is liable to be rather low. Such circumstances render it difficult to define rigorously the boundaries of an industry—should it be canned vegetables or canned meats or canned foods?

A second complication arises from the existence of chains of cross relationships. The cross elasticity between a color TV console and a black-and-white TV console may be high, as might the cross elasticity between black-and-white consoles and black-and-white portables. But console color TVs and portable black-and-white sets may have low cross elasticities, thereby raising issues of just how closely related the markets for console color TVs and portable black-and-white TVs are to one another.

MATHEMATICAL CAPSULE 6

PARTIAL ELASTICITIES OF DEMAND: A MORE RIGOROUS CONCEPT OF DEMAND ELASTICITY

In its most general form, the demand function for a good can be expressed as

$$Q_1 = f(P_1, P_2, \ldots, P_n, I, E, R, N, T, O),$$

where Q_1 = quantity demanded of good 1,
P_1 = market price of the good,
$P_2, \ldots, P_n$ = prices of other goods,
I = level of consumer incomes,

E = consumer expectations regarding future prices, incomes, and product availability,

R = range of goods available to buyers,

N = number of potential buyers, and

O = all other factors relevant in influencing Q_1.

The elasticity of demand with respect to any demand determinant refers to the degree of responsiveness of the quantity demanded relative to some percentage change in that demand determinant *when the values of all other demand determinants are held fixed*.

In mathematical terms, this definition translates into the following expressions for point elasticity:

$$\epsilon_p = \frac{\partial Q_1}{\partial P_1} \cdot \frac{P_1}{Q_1}, \tag{1}$$

which is the partial elasticity of good 1 with respect to its price, P_1, or price elasticity of demand;

$$\epsilon_{12} = \frac{\partial Q_1}{\partial P_2} \cdot \frac{P_2}{Q_1}, \tag{2}$$

which is the partial elasticity of good 1 with respect to the price of good 2, or cross elasticity of demand between good 1 and good 2;

$$\epsilon_{1n} = \frac{\partial Q_1}{\partial P_n} \cdot \frac{P_n}{Q_1}, \tag{3}$$

which is the partial elasticity of good 1 with respect to the price of good n, or cross elasticity of demand between good 1 and good n;

$$\epsilon_I = \frac{\partial Q_1}{\partial I} \cdot \frac{I}{Q_1}, \tag{4}$$

which is the partial elasticity of good 1 with respect to income, or income elasticity of demand; and so on for the other demand determinants. Hence, when given the demand function for a commodity containing more than one variable, the procedure for determining point elasticity requires using the *partial derivative* of the demand function with respect to that demand determinant rather than the first derivative.

Exercises

1. Suppose that the demand function for commodity X is specified by the equation $Q_X = 34 - 0.8P_x^2 + 0.3P_y + 0.04I$.
   (a) Determine the price elasticity of demand for X when $P_x = \$10$, $P_y = \$20$, and $I = \$5000$.

150

*Demand
Functions,
Revenue
Functions,
and Elasticity*

(b) Determine the cross elasticity of demand for X with respect to commodity Y when $P_x = \$10$, $P_y = \$20$, and $I = \$5000$. Are X and Y substitutes or complements?

(c) Determine the income elasticity of demand for X when $P_x = \$10$, $P_y = \$20$, and $I = \$5000$. Is X a normal or an inferior good?

2. Suppose that the demand function for commodity Y is specified by the equation $Q_y = 1665 - 0.5P_y^3 - 0.1P_x^2 - 0.05I$.

(a) Determine the price elasticity of demand when $P_y = \$10$, $P_x = \$20$, and $I = \$2500$.

(b) Determine the cross elasticity of demand for Y with respect to commodity X when $P_y = \$10$, $P_x = \$20$, and $I = \$2500$. Are X and Y substitutes or complements?

(c) Determine the income elasticity of demand for Y when $P_y = \$10$, $P_x = \$20$, and $I = \$2500$. Is Y a normal or an inferior good?

SUMMARY

The analysis of the demand for a product can be approached from the standpoint of an individual consumer (individual consumer demand), from the standpoint of all consumers taken as a group (market demand), or from the standpoint of a particular business firm (product demand or firm demand). Individual consumer demand for a product is determined in the main by (1) the selling price of the item; (2) consumer tastes and preferences; (3) the money income of consumers; (4) the prices of related products; (5) consumer expectations with regard to future prices, income levels, and product availability; and (6) the range of goods and services available for selection. By adding to this listing the number of consumers, we get the seven major determinants of the market demand for a product. Other peripheral considerations include whether the good in question is a luxury or a necessity, whether its demand is derived from the demand for other goods, the extent of market saturation, the price and availability of consumer credit, and the discretionary purchasing power of consumers. The separate impacts of the major and minor demand determinants vary in degree and intensity from product to product; each item has its own unique set of demand determinants.

A firm's demand curve provides the basis for deriving its revenue curves. A firm's average revenue (AR) curve summarizes the relationship between average revenue (average price) and quantity sold; it is identical to the firm's demand curve. A firm's total revenue (TR) equals the total receipts it obtains from the sale of its output. A firm's marginal revenue (MR) is the change in total revenue that results from a very small increase or decrease in output sold. Marginal revenue may be thought of as either *continuous* or *discrete*. Continuous marginal revenue is appropriate when output changes by infinitesimally small amounts. Discrete marginal revenue is used in situations where output changes in amounts of 1 unit (or more). A firm's average revenue can be found by dividing total revenue by the number of units sold. The shapes of the various *TR*, *MR*, and *AR* functions depend on the shape of the demand curve.

Elasticity of demand measures the responsiveness or sensitivity of quantity demanded to changes in a demand determinant. Price elasticity of demand is defined specifically as a ratio of the percentage change in quantity demanded resulting from a percentage change in price. Arc elasticity is an approximate measure of demand sensitivity between two points, while point elasticity measures elasticity at a single point on the demand function. When the coefficient of price elasticity is greater than one, demand is elastic and a price decrease will cause *TR* to rise. When the coefficient of price elasticity is less than one, demand is inelastic and a price decrease will cause *TR* to fall. Total revenue is maximized at the output rate where the price elasticity coefficient is 1. The degree of price elasticity for a product varies according to (1) the region of the demand curve within which price changes, (2) the number and availability of substitutes, (3) the price of the item relative to consumer income, (4) whether the item is a luxury or a necessity, (5) the number of uses for the good, (6) the length of the time period being considered, (7) the durability of the item, and (8) market saturation.

Two other elasticity concepts of particular importance are income elasticity and cross elasticity. High, positive income elasticities characterize luxury-type items; low, positive income elasticities are typical for necessities; and negative income elasticities denote inferior goods. Cross elasticity is a measure of the sensitivity of the demand for one product relative to price changes in another product. When the cross elasticity coefficient is positive, the two goods are substitutes; when the coefficient is negative, a complementary relationship is indicated. The closer the coefficient is to zero, the more independent are the two items.

SUGGESTED READINGS

CLARKSON, G. P., *The Theory of Consumer Demand: A Critical Appraisal* (Englewood Cliffs, N.J.: Prentice-Hall, Inc., 1963).

DEAN, J., *Managerial Economics* (Englewood Cliffs, N.J.: Prentice-Hall, Inc., 1951), pp. 177–210.

HALVORSEN, R., "Residential Demand for Electric Energy," *Review of Economics and Statistics*, Vol. 47, No. 1 (February 1975), pp. 12–18.

SCHULTZ, H., *Theory and Measurement of Demand* (Chicago: University of Chicago Press, 1938).

SUITS, D. B., "The Demand for New Automobiles in the U.S., 1929–1956," *Review of Economics and Statistics*, Vol. 40 (August 1958), pp. 273–280.

WOLD, H., *Demand Analysis* (New York: John Wiley & Sons, Inc., 1953).

PROBLEMS AND QUESTIONS FOR DISCUSSION

1. The following table presents hypothetical data for the market demand for a commodity. Complete the table.

152
*Demand
Functions,
Revenue
Functions,
and Elasticity*

Price	Quantity Demanded	AR	TR	Discrete MR	Coefficient of Price Elasticity
$50	1	‾‾‾	‾‾‾		‾‾‾
40	2	‾‾‾	‾‾‾	‾‾‾	‾‾‾
30	3	‾‾‾	‾‾‾	‾‾‾	‾‾‾
20	4	‾‾‾	‾‾‾	‾‾‾	‾‾‾
13	5	‾‾‾	‾‾‾	‾‾‾	‾‾‾
8	6	‾‾‾	‾‾‾	‾‾‾	‾‾‾

2. Given: The demand equation is $P = 81 - 9Q$.
   (a) What is the equation for MR?
   (b) At what output is $MR = 0$?
   (c) At what output is TR maximum?
   (d) Determine the price elasticity of demand at the output where TR is maximum.

3. Suppose that the demand equation for a commodity is $Q = 20 - 3P$. What is the price elasticity of demand at a price of $1? At a price of $4?

4. If the demand equation for an item is $Q = 16 + 9P - 2P^2$, calculate the price elasticity of demand at a price of $4. At a price of $3.

5. If the demand equation for an item is $P = 1000 + 3Q - 4Q^2$,
   (a) determine price elasticity of demand at $Q = 10$ units.
   (b) determine the equations for TR and MR.

6. Given the following hypothetical data for a consumer, compute *all* meaningful elasticity coefficients (price elasticity, income elasticity, and cross elasticity). Remember that prices must be constant when income elasticity is computed and that income and the prices of other products must be constant when price elasticity is computed, and so on. In other words, the computation of elasticities of any kind is valid *only* when *all other* variables are held constant.

Period	Price of X	Quantity of X Purchased	Price of Y	Income
1	$1.00	200	$.50	$6000
2	1.05	190	.50	6000
3	1.05	200	.52	6500
4	1.05	220	.54	6500
5	1.03	210	.53	6500
6	1.03	215	.55	6500
7	1.03	205	.55	6300
8	1.07	190	.55	6300

7. Given: The market demand equation for widgets is $Q = 840 - 0.50P$, where Q = quantity demanded per period of time and P = price of widgets in dollars.
   (a) If the price of widgets were lowered from $40 to $38, would you expect consumer expenditures for widgets to rise, fall, or remain unchanged?
   (b) If the economy's sole producer of widgets lowered its price from $40 to $38,

what predictions, if any, can you make about the effect the price reduction would have upon the firm's *profits*?

8. Given: The relationship between product A and product B is $Q_A = 80P_B - 0.5P_B^2$, where Q_A = units of product A demanded by consumers each day and P_B = selling price of product B.
   (a) Determine the cross elasticity coefficient for the two products when the price of product B = $10.
   (b) Are products A and B complements, substitutes, or independent, and how "strong" is the relationship?

9. Given the price levels now prevailing for steel products, would you expect that the price elasticity of demand for the output of U.S. Steel Corporation is higher or lower than the price elasticity of demand for the output of the steel industry as a whole? Why?

10. The Tastee Food Company estimates that the demand-income relationships for its line of frozen pies can be represented by the equation $Q = 500 + 0.10I$, where Q = cases of frozen pies and I = average family income.
    (a) Determine the point income elasticity of demand at $I = \$15,000$, $I = \$20,000$, and $I = \$25,000$.
    (b) The calculations in part (a) should show that ϵ_I increases as income increases. Why does this relationship exist? Would the same relationship hold if the demand-income equation were $Q = 0.10I$?
    (c) Would you characterize the demand for Tastee Foods' frozen pie line as susceptible to recessionary influences in the economy? Explain. Would sustained inflation over a period of years tend to alter the demand-income equation because of the effects that inflation has on the purchasing power of the dollar?

11. The Fairfax Apparel Company manufactures leisure shirts for men; during 1980 Fairfax sold an average of 23,000 leisure shirts for $13 per shirt. In early January 1981, Fairfax's major competitor, Lafayette Manufacturing Co., cut the price of its leisure shirts from $15 to $12. The orders Fairfax received for its own leisure shirts dropped sharply, from 23,000 per month to 13,000 per month for February and March 1981.
    (a) Calculate the cross elasticity of demand between Fairfax's leisure shirts and Lafayette's leisure shirts during February and March. Are the two companies' leisure shirts good or poor substitutes?
    (b) Suppose that the coefficient of price elasticity of demand for Fairfax's leisure shirts is -2.0. Assuming that Lafayette keeps its price at $12, by how much must Fairfax cut its price to build its sales of shirts back up to 23,000 per month? (*Hint:* Use the arc formula for price elasticity and substitute the known values into it and solve for the unknown price.)
    (c) Would you recommend that Fairfax cut its price to the value calculated in part (b)? Why or why not?

SIX THE FIRM
AND TECHNOLOGICAL
CHANGE

Having obtained an understanding of the formation of consumer demand and the composition of demand functions, we are ready to examine how best to produce the goods and services that consumers are willing and able to purchase. This chapter surveys some of the properties of a firm's production process and pinpoints the factors governing a firm's choice of production technologies. Specifically, we shall consider (1) types of production processes, (2) the properties of the production functions of firms, (3) the role of technology and technological advance in altering the capabilities of a firm to produce goods and services, and (4) the pressures upon firms for adopting new technologies.

THE CONCEPT OF PRODUCTION

It is common to think of "production" as being synonomous with manufacturing. With a bit of reflection, however, it is clear that quite a large number of economic functions qualify as production. Such diverse activities as collecting taxes, operating a jewelry store, drilling for oil, recruiting new employees, designing a system to measure air pollution, dictating a letter, managing a United Fund drive, discussing with officials of the Federal Trade

Commission the factual basis for claims made in a TV commercial, driving a garbage truck, and interviewing applicants for food stamps can all be properly construed as production of one sort or another. Why? Because each involves some aspect of furnishing a good or service to some economic entity that values it.

In general, *any activity that creates value is production.* In this sense, then, production covers virtually all phases of economic activity except consumption. Nevertheless, because manufacturing activity illustrates the production process so well, we shall find it convenient to couch our discussion of production theory and production decisions largely in a manufacturing context. Still, the principles of production are equally applicable to the whole range of an organization's activities, irrespective of whether it is goods-oriented or service-oriented, profit-oriented or not-for-profit.

PRODUCTION ACTIVITY: TRANSFORMING INPUTS INTO OUTPUTS

If a production engineer were asked how to make a simple product, the reply might well be in terms of the kinds of raw materials needed, the proportions and order in which these ingredients should be combined, and the processing conditions and time needed to produce the desired characteristics. Such an answer would serve as a beginning, although it would be incomplete. Other inputs are needed. Raw material ingredients do not get combined and processed of their own volition; these operations require human intervention or *labor* input. In addition, various tools, machinery, equipment, and physical facilities will probably be required to assist in converting the raw material ingredients into the final product—these types of inputs are from a general category of resources called *capital*. Furthermore, production activity must occur in some location and so occupies space or *land* (this is particularly apparent in the case of agricultural production), and the production process takes *time*—anywhere from a few minutes to a few years. Finally, production activity requires supervision, planning, control, coordination, and leadership, or in other words, an input of *entrepreneurial* or *managerial talent and capability*.

In sum, *production* is a series of activities by which resource inputs (raw materials, labor, capital, land utilization, and managerial talents) are transformed over some period of time into outputs of goods or services. The period requisite for the transformation is variable among products and from recipe to recipe for a given product. Not infrequently, the same basic production process may yield a variety of distinct products. In meat packing, for example, the slaughter of beef cattle produces numerous cuts of meat products, hides for leather goods, and lard for cooking purposes. Outputs produced from the same production process are designated as *joint products*.

Figure 6-1 symbolizes the nature of production activities. Of course, as concerns a specific product or technique, the size of the box and the

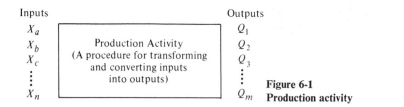

Figure 6-1
Production activity

details of what goes on inside it tend to change over time as a consequence of modifications in technical requirements, the qualities of inputs, and the composition of output. Since production activities are often composed of sequentially organized phases, introducing a change in one of the phases may entail changes elsewhere. Adding a new piece of labor-saving equipment, for example, could have the effect of adjusting materials specifications and of modifying the skill levels of the labor input needed to operate the new equipment. These, in turn, could necessitate changes in procurement patterns and in hiring and training programs. The high productivity of the new equipment could cause bottlenecks at either or both ends of the phase, thereby causing even further adjustments.

BASIC TYPES OF PRODUCTION ACTIVITY

The various types of productive activities can be grouped into four categories: (1) unique-product production, (2) rigid mass production, (3) flexible mass production, and (4) process or flow production.[1] Each type has distinctive features and requirements, and in understanding the production economics of a business it is important to know which type applies and to carry its principles through as efficiently as possible.

Unique-Product Production. This type of production activity is the least advanced. Each product is more or less distinct and made to specific order—a steam turbine, an office building, an aircraft carrier, the services of a law firm or an accounting firm. Production activity is labor intensive in the sense that capital investment tends to be outweighed by labor cost considerations. It makes high demands on skill and craftsmanship. It requires people who are good at technical functions. Unique-product production can operate at a low volume of output and it is amenable to wide fluctuation in output through adjustment in the size of the work force. The trigger for the beginning of production activity is receipt of an order.

Moreover, work is organized more around the stage of production than around craft skill. The model is the telephone installer, who, being neither a skilled carpenter nor an electrician, drills holes, installs electric wiring, makes ground connections, and tests the circuitry—everything needed within

[1]This classification scheme and ensuing discussion is drawn from Peter F. Drucker, *Management: Tasks, Responsibilities, Practices* (New York: Harper & Row, Publishers, 1974), pp. 203–216.

the installation stage. Another example is in the construction of a single-family home, where production is grouped around the stages of putting the foundation in place; framing and roofing; installing the plumbing, wiring, and heating and cooling equipment; and finishing the interior. Craft skills are much in evidence, but they are grouped according to the production stage of the house.

Rigid Mass Production. As the label implies, in rigid mass production both the end product and the tools, materials, and parts used tend to be standardized. When Henry Ford said "The customer can have a car in any color as long as it's black," he expressed the essence of rigid mass production: the manufacture of uniform products in large quantity using a well-defined, proven production method.[2]

Rigid mass production entails a very high and consistent volume of output; minor fluctuations in output adversely affect the economies of the system. It requires high skill in the design of the process, as well as in its maintenance, but very little skilled labor to operate. Production planning and scheduling are of the essence in getting the system to operate at peak efficiency. And because the nature of the final product is tightly constrained by the lack of production flexibility, firms selling standard mass-produced items have to condition customers to adapt their tastes and needs to narrow product variety—otherwise, the low-cost economy of mass production cannot be realized.

Flexible Mass Production. This production type seeks to take advantage of economical mass production by assembling the final product out of mass-produced, standardized components. The result is a diversity of end products which can readily be tailored to meet a diverse range of customer preferences. The key to making flexible mass production a workable approach is systematic analysis of customers, markets, and products to find the patterns around which diversity can be organized; this pattern then becomes the basis for taking the burden of diversity out of manufacturing and shifting it into assembly. General Motors has skillfully practiced the principle of developing as many different products as possible out of fewer and fewer parts. Nearly all comparable makes of GM cars (Chevrolet, Pontiac, Buick, Oldsmobile, Cadillac) use the same frames, bodies, brakes, electrical systems, mechanical parts, and very substantially the same engines. Yet, because of different colors, body styles, fabrics, trim, and interior design, GM cars look different, have different features, and have appeals to different market segments.

Flexible mass production, although generally capital intensive and mechanized, requires a substantial amount of labor input. It also requires

---

[2]Ford realized that it would be easy enough to give buyers a color choice; all that was needed was several paint spray guns instead of one. But his argument was that the uniformity of the product would be lost once he made a concession to product diversity. To him, product uniformity was the key to mass-production economies.

high skill in designing and maintaining the system—especially in terms of balancing product diversity against low-cost production of standard components. Because flexible mass production can turn out a very large variety of products and yet still capitalize upon standardized production techniques, one can predict that rigid mass production methods will become increasingly confined to a fairly small number of end products where basic uniformity is a fundamental customer need and customer specification.

Process Production. Process production is an integrated system whereby a continuous flow of raw material inputs are converted into a continuous flow of output. Typically, the system is highly automated and mechanized, thus requiring a large capital investment in facilities and equipment and utilizing only small doses of labor inputs. The continuous-flow nature of the process makes for high production efficiency as long as it is operated at or near peak capacity 24 hours a day, 7 days a week; the greater the utilization of the facilities, the lower unit costs will be.

The classic example of process production is an oil refinery where crude oil is dispatched through a complex processing system to spawn a variety of refined end products for very different end uses. Process production is also the rule in the chemical industry. Other examples include milk processing, the manufacture of plate glass, and papermaking.

In many instances, process production offers the flexibility of a diverse range of products (gasoline, diesel fuel, fuel oil, motor oil, lubricants). But once built, the process itself tends to be relatively inflexible and can be changed only at major expense. Thus, decisions to invest in process production facilities have to be made with an eye toward the long-range future; in particular, the prospects must be good that a firm will be able to create, maintain, and/or expand the markets for its outputs to whatever extent is needed to utilize plant capacity.[3]

THE PRODUCTION FUNCTION

Economists use the term *production function* to refer to the physical relationship between a firm's input of productive resources (raw materials, labor, capital, land, managerial talents) and its output of goods or services per unit of time. This relationship can be expressed symbolically as

$$Q = f(X_a, X_b, X_c, \ldots, X_n),$$

where $X_a, X_b, X_c, \ldots, X_n$ represent quantities of various types of inputs and Q represents the quantity of output obtainable per period of time from specific combinations of the array of inputs. Such an expression furnishes a

---

[3]A good example of what this means is illustrated by the famous Standard Oil story of the 1890s, where the company distributed kerosene lamps free to Chinese peasants to help create a market for kerosene.

convenient analytical device for indicating that the quantity of a good or service produced per period of time is a function of the quantities of resource inputs used by the firm per period of time.

The specific character of a production function depends partly on the quantities of resources employed and partly on the way in which they are combined (the production technology adopted by the firm). As an illustration, suppose that a firm has two technically feasible ways of combining inputs X_a, X_b, X_c, and X_d:

Production Technology	Resource Inputs (units)	Output (units)
Technology A	50 each of X_a, X_b, X_c, and X_d	5,000
	100 each of X_a, X_b, X_c, and X_d	10,000
	150 each of X_a, X_b, X_c, and X_d	15,000
Technology B	50 each of X_a, X_b, X_c, and X_d	6,000
	100 each of X_a, X_b, X_c, and X_d	12,000
	150 each of X_a, X_b, X_c, and X_d	18,000

By employing technology A, the firm can produce 5000 units of output with 50 units each of inputs X_a, X_b, X_c, and X_d. Using 100 units of each input results in 10,000 units of output, and 150 units of each input yield an output of 15,000 units. However, the input-output relationship is quite different for technology B. Technology B generates more output for the same volume of input than does technology A and consequently is more efficient than A. It follows that there is a corresponding production function for *each* production technique or recipe for producing a product. A firm can alter its quantity of output by varying the amounts of input it combines according to its given production technique, by switching from one production technology to another, or by undertaking both actions. The efficiency of a production technique determines the output yield from each combination of inputs, while the state of technological know-how determines the number of available techniques.

In order to distinguish between the many production techniques available to a firm and the one it actually employs, economists customarily assume that competition and profit incentives induce a firm to utilize the most efficient production technique. Moreover, a firm is presumed to employ the most efficient production technique in such a way as to obtain the maximum output from each alternative combination of inputs it uses. In symbolic language, for a production function of the form

$$Q = f(X_a, X_b, X_c, \ldots, X_n),$$

each numerical value of Q corresponding to specified numerical values of X_a, X_b, X_c, $\ldots$, X_n is interpreted as being the largest possible value of Q

obtainable, given the production technology employed by the firm. For instance, in studying the production function for a firm producing red fireplugs, interest centers only upon the *maximum* number of red fireplugs per period of time that can be produced from specific combinations of machine time, hours of skilled labor, floor space, electricity, hours of managerial input, metal casing, red paint, and so on. The rationale for this presumption is that no firm would knowingly seek to get anything less than the largest possible amount of output for a specified set of inputs, although in reality various frictions and imperfections in the production process may prevent a firm from always realizing its maximum productive capability.

It is equally accurate to conceive of a firm's production function as specifying the *minimum* input requirements for a designated level of output, given its production technology. To use the fireplug example again, the input-output relationship for a firm producing red fireplugs can be estimated by studying the minimum amounts of machine time, hours of skilled labor, floor space, electricity, hours of managerial input, metal casing, red paint, and so on requisite for producing specified quantities of red fireplugs per period of time.

Whichever approach is preferred, the production function for a firm defines the limits of the firm's technical production possibilities. At any point in time, when a firm producing at these limits wishes to increase output, it must use more inputs; similarly, the firm cannot use fewer inputs without decreasing its rate of output. Thus, as long as a firm is using the most efficient production technology currently available, its output rate is dependent upon (1) the quantities of resource inputs employed in the production process and (2) how efficiently it is using these quantities of resource inputs.

Knowledge of a firm's production function permits answers to the following questions:

1. To what extent will total output change if the quantity of one input is increased and the quantity of all other inputs is held constant?
2. To what extent will total output change if the quantity of one input employed is decreased while the quantity of some other input is increased?
3. To what extent will output change if the firm increases some or all of the inputs in either equal or unequal proportions?

A firm can also ascertain from its production function whether its operating rate is technically efficient. Because the production function gives the maximum output obtainable from a given input combination, when the actual output flow is less than the potential maximum flow, the firm can produce its present output with a smaller volume of one or more inputs (and thereby reduce costs), or it can use its present inputs to produce a larger volume of output than it is currently getting. To put it another way, unless a firm is operating at some input-output combination defined by its production function, its output rate is technically inefficient and reorganization of its operations will allow reducing inputs with no loss of output.

THE IMPACT OF TECHNOLOGICAL ADVANCE
UPON PRODUCTION FUNCTIONS

It is a matter of historical fact that technical knowledge and capability have broadened and deepened over time, and presumably they will continue to do so. This kind of technological change is pertinent for production analysis, because an advance in the state of technology increases the number of recipes available and alters the production functions of enterprises as they incorporate new technologies into their production methods. However, the nature of the efficiency improvement associated with technological advance can assume several forms:

1. A new production technology may permit the same amounts of resource inputs to be combined differently so as to yield a greater output than before.
2. A new production technology may utilize the same types of inputs to produce the same type of output as previously known processes but require a *smaller* quantity of one or even several inputs and *no more* of the remaining inputs to produce the same quantity of output as before.
3. A new production technology may employ the same types of inputs to produce the same type of output as previously known processes, using *less* of some inputs and *more* of others, yet with a smaller total cost and rate of input usage, to produce the same quantity of output as before.
4. A new production technology may require inputs, or yield outputs, that are of a kind not heretofore used or available at all.

Needless to say, the discovery of production technologies that are less efficient than those already known seldom has meaningful impact, since enterprises have no motive to implement them.

It is also worth noting that technological proficiency is often not uniform among firms producing the same product. Age differences among the plants of different firms are certain to exist, with newer plants embodying efficiency-increasing technological improvements unavailable to older plants. Also, there may be locational differences in labor efficiency and raw material quality. Managers, engineers, and technical staffs in some firms may simply have failed to keep up with current developments and may not know of better processes that other firms are using. All these factors combine to explain why firms in the same industry may have somewhat heterogeneous production functions.

THE CONSEQUENCES OF TECHNOLOGICAL CHANGE
FOR PRODUCTION PROCESSES

As hinted earlier, the concept of technology encompasses the systematic application of scientific, engineering, administrative, or other organized bodies of knowledge to production activities and product development. The broader and deeper is society's technical capability, the more opportunities there are for breaking down production methods into smaller pieces and bringing the full contribution of each specialized bit of knowledge to bear upon increasing efficiency and lowering costs. In addition, technological advance induces fundamental and persistent changes both in production processes and production functions. Several of these changes have been highly prominent in the twentieth century and deserve brief mention.[4]

First, as elaborate production methods are developed to produce goods more efficiently, an increasing span of time separates the beginning from the completion of production activity. An analogy may be made to the root system of a tree. Production can be thought of as being subdivided into phases that stretch back into time just as the root system of a tree penetrates and spreads through the ground. The bigger the tree, the larger and more complex its root system. Similarly, the more complex the product to be produced or the more sophisticated the production technique, the longer the time span required for its accomplishment and the larger the number of distinct phases of production. Specialized knowledge and technical expertise can then be brought to bear upon the performance of each and every phase of the whole task. As the first-level phases are completed, their results must be combined with the results of related phases so as to effect completion of the second level of the process; these second-level results must be combined again; and so on until the phases have been put together to complete the whole process. The more complex the network, the more steps it takes to complete it and the more individuals with specialized, technical, and managerial skills who are required for staffing the process.

Second, advances in technology are typically accompanied by increases in the use of capital goods. This is because the application of more knowledge to some phase of production often involves the development of specialized tools, machinery, or equipment to perform or assist in performing the function—a trait that tends to increase a firm's dollar investment in its production activity.

Third, the added capital investment—while helping to increase output per unit of input and overall operating efficiency—may have the effect of making production procedures somewhat less flexible or the composition of the final product more rigid. For instance, new equipment may be useful *only* for performing certain well-defined functions; hence, any alteration in the way they are performed may be prohibitively expensive—until a larger portion of the projected life of the specialized equipment is used up and its replacement falls within the range of economic feasibility. In the meantime, a firm finds itself "locked in" by cost to using the production recipe it has already installed.

Fourth, technological advance alters the types of manpower needed to staff the human element of production activity. For example, introducing computers into business operations greatly reduces the need for payroll clerks, billing clerks, bookkeepers, and similar kinds of office staff while it

[4]The following discussion is based largely upon the ideas expressed by John Kenneth Galbraith in Chapter 2 of *The New Industrial State* (Boston: Houghton Mifflin Company, 1967).

creates entirely new demands for keypunch operators, programmers, statistical consultants, systems analysts, computer engineers, and so on. Also, over the last several decades, the character of technological change has dictated that more highly specialized labor be used in conjunction with the introduction of new production techniques and new equipment. The requirement of specialized personnel, however, does not necessarily reflect a need for a higher order of human talent as much as it calls for the specialist to have a deeper knowledge of a smaller range of subjects.

Fifth, with a higher order of technology and more intensive specialization must come more organization and proficient administration. Organization is what brings the work of the specialists in their performance of the various phases of the production process to a coherent result. When a product is complex or the production process is lengthy and complicated, the job of coordinating the work of the many specialists will itself be a major task. Moreover, there is a need to provide for the orderly handling of change and for coping with unscheduled developments and contingencies. Developing the skills and management capability to prevent, offset, or otherwise neutralize the effect of adverse developments and to ensure that the firm's products are in line with market trends become necessary features in structuring complex and time-consuming production processes.[5]

These five technologically related developments have been a major impetus behind the trend to larger-scale enterprises. The technological imperative to subdivide production activities into manageable tasks, the organizational imperative to coordinate these tasks to effect a coherent result, and the market imperative to do so efficiently and profitably help explain why firms in some industries become quite large. Moreover, the long-run impact of technological advance has been to change the production functions of some products in a manner that requires large-scale production to realize maximum efficiency.[6]

CHARACTERISTICS OF TECHNOLOGICAL PROGRESS

Technological advance and innovation have their origins in the internal research efforts of business firms and in knowledge transfer among firms, industries, governments, and educational institutions. A portion of new knowledge originates with basic research—investigations conducted without

[5]In unique-product production, where firms often depend upon a simple and inexpensive technology and lead times are fairly short, long-range predictions and forward planning are much less crucial. It can be assumed that the conditions under which the output is marketed, being near at hand, will be sufficiently similar to the present. Should the product not meet customer approval, it can be readily modified without lasting harm to the producer's reputation. If new developments make the current methods obsolete, the old can be exchanged for the new in a short time and with no undue expense. But similar occurrences for a firm employing capital-intensive mass production or process technologies approaches the intolerable—the correction time is longer, the expense costlier, and the scars on a firm's reputation long in healing.

[6]This is in contrast to the view that the advance of large corporate enterprise is motivated largely by the urge for monopoly power and, ultimately, monopoly profits.

special concern for the usefulness of the results. But many technological discoveries emerge from purposive investigations where the intent is to obtain results for specific uses. Implicit in a firm's search for improved production techniques is the hope that successful research and development activities will increase the productive efficiency of the firm's operations, which in turn will give the firm a cost advantage and ultimately allow for a higher degree of profitability.

The application of *new* production techniques is not, however, the sole means of technological progress. Progress in the form of higher degrees of productive efficiency commonly derives from learning to apply existing techniques more effectively. Obviously enough, as firms obtain more experience with a given process, opportunities will be identified for improving the production technique. Particularly during the early stages of using a new technique is it possible to spot ways to effect improvements. This facet of technological progress is called *learning by doing* and is often neglected as a feature of progress and as a factor causing gradual, yet persistent, shifts in a firm's production function.

Experience in industry has shown that the "bugs" in a new technology survive for sustained periods, even as much as 3 to 10 years. Bits and pieces of complex processes do not always fit as neatly together as was originally envisioned. Parts of the process may have to be torn down and rebuilt; startup and break-in costs may exceed expected forecasts. Meanwhile, output is stymied or not up to acceptable standards, expected revenues from the sale of output are not forthcoming, working capital is used up and not regenerated from the sale of output, with the result that the firm is sometimes caught in a classic, but temporary, profit squeeze. Even with a known technology, new plants may take up to 3 years to get on stream at the level of efficiency originally foreseen.

Another feature of technological progress is that its impact and rate of advance is uneven from firm to firm and industry to industry. Some firms are more financially able to engage in invention and innovation. A number of enterprises are convinced that improvement of their competitive position is more reliably achieved from technological innovation than from the adoption of other competitive strategies that can be duplicated more easily; hence, they place strong emphasis on research and development activities and tend to be technologically progressive. In some cases, advancing technology seems to allow firms to purchase greater amounts of production capacity per dollar of investment. In other instances the dollar investment in production facilities per unit of output is increased. By and large, modern production technology has been associated with substituting machines for labor, thereby raising the overall level of capital intensity in most production processes.

At the same time, firms and industries have displayed a wide disparity in the rates with which they have adopted new technologies.[7] Taking into

[7]F. Lynn, "An Investigation of the Rate of Development and Diffusion of Technology in Our Modern Industrial Society," in *Studies Prepared for the National Commission on Technology, Automation, and Economic Progress*, Appendix, Volume II, Technology and

account a period of 15 years after the discovery of a new technology, it has
been observed that some innovations languish in oblivion for as much as 10 years and then are rapidly adopted, that other innovations never mount a serious challenge to displace predecessor processes and facilities, and that still other innovations come quickly into general use and soon are being used to produce 80% or more of the total output of the industry. The differences in the diffusion rates of new production techniques have several explanations. First, some innovations are slow to be employed because although they are technologically possible, they are risky or are only marginally profitable. An innovation may require resource inputs that are not readily available or have prohibitive costs, thereby undercutting the incentive to adopt it. Second, there is usually ample room for the managers of firms to possess different perceptions of the actual degree of technological superiority of an innovation, thus partially explaining why one firm adopts an innovation and another does not. Unless an innovation has substantial technological and economic superiority over existing methods, firms are likely to switch to the new technology only in the normal course of replacing worn-out equipment. Third, an innovation may require capital commitments beyond the reach of small firms; this may explain why larger firms are, on occasion, technologically superior to smaller firms.

R&D SPENDING AND FIRM SIZE

That large enterprises have a strong financial commitment toward technical development and innovation is readily verified. According to National Science Foundation statistics, while an estimated 11,000 firms engage in research and development work in the United States, a relatively small number undertake the majority of the effort.[8] In 1975 the 116 R&D-performing companies with 25,000 or more employees accounted for 73% of total R&D expenditures (40 companies reported annual R&D budgets above $100 million in 1975). Over 89% of R&D spending was done by the 495 firms having 5000 or more employees; these same firms employed approximately 83% of the scientists and engineers engaged in R&D work. At the other end of the size spectrum, firms with fewer than 1000 employees spend only 4% of total R&D expenditures despite the fact that firms in this size category make up

the American Economy (Washington, D.C., 1966); E. Mansfield, "The Speed of Response of Firms to New Techniques," *Quarterly Journal of Economics* (May 1963), pp. 290–311; E. Mansfield, "Size of Firm, Market Structure and Innovation," *Journal of Political Economy*, Vol. 71 (December 1963), pp. 556–576; John M. Blair, *Economic Concentration: Structure, Behavior, and Public Policy* (New York: Harcourt Brace Jovanovich, Inc., 1972); G. F. Ray, "The Diffusion of New Technology," *National Institute Economic Review* (May 1969), pp. 40–83; A. A. Romeo, "Interindustry and Interfirm Differences in the Rate of Diffusion of an Innovation," *Review of Economics and Statistics*, Vol. 57, No. 3 (August 1975), pp. 311–319.
[8]National Science Foundation, *Research and Development in Industry*, 1975 (Washington, D.C.: U.S. Government Printing Office, 1977).

over 95% of the total number of industrial enterprises. Between 1957 and 1975, companies with fewer than 5000 employees doubled the dollar amount of company funds allocated for R&D, but in companies with more than 5000 employees company-funded R&D increased 400%.

The reasons for the relative lack of R&D effort in small enterprises stem from their financial and organizational constraints in seeking to be innovative and technologically progressive. Small firms cannot afford to staff internally for industrial research programs; they have neither the earning power to pay for such efforts nor the financial power to develop and fully exploit the findings of a comprehensive R&D program.[9] Studies of the innovation process in organizations suggest that R&D is most productive in an "innovative organizational climate" that acts as a catalyst for new ideas. Small, family-based businesses tend to be more tradition-bound and "conservative," thereby offering a less innovative, less progressive climate for new and better ideas. Hence, formal, organized R&D activity is primarily undertaken by bigger firms (those having 5000 or more employees). The only exception tends to be small, technology-based companies specializing in a "high-technology" product that has a small market demand and for which market potential is either unproven or undeveloped.

APPLICATIONS CAPSULE

HOW GENERAL MOTORS MANAGES ITS R&D PROGRAMS

General Motors spends more money on research and development than any other U.S. company. In 1978 General Motors spent $1.5 billion on R&D. For many years, GM has allocated about 3% of its sales revenue to R&D activity, with most of its spending directed toward developing new products rather than new equipment and methods of manufacture.

GM's R&D program is headed by an executive vice-president—one of four corporate executive vice-presidents who, along with the president, vice chairman, and chairman, are members of the company's top policy-making group. The head of R&D at GM has (1) primary responsibility for where and how well the R&D budget is spent, (2) the operations of General Motor's technical center, (3) new-car planning by the divisions, and (4) presiding over monthly meetings with the chief engineers of the divisions. In effect, the head of R&D at GM is deeply

[9] For example, American farmers—entrepreneurs in the classic sense—do almost no research and development on their own behalf. It is taken for granted that technological advance in agriculture is the product of the agricultural experiment stations of state universities, research financed by the U.S. Department of Agriculture, and the R&D efforts of the chemical, seed, and farm implement manufacturers. From a cost/profit standpoint, for a small farm enterprise (even a corporate farm enterprise) to hire and support a staff for conducting agricultural research and experimentation rarely pays off.

involved in everything having to do with future product planning—coordination of designs for new cars, 2, 3, and more years ahead; designing improved engines and transmissions; research on new batteries; designing new-concept cars; fuel economy research; studying alternative ways to meet federally imposed safety and emissions standards; and planning for changes to meet government regulations.

The Tech Center

In 1956 General Motors constructed its impressive Technical Center just outside Detroit. The Technical Center is strong testimony of GM's long-run commitment to R&D—the $200 million-a-year budget of the Tech Center alone puts it among the top 10 corporate research spenders in the United States. The Tech Center is the locus for virtually all of the company's advanced automotive work and is organized into 5 units:

1. *Research* carries out basic research in corrosion, materials, electronics, and environmental sciences.
2. *Engineering* works on advanced designs for engines, transmissions, fuel systems, and accessories, and provides consulting design expertise to the new car divisions when designs for a new part or component are being considered.
3. *Manufacturing Development* brainstorms ways to make more efficient manufacturing processes and equipment.
4. *Design* creates the styling and appearance of new cars, from the early sketches to the final clay model, which is the starting point for engineering and production.
5. *Environmental Activities* coordinates relations with the government on emissions control, noise control, and safety. The staff also sees that GM's manufacturing plants conform to government health and safety standards.

The projects that the Tech Center undertake usually originate from below rather than from above. When a person sees a problem, or perhaps a solution, he or she recommends a portion of the budget be allocated for this particular idea and study. Each project idea has to survive an intense screening from higher-level personnel. Within the Tech Center, each of the five staffs choose those projects which seem to offer the best payoff. These are then presented to the executive vice-president for R&D in corporate headquarters and eventually, if they survive screening, are submitted to the company's executive committee for approval. Generally, GM does not use rigid standards for judging the worth of a project, nor does it use a formal-type approach in selecting research projects. In many cases, the projects stem from a need to figure out how best to comply with new government requirements and regulations. Indeed, about half of GM's research budget is taken up with meeting government regulations and does not relate directly to developing better materials, better manufacturing techniques, and better products. For example, in 1976 GM estimated that its cars had $600 worth of federally required safety and pollution control hardware.

GM's Machine Tool Research Program

One program that GM is giving particular attention to is the development of more efficient machine tools. GM spends $600 to 700 million a year on machine tools, mostly for replacement. A few years ago, GM took a long look at the kinds of machine tools it was using and concluded that the character of the machine tools it was buying was essentially the same as it had been buying 25 or even 50 years ago, except that some of the tools were now equipped with digital controls. Because of the lack of improvement in machine tools, GM estimated that between 1950 and 1975 the productivity of its machine tools had slipped about 40% under what it could be. New and better machine tools were needed because, in GM's view, accounting methods based on conventional measures of labor efficiency had covered up how much productivity had failed to increase. According to one GM executive, "you can be efficient as hell at doing something on equipment that's obsolete, but you're not being productive."

But when GM looked to the machine tool industry to develop new tools, it found none willing to do the necessary research. As a result, GM decided to work on the design of new machine tools itself; the research objective was focused on higher operating speeds and ways to use new materials. The first project was the design of a large parts grinder able to work at three times the speed of current equipment; GM got four machine-tool builders to work with its prototype grinder—a program estimated to cost $20 million.

The Tech Center staff for manufacturing development was also working on the design of new applications for robots. The attempt was to develop robots with rudimentary senses—touch and vision—and to develop the computer logic behind that. The goal was to assemble a robot that had the ability to "see" parts, recognize whether or not they were right-side up, turn them over if necessary, and then install them on the car coming down the assembly line.

Using Computers to Design New Cars

One of GM's principal R&D accomplishments has been its pioneering of new uses for computer-aided design of new cars. GM engineers have figured out ways for computers (1) to design welding fixtures and determine the optimum angle of the welding gun, (2) to simulate automobile crashes and their effects on occupants, (3) to power machine tools to make dies, (4) to simulate the view that a person has from the driving seat, (5) to design trunk space, and (6) to evaluate the structural characteristics of new car designs. This latter computer application has been particularly important to GM and is referred to as the vehicle structural analysis program (VSAP). Using the VSAP, GM puts together mathematical models of the components of a car and then tests the vehicles on a simulated road displayed on computer consoles. The VSAP system was first used on the Cadillac Seville, and was a major factor in allowing GM to design and market the car in near-record time. The VSAP system proved indispensable to GM in trimming 700 to 1000 pounds of weight from GM's full-size line of cars because it allows GM to make large numbers of design changes and learn very quickly what the combined effect of them will be. Prior to VSAP, GM would often not learn whether a design for a new part would work until the prototype stage. So successful is the VSAP system that GM says "it is inconceivable that anyone will ever develop a new vehicle by the old method again."

The Shifting Emphasis in Car Design

In years past the philosophy of GM engineering was to design for lowest cost. Now, however, with the advent of new safety and dimensions standards, increasing cost pressures, and demands for more fuel economy, the design emphasis has shifted to lowest costs within certain weight-range and mileage objectives. According to one GM official, "that's a hell of a difference. It means that if it costs you extra steel waste on a part, you stamp the part out. It means that if you need a high-strength steel bumper bar, you use it. It means that if the car isn't going to make the weight, maybe you tool a new lighter-weight transmission or engine."

Taking these types of changes and translating them into dozens of car designs, thousands of manufacturing steps, and millions of automobiles explains why GM has little trouble figuring out how to spend $1.5 billion a year on R&D. The R&D backup gives GM greater capabilities for maintaining mass production efficiency, avoiding technical foul-ups in designing and producing its cars, and staying in compliance with tougher government regulations.

Source: "How GM Manages Its Billion-Dollar R&D Program" *Business Week* (June 28, 1976), pp. 54–58.

THE MOTIVATION AND PRESSURES FOR INNOVATION

Business firms, even when they are well sheltered from the cold winds of competition, are beset with a multitude of motivations and pressures for seeking out better production techniques and implementing promising innovations.[10] Naturally, the all-encompassing reason for the adoption of new technologies is to improve profitability and, ultimately, to safeguard the firm's market position and chances for survival. But such an explanation is a bit umbrellalike, for it hides the specific forces that tend to make investments in new technology and innovation virtually imperative.

First, new product innovation is a major avenue for increasing profits and, in the face of competition, it becomes a virtual necessity for maintaining consumer favor. Firms consistently attempt to outmaneuver their rivals by introducing more attractive products—in terms of price, quality, service, durability, design, convenience and so on. To successfully defend against such competitive tactics, a firm must be active in seeking new products that can better satisfy consumer demand, protect against shifts to substitute products, and maintain customer loyalty and patronage. In addition, market pressures for quality improvements, for product standardization in terms of sizes or performance, and for lower prices dictate a progressive and efficient technology. In short, technical innovation and virtuosity is a competitive weapon that pervades nearly every industry.

Adverse developments in the market for resource inputs provide added pressures for innovation and technological change. A portion of the trend to automate production originates from the desire of firms to escape rising labor costs and higher raw material prices associated with natural resource scarcity. In the same vein, human safety considerations and the chances of human error provide a strong motivation for technological change in some industries. Furthermore, dwindling supplies of natural resources precipitate the search for technological remedies in the form of substitute resources or the ability to use lower-quality resource inputs (such as lower grades of ore). Rising fuel-oil prices, rising electric rates, and natural-gas scarcity have been major factors in inducing many manufacturers to install energy-saving equipment as fast as possible. The solutions to both energy and environmental pollution are clearly technological in character. Then, too, on occasion, price competition among suppliers of new capital equipment can so reduce the cost of an innovation as to make it feasible on a broader scale. From an internal standpoint, the operating benefits of relieving bottlenecks in the production process can serve to motivate firms to seek technological solutions to their problems.

---

[10]Even firms with a stranglehold on the production of an item cannot long afford to be complacent about technological developments. In a world where the threat of potential substitutes grows more ominous every day and where innovation is proceeding elsewhere at accelerating rates, it is not likely that many firms, even monopolies, will choose to risk the fates of stagnation and obsolescence.

Rare is the firm or industry that can insulate itself successfully from the pervasive pressures to remain technologically up-to-date in the long run. Technical obsolescence spells almost certain disaster for a firm in terms of profitability, subject only to the propensity of government to rescue it by the granting of subsidies, protective tariffs, or regulation. Indeed, there is reason to suspect that government-protected and government-regulated industries are among the least progressive of all industries in terms of the rate of technological advance; the railroad industry provides a classic example. The correlation is as yet unproven but whether a cause-effect relationship exists between government regulation and slow technological progress deserves further study.[11]

Aside from the product market pressures, the resource input pressures, and the operating efficiency requirements that combine to motivate firms to adopt new technologies, there exist several less tangible behavior aspects

APPLICATIONS CAPSULE

THE SOLID-STATE TECHNOLOGY THREAT TO TIMEX

In 1975 Timex ranked as the world's largest maker of finished watches, producing some 40 million watches a year and commanding 50% of the U.S. mechanical watch market and 70% of the electric watch market. Timex's success stemmed from being able to mass-produce a simple pin-levered-movement watch in highly efficient plant facilities and, then, to market them at rock-bottom prices through 150,000 outlets in the United States alone—ranging from auto supply dealers to drugstores. With eye-catching point-of-sale displays and skillful television advertising (the "torture test" ads) to go with its low prices (an average of about $20 in 1975), Timex grew from a tiny company to titan in less than two decades.

Nonetheless, Timex's market position was strongly challenged in the mid-1970s by the growing popularity of digital watches and the technology of solid-state electronics—a technology that was on the verge of sweeping the watch industry and undermining the cost advantage Timex enjoyed with its simple pin-levered mechanical watches. The solid-state revolution in digital display watches was spearheaded not by established watch companies (Timex, Bulova, Benrus, Gruen, and others), but by semiconductor companies, including Texas Instruments, National Semiconductor, Litronix, Hughes Aircraft, and Fairchild Camera & Instrument.

[11]For a survey of the technological progressivity of regulated enterprises, see William M. Capron, ed., *Technological Change in Regulated Industries* (Washington, D.C.: The Brookings Institution, 1971).

The semiconductor manufacturers, although newcomers to the watch industry, moved aggressively to dominate the digital watch market. Several firms originally sought to enter into joint ventures with the traditional watchmakers, but when the latter appeared disinterested, the strategy was changed to one of head-on competition. Traditional watch business practices (such as financing the watch inventories of retail jewelers and considering a 50% margin of selling price over cost as standard) were ignored. Prices were cut sharply even though demand seemed to be outstripping supply. Developments were so fast-paced that by mid-1975 jewelers were worried about the digital watch killing the watch business of quality jewelry stores—not only because of the sharply lower profit margins but also because the semiconductor companies planned to furnish themselves, rather than through jewelers, what little service or repair is needed on digitals.

Digital watches have no moving parts to wear out and are far more accurate (within a minute per year) than the most expensive mechanical watch. A digital watch operates with just four components: a battery, a quartz crystal, an integrated circuit, and a digital display. The battery causes the quartz crystal to vibrate at 32,768 cycles per second (in most watches). The integrated circuit divides the vibrations into one pulse per second; accumulates the pulses to compute minutes, hours, days, and months; and transmits signals to the display to illuminate the digits showing the time and date.

When the first digital watches appeared in 1972, the products were premature—poorly designed, big and ugly, and with 60% defective returns. The biggest problem was in the digital time displays, which were unreliable and often unreadable. Within 3 years, however, the digital watchmakers had made rapid progress in making the displays dependable and easy to read; styling was much sharper; and components had been made much smaller. Then, in a move reminiscent of their strategy in the calculator business, the semiconductor firms in early 1975 slashed the prices of components in half—to as low as $20 per watch. Lower digital watch prices quickly followed (about half of what prices were in 1974), and the move caught the traditional watch manufacturers off guard. The semiconductor firms were said to be pricing their watches and component modules on the "cost learning curve" whereby prices were lowered as production levels were built up. But production costs were also being lowered by reducing the number of parts and squeezing more of the electronic circuitry onto the main circuit.

Digital sales totaled 650,000 watches in 1974 and were forecast to hit more than 2.5 million in 1975 and as much as 10 million in 1976. The rising volume brought prices down from $125 in 1974 to $50 in 1975 and to $20 in 1976, putting digital watch manufacturers in clear head-on competition with Timex. At least seven companies were thought to have the potential of producing 1 million modules in 1976, with Texas Instruments in the lead because of its extremely simple module design and automatic assembly capability.

As late as 1975 Timex had done little more than dip its toe into the digital market, with mediocre results. Solid-state technology was new to Timex. The company had no in-house capacity to produce such components as integrated circuits and digital displays. In 1973 the man Timex hired in 1969 to develop both digital and analog quartz watches left to become director of watch operations for Rockwell International; his departure reportedly was due to Timex's failure to move rapidly in building up a digital capability. Moreover, the company's 1974 operating results suggested the beginnings of a sharp profit squeeze—partly because of inroads being made by the digital watches. Rising materials costs, increased interest charges, production bottlenecks, and higher overhead expenses produced a 33% decline in after-tax profits, even though sales increased 13%. In trying to improve its 1974 earnings picture, Timex reportedly cut its advertising and promotion budget from 8% of sales to $7\frac{1}{2}$% and trimmed new product development operations—notably by extending watchcase design and restyling cycles. The company also increased most of its watch prices an average of 16%, lifting its lowest-priced mechanical watch to $10.95, and raised fees on its watch guarantees by 50%, to $1.50.

Timex introduced its first digital watch in 1972 on a limited basis. However, national sales efforts for these watches were held back until 1973 because of quality-control problems and the slow shipment of components by suppliers. Even then, Timex's digital watches were not well received in the marketplace, mostly because of price—originally $125, later reduced to $85. One of Timex's distributors was quoted by *Business Week* as saying "The consumer will spend money for an inexpensive watch with the Timex name on it, but when you're talking about $85, that's a different consumer." Interestingly enough, at the 1975 Retail Jewelers of America show in New York, Timex's director of sales reportedly refused to be photographed holding a watch from Timex's newest digital line, which consisted of six models priced at $85; he informed the photographer that the company's big push in 1975 was still in mechanized watches.

On several occasions Timex turned down contractual offers from semiconductor firms to supply Timex with digital-watch components. Hughes Aircraft Company, for example, which produced integrated circuits for Timex analog quartz watches, offered in 1971 to build a digital watch to sell under the Timex label if Timex would guarantee a minimum production run of 1 million units. The Hughes offer was for watches with light-emitting-diode readouts, which have to be turned on by pushing a button. Timex rejected the offer. Timex's 1975 digital watches had liquid-crystal displays that showed the time continuously.

One industry observer summed up Timex's situation as follows: "They can produce cases cheaper than anybody else because of their volume and that's a big factor in the low-cost watch market. But they've go to get into the component business. Somewhere along the line they're either going to have to acquire or work closely with an IC (integrated circuit) house."

In mid-1975 Bulova entered into a joint venture with Integrated Display Systems to acquire digital capacity; IDS was also negotiating with Gillette Co. on a digital watch design. In the last half of 1975 Bulova had losses of $526,000 on sales of $107.6 million; in early 1976 Bulova hired a new president and, soon thereafter launched its Computron digital watch line with nine models priced from $99 to $180.

In January 1976, Texas Instruments introduced a $20 digital watch in cases made from a high-performance plastic called polysulfone. Both TI and Fairchild introduced $30 models in metal cases. National Semiconductor announced price cuts on its lowest-price models so they could retail for $25.

Questions for Discussion

1. Why do you suppose Timex did not aggressively develop its own digital-watch-technology capability at an earlier date?

2. Evaluate the seriousness of the competitive threat from digital watches to Timex. Would you expect Timex to eventually commit itself strongly to digital watches? Why or why not? What factors do you think would affect Timex's decision?

3. It has been observed on several occasions that when a new technology shakes up a competitive marketplace, the companies with the established technology do not lead the way. What factors do you think might account for this? Does this observation indicate that big, established firms are not technologically progressive?

Sources: Based upon information in "The Electronics Threat to Timex," *Business Week*, August 18, 1975, pp. 42ff.; "Digital Watches: Bringing Watchmaking Back to the U.S.," *Business Week*, October 27, 1975, pp. 78ff.; "Timex Corporation" in H. Uyterhoeven, R. W. Ackerman, and J. W. Rosenblum, *Strategy and Organization* (Homewood, Ill.: Richard D. Irwin, Inc., 1973), pp. 309–320; and "The $20 Digital Watch Arrives a Year Early," *Business Week*, January 26, 1976, pp. 27–28.

as to why firms are intent upon advancing their levels of technological capability.[12] Some managers are convinced that because the future will undoubtedly differ markedly from the present, a firm has no realistic alterna-

[12]Bela Gold, "Values and Research," in *Values and the Future*, Kurt Baier and Nicholas Rescher, eds. (New York: The Free Press, 1969), pp. 389–430.

tive to participating actively in the stream of innovation even if one is not sure of where it leads and even if attractive estimates of the rates of return from technologically progressive undertakings cannot be contrived. A similar view holds that "technically sound" innovations can be made to pay off eventually even though investment does not seem warranted at the outset. Another bootstrap view holds that innovation is requisite for maintaining the quality and morale of technical and engineering staffs; the reasoning has even been extended to affect the progressive image of the firm and its capacity to attract high-caliber personnel. The point here is that personalities and organizational considerations prevailing inside the firm combine with economic forces from the outside to force the vast majority of enterprises to participate in or even initiate technological change.

SUMMARY

Production, as commonly used in economics, refers to any activity that creates value. Production includes virtually all phases of economic activity except consumption. Four types of production activities are identifiable: unique-product production, rigid mass production, flexible mass production, and process production. A production function indicates, in quantitative terms, the relationship between the unit input of resources and the unit output of goods or services per period of time.

During the twentieth century, technological advance has wrought basic changes in how goods and services are produced, including (1) increasing the span of time separating the beginning from the completion of the production process, (2) broadening and deepening the use of specialized capital goods, (3) rendering production methods less flexible to making rapid adjustments in technology or in the input mix, (4) altering the personnel skills needed to staff the human element of production activity, and (5) requiring a higher order of administrative organization, managerial technology, and long-range planning mechanisms within the firm.

As a general rule, technological change has favored the emergence and growth of large-scale enterprises. This has been reinforced by the fact that the vast majority of industrial R&D activity is now undertaken by large enterprises—a feature that works to their advantage in being on the leading edge of technological know-how.

Rarely can firms insulate themselves from the necessity to remain technologically up to date. Product innovation and progressive production methods are weapons of rivalry that pervade nearly every industry. In addition, pressures to innovate arise from troublesome production breakdowns and inefficiencies, from the desire to escape rising labor or raw material costs, from social pressures to eliminate environmental pollution, from pressure to eliminate hazard to life or human error—all of which ultimately bear upon the profitability, market position, and chances for the survival of an enterprise.

ARROW, K. J., "The Economic Implications of Learning by Doing," *Review of Economic Studies*, Vol. 29 (June 1962), pp. 155–73.

AVERITT, R. T., *The Dual Economy* (New York: W. W. Norton & Company, Inc., 1968), Chapter 3.

BLAKE, S. P., *Managing for Responsive Research and Development* (San Francisco: W. H. Freeman and Company, 1978).

DOUTT, J. T., "Production Innovation in Small Business," *Business Topics*, Vol. 8, No. 3 (Summer 1960), pp. 58–62.

GALBRAITH, J. K., *American Capitalism* (Boston: Houghton Mifflin Company, 1952), Chapter 7.

HALL, W. K., "Strategic Planning, Product Innovation, and the Theory of the Firm," *Journal of Business Policy*, Vol. 3, No. 3 (Spring 1973), pp. 19–27.

HAMBURG, D., *R&D: Essays on the Economics of Research and Development* (New York: Random House, Inc., 1966).

JOHNSTON, R. E., "Technical Progress and Innovation," *Oxford Economic Papers*, (July 1966), pp. 158–176.

KAMIEN, M. I. AND NANCY L. SCHWARTZ, "Market Structure and Innovation: A Survey," *Journal of Economic Literature*, Vol. 13, No. 1 (March 1975), pp. 1–37.

MANSFIELD, E., *The Economics of Technological Change* (New York: W. W. Norton & Company, Inc., 1968), Chapters 2–4.

MANSFIELD, E., *et al.*, *The Production and Application of New Industrial Technology* (New York: W. W. Norton & Company, Inc., 1977), Chapters 1 and 10.

MASON, R. S., "Product Diversification and the Small Firm," *Journal of Business Policy*, Vol. 3, No. 3 (Spring 1973), pp. 28–39.

NELSON, R., M. PECK, AND E. KALOCHEK, *Technology, Economic Growth and Public Policy* (Washington, D.C.: The Brookings Institution, 1967), Chapters 1–5.

NORRIS, K., AND J. YAIZEY, *The Economics of Research and Technology* (London: George Allen & Unwin Ltd., 1973).

ROSENBERG, N., *Technology and American Economic Growth* (New York: Harper & Row, Publishers, 1972).

STEELE, L. W., *Innovation in Big Business* (New York: American Elsevier, 1975).

QUESTIONS FOR DISCUSSION

1. What is a production function? What are its key economic properties?

2. What are several effects that technological change can have upon a firm's production function?

3. Does the pace of technological change seem to be accelerating? Can you cite examples in support of your position?

4. How have technological advances changed the basic nature or production activity during the course of the twentieth century?

5. Why is it important for business firms to keep their production techniques close to the frontier of technological know-how?

6. Do you think that business enterprises on the whole are technologically progressive? Give examples to support your position.

SEVEN PRODUCTION ANALYSIS AND OPTIMAL INPUT COMBINATIONS

Having indicated the influence of technology on production processes, we are now in position to examine the economic principles underlying input-output relationships. Attention will be focused upon the conditions for achieving peak production efficiency and for optimizing the mix of resource inputs in both the short run and the long run. Analyzing the principles of production is of fundamental import because it provides the foundation for estimating production costs and for selecting the most economical production techniques.

FIXED AND VARIABLE INPUTS

To facilitate the exposition of production analysis it is customary to divide inputs into two somewhat artificial categories—fixed inputs and variable inputs. A *fixed input* is defined as one whose quantity cannot *readily* be changed in the short run in response to a desire to alter a firm's rate of output. Admittedly, inputs are seldom fixed in an absolute sense, even for very short periods of time. Practically, though, the costs of varying the use of an input may be prohibitive. Even where they are not, changing the quantity of an input may be severely impeded by the unavailability of additional supplies and/or by the length of time it takes to effect acceptable changes in their usage.[1] Examples of fixed inputs include major pieces of equipment and machinery, the space available for productive activity (buildings, factory size), and key managerial personnel.

In contrast, a *variable input* is one whose usage rate may be altered quite easily in response to a desire to raise or lower the volume of output. Resource inputs whose quantity can be easily varied within a very short time include electric power, most raw materials, transportation services, and the labor services of production and office employees. With respect to raw materials, however, there are a number of products (aspirin, cake mixes, paint, liquid bleach) where the inputs can be changed only in some fixed proportion to one another and to output; otherwise, the product's character is fundamentally changed.

THE SHORT RUN AND THE LONG RUN

Along with the concepts of fixed and variable inputs, economists distinguish between the short run and the long run. The *short run* is a time period so short that the firm is constrained from varying the quantity of its fixed inputs (major pieces of equipment, key managerial personnel, and space for production activities). Yet, the short run is long enough a time period to allow for variation in the firm's variable inputs. Hence, in the short run a firm's output capability must be effected exclusively through changes in its usage of variable inputs.

The *long run* is defined as a period of time sufficiently long to allow *all* inputs to be varied; no inputs are fixed, including technology. Thus, in the long run a firm's output capability can be increased or decreased by altering technology or resource input usage in whatever way may be most advantageous to the firm. For instance, whereas in the short run a firm may be forced to expand production by operating its facilities at overtime rates, in the long run the firm may find it more economical to construct larger facilities or install capital-intensive machinery and avoid overtime wage rates.

The length of the short run varies from industry to industry. In industries where the quantities of fixed inputs are small or where the character of production permits fixed inputs to be changed readily, the short run may not extend beyond a period of several months. The apparel, mobile home, and food-processing industries are cases in point. For other industries the

---

[1]Actually, the fixed inputs are not always as fixed as it might first appear. While a firm may possess a given amount of fixed input, say 10 machines, the operating pattern for the fixed inputs involves a choice among several dimensions of operation. The effective amount of available fixed input can be "changed" by altering (1) the speed at which the machines are operated, (2) the number of hours per day the machines are used, and (3) the number of days of operation per year. However, firms rarely have full flexibility in choosing among these dimensions due to the constraints imposed by maintenance requirements, union work rules, and wage differentials among work shifts.

short run may be 1 to 3 years—automobiles, coal mining, aircraft, aluminum, and paper products. In the electric utility industry it takes as much as 6 to 10 years to design, construct, and start up a new generating plant.

The production significance of differentiating between fixed and variable inputs and between the short and long runs should now be more apparent. The quantities of a firm's fixed inputs determine the size of the firm's plant or its *scale of operations*. The scale of a firm's plant sets an upper limit to the amount of output per period of time that the firm is capable of producing in the short run. Output can, in the short run, be varied up to that limit by increasing or decreasing the usage of variable inputs in conjunction with the amount of fixed input. The limits of output can, in the long run, be raised or lowered by changing the scale of production, the technological character of the production process, and the utilization rate of any and all inputs.

SHORT-RUN PRODUCTION FUNCTIONS

The short-run production function for a firm indicates the output obtainable from combining various amounts of variable inputs with a given amount of fixed input. As stated earlier, the production function may be expressed symbolically as

$$Q = f(X_a, X_b, X_c, \ldots, X_n),$$

where Q refers to the quantity of output per unit of time and is a function of specific quantities of inputs $X_a, X_b, X_c, \ldots, X_n$. In the short run, since the quantity of output (Q) is the result of combining variable input factors (labor and raw materials) with the fixed inputs (size of plant, major pieces of equipment, managerial capacity), the functional relationship should be written as

$$Q = f(X_a, X_b \,|\, X_c, \ldots, X_n).$$

The vertical bar indicates that the input factors to the right are regarded as fixed in the production process, whereas the inputs to the left (labor and raw materials) are variable.

The fundamental problem in the study of short-run production functions is to estimate the quantity of output that can be produced by combining alternative amounts of variable inputs with the available amount of fixed inputs. As an example, consider a firm operating a plant of some given size and having a fixed amount of equipment and managerial capability. Since we shall have occasion to refer to the amount of these fixed inputs, suppose that we arbitrarily designate the amounts of fixed inputs for our fictional firm's plant as constituting 2 "units." Now suppose that we conduct an experiment in which successively larger doses of variable input are combined with the 2 units of fixed input and the resulting output rates are observed and recorded.[2]

A Tabular Illustration

From Table 7-1 we see that when progressively larger doses of variable input are combined with the available fixed inputs, the quantity of output rises more rapidly at first, then more slowly, reaches a maximum, and begins to decline. The exact change in output associated with the use of one more unit of variable input per period is known in economics as the *marginal product of the variable input.*[3] The change in the quantity of output per period

Table 7-1   Data for a Hypothetical Short-Run Production Function

(1) Units of Fixed Input	(2) Units of Variable Input (X)	(3) Quantity of Output $Q = 21X + 9X^2 - X^3$	(4) Discrete Marginal Product of Variable Input	(5) Continuous Marginal Product of Variable Input $MP = 21 + 18X - 3X^2$	(6) Average Product of Variable Input $AP_{vi} = 21 + 9X - X^2$	(7) Average Product of Fixed Input $AP_{fi} = \dfrac{21X + 9X^2 - X^3}{2}$
2	0	0		—	—	0
			29			
2	1	29		36	29	14.5
			41			
2	2	70		45	35	35
			47			
2	3	117		48	39	58.5
			47			
2	4	164		45	41	82
			41			
2	5	205		36	41	102.5
			29			
2	6	234		21	39	117
			11			
2	7	245		0	35	122.5
			−13			
2	8	232		−27	29	116
			−43			
2	9	189		−60	21	94.5

[2]Strictly speaking, the different amounts of variable input are best conceived as being applied to different plants of equal size and type, rather than to a progressively larger application of additional units of variable input to a single plant. Practically, however, real world implementation of this concept of measuring a firm's production function is usually not possible—many identical plants may simply not exist. The sensible alternative, therefore, is to observe the relation between input and output for a single plant operation at various points in time where the rates of variable input usage are different.

[3]It cannot be inferred from the definition of marginal product that the change in output is due just to the efforts and contribution of variable input. An increase in variable input by itself is not *the cause* of changes in output; output changes as a consequence of having more units of variable input employed in conjunction with the fixed input. An example may serve to clarify this point. Suppose a firm has five pieces of machinery, each requiring one skilled operator. As the firm increases its labor inputs from one to five skilled operators to run the five machines, it is clear that the resulting output gains are not due solely to the productive powers of labor but rather are the joint products of using more labor with the five available machines. Economists, however, customarily refer to the gains in output from using more labor as being the marginal product of labor, despite the fact that gains in output from employing more units of labor reflect the *joint* contributions of labor and the other inputs with which it is combined.

of time resulting from a 1-*unit change* in the quantity of that input used per period of time is defined as *discrete marginal product*. In our example the values for discrete marginal product are shown in column (4) of Table 7-1; the reader should verify their derivation. Alternatively, marginal product can be calculated from the first derivative of the equation expressing the mathematical relation between the flow of output and the flow of variable input.[4] Hence, if the relationship between the quantity of output (Q) and the units of variable input (X) is

$$Q = 21X + 9X^2 - X^3,$$

then the marginal product of the variable input is

$$MP = \frac{dQ}{dX} = 21 + 18X - 3X^2.$$

This concept of marginal product is called *continuous marginal product* to distinguish it from discrete marginal product. Continuous marginal product represents the rate of change in total output as the rate of variable input changes per period of time and can be calculated in the manner shown in column (5) of Table 7-1.[5] In a mathematical sense, marginal product is meaningful only for inputs whose rate of usage can be changed; thus, there is no such thing as the marginal product of fixed inputs, since fixed inputs by definition do not change in the short run.

The average product of the variable input is shown in column (6) of Table 7-1. It is found by dividing the output rate by the required number of units of variable input:

$$AP_{vi} = \frac{\text{units of output}}{\text{units of variable input}}.$$

Thus, if $Q = 21X + 9X^2 - X^3$, where X represents the units of variable input, the expression for AP_{vi} becomes

$$AP_{vi} = \frac{Q}{X} = \frac{21X + 9X^2 - X^3}{X} = 21 + 9X - X^2.$$

Likewise, the average product of the fixed input (shown in column 7 of Table 7-1) is defined as the quantity of output divided by the available units of fixed input:

$$AP_{fi} = \frac{\text{units of output}}{\text{units of fixed input}}.$$

---

[4]Should more than one variable input be present in the expression defining the short-run production function, the relevant concept of the marginal product of an input is the partial derivative of the production function. See Mathematical Capsule 7.

[5]The definitions and concepts of discrete and continuous marginal product are analogous to our earlier definitions of marginal utility and marginal revenue. In treating marginal product as a continuous function, we assume that both variable input and output can be varied by extremely small amounts.

DETERMINING MARGINAL PRODUCT
WHEN THE PRODUCTION FUNCTION IS COMPOSED
OF SEVERAL VARIABLE INPUTS

In most production processes the quantity of output in the short run is a function of several variable inputs 'such that

$$Q = f(X_a, X_b, X_c, \ldots, X_n).$$

The marginal product of a specific variable input, say X_a, is found by observing the impact upon Q of a change in the usage of X_a, when the quantities of the remaining variable inputs $(X_b, X_c, \ldots, X_n)$ are held constant. Mathematically, this procedure involves determining the *partial derivative* of the production function with respect to X_a.

Suppose that the production function for a commodity is

$$Q = 7X_a^2 + 8X_b^2 - 5X_a X_b.$$

We can find the effect of a change in the rate of usage of resource input X_a when the usage of X_b is held constant by treating X_b as a constant and differentiating the production function with respect to X_a—this gives the partial derivative of Q with respect to X_a and is symbolized as $\partial Q / \partial X_a$. Thus, we obtain

$$\frac{\partial Q}{\partial X_a} = 14X_a - 5X_b,$$

which is the expression for the marginal product of input X_a. In economic terms it may be interpreted precisely to mean the rate of change in output as the usage of input X_a changes, the usage of input X_b remaining constant. In less formal terms, the expression for the marginal product of X_a tells us how changes in the use of X_a will affect the quantity of output provided X_b does not change.

Similarly, the marginal product for input X_b is the partial derivative of the production function with respect to X_b, or

$$\frac{\partial Q}{\partial X_b} = 16X_b - 5X_a.$$

It shows the impact of changes in X_b upon Q when X_a is held constant.

Exercises

1. Determine the marginal product functions for labor (L) and capital (C) for each of the following production functions.

(a) $Q = 18L^2 + 14C^3 - L^2C$.
(b) $Q = 10L^{0.5}C^{0.5}$.
(c) $Q = 17L + 9C + 0.6L^{0.4}C^{0.5}$.
2. Determine the values for MP_L and MP_C at $L = 10$ and $C = 20$ for each of the following production functions.
(a) $Q = 36L - L^2 + 20C - LC$.
(b) $Q = 5L^2 + 4LC + 6C^2 - 8(L/C)$.

Given that $Q = 21X + 9X^2 - X^3$ and that 2 units of fixed input are present, AP_{fi} can be calculated as follows:

$$AP_{fi} = \frac{Q}{FI} = \frac{21X + 9X^2 - X^3}{2}.$$

Alternatively, AP_{fi} can be computed by dividing the output values in column (3) by the number of units of fixed input given in column (1), yielding the values in column (7) of Table 7-1.

In our example, observe that marginal product increases for the first 3 units of variable input to its maximum value of 48 [column (5)]. Beyond 3 units of variable input marginal product diminishes, reaching zero at an input of 7 units per period of time and becoming increasingly negative past 8 units of variable input. The reasons for this pattern of change in marginal product derives from the *principle of diminishing marginal returns*.

The principle of diminishing marginal returns has to do with the direction and the rate of change in output when increasingly larger amounts of a variable input per period of time are combined with a constant amount of fixed input. Specifically, the principle states that *as the amount of a variable input is increased by equal increments and combined with a specified amount of fixed inputs, a point will be reached (sometimes more quickly and sometimes less quickly) where the resulting increases in the quantity of output will get smaller and smaller*. In other words, as more and more variable input is added to a given fixed input, eventually the marginal product of variable input will begin to diminish. Furthermore, should the amounts of variable input applied to a given fixed input get large enough, output will reach a maximum and thereafter may *decrease* if still additional amounts of variable input are utilized.

Prior to reaching the inevitable point of diminishing marginal returns, the gains in output from larger applications of variable input may either increase at an increasing rate such that marginal product of variable input increases, or the increases in output may increase at a constant rate such that marginal product is constant. For example, in Table 7-1 the first 3 units of variable input cause the quantity of output to increase at an increasing rate. This may occur because when a small amount of variable input is combined with a relatively large dose of fixed input the fixed-variable input proportions are likely to be out of balance, causing production to be inefficient.[6] Hence, whenever variable input is being used in too sparse a proportion to the available fixed input, adding more units of variable input diminishes the associated inefficiencies and causes output to increase at an increasing rate.

A Graphic Illustration

The hypothetical data in Table 7-1 are graphed in Fig. 7-1. Since output is a function of variable input, output is the dependent variable and variable input is the independent variable. Accordingly, output per period of time is plotted on the vertical axis, and the units of variable input are plotted on the horizontal axis. Joining the points by a smooth curve yields a graphical illustration of the firm's production function for the good [Fig. 7-1(a)].

The production function of Fig. 7-1(a) conveys the same input-output relation as does the production schedule in Table 7-1.[7] Note that the production function increases at an increasing rate up to a level of usage of variable input of 3 units per period of time; accordingly, we may say that *increasing returns to the variable input* exist over this range. By this is meant that the increases in output are *more* than proportional to the increases in variable input. As the possibilities for increasing returns to variable input are exhausted, the point of diminishing marginal returns (DMR) is encountered—a point which, mathematically, corresponds to the "inflection point" on the production function. Beyond this point, heavier usage of variable inputs results in a declining marginal product (i.e., extra units of variable input yield successively smaller amounts of extra output). The curvature of the production function becomes such that it rises more slowly (i.e., output increases at a decreasing rate). Thus, between a level of usage of 3 and 7 units of variable input per period of time there exist *decreasing returns to variable input*, or,

---

[6]Examples of this condition are commonplace in manufacturing. Suppose that a plant of a given size has been designed to operate with 400 employees. If an attempt is made to operate with 50 employees, the multiplicity of functions to be performed by each employee with the attendant inefficiencies in execution, coupled with the time lost in changing from job to job, will no doubt cause output to be more than proportionately *less* than might be gotten, say, from 100 employees. Thus, up to some point, equal increments in the amount of labor used may well produce successively larger gains in the quantity of output.

[7]In this example the production function is shown as beginning from the origin of the diagram. This is the case only when the variable input under consideration is absolutely essential to the production of the item and when output may be obtained immediately upon applying variable input. Needless to say, these characteristics do not typify all production processes or all kinds of variable inputs. For variable inputs not essential to the production of the commodity, the production function may begin above the origin (installing carpets in an office building to reduce noise and to enhance the esthetic quality of the working conditions, thereby boosting employee productivity is a case in point). In other situations no output may be forthcoming until substantial amounts of variable input are used with the available fixed inputs. For example, five people in a huge pulp and paper mill can produce nothing. Ten people can do little better. Where a minimum complement of variable input is requisite for any production to take place, the production function or total product curve begins to the right of the origin and at that point on the horizontal axis corresponding to the minimum input requirement.

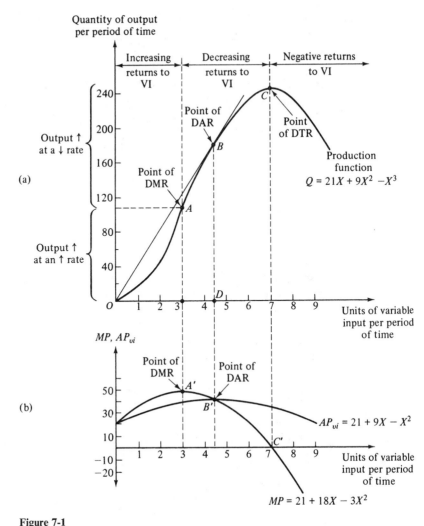

Figure 7-1
Short-run production function and its corresponding marginal and average product functions

to put it another way, the increases in the quantity of output are *less* than proportional to the increases in variable input. Output is maximum when 7 units of variable input per period of time are combined with the fixed input. No further increases in output are possible without employing additional amounts of the fixed inputs in the production process. This is not feasible in the short run. For reference purposes we may label the maximum output rate in the short run as the point of *diminishing total returns* (DTR). Should more than 7 units of variable input per period of time be used in conjunction with the fixed inputs, the quantity of output would actually fall. The rationale for this derives from the existence of a limit to which fixed inputs can accommodate additional variable input and still yield additional output. Past 7 units, variable inputs are present in uneconomically large proportions relative to the available fixed input, and growing inefficiencies in resource usage cause total output to fall.

The marginal product curve corresponding to the production function described above is shown in Fig. 7-1(b). The data for ascertaining the shape and position of the marginal product curve can be obtained from columns (4) and (5) in Table 7-1. Since by the marginal product of the variable input we mean the rate of change in the quantity of output as the usage rate of variable input changes, the slope of the production function at any variable input rate is the value of marginal product at that quantity of variable input. When the quantity of output is increasing at an increasing rate (as it does up to a level of 3 units of variable input), marginal product is increasing. Marginal product attains its maximum value at the point of diminishing marginal returns, which in this example is at 3 units of variable input where $MP = 48$ [point A in Fig. 7-1(a)]. Between 3 and 7 units of variable input, where the quantity of output increases at a decreasing rate, the values of marginal product are positive but diminishing. At 7 units of variable input, total output is maximum, and marginal product is zero. Beyond 7 units, additional units of variable input cause output to decline, meaning that in this range the marginal product of variable input is negative. The negative values for marginal product in the range beyond 7 units reflect the fact that the production function is declining and therefore has a negative slope.

The average product curve for the variable input originates from the same point as does the marginal product curve (in this instance, both assume a value of 21 when $X = 0$). From this point the average product curve rises until it reaches its maximum value at 4.5 units of variable input. It subsequently declines, conceivably becoming zero should variable input ever be added to such an extent that output falls back to zero. The average product curve has a definite relationship to the marginal product curve. As long as the value for MP is greater than the value for AP_{vi}, the average product curve will rise. The value for MP equals the value of AP_{vi} when AP_{vi} is at its maximum value. When the value for MP is less than the value for AP_{vi}, the average product curve falls. The explanation for this relationship is rooted in simple arithmetic; an example may suffice to illustrate it.

Consider a student who after 2 years of college has managed to earn a 2.5 overall grade average in her coursework. If *this term* she earns a 2.8 average in her courses, her new *overall* grade average will rise above the 2.5 level. However, if she earns a 2.0 average *this term*, her overall grade average will *fall* below 2.5. The overall grade average of our hypothetical student is analogous to average product, while the grade average this term is analogous to marginal product. Thus, for average product to be increasing, marginal product must exceed the average. And for average product to be decreasing, marginal product must be less than average product.

The rate of variable input usage at which the AP_{vi} curve reaches its maximum value can be ascertained directly from the graph of the production function. Suppose that a ray is drawn from the origin to point B on the

production function in Fig. 7-1(a). Since average product equals the quantity
of output divided by the units of variable input employed, AP_{vi} at point B
equals distance BD (the quantity of output) divided by distance OD (the
number of units of variable input), or, more simply, BD/OD, which in turn
is equivalent to the slope of the ray OB. As the number of units of variable
input increases from 0 to 4.5 units (point D), the slopes of rays drawn from
the origin to points on the production function become progressively greater.
Since AP_{vi} is mathematically equivalent to the slope of a ray from the origin
to the corresponding point on the production function, AP_{vi} is maximum
at that value of variable input where the slope of such a ray is steepest. This
occurs when the ray from the origin is just *tangent* to the production function
(point B) or at 4.5 units of variable input. We shall designate the peak of
the AP_{vi} curve as the point of diminishing *average* returns to variable input
(DAR).

MATHEMATICAL CAPSULE 8

THE RELATIONSHIP BETWEEN AN INPUT'S MARGINAL AND AVERAGE PRODUCTS

That an input's marginal and average products are necessarily
equal at the maximum value of average product is easily proven mathematically. Let the production function be of the general form $Q = f(X)$.
Then,

$$AP_{vi} = \frac{Q}{X} = \frac{f(X)}{X},$$

$$MP = \frac{dQ}{dX} = f'(X).$$

From Mathematical Capsule 1 in Chapter 3 we know that the condition
which must be satisfied for AP_{vi} to be maximum is that the slope of
AP_{vi} be zero. This in turn means that the derivative of the AP_{vi} equation
must be zero:

$$\frac{dAP_{vi}}{dX} = 0.$$

Using the rule of calculus for finding the derivative of a quotient, and
calculating dAP_{vi}/dX, where $AP_{vi} = f(X)/X$, gives

$$\frac{dAP_{vi}}{dX} = \frac{X \cdot f'(X) - f(X)}{X^2}.$$

For dAP_{vi}/dX to equal zero requires that the numerator of the expression above be equal to zero, or that

$$X \cdot f'(X) - f(X) = 0.$$

Rewriting the condition above yields

$$f'(X) = \frac{f(X)}{X}.$$

Since $f'(X) = MP$ and $f(X)/X = AP_{vi}$, the input rate that makes AP_{vi} maximum is also the value of X at which $MP = AP_{vi}$.

Furthermore, if the expression for dAP_{vi}/dX is rewritten as

$$\frac{dAP_{vi}}{dX} = \frac{f'(X) - [f(X)/X]}{X},$$

it becomes apparent that the slope of the average product function will be positive if $f'(X)$, marginal product, is greater than $f(X)/X$, average product. This reflects the fact that as long as the value for marginal product exceeds the value for average product, the average product curve is rising. Conversely, it is clear that if marginal product is less than average product, the slope of the average product curve is negative and the value of average product is declining.

Some Alternative Types of Short-Run Production Functions

A firm's production function need not exhibit the shape illustrated in Fig. 7-1. Input-output relationships are such that other shapes are quite common. We shall look at three alternative shapes of production functions and their distinctive properties.

Constant Returns to Variable Input. As we shall verify later in this chapter, some production processes have qualities such that the firm's short-run production function is linear over the *normal* ranges of output. A linear production function, along with its corresponding marginal and average product curves, is shown in Fig. 7-2. The general equation for a linear input-output relation is

$$Q = a + bX,$$

where Q is the quantity of output, X represents the units of variable input per period of time, and a and b are constants. For the production function shown in Fig. 7-2(a) it is assumed that variable input is essential for production to occur and that some output can be obtained as soon as variable input

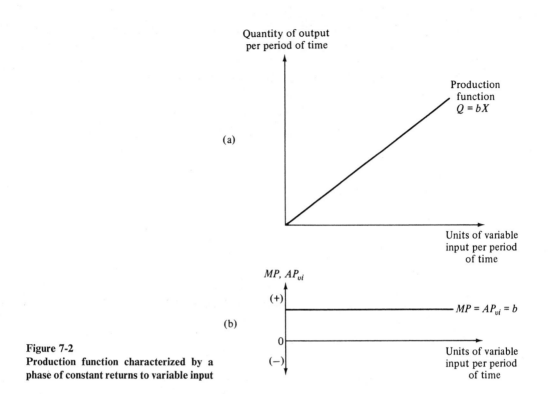

Quantity of output
per period of time

(a)

Production
function
$Q = bX$

Units of variable
input per period
of time

MP, AP_{vi}

(+)

(b)

$MP = AP_{vi} = b$

0

(−)

Units of variable
input per period
of time

Figure 7-2
Production function characterized by a
phase of constant returns to variable input

is combined with the available units of fixed input. The effect of this rather reasonable assumption (and we shall continue to use it in the succeeding illustrations) is that the production function begins at the origin and the value of a in the equation for the production function is zero, thereby reducing the equation of the production function to

$$Q = bX.$$

From the preceding definitions of average and marginal product, we can write

$$AP_{vi} = \frac{Q}{X} = \frac{bX}{X} = b$$

and

$$MP = \frac{dQ}{dX} = b.$$

Thus, in the case of a linear production function both marginal and average product are constants and $MP = AP_{vi}$. These relationships are illustrated in Fig. 7-2(b).

The key properties of the production function in Fig. 7-2(a) and its corresponding MP and AP_{vi} curves are as follows. A linear production function means that as additional units of variable input are combined with the

given units of fixed input, the quantity of output increases at a *constant
rate*—there exist *constant returns to variable input*. Each unit of variable
input contributes just as much to total output as did the previous unit and
as will the next unit. Since successive units of variable input are *equally* productive, their marginal products are necessarily equal. This factor makes
the production function linear, because marginal product is the rate of change
in the quantity of output as variable input changes. When this rate is constant,
the production function is linear. Moreover, with additional units of variable
input being equally productive, the average product of the units of variable
input is itself a constant value equal in size to the value of the marginal
product of the variable input.

It does not follow, however, that a linear production function contradicts the principle of diminishing marginal returns. Rather, linearity implies
that the point of diminishing marginal returns is yet to be reached. There
can be *no doubt* that if *enough* units of variable input are combined with the
given amount of fixed input, diminishing returns will set in. But in production
processes where a standard worker-machine ratio is employed, this point
might not be encountered until the limit of the plant's capacity is approached,
say around 90 to 95% of practical capacity. Thus, up to this limit, experiencing constant returns to the variable input is neither inconceivable nor unrealistic.

Decreasing Returns to Variable Input. Another type of production
function displays *decreasing returns to variable input* as soon as the *first* dose
of variable input is combined with the fixed input. Although several equations
can be used to describe this behavior, the simplest is the quadratic equation:

$$Q = a + bX - cX^2,$$

or, more simply,

$$Q = bX - cX^2$$

if the variable input is essential for production. Here b is a positive constant
and c, as indicated, is negative. The corresponding average and marginal
product functions are

$$AP_{vi} = \frac{Q}{X} = \frac{bX - cX^2}{X} = b - cX,$$

$$MP = \frac{dQ}{dX} = b - 2cX.$$

These three curves are illustrated in Fig. 7-3. Observe that the *MP* curve lies
below the AP_{vi} curve; in fact, it declines at twice the rate of AP_{vi}, as can be
verified from the equations of the two functions (the slope of AP_{vi} is $-c$,
and the slope of *MP* is $-2c$).

Here the nature of the production process is such that each additional
unit of variable input adds *less* to total output than the preceding unit. There-

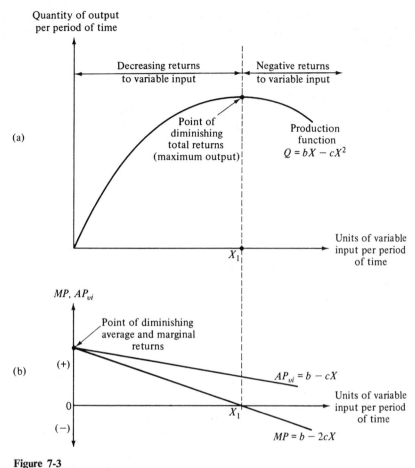

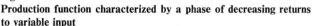

Figure 7-3
Production function characterized by a phase of decreasing returns to variable input

fore, the quantity of output increases at a decreasing rate up to the maximum output. Diminishing marginal returns to variable input are encountered with the first increment of variable input. Increases in the intensity of use of the fixed input brought about by larger doses of variable input yield progressively less and less in additional output. The marginal product of variable input then is a declining, but positive, value up to X_1 units of variable input, at which point the peak of the production function is reached. Since additional usage of variable input lowers marginal product, the average product of variable input is always falling, being pulled downward by the declining values of MP.

When X_1 units of variable input have been combined with the fixed input, the units of fixed input are being utilized to their fullest extent so that no greater output can be gotten until the fixed inputs are increased. Larger applications of variable input beyond the level of X_1 will cause the quantity of output to fall and the marginal product of variable input to become negative, since the fixed input is being *overutilized* to such an extent that all inputs become less efficient and less productive.

Increasing Returns to Variable Input. The last and least likely type of production function has the quantity of output increasing at an increasing rate as large amounts of variable input are used with the fixed input. The simplest form of this function is given by the equation

$$Q = a + bX + cX^2.$$

Again, if $a = 0$ and if b and c are positive constants as indicated, the equation for this production function reduces to

$$Q = bX + cX^2.$$

The general equations for the corresponding average and marginal product curve can be derived as follows:

$$AP_{vi} = \frac{Q}{X} = \frac{bX + cX^2}{X} = b + cX$$

and

$$MP = \frac{dQ}{dX} = b + 2cX.$$

The graph of these three functions is shown in Fig. 7-4.

For production functions of this type, output increases at an increasing rate. Adding extra units of variable input results in larger and larger gains in output as reflected by the rising marginal product of variable input. *Increasing returns to variable input* are said to prevail, because the gains in the quantity of output are *more* than proportional to the increased usage of variable input. The average product of variable input rises persistently, being pulled up by the increases in marginal product.

It is important to note that a production function of this form is likely to describe the behavior of output *only* for relatively small values of variable input, where the fixed input is being utilized far less than it could be. In other words, increasing returns to variable input are likely to prevail only for low rates of output—and then only in those instances where combining more variable input with the fixed input causes a dramatic increase in the productivity of the inputs such that output can be increased at an increasing rate. Situations of this nature can be anticipated only when the fixed inputs are being so grossly underutilized that additional variable input will permit great reductions in inefficiencies, thereby making for disproportionately greater gains in output.

A More General Type of Production Function. When one considers the *entire* range of output of which a firm is capable, the most probable type

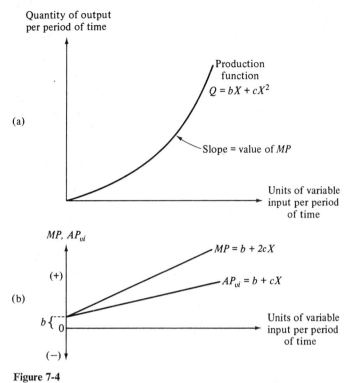

Quantity of output
per period of time

(a)

Production
function
$Q = bX + cX^2$

Slope = value of *MP*

Units of variable
input per period
of time

MP, AP_{vi}

(b)

(+)

$MP = b + 2cX$

$AP_{vi} = b + cX$

$b \Big\{$ 0

Units of variable
input per period
of time

(−)

Figure 7-4
Production function characterized by a phase of increasing returns
to variable input

of input-output relation is that where first is encountered a (short) range of increasing returns to variable input, then a (perhaps long) range of *approximately* constant returns to variable input, and finally a range of decreasing returns to variable input as production capacity is approached. A simple form of a production function which captures these basic elements is like that described earlier and shown in Fig. 7-1. The general equation for a production function of this shape and character is

$$Q = a + bX + cX^2 - dX^3;$$

or, given our assumption that $a = 0$, we have

$$Q = bX + cX^2 - dX^3,$$

where b and c are positive constants and d is a negative constant. The general equations for the corresponding average and marginal product curves are

$$AP_{vi} = \frac{Q}{X} = \frac{bX + cX^2 - dX^3}{X} = b + cX - dX^2$$

and

$$MP = \frac{dQ}{dX} = b + 2cX - 3dX^2.$$

The general applicability of this type of production function is wide. No doubt many production processes contain a stage of increasing returns to variable input at very low output rates, and almost every production process is certain to reflect decreasing returns to variable input as the upper limit to production capacity is approached. Moreover, for many production processes constant returns (or nearly so) to variable input can characterize the range in between. This can be seen from Fig. 7-1(a), where the production function assumes an *almost* linear shape along the range from point *A* to just beyond point *B*.

Because the cubic type of production function does incorporate the key characteristics of other production functions, we shall in future discussions use it to describe input-output relations over the entire range of a firm's output capacity. However, when there is some special reason to expect increasing, decreasing, or constant returns to the variable input to dominate the input-output relationship over the relevant range of output, we shall depart from use of the cubic form of production function and employ instead the indicated form.

THE STAGES OF PRODUCTION

Production functions of the form

$$Q = a + bX + cX^2 - dX^3$$

and the associated average and marginal product curves can be divided into three stages, as illustrated in Fig. 7-5. Stage I extends from zero usage of the variable input to the point where the *average* product of variable input is maximum. Stage II extends from maximum AP_{vi} to where the quantity of output is maximum and *MP* is zero. Stage III coincides with the range of variable input where the total output is falling and marginal product is negative. These stages are of special significance for analyzing the efficiency with which resource inputs are used.

Stage I. Included as stage I is the entire range over which AP_{vi} is increasing. Note that in stage I the point of diminishing marginal returns is reached (point *A*) and passed. Up to the point of DMR, output is increasing at an increasing rate; past this point it increases at a decreasing rate. The marginal product of variable input rises to its peak and begins to fall, yet it remains a greater value than average product throughout the stage. Stage I ends when the point of diminishing *average* returns is reached (point *B*).

What about the efficiency with which the fixed and variable input are

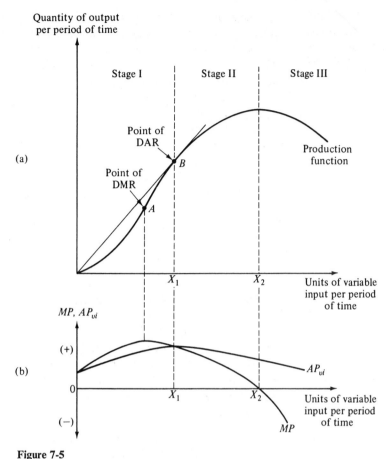

Figure 7-5
The stages of production

being used in stage I? The *efficiency* of an input is best measured by its *average* product, because it indicates the amount of output obtained *per unit* of input. An input's marginal product is a measure of the efficiency of one additional unit of variable input, but it does not reflect the efficiency of *all* the units of variable input taken as a group. Since the average product of variable input is rising throughout stage I, it is evident that variable input is being employed with *increasing* overall efficiency as the end of stage I is approached. Indeed, maximum efficiency of the variable input is attained at the border between stages I and II, where AP_{vi} is maximum. So much for variable input; now what about the efficiency of the fixed inputs in stage I? Although we have no curve representing the average product of fixed input (AP_{fi}), we still know that the quantity of output rises throughout stage I and that the level of fixed input remains unchanged. Thus, because AP_{fi} = units of output/units of fixed input, it follows that the average product of fixed input must also be rising throughout stage I.

Therefore, in stage I increasing the quantity of variable input applied to a given quantity of fixed inputs has the effect of raising the efficiency with which *both* fixed and variable inputs are being utilized. Just *why* the efficiency of both fixed and variable inputs rises in stage I stems from a relative imbalance between the fixed and variable inputs. Throughout stage I the amount of fixed input is excessive compared to the amount of variable input employed. The unduly large proportions of fixed input to variable input in stage I cause the fixed inputs to be *underutilized* and the variable inputs to be *overutilized*. Hence, as more variable input is used, the imbalance is relieved, and the efficiencies of both inputs rise.

The rising efficiencies of fixed and variable inputs have important implications for the costs of production in stage I. As will be demonstrated in the next chapter, when both the average products of fixed and variable inputs are increasing, the *unit* costs of producing more output are declining. Thus, *from the standpoint of efficiency and unit costs, a firm would always prefer to move through stage I to at least the border of stage II before ceasing to use more variable input.*

Stage II. In stage II the quantity of output rises at a decreasing rate; accordingly, the marginal product of variable input is declining, although it remains greater than zero. More significantly, the average product of variable input is falling throughout stage II. The average product of fixed input, however, continues to rise in stage II, because the quantity of output continues to rise even though the amount of fixed input is held constant. In stage II, then, additional units of variable input add to the efficiency of fixed input but diminish the efficiency of variable input.

Stage III. At the boundary between stages II and III, short-run output is maximum, and the fixed input is being utilized to its fullest extent—the efficiency of the fixed input has reached its peak level. With further doses of variable input, the amount of variable input relative to fixed input becomes so large that total output falls. There simply is too little fixed input relative to the amounts of variable input being used. Thus, the use of larger quantities of variable input per period of time reduces AP_{vi} still more, and MP becomes increasingly negative. And with total output falling, AP_{fi} is also decreasing. In sum, the efficiency of variable input and the efficiency of fixed input both diminish as stage III is entered.

The Optimum Stage. The foregoing description of the three stages should make it apparent that operating in stage II is best from the standpoint of efficiency and unit costs. In stage I, variable input is used too sparingly with the available fixed input; increases in variable input will so increase the efficiency of all inputs that the *unit costs* of producing more output will decline. Thus, efficiency and cost considerations will induce the firm to employ at least an amount of variable input sufficient to reach stage II.

Stage III is obviously irrational. It makes no sense whatsoever for a firm to incur the added expense of purchasing and using more units of variable input per period of time when the payoff is a decline in total output and a

reduction in overall operating efficiency.

Therefore, stage II is optimum from the standpoint of overall production efficiency and cost. Just where in stage II is the best rate of variable input usage depends on the prices of fixed and variable input (we shall pursue this point later on in this chapter). However, *stage II is not the stage in which profit is necessarily maximized.* Demand for a firm's product may in the short run be so low that it is actually more profitable in operate in stage I. We shall indicate this more clearly in a later chapter. Additionally, it should be apparent that stage III can never be more profitable than stage I or stage II because the decline in total output is accompanied by rising total costs (because of using more variable input) and potentially lower revenues.

Fixed Inputs and the Short-Run Production Function

In the preceding section it was shown that economical production occurs only in stage II, yet what can a firm do if its level of product demand does not warrant an output sufficiently high to reach stage II? For instance, suppose, as is shown in Fig. 7-6(a), that a firm reaches stage II at an output of Q_2 units but that the quantity demanded at the current selling price is only Q_1 units. Several alternatives are open to the firm. In the short run it can (1) tolerate the production inefficiency of operating in stage I—which may, incidentally, still allow for ample profit to be earned; (2) seek to increase product demand by lowering its selling price and/or increasing promotional and selling efforts; or (3) add new products to its product line to take up the slack in production capacity. If these prove unsatisfactory for a variety of reasons, in the long run the firm can reduce its scale of production operations by cutting back on the size of fixed inputs. Reducing the size of fixed inputs has the impact of shifting the production function down and to the left, as shown in Fig. 7-6(b).[8] Then the firm can reach stage II at a lower output (Q_3 as compared to Q_2) and with a smaller amount of variable input (X_3 as compared to X_1). Demand for the firm's product can be satisfied by using fewer inputs, thereby cutting production costs and widening the firm's profit margin at the current price.

Likewise, when a firm encounters a level of product demand exceeding its total output capability in the short run, several options are again open. If the strong demand for the item is perceived to be temporary, a price increase to ration the available supply among potential buyers may be in order, and no increase in production capacity is warranted. But when demand seems likely to remain above production capacity on a relatively permanent and profitable basis, a price increase in the short run might well

---

[8] In the event that fixed inputs are "lumpy" and can be reduced only by a relatively large proportion, the production function conceivably could shift downward and *to the right*, meaning that the firm can reach stage II at a lower output provided its usage of variable input is increased. Whether the firm would prefer to use less fixed input and more variable input in producing its product would depend on the relative prices of fixed and variable inputs.

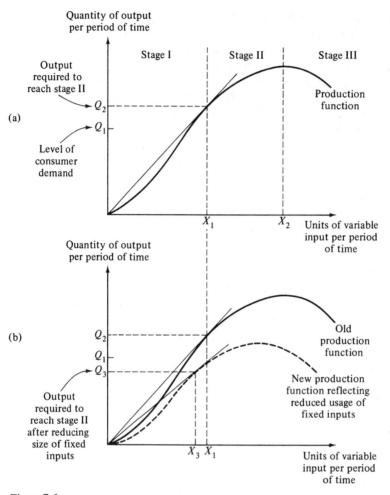

Quantity of output
per period of time

Stage I   Stage II   Stage III

Output
required to
reach stage II

Q_2

(a) Q_1

Level of
consumer
demand

Production
function

X_1 X_2 Units of variable
input per period
of time

Quantity of output
per period of time

(b) Q_2

Q_1

Q_3

Old
production
function

New production
function reflecting
reduced usage of
fixed inputs

Output
required to
reach stage II
after reducing
size of fixed
inputs

X_3 X_1 Units of variable
input per period
of time

Figure 7-6
**Impact of reductions in the use of fixed inputs upon the production
function**

be combined with an expansion of the firm's scale of operations in the long
run. To accomplish this, the size of the fixed inputs must be increased; such
action has the effect of shifting the production function upward and raising
the maximum obtainable rate of total output.

DETERMINING OPTIMAL INPUT PROPORTIONS

So far, the firm has been pictured as changing its rate of output in the short
run by employing more or less units of variable input. In the long run
changes in the usage of fixed inputs may also be undertaken to adjust output

capabilities. Although the fixed-variable input approach to output adjustment helps specify certain fundamental physical relationships of production, it does not permit determination of the precise optimal proportion of different resource inputs within stage II. To pinpoint more exactly the maximum efficiency-minimum cost combination of resource inputs, we must shift our attention away from the relationships between input-output flows to the relationships between resource inputs and resource prices.

The Production Surface

To simplify our analysis of optimal input combinations, let us begin by assuming that capital and labor are the only two types of resource inputs required in producing a good. No disservice to reality is done by this assumption since the relevant principles we shall derive for two inputs apply equally to any greater number of inputs. Capital may be thought of as symbolizing those kinds of resource inputs which are fixed in the short run and labor as symbolizing those kinds of inputs which are variable in the short run. (Letting capital be the proxy for fixed inputs in the short run and labor be the proxy for variable inputs makes it easier to indicate the optimal combination of fixed and variable inputs in the long run.)

In the three-dimensional diagram of Fig. 7-7(a), the coordinates in the horizontal plane show the alternative combinations of capital and labor. The quantity of output associated with each combination of the two types of resource inputs is measured vertically above the plane. Varying the quantities of capital and labor generates the hill-shaped production surface *OCPL*.[9] If *OC* units of capital are used, varying the quantity of labor generates the production function *CDAP*. Similarly, given *OL* units of labor, varying the quantity of capital input gives the production function *LEBP*. Notice that the shapes of the production functions generated by holding the input of one resource constant and letting the other change [lines *CDAP* and *LEBP* in Fig. 7-7(a)] correspond to the cubic type of production function, a type of production relationship which often typifies the entire output range for a plant.

Suppose that we connect all points on the production surface *OCPL* associated with an output of *AA'* units (where *AA'* = *BB'*), obtaining the contour line *AB*. All the points along *AB* are associated with the *same* amount of output (*AA'* = *BB'*). Projecting line *AB* vertically downward onto the horizontal plane gives the dashed contour line *A'B'*. The line *A'B'* defines all the combinations of capital and labor employed per unit of time that will yield an output flow of *AA'* = *BB'*; such a line is called an *isoquant*.[10] For

---

[9]Observe that the concept of the production surface is analogous to the utility surface discussed in Chapters 3 and 4.

[10]The term "isoquant" is derived from the prefix *iso-*, meaning equal, and the word *quantity;* hence, it literally means equal quantity (of output). In the literature of economics isoquants are sometimes referred to as product indifference curves, equal product curves, or isoproduct curves.

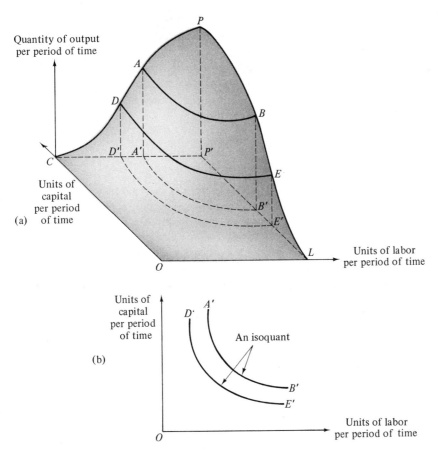

Figure 7-7
Derivation of isoquants from a production surface

movements along an isoquant the rate of output remains constant, but the input ratio (in this case the ratio of capital to labor) changes continuously.

Following the same procedure, suppose we move down the production surface to a lower rate of output, say DD', and connect all points on the production surface $OCPL$ representing an output of DD' (where $DD' = EE'$). This gives the contour line DE, which projected vertically downward onto the horizontal plane traces out the dashed contour $D'E'$. Any point along DE represents constant total output, and all combinations of capital and labor lying on $D'E'$ are capable of producing this amount of output. Contour line $D'E'$ is also an isoquant.

Fig. 7-7(b) illustrates isoquants $A'B'$ and $D'E'$ in a two-dimensional diagram. All input combinations lying on $A'B'$ yield more output than the input combinations on $D'E'$. Higher rates of output are represented by isoquants lying farther from the origin, as indicated by the positions on the production surface of the contour lines from which isoquants are derived.

A complete set of isoquants for a production surface is called an *isoquant map*.[11]

Isoquants may be viewed as analogous to the contour lines on a topographic map. Each isoquant connects all points of the same altitude or output rate. From this standpoint, the entire production surface (of which only a section is shown in Fig. 7-7) can be considered as a "production mountain" with isoquants as the contour lines encircling it.

Although a firm's production function and production surface have been displayed as being continuous, with the isoquants derived therefrom also being continuous, it is more realistic to acknowledge that the "lumpiness" of resource inputs can produce a discrete production surface with correspondingly discrete isoquants. Many resources (especially capital) do not lend themselves to being used in continuously divisible subunits. After all, anything less than a whole machine is less than satisfactory. More importantly, technology is not of such a character that an infinite number of combinations of resources can be used to produce equivalent amounts of output. A firm is necessarily constrained in its selection of resource inputs to the finite number of recipes known to exist for producing an item. Realistically, then, it is more accurate to conceive of an isoquant as a series of points, where each point represents a technically feasible combination of resource inputs that yields the specified level of output. Viewing isoquants as discontinuous or discrete functions keeps the limited potentials of substituting one resource input for another in the forefront. However, as long as the "lumpiness" of resource inputs is recognized, it does little harm to simplify our discussion by drawing isoquants as smooth curves. Certainly, our exposition of the pertinent relationships is made easier by considering a smooth curve instead of a series of points.

The Characteristics of Isoquants

The properties of isoquants are remarkably similar to those of indifference curves: (1) isoquants are nonintersecting; (2) all *rational* combinations of resource inputs lie on that portion of an isoquant which slopes downward to the right; and (3) the rational segments of isoquants tend to be convex to the origin. Each of these properties warrants brief discussion.

For two isoquants to intersect is illogical and contrary to our assumption of efficiency. Intersection would mean that two different amounts of output could be produced with the same combination of resource inputs. This could occur only if a firm uses its inputs so inefficiently that the marginal products of some of the resources are zero or negative—something that a firm is not likely to do knowingly. Hence, an isoquant shows only the maximum output obtainable from resource inputs, which precludes intersection.

---

[11]Suppose that a firm's production function is $Q = f(L, C)$; then a particular isoquant is defined by assigning a value to Q and observing all the different technically feasible values of L and C which will yield that value of Q. The firm's isoquant map is derived by repeating this procedure for many values of Q.

As indicated above, an isoquant map consists of a series of concentric rings around the hill of production. A single such isoquant is reproduced in Fig. 7-8. All the points along the isoquant in Fig. 7-8 represent input combinations capable of producing the same level of output. Although all the combinations of capital and labor lying on this isoquant represent possible recipes for producing this output, some of the combinations are more rational than others. For example, combination B would never be chosen over combination A. Why? Combination A requires the same amount of capital input as B (C_2 units) but requires considerably less labor input (L_1 units as compared to L_3 units); hence, combination A is *cheaper* than B. Similarly, combination D is always preferable to combination C, since it requires much less capital input (C_1 as compared to C_3 units) while using the same amount of labor input (L_2 units). It follows that the economically practical resource combinations fall within the lower left quadrant of the isoquant—the boldly inscribed portion in Fig. 7-8 lying between the vertical and horizontal tangents to the isoquant at points E and F. The remaining points on the isoquant constitute economically foolish resource combinations, even though they represent technically feasible recipes. Thus, for reasons of economy in resource use and in minimizing costs, the rational segment of an isoquant is the portion sloping downward to the right and convex to the origin.

The downward slope of the economic region of an isoquant derives from the possibility of substituting one resource input for another in the production process and still maintaining the same production rate. Consider the *rate* at which one input must be substituted for another to keep output constant. From Fig. 7-9, we see that a change from input combination C_1L_1 to input combination C_2L_2 involves a substitution of labor for capital. The rate at which labor is substituted for capital over this range is

$$\frac{C_2 - C_1}{L_2 - L_1} = \frac{-\Delta C}{\Delta L}$$

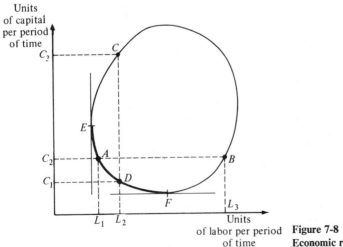

Figure 7-8

Economic region of an isoquant

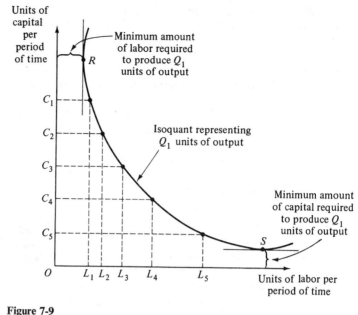

Figure 7-9
Marginal rate of technical substitution

and is called the *marginal rate of technical substitution* of labor for capital. The marginal rate of technical substitution (MRTS) measures the reduction in one input (ΔC) per unit increase in the other (ΔL) that is just sufficient to maintain a constant level of output.

In moving from $C_1 L_1$ to $C_2 L_2$ in Fig. 7-9, the output rate remains unchanged; consequently the "loss" in output from using fewer units of capital input is exactly compensated for by the "gain" in the output from using more units of labor input. The "loss" in output from using less capital equals the reduction in capital usage multiplied by the "average" marginal product of these units, or

$$-\Delta C \cdot MP_C.$$

By the same token, the "gain" in output from using a larger dose of labor equals

$$\Delta L \cdot MP_L.$$

Since the "loss" and the "gain" are equivalent in size, we can say that

$$-\Delta C \cdot MP_C = \Delta L \cdot MP_L.$$

Dividing both sides of this equation by $\Delta L \cdot MP_C$ gives

$$-\frac{\Delta C \cdot MP_C}{\Delta L \cdot MP_C} = \frac{\Delta L \cdot MP_L}{\Delta L \cdot MP_C},$$

which reduces to

$$-\frac{\Delta C}{\Delta L} = \frac{MP_L}{MP_C} \quad \text{or} \quad \frac{\Delta C}{\Delta L} = -\frac{MP_L}{MP_C}.$$

Therefore, it is apparent that between combinations $C_1 L_1$ and $C_2 L_2$,

$$\text{MRTS}_{LC} = \frac{\Delta C}{\Delta L} = -\frac{MP_L}{MP_C}.$$

That MRTS_{LC} is negative derives from the substitution of one resource for the other and the negative slope of the isoquant; however, for our purposes it is the *size* of the ratio that is important, not its sign.

Now suppose that combination $C_1 L_1$ in Fig. 7-9 is moved closer and closer to $C_2 L_2$ so as to merge eventually with it to form a single point. The ratio $\Delta C / \Delta L$ will then approach the value of the slope of the tangent to the isoquant at point $C_2 L_2$. Consequently, we may say that the *marginal rate of technical substitution of one input for another input at any point along an isoquant is equal to the slope of the isoquant at that point.*[12]

The MRTS of labor for capital *diminishes* as more and more labor is substituted for capital because the greater the extent to which labor is substituted for capital, the more labor it takes to compensate for a reduction in the use of capital. The other points along the isoquant in Fig. 7-9 make this clearer. The vertical axis in Fig. 7-9 is measured so that $C_1 C_2 = C_2 C_3 = C_3 C_4 = C_4 C_5 = OC_5 = 1$ unit of capital. Starting at resource combination $C_1 L_1$ and proceeding down the isoquant, we find that it takes a relatively small increase in the use of labor ($L_1 L_2$ units) to compensate for using one less unit of capital and still produce the same quantity of output. But, as we move farther *down* the isoquant and continue to substitute labor for capital, reductions in capital must be offset by progressively larger increases in labor input ($L_1 L_2 < L_2 L_3 < L_3 L_4 < L_4 L_5$). Plainly, then, the MRTS of labor for capital diminishes as the degree of substitution is increased. Where the isoquant becomes horizontal, the substitution of labor for capital has reached its maximum limit, and the $\text{MRTS}_{LC} = 0$. Further reductions in capital will

[12]Mathematically, the MRTS can be found by taking the first derivative of the equation defining an isoquant. For example, if the expression

$$LC = 100$$

defines an isoquant, then the MRTS_{LC} can be found as follows:

$$C = \frac{100}{L} = 100L^{-1},$$

$$\frac{dC}{dL} = -100L^{-2} = -\frac{100}{L^2}.$$

Since $\text{MRTS}_{LC} = dC/dL$, we have

$$\text{MRTS}_{LC} = -\frac{100}{L^2}$$

for any value of L in which interest may focus.

cause output to *fall*; no longer is it possible to reduce the use of capital and maintain output by using more labor. The amount of capital corresponding to point S in Fig. 7-9 is the minimum amount of capital which can be used to produce an output of Q_1. By the same rationale, as we move back up the isoquant toward point R, capital is being substituted for labor, and the ratio of ΔC to ΔL is rising. At point R capital has been substituted for labor to the maximum possible extent; the MRTS of capital for labor is infinity, and the slope of the isoquant is vertical. The amount of labor corresponding to point R is the minimum amount of labor which can be used to produce output Q_1.

It is the changing marginal rate of technical substitution that makes the isoquant convex to the origin. Should two inputs be perfect substitutes for each other, the isoquant is linear and downsloping. Such a relationship between inputs is rare, especially regarding inputs as diverse as labor and capital. That most isoquants are convex is easily demonstrated. Consider labor and capital in making fenders for automobiles. A metal-stamping machine with a single operator can transform a piece of sheet steel into the shape of an automobile fender in a matter of seconds. Within limits, less expensive stamping machines requiring more labor time can be used to make same fender. But the more labor and the less capital used to shape sheet steel into fenders, the more difficult it becomes to carry the degree of substitution further without jeopardizing the quantity and quality of output. The hammering out of the fender, for example, would require an inordinate amount of labor time and cost, as well as entailing a major reduction in fender quality. The same reasoning applies equally well to other resource inputs; consequently, a diminishing marginal rate of technical substitution of one resource input for another is a generally encountered phenomenon in production processes.

The Isocost Curve

Isoquants concern only the possible ways that firms can combine resource inputs—no restrictions, save those of a technical nature, are brought into play. In reality, though, firms are limited in their choice of production techniques by the prices of resource inputs and by the amount of funds available for purchasing these inputs.

An *isocost curve* portrays the various alternative combinations of resource inputs which a firm can purchase, given the prices of resource inputs and the stipulated amount of expenditure on resources.[13] Continuing our assumption of only two inputs, capital and labor, let the price of labor be P_L, the price of capital be P_C, and the stipulated amount of expenditure on resources be TC (total cost). The firm's expenditure for labor equals the price of a unit of labor (P_L) times the amount of labor purchased (L) or $P_L \cdot L$;

[13] The concept of isocost curves is analogous to the concept of lines of attainable combinations (Chapter 4). The only difference is that isocost curves deal with the resource combinations which a firm can purchase, whereas lines of attainable combinations relate to a consumer's ability to purchase goods and services.

similarly, the firm's expenditure for capital is $P_c \cdot C$. With only two resource inputs to choose from, the sum of the firm's expenditures for labor and capital must be equal to or less than the maximum allowable expenditure (TC). Thus, the expression defining the isocost curve may be written as

$$P_L L + P_c C = TC.$$

Provided that P_L and P_c are unaffected by the quantity of labor and capital purchased, if the firm elects to spend all its cost outlay (TC) for labor, a maximum of TC/P_L units can be employed; if the firm elects to spend all its cost outlay for capital, a maximum of TC/P_c can be bought.[14] A straight line joining TC/P_c and TC/P_L shows all the combinations of capital and labor obtainable from an expenditure of TC dollars. Figure 7-10 illustrates such an isocost curve. The slope of the isocost curve may be found by considering points TC/P_c and TC/P_L. Between these two points, the

$$\text{slope of isocost curve} = \frac{(-)TC/P_c}{TC/P_L} = -\frac{TC}{P_c} \cdot \frac{P_L}{TC} = (-)\frac{P_L}{P_c}.$$

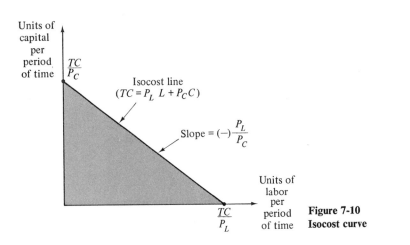

Figure 7-10
Isocost curve

The Optimum Mix of Resource Inputs

A basic objective of firms is to realize the greatest amount of output from a stipulated total cost outlay. In terms of isoquant-isocost analysis this means getting to the highest isoquant permitted by the firm's isocost curve.

[14]Resource prices need not remain constant irrespective of the amounts purchased of labor and capital. A large employer in a tight labor market may have to raise wage rates to attract and hire more labor. A large purchaser of capital goods may be able to squeeze price concessions from suppliers of capital goods as the firm's usage of capital increases. Likewise, quantity discounts may be received on raw material purchases. When the prices of resource inputs fall as the amounts purchased go up, the isocost curve is bowed in toward the origin. In the event that resource prices rise as their levels of usage are increased, the isocost curve is bowed out from the origin.

In Fig. 7-11, the output rate corresponding to isoquant Q_2 is the highest
output which can be attained given an outlay of TC dollars and prices P_L
and P_C. Accordingly, the optimum combination of resource inputs for producing output Q_2 is C_1 units of capital and L_1 units of labor. From a slightly
different viewpoint, this resource combination may also be designated as the
least-cost resource combination, since it represents the minimum cost of
producing Q_2 units of output when the prices of capital and labor are P_C and
P_L, respectively. In other words, the point of tangency between the isocost
and isoquant curves defines the optimum resource combination, whether
interest centers upon (1) finding the maximum output for a given total cost
outlay and at given resource prices, or (2) finding the minimum cost for
producing a given output at given resource prices.

If capital symbolizes fixed input and labor symbolizes variable input,
then the mix of capital and labor at the least-cost resource combination in
Fig. 7-11 defines the optimal proportions of fixed and variable input for
producing Q_2 units of output. This proportion is optimum because, given the
prices of the two inputs, no other combination of fixed (capital) and variable
(labor) input yields Q_2 units as cheaply—hence the term *least-cost* resource
combination.

The Conditions for Optimizing the Resource Mix. There are two conditions for optimizing the combination of labor and capital inputs. First, we
may note that the optimum resource combination of capital and labor lies
on the isocost line rather than inside it. This means the firm must fully
utilize its available dollars in purchasing inputs if it is to maximize output.
Translated into the language of mathematics, we can say that optimization
requires

$$P_L L + P_C C = TC.$$

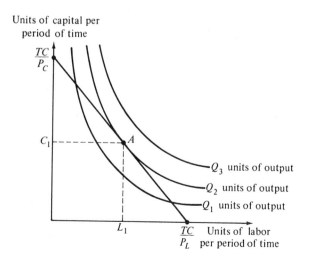

Figure 7-11
**Determining the optimum resource com-
bination**

Second, at the point of tangency between the isocost line and the maximum attainable isoquant, the slope of the isocost line is equal to the slope of the isoquant. From prior discussions the

$$\text{slope of the isoquant} = \text{MRTS}_{LC} = (-)\frac{MP_L}{MP_C}$$

and the

$$\text{slope of the isocost line} = (-)\frac{P_L}{P_C}.$$

Since the slopes are equal, we may write

$$\text{MRTS}_{LC} = (-)\frac{P_L}{P_C}.$$

which states that to optimize the resource mix a firm must allocate its expenditures so that the marginal rate of technical substitution of labor for capital equals the ratio of the price of labor to the price of capital. The interpretation of this result is straightforward. The MRTS_{LC} defines the *rate* at which a firm is *technically able* to substitute labor for capital. The price ratio P_L/P_C shows the *rate* at which a firm is *economically able* to substitute labor for capital. Unless the two rates are equivalent, a firm can alter its resource mix and obtain a larger output or else reduce its costs for a given output. For example, suppose that $\text{MRTS}_{LC} = -\frac{1}{2}$, meaning that a firm is technically able to substitute 2 units of labor input for 1 unit of capital input without changing output. If $P_L = \$10$ and $P_C = \$30$, then a firm is economically able to give up 1 unit of capital in return for 3 units of labor. Giving up 1 unit of capital releases $30, of which only $20 is needed for purchasing labor, since 2 units of labor at $10 each will compensate for a 1-unit reduction in capital input. The remaining $10 can be applied to the purchase of additional resources for increasing output or else to reducing the total costs of the current output rate. In either event the firm will be better off. In general terms, therefore, optimizing the input combination requires equality between the marginal rate of technical substitution for any pair of resource inputs and the ratio of their prices; in the absence of equality some substitution of one resource for another can be initiated to increase output, or else expenditures on resource inputs can be reduced.

However, we can approach this second condition for optimizing the resource mix from another angle. Not only is the slope of the isoquant equal to MRTS at any point, but it is also equal to the ratio of the marginal products of the resource inputs:

$$\text{MRTS}_{LC} = (-)\frac{MP_L}{MP_C}.$$

Thus, we may rewrite the second condition for optimizing the resource combination as

$$(-)\frac{MP_L}{MP_C} = (-)\frac{P_L}{P_C}.$$

This equation states that the firm's total cost outlay should be allocated among labor and capital so as to equate the ratio of their marginal products with the ratio of their prices. Transforming the latter equation still further by cross-multiplying, we get

$$P_L \cdot MP_C = P_C \cdot MP_L.$$

Dividing both sides by $P_L \cdot P_C$ gives

$$\frac{P_L \cdot MP_C}{P_L \cdot P_C} = \frac{P_C \cdot MP_L}{P_L \cdot P_C},$$

which reduces to

$$\frac{MP_C}{P_C} = \frac{MP_L}{P_L}.$$

The latter expression says that a firm should arrange its input purchases so as to obtain an equivalent amount of additional output from the last dollar spent on each input. When the extra outputs per dollar spent on the last unit of each resource are unequal, the quantity of output can be increased (or total costs reduced) by diminishing expenditures where the marginal product per dollar spent is less and by enlarging expenditures where the marginal product per dollar spent is greater. For example, if

$MP_L = 42$ units output for the last unit of labor purchased,
$P_L = \$7$ per unit,
$MP_C = 80$ units of output for the last unit of capital purchased,
$P_L = \$10,$

then

$$\frac{MP_L}{P_L} = \frac{42 \text{ units}}{\$7} = 6 \text{ units of output/\$ spent on labor}$$

and

$$\frac{MP_C}{P_C} = \frac{80 \text{ units}}{\$10} = 8 \text{ units of output/\$ spent on capital.}$$

The firm is realizing more extra output per dollar spent on the last unit of capital than on the last unit of labor. This situation calls for (1) reallocating dollars away from the purchase of labor, thereby raising MP_L and increasing the output per dollar spent on labor, and (2) spending more dollars on the purchase of capital thereby decreasing MP_C and decreasing the output per dollar spent on capital. Substituting capital for labor will tend to equalize the ratios MP_L/P_L and MP_C/P_C.

DETERMINATION OF THE OPTIMUM RESOURCE COMBINATION

Let P_L and P_C be the prices of units of labor (L) and capital (C); let TC symbolize the budget a firm has available for purchasing the two resource inputs; and let $Q = f(L, C)$ represent the firm's production function for a commodity. The issue is how to best allocate the available dollars (TC) among purchases of labor and capital input so as to maximize the quantity of output (Q) subject to the constraint that the total expenditures on inputs just exhaust TC. More formally, what values of L and C will cause $Q = f(L, C)$ to be maximum, yet just meet the constraint that

$$TC - P_L L - P_C C = 0?$$

The mathematical solution requires using the Lagrangian multiplier method of finding the maximum value of a function. A new function is generated which combines the production function to be maximized with the constraint to be met. To keep the solution determinate (as many equations as there are unknowns) an artificial unknown, called a Lagrange multiplier and symbolized by λ, is introduced into the new function, giving

$$Z = f(L, C) + \lambda(TC - P_L L - P_C C).$$

Note that the constraint has been expressed in such a way that it is satisfied when $TC - P_L L - P_C C = 0$. Next, the partial deriviatives of Z are found for each variable and equated to zero to establish the first-order conditions:

$$\frac{\partial Z}{\partial L} = \frac{\partial Q}{\partial L} - \lambda P_L = 0,$$

$$\frac{\partial Z}{\partial C} = \frac{\partial Q}{\partial C} - \lambda P_C = 0,$$

$$\frac{\partial Z}{\partial \lambda} = TC - P_L L - P_C C = 0.$$

These three equations are then solved simultaneously to determine the combination of L and C which will maximize the quantity of output subject to the cost constraint.

As an example of the foregoing, suppose that the production function is

$$Q = 20L + 65C - 0.5L^2 - 0.5C^2$$

and that $TC = \$2200$, $P_L = \$20$ per unit, and $P_C = \$50$ per unit. To find the maximum output obtainable from an expenditure of $2200, we generate the function

$$Z = 20L + 65C - 0.5L^2 - 0.5C^2 + \lambda(2200 - 20L - 50C).$$

Finding the partial derivatives of Z and setting them equal to zero, we have

$$\frac{\partial Z}{\partial L} = 20 - L - 20\lambda = 0,$$

$$\frac{\partial Z}{\partial C} = 65 - C - 50\lambda = 0,$$

$$\frac{\partial Z}{\partial \lambda} = 2200 - 20L - 50C = 0.$$

Solving these three equations simultaneously gives $L = 10, C = 40$, and a maximum Q of 1950 units.

Exercise

1. Determine the optimum resource combination of labor and capital when
   (a) $Q = 140L + 160C - 5L^2 - 2C^2$,
   $P_L = \$12,$
   $P_C = \$24,$
   $TC = \$732.$
   (b) $Q = 6LC,$
   $P_L = \$5,$
   $P_C = \$10,$
   $TC = \$180.$

When There Are More Than Two Resource Inputs.   The preceding conclusions are easily expanded for cases where more than two distinct kinds of resource inputs are used in a production process. In the event that a production process requires multiple types of resource inputs $(X_a, X_b, X_c, \ldots, X_n)$ obtainable at prices $(P_{X_a}, P_{X_b}, P_{X_c}, \ldots, P_{X_n})$, the optimal mix of resource inputs is attained by meeting the following two conditions:

$$P_{X_a}X_a + P_{X_b}X_b + P_{X_c}X_c + \ldots + P_{X_n}X_n = TC, \tag{1}$$

$$\frac{MP_{X_a}}{P_{X_a}} = \frac{MP_{X_b}}{P_{X_b}} = \ldots = \frac{MP_{X_n}}{P_{X_n}}. \tag{2}$$

The Expansion Path

It is not likely that a firm will maintain its output at the same rate for long. Market conditions, particularly demand, change frequently and cause firms to adjust output rates accordingly. For this reason, the firm has an interest in knowing the least-cost resource combinations for several rates of output. Especially pertinent is the issue of how much more of each input to use should market conditions warrant a long-term expansion or contraction of output.

Consider Fig. 7-12, where inputs of C_1 units of capital and L_1 units of labor are being used to produce an output of Q_1 units at a total cost of TC_1 dollars. Now suppose that the firm wishes to expand output to Q_2 units per period of time. Clearly, a greater total cost outlay is required. Assuming that the prices of capital and labor remain constant at P_{L_1} and P_{C_1}, an increase in the expenditure level for resource inputs will shift the isocost curve outward *parallel* to itself. Thus, an outlay of TC_2 dollars using C_2 units of capital and L_2 units of labor represents the least possible cost of producing output Q_2. Similarly, an outlay of TC_3 dollars with inputs of C_3 units of capital and L_3 units of labor is the least possible cost of producing Q_3 units of output. The line joining these and all other least-cost resource combinations is called the *expansion path* of the firm. *The expansion path shows the locus of optimum input combinations for each possible rate of output when the prices of the resource inputs remain constant.*

The shape of the expansion path for labor and capital has a certain amount of economic significance. It is probable that increasing the output of most commodities over the long run entails a technological and economic bias toward using relatively more capital than labor, meaning the expansion path is as shown in Fig. 7-13(a). Support for this stems from the readily observable tendency of large firms to use a more capital-intensive production recipe than do smaller firms producing the same item—presumably because it is almost always more efficient than labor-intensive production techniques. Occasionally, the expansion path may be linear or very nearly so [Fig. 7-13(b)]. A linear expansion path for a product implies that the costs of

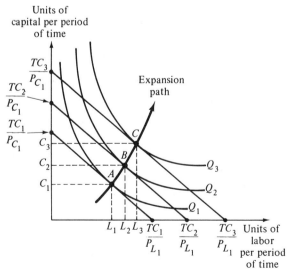

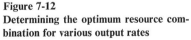

Figure 7-12
Determining the optimum resource combination for various output rates

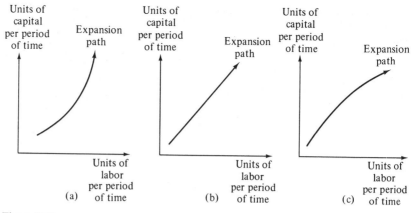

Figure 7-13
Alternative shapes for the expansion path

additional output are minimized by using more of both inputs *in the same proportion* as before, perhaps because technological requirements call for a constant ratio between inputs. In rare cases the expansion path could assume the shape of that in Fig. 7-13(c), where maximum efficiency-minimum cost requires using relatively more labor than capital to expand total output.

The expansion path shows the amounts of resource inputs which the firm should use as it expands its *long-run* rate of output. But in the short run the firm has no alternative to adjusting output rates by using more or less variable input with the given amount of fixed input. To minimize costs in the short run a firm should alter its usage of variable resources so as to keep the ratios of the marginal products per dollar spent on variable inputs equivalent. In other words, if *in the short run* a firm uses four *variable* inputs (X_a, X_b, X_c, and X_d), even though the fixed inputs cannot be changed, then optimal resource usage entails adjusting *variable* input combinations such that

$$\frac{MP_{X_a}}{P_{X_a}} = \frac{MP_{X_b}}{P_{X_b}} = \frac{MP_{X_c}}{P_{X_c}} = \frac{MP_{X_d}}{P_{X_d}}.$$

The Impact of Changes in Resource Prices

The prices of resource inputs, as with the prices of goods and services, are subject to change. When they do change, firms are prompted to alter input combinations. Suppose we examine the effect of an increase in the price of labor upon the optimum mix of capital and labor.

Given the price of labor P_{L_1}, the price of capital P_{C_1}, and the firm's total cost outlay TC_1, the firm will optimize its inputs at an output of Q_1 by combining L_1 units of labor with C_1 units of capital as shown by point A in Fig. 7-14. If the price of labor rises to P_{L_2}, then the isocost curve will pivot to the left about point TC_1/P_{C_1}, restricting the maximum usage of

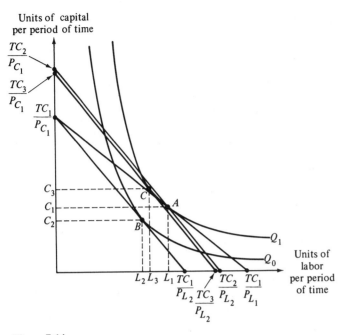

Figure 7-14
Adjusting to changes in resource prices

labor to TC_1/P_{L_2} units were the entire total cost outlay used to buy labor. The new isocost curve will necessarily be tangent to a lower isoquant than previously and it will not be possible to produce Q_1 units of output with an expenditure of TC_1 dollars. The optimum input mix becomes L_2 units of labor and C_2 units of capital (point B in Fig. 7-14) at an output of Q_0 units. The firm must choose between being content with a lower output (Q_0) or else increasing TC to permit maintenance of output at Q_1. If the latter alternative is chosen and assuming the input of capital is fixed *in the short run* at C_1 units (as is truly the case in the real world), then the firm will find it most advantageous *in the short run* to continue to produce Q_1 units of output by using C_1 units of capital and L_1 units of labor (point A). Why? Because when the firm's capital input is fixed at C_1 units, the *smallest* amount of labor that can be used to produce an output of Q_1 units is L_1 units of labor. An examination of Fig. 7-14 verifies this statement. Consequently, *in the short run* point A represents the least cost of producing Q_1 units when no more than C_1 units of capital are available, despite the fact that the price of labor has risen from P_{L_1} to P_{L_2}. But, since the price of labor has gone up, it is clear that the cost of producing Q_1 units of output must be greater than TC_1. The higher cost can be illustrated graphically by drawing a new isocost line with a slope of P_{L_2}/P_{C_1} (so as to reflect the new ratio of resource prices) through point A. The extreme points of this isocost line are TC_2/P_{C_1} and TC_2/P_{L_2}, where $P_{L_2} > P_{L_1}$ and $TC_2 > TC_1$. *In the short run*, therefore, the fixed aspect of capital input may cause the firm to leave its input combination unchanged in response to an increase in the price of labor, provided it elects to continue to produce Q_1 units and provided it can afford to increase its expenditures on resource inputs from TC_1 to TC_2.

However, *in the long run* the firm will wish to change its usage of capital and labor in response to the higher price of labor. As soon as time and money permit, the firm will be induced to produce Q_1 units of output by shifting from point A to point C in Fig. 7-14. Point C is determined by finding the point of tangency between isoquant Q_1 and an isocost line with a slope of P_{L_2}/P_{C_1}; this isocost line is parallel to the isocost line defined by extreme points TC_2/P_{C_1} and TC_2/P_{L_2}, because both lines reflect the resource inputs obtainable when the price of labor is P_{L_2} and the price of capital is P_{C_1}. The shift in the optimum resource mix from point A to point C will reduce the costs of producing Q_1 units of output from TC_2 to TC_3, an amount which is indicated graphically by the distance between the isocost line defined by extreme points TC_3/P_{C_1} and TC_3/P_{L_2} and the isocost line defined by extreme points TC_2/P_{C_1} and TC_2/P_{L_2}.

Thus, in the long run an increase in the price of labor relative to the price of capital will induce the firm to substitute capital for labor. The logic of such action is compelling. Whenever a resource becomes more expensive, it makes sense to use less of it and more of other less expensive inputs. This is precisely what business firms have proceeded to do. In manufacturing, for example, as unions and other wage-increasing forces have combined to drive up the relative price of labor, firms have put forth a concerted effort to substitute capital for labor. Rising labor costs are, in fact, a major motive for introducing automated production processes. Substitution of capital for labor is most evident in the steel, coal-mining, chemical, petroleum, automobile, aluminum, and pulp and paper industries, as well as in the use of computers to perform tasks formerly handled by white-collar employees.

However, the degree to which firms have substituted capital for labor has been obscured somewhat by growing output rates. Suppose that a firm simultaneously experiences a rise in the price it must pay for labor inputs and an increase in the demand for its product. As just explained, the increase in the price of labor, given the price of capital, will eventually precipitate a substitution of capital for labor. This result is shown in Fig. 7-15 as the movement from point A to point C. But should the increase in demand for the firm's product dictate a change in output from Q_1 to Q_2 units, then the firm will find it advantageous to shift from the input mix at point C to the input mix at point D. The movement from point C to point D ultimately calls for using both more capital and more labor than originally. In this case, the labor-increasing effect of raising the firm's output rate more than offsets the labor-decreasing effect of the rise in the price of labor input. But had the price of labor input not risen, the firm would have preferred to use L_4 units of labor instead of L_3 units to produce Q_2 units of output. Thus, the increase in the price of labor input served to restrict the use of labor and caused the firm to select a more capital-intensive production technology (point D) than it otherwise would have selected (point E).

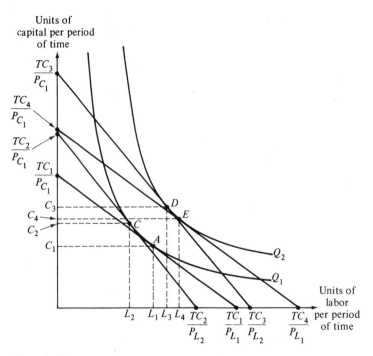

Figure 7-15
Effect of simultaneous changes in resource and output rates upon the optimum resource combination

Insofar as an entire economy is concerned, rising consumer demand is essential to keeping unemployment rates from rising to prohibitive levels as business enterprises shift to more capital-intensive production technologies. Nonetheless, the net effect of increases in labor input prices is still to restrict the growth of employment opportunities to less than what would be realized if rising wages did not further increase the propensity of firms to substitute capital for labor. Fortunately, in the United States the demand for output has usually grown fast enough to override much of the labor-decreasing effect of automation.

RETURNS TO SCALE

Up to now, the firm and its technology have been examined primarily from a short-run point of view, where a portion of the firm's resource inputs are fixed. The concept of *returns to scale* deals with production relationships over a time span sufficiently long to allow changes in any and all inputs, especially those inputs such as plant space, major pieces of capital equipment, and managerial capability, which are typically fixed in the short run. Specifically, the phrase "returns to scale" refers to the character of changes in output when *all* resource inputs are changed in *equal* proportions.

Consider a firm using L units of labor in combination with C units of capital to obtain an output of Q units. Then

$$L + C \longrightarrow Q.$$

Now suppose that the amounts of both labor and capital are increased by some arbitrary proportion a. Plainly, output will rise; the question is by what proportion. Suppose that we designate the proportion by which output increases as b. Then

$$aL + aC \longrightarrow bQ.$$

1. If the change in output is more than proportional to the change in input ($b > a$), *increasing returns to scale* are said to prevail. For example, if the inputs of capital and labor are increased by 20% per period of time, and output rises by 30%, the firm enjoys increasing returns to scale.
2. If the change in output is equal to the proportional change in input ($b = a$), *constant returns to scale* are present. In this case a doubling of the inputs of both capital and labor per period of time leads to a doubling of the number of units produced.
3. If the change in output is less than proportional to the change in input ($b < a$), the firm experiences *decreasing returns to scale*. An illustration of decreasing returns to scale would be where inputs are increased by 40% but output rises by only 30%.

Given the state of technology, it is generally believed that in expanding its scale of operation a firm will pass successively through

1. A short range of increasing returns to scale,
2. A lengthy range of constant returns to scale, and
3. A range of decreasing returns to scale.

Conceivably, a firm can increase its usage of resource inputs to the point where output becomes maximum; subsequent increases in input then would produce a stage of negative returns to scale where output actually falls.

However, if the concept of returns to scale is broadened to permit changes in a firm's technical capabilities as its size increases, firms may well be (and, indeed, are) able by skillful application of new technologies to expand their scale of operations without ever encountering decreasing returns to scale.[15] Constant returns to scale over a wide range of output appear to characterize many manufacturing industries. The reasons for increasing, constant, and decreasing returns to scale are worth exploring further.

Factors Contributing to Increasing Returns to Scale. Five factors combine to produce increasing returns to scale for a firm. The most pervasive

[15]Several recent empirical studies confirm this finding. See, for example, J. Haldi and D. Whitcomb, "Economies of Scale in Industrial Plants," *Journal of Political Economy*, Vol. 75, No. 4 (August 1967), pp. 373–385; and John R. Moroney, "Cobb-Douglas Production Functions and Returns to Scale in U.S. Manufacturing Industry," *Western Economic Journal*, Vol. 6, No. 1 (December 1967), pp. 39–51.

of these five factors originates with opportunities for specializing in the use of resource inputs as a firm's scale of operations is increased. The gains in efficiency from specialized use of production-type labor are well chronicled.[16]

In small-scale operations where the typical employee performs several different and perhaps diverse tasks, it is difficult for workers to attain a high degree of proficiency at each one. Mediocre performance of some tasks, with an attendant loss of efficiency, is almost unavoidable; in addition, time is lost in changing from task to task. As scale increases, however, it becomes easier to assign workers to tasks for which they are particularly adept. In concentrating upon a single, well-defined task, people tend to develop greater speed and accuracy—plus they are better at identifying shortcuts and ways for improvement. Time lost in switching from task to task is eliminated. Also, the costs of training individual workers may be reduced by increased specialization. However, specialization in the use of labor can be carried so far that the monotony of performing assembly line jobs becomes excessively fatiguing and mindless, and efficiency gains are neutralized. Hence, firms must be alert to dividing up work tasks in ways that preserve motivated effort.

Second, the larger the scale of production, the greater the feasibility of utilizing the most advanced productive equipment and technology and obtaining the benefits of using specialized capital equipment.[17] Frequently, the most efficient recipe from a technological point of view involves making

[16]The productive powers of specialized use of labor are amply illustrated in a famous passage from Adam Smith's *The Wealth of Nations*, written over 200 years ago: "To take an example . . . from a very trifling manufacture; but one in which the division of labor has been very often taken notice of, the trade of the pinmaker; a workman not educated to this business (which the division of labour has rendered a distinct trade), nor acquainted with the use of the machinery employed in it (to the invention of which the same division of labour has probably given occasion), could scarce, perhaps, with utmost industry, make one pin in a day, and certainly could not make twenty. But in the way in which this business is now carried on, not only the whole work is a peculiar trade, but it is divided into a number of branches, of which the greater part are likewise peculiar trades. One man draws out the wire, another straights it, a third cuts it, a fourth points it, a fifth grinds it at the top for receiving the head; to make the head requires two or three distinct operations; to put it on, is a peculiar business, to whiten the pins is another; it is even a trade by itself to put them into the paper; and the important business of making a pin is, in this manner, divided into about eighteen distinct operations, which in some manufactories, are all performed by distinct hands, though in others the same man will sometimes perform two or three of them. I have seen a small manufactory of this kind where ten men only were employed, and where some of them consequently performed two or three distinct operations. But though they were very poor, and therefore but indifferently accommodated with the necessary machinery, they could, when they exerted themselves, make among them about twelve pounds of pins in a day. There are in a pound upwards of four thousand pins of a middling size. Those ten persons, therefore, could make among them upwards of forty-eight thousand pins in a day. Each person, therefore, making a tenth part of forty-eight thousand pins, might be considered as making four thousand eight hundred pins in a day. But if they had all wrought separately and independently, and without any of them having been educated to this peculiar business, they certainly could not each of them have made twenty, perhaps not one pin in a day; that is, certainly, not the two hundred and fortieth, perhaps not the four thousand eight hundredth part of what they are at present capable of performing, in consequence of a proper division and combination of their different operations."

[17]M. A. Adelman found that employment among the 200 largest firms was about 60% more capital intensive than in the economy as a whole. See M. A. Adelman, "The Measurement of Industrial Concentration," *Review of Economics and Statistics*, Vol. 33, No. 4 (November 1951), p. 278.

a product via mass production methods. Small enterprises cannot justify the use of such large-volume production technology, let alone raise the money to install it.[18] Thus, small-scale operations often must rely upon multipurpose machinery and equipment, which seldom can attain the speed and precision of the single-purpose pieces of capital equipment used in larger-sized production units. Not only can larger-scale enterprises afford to employ mass production methods and to embrace new technologies, but they also have the organizational ability to market larger volumes of output, to diversify, to integrate vertically and horizontally (when antitrust will allow), and to decentralize. Hence, they are better positioned to capitalize upon more than proportional increases in output from their production, selling, and administrative inputs.

Purely dimensional factors are a third reason for increasing returns to scale. Doubling the diameter of a natural-gas pipeline can more than double the flow through it. A 100-watt light bulb does not require $2\frac{1}{2}$ times as much labor and materials as a 40-watt light bulb. Doubling the labor and materials in a motor can easily more than double the horsepower of the motor. To build and operate a pulp and paper plant capable of producing 5000 tons of paper products per week does not require 5 times as much labor, managerial talent, equipment, and building space as a pulp and paper plant capable of producing only 1000 tons per week. In a somewhat related fashion, tripling the rate of output of an assembly line may require only one additional inspector instead of two; a diesel locomotive may have sufficient power to pull 50 freight cars as adequately as 20; and a bookseller may be able to sell books in both economics and business administration subjects as well as just those in economics with less than a proportional increase in time, effort, and cost.

Fourth, since technologically complex production processes require several major pieces of equipment, the scale of production may have to be large to overcome potential bottlenecks in the process. Suppose two machines A and B are required for packaging a product, machine A being used to fill the package with the proper amount of the product and machine B being used to wrap the package in cellophane. If machine A can fill 15,000 packages per day and machine B can wrap 20,000 packages per day, then at an output of 60,000 units per day, where four type A machines and three type B machines are used, both types of machines can be efficiently utilized. At less than 60,000 units of output full utilization of both machine types is not possible, and some amount of idle capacity will be present.

And, finally, as its size increases a firm can afford to employ management *specialists*, thereby realizing the benefits to be gained from a specialized use of managerial talents (just as from a specialized use of labor). The added presence of management specialists can give larger firms an efficiency edge over smaller firms whose managers, being fewer in number, must spread their time over a wider range of problems. The managers of many small

---

[18]For example, in the mid-1970s the rule-of-thumb estimate for the cost of a new oil refinery was about $2000 per single barrel of capacity. That meant a 100,000-barrel-a-day plant, about the smallest considered economically feasible, would require a capital investment of $200 million.

firms are not skilled enough or equipped for the task of large-scale strategy formulation and organization-building, which increases the chances that they will be "outmanaged." In contrast, larger firms have the flexibility to staff up to just the right range and depth of skills needed. Moreover, they have the ability to apply the skills of specialists in organized, innovative ways. Decentralization, the multidivisional organizational form, matrix organizational structures, project management, and task force concepts have all been employed in their several varieties to bring about improved operating performance and results.[19] At the same time, with larger size comes an ability to utilize the efficiencies of high-speed computers; to initiate and develop new managerial techniques based upon operations research, simulation processes, and other tools of management science; and to experiment with the use of new managerial methodologies. On the whole, therefore, there is a pronounced tendency for the organizational and managerial capabilities of large firms to exceed those of small enterprises. In fact, a large firm may find that one of its strongest competitive weapons is its superior numbers of people and its potential for specializing its personnel more deeply.

Factors Contributing to Constant Returns to Scale. Increasing returns to scale cannot continue indefinitely; the factors responsible for obtaining output at rates more than proportional to the volumes of resource inputs will sooner or later be exhausted—and usually sooner. This is particularly true for the production unit of a firm—the plant. It is no secret in business that certain size plants are more efficient than others. Moreover, experts in technology and engineering can peg quite closely the most efficient plant size for producing a given product. It is then a simple matter for large-scale enterprises to build as many of these optimum-sized facilities as may be necessary to satisfy the firm's need for productive capacity for that product. For example, if the most efficient plant size is one capable of producing 100,000 units per year, a large firm selling 1 million units per year can realize constant returns to scale in producing this item by building 10 plants, each capable of producing 100,000 units. Where a firm produces several products, it can organize itself into divisions and scale them to the most efficient size. In so doing a large firm may be able to realize constant returns to scale for an almost indefinitely large volume of output. And by centralizing purchasing, selling, and administrative activities under one management, it may even be possible to realize increasing returns from these latter inputs, making the firm's overall operations more efficient than that achievable by a smaller enterprise. Since the ability to decentralize into optimum-sized plants and

[19]Alfred D. Chandler, Jr., *Strategy and Structure* (New York: Doubleday & Company, Inc., Anchor Books edition, 1966), pp. 126–127, 156–157, 195–196, 230, 256, 321–323, 369, 382–383; Oliver E. Williamson, *Corporate Control and Business Behavior* (Englewood Cliffs, N.J.: Prentice-Hall, Inc., 1970). Chapters 7 and 8; Jay R. Galbraith, "Matrix Organizational Designs," *Business Horizons*, Vol. 14, No. 1 (February 1971), pp. 29–40; Peter F. Drucker, *Management: Tasks, Responsibilities, Practices* (New York: Harper & Row, Publishers, 1974); Henry O. Armour and David J. Teece, "Organizational Structure and Economic Performance: a Test of the Multidivisional Hypothesis," *Bell Journal of Economics*, Vol. 9, No. 1 (Spring 1978), pp. 106–122.

FORD'S RIVER ROUGE PLANT:
A CASE OF DECREASING RETURNS TO SCALE

One of the most dramatic examples of trying to push size beyond the point of decreasing returns occurred in the 1920s when Ford Motor Company built a gigantic new manufacturing and assembly plant at River Rouge outside Detroit. The River Rouge plant was intended to centralize at one site a broad spectrum of activities relating to automobile production. At this one facility Ford employed 75,000 workers producing coke, pig iron, steel, castings, forgings, and parts and components for cars and tractors, as well as assembly line activities. The plant occupied over 1000 acres and included 93 separate structures, 23 of which were main buildings. The site contained 93 miles of railroad tracks and 27 miles of conveyors. It took a maintenance force of nearly 5000 people to try to keep the plant clean; each year janitorial crews wore out 5000 mops and 3000 brooms and used 86 tons of cleaners on the floors and walls and on the 330 acres of windows.

It soon became evident that the size of the plant was well beyond the optimal point. According to some observers, the plant was so massive and complex that top-level plant managers had little contact with and understanding of what was happening from a plant-wide perspective; lower-level managers were lost in the hubub of so many large and complex activities. The constant and unremitting tempo of the huge quantities of materials coming in and automobiles going out took its toll on both workers and management. According to a former Ford official:

> Everybody was on edge. They ran around in circles and didn't know what they were doing. Physically everybody was going like a steam engine but not so much mentally. As long as their feet were on the go they were working hard. The more a man ran around the better he was. . . . Officials had no offices—only desks in the open factory at which they stood. They couldn't keep records, and lower officials could not discuss their problems together.*

In the final analysis, sheer bigness was the undoing of the giant plant. The coming and going of a virtual army of workers, the incoming shipment of huge volumes of raw materials, the maze of manufacturing and assembly line activities, and the shipping out of thousands of cars—all going on at one centralized site—not only created enormous problems of congestion but became a nightmare to manage and operate.

Ford soon found that it was cheaper to ship parts and components

*Allan Nevins and Ernest Hill, *Ford, Expansion and Challenge: 1915–1933* (New York: Charles Scribner's Sons, 1957) p. 296.

for final assembly to scattered, decentralized plants than it was to try to centralize the manufacturing and assembling of cars at one site. Within a few years Ford Motor Company began establishing branch assembly plants and by 1928 had 35 in the United States alone. For many years now, most of the mighty industrial complex at River Rouge has been shut down; in recent years only the foundry has been in use.

productions is restricted only by a firm's capacity to manage its operations, the range of output for which a firm can experience constant returns to scale in its production activities is virtually unlimited.

Factors Contributing to Decreasing Returns to Scale. The principal factor causing a firm to experience decreasing returns to scale is the limit to which the managerial function can be efficiently performed. As a firm becomes larger, the problems of integrating the many facets of its activities multiply. Decision-making is more complex, and the burdens of administration become disproportionately greater. Conventional wisdom insists that "diminishing returns" to management will be encountered as top management loses touch with the daily routine of operation and finds it increasingly necessary to delegate authority to lower-echelon managers whose level of competence may not be as great. Red tape and paper work expand with size; bureaucratic procedures creep in, causing the managerial hierarchy of larger firms to be sluggish and unwieldy in responding to the operational requirements of the organization.

This view of the limits to managerial efficiency is not without merit, yet it is not altogether valid and convincing. Many of the very large corporate enterprises (General Motors, General Electric, IBM, Procter and Gamble, Xerox, Atlantic Richfield, Sears, International Telephone and Telegraph) are widely noted for being well-managed organizations. Big firms appear to have been quite adept at circumventing and subverting managerial inefficiencies via reliance on a higher order of managerial technology. Innovative organizational schemes, computerized data processing, systems analysis, strategic planning, and operations research models, coupled with superior management talent have had the effect of allowing the management function in billion-dollar corporations to be performed with good results.[20] Hence,

---

[20]The rapid development of analytical and managerial techniques that stimulate and assist enterprises to find more efficient ways of accomplishing their activities is impressive. Operations research, simulation, and mathematical programming are among the more sophisticated of these new forms of managerial technology, but equally significant advances have been made concerning new and more precise accounting and budget-control procedures, better methods of market analysis, more efficient cash management procedures, refinements in business forecasting, and communications techniques. The unifying character of these new developments in managerial technology is that they bring the principles of rational problem solving to bear even more heavily upon sustaining effective organizational performance.

while it is undoubtedly true that limits exist regarding efficient performance of the managerial function, it is just as true that the prevailing limits can be pushed back by the successful application of better managerial technologies. It does not appear that the limits to efficient performance of the managerial function have, in practice, been a significant factor in hindering the growth of enterprises any more than has inefficient performance of other phases of business activity.

Table 7-2 provides summary findings of several investigations of the nature and existence of returns to scale.

Table 7-2 Some Empirical Evidence on Returns to Scale

Analyst/Author	Year	Findings and Conclusions
Moroney[a]	1967	Based upon estimates of production functions made from cross-section statistics in two-digit SIC manufacturing industries, it was concluded that a large majority of these industries were characterized by constant returns to scale.
Bain[b]	1956	In examining the optimum size of plants in the automobile industry, it was found that, in general, a volume of 300,000 cars per year is a low estimate of what is needed for productive efficiency in any one line and that there were probable added advantages to 600,000 units. In assembly alone, a range of 60,000 to 180,000 appeared to be optimal.
Hirsch[c]	1959	It was found that approximately constant returns to scale exist over a considerable range of sizes for public schools and school districts in the St. Louis area.
Riew[d]	1966	In a study of Wisconsin high schools, it was found that there are very significant scale economies up to at least a size of 2400 pupils.
Haldi and Whitcomb[e]	1967	Based upon engineering studies of production functions and scale economies in a variety of industries, it was concluded that (1) there appear to be no great scale economies concerning the use of primary raw materials; (2) efficiency gains for using gas, electricity, and other utilities in larger quantities sometimes occur because larger furnaces, motors, and other such equipment units perform more efficiently than smaller units; (3) large economies of scale in labor costs are possible for process-type plants because labor's chief function is to watch gauges, adjust valves, and perform maintenance tasks—none of which require many extra workers as capacity is added; (4) substantial economies of scale are obtainable in performing supervisory and management functions; (5) there are substantial economies of scale in maintenance performance arising from the fact that maintenance needs do not increase proportionately with capacity, nor do labor costs for this maintenance increase proportionately with output.

Table 7-2 (Cont.)

Analyst/Author	Year	Findings and Conclusions
Blair *et al*[f]	1975	In fitting one linear and three nonlinear functional forms to average administrative costs, there was strong evidence of scale economies in the administrative aspects of a health insurance program.
Miller[g]	1978	Using information from the *1972 Census of Manufactures*, it was found that (1) on average, the four largest firms in an industry had an output per plant employee that was 39% greater than that for all other firms in the industry, (2) on average, the four largest firms had profits per employee that were 57% greater than those for the remainder of the industry, and (3) on average, the top four firms were able to handle 43% more raw material inputs per employee than the remainder of the industry. The study covered 448 industries (at the four-digit SIC level). The conclusion was that the leading four firms are substantially more productive than smaller firms and that there is compelling evidence of large economies of scale at the firm level for a major portion of American industry.

[a]John R. Moroney, "Cobb-Douglas Production Functions and Returns to Scale in U.S. Manufacturing Industry," *Western Economic Journal*, Vol. 6, No. 1 (December 1967), pp. 39–51.

[b]Joe S. Bain, *Barriers to New Competition* (Cambridge, Mass.: Harvard University Press, 1956), p. 244.

[c]Werner Hirsch, "Appendix–Economies of Scale", *Analysis of the Rising Costs of Public Education*, Study Paper No. 4, Materials Prepared in Connection with the Study of Employment, Growth, and Price Levels, for consideration by the Joint Economics Committee, Congress of the United States, November 10, 1959 (Washington, D.C.: U.S. Government Printing Office, 1959).

[d]John Riew, "Economies of Scale in High School Operation," *Review of Economics and Statistics*, Vol. 48, No. 3 (August 1966), pp. 280–287.

[e]John Haldi and David Whitcomb, "Economies of Scale in Industrial Plants," *Journal of Political Economy*, Vol. 75, No. 4 (August 1967), pp 373–385.

[f]Roger D. Blair, Jerry R. Jackson, and Ronald J. Vogel, "Economies of Scale in the Administration of Health Insurance," *Review of Economics and Statistics*, Vol. 47, No. 2 (May 1975), pp. 185–189.

[g]Edward M. Miller, "The Extent of Economies of Scale," *Southern Economic Journal*, Vol. 44, No. 3 (January 1978), pp. 470–487.

MATHEMATICAL CAPSULE 10

DETERMINING RETURNS TO SCALE
FROM THE PRODUCTION FUNCTION

Suppose that a large, diversified enterprise carefully examines the input-output relationships for each of its three major products (X, Y, and Z) and concludes that the production functions for these products are

$$Q_X = 1.6L^{.4}C^{.4}M^{.1},$$
$$Q_Y = \sqrt{0.4L^2CM},$$
$$Q_Z = 10L + 7C + M,$$

where Q represents output per period of time, L is units of labor input, C is units of capital input, and M is units of managerial input. The question immediately arises as to what returns to scale are encountered in manufacturing the three products. The answer can be determined by observing what happens to output when the inputs of labor, capital, and management are increased *in equal proportions*. The production function is "tested" by multiplying each input by a constant factor (say a) and ascertaining whether output changes (1) by an amount greater than a in which case increasing returns to scale are signified, (2) by an amount equal to a in which case constant returns to scale are signified, or (3) by an amount less than a in which case decreasing returns to scale are indicated.

The returns to scale indicated by the production function for product X is found in the following manner. Multiplying each of the three inputs by a, where $a > 1$ so as to indicate an increase in the inputs, we obtain

$$1.6(aL)^{.4}(aC)^{.4}(aM)^{.1},$$

which becomes

$$1.6a^{.4}L^{.4}a^{.4}C^{.4}a^{.1}M^{.1}.$$

Factoring a out of the function gives

$$a^{.4+.4+.1}(1.6L^{.4}C^{.4}M^{.1})$$

or

$$a^{.9}(1.6L^{.4}C^{.4}M^{.1}).$$

The expression in parentheses defines the level of output prior to the change in input, and $a^{0.9}$ represents the proportional change in the output of product X when each input is increased by a. Because the exponent for a is less than 1, increasing the inputs by a results in a *less than proportional* increase in the output of X, and the production function for X may be said to exhibit decreasing returns to scale.

In the case of product Y, increasing each input by an arbitrary proportion a, where $a > 1$, yields

$$\sqrt{0.4(aL)^2(aC)(aM)}.$$

Simplifying this expression, we get

$$\sqrt{0.4a^2L^2aCaM} = \sqrt{0.4a^4L^2CM} = a^2\sqrt{0.4L^2CM}.$$

Hence, increasing each input by a causes output to expand by a^2— obviously, increasing returns to scale are present, since output expands at a rate more than proportional to the input increase. This result is easily confirmed by means of a numerical example. Suppose, originally, that $L = 5$, $C = 5$, and $M = 2$; then

$$Q_Y = \sqrt{0.4L^2CM}$$
$$= \sqrt{0.4(5)^2(5)(2)}$$
$$= \sqrt{100}$$
$$= 10.$$

If all the inputs are doubled ($a = 2$), we have $L = 10$, $C = 10$, $M = 4$, and

$$Q_Y = \sqrt{0.4(10)^2(10)(4)}$$
$$= \sqrt{1600}$$
$$= 40.$$

Consequently, doubling the inputs of labor, capital, and management causes the output of product Y to quadruple (since $a^2 = 4$ when $a = 2$), and increasing returns to scale may be said to characterize the production function for product Y.

Increasing the inputs by a for the production function for product Z gives

$$10(aL) + 7(aC) + aM,$$

or, more simply,

$$a(10L + 7C + M).$$

Here output changes by the same proportion as input, so constant returns to scale are present.* Again, a simple example verifies existence

*The mathematics of production functions is not always as neat and clear-cut as the three cases above might indicate. Consider the production function

$$Q = 16L + 0.5LCM + 1.4L^{.5}C^{.3}M^{.1}$$

Changing the inputs by a yields

$$16(aL) + 0.5(aL)(aC)(aM) + 1.4(aL)^{.5}(aC)^{.3}(aM)^{.1},$$

which simplifies to

$$16aL + 0.5a^3LCM + 1.4a^{.9}L^{.5}C^{.3}M^{.1}.$$

Inspecting the expression above term by term, we find that the first term $(16aL)$ has the characteristic of constant returns to scale, the second term $(0.5a^3LCM)$ has the characteristic of increasing returns to scale, and the third term $(1.4a^{.9}L^{.5}C^{.3}M^{.1})$

of constant returns to scale for product Z. If $L = 15$, $C = 10$, and $M = 5$, then

$$Q_z = 10L + 7C + M$$
$$= 10(15) + 7(10) + 5$$
$$= 225.$$

Doubling the inputs ($a = 2$) so that $L = 30$, $C = 20$, and $M = 10$, we get

$$Q_z = 10(30) + 7(20) + 10$$
$$= 450.$$

Therefore, doubling each input causes the output of product Z to double—a constant-returns-to-scale situation.

The character of the production functions for the three products X, Y, and Z provides a guide to management for choosing the products upon which to concentrate its limited resources. *Other things being equal*, cost and efficiency considerations call for steering resources (financial and otherwise) to those products with the most favorable returns to scale. The most favorable, of course, is increasing returns to scale, followed in order by constant returns and decreasing returns. Hence, products Y, Z, and X in that order yield the enterprise the greatest amounts of output for a given amount of input.

However, a word of qualification must be offered. Returns to scale in no way reflect the demand side of the picture. The mere fact that the output of a commodity is characterized by decreasing returns to scale does not mean that it is unprofitable. The price which can be obtained for product X may be so favorable that it is relatively more profitable than either product Y or Z. In fact, the competitive forces prevailing in the markets for Y and Z could make those commodities unprofitable, even though they can be produced under very favorable conditions. Returns to scale indicate only the direction of change in productive efficiency and unit costs which can be anticipated if the size of the firm's production operations is increased or decreased. Also, the nature of the production function for a product can change over a period of time because of scientific and engineering developments, innovation, and advances in managerial technology. Thus, in the long run the production process for an item can be transformed from decreasing to constant or increasing returns to scale.

---

displays decreasing returns to scale. Whether the entire production function exhibits increasing, constant, or decreasing returns to scale on balance depends on the relative strengths of the three terms. In this instance the strong increasing returns influence found in the second term will overpower the mildly decreasing returns shown in the third term, with the result that the entire production function shows increasing returns to scale.

Exercise

1. Determine the returns to scale implied in each of the following production functions.
   (a) $Q = 0.4A^2 + 0.3AB + 2.0B$.
   (b) $Q = 0.7L^{.8}C^{.3}$.
   (c) $Q = 10 + 4A + 9B$.
   (d) $Q = (10/L) + 6C$.

SUMMARY AND CONCLUSIONS

In analyzing production processes, resources are generally divided into two categories: fixed and variable. Corresponding to the notion of fixed and variable inputs is the notion of the short run and the long run. In the short run, output can be changed only by altering the amount of variable input used in conjunction with the given fixed input. In the long run, output can be changed by altering the scale of production, the technology of the production process, and the rate of usage of any and all inputs.

The principle of diminishing marginal returns states that as the amount of a variable input is increased by equal increments and combined with a specified amount of fixed input, eventually a point will be reached where the resulting increases in the quantity of output will get smaller and smaller. Should the usage rate of variable input get sufficiently large, the quantity of output will reach a maximum and may then decrease as still larger amounts of variable input are employed.

The relationships between the production function, average product, and marginal product can be used to define three stages of production. Stage I covers the range of variable input where AP_{vi} is rising; stage II includes the range where AP_{vi} is falling *and* where MP is declining yet positive; and stage III encompasses the range where MP is negative and total output is falling.

The optimum resource combination is in stage II at the input rate where (1) the firm is fully utilizing its dollars in purchasing inputs and (2) an equivalent amount of extra output is being obtained from the last dollar spent on each input. Graphically, this condition is achieved at the point of tangency between the isocost curve and an isoquant.

If the firm increases all its inputs by a given proportion and output increases by *more* than this proportion, increasing returns to scale prevail. If the firm increases all its inputs by a given proportion and output rises by this *same* proportion, constant returns to scale characterize the production process. If the firm increases all its inputs by the same proportion and output rises *less* than proportionally decreasing returns to scale are present. Increasing returns to scale occur because of increased specialization in use of resources, technological considerations, dimensional factors, and indivisibility of inputs. Constant returns to scale arise when the production process embodies standard man-machine ratios and when it is feasible to assimilate a number of optimum-sized production units under a single management. Decreasing returns to scale occur primarily because of limitations to efficient performance of the managerial function.

SUGGESTED READINGS

COURVILLE, L., "Regulation and Efficiency in the Electric Utility Industry," *Bell Journal of Economics and Management Science*, Vol. 5, No. 1 (Spring 1974), pp. 53–74.

HALDI, J., AND D. WHITCOMB, "Economies of Scale in Industrial Plants," *Journal of Political Economy*, Vol. 75, No. 4 (August 1967), pp. 373–385.

HUETTNER, D. A., AND J. H. LANDON, "Electric Utilities: Scale Economies and Diseconomies," *Southern Economic Journal*, Vol. 44, No. 4 (April 1978), pp. 883–912.

MAXWELL, W. D., "Short-Run Returns to Scale and the Production of Services," *Southern Economic Journal*, Vol. 32, No. 1 (July 1965), pp. 1–19.

MILLER, E. M., "The Extent of Economies of Scale," *Southern Economic Journal*, Vol. 44, No. 3 (January 1978), pp. 470–487.

MILLER, E. M., "Size of Firm and Size of Plant," *Southern Economic Journal*, Vol. 44, No. 4 (April 1978), pp. 861–872.

MOORE, F. T., "Economics of Scale: Some Statistical Evidence," *Quarterly Journal of Economics*, Vol. 73, No. 2 (May 1959), pp. 232–245.

MORONEY, J. R., "Cobb-Douglas Production Functions and Returns to Scale in U.S. Manufacturing Industry," *Western Economic Journal*, Vol. 6, No. 1 (December 1967), pp. 39–51.

SHEN, T. Y., "Economies of Scale, Expansion Path, and Growth of Plants," *Review of Economics and Statistics*, Vol. 47, No. 4 (November 1965), pp. 420–428.

STIGLER, G., "The Economies of Scale," *Journal of Law and Economics*, Vol. 1 (October 1958), pp. 54–71.

PROBLEMS AND QUESTIONS FOR DISCUSSION

1. Fill in the values for discrete MP, AP_{vi}, and AP_{fi} based upon the information given in the table.

Units of Fixed Input	Units of Variable Input	Quantity of Output	Discrete MP	AP_{vi}	AP_{fi}
3	0	0			
3	1	120	___	___	___
3	2	270	___	___	___
3	3	390	___	___	___
3	4	480	___	___	___
3	5	540	___	___	___
3	6	560	___	___	___
3	7	540	___	___	___

2. Given: The production function $Q = 12X$, where $Q =$ units of output per period of time and $X =$ units of variable input.
   (a) Determine the equations for MP and AP_{vi}.
   (b) Assuming 5 units of fixed input are presently being employed in the production process represented by the production function above, determine AP_{fi} when 10 units of variable input are combined with the 5 units of fixed input.
   (c) Graphically illustrate the production function and the corresponding MP and AP_{vi} functions.
   (d) How would you describe the important properties of this production function?

3. Production mangers for the Cosmic Paper Corporation estimate that their production process is currently characterized by the following short-run production function: $Q = 72X + 15X^2 - X^3$, where $Q =$ tons of paper products per production period and $X =$ units of variable input employed per production period.
   (a) Determine the equations for MP and AP_{vi}.
   (b) What is MP when 7 units of variable input are employed?
   (c) By how much does output rise when the usage of variable input is increased from 7 to 8 units per production period?
   (d) At what rate of usage of variable input is the point of diminishing marginal returns encountered?
   (e) What is the maximum output capability per production period? What rate of usage of variable input is required to reach the maximum output level?
   (f) Graphically illustrate this production function and the corresponding MP and AP_{vi} functions. Indicate on your graph the output ranges where output is increasing at an increasing rate and where output is increasing at a decreasing rate. Also indicate the output where the point of diminishing average returns to variable input is encountered.

4. Graphically illustrate the stages of production for each of the following general types of production functions.
   (a) $Q = bX$.
   (b) $Q = bX - cX^2$.
   (c) $Q = bX + cX^2 - dX^3$.

5. The production department of the National Cabinet Corporation employs 20 unskilled laborers, 45 semiskilled workers, and 60 skilled craftsmen. A careful assessment of the productivity of the three types of labor indicates that the marginal product of an unskilled laborer is currently 10 units of output per worker-day, the marginal product of a semiskilled worker is 20 units per worker-day, and the marginal product of a skilled craftsman is 50 units per worker-day. The wage rates for the three types of labor result in labor costs of $20 per worker-day for unskilled labor, $30 per worker-day for semiskilled workers, and $50 per worker-day for skilled craftsmen. Output is currently at the desired level. Would you suggest a change in the labor mix used by the production department? Why or why not?

6. The Fashion Dress Corporation is considering the construction of a new plant. Engineers have submitted the following possible plant designs—all of which are equally capable from a physical standpoint of producing the desired output of 1000 dresses per day:
   (a) Illustrate the technically feasible production alternatives by means of an isoquant.

Plant Design	Units of Capital	Units of Labor
1	50	500
2	75	400
3	150	200
4	250	100
5	350	50

(b) Suppose that the price of capital is $100 per unit and the price of labor is $50 per unit. Which plant design should be selected? Justify your answer with an isocost-isoquant graph.

(c) What will be the required total cost outlay for capital and labor for the selected plant design?

7. Suppose that Apex Manufacturing Corporation has its choice of three production processes for producing its product. With process A, Apex can produce 100 units of output per hour using 5 units of labor and 20 units of capital; by process B, 100 units per hour with 10 units each of labor and capital; by process C, 100 units per hour with 20 units of labor and 5 units of capital. All three processes are characterized by constant return to scale.

(a) Graphically illustrate isoquants for outputs of 100, 200, and 300 units per hour.

(b) If the price of labor is $5 per unit and capital costs $10 per unit, which process should be selected to produce 200 units? *Illustrate* your answer by means of isoquant and isocost curves.

(c) If the price of labor is $8 per unit and the price of capital is $8 per unit, which process should be selected to produce 100 units per hour? Verify your answer with an isoquant-isocost graph.

(d) If the price of labor is $14 per unit and capital is $7 per unit, which process should be selected to produce 300 units per hour? What will be the necessary total cost outlay?

8. Jupiter Products, Inc., has derived the following production function for its operation: $Q = 0.65L^{.42}C^{.38}M^{.20}Z^{.08}$, where Q = units of output per period of time, L = hours of labor, C = hours of machine services, M = hours of managerial input, and Z = miscellaneous resource services.

(a) Assuming that Jupiter's operations are sufficiently flexible to vary the usage of L, C, M, and Z, what kind of returns are indicated by this production function? Why?

(b) What inference, if any, can you make about the firm's unit costs for producing additional units of output?

9. A rapidly developing conglomerate has employed a team of operations researchers to advise it on acquiring prospective enterprises. Four small firms, each producing the same commodity but employing radically different production technologies, are currently being carefully scrutinized for possible acquisition by the conglomerate. The operations research team has initiated investigations of the production, marketing, and financial aspects of the four firms for the purpose of singling out one of them as the best candidate for acquisition. As part of their investigation they have sought to estimate the pro-

duction functions for each of the four firms; their estimates are as follows:

Firm A: $\quad Q_A = 0.8L^{.6}C^{.2}M^{.1}$.

Firm B: $\quad Q_B = \frac{7}{3}L + \frac{3}{2}C + M$.

Firm C: $\quad Q_C = \sqrt{0.09L^{.5}C^{1.0}M^{.5}}$.

Firm D: $\quad Q_D = 6L^2 + 7C^2 - LC + 0.1M^2$.

On the basis of these estimates alone, which of the four firms appears to offer the expansive-minded conglomerate the best prospects? Why?

10. What is the difference between "returns to variable input" and "returns to scale?"

EIGHT ▼ COST FUNCTIONS AND ECONOMIES OF SCALE

The costs of goods and services derive from the technology and the inputs used to produce them. The analysis of cost behavior is founded, therefore, upon the principles of production. In this chapter we shall translate the relationships among production technology, inputs, and outputs into cost functions. After exploring the nature of "cost," the short-run and long-run cost curves will be derived for a variety of possible production functions and production technologies.

THE CONCEPT OF COSTS

Mention of the word *cost* immediately conjures up the thought of "money outlays." In the context of business operations, costs are commonly viewed as a firm's actual or historical expenditures for resource inputs. However, for many decision purposes historical costs are of limited significance. In the first place, the costs that really matter for *business decisions* are future costs; historical costs are useful primarily as bench marks for anticipating future production costs and for estimating the costs of alternative courses of action. But even here past costs should be treated warily since inflation, changing input supply conditions, and so on can make past costs an obsolete indicator of the future. Second, anyone familiar with the vagaries of cost accounting is aware that two manufacturers of physically identical products who use different, but acceptable, methods of measuring cost could differ in their reported costs by 40% or more.[1] Historical cost statistics can thus be misleading unless one knows a great deal about the particular cost accounting system from which they are derived. And, finally, to view costs in exclusively monetary terms is to leave out a sizable portion of what may rightfully be considered as cost. The social costs of noise, congestion, and environmental pollution are not easily reduced to dollar and cents. Nor are psychic costs readily expressed in monetary terms; these involve the mental anguish and mental dissatisfaction associated with such business activities as dismissing employees, moving one's family to accept a transfer in an undesirable location, working on holidays, pressures from one's boss for outstanding performance, and the monotony of repetitious tasks.[2] Plainly, social costs and psychic costs abound in many business situations, yet they never appear in an enterprise's financial accounts.

A thread common to all the many dimensions of cost can be summed up in the word *sacrifice*. All costs entail a sacrifice of some type; the form of the sacrifice may be tangible or intangible, objective or subjective, monetary or nonmonetary. For this reason, it is not always possible in many cases to reduce costs to simple dollars and cents, nor is it possible to arrive at a single, unambiguous and universally acceptable measure of cost.

THE MANY ASPECTS OF COST

As a means of illustrating the multidimensional aspects of cost, consider the apparently innocuous statement: "General Electric's cost of producing an electric toaster in 1980 was $9.45." The most obvious interpretation of this statement is that the costs incurred by General Electric in operating its electric toaster divisional unit amounted to an average of $9.45 in 1980. No doubt the basis for such a figure would be the historical expenses for resources bought outright or hired by GE and which were routinely recorded in its accounts according to GE's scheme of accounting practice. These explicitly incurred expenses might consist of production labor costs, payments for com-

---

[1]Cost differentials can "artificially" be produced by judiciously selecting among the following options for measuring a firm's costs: (1) using an accelerated depreciation schedule instead of the straight-line method; (2) using the first-in, first-out (FIFO) method of inventory valuation instead of the last-in, first-out (LIFO) method; (3) employing a direct costing system rather than a full-cost accounting system; (4) selecting any one of several acceptable rules for determining the time period to which certain kinds of expenses will be charged; and (5) using artificial transfer prices for intermediate goods passing from one operating division to another instead of open market transfer prices.

[2]Psychic costs are not unique to business enterprise, nor can they be lightly dismissed as inconsequential. For example, few students would question that they incur significant psychic costs from preparing for and taking final exams; nor would professors deny the existence of psychic costs in preparing and grading exams and in assigning final grades. The examination process is very painful indeed, and to ignore the psychic costs which it entails would probably mean omitting the greatest of the costs of administering examinations.

ponent parts purchased from suppliers, managerial salaries, interest costs, payments for electric power, transportation costs, telephone services, depreciation charges, administrative expenses, property taxes, and other miscellaneous payments. Such outlays are known as *explicit costs.*

Despite the apparent accuracy and completeness of explicit cost figures, the stated costs of $9.45 per toaster will in all probability not prove to be as definitive and all-inclusive as first appears.[3] To begin with, it is easy to overlook allowances for equity capital supplied by the firm's stockholders as being a valid cost element.[4] If firms borrow money from banks or other financial institutions, the interest costs are shown as an expense on the profit and loss statement; yet if the same funds are raised by selling new issues of common stock, no capital costs are entered in the firm's ledger.[5] Nonetheless, if stockholders fail to receive a return on their invested capital equivalent to what could be earned were they to invest their funds in the best alternative investment of equal risk, then they will understandably be reluctant to supply the enterprise with financial capital in the future. Thus, if General Electric wishes to use equity capital as a source of financing for its activities (including making toasters), then in the long run they must not only cover explicit costs but also have enough revenue left over to reward stockholders with a return on their investment at least equivalent to stockholders' *opportunity costs*—the return GE's owners are sacrificing by not having invested in other ventures of comparable risk. GE must cover this opportunity cost in order to induce continued stockholder participation and confidence in the firm's activities. These opportunity costs represent a minimum acceptable return to stockholders and are just as legitimate a cost as are explicit costs; failure to consider them constitute the chief reason that the stated costs of $9.45 per

---

[3] From a broader social viewpoint, the cost of producing a toaster can be thought of as the utility consumers forego from giving up the commodities that could have been produced had not some of society's existing pool of economic resources been used to manufacture electric toasters. Resources used to produce toasters cannot be used to produce other commodities—commodities from which certain segments of society may derive great satisfaction. Thus, the cost to society of a GE toaster is not $9.45 but is the sacrifice of utility associated with not having more of some other commodity which GE or some other firm could have produced instead.

[4] In the case of entrepreneurial or owner-managed firms the cost of other owner-supplied resources may be overlooked. For example, the proprietor may elect not to pay himself a salary but instead rely upon "profits" as payment for his services. Such a practice clearly understates the operating costs of the enterprise, since the value of the managerial skills furnished by the proprietor is not included. Likewise, if no allowance is made for the costs of land and working capital supplied by the proprietor, total costs will be underestimated.

[5] The concepts governing measurement of total costs in an accounting period are less than logical. For example, if GE were to lease a plant to produce toasters from a second party, the lease payment would generally include a margin for the cost of both debt and equity capital, and such lease payments are allowable expenses in their entirety. If GE were to build its own plant with funds borrowed from the Chase Manhattan Bank, the interest expense for the cost of this debt capital would be allowed. Yet if GE financed the same plant with the proceeds of a common stock issue, no expense for the cost of equity capital would be permitted. The Internal Revenue Service is insistent that explicit costs be the standard upon which profits and, subsequently, corporate profits taxes are computed. The inclusion of implicit costs is strictly illegitimate.

toaster may be a low estimate of the actual costs of producing a GE toaster. The costs of resources supplied by a firm's owners which are not explicitly recorded as expenses according to conventional accounting practices are called *implicit costs*. These could include allowances for rent on company-owned facilities and for fully depreciated property and equipment still in use as well as the costs of equity capital.

In a related vein, for some purposes the best measure of the true economic worth (cost) of a resource input may be the resource inputs' opportunity costs rather than the dollar outlays for the input appearing in historical accounting records. As above, we use the term *opportunity costs* to represent the benefits (monetary or otherwise) foregone by not choosing the best alternative course of action. In other words, opportunity costs are the sacrifices incurred by not having done something else. Several examples may be offered to make the relevance of opportunity cost considerations more apparent. The cost to General Electric of making its own heating elements for use in GE electric toasters can correctly be viewed as the price at which GE could sell these heating elements to other firms were they not to use them in their own toasters. In periods of strong demand for GE products, the cost to GE of using available resources for toaster production is the profit GE gives up by not devoting these resources to the production of other GE appliances and products. The costs to GE of using scarce executive and managerial talents in toaster production is not so much the related salaries as it is the contribution to profits that these executives and managers could make by devoting their time to other GE activities. The cost of building a new $2 million plant to manufacture GE toasters is not just the interest that GE might have to pay on the borrowed money but rather the profits or cost savings that could be achieved by investing the $2 million in making electric skillets, vacuum cleaners, numeric-controlled process equipment, longer-lasting light bulbs, or any other of GE's many products. Opportunity costs are, therefore, a measure of the sacrifice incurred from a decision not to take advantage of an alternative opportunity; putting a dollar value on opportunity costs involves a comparison between the chosen course of action and the best alternative course of action.

Although precise calculation of either implicit or opportunity costs is often subjective, considering these two aspects of cost in conjunction with historical costs can lead to a sounder analysis and determination of costs. Certainly, adjusting historical costs for implicit and opportunity cost elements improves the accuracy with which the profitabilty of an enterprise can be judged. For instance, unless GE's revenues from the sale of toasters exceed both the explicit and implicit costs of toaster production, GE cannot be said to be truly earning a profit on toasters. Moreover, unless GE's return on its dollar investment in toaster production is at least equivalent to what it could earn by putting this investment in another activity, GE should discontinue toaster production and shift its resources into the better alternative. Thus, while the size of a firm's opportunity costs is difficult to determine, some estimate of their size is crucial to key decisions. In this regard it is better to have a rough estimate of the right concept of cost than an accurate estimate of the wrong concept.

But even after adjusting historical costs for implicit and opportunity costs we are left with a cost concept of limited usefulness for business decisions. Given again the stated cost of $9.45 for producing a GE toaster, consider the following questions:

1. How much of the $9.45 represents costs directly related to the production of toasters (direct costs), and how much of the $9.45 represents costs not directly traceable to toasters [e.g., the chief executive's salary and other costs common to the production of several of GE's products (common costs)]?

2. How much of the $9.45 represents fixed charges associated with the plant, equipment, and management needed for toaster production (fixed costs), and how much is accounted for by direct production labor and raw materials (variable costs)?

3. To what extent would the $9.45 cost be altered by a 10% increase in GE's production of toasters (incremental costs)?

4. What portion of the $9.45 represents controllable costs (property taxes as compared to managerial salaries), and what portion represents cuttable costs (the use of skilled union labor as compared to advertising)?

5. How would a labor strike affect the costs of producing a toaster (shutdown costs and startup costs)?

6. To what extent can the $9.45 cost be expected to change in the long run (long-run versus short-run costs)?

7. How is the $9.45 cost of a toaster divided between manufacturing costs and such selling costs as salesmen's salaries and commissions, promotional expenses, maintaining distribution channels, and operating repair centers and warehouses?

8. How would the introduction of a completely automated assembly line alter the $9.45 cost?

9. What portion of the $9.45 could be postponed in the event of a decision to trim the costs of toaster production (postponable costs)?

10. How much of the $9.45 could be avoided if it became necessary to reduce toaster production by 20% (escapable versus unavoidable costs)?

These questions suffice to indicate that no one measure of the costs of production is adequate for decision-making purposes. Different decision problems call for different kinds of cost information. Depending on the purpose at hand, one may wish to determine total costs, average costs, marginal costs, fixed costs, variable costs, direct costs, common costs, explicit costs, implicit costs, opportunity costs, controllable costs, shutdown costs, postponable costs, long-run costs, escapable costs, replacement costs, incremental costs, manufacturing costs, selling costs, administrative costs, labor costs, and so on ad infinitum.[6]

[6] More complete discussions of the many aspects of cost are found in J. M. Clark, *Studies in the Economics of Overhead Costs* (Chicago: University of Chicago Press, 1923), Chapters 4–6; Joel Dean, *Managerial Economics* (Englewood Cliffs, N. J.: Prentice-Hall, Inc., 1951), Chapter 5; and Milton H. Spencer, *Managerial Economics*, 3rd ed. (Homewood, Ill.: Richard D. Irwin, Inc., 1968), Chapter 7.

The fundamental starting point in cost analysis is that a functional relationship exists between the costs of production and the rate of output per period of time. A cost function shows the various costs which will be incurred at alternative output rates; in other words,

$$\text{cost} = f(\text{output}).$$

But, as indicated in Chapter 7, the rate of output is, in turn, a function of the rate of usage of the resource inputs:

$$\text{output} = f(\text{inputs}).$$

Since the production function establishes the relations between input and output flows, once the the prices of the inputs are known the costs of a specific quantity of output can be calculated. As a consequence, the level and behavior of costs as a firm's rate of output changes is largely dependent on two factors:

1. The character of the underlying production function.
2. The prices the firm must pay for its resource inputs.

The former determines the shape of the firm's cost functions, while the latter determine the level of costs. To simplify our examination of cost-output relationships, we shall assume that the prices a firm pays for its resource inputs are not affected by changes in its output rate.

The Short Run and the Long Run

In discussing the relationships between cost and output it is useful to differentiate between cost behavior in the short run and cost behavior in the long run. From Chapter 7 it will be recalled that the short run refers to a period of time so short that the firm cannot readily vary such inputs as the amount of space available for production activity, major pieces of equipment, and key managerial personnel (the so-called fixed inputs); output is alterable only by increasing or decreasing the usage of variable inputs (production labor, raw materials, and so on). In the long run, however, sufficient time exists for modifying the usage of any and all inputs so as to maintain an optimum combination—all inputs are therefore variable in the long run.

The classification of resource inputs as being fixed or variable in the short run and as being all variable in the long run provides a convenient approach to investigating cost behavior. We shall first examine short-run cost functions and then long-run cost functions.

COST-OUTPUT RELATIONSHIPS
IN THE SHORT RUN

239

*Cost-Output
Relationships
in the Short
Run*

The Family of Total Cost Concepts

Three concepts of total cost are important for analyzing a firm's short-run cost structure: total fixed cost, total variable cost, and total cost.

The fixed inputs of a firm give rise to fixed costs, the amount of which depends on the quantity of each of the various fixed inputs and the respective prices paid for them. Salaries of top-management officials, property taxes, interest on borrowed money, depreciation charges, rents on office space, the implicit costs of equity capital, and insurance premiums are examples of fixed costs. As indicated above, costs may be explicit or implicit. A firm's explicit fixed cost is simply a summation of the dollar value (or economic worth) of the explicit fixed inputs. Because the amounts of explicit fixed input do not vary with output in the short run, it follows that explicit fixed costs also do not vary with output. Likewise, implicit costs are not a function of short-run output, and they, too, are properly a part of the firm's short-run fixed cost structure. In formal terms, *total fixed cost (TFC)* may be defined as the sum total of the explicit costs of all the fixed inputs plus the implicit costs associated with the firm's operations.[7] Because the firm's fixed input quantities are not subject to change in the short run, *TFC* is constant unless the *prices* of the fixed inputs change (higher property taxes, increases in insurance rates or rents, and so on). Moreover, total fixed costs continue even if production facilities are idle.

Similarly, those inputs that are variable in the short run give rise to short-run variable costs. Since in the short run a firm modifies its output rate by buying more or less units of variable input, variable costs depend on and vary with the quantity of output. *Total variable cost (TVC)* is the sum of the amounts a firm spends for variable inputs employed in the production process.[8] Examples of variable costs include payroll expenses, raw material outlays, power and fuel charges, and transportation costs.[9] Total variable

---

[7]In terms of more formal mathematics, total fixed costs may be defined as

$$TFC = \sum_{i=1}^{n} p_i x_i,$$

where p_i = price of a specified fixed input,
x_i = quantity of the specified fixed input, and
n = number of various kinds of fixed inputs (explicit as well as implicit).

[8]Total variable costs may be defined in mathematical terms as

$$TVC = \sum_{j=1}^{m} p_j x_j,$$

where p_j = price of a specified variable input,
x_j = quantity of the specified variable input, and
m = number of various kinds of variable inputs.

[9]A variety of expenses incurred by firms has both fixed and variable aspects. These include telephone service, advertising outlays, research and development costs, office supplies, expense account allowances, payroll taxes, and fringe benefit costs.

cost (*TVC*) is zero when output is zero because no variable inputs need be employed to produce nothing. However, as output increases, so does the usage of variable input; thus, *TVC* increases directly with output.

The *total cost* of a given output rate in the short run is the sum of total fixed cost and total variable cost:

$$TC = TFC + TVC.$$

At zero output, total variable cost is zero and total cost is equal to total fixed cost. As soon as output rises above zero in the short run, some variable inputs must be used, variable costs are incurred, and total cost is the sum of the fixed and variable expenses.

The Family of Unit Cost Concepts

There are four major *unit cost concepts*: average fixed cost (*AFC*), average variable cost (*AVC*), average total cost (*ATC*), and marginal cost (*MC*). All these may be derived from the total cost concepts discussed above.

Average fixed cost is defined as total fixed cost divided by the units of output, or

$$AFC = \frac{TFC}{Q}.$$

Since total fixed cost is a constant amount, average fixed cost declines continuously as the rate of production increases. For example, if $TFC = \$1000$, at an output of 10 units $AFC = \$1000/10 = \$100$; at an output of 20 units $AFC = \$1000/20 = \$50$; at an output of 50 units $AFC = \$1000/50 = \$20$; and so on. The reduction of *AFC* by producing more units of output is what businessmen commonly call "spreading the overhead." The calculation of average fixed cost can also be approached from a slightly different direction. If we conceive of a firm's inputs as consisting of a number of identical units, then total fixed cost equals the number of units of fixed input (*FI*) multiplied by the unit price of the fixed input (P_{fi}), or $TFC = (P_{fi})(FI)$. Substituting into the expression for *AFC* gives

$$AFC = \frac{TFC}{Q} = \frac{(P_{fi})(FI)}{Q} = P_{fi}\left(\frac{FI}{Q}\right).$$

Recalling that in Chapter 7 we defined average product of the fixed input as total output (*Q*) divided by the number of units of fixed input (*FI*), it follows that the term FI/Q equals $1/AP_{fi}$ and that

$$AFC = P_{fi}\left(\frac{1}{AP_{fi}}\right).$$

Average variable cost is total variable cost divided by the corresponding number of units of output, or

$$AVC = \frac{TVC}{Q}.$$

As with *AFC*, the concept of *AVC* may be related to the underlying production function. Total variable cost equals the units of variable input employed (*VI*) multiplied by the price per unit of variable input (*P_{vi}*). Assuming a single type of variable input is used, $TV\dot{C} = (P_{vi})(VI)$. Hence, we have

$$AVC = \frac{TVC}{Q} = \frac{(P_{vi})(VI)}{Q} = P_{vi}\left(\frac{VI}{Q}\right).$$

Since the average product of variable input is defined as Q/VI, then

$$AVC = P_{vi}\left(\frac{1}{AP_{vi}}\right).$$

Average total cost is defined as total cost divided by the corresponding units of output, or

$$ATC = \frac{TC}{Q}.$$

However, since $TC = TFC + TVC$,

$$ATC = \frac{TC}{Q} = \frac{TFC + TVC}{Q} = \frac{TFC}{Q} + \frac{TVC}{Q}.$$
$$= AFC + AVC.$$

Last, *marginal cost* is the change in total cost associated with a change in the quantity of output per period of time. As with previous marginal concepts, we can make a distinction between discrete marginal cost and continuous marginal cost. *Discrete marginal cost* is the change in total cost attributable to a 1-unit change in the quantity of output. For example, the marginal cost of the 500th unit of output can be calculated by finding the difference between total cost at 499 units of output and total cost at 500 units of output. Hence, the increase in total cost of producing one additional unit of output equals the marginal cost of that unit. *Continuous marginal cost* may be thought of as the *rate* of change in total cost as the quantity of output changes, and it can be claculated from the first derivative of the total cost function. Thus,

$$MC = \frac{dTC}{dQ}.$$

However, because in the short run all output-related changes in total cost are attributable *solely* to changes in total variable cost (*TFC* is constant), it is equally accurate to measure discrete marginal cost by observing changes in total variable cost—the marginal cost of the 500th unit of output equals the difference between TVC at 499 units of output and TVC at 500 units of output. And continuous marginal cost can be calculated from the first derivative of the TVC function:

$$MC = \frac{dTVC}{dQ}.$$

As with the other unit cost concepts, the value of marginal cost is related to the underlying production function. Marginal costs stem from the changes in variable costs associated with altering the quantity of output. Since in the short run output is altered by increasing or decreasing the usage of variable inputs, changes in total variable cost (ΔTVC) may be calculated by multiplying the price of variable input (P_{vi}) by the associated change in variable input (ΔVI), giving

$$\Delta TVC = P_{vi}(\Delta VI).$$

As indicated above, $MC = \Delta TVC$ for a 1-unit change in output, or if output changes by several units, then

$$MC = \frac{\Delta TVC}{\Delta Q}.$$

But since $\Delta TVC = P_{vi}(\Delta VI)$, we have

$$MC = \frac{P_{vi}(\Delta VI)}{\Delta Q} = P_{vi}\left(\frac{\Delta VI}{\Delta Q}\right).$$

In Chapter 7, marginal product (MP) was defined as the change in output attributable to a change in variable input, or $MP = \Delta Q/\Delta VI$. It follows, therefore, that

$$MC = P_{vi}\left(\frac{1}{MP}\right).$$

Marginal cost is of central interest because it reflects those costs over which the firm has the most direct control in the short run. More particularly, MC indicates the amount of cost which can be "saved" by reducing output by 1 unit or, alternatively, the amount of additional cost which will be incurred by increasing production by 1 unit. Average cost data do not reveal this valuable bit of cost knowledge.

Now let us use these definitions to investigate the behavior of a firm's costs for a variety of production functions. Specifically, we shall examine the total, average, and marginal cost functions for each of the following types of short-run production functions:

1. $Q = a + bX + cX^2$ (increasing returns to variable input).
2. $Q = a + bX$ (constant returns to variable input).

3. $Q = a + bX - cX^2$ (decreasing returns to variable input).
4. $Q = a + bX + cX^2 - dX^3$ (increasing and decreasing returns to variable input).

Here Q is the quantity of output and X the units of variable input.

Cost Behavior under Increasing Returns to Variable Input

When a firm's production function exhibits increasing returns to variable input, each additional unit of variable input adds more to total output than does the previous unit. Graphically, then, the production function increases at an increasing rate and has, in the simplest case, the general equation $Q = a + bX + cX^2$, where $a = 0$, provided that variable input (X) is essential for any output (Q) to be produced. Figure 8-1(a) illustrates this type of production function. The corresponding marginal and average product functions are shown in Fig. 8-1(b).

As previously indicated, a firm's fixed inputs, not being easily susceptible to change in the short run, give rise to a constant amount of cost. Hence, graphically, the firm's *TFC* function is a horizontal line, reflecting the fact that *TFC* does not vary with the quantity of output—as depicted in Fig. 8-1(c). Note that, in drawing the *TFC* curve, costs (in dollars) are plotted on the vertical axis and the quantity of output is on the horizontal axis. Algebraically, the dollar amount of *TFC* can be represented by a constant, say a, making the general equation for the total fixed cost function

$$TFC = a.$$

The total variable cost (TVC) function gets its shape directly from the production function. To illustrate the tie between the production function and TVC, consider the behavior of TVC as successive units of variable input per period of time are added to the given amount of fixed inputs. Suppose that the price of variable input is \$100 per unit. From Fig. 8-1(a) it can be seen that employing 1 unit of variable input with the given fixed input will yield an output of Q_1 units; this translates into TVC of \$100 for Q_1 units of output [Fig. 8-1(c)]. Similarly, employing 2 units of variable input yields Q_2 units of output and results in TVC of \$200. Note that in panel (a) the marginal product of the second unit of variable input is larger than the marginal product of the first unit (distance $Q_1 Q_2 >$ distance $O Q_1$) in accordance with increasing returns to the usage of variable input. Adding the third unit of variable input causes the quantity of output to increase even faster to Q_3 units (distance $Q_2 Q_3 >$ distance $Q_1 Q_2$), and TVC at Q_3 is \$300. When the fourth unit of variable input per period of time is employed, output rises by yet a greater increment to Q_4 units (distance $Q_3 Q_4 >$ distance $Q_2 Q_3$), and TVC becomes \$400. From Figs. 8-1(a) and (c) it is apparent that when the quantity of output increases at an increasing rate, TVC must necessarily increase at a decreasing

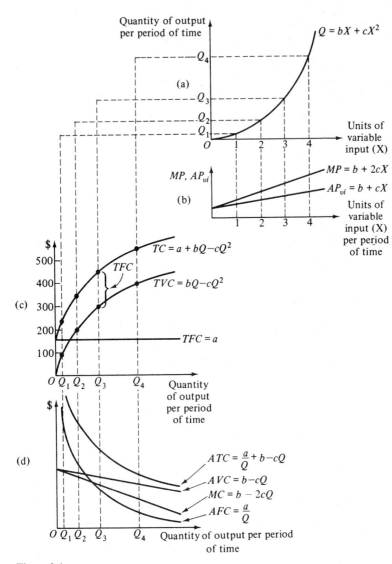

Figure 8-1
Production and cost behavior for an increasing-returns-to-variable-input situation

rate. With each additional unit of variable input, TVC rises by a constant amount equal to the price per unit of variable input, yet the associated increases in output get larger and larger owing to the rising productivity of additional variable input. To put it another way, when increasing returns to variable input characterize the production function, the quantity of output rises faster than does total variable cost. The simplest equation for representing *TVC* which captures the properties of such cost behavior is

$$TVC = bQ - cQ^2.$$

[It must be emphasized that while the equations for the production function $(Q = bX + cX^2)$ and the *TVC* function $(TVC = bQ - cQ^2)$ are very similar in form, the values of the constants *b* and *c* in the production function *are not equal* to the values of *b* and *c* in the *TVC* equation—except in the rarest of coincidences.] Notice that *TVC* equals zero at zero output and that the *TVC* function begins at the origin. Also, the greater is the usage of variable input, the greater is both the quantity of output and the level of total variable costs.

Given that $TC = TFC + TVC$, the total cost curve is found by vertically summing the *TFC* and *TVC* functions. The equation for the total cost function in this case is

$$TC = a + bQ - cQ^2,$$

where *a* represents the *TFC* component of *TC* and $bQ - cQ^2$ represents the *TVC* component. From Fig. 8-1(c), it can be seen that the shapes of the *TVC* and *TC* curves are identical. At every rate of output their slopes are equal and the two curves are separated by a constant vertical distance equal to the amount of *TFC*. At zero output, $TVC = 0$ and $TC = TFC$.

The *AFC* curve decreases continually as the quantity of output increases —as indicated in Fig. 8-1(d). Its equation is

$$AFC = \frac{TFC}{Q} = \frac{a}{Q}.$$

As explained earlier, the decline in *AFC* derives from the spreading of *TFC* over a greater number of units of output. Geometrically speaking, the *AFC* curve is a rectangular hyperbola, meaning that the curve approaches the vertical and horizontal axes asymptotically. In addition, were we to pick any point on the *AFC* curve, draw lines perpendicular to the two axes, and calculate the area of the resulting rectangle, this area will be the same irrespective of the point chosen. Why? Because this area measures $AFC \times Q$ and because $AFC \times Q = TFC = $ a constant value.

The nature and behavior of average variable cost can be deduced from the total variable cost function. When the production function exhibits increasing returns to variable input and *TVC* is represented by the equation $TVC = bQ - cQ^2$, then

$$AVC = \frac{TVC}{Q} = \frac{bQ - cQ^2}{Q} = b - cQ.$$

The *AVC* curve corresponding to this type of production function is shown in Fig. 8-1(d). The significant point here is that increasing returns to variable input cause unit variable costs to *fall* as output increases. That this is so can be verified by means of the relationship between AVC and the production function:

$$AVC = P_{vi}\left(\frac{1}{AP_{vi}}\right).$$

Given increasing returns to variable input, the average productivity of variable input rises as more units of variable input are added [see Fig. 8-1(b)]. As AP_{vi} goes up (and provided the price of variable input does not change), then AVC must necessarily fall.

The average total cost function can be derived by dividing the equation for total cost by the units of output, obtaining

$$ATC = \frac{TC}{Q} = \frac{a + bQ - cQ^2}{Q} = \frac{a}{Q} + b - cQ.$$

The equation for ATC could just as well have been found by adding together the equation for AFC (a/Q) and the equation for AVC $(b - cQ)$ since $ATC = AFC + AVC$. The shape of the average total cost curve is obtained by vertically summing the AFC and AVC curves at every rate of output, as illustrated in Fig. 8-1(d). Here, ATC declines throughout because both AFC and AVC are decreasing. Observe that the ATC curve is asymptotic to the AVC curve. Why? The difference between ATC and AVC is the amount of AFC. At low rates of output AFC is relatively large, and the values of ATC are well in excess of the AVC values; however, as output increases, the values of AFC decline and the values of ATC more closely approach the values of AVC. Thus, while ATC always exceeds AVC, the greater the quantity of output, the smaller the value of AFC and the smaller the distance between the AVC is not unique to cost behavior in the instance of increasing returns to variable input but rather is a general and necessary trait for all types of production and cost situations.

The marginal cost function is obtained by finding the first derivative of the TC function (or TVC function—the result is the same in either event). If $TC = a + bQ - cQ^2$ and $TVC = bQ - cQ^2$, then

$$MC = \frac{dTC}{dQ} = \frac{dTVC}{dQ} = b - 2cQ.$$

The MC curve is, therefore, both linear and downsloping, as shown in Fig. 8-1(d). The MC curve decreases here because under increasing returns to variable input the marginal product of successive units of variable input rises. In other words, since

$$MC = P_{vi}\left(\frac{1}{MP}\right),$$

it follows that if MP is increasing and if P_{vi} remains constant, then MC must necessarily be falling. Moreover, note that the slope of the MC curve $(-2c)$ is twice as large as the slope of the AVC curve $(-c)$; both curves originate at a common point (b). Further, the value of MC at a given output is equal to the slopes of the TVC curve and the TC curve at that output rate.

The salient feature of increasing returns to variable input is that the efficiency with which resource inputs are used rises as the quantity of output increases, with the concomitant result of declining unit costs. In other words, the larger the quantity produced, the lower the costs of each unit—clearly, a most favorable set of circumstances. But unfortunately for the firm, increasing returns to variable input are not likely to be realized except at output rates well below the normal operating range.

Table 8-1 presents hypothetical production and cost data for a production function exhibiting increasing returns to variable input. (Before proceeding, you would do well to examine the cost figures in this table to be sure that you fully understand how each one is computed.)

Table 8-1   Hypothetical Production and Cost Data for Increasing Returns to Variable Input

Units of Fixed Input	Units of Variable Input	Quantity of Output	TFC[a]	TVC[b]	TC	AFC	AVC	ATC	"Average" MC
2	0	0	$100	$ 0	$100	—	$ 0	—	
2	1	10	100	40	140	$10.00	4.00	$14.00	$4.00
2	2	25	100	80	180	4.00	3.20	7.20	2.67
2	3	45	100	120	220	2.22	2.67	4.89	2.00
2	4	70	100	160	260	1.43	2.29	3.72	1.60
2	5	100	100	200	300	1.00	2.00	3.00	1.33

[a]The price of fixed input is assumed to be $50 per unit.
[b]The price of variable input is assumed to be $40 per unit.

Cost Behavior under Constant Returns to Variable Input

When a firm's production process is characterized by constant returns to variable input, each additional unit of variable input used per period of time adds the same amount to total output as the preceding unit. The quantity of output increases at a constant rate, and the production function is linear. The related MP and AP_{vi} functions are horizontal lines, indicating that the values of MP and AP_{vi} are the same for every unit of variable input. The general equation for the production function is

$$Q = a + bX,$$

where $a = 0$. The related equations for marginal and average product are

$$MP = b, \qquad AP_{vi} = b,$$

where b is a constant equal to the slope of the production function. Panels

(a) and (b) in Fig. 8-2 illustrate the family of product curves corresponding to a constant-returns-to-variable-input situation.

The *TFC* curve for a production process displaying constant returns to variable input is again a horizontal line [see Fig. 8-2(c)]. As before, this is because *TFC* is determined by the prices and quantities of fixed input, not by the relationship between variable input and output. The equation for total

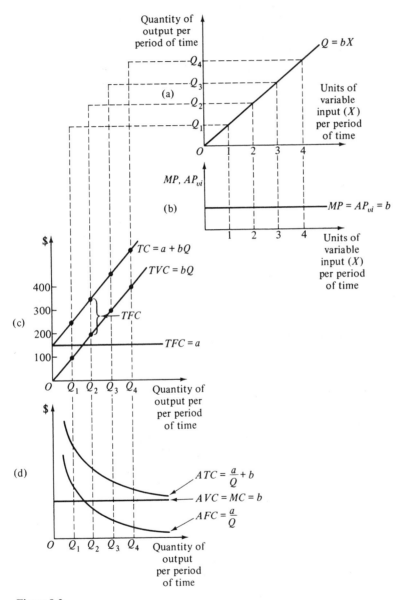

Figure 8-2
Production and cost behavior for a constant-returns-to-variable-input situation

fixed cost thus remains

$$TFC = a,$$

where a is a given amount of dollars and is determined by the amount and prices of fixed inputs present.

To discuss the shape of the TVC curve given constant returns to variable input, consider how TVC and output are affected when additional variable input is used. From Fig. 8-2(a) it can be seen that combining 1 unit of variable input per period of time with the given amount of fixed inputs will yield an output of Q_1 units; accordingly, the total variable cost of Q_1 units is \$100, as shown in Fig. 8-2(c). Combining 2 units of variable input with the available fixed input yields an output of Q_2 units [Figure 8-2(a)]; the marginal product of the second unit of variable input equals the marginal product of the first unit ($OQ_1 = Q_1Q_2$) in accordance with the condition of constant returns to variable input [Fig. 8-2(b)]. TVC at Q_2 units of output is \$200 [Fig. 8-2(c)]. Adding the third unit of variable input causes the quantity of output to rise to Q_3 ($OQ_1 = Q_1Q_2 = Q_2Q_3$), and the total variable cost of Q_3 units is \$300. And so it goes. Each additional unit of variable input produces an equivalent rise in output (MP is constant), and TVC rises by a constant amount (\$100 in this case) with each unit increase in variable input. Plainly then, the TVC curve is *linear*, begins from the origin, and has the general equation

$$TVC = bQ.$$

The TVC function is illustrated in Fig. 8-2(c).

Since $TC = TFC + TVC$, the shape of the total cost curve is derived by vertically adding the TFC and TVC curves [see Fig. 8-2(c)]. It follows that the equation for TC may be found by adding together the expressions for TFC and TVC:

$$TFC = a, \qquad TVC = bQ,$$
$$TC = TFC + TVC = a + bQ.$$

Since all changes in total cost are solely attributable to changes in variable cost items, the shape of the TC curve is identical to the shape of the TVC curve. Given constant returns to variable input, the TC curve is therefore a linear function with a slope equivalent to the slope of TVC; the two curves are separated by a constant vertical distance equal to the amount of TFC. At zero output, $TVC = 0$ and $TC = TFC$.

As before, the AFC curve decreases continually as the quantity of output increases, and it assumes the shape of a rectangular hyperbola. Its equation is

$$AFC = \frac{TFC}{Q} = \frac{a}{Q}.$$

The reasoning is the same as previously. As a constant value (TFC) is divided by an increasing value (Q), the resulting values (AFC) get smaller and smaller, as depicted in Fig. 8-2(d).

The equation for AVC can be derived from the expression for total variable cost as follows:

$$AVC = \frac{TVC}{Q} = \frac{bQ}{Q} = b.$$

This means that with constant returns to variable input AVC is a constant value. That this is so can be confirmed from the relationship

$$AVC = P_{vi}\left(\frac{1}{AP_{vi}}\right).$$

With constant returns to variable input, AP_{vi} is also a constant, and assuming a given price for variable input, AVC must necessarily be a constant. To illustrate, suppose that variable input costs \$100 per unit and that AP_{vi} is fixed at 50 units of output. Then,

$$AVC = P_{vi}\left(\frac{1}{AP_{vi}}\right) = \$100\left(\frac{1}{50}\right) = \$2,$$

and it is \$2 at each and every output rate. Graphically, the AVC curve is a horizontal line with a height of b dollars above the horizontal axis [see Fig. 8-2(d)].

Since, by definition, average total cost equals total cost divided by the units of output, the equation for ATC under conditions of constant returns to variable input becomes

$$ATC = \frac{TC}{Q} = \frac{a + bQ}{Q} = \frac{a}{Q} + b.$$

Observe that since a/Q is AFC and b is AVC, the equation for ATC can be found by adding the equation for AFC to the equation for AVC. Also, because AVC is a fixed value when there are constant returns to variable input, the associated ATC curve assumes a shape precisely identical to that of the AFC curve and lies above it by the amount of AVC [see Fig. 8-2(d)]. The ATC curve is, therefore, asymptotic to the horizontal AVC curve and decreases throughout.

With marginal cost being equal to the first derivative of the TC function (or the TVC function) and the equation for TC being $TC = a + bQ$, the equation for MC becomes

$$MC = \frac{dTC}{dQ} = \frac{dTVC}{dQ} = b,$$

where b is a constant. That MC is a constant value when constant returns to variable input prevail follows from its relationship with marginal product:

$$MC = P_{vi}\left(\frac{1}{MP}\right).$$

With constant returns, MP is itself a fixed value, and if P_{vi} is also a given, then MC becomes the product of a constant times a constant. For example, if $P_{vi} = \$100$ and if the marginal product of every additional unit of variable input equals 50 units of output, then

$$MC = P_{vi}\left(\frac{1}{MP}\right) = \$100\left(\frac{1}{50}\right) = \$2.$$

Thus, with constant returns to variable input, $MC = AVC = b$, and the MC curve is a horizontal line. The value of MC equals the slope of the TVC and TC curves.

Figure 8-2(d) illustrates how the unit cost curves are related to one another. Table 8-2 presents hypothetical production and cost data for a pro-

Table 8-2 Hypothetical Production and Cost Data for Constant Returns to Variable Input

Units of Fixed Input	Units of Variable Input	Quantity of Output	TFC^a	TVC^b	TC	AFC	AVC	ATC	"Average" MC
2	0	0	$100	$ 0	$100	—	$ 0	—	
2	1	10	100	40	140	$10.00	4.00	$14.00	$4.00
2	2	20	100	80	180	5.00	4.00	9.00	4.00
2	3	30	100	120	220	3.33	4.00	7.33	4.00
2	4	40	100	160	260	2.50	4.00	6.50	4.00
2	5	50	100	200	300	2.00	4.00	6.00	4.00

^{a}The price of fixed input is assumed to be $50 per unit.
^{b}The price of variable input is assumed to be $40 per unit.

duction function exhibiting constant returns to variable input. Observe that the greater the output rate, the lower is average total cost. This occurs because total fixed costs are being spread over a larger volume of output and AVC and MC are constant. A number of industry studies show that constant MC and AVC and slowly declining ATC typify many production processes over the "normal" range of output (more about this presently).

Cost Behavior under Decreasing Returns to Variable Input

With a production process characterized by decreasing returns to variable input, the marginal product of variable input declines as output rises. Each additional unit of variable input used per period of time with the available fixed input adds less to total output than the previous unit, and the quantity of output increases at a decreasing rate. Both the marginal and average product functions are downsloping. The product curves are illustrated in panels (a) and (b) of Fig. 8-3.

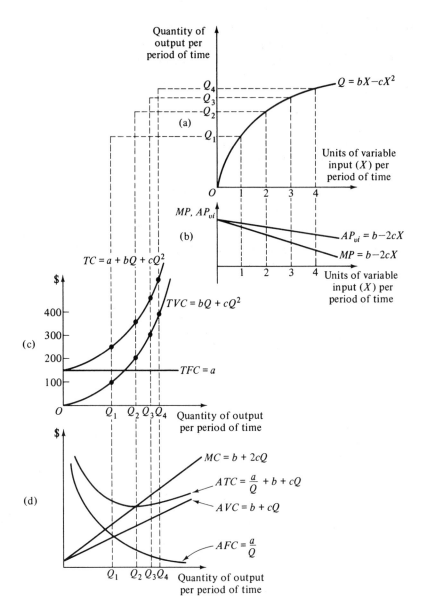

Figure 8-3
Production and cost behavior for a decreasing-returns-to-variable-input situation

As is the case with all types of short-run production functions, the *TFC* curve associated with decreasing returns to variable input is again a horizontal line having the equation

$$TFC = a,$$

where a is a constant [see Fig. 8-3(c)]. *TFC* is a constant dollar value because neither the amount nor the cost of the available fixed inputs is affected by the nature of the returns to variable input embodied in the production function.

However, the shape of the *TVC* curve is very definitely affected by the nature of the underlying production function. Letting $P = \$100$ per unit, each additional unit of variable input employed will cause *TVC* to rise by $100. From Fig. 8-3(a) it is evident that combining 1 unit of variable input per period of time with the given fixed input yields an output of Q_1 units. This translates into a *TVC* of $100 at an output of Q_1 units, as shown in Fig. 8-3(c). Combining 2 units of variable input with the fixed input produces a less-than-proportional increase in output to Q_2 units ($OQ_1 > Q_1Q_2$), and *TVC* becomes $200 at an output of Q_2. Adding the third unit of variable input yields yet a smaller increment in the quantity of output ($Q_1Q_2 > Q_2Q_3$); *TVC* rises to $300. Successive additions of variable input produce similar results. The declining marginal product of variable input causes output to rise ever more slowly, while *TVC* increases by a given amount ($100 in this example) with each unit increase in variable input. Such behavior produces a *TVC* curve which increases at an increasing rate with output, as indicated in Fig. 8-3(c). The simplest equation to represent this type of function is

$$TVC = bQ + cQ^2.$$

Since $TC = TFC + TVC$, the equation for *TC* under conditions of decreasing returns to variable input becomes

$$TC = a + bQ + cQ^2.$$

The graph of this function, shown in Fig. 8-3(c), starts from the point where the *TFC* curve intersects the vertical axis and thereafter increases at an increasing rate. The shape of the *TC* curve is identical to the shape of the *TVC* and lies above it by a constant amount equal to *TFC*.

As is the case irrespective of the character of the production function, the *AFC* curve is a decreasing function that is asymptotic to the horizontal axis [see Fig. 8-3(d)]. Its equation is

$$AFC = \frac{TFC}{Q} = \frac{a}{Q}.$$

The nature and behavior of *AVC* are easily established. Since the equation for *TVC* is

$$TVC = bQ + cQ^2,$$

the equation for *AVC* becomes

$$AVC = \frac{TVC}{Q} = \frac{bQ + cQ^2}{Q} = b + cQ.$$

The graph of the *AVC* function is linear with a positive slope equal to the value of *c*. Thus, when the production function exhibits decreasing returns to variable input, *AVC* rises as output is increased. That *AVC* rises throughout can be confirmed by examining the expression

$$AVC = P_{vi}\left(\frac{1}{AP_{vi}}\right).$$

With decreasing returns to variable input, AP_{vi} decreases over the entire output range [see Fig. 8-3(b)]. Assuming a constant price for variable input, as output is increased the smaller and smaller values of AP_{vi} result in larger and larger values of *AVC*. Aside from the mathematics of the situation, the logic for rising *AVC* is compelling. When the production function displays decreasing returns to variable input, both the marginal and average productivity of variable inputs decline as output is increased. Hence, the efficiency of variable input falls as more variable input is added and as output rises. Lower efficiency in the usage of variable input clearly implies higher variable costs per unit of output.

Since $ATC = TC/Q$, the equation for average total cost is

$$ATC = \frac{TC}{Q} = \frac{a + bQ + cQ^2}{Q} = \frac{a}{Q} + b + cQ.$$

However, the graph of *ATC* is somewhat less obvious. Whereas the *AFC* component of *ATC* (a/Q) decreases as the quantity of output rises, the *AVC* component of *ATC* ($b + cQ$) rises continuously as output rises. Hence, whether *ATC* rises or falls hinges upon the decreases in *AFC* relative to the increases in *AVC*. At low output rates the declines in *AFC* are larger than the increases in *AVC*, so the *ATC* curve declines up to an output of Q_2 units. At Q_2 the decline in *AFC* is exactly offset by the increase in *AVC*, and *ATC* is a minimum. Beyond Q_2, the increases in *AVC* override the decreases in *AFC*, with the result that the *ATC* curve turns upward. But despite the U-shaped behavior of *ATC*, the *ATC* curve is still asymptotic to the *AVC* curve for the reason previously given.

A production function displaying decreasing returns to variable input is associated with a rising marginal cost function. Given that $TC = a + bQ + cQ^2$ (and that $TVC = bQ + cQ^2$),

$$MC = \frac{dTC}{dQ} = \frac{dTVC}{dQ} = b + 2cQ.$$

The graph of such an equation is a linear function with a positive slope equal to $2c$ [see Fig. 8-3(d)]. The increasing aspect of *MC* stems from its relationship to marginal product:

$$MC = P_{vi}\left(\frac{1}{MP}\right).$$

By definition, decreasing returns to variable input means that the marginal product of additional units of variable input is a declining, yet positive, value. With *MP* falling as output rises, *MC* must necessarily rise. Note that in this instance the slope of the *MC* curve (2*c*) is twice as great as the slope of the *AVC* curve (*c*). Also, the *MC* curve passes through the minimum point of the *ATC* curve. The latter property is an inherent feature of the mathematical relationship between average and marginal values. *MC* is the additional cost for 1 unit of output; *ATC* is the average for all the units produced up to that point. As long as *MC* is below *ATC*, *ATC* is pulled down by the lower cost of the additional output. When the cost of an additional unit is greater than the average cost of previous units, *ATC* is pulled up by the higher cost of the incremental output. At the point of intersection of *MC* and *ATC*, *ATC* has ceased declining but has not begun to rise; this, then, is the minimum point on the *ATC* curve.

A production-cost structure predicated on decreasing returns to variable input (as in Fig. 8-3) is not likely to typify a firm's entire output capacity. But decreasing returns to variable input are typical of production and cost behavior at near-capacity rates of output, because the closer capacity is approached, the harder it becomes to increase production without encountering the point of diminishing marginal returns; as this happens *MC*, *AVC*, and *ATC* will begin to rise.

Table 8-3 illustrates production and cost behavior for a situation characterized by decreasing returns to variable input throughout the indicated output range. Note that the patterns of change in the total and unit cost values parallel exactly the shapes of the cost curves in panels (c) and (d) of Fig. 8-3.

Table 8-3 Hypothetical Production and Cost Data for Decreasing Returns to Variable Input

Units of Fixed Input	Units of Variable Input	Quantity of Output	TFC[a]	TVC[b]	TC	AFC	AVC	ATC	"Average" MC
2	0	0	$100	$ 0	$100	—	$ 0	—	$ 2.00
2	1	20	100	40	140	$5.00	2.00	$7.00	2.50
2	2	36	100	80	180	2.78	2.22	5.00	3.33
2	3	48	100	120	220	2.08	2.50	4.58	5.00
2	4	56	100	160	260	1.79	2.86	4.65	10.00
2	5	60	100	200	300	1.67	3.33	5.00	

[a]The price of fixed input is assumed to be $50 per unit.
[b]The price of variable input is assumed to be $40 per unit.

Cost Behavior with Increasing and Decreasing Returns to Variable Input

As stated in Chapter 7, the most general and pervasive type of short-run production function is the one illustrated in Fig. 8-4(a) having the general equation

$$Q = a + bX + cX^2 - dX^3,$$

and having MP and AP_{vi} functions, as shown in Fig. 8-4(b). Up to X_1 units of variable input, output increases at an increasing rate. From X_1 to X_3 units of variable input, output increases at a decreasing rate.

Again, the TFC curve is a horizontal line with the equation $TFC = a$ [see Fig. 8-4(c)]. The TVC curve for this type of production function combines the shapes of the TVC curves for both increasing and decreasing returns to variable input. From panels (a) and (c) of Fig. 8-4 it can be seen that over the range of output where increasing returns to variable input prevail (O to Q_1) the TVC curve increases at a decreasing rate, whereas over the range of output where decreasing returns to variable input are encountered (Q_1 to Q_3) the TVC curve increases at an increasing rate. At the short-run capacity rate of output (Q_3) the slope of the TVC curve becomes vertical. The explanation for this behavior of TVC rests with the principle of diminishing marginal returns. Where the quantity of output increases at an increasing rate, marginal product is also increasing, and smaller and smaller increases in variable inputs are required to produce successive units of output. This means that TVC will increase by progressively smaller amounts as output rises. But when the point of diminishing marginal returns is encountered and marginal product begins to decline, it becomes necessary to use increasingly larger amounts of variable input to obtain the same-sized output gain. Total variable costs therefore increase at an increasing rate over this output range. The general equation for a TVC curve with these traits is

$$TVC = bQ - cQ^2 + dQ^3.$$

Total cost equals the sum of TFC and TVC at each output rate and has the equation

$$TC = a + bQ - cQ^2 + dQ^3,$$

where a equals the amount of TFC and the expression $bQ - cQ^2 + dQ^3$ equals the amount of TVC at each value of Q. At zero output, $TC = TFC$, and for each successive unit produced TC varies in precisely the same fashion and at precisely the same rate as does TVC. As indicated in Fig. 8-4(c), the TC curve is the same shape as the TVC curve but lies above it by the amount of TFC.

The graph and equation of the AFC curve are identical to the preceding cases and are shown in Fig. 8-4(d). The behavior of AVC can be determined from TVC. Since $TVC = bQ - cQ^2 + dQ^3$, the average variable cost equa-

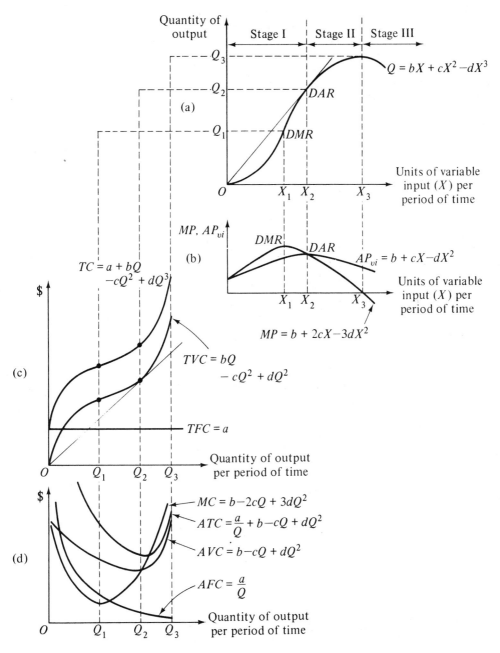

Figure 8-4
Production and cost behavior where both increasing and decreasing returns to variable input are present

tion is

$$AVC = \frac{TVC}{Q} = \frac{bQ - cQ^2 + dQ^3}{Q} = b - cQ + dQ^2.$$

When plotted on a graph, an equation of this type produces a curve which declines initially, reaches a minimum, and then increases. The AVC curve is therefore U-shaped, as shown in Fig. 8-4(d). The rationale for this behavior of AVC can be seen from its relationship with AP_{vi}:

$$AVC = P_{vi}\left(\frac{1}{AP_{vi}}\right).$$

Given a fixed price for units of variable input, when AP_{vi} is rising [Fig. 8-4(b)] AVC must be falling; when AP_{vi} is declining AVC must be rising. Minimum AVC (an output of Q_2) corresponds to the output rate where AP_{vi} is maximum (X_2 units of variable input). At Q_2 the point of diminishing average returns is encountered, and the stage II phase of production begins. Thus, stage I rates of output correspond to the output range where AVC is declining, whereas stage II quantities correspond to the range of output where AVC is rising.

As previously indicated, ATC is calculated by dividing total cost by the quantity of output—or, more simply, by adding AFC and AVC at each rate of output. Here the equation for ATC is

$$ATC = \frac{TC}{Q} = \frac{a + bQ - cQ + dQ^3}{Q} = \frac{a}{Q} + b - cQ + dQ^2,$$

where a/Q is the AFC component of ATC and $b - cQ + dQ^2$ is the AVC component of ATC. As before, the vertical distance between ATC and AVC reflects the value of AFC at any output. Because AFC decreases as output expands, the distance between ATC and AVC gets progressively smaller. Thus, the ATC curve is asymptotic to the AVC curve and U-shaped [see Fig. 8-4(d)]. Note that the minimum point on the ATC curve corresponds to a quantity of output in stage II. This result is in accord with the rationale for operating in stage II presented in Chapter 7. Also, the minimum point of the ATC curve is at a larger volume of output than is the minimum point of the AVC curve. Why? ATC continues to fall beyond the output where AVC is minimum because the continuing declines in AFC more than offset the slight increases in AVC. As output expands further, however, the increases in AVC begin to override the decreases in AFC, and ATC turns upward. The minimum point on the ATC curve defines the most efficient and economical rate of operation in the short run.

Marginal cost can be determined by calculating the first derivative of the equation for either TC or TVC:

$$MC = \frac{dTC}{dQ} = \frac{dTVC}{dQ} = b - 2cQ + 3dQ^2.$$

The *MC* function in this instance is a quadratic equation which, when graphed, assumes the U-shape shown in Fig. 8-4(d). The curvature of the *MC* function reflects its relationship with marginal product. Since

$$MC = P_{vi}\left(\frac{1}{MP}\right),$$

then as long as *MP* is rising, *MC* must be declining. But when diminishing marginal returns set in and *MP* is falling, then the marginal cost of the extra unit of output is rising. Hence, assuming a constant price for variable input, increasing returns to variable input result in declining marginal costs, and decreasing returns are associated with rising marginal costs. Marginal cost is minimum at the point of diminishing marginal returns where *MP* is maximum (note that this quantity of output is in stage I). Furthermore, the *MC* curve intersects the *AVC* and *ATC* curves at their minimum points—a relationship of mathematical necessity.[10] As long as the cost of producing an additional unit is less than the average total cost of previously produced units, the newly computed values of *ATC* will fall, being pulled down by the lower *MC*. Similarly, when the cost of producing an additional unit is greater than the average total cost of the preceding units, the new value of *ATC* rises, being pulled up by the higher value of *MC*. It follows that *ATC* is minimum at the point of intersection of *MC* and *ATC*. By analogous reasoning the *MC* curve must pass through the minimum point of the *AVC* function.

Table 8-4 illustrates the patterns of change in the total and unit cost values for a production function having phases of both increasing and decreasing returns to variable input.

[10]The mathematical proof of this point is relatively simple and follows the procedure presented earlier in Mathematical Capsule 8. Let *TC* be some function of the quantity of output:

$$TC = f(Q).$$

Then, by definition,

$$MC = \frac{dTC}{dQ} = f'(Q) \quad \text{and} \quad ATC = \frac{f(Q)}{Q}.$$

For *ATC* to be a minimum value, it is necessary that the slope of the *ATC* curve be zero, which, in turn, requires that the derivative of the *ATC* equation be equal to zero:

$$\frac{dATC}{dQ} = \frac{Q \cdot f'(Q) - f(Q)}{Q^2} = 0.$$

For $dATC/dQ$ to equal zero, the numerator of the above expression must be zero, or

$$Q \cdot f'(Q) - f(Q) = 0.$$

This can be rewritten as

$$f'(Q) = \frac{f(Q)}{Q}.$$

Since $f'(Q) = MC$ and $f(Q)/Q = ATC$, then the output rate that makes *ATC* minimum is also the value of *Q* at which $MC = ATC$.

By analogous logic, it can be shown that $MC = AVC$ at the minimum point of the *AVC* curve when the equation for total variable cost is of the form $TVC = f(Q)$.

Table 8-4 Hypothetical Production and Cost Data for Increasing and Decreasing Returns to Variable Input

Units of Fixed Input	Units of Variable Input	Quantity of Output	TFC[a]	TVC[b]	TC	AFC	AVC	ATC	"Average" MC
2	0	0	$100	$ 0	$100	—	$ 0	—	
									$4.00
2	1	10	100	40	140	$10.00	4.00	$14.00	
									2.00
2	2	30	100	80	180	3.33	2.67	6.00	
									1.14
2	3	65	100	120	220	1.54	1.85	3.39	
									1.33
2	4	95	100	160	260	1.05	1.68	2.73	
									1.60
2	5	120	100	200	300	.83	1.67	2.50	
									2.00
2	6	140	100	240	340	.71	1.71	2.42	
									2.67
2	7	155	100	280	380	.65	1.81	2.46	
									4.00
2	8	165	100	320	420	.61	1.94	2.55	
									8.00
2	9	170	100	360	460	.59	2.12	2.71	

[a]The price of fixed input is assumed to be $50 per unit.
[b]The price of variable input is assumed to be $40 per unit.

APPLICATIONS CAPSULE

USING MARGINAL COST CONCEPTS TO DISPATCH ELECTRIC POWER

Electric utility firms have, for more than two decades, used marginal product-marginal cost concepts to generate and dispatch electric power in a more efficient, lower-cost manner. Southern Company, the nation's third largest utility, employs a load dispatching method that is designed to provide automatic, computerized control of all the company's power production and transmission facilities. The marginal cost of delivering additional kilowatts of electricity to Southern Company customers anywhere in the company's service area is continuously calculated; then, as electricity demand rises or falls at points throughout the system, computers transmit "raise" or "lower" impulses to the company's generating units and route the correct amount of electricity along the most economical transmission path to the end user.

Periodically, Southern Company engineers test the operating efficiency of every piece of power-generating equipment the company has in service. The purpose of the test is to determine how much fuel, labor, and other variable inputs are required to produce electricity with that unit and, subsequently, to calculate a production function for that generating unit. Experience has shown that revised production function equations must be calculated from time to time because normal wear and tear, maintenance problems, and mechanical efficiency vary over time and from generator to generator, depending on who manufactured it, when it was purchased, how long it has been in service, and the reliability with which it has performed. In other words, the production function for a given generating unit shifts by sufficiently large amounts over time to make it worthwhile to update the input-output equation. The equations for the production functions of each generating unit are then fed into the computer and combined with information as to fuel prices, wage rates, and other variable input prices to obtain marginal cost functions; from these, *MC* values can be calculated for a particular generating unit at whatever rate it is being operated.

In addition, because there is a loss of electricity in the course of "shipping" it through the transmission wires, Southern engineers make studies to determine the transmission loss coefficients from generating units to distribution substations. These, too, have to be updated several times a year since the transmission loss depends not only on the distance factor but also on the varying load characteristics of the system and changes in the transmission grid.

The marginal cost equations, together with the transmission loss coefficients, are the nucleus for computerized control of power generation and transmission. When, during the course of a day, the demand for electricity picks up, the computer system is programmed to compare the marginal costs of generation at each on-line unit and then to send impulses to raise the electricity output of the unit (or units) where *MC* is lowest. Simultaneously, another computer program analyzes the transmission loss coefficients to calculate how best to allocate the increased load on the transmission grid so as to minimize transmission loss to the many substations and end-user locations. In similar fashion, when electricity demand falls off (as work shifts end and businesses close at the end of the day), the dispatch system automatically sends impulses to reduce electricity generation at those power units where *MC* is highest and reroutes the remaining load to maintain maximum transmission economy and load-generation balance. At periods of peak demand, when on-line generating units are already operating at or near their minimum cost points, and assuming that water levels in Southern's dammed reservoirs are ample, the computer sends impulses to Southern's hydroelectric facilities to open the gates and generate enough power to get across the peak.

Southern's power dispatch control center is also equipped to forecast short-term loads for the next hour, day, or week. For example, weather data from all around Southern's four-state service area are fed into the computer network several times a day to help forecast heating and air-conditioning loads. The hourly, daily, and weekly forecasts of upcoming load demands are used to preplan the mix of generating units to put on line and those to put on standby, to schedule maintenance, and to determine whether to exchange blocks of electricity with neighboring utilities. For instance, approximately 15 minutes prior to the beginning of an hour, calculations as to the next hour's generating and transmission costs are made; this information is then compared immediately with similar information obtained from adjoining utilities having interconnections with Southern's transmission network. If it is determined that it would be more economical for Southern to buy a "block" of electricity from an adjacent company than to generate the electricity needed itself (because at the forecasted generating rates the other company will have lower *MC* than Southern), then an order is placed for that unit at a price set forth in the interchange agreement between the two companies. On the other hand, if Southern's marginal costs are lower than those of its neighbors, then it may agree to sell a block. The exchange of electricity among interconnected companies based upon marginal cost calculations is common throughout the electric utility industry.

As bigger and faster computers have become available, the functions of the dispatch system have been expanded to permit

1. Reductions in unnecessary "load-chasing," with resultant savings on maintenance;
2. Monitoring the current operating status of generating units, line flows, voltages, station breakers, and switches as a basis for assessing the prevailing degree of security (reliability) within the system;
3. Altering the dispatch criteria to allow for reducing power output at a particular facility because of unexpected air or thermal pollution, yet doing so in a way which entails the least increased costs to the system;
4. Operating hydro, steam, combustion, and nuclear generating units in a mix which seeks to minimize fuel costs; and
5. Monitoring temperatures, oil pressures, stream flows, and so on at unattended hydro stations to give early notification of potential troubles.

Questions for Discussion

1. Suppose you were the head of a group charged with developing estimates of the production functions and marginal cost functions for power generators. What data would you want, and how would you go about conducting a test of the equipment to obtain the production function?
2. What is your judgment as to how the *MC* of power output from hydroelectric units compares with the *MC* of coal-fired steam generators? Why? If a utility served an area where there were not many rivers and streams to dam up and thus it had only limited hydroelectric generating capability, would it be more economical to use the hydro units primarily for "peaking"—meeting the demand for electricity at peak periods? Why? What factors would you need to consider?

263
*Short-Run Cost
Functions in
the Real
World: the
Empirical
Evidence*

SHORT-RUN COST FUNCTIONS IN THE REAL WORLD: THE EMPIRICAL EVIDENCE

Economists have conducted a great many studies of the short-run cost functions of particular firms and industries. A wide variety of accounting, engineering, and econometric methods have been used to analyze historical cost and output data. Although both the methods employed and the data used suffer from a number of deficiencies, the results of these studies point consistently to one conclusion: *In the short run a linear TC function with constant marginal cost is the pattern that best seems to describe actual cost behavior over the "normal" operating range of output.* U-shaped marginal and average cost curves have been found to exist but seem to be less general than commonly thought. Table 8-5 summarizes the findings of a number of these studies.

Despite a lack of strong empirical confirmation for a U-shaped cost structure, there is still ample reason for asserting that the closer a firm approaches its short-run maximum rate of production, the greater becomes the pressure for rising marginal and average costs. As a firm attempts to squeeze more and more output from its production facilities, the chances increase that some wage premium for overtime will be incurred. If second and third shifts are used, the productivity of labor tends to be noticeably lower than on the day shift. Intensive use of equipment induces more breakdowns, leaves less time for maintenance, and induces production bottlenecks.

Table 8-5   Results of Empirical Studies of Short-Run Cost Functions

Name	*Type of Industry*	*Finding*
Lester (1946)	Manufacturing	*AVC* decreases up to capacity levels of output.
Hall and Hitch (1939)	Manufacturing	Majority have decreasing *MC*.
Johnston (1960)	Electricity, multiple-product food processing	"Direct" cost is a linear function of output, and *MC* is constant.
Dean (1936)	Furniture	Constant *MC* which failed to rise.
Dean (1941)	Leather belts	No significant increases in *MC*.
Dean (1941)	Hosiery	Constant *MC* which failed to rise.
Dean (1942)	Department store	Declining or constant *MC*, depending on the department within the store.
Ezekiel and Wylie (1941)	Steel	Declining *MC* but large variation.
Yntema (1940)	Steel	Constant *MC*.
Johnston (1960)	Electricity	*ATC* falls, then flattens, tending toward constant *MC* up to capacity.
Mansfield and Wein (1958)	Railways	Constant *MC*.

Source: A. A. Walters, "Production and Cost Functions," *Econometrica*, Vol. 31, No. 1 (January 1963), pp. 1–66.

Marginal, and perhaps obsolete, pieces of equipment may have to be brought on stream to achieve rated capacity. Hiring standards may have to be lowered to obtain the needed labor. Hence, in striving to push output toward the limit there is a tendency for a firm to utilize less efficient and/or marginal capital and labor inputs. As this occurs, increases in *MC* and *ATC* can be expected.

Evidence to this effect comes from McGraw-Hill's annual survey of manufacturing firms regarding (1) what percentage of production capacity is currently being used and (2) at what percentage they would prefer to operate. The preferred rates of operation usually range in the neighborhood of 90%, which strongly implies that many firms achieve maximum efficiency-minimum *ATC* at about 90% of the capacity rate of production. Apparently, producing within the 90 to 100% range would entail, as argued, rising marginal and average costs. It could be, therefore, that the failure of empirical studies

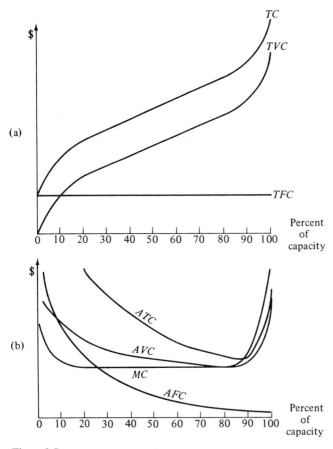

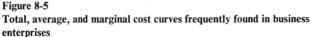

Figure 8-5
Total, average, and marginal cost curves frequently found in business enterprises

to detect rising unit costs is because the cost-output data of the firms and industries examined were, for the most part, below the output range where the pressures on capacity cause unit costs to increase.

If one combines the results of empirical cost studies with the implications of the McGraw-Hill survey, then the cost functions shown in Fig. 8-5 may represent a generalized cost structure for a number of firms and production processes. The properties of these cost functions suggest increasing returns to variable input at exceptionally low production rates, constant returns to variable input thereafter up to about 90 or 95% of capacity, and decreasing returns to variable input beyond the 90 to 95% level. Thus, while the marginal cost curve is U-shaped, the bottom of the U has a wide, flat range that encompasses the "normal" and "preferred" rates of output. AVC continues to fall over this entire range because MC is below AVC. This follows from the fact that the slope of TVC in the linear portion is a smaller value than the slope of a ray drawn from the origin of the diagram in Fig. 8-5(a) to the TVC curve; the former slope value equals MC, while the latter equals AVC.

COST-OUTPUT RELATIONSHIPS IN THE LONG RUN

In the long run all resource inputs are variable; a firm can alter its usage of major capital equipment, change top-management personnel, build new plant capacity, close down obsolete facilities, update its use of technology, or in any other way modify its production process and use of resources per period of time.

Such decisions are important because they determine the character of the short-run positions the firm will occupy in the future. For instance, before a firm makes a decision to change its productive potential, the firm is in a long-run position, with several options as to equipment, technology, and capital-labor mix. But once commitments are made and the new production capacity is installed, the firm's situation reverts to the short run, where the types and amounts of certain inputs are, for the time being, frozen.

Generally, a firm's long-run cost objective is to be in a position to produce the desired output at the lowest possible cost. This means adjusting its scale of production so as to be "the right size." Sometimes economies can be attained by dividing the production process into smaller production units. On other occasions lower unit costs can be achieved by enlarging the scale of production. In examining how efficiency and costs are affected by the scale of production, it is important to distinguish between *plants* and *firms* because the cost-efficiency advantages and disadvantages of each are different. Moreover, because there are no fixed inputs in the long run, the distinction between fixed and variable costs disappears—there are no TFC and AFC curves, and, in fact, we need look only at the nature and shape of the long-run average cost curve.

Suppose that technological constraints allow a firm the choice of constructing any one of three plant sizes: small, medium, and large. The short-run average cost curve for each of these plant sizes is represented by $SRAC_S$, $SRAC_M$, and $SRAC_L$ in Fig. 8-6. Whatever size plant the firm has currently, in the long run it can convert to or construct any one of these three plant scales. Obviously, the firm's choice of plant size is conditioned by its estimate of the production capacity needed to meet the demand for its products. For example, if the anticipated demand is OQ_1, the firm should elect to build the small-sized plant since it can produce OQ_1 units of output per period of time at a cost of AC_1, which is well below either the unit cost of the medium-sized plant (AC_2) or the unit cost of the large-sized plant (AC_3). If the expected demand is OQ_2, the medium-sized plant plainly offers the lowest unit cost. On the other hand, at a demand of OQ_3 the medium-and large-sized plants are equally efficient from a unit cost standpoint. Here the final choice of plants might depend on the forecasted *trend* in consumer demand, with an expectation of strong growth tipping the scales in favor of the large plant. Otherwise, the medium-sized plant is likely to be the more attractive because of its smaller capital investment requirements.

The portions of the three short-run average costs curves which identify the optimum plant size for a given output are indicated by the solid, scalloped line in Fig. 8-6. This line is called the *long-run average cost curve* (*LRAC*) and shows the minimum cost per unit of producing at each output rate when all resource inputs are variable and any desired scale of plant can be built. The dashed line segments of the *SRAC* curves all entail higher average costs at each output rate than is capable of being achieved with some other plant scale.

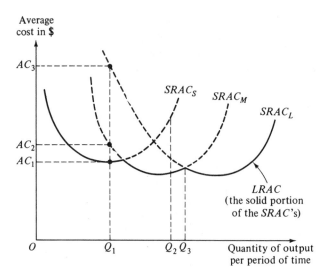

Figure 8-6 Long-run average cost curve when only three plant sizes are available

Usually, a firm will have more than just three plant sizes to choose from. When the number of alternative plant sizes approaches infinity, the $LRAC$ curve is an "envelope" of the short-run curves that is tangent to each of the short-run average cost curves (see Fig. 8-7). Here, again, the $LRAC$ curve should be interpreted as representing the *least unit cost attainable for a given output rate when the firm has time to change the rate of usage of any and all inputs.* Suppose the firm estimates that an output of OQ_1 is most desirable; then the plant represented by $SRAC_1$ is the most efficient because it can produce OQ_1 units at a lower cost per unit than can a plant of any other size. If consumer demand should expand sufficiently to warrant an output of OQ_2 units, the output of the plant represented by $SRAC_1$ could be increased to meet this demand in the short run. Nevertheless, in the long run the firm would prefer to construct the plant represented by $SRAC_2$ because this slightly larger plant is capable of producing OQ_2 units at a lower cost. Should the level of demand expand even further to OQ_3, although the plant represented by $SRAC_2$ is capable of producing OQ_3 units, the plant represented by $SRAC_3$ is preferable because of its ability to produce OQ_3 units at a lower average cost.

Of all the possible plant sizes, the one which is most efficient of all is the one whose $SRAC$ curve is tangent to the $LRAC$ curve at the *minimum point* of the $LRAC$ curve.[11] The plant capable of producing the product at the lowest unit cost of all the other plants is termed the *optimum plant*

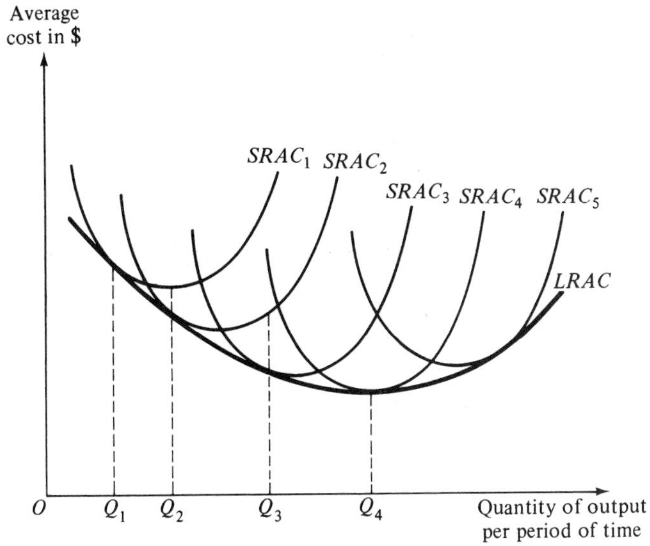

Figure 8-7
Long-run average cost curve for alternative plant sizes

[11]In the event that the $LRAC$ curve has a horizontal segment, there will be several plant sizes which qualify as the most efficient.

size. In Fig. 8-7 the optimum plant size is the one corresponding to $SRAC_4$ —no other plant is capable of producing the item at as low an average cost as is the plant associated with $SRAC_4$. It is in this sense that $SRAC_4$ represents the optimum plant size.

Observe that the *LRAC* curve is *not* tangent to the *SRAC* curves at their minimum points except in the one case of the optimum plant size. When the *LRAC* curve is decreasing (up to an outpout of OQ_4 in Fig. 8-7) the *LRAC* curve is tangent to the *SRAC* curves to the left of their minimum cost points. Therefore, for outputs smaller than OQ_4, it is more economical to produce the desired output by "underusing" a slightly larger plant operating at *less* than its minimum cost output than it is to construct a plant that will produce the desired output at the minimum point of its *SRAC* curve. However, when the *LRAC* curve is rising (past an output of OQ_4 in Fig. 8-7), the *LRAC* curve is tangent to the *SRAC* curves to the right of their minimum cost points. Hence, at outputs greater than OQ_4 it is more economical to produce the desired output by overusing a slightly smaller plant than it is to build a larger plant to produce the desired output at the minimum point of its *SRAC* cruve.

The U-shape of the *LRAC* curve clearly implies that up to a certain output constructing larger-sized plants results in greater efficiency and lower unit cost, but that beyond this output larger plants become progressively less efficient and entail higher unit costs. There are a host of factors which underlie *economies of scale* and *diseconomies of scale*.

Reasons for Economies of Scale at the Plant Level. At the plant level, lower unit costs basically derive from the economies of mass production. Up to a point, larger-operations allow greater subdivision of the production process and greater specialization in the use of resource inputs (labor, capital equipment, and supervision). Almost invariably, specialization along functional or task-specific lines maximizes the efficiency gains and cost savings to be had from "the learning curve" (or the "experience curve") and from machine execution of simplified work elements. For example, in the automobile industry the huge presses which stamp out automobile bodies in a matter of seconds, the automatic equipment which drills holes in the cylinder block in one operation, the large ovens which spray and bake paint on the car, the miles of computerized assembly lines, and the mechanized equipment used to transport materials and finished parts from station to station on the production floor are quite efficient. Moreover, the greater the volume of production and the more intensive the utilization of such facilities, the lower are the unit fixed costs per car because the fixed investment costs of capital-intensive techniques are being spread out over a larger number of units of output. This, together with the fact that the cost of purchasing and installing larger machines and equipment is usually *not* proportionately greater that the costs of smaller machines with less capacity, means that large-sized plants have an inherent ability to achieve lower average fixed costs, since they produce more units of output over which to spread proportionately smaller overhead costs.[12]

Centralizing and integrating manufacturing stages into a single continuous process offers another avenue for achieving scale economies at the plant level. For instance, steel firms have found it advantageous to have pig iron, raw steel, and semifinished steel products produced in one continuous operation in order to economize on reheating materials between phases of the production process.

Also, the larger a plant, the greater the opportunities for taking advantage of and utilizing by-products. Take the case of naphtha; naphtha is a by-product of producing coke from coal and can be commercially marketed by steel plants having a large enough coking facility to make the capture of naphtha worthwhile. Other industries where by-products come into play include petroleum refining, meat packing, chemicals, and paper products. The advantage of building on a scale large enough to capture by-products is that, by gaining salable output which otherwise is waste, firms have added revenues to apply against production costs associated with the primary product.

Large-scale plants are in a position to take advantage of quantity discounts on their purchases of raw materials and utility services. Similarly, larger plants can realize transportation savings by instituting their own shipping.

Eventually, of course, plants can be enlarged to the point where all economies of scale are taken full advantage of; larger plants then bring no additional savings in unit costs. It is here that the minimum level of the *LRAC* curve for plants is reached. Whether the *LRAC* curve begins to rise immediately with further increases in plant size or whether it has a flat portion before turning upward varies from industry to industry, depending on return-to-scale considerations and whether an industry's production technology requires large and indivisible units of capital input for low-cost production. Given the apparent prevalence of constant returns to scale, the *LRAC* curve is likely to have a flat bottom, thereby giving rise to a number of optimum-sized plants, each capable of producing at the lowest achievable unit cost. But there can be little doubt that, at some juncture, continued increases in plant size will produce diseconomies and cause *LRAC* to rise.

Generally, the production units in aircraft, electric power production,

[12]One of the major reasons for lower electric rates during the 1950s and 1960s was the substantial savings in investment costs which electric utility firms realized by increasing generating unit sizes from 40 megawatts to 60, 80, 120, 150, and 250 mw. As of 1976, a generating plant with two 300-mw coal-fired units could be installed for an investment of about $330 per kilowatt ($198 million total); doubling the size to two 600-mw units involved an investment of about $268 per kilowatt; and doubling again to two 1200-mw units entailed an investment of approximately $245 per kilowatt. However, past sizes of 800 to 900 mw, there were offsets against part of the investment savings because of higher transmission and maintenance costs and because of the need to maintain larger reserve margins as a hedge against unexpected breakdowns. Thus, the net savings associated with an increase in size from 880 mw to 1000 mw was only about $3 per kilowatt.

ECONOMIES OF SCALE IN THE PIPELINE BUSINESS

The operation of oil and natural gas pipelines typically entails substantial economies of scale. According to studies made by Exxon, the relative costs of oil pipelines fall rapidly as the diameter of the pipeline increases—as shown in the diagram.

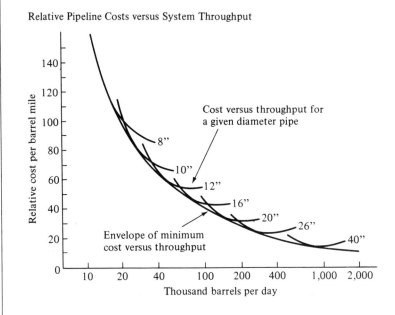

Relative Pipeline Costs versus System Throughput

The scale economies in the pipeline business are so large that they extend the efficient size beyond the level which a single company may be able to utilize. As a result, most interstate pipelines in the United States are owned by more than one company and the same pipeline system is often jointly used by many companies, owners, and nonowners. This joint use allows the most efficient-size pipeline to be built and full advantage to be taken of scale economies. It has also resulted in interstate pipelines being designated as "common carriers" subject to regulation by the Interstate Commerce Commission (ICC).

The presence of large economies of scale has dictated a number of operating practices. For example, in the case of oil pipelines, owners may require throughput guarantees or some other provision for the recovery of costs incurred before they will connect a new shipper to the system. The cost of a new connection may include laying a pipeline to the new shipper or installing new metering facilities to account for shipments or building additional working tankage. Throughput guarantees commit the shipper who is requesting the connection to either ship sufficient volumes or pay sufficient tariffs to provide some reasonable assurance that the added investment by the pipeline owner will be paid off. The ICC has authority to address any abuses, including the prevention of excessive throughput guarantees. Small nonowner firms are guaranteed access to pipelines on an equal basis with large owner-users and thus crude and product transportation is available to producers, refiners, and marketers alike.

Pipeline practices such as minimum tender requirements are dictated by considerations of efficiency. Crude oils vary greatly in quality, as do the different types of refined products. To minimize mixing and contamination at the interface between sequential batches of crude or product, the pipeline sets minimum batch sizes. When a full batch is accumulated, it is pumped through the pipeline.

Whenever common carrier pipeline capacity is inadequate to meet volumes tendered, government regulations require that available capacity be allocated equitably. Pipeline proration rules allocate capacity in proportion to recent shipments or current tenders of new shippers and historic shippers alike. Deviation from the pipeline's proration rules in favor of an owner company is a violation of the law. Under ICC regulations and the common carrier status of the interstate pipelines, users have the right to appeal for relief to the ICC if they feel they have been treated unfairly.

Pipeline tariffs are regulated by the ICC and have fallen steadily since the early 1950s, mainly because new technology has allowed larger and larger diameter pipelines with their resultant economies of scale and greatly reduced costs. According to ICC statistics, the average industry revenue per barrel moved 1000 miles fell from 65 cents in 1955 to 50 cents in 1971.

automobiles, steel, oil refining, paper, tires, glassware, aluminum, and inorganic chemicals all involve large-scale, multimillion-dollar plant investments. On the other hand, the manufacture of garments, mobile homes, shoes, furniture, sporting goods, and precision instruments, as well as printing and publishing, coal mining, and farming, can be efficiently conducted in relatively small production units.

Reasons for Diseconomies of Scale at the Plant Level. The more space over which a plant is spread, the greater the bottlenecks and costs of getting labor, materials, and semifinished goods from one place in the plant to another. Moreover, the larger the plant, the more likely that needed raw materials will have to be shipped from more distant suppliers, thereby driving up the transportation costs of incoming materials. Similarly, the larger the output of a plant, the farther distances outputs may have to be shipped to reach potential buyers, thereby raising the costs of transporting the product from the point of manufacture to the final consumer. To these must be added the growing difficulties of maintaining efficient supervision and coordination. As an extreme example, imagine the incredible problems that would beset General Motors were it to try to produce some 5 million Buicks, Cadillacs, Chevrolets, Oldsmobiles, and Pontiacs at a single plant site—the logistics of managing 850,000 employees, millions of component parts, and hundreds of thousands of inventoried cars would entail a colossal logjam and gross inefficiency.

Cost Behavior and Firm Size

Even after plants have been expanded to their most efficient size and all economies of plant size taken advantage of, there may arise additional cost-efficiency gains from putting a number of plants under common management. The separate units of a multiplant enterprise may perform the same kind of operation and thus be horizontally integrated—a chain of motels or a series of garment plants. Or the plants may be vertically integrated to perform successive phases of the same overall production process. Or they may involve the production of a number of unrelated commodities, as with conglomerate enterprises. In all three situations, opportunities for realizing scale economies may exist.

Reasons for Economies of Scale at the Firm Level. To begin with, putting several plants under common management economizes on top-management costs. Spreading the salaries of key executives and administrative staff over 5 million units of output a year instead of 1 million units lowers average cost. Second, multiproduct firms may derive a number of economic advantages from specializing in serving the full range of needs of a particular customer segment or market, or from using the same distribution channel to market their outputs, or from using a common technology to produce a number of different products. Third, there are mass-marketing economies associated with nationwide distribution systems and sales promotion compaigns which provide a more effective canvassing of markets and consumers per dollar spent.[13] For example, General Motors in selling 5 million cars annually can well afford to spend $90 million advertising its cars (a paltry advertising cost of only $18 per car), but for American Motors to spend $90 million on advertising to sell 300,000 cars ($300 per car) would place them at a distinct price disadvantage. Fourth, a large enterprise is better able to afford expert specialists for research, development, design, and production engineering, thereby keeping it in position to introduce new and

[13]This contention is documented in a study by William S. Comanor and Thomas A. Wilson, "Advertising and the Advantages of Size," *American Economic Review, Papers and Proceedings*, Vol. 59, No. 2 (May 1969), pp. 87–98.

improved products and to embrace new technologies. Fifth, with large size comes greater market visibility and recognition, which, if accompanied by growth and above-average profitability, can translate into lower borrowing and capital costs. Some large corporations are able to borrow at interest rates 1 to 3 percentage points below small- and medium-sized firms. Sixth, the debt capacity and capital-raising potential that tends to accompany large size is available for (1) pioneering the development and implementation of cost-saving technological innovations; (2) withstanding the risk of cyclical downturns, sour investments in a new project, or secular decline in demand for some of its products; and (3) investing in specialized management talent proficient in solving problems and developing better managerial technologies. When fully exploited, the outcome is an *organizational economy of scale* that can produce sizable reductions in unit costs and effective strategies for competing in the marketplace.[14]

Last, but far from least, large size achieved via vertical integration and/or diversification can be a distinct asset in surviving fundamental market changes occasioned by abrupt increases in input prices, disruptions in raw material supplies (bad harvests, trade boycotts), the ups and downs of the business cycle, technological breakthroughs, shifts in consumer demand, and changing life-styles. An unintegrated, undiversified, single-plant enterprise is vulnerable to unexpected market developments. But with vertical integration, diversification, or both, an enterprise obtains a measure of security. Integrating vertically allows a firm to *internalize* the problems of securing reliable supplies of essential inputs at reliable prices and of marketing the firm's outputs. Thus, it is not without design that heavy users of coal buy and operate coal mines; that major steel firms have their own sources of iron ore; that major oil refiners maintain divisions to search out deposits of crude oil on the one hand and to market refined products at retail on the other hand; that Sears has an ownership interest in an appliance manufacturer; that General Motors has its own divisions to supply it with batteries, shock absorbers, air-conditioning units, and various other automobile parts; that A&P has a division to supply it with bakery products and canned goods; and that Goodyear, Firestone, and B. F. Goodrich all give special attention to maintaining an effective chain of retail stores, including a number of company-owned and -operated outlets. Diversifying into a variety of products and markets spreads risk and lessens the dependence a firm has on any one product, customer, market, or line of business. Both integration and product-market diversification, therefore, help to insulate a firm from adverse developments and to stabilize its base of operations.

However, one other advantage of large size is not to be minimized in explaining the success of corporate enterprise. As a firm gets larger, its *absolute* size gives it a measure of *control* or leverage over its costs, its selling prices, its production technology, its sources of financial capital, the attitudes

[14]This point is developed in more detail in Oliver E. Williamson, *Corporate Control and Business Behavior* (Englewood Cliffs, N.J.: Prentice-Hall, Inc., 1970), especially Chapters 8 and 9.

and buying propensities of its customers, its relationships with government, and whatever other factors are crucial to successful enterprise. The mere size of a firm breeds power or, at the very least, an ability to throw its weight around on its own behalf. Motivated by an instinct for self-protection and risk avoidance, large firms often take deliberate steps to achieve some degree of control over the stability of operations. Max Weber, years ago, observed the tendency of large-scale organizations to construct buffers and control devices that guard against market and competitive adversity. To be sure, the power and influence of the giant corporation is far from absolute or unfailing in application, but where it can be brought into play it *partially* frees a firm from the grip and sometimes harsh discipline of competitive market forces.

Moreover, with bigness comes an opportunity to exercise political influence and thereby win undue favors and privileges via the governmental process. Usually, the large corporation is careful not to flaunt its power publicly, but there can be little doubt that where such power exists it will be used to protect and enhance the firm's interests. As a consequence, the economic benefits of large size can accrue to several groups in varying proportions—to consumers in the form of better and lower-priced commodities and/or to stockholders in the form of higher profits, dividends, and stock prices and/or to corporate management in the form of higher salaries, luxurious office accommodations, social prestige, and political clout and/or to rank-and-file employees in the form of higher wages, more fringe benefits, and better working conditions.

Reasons for Diseconomies of Scale at the Firm Level. The chief reason why a firm's long-run average cost curve supposedly turns upward relates to the increasing difficulties and costs of managing ever-larger enterprises. Conventional wisdom instructs that beyond some size the larger a firm gets, the more likely it will become burdened down with bureaucratic red tape and unwieldy decision-making procedures; as a result, approval of key recommendations gets bogged down in costly layers of management and the time it takes for the firm to respond to new developments becomes inefficiently long. In addition, large firms may be at a price disadvantage in obtaining the services of blue-collar labor. Unions have had their greatest success in dealing with large enterprises; large firms often pay higher hourly wage rates than do small-and medium-sized firms. Thus, to the extent that larger size is accompanied by an increase in the ability of unions to secure higher wage rates, the large enterprise may find itself confronted with diseconomies of scale unless it takes steps to offset them by means of automation or some other productivity-increasing strategy.

The Long-Run Average Cost Curve for Firms. In some industries economies of scale are negligible and diseconomies assume paramount importance at relatively low outputs. Figure 8-8(a) shows a long-run average cost curve for firms in such situations. The points on the curve show the lowest feasible unit cost of production for various *firm* sizes when the *firm* has

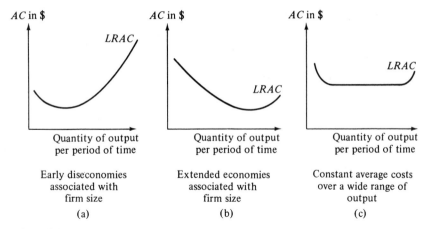

Early diseconomies associated with firm size

(a)

Extended economies associated with firm size

(b)

Constant average costs over a wide range of output

(c)

Figure 8-8
Alternative shapes for the long-run average cost curve

APPLICATIONS CAPSULE

LOWERING THE HIGH COST OF DYING

In 1975 the average cost for funeral and burial arrangements in the United States (including cemetery plot and grave marker) approximated $2000. The National Funeral Directors Association estimated that the average adult funeral purchased in 1974 cost $1200, of which the casket accounted for approximately $200 and funeral service charges $1000; this compares with average costs per adult funeral of about $650 in 1958. The vast majority of these funerals were handled by small owner-managed funeral homes serving a local area. However, in Alabama, the average price of funerals historically has run 40 to 60% *below* the national average. A major explanation for this is the competitive alternative of burial insurance and the low-cost economics of providing large numbers of funerals through a vertically integrated burial insurance system.

The leader in burial insurance in Alabama is Liberty National Life Insurance Company—one of the fastest-growing and largest insurance companies in the country. In 1974 it ranked 35th in assets on *Fortune*'s list of the 50 largest life insurance companies. As of 1975, Liberty National had approximately 2.5 million burial insurance policies in force, almost all involving residents of Alabama. (The company has not chosen to sell burial insurance in any other of the 34 states in which it is licensed to do business even though it could, under the laws of several states, issue burial policies of the type it has sold in Alabama.)

Over the past 20 years, approximately 70% of all white persons and 17% of all black persons who died in Alabama have owned a Liberty National burial policy and have had all or part of their funeral costs covered by such policies. These percentages result in Liberty National policies being involved in the handling of about 19,000 funerals annually in Alabama (out of nearly 35,000 resident deaths). From an economic viewpoint, the widespread public acceptance of Liberty National's burial insurance policies stems from the fact that policyholders are able to purchase a complete funeral on a pre-need basis at a substantial discount from prevailing retail funeral prices.

The most numerous of the burial policies issued by LNL are those providing for benefits of a *retail value* of $300 or $600. Unlike most insurance policies the benefits are not payable in cash but rather take the form of *funeral merchandise* (casket and burial clothing) and *funeral services* (transportation of the remains to the funeral home, embalming and preparation of the body, use of viewing room and chapel, assistance in conducting the funeral service, and transportation of the body to the place of interment). The funeral services provided in all LNL burial policies are the same, only the casket differs; for example, the $300 policy provides for a wooden cloth-covered casket, whereas the $600 policy provides a metal casket.

The "cash value" of the insurance provided in LNL policies and the basis on which policy premiums are based is *not* the "retail value" ($300 or $600) of the funeral benefits, but instead Liberty National's cost of providing the policy benefits. In the case of many of the policies issued by LNL, a policyholder could buy a $300 funeral by paying premiums keyed to a $150 cash value; similarly, the premiums on many $600 policies were based on a $300 cash value. In effect, then, taking out a LNL burial policy allowed a person to purchase a complete funeral at much less than its retail value and, given inflation, much less than future prices likely to prevail at the time of death. Moreover, LNL burial policies contain all the usual provisions found in industrial life insurance policies, including nonforfeiture benefits, a grace period for the payment of premiums, provisions for designations of beneficiary, and maintenance of cash reserves by the issuing company.

To fulfill its obligation under the burial policies, Liberty National has a wholly owned subsidiary, Brown-Service Funeral Homes Company, whose sole function is to see that the appropriate merchandise and services are made available to policyholders upon death. For performing these tasks, LNL pays to Brown-Service the cash value of the insurance provided under each policy on which claims are filed ($150 in case of a $300 policy and $300 in case of a $600 policy).

Brown-Service has entered into renewable long-term *contracts* with independently owned funeral home businesses throughout

Alabama to provide the funeral *services* at the time of the death of an insured person. These "authorized" funeral homes, when called upon by the family of a deceased policyholder, furnish a complete funeral service (use of funeral coach, embalming, viewing, chapel, and so on) for an agreed-upon service fee paid to them by Brown-Service (approximately $95 for a $300 policy and $180 for a $600 policy).

Brown-Service owns and operates a plant to manufacture the various models of wooden and metal caskets provided under the terms of LNL burial policies. Because the policy caskets are produced in sizable quantities and do not have elaborate trimmings, the average cost of producing a policy casket (wood or metal) is substantially below the wholesale cost of comparable caskets on the open market. Consequently, Liberty National is able to furnish policy caskets to authorized funeral homes at a cost well below what a funeral director would pay for a comparable casket bought from other casket manufacturers. The burial garments are acquired by Brown-Service from several suppliers in the open market. Brown-Service then consigns and delivers caskets and garments to each authorized funeral home so that they will be on hand when needed for a policyholder's funeral.

In 1976 Brown-Service had contracts with 221 out of approximately 273 funeral homes doing business in Alabama. Only one Alabama funeral home serving primarily white persons did not have a contract with Brown-Service to service Liberty National policyholders. The family of a deceased policyholder has the option of calling upon any authorized funeral home within a 35-mile radius to provide the services without incurring extra transportation charges; over 98 percent of Alabama's population resides within 35 miles of at least one authorized funeral home.

Under the terms of the funeral service contract, Brown-Service requires its authorized funeral directors to inform persons making funeral arrangements for a deceased policyholder of the services provided by the policy and to be shown the funeral merchandise provided under the policy. It also requires the authorized funeral director to post plainly the prices of all funerals and to give full credit for the *retail value* of the policy ($300 or $600) in the event the deceased's family elects to buy a more expensive casket or wishes additional services (referred to as an "oversale"). When the funeral director makes an oversale, he receives the usual service fee from Brown-Service and either is assigned ownership of any unused merchandise or given a cash allowance therefor, the same as if a regular policy funeral was provided. The deceased's family is, of course, responsible for paying the difference between the cost of the more expensive casket and services and the retail value of the burial policy.

While neither Liberty National nor Brown-Service owns any

funeral home business in Alabama or any interest therein, they do own approximately 63 funeral home buildings throughout the state which are leased to authorized funeral directors. From time to time Liberty National and Brown-Service make secured loans to authorized funeral directors for the purchase of funeral vehicles, furniture, and equipment. The interest rate charged on these loans is generally lower than prevailing bank rates but higher than the rate of return which Liberty National is earning on invested assets at the time the loans are executed.

Questions for Discussion

1. To what extent is Liberty National's backward integration into casket manufacturing and into the establishment of long-term contractual relationships with independently owned funeral homes crucial to its being able to issue fixed premium burial insurance policies with some confidence that the cash reserves available for paying for the policy benefits will cover the costs of providing merchandise and services?

2. Why do you suppose so many Alabama residents have purchased a Liberty National burial policy? Are such policies "a good buy?" Explain.

3. Do you suppose that Liberty National realizes the benefits of any economies of scale in its burial insurance business? Is there any reason to believe that any such economies have been passed on to policyholders in the form of lower premiums and, ultimately, lower funeral expenses?

sufficient time to adjust its input combinations to optimum levels.[15] Examples where small-scale firms sometimes have cost advantages over large-scale enterprises include farming, many of the retail trades, printing, and certain types of light manufacturing such as baking, electronics, instruments, concrete products, and soft-drink bottling.

In other industries economies of scale are extremely important, and the firm's *LRAC* curve declines significantly over a long range of output, as depicted in Fig. 8-8(b). Here a firm must be big in an absolute sense if it is to stay competitive. The automobile, aluminum, steel, railroad, aircraft, paper products, and farm implement industries are cases in point.

In still other industries the *LRAC* curve of firms is virtually horizontal over a wide range of output [see Fig. 8-8(c)]. Economies of scale are quickly exhausted, yet diseconomies are not forthcoming until very large outputs are produced. Or, alternatively, economies and diseconomies cancel each other out over an extended range of output. The result is that small, medium, and large firms can operate with roughly an equivalent degree of efficiency. The

---

[15]It is worth noting that cost curves can vary between plants and firms in the same industry because of (1) differences in the firms' products and the impact this can have on costs; (2) age differences in production facilities, with newer facilities incorporating more efficient and cheaper technology-related improvements; and (3) differences in geographic locations—where wage rates, labor productivity, transportation costs, and taxes vary from area to area.

meat packing, apparel, furniture, oil, household appliance, coal mining, textile, food products, rubber, and chemical industries are representative of this type of long-run cost behavior.

Table 8-6 summarizes the results of several major studies of long-run cost functions. None of these studies present conclusive evidence that large firms actually encounter significant diseconomies of scale in the range of observed data. Rather, the long-run average cost curve has generally been found to decrease and then level off as output rises. However, the failure to find much evidence of diseconomies of large size does not warrant concluding that *LRAC* curves in these industries fail to turn upward at some point. Firms may simply have been wise enough to avoid becoming so large as to incur rising unit costs. Moreover, the lack of truly large firms in several industries indicates that diseconomies do exist, although it does appear that diseconomies do not begin at so small a firm size as some might have imagined.

Table 8-6 Results of Empirical Studies of Long-Run Cost Functions

Name	Type of Industry	Finding
Bain (1956)	Manufacturing	Small economies of scale for multiplant firms.
Holton (1956)	Retailing	*LRAC* is L-shaped.
Alpert (1959)	Metal	Economies of scale up to an output of 80,000 lbs per month; constant returns to scale and horizontal *LRAC* thereafter.
Moore (1959)	Manufacturing	Economies of scale prevail quite generally.
Lomax (1951) and Gribbin (1953)	Gas (Great Britain)	*LRAC* of production declines as output rises.
Lomax (1952) and Johnston (1960)	Electricity (Great Britain)	*LRAC* of production declines as output rises.
Johnston (1960)	Life assurance	*LRAC* declines.
Johnston (1960)	Road passenger transport (Great Britain)	*LRAC* either falling or constant.
Nerlove (1961)	Electricity (U.S.)	*LRAC* (excluding transmission costs) declines and then shows signs of increasing.

Source: A. A. Walters, "Production and Cost Functions," *Econometrica*, Vol. 31, No. 1 (January 1963), pp. 1–66.

SUMMARY AND CONCLUSIONS

Measuring the cost of an activity means assessing the amount of sacrifice associated with conducting that activity. Completeness requires that the nature of the sacrifices considered be both tangible and intangible, objective and subjective, monetary and nonmonetary.

No one measure of cost is adequate for managerial or economic purposes. Depending on the type of problem, one may wish to determine explicit costs, implicit costs, opportunity costs, total costs, average costs, marginal costs, fixed costs, variable costs, direct costs, common costs, long-run costs, short-run costs, labor costs, controllable costs, shutdown costs, escapable costs, replacement costs, incremental costs, production costs, selling costs, administrative costs, and so on.

The cost-output relationships for a firm in the short run are governed by the character of the underlying production function. When the production function exhibits increasing returns to variable input, as output rises *TFC* remains constant, *TVC* and *TC* increase at a decreasing rate, and unit costs (*AFC*, *AVC*, *ATC*, and *MC*) decline.

When the underlying production function displays constant returns to variable input, rising output is associated with the following cost behavior: *TFC* is a fixed value, *TVC* and *TC* rise at a constant rate, *MC* and *AVC* are equal and constant, and *AFC* and *ATC* decline.

When the underlying production function is characterized by decreasing returns to variable input, increases in the output rate generate cost functions such that the *TVC* and *TC* functions increase at an increasing rate, *TFC* remains fixed, *AVC* and *MC* rise, *AFC* decreases, and *ATC* is U-shaped.

When the production function has a range first of increasing returns and then of decreasing returns to variable input, the firm's *TFC* function is again a horizontal line, but the *TVC* and *TC* functions both increase at a decreasing rate over the range of output where increasing returns to variable input prevail, then increase at an increasing rate over the output range where decreasing returns prevail. As usual, *AFC* decreases with increases in output irrespective of the nature of the returns to variable input. And the *AVC*, *ATC*, and *MC* are U-shaped functions, with the *MC* curve intersecting the *AVC* and *ATC* curves at their minimum points.

According to the best available empirical evidence, the behavior of total, average, and marginal costs in many firms embraces elements of the four preceding basic types of production-cost-output relationships. At output rates well below "normal," increasing returns to variable input are encountered, and unit costs fall as output rises. Beyond these abnormally low output rates, constant returns to variable input prevail up to approximately 85 to 90% of capacity; over this output range total costs rise linearly, *MC* is a constant, and *ATC* declines. Past 90% of capacity, decreasing returns to variable input are encountered, *TVC* and *TC* begin to rise disproportionately to the additional increases in output, and *AVC*, *MC*, and *ATC* rise sharply.

In the long run when there is time to alter the usage of any and all inputs, a firm will seek to become the right size to produce the desired output at the lowest possible cost. The *LRAC* curve for a *plant* shows the minimum average cost of producing a commodity for various *plant* sizes when all resource inputs are variable and any desired scale of *plant* can be built. The

LRAC curve for a *firm* shows the minimum average cost of producing a commodity for various firm sizes when the firm has adequate time to adjust any and all of its inputs to optimal levels. By and large, the *LRAC* curves for both plants and firms are U-shaped.

The behavior of long-run costs is a key force in determining the number and size of firms in a particular industry. Generally speaking, where significant economies are associated with mass production technologies, the structure of the industry will consist of a small number of large-scale producers. When there are few cost advantages to producing in large quantities and many cost disadvantages, production units will be large in number and small in size. In those cases where unit cost is virtually unaffected by the output rate, small, medium, and large firms may be able to compete on fairly equal terms.

SUGGESTED READINGS

ALCHIAN, A. A., "Costs and Outputs," *The Allocation of Economic Resources*, Moses Abramovitz *et al.*, eds. (Stanford, Calif.: Stanford University Press, 1959), pp. 23–40.

APEL, H., "Marginal Cost Constancy and Its Implications," *American Economic Review*, Vol. 38, No. 5 (December 1948), pp. 870–885.

BECKENSTEIN, A. R., "Scale Economies in the Multiplant Firm: Theory and Empirical Evidence," *Bell Journal of Economics*, Vol. 6, No. 2 (Autumn 1975), pp. 644–657.

CLARK, J. M., *Studies in the Economics of Overhead Costs* (Chicago: University of Chicago Press, 1923), Chapters 4–6.

DEAN, J., *Managerial Economics* (Englewood Cliffs, N.J.: Prentice-Hall, Inc., 1951), Chapter 5.

EITEMAN, W. J., "Factors Determining the Location of the Least Cost Point," *American Economic Review*, Vol. 37, No. 5 (December 1947), pp. 910–918.

JOHNSTON, J., *Statistical Cost Analysis* (New York: McGraw-Hill Book Company, 1960), Chapters 4 and 5.

KOOT, R. S., AND D. A. WALKER, "Short Run Cost Functions of a Multiproduct Firm," *Journal of Industrial Economics*, Vol. 18, No. 2 (April 1970), pp. 118–128.

SHERER, F. M., A. R. BECKENSTEIN, E. KAUFER, AND R. D. MURPHY, *The Economics of Multiplant Operation: An International Comparison Study* (Cambridge, Mass.: Harvard University Press, 1975).

TANGRI, O. P., "Omissions in the Treatment of the Law of Variable Proportions," *American Economic Review*, Vol. 56, No. 3 (June 1966), pp. 484–493.

VINER, J., "Cost Curves and Supply Curves," reprinted in *Readings in Price Theory* (Homewood, Ill.: Richard D. Irwin, Inc., 1952), pp. 198–232.

WALTERS, A. A., "Production and Cost Functions," *Econometrica*, Vol. 31, No. 1 (January 1963), pp. 1–66.

WILLIAMSON, O. E., "Hierarchical Control and Optimum Firm Size," *Journal of Political Economy*, Vol. 75, No. 2 (April 1967), pp. 123–138.

1. Complete the following table:

Units of Output	TFC	TVC	TC	AFC	AVC	ATC	"Average" MC
0	___	___	$ 500	___	___	___	
100	___	___	750	___	___	___	___
200	___	___	1100	___	___	___	___
300	___	___	1500	___	___	___	___
400	___	___	2000	___	___	___	___
500	___	___	2600	___	___	___	___

2. Complete the following table. Assume that units of fixed input cost $10 each and that units of variable input cost $20 each.

Units of Fixed Input	Units of Variable Input	Units of Output	"Average" Marginal Product of Variable Input	Average Product of Variable Input	TFC	TVC	TC	AFC	ATC	"Average" MC
100	0	0			___	___	___	___	___	
100	20	600	___		___	___	___	___	___	___
100	40	1500	___		___	___	___	___	___	___
100	60	2000	___		___	___	___	___	___	___
100	80	2200	___		___	___	___	___	___	___
100	100	2300	___		___	___	___	___	___	___

3. Given the total cost function $TC = 10,000 + 9Q$, where $Q =$ units of output:
   (a) Determine the equations for TFC and TVC, and illustrate graphically the relationships among TFC, TVC, and TC.
   (b) Determine the equations for AFC, AVC, ATC, and MC. Graphically illustrate their relationships to one another.
   (c) What, if anything, can you infer about the nature of the underlying production function?
   (d) How much is the marginal cost of the 100th unit of output? How much is AVC at an output of 100 units? Explain why $MC = AVC$ at each rate of output.

4. Given the total cost function $TC = 20,000 + 4Q + 0.5Q^2$, where $Q =$ units of output:
   (a) Determine the equations for TFC and TVC. Graph the TFC, TVC, and TC functions, and graphically show their relationships to one another. How would you describe the behavior of TVC as output increases?

(b) Determine the equations for *AFC*, *AVC*, *ATC*, and *MC*. Graph each of these functions, and graphically show their relationships to one another.

(c) What is the nature of the underlying production function? What will its shape be?

5. Given the following information:
   (a) $Q = 6X$, where $X =$ units of variable input and $Q =$ units of output.
   (b) There are 10 units of fixed input.
   (c) Price of the fixed inputs $= \$10$/unit.
   (d) Price of the variable inputs $= \$5$/unit.
   Determine the corresponding equations for *TFC*, *TVC*, *TC*, *AFC*, *AVC*, *ATC*, and *MC*.

6. The total cost function of a shirt manufacturer is $TC = 10 + 26Q - 5Q^2 + 0.5Q^3$, where *TC* is in hundreds of dollars per month and *Q* is output in hundreds of shirts per month.
   (a) What is the equation for *TVC*?
   (b) What is the equation for *AVC*?
   (c) What is the equation for *ATC*?
   (d) What is the equation for *MC*?
   (e) Plot (or sketch) the relationships among *TFC*, *TVC*, and *TC*.
   (f) Plot (or sketch) the relationships among *AFC*, *AVC*, *ATC*, and *MC*.
   (g) What, if anything, can you infer about the nature of the underlying production function?

7. Given $TC = 2000 + 15Q - 6Q^2 + Q^3$, where $Q =$ units of output:
   (a) How much is *TFC* at an output of 2000 units? At 5000 units?
   (b) How much is *AFC* at an output of 2000 units? At 5000 units?
   (c) How much is *AVC* at an output of 20 units?
   (d) How much is *MC* at an output of 20 units?
   (e) How much is *ATC* at an output of 20 units?
   (f) At approximately what output rate is the point of diminishing marginal returns to variable input encountered?
   (g) At approximately what output rate does diminishing average returns begin?

   (h) At approximately what rate of output does stage II begin?

8. Given the production function $Q = 15X$, where $X =$ units of variable input and $Q =$ units of output. Units of variable input cost $30 each and units of fixed input cost $100 each. Ten units of fixed input are available.
   (a) Determine *AFC* at an output of 400 units.
   (b) Determine *AVC* when 10 units of variable input are combined with the 10 available units of fixed input.
   (c) How much is *MC* at an output of 300 units?

9. Prove that $MC = AVC$ at the minimum point of the *AVC* curve when the equation for *TVC* is of the general form $TVC = bQ - cQ^2 + dQ^3$. (*Hint:* See footnote 10.)

10. What is the relationship, if any, between marginal costs and fixed costs?

11. Given the following cost information:
    (a) *AFC* for 5 units of output is $2000.
    (b) *AVC* for 4 units of output is $850.
    (c) *TC* rises by $1240 when the sixth unit of output is produced.
    (d) *ATC* for 5 units of output is $2880.
    (e) It costs $1000 more to produce 1 unit of output than to produce nothing.
    (f) *TC* for 8 units of output is $19,040.
    (g) *TVC* increases by $1535 when the seventh unit of output is produced.
    (h) *AFC* plus *AVC* for 3 units of output is $4185.
    (i) *ATC* falls by $5100 when output rises from 1 to 2 units.

Using this information, complete the following table:

Output	TFC	TVC	TC	AFC	AVC	ATC	MC
0	——	——	——	——	——	——	
1	——	——	——	——	——	——	——
2	——	——	——	——	——	——	——
3	——	——	——	——	——	——	——
4	——	——	——	——	——	——	——
5	——	——	——	——	——	——	——
6	——	——	——	——	——	——	——
7	——	——	——	——	——	——	——
8	——	——	——	——	——	——	——

12. Midwest Foundry Corp. was exploring the construction of one of three types of facilities for manufacturing a new type of cast iron pipe. Estimated costs for each of the three facilities are indicated below:

Cost Component	Plant A	Plant B	Plant C
Cost of materials per unit	$3.00	$3.00	$3.00
Labor costs per unit	$0.25	$0.50	$0.75
Equipment cost (10-year life)	$750,000	$600,000	$250,000
Fixed overhead expenses	$100,000	$60,000	$20,000
Maintenance and variable overhead expense per unit	$0.15	$0.20	$0.40
Annual output capacity (in units)	500,000	375,000	125,000

(a) Determine which plant is capable of achieving the lowest *ATC* at an output of 300,000 units. (For outputs greater than the annual capacity of plant C, assume that Midwest would simply build as many type C plants as necessary to obtain the desired output.)

(b) What is the lowest-cost plant arrangement for an output of 1 million units?

NINE THE FIRM AND ITS GOALS

A major task of microeconomic theory is to explain and to predict changes in prices and outputs as a consequence of changes in particular economic forces and public policies. This is not a simple matter in a trillion-dollar economy where the forms of business enterprise range from the free-wheeling independent proprietorship to the multiproduct, billion-dollar modern corporation and where the competitive mix varies from one industry to the next. However, economists have developed two complementary approaches to studying business behavior. One approach is to try to explain business behavior through the goals of the firm, the argument being that decision makers are prone to select the market strategies which they perceive best contribute to achieving the firm's goals. The other approach holds that market conditions and competition are the chief factors underlying (or constraining) a firm's behavior. The two are by no means exclusive and we shall find it useful to use both.

In this chapter we shall examine the goals of business enterprises, concentrating mainly on the profit motive. Particular consideration will be given to the character, source, and use of profit, the role and functions of profit in a modern economy, and whether firms seek to maximize profit. In the last section of the chapter some major alternatives to profit maximization will be presented.

Profit is typically defined as the difference between total revenue and total cost. In terms of symbols, $\pi = TR - TC$, where π represents profit. This definition of profit, although widely accepted and seemingly straightforward, is nonetheless ambiguous in its application. To the accountant, "profit" usually means total revenue minus explicit costs; thus *accounting profit* is an *ex post* concept based upon past transactions and historical fact.[1] To the economist "profit" means total revenue minus *all* costs—not just the money expenses incurred by the firm but implicit costs as well as an allowance for a "normal" profit. The various approaches to what constitutes a cost and how cost should be measured give rise to the concepts of accounting profit, normal profit, and economic profit.

The most significant element of discrepancy between accounting and economic measures of profit relates to the treatment of the stockholders' capital investment in an enterprise. Suppose that we explore this point briefly. In a capitalistic economy the owners of an enterprise must over the long run receive a return on their investment of sufficient magnitude to induce the enterprise to remain in business. Whenever the profitability of a business consistently is below what can generally be earned in other enterprises of equivalent business risk, the stockholders can be expected to seek greener pastures for their investment funds. Because additional resources and capital will tend to be withheld from an enterprise if and when realized accounting profits fall below "minimum acceptable levels" for sustained periods, it is appropriate to conceive of this minimum profitability as a "cost." It is a cost in the sense that unless revenues from a firm's operations are adequate to provide acceptable rewards to stockholders, the enterprise will be denied additional venture capital and, in time, will wither and die.[2] In other words, in the long run, *profit is a condition of survival.*

How large is this minimum acceptable degree of profitability? a 10% after-tax return on equity investment? or 15%? Actually, a hard and fast standard does not exist; how much profit is enough varies with the circumstances—the risk involved, the time period, the amount of required capital investment, inflation rates, the health of the economy, the type of industry, the long-run potential of the enterprise, what other firms are earning, and so on. But whatever the size of the minimum, it provides a benchmark for

[1]However, accounting measures of profit are by no means exact just because they are based upon past events with known monetary values. Indeed, several acceptable accounting alternatives exist for determining the "correct" revenues and costs to attribute to a given time period. There are a number of alternative techniques for calculating depreciation, valuing inventories, deciding when to write overdue accounts receivable off as bad-debt losses, and deciding how to adjust the costs of fixed assets for price level changes. In addition, while it is customary to count the costs of advertising, public relations, research and development, and training in the period in which they occur, it is clear that they affect *future* sales, production, and profits. Hence, accounting profit calculations are estimates rather than absolute truth.

[2]The actual or realized return to stockholders takes two forms: (1) dividends and (2) capital gains—increases in the value of a stock in terms of price per share.

judging whether to remain in business or get out. Firms that cannot earn an
acceptable profit doing what they are doing should "get out" and divert capital and resources into activities where *at least* a minimum acceptable profit can be earned. Accordingly, it has become customary in economics to think of the *minimum profit* that is necessary to keep a firm in business in the long run *as being a genuine cost of production*. We shall refer to this minimum return to ownership as *normal profit*. On the other hand, *economic profit* can be construed as a return over and above a normal profit. The following examples illustrate how accounting profit, normal profit, and economic profit are related.

Example 1: Company A owns production facilities valued at $100 million. Its net earnings after taxes were $12 million—as determined by standard accounting techniques. Assuming that the "normal" rate of return for firms of comparable position is 8%, the company's normal profit should approximate $8 million (8% of $100 million). Company A's *economic profit* is thus $12 million—$8 million = $4 million. The $4 million represents that portion of the overall return to owners (stockholders) *over and above* what could be earned in comparable alternative ventures.

Example 2: Company X has made an equity investment of $50 million in facilities to produce high-speed copying equipment. According to conventional accounting measures, its earnings after taxes were $5 million or 10% on investment. However, an evaluation of the alternatives open to company X indicate that had the firm directed its energies to producing electronic desk calculators net earnings after taxes could have been $6 million. Hence, even though company X realized 10% return on its investment, it turned down the opportunity of earning 12%, thereby resulting in an *opportunity loss* of 2%.

Henceforth we shall endeavor to use the term "profit" to mean economic profit; a normal return or normal profit will be treated as part of total cost. One final point: insofar as both decision making and the analysis of firm behavior are concerned, interest centers more on *expected* profit than upon *realized* profits.[3] Realized profits are relevant as a guide to action and to behavior only to the extent that they influence future profit expectations. Realized profits can also serve as the yardstick for measuring performance. Nonetheless, expected profit considerations must in the final analysis serve as the basis for making decisions and for predicting business behavior.

THEORIES OF PROFIT

The profit-oriented capitalistic type of economic system has provoked a wealth of controversy and discussion about profit—from whence it derives,

[3]More precisely, managers are primarily interested in the size of the time-discounted profit flow, or to put another way, the *present value* of the expected stream of profits. The present value of the stream of profits flowing in from an investment is the amount of money that must be invested *now*, at some rate of return, to produce a cash flow equivalent to the expected profit flow.

the economic functions it performs, its ethical and moral qualities, and whether profit is socially justified. The various theories about profit and its economic role can, for convenience, be grouped into three broad categories:

1. Compensatory and functional theories of profit.
2. Friction and monopoly theories of profit.
3. Technology and innovation theories of profit.

This grouping is indicative of historical patterns of thinking on profit issues and for our purposes offers a logical approach to examining the whys and wherefores of both normal and economic profit.

Compensatory and Functional Theories of Profit

As applied to owner-managed firms, the compensatory and functional theories of profit regard normal profit as a payment to the entrepreneur in return for services performed in coordinating and supervising the many facets of the firm's activities and in bearing the risks of enterprise. The entrepreneur is the key force in initiating, integrating, and guiding the course of production to a successful conclusion. It is entrepreneurial alertness to unnoticed product-market-customer-technological opportunities that catalyzes and drives market processes. The entrepreneur is held to be *the* human action element crucial to making the firm a success and to stimulating economic activity in general. Profit, therefore, arises partly as a justifiable compensation and reward to the entrepreneur for fulfilling the various economic and managerial functions successfully. Losses are the penalty for entrepreneurial failure.

From this perspective, the entrepreneur appears as a laborer of a particular type and talent. Profit becomes the special creation of the gifted entrepreneur, who, by his or her comprehension of the marketplace, capacity for organization, administrative ability, and energy, wisdom, and economy, is most responsible for generating an excess of total revenue over total cost—an excess that may result in the realization of economic profits as well as normal profits. Profit, then, is more than something that just happens to be left over after all costs are covered; rather its existence signals astute entrepreneurship, a vitality of enterprise, and economic progress.

While this explanation of profit provides a plausible rationale for justifying and explaining why individual proprietorships, partnerships, and small entrepreneurial corporations are entitled to at least a normal profit, it is at considerable variance with the realities of large corporate enterprise. In large corporations, salaried managers perform much of the entrepreneurial function, but the profits accrue to "absentee" stockholders, who are primarily "capitalists" rather than entrepreneurs. Consequently, other functional and compensatory reasons must be found for justifying why corporations should earn a normal profit.

One such basis pertains to the risk-taking function which stockholders perform even though they are absentee owners. In furnishing the corporation with money capital, the stockholder receives no assurance of a return on his or her investment in the form of dividends and/or capital gains. The stockholder can and does lose money when the corporation's activities prove to be unprofitable. Unpredictable changes in the general economic environment combine with sudden changes in consumer tastes, resource supplies, government policy, and technology to produce an abundance of uncertainty that tends to enrich some firms and impoverish others. Persons willing to accept the uncertainties of enterprise are entitled to a reward for the use of their capital—a reward that rightly should be keyed to the degree of uncertainty borne by the investor. The reward for bearing risk and uncertainty is most properly considered as constituting normal profit and not economic profit.

At least a portion of corporate profits, then, can be looked upon as a reward to stockholders for bearing uncertainty and supplying venture capital to the enterprise. Naturally, though, a 20% *expected* return will not be valued as highly as a 20% *guaranteed* return. Depending upon the confidence investors place in the estimated profitability of a venture and depending upon their immediate inclinations toward either taking risks or avoiding them, they may evaluate a 20% expected return as equivalent to 10% on a sure thing, or just 8%, or even just 5%. Hence while stockholders are indeed absentee owners, they still perform the essential entrepreneurial functions of bearing the uncertainties of enterprise and of supplying capital—both of which are crucial to the survival and success of the corporation. And the element of uncertainty explains why business firms must sometimes earn "high" profits if they are to keep investors willing to supply risk capital—the greater the degree of uncertainty, the greater must be the prospect of reward to justify going ahead with a venture.

Another compensatory explanation as to how profit arises attaches to the service that a firm renders to its customers. To some extent, a firm's profit (normal or economic) may derive from the fact that many buyers are willing to pay a price that more than covers the cost of labor, materials, capital, taxes, and other expenses involved in furnishing the good or service because of the time it saves, or its usefulness and convenience, or status and prestige, or other utility-related reason. The excess of price over cost thus represents compensation to the supplier for having the skill and foresight to give buyers the kind of value they wanted. The proponents of this viewpoint observe that when firms are adequately rewarded with profit for fulfilling society's material wants in the face of market uncertainties, they tend to be more efficient, more willing to innovate, more venturesome, and therefore more progressive. Why? Because when the stakes are more attractive, enterprises are more daring and their entrepreneurial spirit more vibrant. Moreover, the earning of economic profit enhances the financial ability of firms to invest in new activities and to make up for the periodic losses of those ventures that turn sour.

Friction and Monopoly Theories of Profit

A second group of theories maintains that profit can result from luck, good fortune, positions of advantage, various market frictions, and/or a lack of vigorous competition. These have the effect of allowing firms to earn "monopoly" profits. Ideally, competition is always sufficiently strong to preclude firms from "exploiting" consumers; when it is, firms are generally unable to maneuver themselves into the position of being able to influence prices or otherwise "rig the market" to their own advantage.

In the real world, of course, competition is not always powerful and responsive enough to foreclose any and all elements of monopolistic advantage. For example, unusually favorable locations for motels, service stations, restaurants, and similar establishments give them distinct locational advantages over less fortunately situated rivals. International trade barriers may give domestic producers a more strategic position in domestic markets. Military and other government installations may bring profit bonanzas to adjacent localities. Windfall profits may be obtained for short periods of time as the result of circumstances (labor strikes, extreme weather conditions, natural disasters) which temporarily create a sellers' market. The granting of patents, trademarks, and copyrights enables the holder to legally exclude competitors. Hence, being in a position to exercise monopoly power and thereby realize "monopoly profits" explains how and why some firms have above-normal degrees of profitability.

However, the ability of firms to extort monopoly profits from their customers is often exaggerated. Competition is seldom absent long enough for great numbers of firms to grab positions of monopoly power. Nor is it valid to conclude that monopoly profits are always socially undesirable relative to the alternatives. For example, society undoubtedly benefits from the practice of granting patents (a legal monopoly); to do otherwise would surely discourage inventive and innovative activities.

Technology and Innovation Theories of Profit

The unifying feature of the third group of profit theories is the potential of technology and innovation for providing the impetus for above-average profitability.[4] New methods of production and distribution enhance profits by lowering costs or else neutralizing cost-increasing factors. New and improved products raise profits by generating favorable changes in demand and/or prices. New managerial, financial, marketing, or accounting practices promote higher profits through operating economies. Taken together, the

---

[4]The "innovation theory of profit" is chiefly associated with the late Joseph A. Schumpeter. He made a distinction between invention and innovation; the former he termed as the creation of something new, whereas the latter he viewed as the actual application of an invention in the production process. As originally expounded, Schumpeter used innovation theory to explain business cycles rather than to identify the causes and character of profits. See especially his *Theory of Economic Development* (Cambridge, Mass.: Harvard University Press, 1934), Chapter 6.

various forms of innovation constitute perhaps the most powerful and pervasive weapon business firms have for earning sustained economic profits.

That technologically superior production techniques and product innovations are capable of producing attractive economic profits is confirmed by the profit performance of IBM, Xerox, Polaroid, DuPont, General Electric, and Eastman Kodak—all of which have emphasized innovation-related strategies. However, innovation-related profits are subject to attacks over the long run. As an innovation becomes widely adopted and/or imitated, the innovating firms gradually lose their initial advantage; competitive pressures stiffen, product prices are shaved in response to rising supply capabilities, and profits drift back down to "normal" levels. Hence, for a firm to continue to profit from innovation, it must be able to bring forth new innovations to replace the shrinking profits of previous innovations. In a technologically dynamic environment, the pursuit of innovation profits creates "a perennial gale of creative destruction" whereby something new, something better, and something different is constantly being introduced to replace older innovations whose associated profitability has already been undermined.[5]

A Perspective View of Profit Theories

The diversity among the three groups of profit theories suggests that, in practice, profit (both normal and economic) results from a variety of influences, with the mix varying from firm to firm and time to time. In a sense, profit results from any of several elements either within the firm or in its environment which differentiates it from other firms in the marketplace; or, to put it another way, *profit arises from the differential advantages among firms.* Since there are any number of kinds and degrees of advantages a firm can assemble, no single theory of profit can adequately justify or explain profit. Furthermore, the various theories themselves are not mutually exclusive. For example, the profit earned by an innovating firm derives in part from the monopoly which the superiority of its innovation provides. At the same time, innovation-related profits may be viewed partly as compensation for successful risk-taking, since, after all, a firm cannot know in advance whether an innovation will produce the results the blueprints predict.

THE SOCIAL BENEFITS OF PROFIT

Traditional capitalist theory holds that the owners of enterprise are not the sole beneficiaries of profit—major benefits accrue to society as well. The

---

[5]The chemical and pharmaceutical industries offer classic examples of the process of creative destruction. In both these industries the pace of technological progress is rapid and competition is keen. Large profits are earned for short periods of time as new products are introduced, but the forces of competition soon cut severely into earnings as other firms develop similar products or as patents expire. Hence, the maintenance of high earnings is almost entirely dependent upon a firm's ability to sustain a steady flow of new products.

argument that private self-gain benefits society proceeds as follows. Profit-seeking enterprises find the rewards greatest for doing what society most wants done simply because it is virtually impossible for a firm to earn profits doing something for which consumer demand is lacking. The size of the profit flow acts as a feedback mechanism, informing firms clearly and quickly of what is being well received in the market and what is not. Rising profits serve as society's signal for an industry to expand. At the same time, rising profits help provide firms with the earning power needed to obtain capital and resource inputs for expansion. When profits are less than satisfactory, a reevaluation of the firm's market offering is warranted and if the low profitability is viewed as permanent, a reallocation of the firm's resources to other more profitable ventures is in order. Thus, profit is *the* supreme test of a firm's performance. Profit feedback automatically regulates market processes, signaling how society's resource pool is to be allocated among alternative uses.

With a profit-minded business sector there is an almost ironclad guarantee that production will be in harmony with demand. One might even say that business firms behave responsibly by seeking to earn the largest practicable amount of profit, for by so doing firms will be producing what society is most desirous of having performed.[6] To put it a little differently, socially responsible business behavior requires that firms vigorously pursue the earning of profit, for it is through the profit mechanism that society signals business firms just which goods and services are most preferred by consumers. Moreover, the profit-loss discipline is extremely reliable in inducing economic resources to be used in accordance with the tastes and preferences of consumers.

Society is also a prime beneficiary of the profit stemming from innovation. Innovation is a fundamental contributor to the process of economic growth and to advances in the standard of living, and it is, of course, the prospect of profit that stimulates innovative activity. Innovation acts as a spur to expanded production capacity, to higher levels of output, and to growth in employment. These socially beneficial spinoffs from innovative activities are critical to the realization of economic progress and cannot be lightly dismissed.

But perhaps the strongest argument for profit relates to its role in allowing a firm to better serve as a useful social and economic vehicle. A firm that does not earn at least a normal profit is not a healthy firm. Firms which are losing money or which are earning subpar profits are weakly positioned to grow and prosper; the job prospects they offer are dim; they are less able to pay higher wages and salaries; they find it difficult to obtain credit; they are financially unable to commit substantial resources to innovation and technological advance; and they are thrust, sooner or later, into a weak competitive position. Consequently, they have little to contribute in terms of providing new jobs and expanding career opportunities, implement-

---

[6]For a more thorough discussion of this issue, see Milton Friedman, *Capitalism and Freedom* (Chicago: University of Chicago Press, 1962), pp. 133–136.

ing new technologies, marketing important new commodities, raising living
standards, and meeting societal needs—all of which are crucial to enhancing society's overall economic welfare. The earning of what is generally considered to be at least adequate profits is, therefore, an essential prerequisite for business to be able to respond to society's needs in a positive and efficient fashion.

THE PROFIT RECORD OF BUSINESS ENTERPRISES

On the whole, the profit ethic and profit-seeking enterprises are not totally deserving of the low esteem, irrespectability, and contempt which they have come to inherit. For instance, before-tax manufacturing profits as a percentage of sales have ranged in the neighborhood of 7 to 12% since 1950 (see Table 9-1); only 4 to 6 cents out of every sales dollar ends up as profit after taxes—based on accounting definitions of profit. The rate of return before taxes on stockholders' ownership has fluctuated from 16 to 22%, depending upon overall economic conditions; the rate of return after taxes has usually been 8 to 12%—amounts that do not seem unduly excessive considering the risks and uncertainties that go with enterprise and considering the interest rates that prevail on virtually risk-free savings accounts and U.S. Treasury bonds. The cynical view of business executives as cigar-smoking fat cats who

Table 9-1   Profits as a Percentage of Sales and as a Percentage of Stockholders' Equity, All Manufacturing Corporations, 1950–1979

	PROFITS AS A PERCENTAGE OF SALES		PROFITS AS A PERCENTAGE OF STOCKHOLDERS' EQUITY	
Year	*Before Federal Income Taxes*	*After Federal Income Taxes*	*Before Federal Income Taxes*	*After Federal Income Taxes*
1950	12.8	7.1	27.9	15.4
1955	10.3	5.4	23.8	12.6
1960	8.0	4.4	16.6	9.2
1965	9.4	5.6	22.0	13.0
1970	6.8	4.0	15.7	9.3
1971	7.1	4.1	16.6	9.7
1972	7.4	4.3	18.4	10.6
1973	8.0	4.7	21.8	12.8
1974	8.7	5.5	23.3	14.9
1975	7.5	4.6	18.9	11.6
1976	8.7	5.4	22.7	13.9
1977	8.7	5.3	23.2	14.2
1978	8.9	5.4	24.6	15.0
1979	9.2	5.8	26.4	16.7

Sources: *The Economic Report of the President*, February 1980, pp. 300–301, and Federal Trade Commission, *Quarterly Financial Report for Manufacturing Corporations*, 1979 and 1980.

exploit helpless consumers to raise their firm's already high rate of return is thus at variance with the evidence—they exist, but they are not the dominant type.

DO BUSINESS FIRMS SEEK TO MAXIMIZE PROFITS?

Because of the strong profit orientation in a capitalistic economy, it is usually accepted as an article of faith that business firms seek to earn the largest possible profits. Most theories of the firm do not just postulate that profit is *a* goal or the *chief* goal, they state unequivocally that *the* goal is *maximum* profit and that firms can be counted upon to behave *as if* they are profit maximizers. Although it would be an exaggeration to view profit maximization as meaning a firm will point its *every* action and decision in a direction coldly calculated to obtain the largest excess of revenue over cost, it does imply that *a firm faced with several alternatives having different expected profit outcomes can usually be counted upon to select the alternative with the greatest expected profit.*

A wealth of literature has sprung up regarding the validity of relying upon the assumption of profit maximization in constructing theoretical models to explain and to predict business reponses to market forces.[7] Both sides have argued from positions of strength, although each appears vulnerable on certain points. Table 9-2 summarizes the main arguments in support of profit maximization. Table 9-3 presents the chief criticisms of the assumption that firms behave as if they seek to maximize profits.

A Sense of Proportion

Although a close examination of Tables 9-2 and 9-3 suggests that both the critics and the defenders of the profit maximization assumption have persuasive arguments in their favor, choosing between full acceptance or all-

---

[7]The interested reader may wish to consult the discussions by Lester, Machlup, Oliver, Blum, and Gordon beginning in the *American Economic Review* in 1946. Pertinent literature of more recent vintage includes Joseph W. McGuire, *Theories of Business Behavior* (Englewood Cliffs, N.J.: Prentice-Hall, Inc., 1964); H. A. Simon, "Theories of Decision Making in Economics and Behavioral Science," *American Economic Review*, Vol. 49, No. 3 (June 1959), pp. 253–283; William Baumol, *Business Behavior, Value and Growth*, 1st ed. rev. (New York: Harcourt Brace Jovanovich, Inc., 1967); Edith Penrose, *The Theory of the Growth of the Firm* (New York: John Wiley & Sons, Inc., 1959); Robin Marris, "A Model of the 'Managerial' Enterprise," *Quarterly Journal of Economics*, Vol. 77, N.o 4 (May 1963), pp. 185–209; R. M. Cyert and J. G. March, *A Behavioral Theory of the Firm* (Englewood Cliffs, N.J.: Prentice-Hall, Inc., 1963); O. E. Williamson, *The Economics of Discretionary Behavior: Managerial Objectives in a Theory of the Firm* (Englewood Cliffs, N.J.: Prentice-Hall, Inc., 1964); R. F. Lanzilotti, "Pricing Objectives in Large Companies," *American Economic Review*, Vol. 48, No. 5 (December 1958), pp. 921–940; William L. Baldwin, "The Motives of Managers, Environmental Restraints and the Theory of Managerial Enterprise," *Quarterly Journal of Economics*, Vol. 78, No. 3 (February 1964), pp. 238–256; and Gerald L. Nordquist, "The Breakup of the Maximization Principle," *Quarterly Journal of Economics and Business*. Vol. 5, No. 3 (Fall 1965), pp. 33–46.

Table 9-2 Summary of Arguments as to Why Firms Behave as If They Seek to Maximize Profits

Arguments for Profit Maximization	*Supporting Rationale*
1. The profit motive is the strongest, the most universal, and the most persistent of the forces governing business behavior.	Although firms may pursue goals other than profit, the impact of such goals upon behavior is quite small. Hence, imputing "more realistic" goals to the firm yields no *significant* improvement in explanation or prediction while greatly increasing the complexity of the analysis.
2. Competition forces firms to adopt a goal of maximum profits.	Where competition is keen, firms must display a behavior pattern very closely akin to profit maximization in order to stand a chance of earning any profit at all. Knowledge that only the fittest will survive is a powerful incentive for all firms to direct their energies in profit-maximizing directions, learning whatever skills are required and emulating firms which are visibly successful in the battle for survival.
3. Assuming that business firms behave as if they seek to maximize profits is an appropriate theoretical approach as long as such an assumption allows accurate predictions to be made about behavior.	The only valid test of a theory is its predictive power. Whether an assumption is realistic enough can be settled only by examining the predictive ability of the theory. Since economists have had considerable success in using the profit-maximizing assumption as a basis for predicting the price and output behavior of business firms, the merit of using this assumption in theoretical models is well established.
4. The profit-maximizing assumption is a useful aid in obtaining a general understanding and explanation of the behavior of groups of firms.	Microeconomic theory is not designed to explain and predict the behavior of *particular* firms; instead it is designed to explain and predict changes in observed prices and outputs as consequences of particular market forces (such as changes in wage rates, resource prices, or taxes). In accomplishing this purpose, the firm serves only as a theoretical link for identifying how one gets from the causes of business behavior to the effects of business behavior. This is altogether different from conceiving of the firm as an object of study in itself and of trying to predict and explain the behavior of Texaco or Holiday Inns.

References: 1. Milton Friedman, "The Methodology of Positive Economics," *Essays in Economics* (Chicago: University of Chicago Press, 1953), pp. 22–23.
2. Fritz Machlup, "Theories of the Firm: Marginalist, Behavioral, Managerial," *American Economic Review*, Vol. 57, No. 1 (March 1967), p. 9.
3. Melvin W. Reder, "A Reconsideration of the Marginal Productivity Theory," *Journal of Political Economy*, Vol. 55, No. 5 (October 1947), pp. 453–454.
4. George J. Stigler, *The Theory of Price* (New York: The Macmillan Company, 1952), pp. 148–149.

Table 9-3 Summary of Arguments as to Why Firms Do Not or Cannot Maximize Profits

Arguments against Profit Maximization	Supporting Rationale
1. Uncertainty prevents firms from maximizing profits, even if they wish to do so. Because of imperfect information and uncertainty, it is usually not possible to say unequivocally which of several courses of action appears to be the profit-maximizing alternative. Hence, profit maximization becomes a meaningless goal and prescription for decision making.	Business decisions are made in a fog of uncertainty; managers are not aware of all the alternative courses of action, much less the possible outcomes associated with each known alternative. Consequently, the path along which profit can be maximized is not easily identified because of imperfect information about demand, costs, competitive responses of firms, and general economic conditions. Moreover, the "best" rule for a firm in one decision situation may not be "best" in another decision situation. Nor is the "best" rule for one firm necessarily identical to the "best" rule for another firm. If, because of uncertainty, each firm concludes that profit maximization can be attained by a different route, then the profit-maximizing assumption has little utility in predicting business behavior.
2. In the large corporation the separation of control from ownership gives managers the discretion to pursue goals other than maximum profit.	Why should managers assume the onerous task of maximizing the monetary gains of stockholders? What motive is there for them to do so? Managers rarely encounter interference from stockholders as long as earnings remain "acceptable" and show a persistent tendency to increase. Furthermore, competitive pressures are often neither powerful nor quick enough to keep firms on the tightrope of economic survival; this gives corporate managers the discretion to pursue goals other than profit.
3. Many readily observable business practices are inconsistent with profit maximization.	Separation payments to discharged employees, beautification projects around plant facilities, donations to charity, the failure of executives to spend their whole day hard at work, and the failure of cost accounting practices to generate the data required for maximizing profits are all examples of deviations from profit-maximizing behavior. Also, managers may be anxious to maintain such harmonious relations with employees that they tolerate lax work habits and agree to restrictive work practices and cost-increasing union work rules.
4. Firms find it advantageous to avoid making as large a profit as possible.	Some of the most important reasons for not maximizing profits include (1) a fear of attracting competition from firms which have the potential to enter the industry, (2) a fear of provoking antitrust action, and (3) a belief that holding profits down to "satisfactory" levels will restrain union wage demands and will promote stronger public relations.
5. Maximizing profit is too difficult, unrealistic, and immoral.	Strictly speaking, profit maximization requires businessmen to use every trick in the trade to keep wages and fringe benefits down, to charge as high a price as the consumer can and will pay, to sell as low a quality of merchandise as they can legally hoodwink the consumer into buying, to disclaim any community responsibility, to finagle the lowest prices from suppliers, and so on. Firms seldom pursue these tactics as zealously as is suggested by profit-maximizing behavior.

References: 1. R. N. Anthony, "The Trouble with Profit Maximization," *Harvard Business Review*, Vol. 38, No. 6 (November–December 1960), pp. 126–134.
2. Neil W. Chamberlain, *Enterprise and Environment* (New York: McGraw-Hill Book Company, 1968), Chapter 4.
3. John Kenneth Galbraith, *The New Industrial State* (Boston: Houghton Mifflin Company, 1967), p. 117.
4. Melvin W. Reder, "A Reconsideration of the Marginal Productivity Theory," *Journal of Political Economy*, Vol. 55, No. 5 (October 1947), p. 452.

APPLICATIONS CAPSULE

297

*Do Business
Firms Seek to
Maximize
Profits?*

HOW BUSINESS EXECUTIVES DEFINE WHAT IS A "REASONABLE" PROFIT

Several top-level business executives were recently asked what they considered to be a "reasonable" profit. Excerpts of their answers are indicated below:

Irving S. Shapiro
Chairman of the Board
DuPont Corp.

Asking how much profit is reasonable is like asking how many eggs you should buy for breakfast. It depends on the size of your family and other factors.

By the same token, what is a reasonable profit depends on an industry's needs. Most Americans will agree that a fair profit is essential to a strong economy, but the idea that there are "needs" for earnings may be difficult to accept. It helps to understand the functions of profit.

Profits are not pools of money that sit idle. In all business firms, profits are used—put to work—as soon as they are earned. They are plowed back into the economy through investment in new manufacturing plants and new equipment. They are used to expand production and create jobs. They improve efficiency. In sum, profits are "seed money," the means to insure a healthy, growing economy.

Profits have a second function. A portion is paid out in dividends to the stockholders or owners. These dividends are, essentially, payment for the use of stockholders' money, which has been invested in the company.

To return to the original question, a reasonable profit is an amount that allows a company to meet its obligation to its stockholders and to acquire the facilities it must have to provide goods, services, the jobs in the future.

These needs will vary among industries. In the chemical industry, stiff competition and new technology mean plants become obsolete quickly. Bigger manufacturing units are required to supply growing markets. These conditions add up to a huge demand for capital investment.

All business—not just the chemical industry—has been suffering from a shortage of capital, due in large part to a decline in profits in recent years. This situation cannot go on indefinitely. At some point, additional borrowing becomes too risky. Our economic system must be able to generate reasonable profits so we can continue to improve our standard of living.

Fletcher L. Byrom
Chairman of the Board
Koppers Company, Inc.

A profit is reasonable when it provides for the survival of an enterprise.

Survival is possible only when profits are sufficient to perform their two life-giving functions . . . to pay investors for the use of their savings and to increase the productive base of an enterprise so that it can remain a useful entity. These two functions are essential regardless of whether the enterprise is privately held or state-owned.

Marshall McDonald
President
Florida Light and Power Company

What's a reasonable profit? Let's start the answer with another question.

What does it take to keep a company in business? It takes capital—money to buy the facilities that bring in income. You must pay for the use of this money, and what you pay with is income left over after meeting expenses.

This "left-over" income is what most call "profit"; but since you must pay it to attract capital, business analysts consider it a cost—the "cost of capital." Out of this profit comes capital for reinvestment in the business. Out of profit comes the dividend that attracts shareholder capital. Out of profit comes the ability to borrow additional capital at reasonable (there's that word again) interest rates.

All this is especially critical for an electric utility because it takes a lot of capital to keep us in business. About four dollars in facilities for each dollar we collect in revenue.

Now the key question: How much profit does it take to attract this necessary capital? That depends on the relation between earnings and the risk of their loss, for one thing, and on competition for investors' money, for another. Recently, the United States government issued some securities offering about $9\frac{1}{2}$ percent interest. That's tough competition for a private company that must bid even higher for an investor's savings.

Indications are that what investors consider reasonable for an electric utility company is a return on common shareholders' equity in the 14 to 16 percent range. When the United States government must offer so high a return on a virtually risk-free investment, you can see why private business has to offer 14 percent or more to attract equity capital.

Hamer H. Budge
President
Investors Group of Companies

[A reasonable profit is] one which is somewhat above a rate that will attract investors to a similar enterprise, entailing a similar risk.

Thomas A. Murphy
Chairman of the Board
General Motors Corp.

In my view, many labels have been attached to the word profit, such as reasonable, fair, and equitable, which reflected a misunderstanding of the nature of profit itself. To be specific, I view profit as a resultant of the complex of activities carried on by a business.

Profit varies from one year to the next depending upon general economic conditions, the acceptability of the products in the market, and the ability of the enterprise to produce those products efficiently.

I would underscore the fact that our market economy requires that each business must compete for customer favor both in terms of price and product. If it is successful in this competitive effort it earns a profit and if it is successful it can generate the resources for growth. Obviously, no business can maintain itself unless its earnings are adequate to attract investment.

There is one further consideration and this is the risk factor. A company may generate above-average earnings, but when consideration is given to risk its above-average earnings may be no more than is necessary to sustain the investment.

Put in other words, a "high" profit relative to some average of all profits may well be inadequate for growth when risk is considered. If, as I believe, profits are a resultant of the operation of the business, then it follows that descriptive labels such as reasonable, fair, or equitable have little or no meaning.

David Rockefeller
Chairman of the Board
Chase Manhattan Corp.

In a free economy, growing business profits are the key to reaching and sustaining a satisfactory rate of private capital spending. Profits retained by business provide capital for growth. Profits paid out as dividends make it possible for business to raise additional funds for capital investment through the private capital markets. A good profit trend makes it easier for a business to obtain financing through the commercial banking system; this can be especially important for smaller and medium-sized companies.

These views can be summed up in the following way:

1. What size profit is "reasonable" varies from industry to industry, depending on risk, business cycles, and capital needs.
2. A reasonable profit is an amount that allows a company to meet its obligation to its stockholders and to acquire the facilities it must have to provide goods, services, and jobs in the future.
3. The essential function of profit is to allow a firm to attract enough capital to enable it to meet the needs of customers for its products and services.

Source: Downs Matthews, "Just What Is a Reasonable Profit?" *Exxon USA*, Vol. 16, No. 3 (Third Quarter 1977), pp. 27–31.

out condemnation of the profit-maximizing assumption is not necessary. There is merit in a intermediate position which recognizes that there are circumstances where the profit maximization assumption will suffice and circumstances where other business goals should be recognized and incorporated into the analysis of the firm.

Profit is sure to be a goal of nearly every enterprise—probably the predominant goal. Profit is a universal measure of business performance and few firms will pursue a course of action that will deliberately lead to lower long-run profits than otherwise could be earned. Nonetheless, there is room for some firms to evidence more profit-conscious and profit-oriented behavior than for others.[8]

In general, firms confronted with severe and sustained competitive pressures are prone to exemplify short-run profit-maximizing behavior, whereas nonprofit goals are most likely to surface in firms where profits are expected to be ample enough to please stockholders, thereby opening the door for other considerations to influence managerial decisions. There are several reasons why this tends to be so. In highly competitive markets where profit margins are thin, security is shaky, and the ability of firms to absorb losses is weak, there exists (as Darwin's thesis maintains) a fierce struggle in which only the fittest will survive. Market forces allow little room for discretionary action. Under such conditions earning even a normal profit is far from a sure thing and short-run profit considerations rise to dominate the firm's economic decisions. The elected courses of action are extremely likely to be those *perceived* to have the greatest expected profit because to do otherwise is to endanger the firm's survival. Thus, strong competitive forces can so constrict a firm's market behavior that it may have little alternative but to pursue a strategy of short-run profit maximization. A similar condition emerges when recession or inflation weaken consumer demand to such an extent that profits plunge. In methodological terms, the profit-maximizing assumption, although not always an exact representation of reality, is nevertheless a sufficiently good approximation to the actual behavior of most enterprises confronted with these situations. Certainly, it is the best *single* assumption that can be made about the goals of these firms.

On the other hand, firms enjoying adequate profits are in the best position to deviate from a short-run profit-maximizing pattern of behavior. The reason for this is that so long as profits and earnings trends are adequate to satisfy stockholders, management has some leeway to pursue objectives other than higher short-run profits. One cannot stretch this ability too far, though.[9] It would be a gross exaggeration to presume that nonprofit goals govern the market behavior of firms with above-average profits or that management loses sight of the impact that satisfaction of other goals will have on profits. All that is being implied here is that once minimum acceptable profit levels are within reach, then management has some ability and some discretion to give more emphasis to long-run profit maximization and to nonprofit goals. There is some evidence, for instance, that the pursuit of

[8]Conceivably, there are firms where the profit goal is consistently subordinate to the achievement of other goals. But the list of firms that can afford the luxury of relegating profit to positions of lesser importance in the goal hierarchy is very short and their role in the private sector of the economy is doubtless minimal.

[9]Witness, for instance, the wave of cost-cutting campaigns, reorganizations, and overall belt tightening that transcends the business community when business turns sour and profits fall. Often, it is when profits turn into losses that management discovers how much inefficiency it has overlooked or been tolerating.

nonprofit goals is more likely to occur in large, single-product, vertically integrated firms than in large multiproduct enterprises. The former tend to be organized along functional lines and the heads of functional units appear more prone to disagree over priorities, to resist full organizational coordination, and to bend organizational goals to their own interests.[10] On the other hand, diversified firms with decentralized, quasi-autonomous divisions (organized along product or geographic lines) seem to have comparatively stronger profit orientations; divisional units are generally run as profit centers and division managers are rewarded largely on the basis of short-run performance.

To summarize, then, the assumption of profit-maximizing behavior is especially suitable in those situations where (1) large groups of firms are involved and nothing has to be predicted about the behavior of individual firms; (2) competitive forces are relatively intense; (3) the *effects* of a specified change in conditions upon prices, outputs, and resource inputs are to be explained and predicted rather than the values of these magnitudes before or after the change; and (4) only the directions of change are sought rather than precise numerical results.[11] But when the behavior of specific firms is at issue, where the number of firms is small and the behavior of any one firm affects the behavior of others, where competitive pressures are slack, where profits are ample, and/or where precise numerical estimates are called for, an explicit identification of firm goals is needed before a firm's behavior can be explained and predicted.

THE ALTERNATIVES TO PROFIT MAXIMIZATION

Dissatisfaction with profit maximization as the sole basis for motivating business behavior had led observers of contemporary corporate capitalism to propose a number of alternative goals. These alternatives are held to provide a more realistic underpinning for explaining and predicting the behavior of the firm, especially large corporations.

Satisficing Behavior

One of the most persuasive alternatives to profit maximization is the suggestion that firms aim for a "satisfactory" rate of profit rather than a "maximum" profit.[12] Said differently, firms *satisfice* rather than maximize

[10]See Oliver E. Williamson, *Corporate Control and Business Behavior* (Englewood Cliffs, N.J.: Prentice-Hall, Inc., 1970).

[11]Fritz Machlup, "Theories of the Firm: Marginalist, Behavioral, Managerial," *American Economic Review*, Vol. 57, No. 1 (March 1967), p. 31.

[12]For example, see Herbert A. Simon, *Models of Man* (New York: John Wiley & Sons, Inc., 1957); Simon, "Theories of Decision Making in Economics and Behavioral Science"; Cyert and March, *A Behavioral Theory of the Firm,* and other works by the same authors. Also, see Julius Margolis, "The Analysis of the Firm: Rationalism, Conventionalism, and Behaviorism," *Journal of Business*, Vol. 31, No. 3 (July 1958), pp. 187–199.

in pursuing profitability. The thesis is that management decision makers are content to go with workable or satisfactory solutions and courses of action rather than undertaking the more burdensome chore of figuring out the very *best* alternative at each and every fork. According to Herbert Simon: "Administrative theory is peculiarly the theory of intended and bounded rationality—of the behavior of human beings who *satisfice* because they have not the wits to *maximize*."[13]

Briefly, the advocates of satisficing view the modern corporation as aspiring to earn future profits at least as great and probably greater than current profits. When confronted with a profit-related decision, corporate managers draw upon their experiences, decision-making conventions, and whatever information is available to select an alternative from among these known to exist that is expected to produce a *satisfactory* stream of profits. But, it is contended, decision makers typically make no attempt to identify *every* possible alternative in search of *the* most profitable alternative because the search process for finding the maximizing alternative, given market uncertainty and imperfect information about demand, costs, competitive responses of rival firms, and future economic conditions, will be too complicated, time-consuming, and futile.[14]

There also exists another rationale for satisficing behavior. Contemporary corporate theory views top management as trustees of the organization, with responsibilities not only to stockholders but to employees, customers, creditors, suppliers, communities, government, and society as well. Corporate executives should, it is said, seek a statesmanlike balance among the claims of stockholders for dividends and higher stock prices, the demands of employees for higher wages and more economic security, the pressures from consumers for lower prices and higher quality products, the requests of retailers for comfortable profit margins and of suppliers for more stable purchasing arrangements, and the insistence of the public for a cleaner environment—all within a framework that is constructive and acceptable to society. According to the satisficing theorists, these considerations lead management to adopt a posture of trying to resolve organizational conflicts and competing claims and, where feasible, to advance the welfare of *all* groups who have a stake in the organization.

Moreover, within the management group itself, there are large numbers of people in middle management as well as in top management who occupy key decision-making and policy-formulating positions. Many of these people share vested interests in production, sales, personnel relations, finance, or research and development and form coalitions to promote their cause. For example, production managers (and production employees) are prone to exert organizational pressure for stable employment, ease of production

[13]Herbert A. Simon, *Administrative Behavior*, 2nd ed. (New York: The Macmillan Company, 1957), p. xxiv.
[14]Satisficing has been tested in experimental goal-seeking and problem-solving situations and appears to be a verifiable trait of human behavior. See J. G. March and H. A. Simon, *Organizations* (New York: John Wiley & Sons, Inc., 1958), pp. 140–141, and R. M. Cyert and J. G. March, "Organization Factors in the Theory of Oligopoly," *Quarterly Journal of Economics*, Vol. 70, No. 1 (February 1956), pp. 44–64.

scheduling, reasonable cost standards, and output expansion. The sales department and those who view marketing as critical to the firm's success can be counted upon to focus upon the importance of sales effectiveness—including sales volumes and the firm's market share. Similarly, other coalitions of interest in the corporation press for goals relating to higher wages and salaries, better inventory control, higher dividends, bigger pensions, nicer offices, larger expense accounts, more power and status in decision making, greater financial liquidity, technological superiority, and so on. In many respects, these various constituencies within an organization pursue their own interests and attempt to maximize their own utility subject to whatever constraints prevail.

In effect, then, the large corporation contains many centers of power of varying potency over which top management presides. According to the satisficing theorists, the outcome is to reduce corporate goals and decisions to a matter of politics, trade-offs, and compromises. In such an environment, maximizing the monetary well-being of stockholders is not feasible because the pursuit of profit is constrained by the requirement to *satisfy*, at least minimally, the demands of other competing interests. No one center of power, least of all absentee stockholders who may have no more knowledge about the organization than is contained in the annual report, normally has the organizational support needed to impose its goal on all the others and thereby *maximize* its attainment. As a consequence, satisficing behavior becomes the rule rather than the exception and is exemplified in such performance standards as seeking to earn a "satisfactory profit," charging "fair prices," obtaining a "satisfactory share of the market," and growing at an "acceptable rate."

Revenue Maximization

A second frequently mentioned alternative to profit maximization is that of constrained revenue maximization.[15] Here it is contended that once profits reach acceptable levels some firms are inclined to place higher dollar sales ahead of higher profits as the main object of concern. They are allegedly moved to do so because sales revenue is such a key yardstick of business performance. Sales revenue trends reflect consumer acceptance of a firm's products, its competitive position in the marketplace, and growth—all of which are indicative of the firm's vitality. Any position of advantage a firm has in its markets is undermined and its ability to respond effectively to competitive pressures is weakened when sales fall off. In such cases, firms become particularly vulnerable to a deterioration in general business conditions. At the same time, managerial self-interest underlies an expansive sales strategy to the extent that executive salaries evidence closer correlation with the scale of a firm's operations than with its profitability.

[15]This goal was first proposed by William Baumol. Baumol's thesis is fully developed in Chapter 6 of his *Business Behavior, Value and Growth*, previously cited. This section draws heavily from his discussion therein.

Nonetheless, revenue maximization is pursued with a watchful eye toward profits. Profits must be kept high enough to satisfy stockholders and to help finance an expansion of sales and output. Funds for expansion can be gotten internally from retained earnings, or they can be obtained externally from new stock issues and borrowing. However, the willingness of bankers and investors to supply the firm with money capital depends directly on the firm's earning power—the larger are profits (current and expected), the more funds a firm can attract from the capital market. Thus, while a firm is motivated to sell more output and push sales revenues to new peaks, it is constrained from pursuing revenue maximization to such an extent that profits are seriously impaired and the firm is denied the funds it needs for sustained growth and expansion into new markets.

Market Share Goals

Many firms profess to have targets relating to sales effectiveness and market share.[16] Obviously, good market position can be a valuable asset—not only because being on top or near the top in the market share pecking order is an enviable position to defend but also because it reflects a firm's ability to compete effectively and to cope with market uncertainties. However, it is clear that achieving a strong market position supports attainment of profit and sales goals; by itself a bigger market share is without significance. For this reason, market share is not likely to be the principal goal of the firm. In fact, aggressive pursuit of a higher market share may endanger profitability.[17] Too successful a pursuit of an ever-larger market share may produce a market dominance that invites antitrust action.[18]

Long-Run Survival Goals

Some economists have argued that business firms, like most other organizations and individuals, have a compelling instinct and motivation to survive.[19] The urge to survive is, allegedly, more fundamental than the profit

[16]Robert F. Lanzilotti, "Pricing Objectives in Large Companies," *American Economic Review*, Vol. 48, No. 5 (December 1958), pp. 921–940; A. D. H. Kaplan, J. B. Dirlam, and R. F. Lanzilotti, *Pricing in Big Business: A Case Approach* (Washington, D.C.: The Brookings Institution, 1958), pp. 181–200; Burnard H. Sord and Glenn A. Welsh, *Business Budgeting* (New York: Controllership Foundation, 1958), p. 149; and Paul N. Bloom and Philip Kotler, "Strategies for High Market Share Companies," *Harvard Business Review*, Vol. 53, No. 6 (November–December 1975), pp. 63–72.

[17]See William E. Fruhan, Jr., "Pyrrhic Victories in Fights for Market Share," *Harvard Business Review*, Vol. 50, No. 5 (September–October 1972), pp. 100–107, and R. D. Buzzell, B. T. Gale, and R. Sultan, "Market Share—A Key to Profitability," *Harvard Business Review*, Vol. 53, No. 1 (January–February 1975), pp. 97–106.

[18]General Motors is said to exercise care that its share of the automobile market does not go much beyond the 55% level. General Electric officials have stated they do not wish to exceed 50% of any given market; moreover, "the company would rather be pushing to expand a 25% share than defending a 50% share." See Lanzillotti, "Pricing Objectives in Large Companies," p. 933.

[19]Kenneth E. Boulding, *A Reconstruction of Economics* (New York: John Wiley & Sons, Inc., 1950), pp. 26–27; Galbraith, *The New Industrial State*, p. 167.

motive because a firm could maximize profit and still not survive. An inadequate cash flow, shrinking markets, takeovers by acquisition-minded firms, and so on may spell the end, even for profitable firms. In the view of these economists, higher sales, profits, and market share are relevant because they contribute to the long-run survival and viability of the firm. Thus, it is contended, survival goals take precedence over other goals, particularly in stress situations.

The importance of long-run survival is apparent. But, as a goal, it is not very helpful in predicting and explaining business behavior. At any one time, there exist many avenues for survival, and thus the choice of one necessarily tends to hinge on other factors. And once survival over the near term seems assured, other goals are sure to motivate managerial decisions. The primary significance of a survival goal is that it is a precondition for accomplishing other goals and objectives. As an explanation of behavior, its relevance is limited to those occasions where the firm's situation is so grave that every effort must be directed toward getting through the period ahead.

Personal Goals of Corporate Managers

The separation of ownership and control in corporations allows executives some measure of freedom to fulfill personal goals. Such motives as the glory of being the industry leader, personal vanity, the pride of being at the head of a large business empire, the desire for professional recognition in executive circles, an affinity for luxurious office accommodations, and the quest for larger salaries may divert managerial decisions down avenues other than profit maximization. The desires of managers for a quiet, easy life and for more leisure time have also been said to blunt the drive for maximization, since managers with "normal" preferences will attempt to maximize their satisfactions from both money income and leisure.[20]

Fellner has observed the tendency for there to be asymmetry in the rewards to managers.[21] In his view, when risky investments turn out badly, stockholders lose their assets and managers their jobs. But when aggressive moves turn out well, the rewards that managers receive are not always in close proportion to stockholder gains. Faced with this imbalance, Fellner asserts that managers are inclined to forgo high-risk/high-profit ventures for more secure (although still acceptable) profits associated with lower-risk endeavors. A related manifestation is the preference of managers for steadily rising profits over widely fluctuating profits, even though the latter may average higher than the former. This is because sharp earnings' declines may arouse stockholders' demands for a management change, while an outstand-

[20]Tibor Scitovsky, "A Note on Profit Maximization and Its Implications," *The Review of Economic Studies*, Vol. 11, No. 4, (Winter 1943), pp. 57–60, and John R. Hicks, "Annual Survey of Economic Theory: The Theory of Monopoly," *Econometrica*, Vol. 3, No. 1 (February 1935), p. 8. Such a characterization may do considerable justice to some European business managers of past generations, but whether it describes the psychology of present-day corporate executives in either the United States or Europe is dubious indeed.

[21]William Fellner, *Competition among the Few* (New York: Alfred A. Knopf, Inc., 1949), pp. 172–173.

ing rise in earnings may produce investor expectations of repeat performances and embarrassing questions when the gains are not duplicated.

In the same vein, a pride of workmanship, the urge to create, a pervasive interest in technological feats, and an ambition to demonstrate professional excellence may lead to managerial actions in conflict with the greatest possible profits. Achieving technological superiority and a leadership position in product engineering in spite of possible adverse effects on profits is said to appeal especially to executives with technical and scientific backgrounds and to firms in "high-technology" industries. Technological virtuosity meshes well with the needs of those members of the firm (engineers, technical specialists, research scientists) concerned with keeping the firm on the frontiers of technical know-how and product capability because it means opportunities for the technologists to pursue their favorite interests, as well as opportunities for personal advancement in the form of better jobs, higher salaries, and promotions.

The Goal of Social Responsibility

In recent years much has been said and written about the need for firms, particularly large corporations, to behave in a "socially responsible" manner.[22] Social responsibility has come to mean many things: having a number of diverse interest groups represented in the corporation's governance structure and decision-making process; relating the entire enterprise to the changing needs of society; balancing stockholder interests against the larger interest of society as a whole; revamping corporate policies and practices so as to promote the public welfare in a positive way; and urging firms to help solve the social ills of society while going about their regular business. In essence, the function of social responsibility is to create a "corporate conscience."

The philosophy underlying social responsibility goals is that stockholder interests in the long run are best served by corporate policies that contribute to developing the kind of society in which business can grow profitably. In fact, the pursuit of profit and the pursuit of social objectives are held to be mutually reinforcing. Profits can be earned performing functions that entail primary or secondary social benefits. At the same time social objectives can be achieved more rapidly and more efficiently by enlisting the productive power of business firms through the opportunity for profit and by imposing harsh penalities for business activities that are deemed socially harmful.

Adoption of social responsibility goals probably has the ultimate effect of containing the drive for greater short-run profits. Very likely, it makes a satisficing approach to goal formation an even more viable and more attractive managerial practice. But by no means does social responsibility

---

[22]See *Social Responsibilities of Business Corporations*, issued by the Research and Policy Committee of the Committee for Economic Development, New York, June 1971.

mean that a firm's profitability is secondary; the earning of adequate profit is a prerequisite for giving a firm the organizational ability and the financial wherewithal to respond to social objectives.

Exhorting business firms to be socially responsible has met with resistance from some business managers and several public interest groups. It has been observed, perhaps correctly, that "the business of business is business." Corporate executives, it is said, are neither equipped to be social engineers nor is it proper for them (or their firms) to usurp stockholder interests and act as philanthropists. Still, a number of firms appear to have adopted social responsibility goals and, in the majority of others, more careful consideration is being given to how corporate policies affect society. Nonetheless, they may be doing this to reduce the chances of more government interference—which, if true, may make social responsibility part of a profit-maximizing strategy.

Security, Autonomy, and Growth

John Kenneth Galbraith in *The New Industrial State* imputes a specific hierarchy of goals to the large corporate enterprise. In Galbraith's view, the directing force of the large corporation consists not only of those persons plainly identified with management (the chairman of the board, the president, vice-presidents and their staffs, division and department heads) but also of all the technicians, engineers, scientists, and specialists who bring specific knowledge, talent, and experience to the organization.[23] He argues that corporate decisions are not the product of top executives but of a complex of groups, teams, and committees which contains individuals possessed of expert information bearing on the particular decision at hand. Galbraith calls this decision-making system the "technostructure."

The goals of the technostructure and therefore the goals of the corporation, argues Galbraith, are its own security, autonomy, and self-interest.[24] The first concern of the corporate technostructure is to preserve the autonomy on which its decision-making power depends; this means that the firm must have a secure minimum of earnings sufficient to free the firm both from close stockholder scrutiny and from the need to make appeals to bankers and other monied interests who may ask questions, impose conditions on the capital they supply, and thereby compromise the autonomy of the technostructure. However, the effects of low and high earnings on the technostructure are not symmetrical. With low earnings or losses the technostructure becomes vulnerable to outside influence and its autonomy dissipates. But once profits reach a certain level and show a persistent tendency to increase, higher profits add little or nothing to the technostructure's security, and its autonomy becomes nearly absolute.

Once profit security is achieved, the technostructure's next chief concern is realizing the greatest possible rate of sales revenue growth. This goal

[23]Galbraith, *The New Industrial State*, Chapter 6.
[24]*Ibid.*, Chapter 15.

commends itself strongly to the self-interest of the technostructure since expansion of sales and output means expansion of the technostructure in the form of more jobs with more responsibility, more promotions, and higher salaries. Growth is also the best tactic to protect against contraction of the firm's activities. Any contraction of output is painful and damaging to the technostructure, for it entails such distasteful consequences as dismissal, curtailment of pet projects, and possible loss of autonomy.

Associated with the technostructure's growth goal is technological virtuosity. Progressive technology means more and better jobs and promotions for the technologists. It is also the best pathway to growth, since innovation allows a firm to hold and recruit customers for its existing products and to open up entirely new markets for its products. However, the pursuit of technological virtuosity cannot be so aggressive that it prejudices the minimum level of profits.

Next in technostructure's goal hierarchy comes a progressive rise in the dividend rate. This goal is clearly secondary but is sought as an added means of enhancing the technostructure's autonomy from stockholder interference.

Thus, in Galbraith's scheme of things, large corporations have a distinct goal hierarchy based upon the self-serving desires of the technostructure. A secure level of earnings and a maximum rate of growth consistent with providing adequate retained earnings to finance expansion are the prime goals. Technological virtuosity and a rising dividend rate are secondary in the sense that they are not pursued to the detriment of the prime goals. After these ends are achieved to some adequate extent, satisfaction in other lesser goals may be sought.

Growth and Expansion Goals

Business firms are usually alert to the organizational dangers of stagnation and of the need to remain aggressive at seizing new opportunities. The firm's present activities will in time lose their sustaining power, through changes in consumer tastes, technological change, the appearance of superior products, increased competition from domestic rivals and importers, and growth in the market power of suppliers and customers. The company that does not innovate and grow will eventually find itself managing a tired product line. Although a corporation may elect to maintain the status quo and gradually divert the firm's inputs from declining activities into expanding activities, profits can be expected to show little movement, and progress in achieving the firm's other goals is likely to be slim. Not many firms will willingly choose "coasting along"—the only thing more damning in the business world than the status quo is decline.

There are several specific appeals for growth being a major corporate goal. To begin with, growth is a good defense against adversity. Growth via greater market penetration offers a firm a stronger, more secure market position vis-à-vis competitors, suppliers, and customers. To the extent a firm can gain on or overtake its rival, it has greater freedom for maneuver and more influence over important industry decisions. Growth by diversification into a wider range of products frees firms from too much dependence on one or a few products and serves as a hedge against the possible demise of bread-and-butter products. If one product or phase of a firm's operations slows down and becomes unprofitable, it can survive and even grow on the strength of its other activities. If research and development ventures in one area prove fruitless, as recurringly can be expected, other projects may reveal new vistas of opportunity. Thus, growth and diversification can help firms withstand short-term setbacks and overcome the uncertainties of enterprise.

Second, no other measure of business success has such almost unanimous acceptance as long-term growth (i.e., rising sales, rising production, and rising profits). Growth and expansion (realized and expected) comprise a recurrent theme in the annual reports of large corporations and receive constant emphasis on financial pages and in journals devoted to business affairs. Investors and financial analysts tend to judge the worth of an enterprise not so much by current sales and profits as by growth potential. In almost all cases, more attention is given to the rates at which sales and profits have grown than to the absolute size of current sales and profits. Consequently, many firms have a strong compulsion to achieve a high growth rate; they almost always are eager to get into a lively market, and once they are in, many want nothing short of first place.

Finally, growth and expansion provide an effective means of pursuing other corporate goals and objectives. A growth strategy can be very consistent with earning higher profits, expanding sales, defending and strengthening the firm's competitive position, paying higher dividends to stockholders, achieving higher stock prices, acquiring superior technological capabilities, creating a "sound corporate image," and so on. Although growth just for the sake of growth is suspect as a goal, there is still a pervasive tendency for growth to complement and support the achievement of other goals. This alone suffices to put growth near the top of the priority list of goals and objectives.

Conflicts and Trade-Offs among Alternative Goals

Judging from the statements of corporate executives, many companies have multiple objectives and goals. None are usually singled out as predominant. Typical statements include:

1. We want to increase sales and profits by 10% each year, while minimizing stockholder exposure to risk and striving for the most effective use of capital.
2. We intend to grow at a 15% annual rate and improve our market position in each of our product lines.
3. We seek to provide a quality product that will maximize customer satisfaction, provide an adequate return on investment, and increase our market share.
4. Our objective is to be the best firm in the industry.

PROFIT STRATEGY AT IBM

IBM's System/360 computer models included a wide range of central processing unit (CPU) sizes, together with numerous options for tying in input-output equipment (printers, readers) and memory storage. IBM priced its memory and input-output equipment separately from its central processing computer units so as to allow customers maximum flexibility in choosing the best equipment combinations. The design characteristics of the System/360 models, however, allowed rival computer manufacturers to produce almost identical copies of the IBM input-output units and memories; they could then sell these at lower prices directly to users having IBM central processing units. Generally, IBM's central processing units were protected from the competition of rival computer firms because IBM customers were very reluctant to discard their investment in specialized programming and because of the difficulty in manufacturing a CPU having programming logic compatible with IBM processors. There was no such compatibility problem with input-output equipment or with memory units. Potter Instrument Company in 1967 initiated competition with IBM by introducing a replacement for IBM tape drives; a short time later, other peripheral equipment manufacturers came out with replacements for IBM disc drives and then for main memory units.

Because sales of input-output equipment and memory units accounted for over half of IBM's computer revenue, IBM was concerned in early 1970 about the threat posed by the competitive products of the peripheral equipment manufacturers and the great success they were having in getting IBM users to switch to lower-priced non-IBM equipment. At the time, IBM was preparing to introduce its new System/370 line, and while the company felt it could safely ignore the threat to the System/360 memories, it wanted to avoid losing the new System/370 memories to rival firms. IBM assembled a task force to assess how well rival firms would fare in selling IBM-compatible memory units against IBM at various IBM prices; the study was done for a hypothetical new company and also for an established company having the capacity to produce IBM-compatible memory units. Insofar as the hypothetical new company was concerned, the analysis showed that IBM's primary protection from competition was the time required for a new company to become established in the marketplace. The IBM task force estimated that if IBM established a lease price of $16,000 to $18,000 per month per megabyte of memory (with initial shipments to begin in 1972), then a new company could not break even competing with IBM until around 1974, and, further, if the IBM lease price was $12,000 and above, the task force projected good profitability for a new company beyond 1976 but at prices of $10,000 and below no break-even point was envisioned until the far future.

For an established company, the task force projected that a firm could enter memory competition and reach the break-even point by 1973 at an IBM lease price of $18,000 per month per megabyte, and by 1975 with a price of $10,000 to $12,000, with high profitablitity in later years for all lease rentals of $12,000 and above. The task force concluded that if IBM went ahead with its planned $12,000-per-megabyte monthly fee that a new company could be only marginally profitable but that an established peripheral equipment company would be very likely to enter the field because they could make a 20% return on investment for a $10 million investment and would enjoy a healthy 23% profit margin.

However, additional studies indicated that of the $61 million-per-month rental value which IBM expected to have from its memory units by 1976, that 26% would be protected through minimum memory sizes tied directly to the CPU, 36% through customers who would resist mixing IBM equipment with that of other manufacturers, and 15% because of locations in outlying geographical areas where the smaller firms were not expected to compete. This left only 23% of IBM's memory business as a possible competitive target, regardless of the exact price set by IBM. Thus, based upon the expected customer resistance to using non-IBM equipment and upon the estimated lag time between IBM's introduction to System/370 memory units and the availability of competitive memory units, IBM decided to go ahead with its planned price of $12,000 per month per megabyte for memory units on its 155 and 165 System/370 models. The 370/155 and 165 memory units utilized magnetic cores—the standard computer memory technology. But when IBM came out with its next System/370 model, the 145, a new all-semiconductor memory was used; this semiconductor memory was much faster than magnetic cores, and because it was a new technology, it was not considered subject to immediate competitive attack. As a result, IBM priced its new semiconductor memory units 60% higher than its magnetic core memory units. Within less than a year, though, IBM became concerned about the ability of rival firms to introduce not only magnetic core replacements for the earlier System/370 models but also replacement equipment for the new semiconductor unit.

Meanwhile, IBM studies indicated lower prices for central processing units prompted users to install the largest possible system and thus generate the maximum demand for memory and input-output equipment (subject to replacement by competitors), while higher prices on central processing units increased CPU profits but reduced the demand and profit earned on peripheral equipment sales and leases. IBM's solution to this profit trade-off was to package a large amount of memory with a central processing unit and charge a lower CPU price. This had the advantage of raising overall profits, while protecting at least the packaged portion of memory from competition.

Even so, within a few months, IBM saw that its previous forecast had underestimated the ability of rival firms to keep pace, and still another task force was set up to study alternatives for reducing the competitive threat. Basically, the plans the task force considered were various combinations of minimum memories, lower memory unit prices, and increased CPU prices. The task force also looked at reducing the number of memory options obtainable with a central processing unit and then refusing to sell CPUs without at least the minimum memory. Nonetheless, the final decision was to raise the central processing unit prices by a maximum of 8%, cut the purchase price of memory units on 155 and 165 models, and make no change on the rental price of memory units.

This action shortly proved to be ineffective, and IBM reviewed the strategy of introducing upgraded 155 and 165 models as new machines having higher CPU prices and lower memory prices. This was to be accomplished by tying the announcement of "virtual memory" for CPU to the new 145 model semiconductor memory announcement, thus justifying the higher CPU prices through increased performance and the lower memory price through the reduced manufacturing cost of semiconductor memory. Accordingly, IBM in August 1972 announced new versions of its 155 and 165 models, to be known as the 158 and 168 models (a revision known inside IBM as the SMASH program). The basic CPU price was raised 36% on the 165 model and 54% on the model 155. The memory price was cut 57% and a larger minimum memory size was tied to the basic central processing unit on both models, neither of which could be acquired without the memory units. The effect of the changes was to make the total price of the 158 and 168 models higher in small configurations and lower in large configurations than the original 155 and 165 models. The semiconductor memory was not made available to users of the original 155 and 165 models, thereby prohibiting users from buying the cheaper central process unit and putting on the cheaper memory as well. The SMASH program effectively foreclosed rival firms from the memory market for several months.

In trying to unravel IBM's actions it is important to understand that there are high barriers to entry in the full-line computer systems market but low barriers to entry in the peripheral equipment market. The barriers that do exist in the peripheral equipment market are related primarily to brand loyalty to IBM (including a fear of problems of mixing the equipment of different manufacturers) and the difficulty of producing IBM-compatible products which will match IBM interface specifications. The latter problem causes a lag between the time IBM introduces a product and the time it can be copied. This time lag reduces the rental life of the product of rival firms and gives IBM some time after a new product introduction without competition. Additional barriers to entry in the peripheral market include raising enough working capital to finance a rental business and some small manufacturing economies of scale. However, the disadvantages of small size are not so large as to preclude a satisfactory profit by undercutting IBM's existing price—unless and until IBM also cuts prices.

A second aspect of the computer equipment market is the disruption caused by equipment installation and removal, even if compatibility is not a problem. Normally, lower-priced equipment is introduced as a "new" product having essentially identical performance specifications as existing products. The customer can get the price cut only by physically removing the old model and installing the new one. The freight charges and disruption involved, as well as lack of information or lethargy on the part of some computer users, means IBM can come out with a competitive low-priced product while still receiving the higher rent from many users for some time after the price cut.

A third feature which IBM used to good advantage related to the time lag between IBM's introduction of a new product and a rival's introduction of its equivalent. As part of its introductory scheme, IBM induced users to agree to a fixed-term lease period, with heavy penalties for early termination. This effectively locked out competitors until users completed their lease agreements. Then, too, by making periodic design changes in its products (such as switching control functions between drive and control units), IBM was able to further reduce the marketing effectiveness of its competitors without reducing its own prices.

Question for Discussion

1. Based upon the description above, what would you say IBM's principal goal was? Why?

Sources: Based upon documents released in the antitrust litigation between Telex and IBM and upon Gerald Brock, *The U.S. Computer Industry: A Study of Market Power* (Cambridge, Mass.: Ballinger Publishing Company, 1975).

5. We plan to maximize sales, profits, growth, and market share through product innovation and diversification into new fields.

While such statements make good rhetoric, they often involve operational ambiguity, conflict, or trade-offs among competing goals. For example, simultaneously maximizing sales and profits may not be possible because revenue maximization may occur at a different price and output rate than does profit maximization (as we shall see in Chapter 15). Every firm is confronted with choosing among a host of strategic trade-offs and options:

1. To pursue short-run profits or long-run profits.
2. To improve profit margins or increase market share.
3. To increase penetration of existing markets or to enter new markets.
4. To diversify into related products or into unrelated products.
5. To compete in only low-risk environments or to move into high-risk markets.
6. To emphasize profit goals or nonprofit goals.
7. To seek out faster growth or more stability.

How a firm goes about compromising and balancing these competing goals and considerations obviously varies from firm to firm and time to time. And the choices can be very tough. For example, a firm whose profits are plunging may be tempted to reduce or eliminate expenditures for R&D, advertising and promotion, investment in new ventures, facilities and equipment, or product innovations—the very things on which long-term profits and growth are built. Evidence also exists to the effect that there is an inverse relationship between profits and profit margins, on the one hand, and growth and market share, on the other hand. Several years ago, DuPont and Union Carbide appear to have followed a strategy aimed at maintaining profit margins significantly above the chemical industry as a whole.[25] To do this, however, the companies had to be highly selective in their choices of markets, resulting in subpar rates of growth. Allied Chemical also sacrificed growth in order to improve its below-average profit rates. The trade-offs among profits, growth, and competitive market position thus pose a very difficult choice of goals. Firms with above-average profit margins are likely to attract strong competition. Rival firms may well be willing to accept initially lower profits and therefore charge lower prices or spend more on promotion in order to gain a stronger market foothold and build a clientele. As they pull sales away, the leaders have two recourses: (1) try to maintain profit margins and tolerate eroding sales and market shares or (2) retaliate with price cutting, product innovation, or increased promotion (more and better ads)—any and all of which tend to lower profit margins.

The trade-offs between other alternative goals can be equally serious. Hence, firms with multiple goals should be alert to inconsistency and conflict between competing goals and seek to develop analytical mechanisms for resolving trade-offs and balancing competing interests. In any event, the effect of conflicting goals is probably to force multiple-goal enterprises to adopt *satisficing* rather than *maximizing* criteria as the basis for decision making.

[25]Cited in Philip Kotler, *Marketing Management: Analysis, Planning, and Control* (Englewood Cliffs, N.J.: Prentice-Hall, Inc., 1976), p. 56.

Few economic concepts are used with a more bewildering variety of well-established meanings than profit. Not only is there accounting profit, normal profit, and economic profit, but each of these may be measured in several ways, depending on the specific accounting conventions employed and depending upon whether the desired profit measure is a dollar amount or a rate of return. Accounting profit is based upon a firm's income statement and is conceived as the excess of revenue over historical costs after corporate taxes have been deducted. Normal profit is the minimum amount of profit (or rate of return) sufficient to keep the firm in business in the long run; normal profit is considered by the economist as part of total cost. Economic profit is a return over and above a normal profit. It is economic profit which business firms really seek and which governs much of their behavior.

Profit (both normal and economic) is a mixture resulting from a variety of influences, including business acumen, successful performance of the entrepreneurial function, services rendered to the consumer, a fortuitous coping with uncertainty, the presence of market frictions that inhibit a quick response of competitive forces, monopoly power and positions of advantage, technological superiority, and new product innovation.

Wide disagreement exists among economists over whether business firms, especially large corporations, behave as if they seek to *maximize* profits. Diffused ownership, conditions of uncertainty, and insulation from heavy competitive pressures are held to allow firms to pursue goals other than profit maximization. Among the most prominent alternatives to profit maximizing behavior are satisficing, revenue maximization, and growth. Lesser and/or corollary goals include a target market share, long-run survival, satisfactory and secure profits, a rising dividend rate, financial liquidity, technological virtuosity, autonomy of the "technostructure," attainment of a "good" image, behaving in a "socially responsible" manner, maintaining a strong competitive image, and achievement of personal goals of top management (power, prestige, sense of accomplishment, professional recognition, and high incomes). An aggressive growth strategy offers firms an effective means of simultaneously pursuing and achieving many of these goals.

Doubtless, there can be no *single* goal that captures the *whole* truth about what underlies business behavior simply because there are too many subtle shadings of behavior and the decision constraints are far too complex. Furthermore, diversity of goals and variations in motivations are a natural outgrowth of a dynamic trillion-dollar economy populated by a variety of business firms ranging from the small proprietorship to the giant multiproduct corporation. The sizable differences among firms regarding market position, ownership and control, size, competition, uncertainty, technological capabilities, personalities of owners and managers, profitability, and growth opportunities make it highly improbable that all firms pursue the *same* set of goals with the *same* degree of intensity and priority.

Even so, the profit motive is deeply ingrained in the folklore of modern business behavior, and rightly so. The imperatives of earning profits are pervasive and powerful influences. Certainly, profit stands foremost in the goal hierarchy of most firms and if one were forced to choose a single goal to characterize business behavior, then the choice would have to be long-run profit maximization. However, in the following chapters we shall find it helpful to use models that incorporate goals other than pure profit maximization in order to predict and to explain the full range of business behavior.

SUGGESTED READINGS

FARMER, R. N., "Two Kinds of Profit," *California Management Review*, Vol. 8, No. 2 (Winter 1965), pp. 21–28.

FRUHAN, W. E., JR., "Pyrrhic Victories in Fights for Market Share," *Harvard Business Review*, Vol. 50, No. 5 (September–October 1972), pp. 100–107.

FURUBOTN, E. G., AND S. PEJOVICH, "Property Rights and Economic Theory: A Survey of Recent Literature," *Journal of Economic Literature*, Vol. 10, No. 4 (December 1972), pp. 1137–1162.

GALBRAITH, J. K., *The New Industrial State* (Boston: Houghton Mifflin Company, 1967), Chapters 6, 7, 8, 10–15.

KIRZNER, I. M., *Competition and Entrepreneurship* (Chicago: University of Chicago Press, 1973), Chapter 2.

LANZILOTTI, R. F., "Pricing Objectives in Large Companies," *American Economic Review*, Vol. 48, No. 4 (December 1958), pp. 921–940.

MACHLUP, F., "Theories of the Firm: Marginalist, Behavioral, Managerial," *American Economic Review*, Vol. 57, No. 1 (March 1967), pp. 1–33.

NORDQUIST, G. L., "The Breakup of the Maximization Principle," *Quarterly Journal of Economics and Business*, Vol. 5, No. 3 (Fall 1965), pp. 33–46.

SIMON, H. A., "Theories of Decision Making in Economics and Behavioral Science," *American Economic Review*, Vol. 49, No. 3 (June 1959), pp. 253–283.

Social Responsibilities of Business Corporations: A Statement on National Policy by the Research and Policy Committee of the Committee for Economic Development (New York: Committee for Economic Development, 1971).

WHITE, C. M., "Multiple Goals in the Theory of the Firm," in K. E. Boulding and W. A. Spivey, *Linear Programming and the Theory of the Firm* (New York: The Macmillan Company, 1960), pp. 181–201.

WILLIAMSON, O. E., *Corporate Control and Business Behavior* (Englewood Cliffs, N.J.: Prentice-Hall, Inc., 1970).

PROBLEMS AND QUESTIONS FOR DISCUSSION

1. (a) The Vista Corporation has invested $10 million in producing greeting cards. Its after-tax profits according to conventional accounting measures amounted to $800,000. During the same period an average return of 6% would have been obtained by purchasing government securities. Do you think Vista Corporation earned an economic profit? Why or why not? Explain.

(b) Suppose that the financial vice-president of Vista Corporation conducts a thorough study and finds that the prospects are excellent (90% chance of success) that an annual profit of $900,000 could be earned by shifting Vista's $10 million investment into the production of business forms. What implications, if any, does this estimate have for evaluating the profitability of Vista's greeting card operations? for future resource allocation within the firm?

2. How should an enterprise go about estimating normal profit?

3. In which of the following circumstances would an assumption of profit maximization be appropriate and in which would the analysis probably be improved by a consideration of goals other than profit? Justify your answer in each case:
   (a) The effect of steel import quotas on steel prices.
   (b) The effect of the UAW's winning a lucrative wage increase from General Motors upon the prices of GM cars.
   (c) The effect of increased liquor taxes upon the price of liquor.
   (d) The effect of the ban on cigarette advertising upon the sales strategy of the three largest cigarette producers.
   (e) The effect upon coal prices of the major oil firms' acquiring producers of coal and thereby gaining control over a large segment of the nation's coal deposits.
   (f) The effect of strong antipollution laws upon the prices of paper products, chemicals, steel, and other products produced by processes with a heavy pollution by-product.

4. "No single goal of business enterprise is pure in its purpose. Goals tend to be overlapping and interdependent." Discuss the validity of this viewpoint and give examples in support of your answer.

5. Is it possible to determine whether or not a particular firm is maximizing profits? Or, to put it another way, is it possible to ascertain at some moment of time what the maximum potential profit performance of a firm is, thus allowing a comparison with the firm's actual profit performance to see if the firm is maximizing profits? Justify your answer.

6. The Hall-Prentiss Corporation is weighing two alternative projects costing $50 million, one offering a best-guess profit expectation of $10 million with a 10% chance of losing $5 million, the other offering an expected profit of $20 million with a 30% chance of losing $5 million. Which is the profit-maximizing alternative? How does this decision situation illustrate the problem of trying to maximize profits under conditions of uncertainty?

7. Is there any difference between a firm's having "monopoly power" and having a "position of advantage" in the markets for its products?

8. Henry Ford II, in an address before the Michigan State Chamber of Commerce on October 2, 1962, made the following statements:

> There is no such thing as planning for a minimal return less than the best you can imagine—not if you want to survive in a competitive market. It's like asking a professional football team to win by only one point—a sure formula for losing. There's only one way to compete successfully— all-out. If believing this makes you a greedy capitalist lusting after bloated profits, then I plead guilty. The worst sin I can commit as a businessman is to fail to seek maximum long-term profitability by all decent and lawful means. To do so is to subvert economic reason.

(a) What do you suppose Ford meant when he claimed that to fail to try to maximize long-term profitability is a "sin" and subverts "economic reason"?
(b) Do you agree with Ford's viewpoint? Why or why not?

9. It has been observed by Milton Friedman, one of the nation's most eminent economists, that "few trends could so thoroughly undermine the very foundations of our free society as the acceptance by corporate officials of a social responsibility other than to make as much money for their stockholders as possible."

   (a) What is the economic basis for such a statement?

   (b) Do you agree with this view? Why or why not?

10. According to Peter Drucker, noted professor of management and business consultant, "there is *no* justification and no rationale for profit as long as one talks the nonsense of profit motive and profit maximization." But he goes on to say: "Profit . . . is not the whole of business responsibility; but it is the first responsibility. The business that fails to produce an adequate profit imperils both the integrity of the resources entrusted in its care and the economy's capacity to grow. . . . Business needs a minimum of profit: the profit required to cover its own future risks, the profit required to enable it to stay in business and to maintain intact the wealth-producing capacity of its resources."

    Is Drucker's view in conflict with how economists view profit? With whom do you agree?

TEN HOW MARKETS FUNCTION: THE MODEL OF PERFECT COMPETITION

Of critical importance in examining the market for a product is the structure of competition—whether there are *many* or *few* sellers in the industry. The terms "many" and "few" are delineated not so much by the numbers of firms as by the competitive interaction among firms. There are "many" sellers of a product when no one firm has a big enough volume of business or market share for the remaining firms to react to its actions. And with so many firms, each is virtually an anonymous entity, hidden by sheer numbers from the watchful eyes of other firms. In contrast, we say there are "few" sellers of a product whenever the actions of any one firm will be noticed and reacted to by rival sellers. "Few" means few enough so that firms find it imperative to follow each other's moves closely. Fewness of sellers also means that each firm is large relative to the size of the market in which it operates; often, when firms are few in number each firm is large in absolute size as well.[1] The single-firm industry, or monopoly, is the limiting case of fewness.

A second key element in market behavior relates to whether the products of sellers are identical or differentiated. The products of sellers may be

---

[1]Fewness does not always mean bigness. A small community has only a few banks, dry cleaners, movies, florists, doctors, lawyers, and hairdressers—none of which are big in an absolute sense. General Motors, however, is big from both an absolute and a relative standpoint.

320

*How Markets
Function: The
Model of
Perfect
Competition*

considered to be identical whenever and wherever customers evidence no particular preference for one firm's product over that of another firm. This may arise because the item is produced by a process that confers certain measurable qualities which can be graded and which are unrelated to the seller producing it. For instance, choice-grade beef is choice-grade beef, and one cannot tell (nor does it really matter) whether it came from ranch A or ranch B. In such cases, the products of firms in an industry tend to be perfect substitutes; examples include cotton, sulfuric acid, natural gas, coal, cement, and coffee beans.

On the other hand, where the products of firms are distinctive and somewhat unique, they are not perfect substitutes for one another, and buyers may have good reason to prefer the product of one firm over that of another. However, the ultimate test of differentiation is in the mind of the buyer, and the perceived differences in the products of various firms may be either real or contrived. "Real" differences involving performance, materials, design, workmanship, and service are obviously important aspects of product differentiation. But "contrived" differences brought about by brand names, trademarks, packaging, and advertising can also be important to buyers; for example, even though all brands of aspirin are chemically alike, many buyers evidence preferences for one brand over others.

In addition, it should be recognized that a firm's product extends beyond the physical and functional characteristics of the item itself. Although a large number of retailers in an area may sell Crest toothpaste, they may not be viewed as equally attractive to buyers of Crest. The sales clerks in one store may be more courteous, or its location more convenient, or its checkout system faster, or its delivery service more dependable, or its credit terms more accommodating. Such factors can cause buyers to prefer one seller over another, even though the item purchased is the same. The various brands of shoes, wines, cereal, cosmetics, tires, and soft drinks are all examples of differentiated products.

As might be expected, competition proceeds along different lines, depending on whether there are "many" or "few" firms and whether their products are identical and differentiated. Viewed from this perspective, four main forms of market structure and types of competition stand out:

1. *Perfect competition*—Many sellers of a standardized product.

2. *Monopolistic competition*—Many sellers of a differentiated product.

3. *Oligopoly*—Few sellers of either a standardized or a differentiated product.

4. *Monopoly*—A single seller of a product for which there is no close substitute.

In this chapter we shall present the model of perfect competition. Chapters 11 to 13 concern pricing and production under conditions of monopolistic competition, oligopoly, and monopoly.

THE CHARACTERISTICS OF PERFECT COMPETITION

321

The
Characteristics
of Perfect
Competition

A perfectly competitive market environment is distinguished by four main features. First, the products of firms in the industry are identical or at least so much alike that buyers do not care whether they buy the product of one firm or another. Since the products of the firms are indistinguishable and therefore homogeneous, no buyer is willing to pay one firm a higher price than that charged by rival firms. Buyers are totally indifferent as to the firm from which they purchase as long as price is the same. In fact, differences in price constitute the *only* reason a buyer might prefer one seller to any other.

Second, in perfect competition each and every buyer and seller is without power to affect the going market price of the product. This means that a buyer's purchases must be such a sufficiently small portion of the total bought by all buyers that he cannot wrangle a lower price from sellers than can any other buyer. Likewise, the sales made by a particular firm must be such a sufficiently small portion of the total sold by all firms that the price of the product is not materially affected by any one firm's decision to increase or decrease its output rate. Only if many buyers or sellers act in concert can market conditions be influenced materially.

Third, in a perfectly competitive market resource inputs of all kinds are completely mobile. In the long run, there are no important restrictions upon the freedom of firms to enter or leave the industry. Resources can be switched from one use to another very readily. Workers are willing and able to move from region to region in response to new job opportunities and changing wage rates. The supplies of raw materials are in no way monopolized but are made freely available to the highest bidders.

Fourth, perfect competition is characterized by a state of perfect knowledge. Decisions are made under conditions of *certainty*. Firms know exactly what their revenue and cost functions are. They also know the prices of all resource inputs and the various alternative technologies which can be used to produce their products. Consumers are aware of the prices charged by all firms. Resource owners are aware of the prices firms are paying for resource inputs and all relevant opportunity costs.

Obviously, these four conditions are so stringent that no market in the real world ever has or ever can meet them. A few markets come close to satisfying the first three requirements (numerous agricultural products and some stocks and bonds), but naturally none meet the fourth requirement of perfect knowledge. Nonetheless, the study of perfectly competitive markets is not without value. Recall from the introductory chapter that a model may yield valid conclusions even though its assumptions are "unrealistic." As we shall see, the perfectly competitive model captures the essence of real-world markets where large numbers of relatively small firms sell identical products. In addition, it illuminates several basic principles underlying the economics of business behavior. For these reasons perfect competition is worthy of study even though the assumptions upon which it rests are not always

322

*How Markets
Function: The
Model of
Perfect
Competition*

accurate reflections of real-world conditions. We shall, however, be careful not to claim too much for the model of perfect competition, and we shall be especially judicious in applying its conclusions to the behavior of firms in actual situations. With these points fixed firmly in mind, suppose we examine how a representative firm behaves in a perfectly competitive market.

SHORT-RUN EQUILIBRIUM OF A FIRM IN A PERFECTLY COMPETITIVE MARKET

In perfect competition the prevailing market price of a product is established in classic fashion by the interaction of the market forces of demand and supply. Given the market demand and supply curves in Fig. 10-1(a), a short-run market equilibrium is attained at a price of P_1 dollars and at a total industry output of Q_T units.[2] If price were higher than P_1, then excess supply conditions would drive it downward. By the same token, if price were lower than P_1, then excess demand conditions would force it upward.

Under conditions of perfect competition, each firm has a *horizontal* demand-AR curve which intersects the vertical axis at the price established by market supply and market demand conditions. This is illustrated in Fig. 10-1(b). No firm can sell its output at a price even slightly higher than P_1 dollars because buyers will immediately shift their purchases to other firms selling the same item at a lower price. And since each firm is so small relative to the total market, it can sell its entire output at the market price of P_1; hence, there is no inducement whatsoever to sell at a price lower than P_1. The result is that all firms sell at the going price. At any one time a *single* price prevails throughout the market, as determined by the balance between demand and supply.

When the firm's demand-AR curve is horizontal, it can sell additional units of output without reducing price. Thus, marginal revenue equals price at every output rate since each additional unit sold will cause total revenue to rise by an amount equal to the price of the product. For example, if price is fixed at $10, then the sale of each additional unit causes total revenue to rise by $10; MR is therefore constant and equal to $10. The firm's MR function corresponds precisely to its demand-AR curve, as shown in Fig. 10-1(b). Both marginal and average revenue are equal to the market price of the product at all possible outputs of the firm.

Since the firm can sell whatever amount it wishes at the going price, its total revenue (TR) function will be a linear, upward-sloping curve starting from the origin, as depicted in Fig. 10-1(c). Each and every unit sold will increase TR by an amount equal to the selling price. Marginal revenue (MR) is constant, so the TR curve rises at a constant rate (equal to MR and price).

[2]The total industry output, Q_T, is the sum of the outputs of all the firms in the industry. It is important to remember that no one firm's output constitutes a significant portion of Q_T.

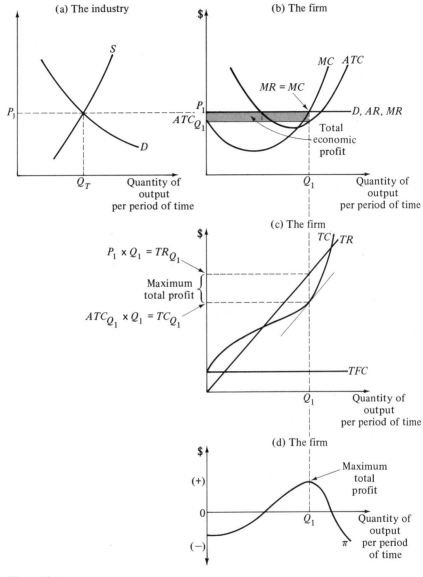

Figure 10-1
Profit-maximizing price and output for a firm operating in a perfectly competitive market environment

The general equation for the TR function can be written as

$$TR = P \cdot Q.$$

Now suppose that the firm has a cost structure represented by the average total cost (ATC) and marginal cost (MC) curves in Fig. 10-1(b) and by the associated total cost (*TC*) curve in Fig. 10-1(c).[3] How much should the firm decide to offer for sale? How will the firm fare at the going price? To answer these questions first requires a consideration of the goal or goals of business enterprises in an environment of perfect competition. As was indicated in Chapter 9, profit is the single strongest goal of most firms, so suppose we assume that the prime objective of perfectly competitive firms is to *maximize profits* (or to minimize losses if they cannot make profits). Whether this assumption is valid will be seen shortly.

Since price is established by the market, a perfectly competitive firm has no pricing decision to make. It is a *price-taker*. The determination of price in a perfectly competitive environment is well beyond the control of any one firm; rather, each firm must live with whatever price that market demand and supply conditions establish. However, alternatives do exist regarding the firm's short-run output. The firm *is* able to exert some measure of control over its destiny by adjusting its output to any rate it is capable of producing. Assuming, then, a goal of profit maximization, consider the optimum output decision of a perfectly competitive firm.

Profit Maximization: The Total Cost–Total Revenue Approach

The easiest and most direct way to determine where profits are maximum is to compare total revenue and total costs. Logic dictates that *total profits are maximized at the output rate where TR exceeds TC by the greatest amount.* In Fig. 10-1(c) the profits of the firm are maximum at an output of Q_1 units, where the *vertical distance* between *TR* and *TC* is greatest. Geometrically, it so happens that the maximum vertical distance between *TR* and *TC* occurs at the output rate where a tangent to the *TC* curve has the same slope and is parallel to the *TR* curve, as indicated on the diagram.

The firm's profit function [Fig. 10-1(d)] is derived by subtracting *TC* from *TR* at each rate of output. It indicates how the firm's short-run profits vary with its output rate. The peak of the total profit (π) curve defines the output rate corresponding to maximum short-run profits.

Profit Maximization: The Unit Cost–Unit Revenue Approach

On a unit cost and unit revenue basis, *maximum profits are obtained at the output rate where marginal cost equals marginal revenue.* The validity of

---

[3]It should be recognized that the cost curves portrayed in Figs. 10-1(b) and (c) represent just one of the several types of short-run cost functions which firms may possess. As was discussed in Chapter 8, the cubic type of *TC* function is viewed by many economists as representative of the most typical type of cost behavior. However, firms may well possess other types of cost functions depending on the character of the technology employed in the production process. The chapter-end exercises incorporate other types of cost functions to illustrate the perfectly competitive firm's output decision under a variety of cost circumstances.

this proposition may be established as a matter of common sense. If the production and sale of one more unit of output will add more to a firm's total revenue than to its total costs, the sale of the unit must necessarily add something to the firm's total profits. If, however, the extra cost of producing and selling one more unit is greater than the extra revenues the firm gains, the firm's total profits will be reduced by selling that unit. Marginal revenue (*MR*) is defined as the *addition* to total revenue attributable to the sale of one more unit of output, while marginal cost (*MC*) is defined as the addition to total cost resulting from the production and sale of one more unit of output. Hence, to maximize profits the firm must be cognizant of the marginal revenue and the marginal cost of each successive unit of output.

Thus, in Fig. 10-1(b) the most profitable output level is at Q_1 units, where the *MC* curve intersects the *MR* curve. If the firm stops short of selling Q_1 units, then the revenue from selling an additional unit will exceed the cost of selling another unit. Plainly, the firm can increase profits by increasing its rate of output to Q_1. Should the firm produce beyond an output rate of Q_1 units, the marginal costs of all the units in excess of Q_1 will exceed the additional revenue which the firm can obtain from selling them. The firm will lose money on all the units sold past an output of Q_1 units, thereby causing total profits to be smaller than that obtainable at lesser outputs.

The profit-maximizing output rate in Fig. 10-1(b) corresponds exactly to the output rate in Fig. 10-1(c) where *TR* exceeds *TC* by the greatest amount. How do we know? Because at an output of Q_1 units in Fig. 10-1(c), the slope of the *TR* curve equals the slope of the *TC* curve. *MR*, by definition, equals the slope of *TR*, and *MC*, by definition, equals the slope of the *TC* function. Hence, since the values of the slopes are equal, *MC* must necessarily equal *MR* at the same output where total revenue exceeds total cost by the largest amount. Logical consistency requires further that the profit-maximizing output rate in Fig. 10-1(b) coincide with the output rate in Fig. 10-1(d) where the total profit function reaches its maximum height.

The profit-maximizing rule may be stated in yet another way: *Total profit is maximum at the output rate where marginal profit equals zero.* Marginal profit is the change in total profit resulting from a 1-unit change in output; this is equivalent to saying that

$$M\pi = MR - MC,$$

where $M\pi$ is marginal profit. More technically, marginal profit equals the rate of change in total profit as the rate of output changes, or

$$M\pi = \frac{d\pi}{dQ}.$$

Marginal profit is, therefore, geometrically equal to the slope of the total profit function. At the peak of the total profit function, its slope equals zero —hence the rationale for saying that total profit is maximized where $M\pi = 0$. As long as marginal profit is positive, the total profit function is rising, and

326

*How Markets
Function: The
Model of
Perfect
Competition*

it pays to increase output. When the profit earned on the next unit of output has shrunk to zero ($M\pi = 0$), the peak of the total profit function has been reached. If the firm produces beyond the output rate associated with zero marginal profit, marginal profit becomes negative, and the loss incurred on each of these extra units causes the total profit function to turn downward. This is evident from inspection of the total profit function in Fig. 10-1(d).

Calculation of the Profit-Maximizing Output

It is useful to examine the mathematics of determining the perfectly competitive firm's optimum output decision. Suppose the going market price for the commodity is \$20 and the firm's total cost function is $TC = 75 + 17Q - 4Q^2 + Q^3$. From the preceding discussion we know that profit is maximized at the output where $MR = MC$. Both the MR and MC functions can be obtained from the information given. At a constant price of \$20, MR is also \$20 at every output rate. The MC function is the first derivative of the TC function, giving

$$MC = \frac{dTC}{dQ} = 17 - 8Q + 3Q^2.$$

Equating MR with MC, we have

$$20 = 17 - 8Q + 3Q^2.$$

Solving for Q yields the two roots $Q = -\frac{1}{3}$ and $Q = 3$. Since output can never be negative, the profit-maximizing rate of output is 3 units. Actually, it can be proved that the larger of the two roots is always the profit-maximizing (or loss-minimizing) output rate. It is a simple matter, however, to resolve the issue by calculating total profit at each of the values of Q for which $MR = MC$ and observing firsthand which Q yields the greatest total profit.

The profit-maximizing output can also be determined using the rule that total profit is maximum where marginal profit is zero. Again, let $P = MR = \$20$ and $TC = 75 + 17Q - 4Q^2 + Q^3$. Total profit is defined as

$$\pi = TR - TC.$$

Total revenue, being equal at every output to $P \cdot Q$, can in this case be represented by the expression $20Q$. Substituting into the expression for total profit, we have

$$\pi = 20Q - (75 + 17Q - 4Q^2 + Q^3).$$

Since marginal profit is precisely defined as the rate of change in total profit as the rate of output changes, the expression for marginal profit becomes

$$M\pi = \frac{d\pi}{dQ} = 20 - (17 - 8Q + 3Q^2).$$

Given that total profit is maximum where $M\pi = 0$, the expression above is set equal to zero, yielding

$$20 - (17 - 8Q + 3Q^2) = 0,$$
$$20 - 17 + 8Q - 3Q^2 = 0,$$
$$3 + 8Q - 3Q^2 = 0.$$

Solving for Q gives the roots $Q = -\frac{1}{3}$ and $Q = 3$, the same results given by the $MR = MC$ approach.

Total Profit or Loss

Whether the firm realizes a profit or a loss depends on the relationship between price and average total cost at the intersection of MR and MC. If price exceeds ATC, the firm will enjoy short-run profits, whereas if price is less than ATC, losses will be incurred.

In Fig. 10-1(b), selling price is P_1 dollars, and ATC at the profit-maximizing output of Q_1 units is ATC_{Q_1} dollars. Profit per unit is therefore $P_1 - ATC_{Q_1}$ dollars at an output of Q_1 units. Total profit is profit per unit multiplied by the number of units sold, or

$$\pi = (P_1 - ATC_{Q_1})Q_1,$$

which is numerically equivalent to the size of the shaded area in Fig. 10-1(b). This shaded area has a numerical dollar value equal to the vertical distance between TR and TC at an output of Q_1 units in Fig. 10-1(c) and equal to the height of the total profit function in Fig. 10-1(d). It should also be clear from Figs. 10-1(b) and (c) that multiplying P_1 by Q_1 gives TR_{Q_1} and that ATC_{Q_1} times Q_1 equals TC_{Q_1}.

Observe that at output Q_1, profit *per unit* is *not* maximized; in other words, total profit is not maximum at the same output at which profit per unit is maximum. Profit per unit is maximized at the output rate where price exceeds ATC by the greatest vertical distance, whereas total profit is maximized where $MR = MC$. These two output rates do not coincide, as an examination of Fig. 10-1(b) will confirm.

Minimizing Short-Run Losses

It does not, of course, always work out that perfectly competitive firms can earn positive economic profits in the short run. The equilibrium market price in the short run may fall below the firm's ATC curve at every rate of output, thereby making it impossible for the firm to cover all its costs in the short run. What, then, is the firm's optimum output decision? Should it shut down operations and wait for price to return to a more profitable level, or should it produce at a loss? If it continues to operate, at what output will the firm's losses be minimized?

328

*How Markets
Function: The
Model of
Perfect
Competition*

The firm's decision rests on whether or not the market price is high enough to cover the firm's average variable costs (or whether enough total revenue can be obtained to cover total variable costs) at some output rate. Suppose we define *unit contribution profit* as the difference between price and average variable cost:

$$\text{unit contribution profit} = P - AVC.$$

The relevance of unit contribution profit is easily demonstrated. If a product sells for $10 per unit and average variable cost is $6, the firm is able to cover all the expenses associated with the variable inputs needed to produce the product and has $4 left over to help pay total fixed costs and to contribute to the earning of profit. Hence, even though price may not be sufficient to cover ATC, as long as the prevailing price is high enough to permit the firm to obtain a margin over and above AVC, it pays the firm to produce in the short run. Covering part of AFC is better than covering none of AFC.

A related concept is that of *total contribution profit*. Total contribution profit is the difference between total revenue and total variable costs:

$$\text{total contribution profit} = TR - TVC.$$

It should be apparent that even if TR is not sufficient to cover TC, as long as TR more than covers TVC, the firm earns some amount of total contribution profit, which can be used to pay at least a portion of the firm's total fixed costs. This is a superior outcome to the situation of shutting down. When the firm ceases selling in the short run, TR falls to zero, and the firm's loss will be equal to its total fixed costs. Furthermore, it stands to reason that the larger the amount of total contribution profit a firm can obtain, the better will be its short-run profit and loss position. The greater the amount by which TR exceeds TVC, the more dollars the firm will have to pay fixed costs. And when total fixed costs have all been paid, then any remaining total contribution profit represents economic profit.

We are now ready to use the concepts of contribution profit in determining a firm's optimum output decision when price temporarily falls below average total cost. Consider Fig. 10-2. Suppose supply and demand conditions establish an industrywide price of P_1 dollars. Given the firm's MC, AVC, and ATC curves, what is the optimum output rate? Clearly, the firm cannot make a profit because the ATC curve lies above price P_1 at every output rate; the firm's decision then turns on how to minimize its losses. Observe that between output Q_1 and Q_3 in Fig. 10-2(b) price exceeds AVC; similarly, between the same outputs in Fig. 10-2(c), TR exceeds TVC. Thus, there are a number of output rates at which both unit and total contribution profits are positive. The significance of this finding is that the firm will minimize its losses by producing somewhere between Q_1 and Q_3, since in this output range TR will exceed TVC, and the resulting total contribution profit can be applied to the payment of total fixed costs. Common sense tells us that the firm will want to obtain as much total contribution profit as possible, so as to

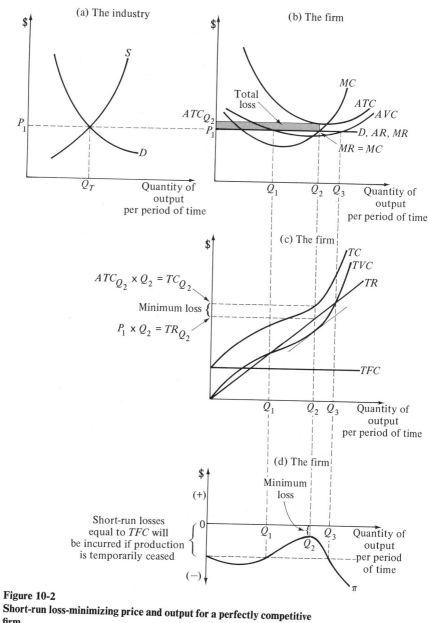

Figure 10-2
Short-run loss-minimizing price and output for a perfectly competitive firm

have the maximum number of dollars available for covering total fixed costs and thereby keeping losses to a minimum. Note in Fig. 10-2(c) that the output at which TR exceeds TVC by the greatest vertical distance occurs at output Q_2, where a tangent to the TVC curve is parallel to the TR curve; this is the output rate associated with maximum total contribution profit. It is also

330

*How Markets
Function: The
Model of
Perfect
Competition*

apparent from Fig. 10-2(c) that the vertical distance by which TC exceeds TR is less at Q_2 than at any other output rate, meaning that here the firm's short-run losses are minimized. Thus, from the standpoint of TC-TR analysis, *short-run losses are minimized at the output where TC exceeds TR by the smallest vertical distance.* In Fig. 10-2(d) the total profit function reaches its highest level at an output of Q_2 units; short-run losses are measured by the vertical distance from the peak of the profit function to the horizontal axis. Insofar as the firm's unit costs and revenues are concerned [Fig. 10-2(b)], an output of Q_2 units per period of time corresponds exactly to the output where $MR = MC$ and $M\pi = 0$. Thus, we find that the $MR = MC$ rule and its corollary, $M\pi = 0$, not only identify the short-run profit-maximizing output but also identify the short-run loss-minimizing output.

Now consider Fig. 10-3, where the forces of supply and demand combine to establish a short-run equilibrium price of P_1 dollars such that the firm's demand-AR-MR curve is just tangent to the minimum point of its AVC curve. Again, there exists no opportunity for earning a normal profit, much less an economic profit, and the firm's output decision must be aimed at minimizing short-run losses. If the firm elects to produce where $MR = MC$ and where $M\pi = 0$, then it will produce Q_1 units [Fig. 10-3(b)] and will obtain total revenues of TR_1 dollars [Fig. 10-3(c)]. Price will be just equal to AVC [Fig. 10-3(b)], and total variable costs will be equal to total revenue [Fig. 10-3(c)]. Unit contribution profit will be zero, and total contribution profit will be zero. The firm's revenues will just cover variable expenses, and the firm's losses will be equal to total fixed cost. Insofar as minimizing losses is concerned, the firm will be indifferent as to producing and selling Q_1 units or closing down its operations in the short run. In either case, short-run losses will equal total fixed costs, and this is the best the firm can do. At any other output rate revenues will not even be sufficient to cover TVC, contribution profit will be negative, and losses will exceed TFC by the amount of TVC not covered by TR. However, given that short-run losses will be no more by operating at Q_1 than by closing down, the firm will in all probability elect to produce and sell Q_1 units. By so doing, the firm continues to serve its customers and to offer employment to its workers, with no difference in losses from that of the shutdown case.

However, Fig. 10-4 shows a situation where the short-run equilibrium market price falls below even minimum AVC. Should the firm again follow the rule of producing at the point where $MR = MC$ [Fig. 10-4(b)], then total losses will be equal to the vertical distance between TR and TC in Fig. 10-4(c). Observe that TR will not even cover TVC at this output—or any other output for that matter. The vertical spread between TR and TC is always greater at outputs above zero than at zero. Both unit and total contribution profits are negative at every output above zero. Therefore, in this instance the firm will minimize short-run losses by discontinuing production and selling nothing; losses will equal total fixed costs.

The following principles summarize the analysis: The relationship between price and AVC tells the firm *whether* to produce; the firm will find it

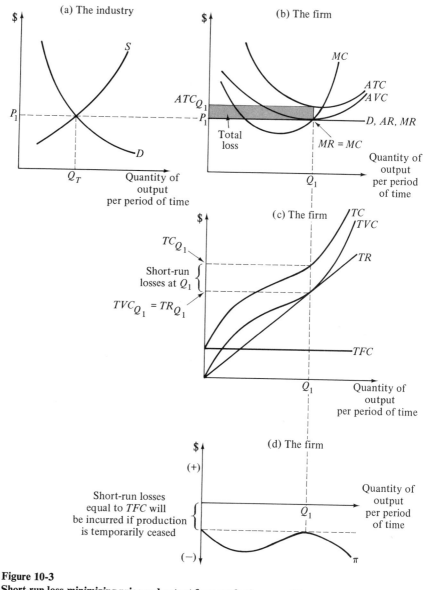

Figure 10-3
Short-run loss-minimizing price and output for a perfectly competitive firm when the demand curve is just tangent to the *AVC* curve

advantageous to continue production if price equals or exceeds *AVC* at one or more output rates and to cease production if price falls below *AVC* at every output rate. The relationship between marginal revenue and marginal cost indicates *how much* the firm should produce when price equals or exceeds *AVC*; profits are maximized or losses are minimized at the output rate where $MR = MC$ and $M\pi = 0$. The relationship between price and *ATC* indicates

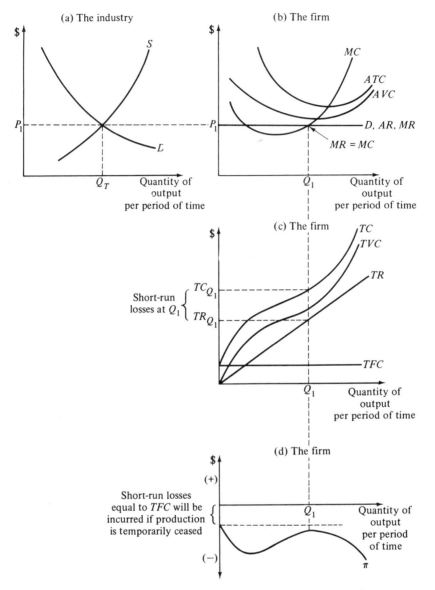

Figure 10-4
Short-run close-down position for a perfectly competitive firm

the *amount of profit or loss* that results from the decision to produce; total profit or loss equals the difference between price and *ATC* multiplied by the quantity produced and sold. Thus, the firm maximizes short-run profits or minimizes short-run losses by producing and selling the output at which $MR = MC$ and $M\pi = 0$. There is only one exception. When the prevailing market price is below the firm's minimum average variable costs at every output rate, losses will be minimized by stopping short-run operations altogether, holding losses to the amount of total fixed costs. As will be indicated shortly, these same principles also hold true for firms operating under conditions other than perfect competition.

THE PERFECTLY COMPETITIVE FIRM'S SHORT-RUN SUPPLY CURVE

We have just seen that a perfectly competitive firm incurring a loss in the short run will continue to produce in the short run provided it loses no more by producing than by shutting down production entirely. This proposition is useful for deriving the short-run supply curve of an individual firm in a perfectly competitive environment. The procedure is illustrated in Fig. 10-5. Suppose that market price is P_0 dollars and the firm's AVC, ATC, and MC curves are as shown in Fig. 10-5(a). Since P_0 is below the minimum AVC which the firm can achieve, the firm's short-run equilibrium rate of output is zero. Next, suppose market price is P_1. The corresponding equilibrium rate of output for the firm is Q_1 units, as this is the output at which $MR = MC$ and at which losses are minimum. Thus, the firm is ready, willing, and able to supply Q_1 units at a price of P_1 dollars; the values (P_1, Q_1) define a point (S_1) on the firm's supply curve in panel (b). Now suppose market price is P_2, generating D_2, AR_2, and MR_2. In this case, the firm's optimum output decision is to produce Q_2 units and thereby minimize its short-run losses. The values (P_2, Q_2) are associated with point S_2 in Fig. 10-5(b). Similarly, a price of P_3 leads to a profit-maximizing output of Q_3 units and point S_3. Other supply points can be derived in like fashion.

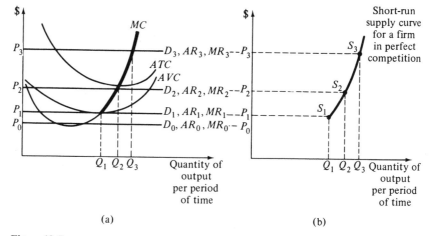

(a)   (b)

Figure 10-5
Derivation of the short-run supply curve for a perfectly competitive firm

334

*How Markets
Function: The
Model of
Perfect
Competition*

Connecting the price-output combinations in Fig. 10-5(b) gives the short-run supply curve of the perfectly competitive firm. The supply curve indicates the quantity of output per period of time which a profit-maximizing firm would supply at various alternative prices under conditions of perfect competition. It should by now be apparent that the firm's supply curve is identical in shape and position to that portion of the firm's *MC* curve lying above its *AVC* curve. This is illustrated in Fig. 10-5(a) as the boldly inscribed portion of the firm's *MC* curve. In other words, *the short-run supply curve for a perfectly competitive firm coincides with its marginal cost curve for all rates of output equal to or greater than the output at which AVC is minimum.* The firm's supply of output drops to zero at any price below *AVC*. Herein lies the link between production costs and output rates in the short run for a perfectly competitive enterprise.

THE PERFECTLY COMPETITIVE INDUSTRY'S SHORT-RUN SUPPLY CURVE

In Chapter 4 the market demand curve was derived by horizontally adding together the demand curves of individual consumers. However, factors are present which may preclude a similar determination of the short-run industry supply curve for the commodity in question. The perfectly competitive firm's marginal cost curve is derived from the underlying production function (Chapter 8) on the assumption that the price of variable input is constant, no matter how many or how few units the firm purchases. This is a reasonable assumption in the case of perfectly competitive firms, because any one firm uses such a small amount of the total supply of the variable input that changes in its rate of input usage have no perceptible effect on the market price of the variable input. In other words, a single firm can expand or reduce its output rate, and consequently its variable input usage, without affecting the price it pays for variable input.

Yet, should *all* firms in a perfectly competitive industry simultaneously decide to expand or to reduce output, there may be a marked effect upon the supply price of the variable input. For example, suppose one chicken producer decides to raise more chickens and therefore buys more chicken feed. The prevailing price of chicken feed is quite unlikely to be affected. But if all chicken producers decide to raise more chickens, upward pressure on the price of chicken feed becomes a distinct possibility, particularly in the short run when the supplies of chicken feed are limited by the available production capacity.

As a consequence, the short-run supply curve for the product of a perfectly competitive industry cannot necessarily be obtained by horizontally summing the relevant portion of the marginal cost curves of each firm. It all depends on what happens to the price of variable input when *all* firms in the industry alter their usage of variable input. In the event that the supplies of variable input to a perfectly competitive industry are perfectly elastic (the input supply curves are horizontal), then it is valid to conceive of the short-run industry supply curve for the product as being the horizontal summation of the relevant portions of the *MC* curves of the individual firms. If the use of more variable input by all firms in the industry precipitates an increase in the price of variable input, then the marginal cost curve of each individual firm will shift upward by the increase in input price, and the short-run industry supply curve will be *more steeply sloped* than had input prices remained constant. If the use of more variable input by all firms in the industry causes the price of variable input to decline (perhaps because it can be supplied more economically in larger quantities), then the marginal cost curve of each individual firm will shift downward by the decrease in input price, and the short-run industry supply curve will be *less steeply sloped* than had input prices remained constant.

But whatever happens to the price of variable input when all firms use more or less of it, we can be confident that the short-run industry supply curve is upward sloping. How steeply sloped it is depends on the factors determining the shape of the marginal cost curve of each firm and on the effect of changes in industrywide output on variable input prices. Suffice it to say at this point that to induce greater supplies of output in the short run from a perfectly competitive industry, higher prices will have to be offered. This characteristic gives rise to a short-run industry supply curve that slopes upward to the right—such then is the basis for the industry supply curves drawn in Figs. 10-1 through 10-4.

LONG-RUN EQUILIBRIUM OF A FIRM IN A PERFECTLY COMPETITIVE MARKET

Although a perfectly competitive firm finds its short-run output decision constrained by the limitations of the fixed inputs, in the long run the options are more numerous. An established firm can alter its plant size, implement new technologies, or modify the character of its products in line with changing consumer tastes. More importantly, the firm can abandon production entirely and leave the industry if below-normal profits are being earned and the prospects are dim for any improvement. On the other hand, new firms may enter the industry if the profits of established firms are sufficiently attractive. Consider now the transition of a firm from short-run to long-run equilibrium in a perfectly competitive market.

Two assumptions will greatly simplify the analysis without invalidating the important conclusions:

1. We shall suppose that all firms in the industry have comparable cost structures. By so doing we can talk in terms of a typical firm with the knowledge that all other firms in the industry will be similarly affected. (This assumption is not implausible, given that all the firms are producing identical products.)
2. We shall assume for the moment that the prices of resource inputs are unaffected (a) by changes in the long-run output rates of existing firms, (b) by the entry of firms into industry, or (c) by the exodus of firms from the industry. In other

336

*How Markets
Function: The
Model of
Perfect
Competition*

words, the firms in the industry can, singly or as a group, alter their input requirements without affecting the prices they pay for them.

Let the short-run forces of market demand (D_1) and supply (S_1) result
in a market price of P_1 dollars [Fig. 10-6(a)]. Further suppose that the typical
firm has a short-run cost structure represented by $SRAC_1$ and $SRMC_1$ at the
indicated position on the $LRAC$ curve [Fig. 10-6(b)]. With these revenue and
cost functions, short-run equilibrium output for the firm is Q_1 units. At this
output rate the firm realizes an economic profit because price exceeds $SRAC$
at Q_1 units. Recall from Chapter 9 that an economic profit means the firm is
receiving a rate of return on its investment greater than it could earn by
diverting its resources into the production of other commodities. Under these
circumstances the earning of an economic profit will have two significant
effects. First, it will encourage the firm (if it has not already done so) to
expand its production capability and take advantage of any available economies of scale indicated by the firm's $LRAC$ curve. Expanding its long-run
output potential (to the position defined by $SRAC_3$ and $SRMC_3$) offers the
firm the prospect of even greater economic profits. Second, the existence of
above-normal profits in this industry will induce new firms to initiate production of the commodity. The process of new entry may be very slow or very
rapid, depending on the amount of economic profits being earned by established firms and on the length of time it takes new entrants to begin their
production operations.

As time elapses and these two effects take hold, the industry supply
curve will shift to the right, say from S_1 to S_3, thereby driving the market
price from P_1 down to P_3 and increasing the equilibrium industry output
from Q_{T_1} to Q_{T_3}. The larger volume of industry output is a result of both the
entry of new firms and the expansion of firms already in the industry.

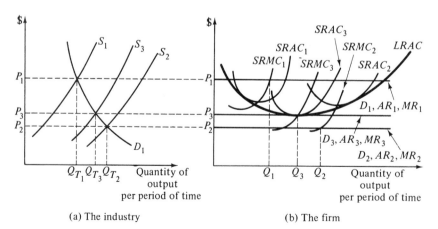

(a) The industry   (b) The firm

**Figure 10-6
Transition to long-run equilibrium for a firm operating
in a perfectly competitive market environment**

However, it is also possible that the profit attraction could be strong enough to induce the typical firm to expand its production capacity beyond $SRAC_3$ and $SRMC_3$ to the output range where it has a cost structure represented by $SRAC_2$ and $SRMC_2$. In such a case, the greater output capabilities of firms would mean a shift of the industry supply to S_2 rather than to just S_3, and the industry price would be at P_2 where D_1 intersects S_2. It is apparent from Fig. 10-6(b) that a price of P_2 dollars the typical firm will sustain losses in the short run, since market price is below $SRAC_2$ at every output rate. Obviously, then, the typical firm and the industry would have both *overexpanded*; no longer would it be possible for firms to earn normal profits. The result will be a readjustment in the industry's production rates. Given that firms can earn higher rates of return in other industries, some firms— most likely the least efficient firms, which are incurring the greatest losses— will elect to cease production of the commodity in question and shift their energies into the production of products where the profit outlook is brighter. The firms that choose to remain in the industry will find it advantageous over the long term to reduce costs by adjusting their production capabilities to the optimum size—where the $SRAC$ curve is tangent to the minimum point of the $LRAC$ curve. In terms of Fig. 10-6(b), the typical firm would be induced to construct production facilities having a cost structure represented by $SRAC_3$ and $SRMC_3$. The outmigration of firms, coupled with the retrenchment of the production capacity of the remaining firms, would then cause the industry supply curve to shift to the left, eventually to S_3. As the industry supply curve moves leftward, market price will rise to P_3 and total industry output will contract to Q_{T_3}. Again, the optimum output rate for the typical firm becomes Q_3 units, where MR_3 intersects $SRMC_3$.

Observe that at this output price is just equal to short-run average total cost and to long-run average cost. The typical firm earns no economic profit but is able to squeeze out a normal profit. Taken together, these conditions define long-run equilibrium for a perfectly competitive market. Given our initial assumptions of (1) perfect mobility of resources into and out of the industry and (2) a goal of profit maximization, the position of long-run equilibrium is necessarily ordained to occur at the point where price equals the minimum value of long-run average cost and where the typical firm earns no more and no less than a normal profit. This is, indeed, the only conceivable point of long-run equilibrium. The reasoning is straightforward. As long as market price is above the long-run average costs of the typical firm, economic profits can be realized. Established firms will be induced to expand provided it is profitable to do so, and new firms will be attracted into the industry. Over time the market supply curve will be shifted to the right, thereby driving market price down and lowering the horizontal demand-AR-MR curve confronting each firm. Economic profits will tend to vanish. On the other hand, whenever price is below the long-run average costs of the typical firm, losses will be incurred. As their plants and equipment depreciate, some firms will leave the industry, being attracted by the higher profit prospects elsewhere; the remaining firms will attempt to lower their

338

*How Markets
Function: The
Model of
Perfect
Competition*

costs by constructing more economically sized facilities. The industry supply curve shifts leftward, and market price is raised along with the horizontal demand, AR, and MR curves for the individual firms. Losses will gradually be eliminated. The number of firms in the industry and the production capacity of each firm will stabilize only when the opportunities for earning an economic profit are exhausted and when economic losses can be avoided. Therefore, since the position of long-run equilibrium must be consistent with *zero* economic profit and *zero* economic loss, it is necessary that the long-run equilibrium price be exactly equal to minimum short-run average cost and to minimum long-run average cost. Unless $P = MR = SRAC = LRAC$, a change in firm size or in the number of firms will lead to the appearance of either economic profits or economic losses, in which case the forces of adjustment will spring into motion.[4]

It should now be apparent that we are entirely justified in our assumption made earlier that perfectly competitive firms will seek to maximize profits. Actually, perfectly competitive firms have no choice—they are placed in a position of *forced profit maximization*. Under conditions of long-run equilibrium a firm which operates at any output rate other than minimum $LRAC$ will not earn a normal profit. With dismal earnings (or even losses), few firms are likely to pursue alternative goals; they simply cannot afford it. For this reason, it seems justifiable to assume that perfectly competitive firms will behave as if they seek to maximize profits.

In practice, of course, it is not really expected that a perfectly competitive industry will reach and thereafter maintain a state of long-run equilibrium. The market demand curve will certainly undergo frequent shifts as consumer tastes and preferences, incomes, and so on change. Likewise, technological progress, changing input prices, and new product availability cause periodic shifts in the firm's $SRAC$ and $LRAC$ curves and the industry supply curve. As a consequence, long-run equilibrium is a moving target that a perfectly competitive industry continually chases but never catches. The process of market adjustment to long-run equilibrium is dynamic and always unfolding, in response to new market circumstances of demand, supply, and prices.

Furthermore, the continual process of adjusting toward a long-run equilibrium position imposes severe constraints on perfectly competitive firms. The impersonal market forces of supply and demand are so powerful that in the long run firms are unable to make a profit any larger than that just sufficient to induce them to remain in business. The only discretionary

---

[4]In practice, however, the profit thermostat regulating the number of firms and the outputs they produce works much better for expansion than contraction. Economic profits and free entry are reliable stimulants for increasing industry output, given sufficient time for firms to construct new facilities and bring new production capacity on stream. But to squeeze firms out of an over-expanded industry where profits are below normal or negative can be a slow and painful process. It takes time for entrepreneurs to accept the harsh fact that profit prospects are bleak, time for production facilities to wear out, and time to shift into the production of other commodities or else go out of business entirely. The long death of the small farmer is a case in point.

AGRICULTURAL MARKETS: AN ILLUSTRATION OF *SOME* OF THE CHARACTERISTICS OF PERFECT COMPETITION

The biggest sector of the American economy where perfectly competitive conditions are reasonably approximated is that of agriculture. This is so for three reasons:

1. The supply side of the markets for many agricultural commodities (wheat, corn, soybeans, tobacco, cattle, hogs, cotton) is comprised of literally thousands of firms—each of which tends to be small absolutely and also relative to the market as a whole. True, some farms are much larger than others in terms of acreage, but even the largest farms are seldom as big as a moderately sized manufacturing enterprise. More important, there is virtually no instance in which a single farm produces a large enough fraction of an agricultural product to put it in a position to exert meaningful influence over either price or the total quantity supplied. Indeed, suppliers of most farm commodities are so great in number and so sufficiently equal in size that the chance to act independently and exercise market power is for all practical purposes nil.

2. Agricultural products are essentially identical from farm to farm—at least in terms of each grade and variety. Wheat, for example, is not a branded product at the farm level and carries no identification as to the farm on which it was grown. Meats, dairy products, fruits, and vegetables may carry the brand of a processor or store, but usually not the name of the farmer who raised them (exceptions where the producer's brand name does appear include eggs, bananas, and pineapples). As a result, agricultural products within the same class or grade are *highly* substitutable—so much so that each producer can rightly regard its demand curve as being horizontal at the going market price.

3. Compared to other industries, there are few barriers to the entry of new firms into the production of agricultural products. At the same time, a farmer often finds it easy to shift acreage out of the production of one item (where profit prospects are dim) into the production of another item (where profit opportunities are brighter); in such cases barriers to entry and exit are extremely low since as each new growing season rolls around farmers can readily adjust their production mix in whatever directions market conditions seem to warrant.

A combined effect of these three aspects is to make the markets for agricultural commodities very sensitive to shifts in market conditions. When bad weather produces a smaller than expected crop, market prices rise sharply. If there is an unusually bountiful harvest, the prices that farmers receive can fall drastically. A trade deal with another country can dramatically boost farm export opportunities and thus the prices of the affected products. Prices can and do fluctuate daily on the commodity exchanges, often in response to fleeting demand-supply conditions. Thus, "the market" in its role as the governing force

340

*How Markets
Function: The
Model of
Perfect
Competition*

is liable to be volatile, causing sometimes sharp swings in farm prices and farm profits. The competitive struggle becomes a contest where each seller, under conditions of considerable uncertainty, must decide whether and how it can profitably survive at the expected market prices.

The Case of Soybeans

In 1973–1974, when higher energy costs and economic recession cut into household food budgets, livestock producers began trimming back output as meat sales slacked off and, consequently, reduced their purchases of livestock feeds. Soybean meal prices tumbled from $400 a ton in 1973 to as low as $100 a ton in June 1974 and then recovered slightly to around $125 a ton throughout most of 1975. Soybean oil prices sank to around 20 cents a pound in 1975 from a peak of more than 50 cents in 1974, mainly because cautious processors starting switching to competing products such as palm oil.

At planting time in spring of 1975, farmers were confronted with a hard choice of which crop to plant. Prospects for higher prices for corn, cotton, and soybeans were discouraging and the federal government offered no subsidy programs to farmers to take land out of production. Many farmers chose to plant soybeans, saying at the time that soybean prices seemed less vulnerable to a sharp decline. The soybean crop flourished because of good weather, and 1975's crop was 20% greater than 1974's. Brazil's crop, stimulated by planting newly available acreage, exceeded 350 million bushels compared to only 24 million bushels in 1968. Meanwhile the record-high soybean-product prices of previous years spurred production not only of soybeans but also of other oils and meals—from sources like cottonseed, linseed, corn, peanuts, palms, olives, and sunflowers. Particularly was soybean oil under competitive pressure from palm oil; palm oil imports were up 145% during the first 8 months of 1975.

In addition, soybean growers had another problem to contend with: because of differing production features, a farmer could grow more bushels of corn than soybeans on an acre of land. Consequently, the price of soybeans had to be higher than corn to get the same financial return per acre (many observers contended that soybeans had to be worth 2.5 to 3 times per bushel more than corn to be equally profitable). Thus, the dilemma was whether the market price of soybeans would be low enough to compete with foreign imports and substitute products and yet high enough to justify growing soybeans as opposed to alternative crops.

As the 1976 growing season approached, analysts predicted:

1. Between 2 and 3 million acres planted to soybeans in 1975 would be planted in other crops in 1976—a move that would stabilize soybean-product prices near 1975 levels, given the large inventory of soybeans in storage.
2. Soybean meal demand would improve because cattle and broiler producers were gearing up to increase outputs and consequently would need more meal for protein supplements.
3. Soybean growers would elect to be more "orderly" in marketing their soybean crops because the high prices of past years put them in a stronger financial position to hold on to their beans and finance their inventories in the hope that higher prices would return.

Questions for Discussion

1. What economic factors are apparent in influencing short-run changes in the equilibrium price of an agricultural commodity (say soybeans)? What about the long-run equilibrium price?
2. Using the soybean market as an example, explain how "the price mechanism" acts to bring market supply and demand into balance. In what ways is competition a factor in this adjustment process?

Source: Adapted in part from *The Dow Jones Commodities Handbook 1976*, pp. 39–46.

action a firm has relates to its output decision. And in the long run even here the firm's option is taken away; it is forced to produce where $P = MR = SRAC = SRMC = LRAC$ if it wants to earn at least a normal profit. Thus, *the firm is truly a captive servant of the market.* All of this, according to conventional wisdom, works to the advantage of consumers and society as a whole. Under long-run equilibrium conditions the consumer pays a price no higher than is required to cover all costs of production, thereby obtaining products at as low a price as is economically feasible. Moreover, all firms produce at the minimum points of their cost curves, thus utilizing in the most efficient manner the pool of resources that society makes available to the industry.

A Constant-Cost Industry

In the preceding section it was assumed that the expansion or contraction of industry output had no effect on *input* prices. An industry having this characteristic is referred to as a *constant-cost* industry. The existence of such an industry has several implications which merit further exploration.

Figure 10-7 depicts long-run equilibrium under conditions of constant costs. Let D_1 and S_1 be the original short-run market demand and supply

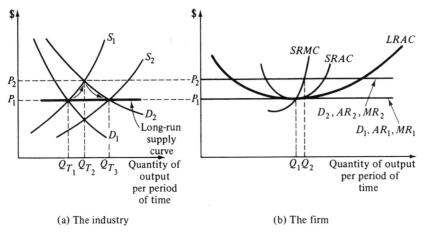

(a) The industry   (b) The firm

Figure 10-7
Long-run supply curve for a constant-cost industry

curves, with an equilibrium price at P_1 dollars. Assume that each firm in the industry is in long-run equilibrium at Q_1, where the firm's horizontal demand-AR-MR curve is just tangent to the minimum points of the firm's $SRAC$ and $LRAC$ curves, as shown in Fig. 10-7(b). Now consider the impact of a shift in the short-run market demand curve to D_2. The market price will rise to P_2 dollars, and the profit-maximizing output for the firm becomes Q_2 units per period of time. However, at a price of P_2 dollars and an output of Q_2 units each firm will earn an economic profit, thereby triggering the entry of new firms into the industry and shifting the industry supply curve rightward, eventually to S_2. In the case of a constant-cost industry the entry of new firms and the expansion of industry output will not affect the costs of the existing firms. The reason is that the resource inputs employed by this industry are available in such sufficiently large quantities that the appearance of new firms does not bid up the prices of the inputs and raise the costs of the existing firms. As a consequence, the $LRAC$ curve of established firms remains fixed, and the new firms can operate with an identical $LRAC$ curve.

Long-run equilibrium adjustment to the shift in demand is accomplished when the entry of new firms has caused the market price to fall back to P_1, where $P_1 = MR_1 = SRAC = SRMC = LRAC$, and each firm is producing Q_1 units and earning only a normal profit. The important point here is that the industry has a *constant long-run supply price*, which means industry output can be expanded or contracted in accordance with market demand conditions without altering the *long-run* equilibrium price charged by the firms. To put it another way, *a constant-cost industry operating under conditions of perfect competition has a horizontal long-run supply curve*. Such a curve is illustrated in Fig. 10-7(a).

An Increasing-Cost Industry

343

*Long-Run
Equilibrium of
a Firm in a
Perfectly
Competitive
Market*

Obviously, a situation can easily arise where changes in the output rate of an industry can cause the prices of resource inputs to change. In this section we examine the case where the expansion of industry output has the effect of *raising* input prices, thereby giving rise to an *increasing-cost industry*.

As illustrated in Fig. 10-8, suppose that the industry is in long-run equilibrium. D_1 and S_1 portray the initial market demand and supply conditions, market price is P_1 dollars, and each firm is operating at the output rate where price equals minimum $SRAC$ and minimum $LRAC$. Now suppose that market demand increases to D_2, temporarily causing an increase in market price to the level where D_2 intersects S_1. The higher price allows established firms to earn an economic profit, which in turn attracts the entry of new firms. As output expands more resources are needed; at this point resource input prices are bid up by firms competing for the available resource supplies. The effect of rising input prices is to increase the operating costs of both established firms and new entrants. As industry output expands and input prices rise, the marginal and average cost curves for the typical firm all gradually shift upward from $SRMC_1$, $SRAC_1$, and $LRAC_1$, say to a position represented by $SRMC_2$, $SRAC_2$, and $LRAC_2$. Moreover, the short-run industry supply curve is shifted to the right by the expansion of industry output. The process of adjustment continues until all economic profits have been eliminated. In Fig. 10-8, this is depicted by the intersection of D_2 and S_2 and its associated price of P_2 dollars. Each firm selects the rate of output where $P_2 = MR_2 = SRMC_2 = SRAC_2 = LRAC_2$. The long-run industry supply curve is found by joining the points of long-run equilibrium; in Fig. 10-8 these points are represented by the intersection of D_1 and S_1 and the intersection of D_2 and S_2.

The salient feature of an increasing-cost industry is the presence of a

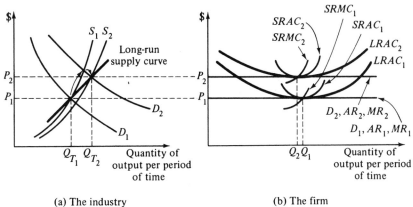

(a) The industry

(b) The firm

Figure 10-8
Long-run supply curve for an increasing-cost industry

344

*How Markets
Function: The
Model of
Perfect
Competition*

positively sloped long-run supply curve. Whereas in a constant-cost industry the expansion of industry output has no effect on the long-run price of the industry's product, in an increasing-cost industry the effect of greater industry output is a higher product price. The long-run supply curve of an increasing-cost industry slopes upward, because greater rates of output entail rising input prices and hence rising costs. Under these circumstances, higher market prices will be required to give firms the incentive to expand output.

A Decreasing-Cost Industry

Price and output behavior in a *decreasing-cost industry* is depicted in Fig. 10-9. The initial long-run equilibrium is given by the market demand curve D_1, the short-run industry supply curve S_1, a market price of P_1 dollars, and each firm producing at the minimum points of $SRAC_1$ and $LRAC_1$. As before, suppose that market demand increases to D_2. Market price rises to the point where D_2 intersects S_1, and established firms find themselves in the position of being able to earn an economic profit. New firms are induced to enter the industry, and the short-run industry supply curve shifts rightward, say to S_2. In a decreasing-cost industry the expansion of output results in *lower* input prices and hence lower costs for the firms in the industry. Thus, as the entry of new firms causes input prices to fall, the short-run and long-run cost curves of the firm shift downward. The adjustment process will continue until a new long-run equilibrium is established. In Fig. 10-9 this occurs at the intersection of D_2 and S_2, where the resulting price of P_2 dollars is just equal to the minimum points of $SRAC_2$ and $LRAC_2$. Connecting the two points of long-run equilibrium gives the long-run industry supply curve.

Clearly, a decreasing-cost industry has a negatively sloped long-run supply curve, meaning that the equilibrium price of the industry tends to fall as industry output increases. Although it is rare for input prices to fall when

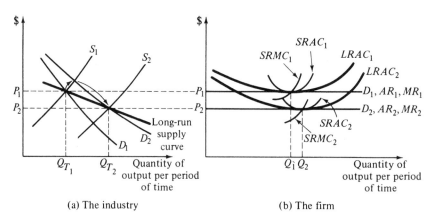

(a) The industry   (b) The firm

Figure 10-9
Long-run supply curve for a decreasing-cost industry

industry output expands, it does occur. One example is the case of a young industry which springs up in a relatively underdeveloped area, where resource markets are poorly organized, marketing facilities are primitive, and transportation is inadequate. An increase in the number of firms and in the output of the industry may stimulate the development of marketing and transportation facilities that reduce the costs of individual firms; in addition, supplies of labor and other support services may become more dependable and more efficient. Another example arises in the case of capital goods purchases. The more firms there are in an industry and the larger its output, the more economically suppliers of capital goods may be able to provide these firms with specialized machinery, continuous-process equipment, and higher-quality tools because of their own economies of scale in producing them. By and large, the individual firm has little control over these sorts of decreasing costs; consequently, cost reductions of this type are often referred to as external economies of increasing production, or, more simply, just *external economies*. They result solely from growth of the industry and from forces outside the control of the individual firm. External economies should not be confused with the internal economies of scale, which are under control of the firm and which can be secured by enlarging the scale of the firm's operations.

In the absence of technological change, most economists regard increasing-cost industries as being the most prevalent of the three types. Decreasing-cost industries are perhaps the most unusual situation. Both decreasing- and constant-cost industries are likely to evolve gradually into industries of increasing cost as they grow larger and become more mature. However, if technological change is admitted to the picture, a downsloping long-run industry supply curve becomes more probable. Technical progress in an industry can cause costs of production to fall over time, thus giving rise to a downsloping long-run industry supply curve.[5] Indeed, the industries which are most successful in lowering costs and relative prices tend to show the most dramatic increases in output over time. Technological progress can also neutralize rising input prices, thereby transforming an otherwise increasing cost industry into a constant- or decreasing-cost industry.

IMPLICATIONS AND SIGNIFICANCE OF THE PERFECTLY COMPETITIVE MODEL

The behavior of firms and markets under conditions of perfect competition has the following features and results:

1. The chief feature of perfect competition is the existence of powerful market forces which tend to drive price to a level where each firm earns no more and no less than a normal profit and return on investment. Whenever demand and supply conditions allow firms in the industry to earn more than

[5]The manufacture of transistors and solid-state components is an excellent example of an industry which has experienced declining costs as a result of new technologies.

346

*How Markets
Function: The
Model of
Perfect
Competition*

a normal profit, new firms are induced to enter, and where economies of scale permit, existing firms are induced to expand. Subsequently, price is driven down to the point of minimum $SRAC$ and minimum $LRAC$, thereby foreclosing the opportunity to earn more than a normal return. Should demand and supply conditions result in a price that inflicts losses upon the firms in the industry, then some firms are induced to shift into the production of other commodities where the profit prospects are more favorable; the remaining firms seek to adjust their scale of operations in the direction of minimum long-run average cost. As a consequence, market forces move firms toward a "no-profit/no-loss" situation where firms earn only an accounting profit sufficient to induce them to continue in business in the industry.

2. Since every firm is subject to the discipline of the market, it must remain as efficient as the average firm in the industry, or eventually the losses that accompany inefficiency and high unit costs will force it out of business. The process of adjusting to long-run equilibrium *compels* all firms to try to produce at the lowest possible long-run average cost.

3. Perfectly competitive firms are *price-takers and quantity-adjusters.* They have absolutely zero market power. A single firm exercises no control whatsoever over the going market price, and its only discretionary judgment is how much to produce at the prevailing market price. But even here, as long-run equilibrium adjustment occurs, the discretion over output erodes; firms which wish to earn at least normal profit find their best chance of doing so at the minimum point of the $LRAC$ curve where $P = MR = SRMC = SRAC = LRAC$.

4. Both the output of specific firms and the capacity of the industry are responsive to changes in demand. If market demand increases in relation to the supply capability of the industry, market price is bid up, entry and expansion are induced, and over time additional output capacity is created. Conversely, if market demand falls or if the industry overexpands, then market price falls, expansion is discouraged, and firms may even leave the industry.

5. Perfect competition is a unique form of competition. It does not pit rival against rival; rather, it pits the firm against the market. The firm's competitive struggle is one of responding to changing market conditions and trying to stay in a cost-efficiency position to earn at least a normal profit at the going market price. Only the fittest survive the struggle—in the long run.

6. With identical products, the competitive focus is on price but most particularly on the ability of firms to compete at lower market prices. In perfect competition, prices are very flexible downward. Prices fall whenever the quantity offered for sale exceeds the quantity purchased and also whenever efficiency gains, technological improvements, or lower input prices (all of which mean lower unit costs) allow firms to earn attractive profits selling at lower market prices.

7. Perfect competition provides consumers maximum protection from "exploitation" by business firms. The outcome in the marketplace results from freely made decisions of consumers to buy and freely made decisions of

producers to sell. Neither is able to control the other or rig the market to his own advantage. Therefore, there can be no question of an abuse of power and, thus, no need for government intervention or regulation. In short, perfect competition is the epitome of what is meant by a *free market*.

8. The perfectly competitive model takes an overly narrow view of the competitive process because, in a sense, the entire spotlight is on price and price competition. The model takes no formal cognizance of product competition (because the products of all firms are assumed to be identical) or of technological competition (because all firms are forced to adopt the most efficient production techniques) or of promotional competition (what is there to promote?). In fact, it is fair to say, that the model of perfect competition looks upon the only "valid" and "lasting" form of competition as being competition based upon price. Such a view of competition is too restrictive.

In conclusion, the major economic significance of the model of perfect competition concerns the benefits to consumers of perfect competition and the efficiency with which it allocates resources. Under conditions of long-run equilibrium, consumers are able to buy the product at the lowest price consistent with covering all costs of production. Since price is barely sufficient to give the firm a normal profit and keep it in business in the long run, the consumer obtains the product at as low a price as is economically feasible. In addition, every firm is forced to produce at the most efficient output rate. All scale economies are realized, and all diseconomies of size are avoided. Thus, perfectly competitive firms utilize resources in the most efficient manner possible—full production efficiency is attained. Society obtains the greatest output from the resources used in producing the commodity and at the lowest feasible price. Herein lies the social justification for a free market (or capitalistic) economy. The perfectly competitive model is indeed how pure capitalism is supposed to work in theory; in other words, the model describes how a market economy is supposed to operate and provides the theoretical underpinning for laissez-faire capitalism. The model is, at least, an excellent starting point for assessing the benefits which society gains from a competitive marketplace.

SUGGESTED READINGS

CLARK, J. M., *Competition as a Dynamic Process* (Washington, D.C.: The Brookings Institution, 1961), Chapters 2 and 3.

KIRZNER, I. M., *Competition and Entrepreneurship* (Chicago: University of Chicago Press, 1973), Chapters 1 and 2.

MCNULTY, P. J., "A Note on the History of Perfect Competition," *Journal of Political Economy*, Vol. 75, No. 3 (August 1967), pp. 395–399.

———, "The Meaning of Competition," *Quarterly Journal of Economics*, Vol. 82, No. 4 (November 1968), pp. 639–656.

SCHERER, F. M., *Industrial Market Structure and Economic Performance* (Chicago: Rand McNally & Company, 1970), Chapter 2.

348

*How Markets
Function: The
Model of
Perfect
Competition*

STIGLER, GEORGE J., "Perfect Competition, Historically Contemplated," *Journal of Political Economy*, Vol. 65, No. 1 (February 1957), pp. 1–17.

PROBLEMS AND QUESTIONS FOR DISCUSSION

1. (a) A firm's total revenue can be determined by adding the values of MR for each unit sold. True or false? Explain.
   (b) A firm's total cost can be determined by adding the values of MC for each unit produced. True or false? Explain.
   (c) A firm's total profit can be determined by adding the values of $M\pi$ for each unit produced and sold. True or false? Explain.

2. Total profit is maximum at the same output at which total contribution profit is maximum. True or false? Explain.

3. Unit contribution profit $(P - AVC)$ is greatest at the same output that total contribution profit $(TR - TVC)$ is greatest. True or false? Explain.

4. Why is competition said to be "perfect" in a perfectly competitive market? Just what is so perfect about perfect competition?

5. How do perfectly competitive firms compete? In what form is "competition" present in a perfectly competitive market?

6. Graphically illustrate the short-run supply curve for a perfectly competitive firm which has a short-run production function characterized by decreasing returns to variable input over the entire range of its output capability.

7. Suppose in a perfectly competitive industry that market supply and demand forces combine to produce a short-run equilibrium price of $70. Suppose further that a firm in this industry has a weekly total cost function expressed by the equation $TC = 200 + 25Q - 6Q^2 + \frac{1}{3}Q^3$. Determine the perfectly competitive firm's profit-maximizing output rate and the amount of its short-run profits or losses.

8. Using the unit cost and unit revenue curves, graphically illustrate the short-run profit-maximizing price and output for a perfectly competitive firm which has a production function that exhibits decreasing returns to variable input over its entire range of output capability. (*Hint:* Determine the shape of the ATC and MC curves that correspond to a production function characterized by decreasing returns to variable input and then locate the price and output at which $MR = MC$.) Indicate on your graph the area that represents the firm's total profits.

ELEVEN HOW MARKETS FUNCTION: THE MODEL OF MONOPOLISTIC COMPETITION

In most real-world markets the products of firms are not homogeneous. Ordinarily, the product of each firm is in some way *differentiated* from the product of every other firm. In fact, most enterprises devote considerable time and effort to engineering special features into their products and to making their products unique through advertising, packaging, brand names, terms of credit, service, and so on. The particular concern of this chapter is with the economics of the firm in a market environment comprised of *many* firms selling products that are very close (but not perfect) substitutes for each other. Such a market structure is labeled by economists as *monopolistic competition*.

THE DISTINCTIVE FEATURES OF MONOPOLISTICALLY COMPETITIVE MARKETS

Three factors combine to set monopolistic competition apart: (1) product differentiation, (2) the presence of large numbers of sellers, and (3) nonprice competition.

Introducing the element of product differentiation into the marketplace causes some consumers to prefer the products of particular firms over those of other firms. Each firm in producing its own unique version of the product obtains a kind of limited monopoly. There is only one producer of Schlitz beer, only one manufacturer of Hart, Schaffner, and Marx suits, and only one publisher of *Playboy*; even so, each of these firms faces competition from rival firms—hence, the label "monopolistic competition." Ultimately, product differentiation has the effect of giving a monopolistically competitive firm limited influence over the price it charges for its output—the firm in a very restricted sense is a "price-maker." It derives this power from the fact that some consumers are willing, within limits, to pay a higher price to satisfy their preferences for the products of specific firms. The price differential which a firm is able to charge is a function of the firm's success in differentiating its product in the minds of consumers, thereby creating "brand loyalties" and "company loyalties." However, the price differential obtainable by any one firm is likely to be slight since close similarity among the products of rival firms makes it quite difficult to create strong brand attachment when price differences are sizable. In more formal terms, we can say that the cross elasticity of demand between products of monopolisitcally competitive firms is quite high; so also is the price elasticity of demand for any one firm's product.

Like perfect competition, monopolistic competition is characterized by such a sufficiently large number of firms that no one firm has the production capacity to supply a significant share of the industry's output. Monopolistically competitive firms are typically small-sized firms, both absolutely and relatively. Entry into monopolistically competitive industries is usually easy, though it is a bit more difficult than in perfect competition, because of product differentiation. A new firm must not only possess the capacity for producing the product but it must also be able to win customers away from established firms. Securing a niche in the market is likely to entail research and development costs by the new firm to discover features which will distinguish its product from products already on the market. Moreover, unlike perfection competition, advertising and sales promotion may be necessary to inform consumers of the availability of a new brand and to persuade enough customers to switch to the new brand. Therefore, a newcomer into a monopolistically competitive industry faces somewhat greater financial and marketing obstacles than a newcomer into a perfectly competitive market.

The final feature of monopolistic competition is the presence of vigorous *nonprice competition* among the firms. Economic rivalry is based partially upon price and partially upon product quality, service and other conditions of sale, and sales promotion. A firm operating under conditions of monopolistic competition can simultaneously undertake three strategies for influencing its sales volume. First, the firm can change the price it charges—the strategy of *price competition*. Second, the firm can modify the nature of its product—the strategy of *product competition*. Third, the firm can revise its sales promotion tactics—the strategy of *promotional competition*. The first strategy represents an attempt to move along the demand curve confronting the firm, whereas the last two strategies involve an attempt to shift the firm's demand curve. From a theoretical standpoint all three strategies can be pursued without explicit regard for the behavior of rival firms and without much concern for retaliation by rival firms. The reason? With a large number of firms in the industry, the impact of the strategy of a single firm spreads itself over so many of its rivals that the effect felt by any one rival is greatly diluted and does not usually lead to the formulation of a counterstrategy or a readjustment. Accordingly, each firm may expect its actions to go unnoticed by its competitors and to be unimpeded by counter-measures on the part of any one firm.[1]

We shall examine each of the foregoing three strategies in the sections immediately following.

PRICE AND OUTPUT DECISIONS OF MONOPOLISTICALLY COMPETITIVE FIRMS

Under conditions of monopolistic competition, each firm is confronted with a downsloping demand and average revenue curve. Herein lies the fundamental difference between the model of perfect competition and the model of monopolistic competition, and it stems from the presence of differen-tiated products. Because the particular product of each firm has certain distinguishing features which set it apart from those of other firms, a monop-olistically competitive firm has a small measure of discretion in establishing the price of its product. By shaving its price to levels somewhat below the prices of rival firms, a firm can usually induce proportionately more customers to buy its product because it is a good substitute for the products of its com-petitors. On the other hand, a firm which raises its price can expect a signifi-cant decline in sales as many of its customers switch to lower-priced brands. Accordingly, the firm must have a downsloping demand curve, for it can sell more of its product at lower prices than at higher prices. The firm cannot raise price without losing sales, and it cannot gain sales without charging a lower price (assuming, of course, the demand curve does not shift). Moreover, the presence of large numbers of good substitutes makes the demand curve of a particular firm highly elastic over the relevant range of possible prices.[2]

[1]Some economists challenge the view that a firm can rationally assume its actions will go undetected by rival firms. From a behavioral standpoint a firm can be expected to learn, sooner or later, that its strategies will in fact invoke retaliation from competitors—especially if its strategies prove successful. One must search long and hard to find a business-man who does not believe his actions will be noticed by his competitors and who, in turn, does not keep close tabs on what rival firms are doing—irrespective of how many rivals he may have. Thus, the ability to act independently is relative, not absolute. But despite this legitimate objection, it still seems fair to conclude that the larger the number of firms in an industry, the more able a firm will be to implement new strategies without provoking direct retaliation from rival firms. The fact that a firm with many rivals can act more independently than a firm with few rivals does indeed lead to differences in firm and market behavior.

[2]The results of one study showed a coefficient of price elasticity of -5.7 for different brands of frozen orange juice, -5.5 for instant coffee, -4.4 for regular coffee, and -3.0 for margarine. Indirect evidence of high elasticity also stems from the fact that rival firms in monopolistic competition act as though they believe that their demand curves are highly price elastic. They usually sell their products at very nearly the same price and display a

352

*How Markets
Function: The
Model of
Monopolistic
Competition*

Graphically, this means that the firm's demand curve tends to be *gently* downsloping, as depicted in Fig. 11-1(a); the demand curve is drawn as a straight line merely for simplicity and convenience. Generally speaking, the exact degree of price elasticity reflected in a monopolistically competitive firm's demand curve is a function of the number of rival firms and the degree of product differentiation. The larger the number of competitors and the weaker the product differentiation, the greater the price elasticity of demand for a firm's product over the relevant price range.

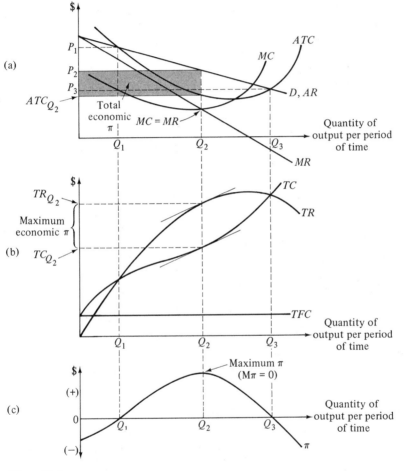

Figure 11-1
Short-run profit maximization for a firm in monopolistic competition

distinct hesitancy to test consumer loyalty by pricing their products much above the prices charged by rival firms. For some empirical evidence as to the degree of consumer loyalty see two articles by Lester G. Telser: "The Demand for Branded Goods as Estimated from Consumer Panel Data," *Review of Economics and Statistics*, Vol. 44, No. 3 (August 1962), pp. 300–324; and "Advertising and Cigarettes," *Journal of Political Economy*, Vol. 70, No. 5 (October 1962), pp. 471–499.

When the firm's demand curve is downsloping, the firm's marginal revenue function does not coincide with the demand-average revenue function; rather, it lies below the demand-AR curve.[3] If the firm's demand-AR curve is linear and downsloping, the firm's MR curve is also linear and downsloping and has a slope twice that of the demand-AR curve. Recall from Chapter 5 that if the demand function is given by the general linear equation

$$P = a - bQ,$$

then the equation for TR becomes

$$TR = P \cdot Q = (a - bQ)Q = aQ - bQ^2.$$

Since the expression for marginal revenue is found by taking the first derivative of the TR equation, the general equation for MR is

$$MR = \frac{dTR}{dQ} = a - 2bQ.$$

Both the demand-AR curve and the MR curve originate at the same value a, but the slope of the MR function is twice as great as that of the demand-AR curve ($-2b$ as compared to $-b$). In geometric terms, the MR curve is located by drawing it so as to bisect the horizontal distance between the demand-AR curve and the vertical axis [Fig. 11-1(a)]. The total revenue function corresponding to the demand-AR and the MR functions is depicted in Fig. 11-1(b).

Suppose that the cost structure of a typical firm in a monopolistically competitive industry is given by the ATC and MC curves in Fig. 11-1(a) and by the corresponding TC curve in Fig. 11-1(b). What, then, are the firm's optimal price and output levels? Since monopolistically competitive industries are composed of numerous firms that, in the main, are both small and owner-managed, it is appropriate again to assume that the firm's decisions are motivated by the desire to maximize profits. However, we cannot be completely confident about assuming firms will behave as if they seek to maximize profits, because the element of product differentiation gives each firm somewhat more discretionary decision-making power than was the case in perfectly competitive environments. As we shall see shortly, there are more variables to be considered, a greater degree of uncertainty is present, and market forces operate in ways which allow firms a modest leeway in deviating from profit-maximizing behavior. Nevertheless, a goal of profit maximization is a reasonable approximation of reality because of the close ties between ownership and control which typifies relatively small firms. Suppose, also, we assume for the moment that the firm produces a fixed product and engages in a given amount of sales promotion activity; this will allow us to pinpoint the principles underlying the price and output behavior of a monopolistically

[3]The reader is urged to refresh his memory on this point by reviewing the section on "Average, Total, and Marginal Revenue" in Chapter 5.

354

*How Markets
Function: The
Model of
Monopolistic
Competition*

competitive firm. Following this, we shall relax this assumption and examine the effect of product variation and promotional expenditures upon price-output behavior.

Profit Maximization: The Total Cost–Total Revenue Approach. A firm in monopolistic competition, like the perfectly competitive firm, will maximize short-run profits at the output where total revenue exceeds total cost by the greatest amount. Given the TR and TC functions in Fig. 11-1(b), the firm will be able to earn an economic profit at any output rate between Q_1 and Q_3 units, but short-run profits will be maximum at an output of Q_2 units, where the vertical distance between TR and TC is the greatest. Geometrically, TR exceeds TC by the greatest amount at the output rate where a tangent to the TC curve has the same slope and is parallel to a tangent to the TR function. The total profit function in Fig. 11-1(c) is again derived by subtracting TC from TR at each output rate. Logic dictates that the peak of the total profit function correspond to an output rate of Q_2, where TR exceeds TC by the largest amount.

Profit Maximization: The Unit Cost–Unit Revenue Approach. On a unit cost and unit revenue basis, short-run profits are maximized at the output where $MC = MR$ and $M\pi = 0$. The reasoning is precisely the same as in the case of perfectly competitive firms. As long as an additional unit of output adds more to the firm's revenues than it does to the firm's costs, profit on that unit will be positive and total profits will be increased (or losses decreased) by producing and selling the unit. Alternatively, when MC exceeds MR and $M\pi$ is negative, total profits can be increased (or losses decreased) by decreasing the rate of output. In Fig. 11-1(a) short-run profits are maximum at an output of Q_2 units per period of time. This is the output rate at which the marginal cost curve intersects the marginal revenue curve. Moreover, it corresponds exactly to the value of Q_2 in Fig. 11-1(b). At Q_2, the tangents to TR and TC have identical slopes. Since the slope of TC equals MC and the slope of TR equals MR, MR must equal MC at exactly the output where TR exceeds TC by the greatest amount.

The highest price which the firm can charge and still sell Q_2 units is P_2 dollars. The profit-maximizing price thus corresponds to the point on the demand-AR curve associated with the output at which $MC = MR$. Average total cost at Q_2 units of output is ATC_{Q_2}. Total economic profit in the short run equals $(P - ATC_{Q_2})Q_2$, or the shaded area in Fig. 11-1(a). At outputs smaller than Q_2 units, MR exceeds MC, and larger outputs up to Q_2 will add more to total revenue than to total costs; accordingly, total profit will rise as the output rate is raised. At an output rate beyond Q_2, MC exceeds MR, and additional sales cause total costs to rise faster than total revenue, thereby decreasing total profit. Note that the firm can realize at least a normal profit by selling at a price as high as P_1 or as low as P_3 but that a price of P_2 dollars will yield the greatest economic profit. Prices P_1 and P_3 may be thought of as the "break-even" prices and outputs Q_1 and Q_3 may be thought of as the "break-even" output rates.

355
Price and
Output
Decisions of
Monop-
olistically
Competitive
Firms

Calculating the Profit-Maximizing Output. The mathematical procedure for determining the profit-maximizing price and output for a firm with a downsloping demand function is analogous to the calculations for a firm in perfect competition. Suppose the firm's demand function is given by the equation $P = 11,100 - 30Q$ and the firm's total cost function is given by the equation $TC = 400,000 + 300Q - 30Q^2 + Q^3$. From the preceding discussion we know that profit is maximized at the output where $MR = MC$. Both MR and MC can be obtained from the information given. If the demand function is $P = 11,100 - 30Q$, then

$$TR = P \cdot Q = (11,100 - 30Q)Q = 11,100Q - 30Q^2,$$

and

$$MR = \frac{dTR}{dQ} = 11,100 - 60Q.$$

The MC function, being the first derivative of the TC function, is

$$MC = \frac{dTC}{dQ} = 300 - 60Q + 3Q^2.$$

Equating MR with MC gives

$$11,100 - 60Q = 300 - 60Q + 3Q^2,$$

which reduces to

$$3Q^2 = 10,800.$$

Solving for Q yields the two roots $Q = -60$ and $Q = 60$. Obviously, output can never be negative; hence, the profit-maximizing rate of output is 60 units. As indicated earlier, it can be proved that the larger of the two roots is always the profit-maximizing (or loss-minimizing) output rate. It is a simple matter, however, to calculate total profit at each positive value of Q for which $MR = MC$ and see which root is associated with the greatest profit.

The profit-maximizing price is found by substituting the profit-maximizing output rate into the demand function and solving for P. In terms of our example, the profit-maximizing price is

$$P = 11,100 - 30Q$$
$$= 11,100 - 30(60)$$
$$= 11,100 - 1800$$
$$= \$9300.$$

Total profit at this price and output can be calculated by subtracting TC at

60 units of output from *TR* at 60 units of output. The reader should verify that total profit at 60 units of output will be $32,000 per period of time.

Total Profit or Loss. If demand is weak, then the monopolistically competitive firm may be unable to make an economic profit or even a normal profit. In such cases the firm must decide whether to shut down its operations in the short run and wait for demand conditions to become more favorable or whether to continue operating at a loss. The firm's short-run price and output decision hinges upon whether or not demand is strong enough to allow the firm to cover variable costs at some output rate.

Consider Fig. 11-2(a). Between outputs of Q_1 and Q_3 units per period, the firm's demand-*AR* curve lies above its *AVC* curve; hence, unit contri-

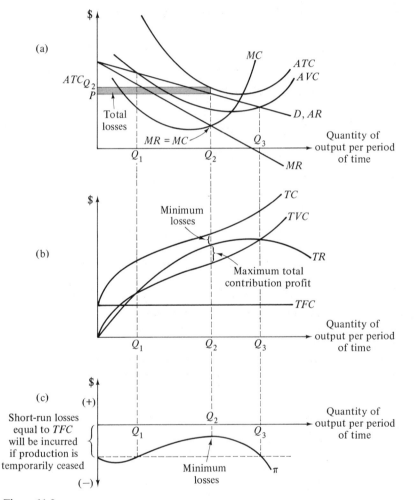

Figure 11-2
Short-run loss-minimizing price and output for a monopolistically competitive firm

bution profit $(P - AVC)$ is positive at all outputs greater than Q_1 and less than Q_3. As a consequence, between these outputs the total revenues obtained by the firm are more than sufficient to cover total variable costs, and some total contribution profit can be earned to pay at least a portion of the firm's total fixed costs [see Fig. 11-2(b)]. The firm should definitely continue to operate in the short run, since losses will be less than the amount of TFC—the amount it will lose if production and sales are temporarily discontinued. The question now is where between Q_1 and Q_3 to operate. Clearly, the firm is motivated to obtain as much total contribution profit as possible and thereby cover as large a portion of its total fixed costs as conditions will permit. Total contribution profit is maximum at the output where TR exceeds TVC by the greatest vertical distance. In Fig. 11-2(b) this occurs at an output rate of Q_2 units, where a tangent to the TR curve has the same slope as a tangent to the TVC curve. By inspection, the vertical distance by which TC exceeds TR is a minimum at Q_2, meaning that at Q_2 the firm's short-run losses are minimized. Therefore, from the standpoint of $TC\text{-}TR$ analysis, short-run losses are minimized at the output rate where total contribution profit is the greatest. This output coincides exactly with the output where the vertical spread between TC and TR is smallest. The corresponding total profit function reaches its highest level at Q_2, although it still lies entirely in the negative (loss) range. Insofar as unit costs and unit revenues are concerned [Fig. 11-2(a)], an output of Q_2 units corresponds exactly to the intersection of marginal cost and marginal revenue, where marginal profit equals zero. The loss-minimizing price is P dollars. At an output of Q_2 units, average total cost is ATC_{Q_2}; the firm's short-run losses will equal $(P - ATC_{Q_2})Q_2$—which is shown as the shaded area in Fig. 11-2(a). Thus, provided at least a portion of the demand-AR curve lies above the AVC curve (so that $P > AVC$), we see that the $MR = MC$ rule, along with its corollary, $M\pi = 0$, identifies not only the short-run profit-maximizing output but also the short-run loss-minimizing output.

Figure 11-3 illustrates a situation where the firm's demand-AR curve again lies below the ATC curve, foreclosing the opportunity for earning a normal profit in the short run. Note that the demand-AR curve is tangent to the AVC curve at a single output—Q_1 units. At Q_1, demand is just strong enough to permit the firm to sell at a price that will cover AVC. Unit contribution profit equals zero at Q_1; likewise, total contribution profit is zero, since $TR = TVC$ [see Fig. 11-3(b)]. From a profit-loss standpoint the firm will be indifferent as to producing and selling Q_1 units or closing down production in the short run. In either event, short-run losses will equal TFC, and this is the best the firm can do [see Fig. 11-3(b) and (c)]. At any other price and output combination TR will be insufficient to cover even TVC, both total and unit contribution profit will be negative, and short-run losses will exceed TFC by the amount of TVC not covered by TR. Given that selling Q_1 units at a price of P_1 dollars will have no adverse effects on its profit-loss position (as compared to temporarily closing down operations), the firm will undoubtedly elect to continue production. In doing so, the firm will protect its market

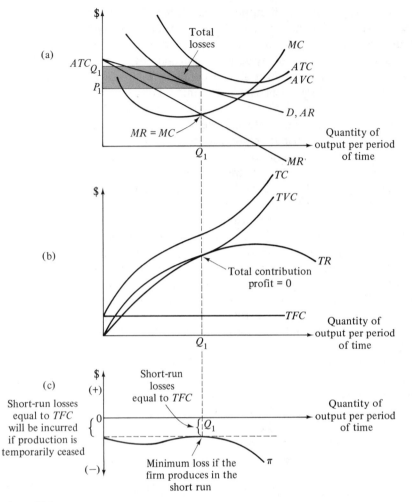

Figure 11-3

Short-run loss-minimizing price and output for a monopolistically competitive firm when the demand curve is just tangent to the AVC curve

share and, by continuing to place its product before the public, stand a better chance of realizing a favorable shift in demand conditions in the future.

Now consider Fig. 11-4, where the firm's demand-AR curve lies entirely below the AVC curve. At no output rate can sufficient revenues be accumulated to cover the variable costs of production. The vertical spread between TR and TC is always greater at output rates above zero than at zero. Both unit and total contribution profits are negative at all positive outputs. The total profit function is even more negative at positive output rates than at zero output. Therefore, in this instance the firm will minimize short-run losses by temporarily ceasing production and waiting for a favorable shift of the demand-AR curve; short-run losses will equal total fixed costs.

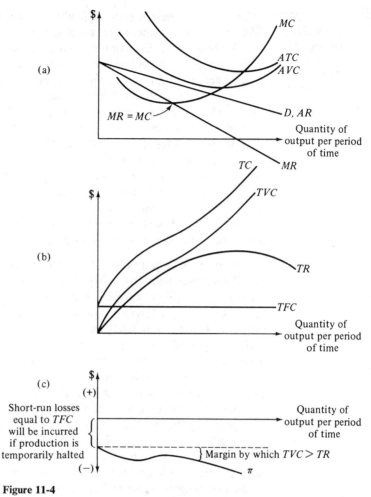

(a)

MC

ATC

AVC

$MR = MC$

D, AR

Quantity of output per period of time

(b)

TC

MR

TVC

TR

TFC

Quantity of output per period of time

(c)

$(+)$

Short-run losses equal to TFC will be incurred if production is temporarily halted

Quantity of output per period of time

} Margin by which $TVC > TR$

$(-)$

π

Figure 11-4
Short-run close-down position for a monopolistically competitive firm

Of course, if the weak demand conditions are perceived as permanent and if over time the firm's costs cannot be lowered sufficiently to allow a normal profit to be earned, then the firm should begin to divert its energies and resources into the production of other more profitable commodities or else dissolve entirely. Short-run losses can be sustained only temporarily. As the time perspective lengthens, some sort of readjustment must be made.

Market Demand and Supply Curves in Monopolistic Competition. Under conditions of monopolistic competition, representing industry supply and demand conditions by means of industry supply and demand *curves* is not satisfactory. Product differentiation makes the product units sold by one firm somewhat different from the product units sold by another. Bottles of hair oil differ from tubes of hair cream. Aerosol cans of hair spray are still

360

*How Markets
Function: The
Model of
Monopolistic
Competition*

different. Thus, there is some difficulty in constructing the quantity axis for industry curves. Furthermore, no single price prevails for the products of firms in the industry. Each firm may charge a slightly different price, according to the costs of producing its particular product and the strength of consumer demand for it. As a result of the price and product variations among firms, it is difficult to speak of a specific amount of output being supplied or demanded at a specific price. Moreover, what a firm is willing to produce at a given point in time hinges upon both *MR* and *MC*—the former varies with the demand for the product, and the latter is a function of input prices and the firm's technology. There is no unique price for each alternative output; it all depends on the shape and position of the demand-*AR* curve as to what the profit maximization price is for any given output a which *MR* = *MC*. Thus, the price-output decisions of firms cannot be meaningfully translated into an industry supply curve. The market as a whole is there, but it is better described in words than graphs.

Long-Run Adjustments of Monopolistically Competitive Firms. We saw earlier that with free entry and exit firms in a perfectly competitive industry are unable to earn more than a normal profit. Under monopolistic competition similar forces are present, though they are not quite so powerful as to eliminate completely the earning of economic profit or to guarantee each firm as much as a normal profit. The most which can be said is that *a tendency exists* for profits to move toward normal rates of return.

The process of long-run adjustments in a monopolistically competitive industry is analogous to that of perfect competition. New firms can enter the industry without undue difficulties. When short-run economic profits exist generally throughout the industry, established firms can be expected to pursue additional economies of scale, new technologies, and other profit-enhancing, cost-reducing options. New firms, attracted by the above-normal rates of return, will be motivated to enter the industry.[4] The entry of new rivals, assuming constant market demand for the products of the industry, will cause the demand curve of each firm to shift to the left. Why? Because each firm will necessarily have a smaller market share, since more firms will be dividing the relatively constant total market among themselves. Moreover, the demand curve will become somewhat more elastic, owing to the presence of a larger number of close-substitute products. These shifts in demand will tend to narrow profit margins and cause economic profits gradually to dissipate. Provided the attraction of economic profits is sufficiently strong to induce the entry of enough new firms and provided established firms are unable to discover innovative means of earning economic profits, there will exist a tendency for all economic profits to be eliminated in the long run.

Figure 11-5 illustrates the long-run equilibrium position of the representative firm. In panel (a) the demand-*AR* curve is shown tangent to the *SRAC*

[4]For simplicity, we shall assume that the entry and exit of firms has no effect on input prices and, consequently, upon the *SRAC* and *LRAC* curves of the firms. In other words, the long-run adjustment process is presumed to take place in a constant-cost environment. Shifts in the *SRAC* and *LRAC* curves as firms enter or leave the industry would unduly complicate the discussion without altering the conclusions.

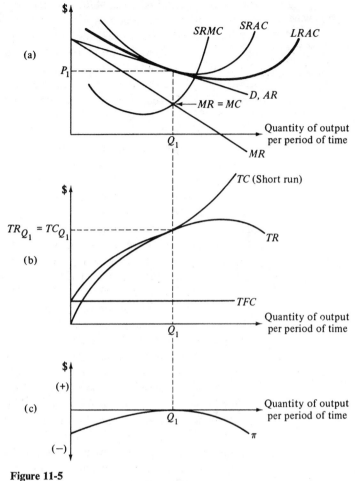

Figure 11-5
Long-run equilibrium for a monopolistically competitive firm

curve and the *LRAC* curve at the profit-maximizing output. Output Q_1 is the long-run equilibrium output, and price P_1 is the long-run equilibrium price. Since price equals *SRAC* at Q_1 units of output, the firm is just covering *all* its costs, including implicit and opportunity costs. The accounting profit reported by the firm will be equal to a normal profit or a normal rate of return in the economic sense. In panel (b) the *TC* curve is tangent to the *TR* curve at an output of Q_1 units. The total profit function in Fig. 11-5(c) climbs just to the zero-economic-profit level at Q_1 units. Plainly, any deviation from an output of Q_1 and a price of P_1 will yield revenues which are insufficient to cover *all* production costs including a normal profit. And since economic profits have dwindled to zero, no incentive exists for additional firms to enter the industry.

Should weak demand conditions preclude established firms from earning a normal profit (as previously illustrated in Figs. 11-2, 11-3, and 11-4),

362

*How Markets
Function: The
Model of
Monopolistic
Competition*

the least-efficient, highest-cost firms which are sustaining the largest losses are the most probable candidates for leaving the industry. The remaining firms can be counted upon to seek out ways to increase efficiency, reduce costs, stimulate demand, and thereby trim their losses. The exodus of firms from the industry will tend to shift the demand-*AR* curves of the remaining firms to the right, since the now fewer firms can divide the total market into larger pieces. Also, the reduction in the number of good substitutes will make the demand-*AR* curve a little less price elastic. The net result will tend to be an improvement in the profit-loss position of the representative firm to the point where at least a normal profit can be earned.

Observe that at the long-run equilibrium position, the representative firm is operating short of the minimum point on the *LRAC* curve. Each company is too small to achieve the lowest possible unit cost. In one sense there are too many firms in the industry. The same total output could be produced by a smaller number of firms, each operating at capacity. Thus, *excess production capacity* may be said to exist in the industry. Also, the long-run equilibrium price is higher than the minimum value of *LRAC*. Economists have made much of these two results; however, it is debatable how significant a criticism they consitute. The apparently excessive number of firms derives from consumer preferences for one brand over another, as reflected in the downsloping demand-*AR* curve. Consumers evidently believe they *gain* by being able to exercise their preferences for a brand or a store; otherwise, brand and store loyalty would vanish and the demand-*AR* curves of firms would tend to be horizontal (perfectly elastic).

However, the forces of long-run equilibrium adjustment in monopolistic competition are not so powerful as in perfect competition. The sequence of events leading to long-run equilibrium in monopolistic competition is readily interrupted. In the first place, some firms may be able to develop unique features in their product which are patentable and which give them a significant marketing edge over competitors, even over the long term. Second, some firms may obtain an especially favorable location for their business which allows them to earn sustained economic profits; this arises often in the case of motels, service stations, restaurants, and shopping centers. Third, through ongoing product innovation and the implementing of new technologies, firms may be able to gain advantages over their rivals which are sustainable for long periods. Finally, entry is not totally unrestricted; the added financial investment associated with product differentiation and sales promotion activities may pose some barrier to the entry of new firms, thereby allowing modest economic profits to persist in the long run. At the other end of the ladder, below-normal profits may also persist in the long run. The suburban florist may accept a return less than he could earn elsewhere because he likes living near a metropolitan area and because he likes designing floral arrangements. The proprietor of the corner grocery store may reluctantly accept subpar profits because his business is a way of life to him. Consequently, market forces will seldom be powerful enough in monopolistic competition to drive price all the way to equality with short-run and long-run average cost. Nevertheless, a *tendency* will exist for market forces to *limit* the profits and to *restrict* the losses of monopolistically competitive firms.

PRODUCT VARIATION DECISIONS

In monopolistic competition firms have the option of changing the characteristics of their product as well as price and output rates. Indeed, seeking to differentiate one's product from those of rival firms can be a potent sales-increasing strategy. Leadership in offering better values, improved quality and performance, new or greater convenience, or more selection is very apt to meet with buyer approval. In effect, successfully differentiating one's products from those of rival firms affords a firm breathing space to refrain from meeting or beating the prices of competing items. And from a broader social viewpoint, *product competition* is an important stimulant to technological innovation and living standards over a period of time.

Given a goal of profit maximization, our representative firm in monopolistic competition can be expected to search among the various possible product variations for the one it perceives to be the most profitable. The problem is to select it under conditions of less than perfect knowledge. One approach is to estimate from available market information the profitability of each of several product differentiation approaches, given the prices and product characteristics of rival firms. The firm then maximizes expected profit by choosing the product variation theme with the highest expected profit and operating at the price and output where MC equals MR.

However, from time to time rival firms can be counted upon to adopt new variations of their own products. When they do, a firm may find further product modifications necessary to remain competitive. A continuous sequence of product variation moves and countermoves is set in motion, made feasible by research and development efforts to come up with a steady stream of potentially profitable opportunities for modifying product offerings. Firms are prompted to incorporate new product features because they hope to gain a profitable, albeit temporary, competitive edge. The edge tends to be temporary because if the variation catches on in the market, other firms either begin to imitate the variation or to try to go it one better, in hopes of leapfrogging the competitive edge of the leaders.

In the course of this product-differentiating struggle, some firms will perceive it more profitable to adopt product variations which appeal to price-conscious consumers, with the result that their products are slightly less expensive and of lower quality. Other firms will view it advantageous to cater to the market segment desirous of superior-quality goods, with the result that their products carry above-average prices and are claimed to have above-average features or performance standards. Still other firms may pursue an intermediate strategy, positioning their products in between the high and low ends of the market. A few firms may be content to base their product strategy on "gimmicks," styling, and image-related features. These strategy differences reflect the fact that markets are diverse—being comprised in part by consumers who are strongly quality-conscious but not especially price-conscious, in part by consumers willing to sacrifice quality to get a lower price, and in part by consumers who are susceptible to gimmickry and clever sales promotion schemes. Because consumer tastes and preferences are not uniform, it is feasible and profitable for firms in the same industry to pursue slightly different product variation strategies aimed at appealing to specific buyer traits and market segments. This sort of product competition provides consumers with a wider range of product qualities, performance features, and prices, thereby permitting each consumer to select the product which appears best-suited to his preferences.[5]

Product competition can cause a firm's *SRAC* and *LRAC* curves to shift either up or down, according to the amounts and prices of the resource inputs needed to implement product differentiation themes. In the process, the demand-*AR* curves of each firm can shift both in position and slope as consumers respond to new product variations. One effect of the differences in the products and cost curves of monopolistically competitive firms is to make the long-run equilibrium positions differ from firm to firm. Higher-quality firms can exist alongside lower-quality firms. Higher-priced firms can exist alongside lower-priced firms. This condition is readily observed in the sale of drugs and cosmetics where retailers display on the same shelf the high-priced, better known brands and the lesser-known, cut-price varieties. Moreover, at a given moment, some monopolistically competitive firms may be earning sizable economic profits, others may be earning only a normal profit, and others may be sustaining losses.

PROMOTIONAL EXPENSE DECISIONS

The third basic type of strategy which monopolistically competitive firms may employ to strengthen their market position concerns sales promotion. Advertising and promotional campaigns are a strong complement to a firm's pricing and product variation strategies. True, sales promotion adds to

---

[5]Product differentiation is not, however, without its drawbacks. Critics warn that the proliferation of product varieties may so confuse the consumer that the exercise of rational choice becomes virtually impossible. Some consumers, confronted with a myriad of similar products, may fall into the "trap" of judging quality by price alone. Critics also point out that many product alternations consist of frivolous and superficial changes which are of dubious value in improving durability, efficiency, or usefulness. In the case of durable and semidurable consumer goods, the process of product development seems to follow a pattern of "planned obsolescence"; firms make gradual but regular changes in their products aimed at increasing the frequency with which consumers become dissatisfied with their present model and trade it in on the new model. As partial remedies for product proliferation, a number of economists propose that information about products be provided to consumers in greater amounts and that laws and penalties regarding infringement on brands and trademarks be relaxed. Increased information and a weakening of trademark protection are held to increase "competition" by promoting a greater degree of products standardization and thereby lessening the powers of producers to vend differentiated products. The end result should be a movement in the direction of perfect competition. For a more thorough argument of this point, see Edward H. Chamberlin, *The Theory of Monopolistic Competition* (Cambridge, Mass.: Harvard University Press, 1933), pp. 271–274, and George J. Stigler, "The Economics of Information," *Journal of Political Economy*, Vol. 69, No. 3 (June 1961), pp. 213–225.

the firm's costs. But if well conceived, demand can be increased by drawing

new customers away from other brands; at the same time, buyers may be
persuaded that the firm's product is worth paying more for. In short, promotional expenditures can shift the firm's demand-AR curve to the right and
make it slightly *less* elastic as well. As long as revenues increase by more than
enough to compensate both for promotional expenses and for extra production costs associated with greater outputs, the firm will have improved its
profit position.

Suppose we look closer at the possible effects of promotional expenses
upon a firm's long-run average costs. Initially, for the sake of argument,
suppose promotional outlays substantially increase the demand for the firm's
product and, consequently, the firm's most profitable long-run output rate.
What, then, is the effect on the firm's long-run average costs? As depicted in
Fig. 11-6, it is obvious that sales promotion outlays will shift the $LRAC$
upward. However, if the demand-AR curve shifts such that production is
more profitable at Q_2 than at Q_1, units costs will decline from $LRAC_{Q_1}$ to
$LRAC_{Q_2}$ because of the economies of scale which the firm can take advantage
of. Greater production efficiency more than offsets the increase in unit costs
associated with promotional expenses. On the other hand, increased demand
realized from sales promotion may force diseconomies of scale upon the firm,
as indicated by the movement from Q_1 to Q_3; in this case, unit costs would
rise from $LRAC_{Q_1}$ to $LRAC_{Q_3}$. In some cases a great portion of sales promotion efforts by firms are self-cancelling; one seller's stepped-up advertising
campaign is matched by rival firms, resulting in only slight gains in sales and
output—as is suggested by the movement from Q_1 to Q_4.[6] In this instance,

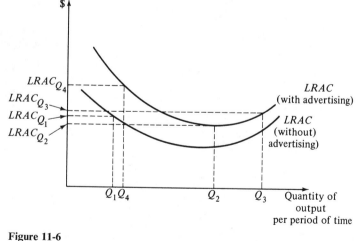

Figure 11-6

Effect of sales promotion expenditures upon unit costs and output rates

[6]The cigarette, soap, beer, and toiletries industries are good cases in point. Like the
Red Queen in *Alice Through the Looking Glass*, each firm has to run as fast as it can in its
promotional activities just to keep up with where it is. This correctly recognizes that some
promotional activity is defensive in nature and is undertaken to protect a firm's position
as well as to enhance it.

unit costs may be driven up substantially by the decision to adopt an agressive sales promotion strategy. Plainly, all three outcomes are possible; which one will actually occur in a particular situation varies with the shape of the $LRAC$ curve and the size of the effect of sales promotion upon demand and output.

A somewhat more interesting question relates to the effect of sales promotion activity upon a firm's price and profits. Consider Fig. 11-7. In panel (a) is illustrated a situation where sales promotion outlays have the effect of *lowering* a firm's price and *raising* a firm's profits. In the absence of promotion, the profit-maximizing price and output are P_1 and Q_1, respectively, and total profit equals $(P_1 - SRAC_{Q_1})Q_1$. Initiating promotional activity shifts the demand-AR curve rightward from (D_1, AR_1) to (D_2, AR_2) and the $LRAC$ curve upward from $LRAC_1$ to $LRAC_2$. The firm will find it advantageous to expand output to Q_2 and to lower price to P_2; total profit will be $(P_2 - SRAC_{Q_2})Q_2$ dollars—an amount that dwarfs the profits

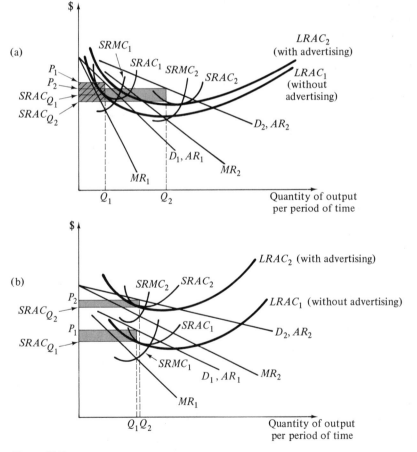

Figure 11-7
Possible effects of sales promotion activity upon prices and profits

DETERMINING THE PROFIT-MAXIMIZING OUTPUT RATE
AND LEVEL OF ADVERTISING EXPENDITURE

Advertising and promotional outlays necessarily affect the firm's profitability. Thus, we may say that

$$\pi = f(\text{output, advertising outlays}).$$

Suppose empirical analysis of a firm's operations indicates that the following relationship exists:

$$\pi = 600 - 4Q - Q^2 + 2QA + 116A - 5A^2,$$

where π = total profit per period of time, Q = the firm's output rate, and A = the firm's advertising outlay (in dollars) per period of time.

How can we determine the profit-maximizing output rate and the profit-maximizing amount of advertising expenditure? The answer to this question involves use of partial derivatives (Mathematical Capsule 2) and the principles of profit maximization. In mathematical terms we need to find the specific combination of values of Q and A that will maximize the value of π.

The first-order conditions for maximizing a multivariable function of this type are that

$$\frac{\partial \pi}{\partial Q} = 0 \quad \text{and} \quad \frac{\partial \pi}{\partial A} = 0.$$

Thus, the first step is to find the partial derivatives of π with respect to Q and A and set them equal to zero; this gives

$$\frac{\partial \pi}{\partial Q} = -4 - 2Q + 2A = 0,$$

$$\frac{\partial \pi}{\partial A} = 2Q + 116 - 10A = 0.$$

Solving these two equations simultaneously gives $Q = 12$ and $A = 14$.

To prove that these values represent maximum π rather than minimum π, we must check to see that the second-order conditions are met at $Q = 12$ and $A = 14$. The second-order conditions are that

$$\frac{\partial^2 \pi}{\partial Q^2} < 0, \quad \frac{\partial^2 \pi}{\partial A^2} < 0 \quad \text{and} \quad \left(\frac{\partial^2 \pi}{\partial Q^2}\right)\left(\frac{\partial^2 \pi}{\partial A^2}\right) > \left(\frac{\partial^2 \pi}{\partial Q \, \partial A}\right)^2.$$

368

*How Markets
Function: The
Model of
Monopolistic
Competition*

Since

$$\frac{\partial^2 \pi}{\partial Q^2} = -2,$$

$$\frac{\partial^2 \pi}{\partial A^2} = -10,$$

$$\frac{\partial^2 \pi}{\partial Q \, \partial A} = 2,$$

it is quickly verified that the profit-maximizing output rate is 12 units per period of time and the profit-maximizing advertising outlay is \$14 per period of time.

Exercise

1. Suppose that the functional relationship among profit, output, and advertising is given by the expression

$$\pi = 1000 - 3Q^2 - 6Q + 6QA + 90A - 10A^2.$$

Determine the profit-maximizing rates of output and advertising expenditure.

APPLICATIONS CAPSULE

THE DOCTOR BUSINESS: A CASE WHERE MORE COMPETITION IS BETTER

In the Twin Cities of Minneapolis–St. Paul and their suburbs, the market for health care has recently gone through a competitive upheaval. In 7 years the proportion of the area's 1.9 million residents enrolled in health-maintenance organizations (HMOs) rose from 2% to 12%. An HMO is an organization that offers comprehensive medical care for a flat annual fee; it has professional management and is staffed with doctors who agree to tie their remuneration to each year's subscription income. The alleged advantage of an HMO is the incentive it provides to avoid waste and inefficiency of conventional fee-for-service medicine where a "spare no expense" mentality is nurtured by the fact that most medical and hospitalization bills are reimbursed by Medicare-Medicaid and private insurance plans (such as Blue Cross–Blue Shield). Moreover, the mere presence of the HMO alternative tends to act as a competitive check on the prices of conventionally provided health care services.

The well-known Kaiser-Permanente medical plans, operating in Hawaii and California for decades, have shown how HMOs can hold down medical costs, but they failed to trigger the kind of competitive free-for-all and price war that sprung up in the Twin Cities area. In 1979 eight HMOs existed in Minneapolis–St. Paul; each competed not only with the other seven but also, and perhaps more important, with conventional health insurance plans and with the hundreds of independent doctors in the area. According to some observers, the competitive atmosphere was "cutthroat" and some of the HMOs were said to be "underpricing their product." Even so, most of the HMOs were operating in the black, and all were characterized as offering more product for the money. In fact, it was estimated that the same coverage provided by a flat-fee HMO would cost 15 to 20% more under conventional health insurance plans (mainly because a lot of unneeded services tend to be rendered under the latter). Whereas in recent years, the cost of annual health insurance has risen at double-digit rates, HMOs in the Twin Cities areas have managed to hold fee increases to a single digit.

One explanation for the popularity of HMOs in the Twin Cities is the extra coverage and convenience. There is no deductible amount below which a family pays everything; childrens' checkups and immunization shots, excluded from most conventional plans, are included. Except for prescription drugs and a few extras for out-of-the-ordinary services, subscribers never see a medical bill; everything is paid in advance—mainly by employers who foot most or all of the subscription fee as a fringe benefit. And there are no complex forms to fill out every time a service is rendered.

The attractiveness of HMOs as a competitive alternative has not gone unnoticed by major employers in the area. Honeywell first offered the HMO option to its 15,000 workers in 1978 and used two selling points: (1) less paperwork and (2) as much as a $9.60 per month reduction in the cost to an employee with dependents; 31% of Honeywell's employees elected the HMO option at the first opportunity. About 30% of Control Data's area employees elected the HMO option after it had been available for a year and the figure was expected to grow to 40 to 50% the next time workers were given a chance to choose which option they wished. At General Mills, where the HMO option had been offered for 5 years, 60% of the area employees were HMO subscribers.

Interestingly enough, when health care groups in the Minneapolis–St. Paul area began to seriously consider the formation of HMOs, the local business community was, at the same time, beginning to discuss

370

*How Markets
Function: The
Model of
Monopolistic
Competition*

ways to slow down annual, double-digit increases in health insurance costs. The first concrete proposal was for a single HMO controlled by doctors and hospitals. The business community, led by General Mills, objected strenuously to a single-provider organization because it did not offer the prospect of sufficient competition. The multiple-HMO approach, because it did interject a new and much stronger competitive force, won out.

The most interesting HMO, but also the one with the rockiest experience, is the one formed in "desperation" by doctors left out of the other HMO plans. Called the Physicians Health Plan, it was organized in 1975 when the local medical society became alarmed by the market inroads being made by HMOs; it differed, however, from the others in that it was an open-panel HMO, or "independent practice association," whereby participating doctors used their regular private office to treat HMO patients as well as their own private patients. This offered doctors the distinct advantage of being in position to straddle both market segments at once; they could continue a normal private practice and charge "regular" patients a conventional fee based on service rendered and, simultaneously, take on HMO subscribers on a fixed-fee basis. In addition, this arrangement got around a widespread objection to closed-panel HMOs; under the Physicians Health Plan patients could chose among any of the participating doctors rather than being restricted to seeing one of the more limited number of doctors connected with one HMO clinic or hospital. Within 3 years, the Physicians Health Plan became the third-largest HMO in the Twin Cities.

Whatever the future of HMOs, the Twin Cities experience illustrates three important aspects of markets and competition:

1. If a product or service is good and its price is competitive, then consumers can be attracted to purchase it.
2. Markets function best in a competitive atmosphere where suppliers are forced to scramble and scrap for each customer's patronage.
3. Competition is enhanced when new types of firms offering a new type of product decide to enter the market.

Source: Adapted by the author from information in "Where Doctors Scramble for Patients' Dollars," *Fortune*, November 6, 1978, pp. 114–120.

earned when no promotional activity is undertaken. In panel (b) is shown a situation where promotional activity causes price to rise and profits to fall. Prior to initiating a promotional strategy, profit maximization occurs at P_1 and Q_1 with a resulting total profit of $(P_1 - SRAC_1)Q_1$ dollars. With promotion activity the profit-maximizing price and output are P_2 and Q_2 and total profit is only $(P_2 - SRAC_{Q_2})Q_2$ dollars. Other possibilities exist: Promotional activity can cause price to rise and profits to rise, price to fall and profits to fall, and so on. No general answer can be given as to the effect of promotional strategies upon a firm's costs, price, output, or profits. It all depends on the effect which promotional expenditures have upon the position and shape of the firm's demand-AR curve and its $LRAC$ curve.

SUMMARY OF THE MODEL OF MONOPOLISTIC COMPETITION

The distinguishing features of monopolistic competition are (1) many small, entrepreneurial firms selling differentiated, yet similar, products; (2) the ability of each firm to influence its sales by changing its price; (3) down-sloping, but highly elastic, demand-AR curves for the relevant output range of the firms; (4) the relative ease with which firms can enter and leave the industry; (5) the small effect the actions of any one firm have upon rival firms; and (6) firms which behave as if they seek to maximize profits.

Monopolistically competitive firms may earn short-run economic profits or incur short-run losses. The relative ease with which firms can enter the industry limits the opportunities for earning large economic profits over the long run. The exodus of firms from the industry tends to elimiate or at least reduce economic losses in the long run.

The firm in monopolistic competition has three basic strategies for pursuing its principal goal of maximum profits: price changes, variations in its product, and promotional activity. Just what specific variation of the product, selling at what price, and supplemented by what amount of promotional expenses will actually maximize profits is a complex issue. Each possbile combination of price, product variation, and promotional outlay poses a different demand and cost situation for the firm, some one of which will yield the firm maximum profits. A trial-and-error procedure is virtually imperative in arriving at an optimum combination of price, product features, and promotional outlays.

Thus, the competitive strategies of firms can assume a variety of forms. Some firms may seek to compete mainly on price, while others aim at quality, and still others use heavier than usual advertising. Product differentiation themes may be aimed at making the item more durable or less durable; various performance features may be made standard or optional; the range of colors and styles may be expanded or contracted; chrome trim may be added, removed, or rearranged; packaging may be made more or less elaborate and colorful. A stepped-up advertising campaign by one seller may be countered by another seller with improved guarantees to buyers. Lower prices may be met by improved customer services or adding new convenience features. Some products are so obviously different that sellers feel little pressure or derive little advantage from further promoting and proclaiming differences which most buyers are already well aware of. On the other hand, promotional activity plays a bigger role in industries where product differentiation is slight or not readily apparent; here, rival firms are easily led to try to exploit and bolster the importance of differences.

372 COMPETITION AMONG THE MANY—IN PRACTICE

*How Markets
Function: The
Model of
Monopolistic
Competition*

It turns out that the theoretical models of perfect competition and monopolistic competition are reasonably descriptive of firm and market behavior in certain industries. Where large numbers of relatively small firms sell a homogeneous product, market patterns *tend* to be in accord with the perfectly competitive model. Where large numbers of small firms sell differentiated products, firm behavior regarding prices, outputs, product variation, and promotion parallels the model of monopolistic competition.

Real-world examples of industries where near perfectly competitive conditions prevail include such agricultural markets as corn, wheat, cotton, wool, barley, oats, and livestock; the manufacture of cotton cloth; and some financial markets involving stocks, bonds, and loans to business. Conditions approaching monopolistic competition are found in such industries as machine tools, valves and pipe fittings, brick, wood and upholstered furniture, sawmills, screw machine products, paperboard boxes, shoes, paints and varnishes, millinery, costume jewelry, lighting fixtures, men's and boys' suits and coats, and women's dresses, suits, coats, and skirts; monopolistic competition also typifies the wholesaling and retailing trades in more populated urban centers.

In addition, segments of other industries exhibit the characteristics of these two models. As we shall see in Chapter 12, in industries where numerous, comparatively small firms operate alongside a few large corporations, the competitive and market relationships between the two sets of firms often result in the small firms exhibiting behavior patterns closely akin to that of perfect or monopolistic competition—conditions in the steel, tire, dairy, retail grocery, soap, petroleum refining, plumbing fixtures, machinery, and electrical appliance industries serve as examples.

The behavior of prices, outputs, and profits in the above-mentioned industries (or segments thereof) compares favorably with the conclusions drawn from the two theoretical models of perfect and monopolistic competition. Rates of return on stockholder investment tend to run a bit below average. However, as might be anticipated, profits tend to be somewhat higher in the faster-growing industries and somewhat lower in the slow-growth industries. Supply is generally responsive to changes in consumer demand, rising most dramatically where market demand curves are shifting rapidly to the right. Outputs and prices respond rapidly to cost changes. Industries where technological change has tended to reduce unit costs show a relative decline in prices and a relatively large expansion of output. Consumer demand, output, and cost movements are correlated. Where consumer demand and output are vigorously expanding, technical progress is stimulated, and firms take advantage rather quickly of expansion opportunities. Unless scale economies dictate otherwise, the number of firms in the industry increases with demand. Cost reductions coupled with expanding production capabilities give rise to price cuts, which, in turn, reinforce the expansion process by triggering higher sales and output; this is a familiar cycle during the early and intermediate stages of the life cycle of a product or product group. It is clear, then, that the models of perfect and monopolistic competition have empirical validity; both are able to predict and explain market behavior in certain circumstances.

The Benefits of Competition among the Many

The conventional wisdom in economics is that market conditions of perfect competition and monopolistic competition offer consumers the best of all possible worlds. If consumers are willing to accept homogeneous products, a perfectly competitive market structure will give it to them at the lowest possible price consistent with the costs of production. Under conditions of long-run equilibrium each firm operates at the minimum point of its short-run and long-run average cost curve and thus achieves maximum production efficiency. Price is driven to the level of minimum average cost, and investors receive a rate of return just sufficient to induce them to maintain their investment at levels adequate for producing the industry's equilibrium output most efficiently. Firms which fail to attain the lowest possible unit cost incur losses and eventually are driven from the industry. Consequently, resources *tend* to be employed at maximum production efficiency in a perfectly competitive industry.

If consumers exhibit a preference for differentiated products, as usually they do because of the diversity of tastes among individuals, then monopolistically competitive conditions are held to produce optimum consumer benefits. Competition is strong enough to keep prices down close to costs and profit margins slim. Although monopolistically competitive firms may not quite achieve maximum production efficiency (because at long-run equilibrium the demand-AR curve is tangent to the $LRAC$ curve just short of the minimum point), unit costs still tend to be as low as can be achieved with differentiated products.

In both perfect and monopolistic competition, the output of goods and services automatically stays in close accord with consumer demand. Prices are no higher than necessary to maintain production. The market power of any one firm is negligible. For these reasons the market structures of perfect and monopolistic competition are commonly thought to yield an overall economic outcome that is most advantageous to consumers.

Because of the prominent role which "the market" and market processes play in competition among the many, it is descriptively fair to use the term *market capitalism* to refer to firms and industries where conditions of perfect or monopolistic competition are approximated. The key feature of market capitalism is many relatively small firms competing under conditions where market forces are so dominant that consumers are well protected from exploitation by business firms and abuses of economic power on the supply side of the market. Firms are, for the most part, price-takers, not price-makers.

Some Disadvantages of Competition among the Many

However, competition among the many can produce some subtle disadvantages. To see why we have to go beyond industrywide prices, outputs, and profits and look critically at the specific traits that an environment of market capitalism can *sometimes* impose upon individual firms. Almost every real-world example of market capitalism involves industries where firms are small both relatively *and* absolutely. There is, in other words a very close correspondence between (1) the existence of near-perfect competition and of monopolistic competition and (2) the presence of small, entrepreneurial enterprises. This is more than mere circumstance. The representative firm operating under conditions of perfect or monopolistic competition *must* be small relatively because both models are predicated on the presence of large numbers of firms, no one of which has a sizable share of the market. In practice, the size of the representative firm is also absolutely small. Firm size is severely limited by the relatively quick appearance of diseconomies of scale. Were significant economies of scale present, firms would tend to be large—not small—relative to the total market because demand is seldom big enough to accommodate the competitive existence of *large* numbers of *large* firms. Moreover, once existing firms take full advantage of scale economies, increased industry output is likely to be achieved *by the entry of new firms rather than by the expansion of existing firms*. In other words, the economic limitations on firm size tend to guarantee an atomistic structure of many small firms. This is not to say that conditions of perfect or monopolistic competition prevail wherever small firms exist, but it does say that perfect and monopolistic competition are found almost exclusively in markets comprised of firms that are small in an absolute sense. Billion-dollar corporations, commonplace in many industries, are seldom found in industries approximating perfect and monopolistic competition.

The small size and enterpreneurial character of firms that operate in an environment of market capitalism, in conjunction with the fundamental nature of competition among the many, are what gives rise to the disadvantages. To begin with, the representative firm in market capitalism is thrust into a position of *reacting* and *responding* to changing market conditions. "The market" calls the shots, with the winds of change just as prone to blow in the direction of lower profits as in the direction of higher profits. Market forces can be harsh and unrelenting. Much like a small boat caught in the midst of a hurricane, the firm's security and survival is extremely tenuous— witness the comparatively precarious condition of many small businesses during recession and times of natural disaster. As a consequence, the actions of such firms come to be aimed mainly at short-run profit maximization. Profit margins are too slim and too uncertain to allow otherwise. Falling demand may force severe financial retrenchment, bankruptcy, or exit from the industry. Rising demand, on the other hand, may offer limited prospects for above-average profits and growth because of the ease of entry of new firms and because of a lack of financial strength to pursue a large expansion program.

In such an environment, profit incentives and financial capacities for risk-taking, for research, and for innovation are definitely impaired—both by the firm's small size and by its susceptibility to stringent treatment by market forces. There is, therefore, an increased likelihood that the pace of technological advance will be slower, not faster, where firms are small as compared to where they are large. A little bit of bigness—sales levels of $100 million to $250 million in most industries—is good for R&D and innovation. Firms of this size and larger find a well-rounded research and development program and the new ideas it generates to be an asset in maintaining their viability and growth. Moreover, they can better afford the talent needed to staff such an effort. Naturally, exceptions exist; some small entrepreneurial firms are known for their technological prowess, being extraordinarily prolific in generating new ideas and in developing relatively uncomplicated processes and products.[7] But, *generally*, small owner-managed firms tend not to be especially innovation-minded or technologically advanced. This is partially because the dominance of the market, competition, and ease of entry keep profits so slim and uncertain that firms are deprived of the venture capital requisite for financing technological research and for instituting sustained expansion. And it is partially because such firms operate on too small a scale to justify spending funds for formal research and development activities; R&D may not pay off from a short-run profit-and-loss viewpoint—the criterion employed by firms in atomistically competitive market environments. Even more significantly, a small firm may not be able to absorb the risk of failure that goes with venturesome R&D efforts.

This argument is supported by the fact that most industries exemplifying the characteristics of market capitalism are low-wage, low-skill industries, having low productivity and below average rates of productivity increase. Their levels of technological sophistication are minimal and capital investment requirements are small. They evidence a distinct propensity to lag behind the technological progress achieved in markets where firms are bigger. Indeed, the *comparatively* slow pace of technological advance in sawmill operations, apparel, and segments of the food products, textile, fabricated metal products, and leather industries suggests that technological progress is more rapid where the rigors of short-run competitive forces are not so relentless as to make firms unwilling and unable to bear the risks and costs of research and innovation. Market capitalism has spawned none of the showcases of American ingenuity and technological achievement.

Furthermore, it is questionable whether the instability and insecurity of firms in a market-dominated environment promotes rising incomes and noninflationary full employment. Less-advanced technology, low profits, and limited capital availability translate into low and slowly rising incomes for

[7]Control Data Corporation was a tiny firm when it led the way to very high speed digital computers for scientific applications.

376

*How Markets
Function: The
Model of
Monopolistic
Competition*

employees. Moreover, adjusting to market decline or stagnation is often a long, painful process—the prolonged death throes of the New England textile industry and the small farmer serve as cases in point. Over the long haul, it is the rates and quality of economic growth and technical progress, not low profits and maximum production efficiency, that *most* affect society's overall economic welfare.

Thus, upon closer examination market capitalism has some side effects and long-term drawbacks that make the case for perfect competition and monopolistic competition weaker in actual practice than the theory seems to suggest. Basically, this is because rapid technical progress, increases in productive capability, and higher personal incomes are not always forthcoming on a long-term basis in a market environment where firms are thrown into a life-or-death competitive struggle, profits are minimal, risks are high, firms have less chance of long-term survival (owing either to competitive failure or death of the owner-entrepreneur), capital investment is low, and little or no R&D efforts are undertaken.

Still, the two models of market capitalism do convincingly indicate the social value of a competitive market environment. The case for more competition *typically* outweighs the case for less competition.

SUGGESTED READINGS

ARCHIBALD, G. C., "Chamberlin *versus* Chicago," *Review of Economic Studies*, Vol. 29 (1961), pp. 2–28.

BISHOP, R. L., "The Theory of Monopolistic Competition after Thirty Years: The Impact on General Theory," *American Economic Review*, Vol. 54, No. 3 (May 1964), pp. 33–43.

CHAMBERLIN, E. H., *The Theory of Monopolistic Competition* (Cambridge, Mass.: Harvard University Press, 1933).

DOYLE, P., "Economic Aspects of Advertising: A Survey," *Economic Journal*, Vol. 78, No. 311 (September 1968), pp. 570–602.

KALDOR, N., "The Economic Aspects of Advertising," *Review of Economic Studies*, Vol. 18 (1949–1950), pp. 17–21.

KIRZNER, I. M., *Competition and Entrepreneurship* (Chicago: University of Chicago Press, 1973), Chapters 3 and 4.

ROBINSON, J., *The Economics of Imperfect Competition* (London: The Macmillan Company, 1933).

SCHERER, F. M., "Research and Development Resource Allocation under Rivalry," *Quarterly Journal of Economics*, Vol. 81, No. 3 (August 1967), pp. 359–394.

———, *Industrial Market Structure and Economic Performance* (Chicago: Rand McNally & Company, 1970), Chapter 14.

STIGLER, G. J., "Monopolistic Competition in Retrospect," *The Organization of Industry* (Homewood, Ill.: Richard D. Irwin, Inc., 1968), pp. 71–94.

———, "Price and Non-price Competition," *Journal of Political Economy*, Vol. 76, No. 1 (January–February 1968), pp. 149–154.

TELSER, L. G., "Advertising and Competition," *Journal of Political Economy*, Vol. 72, No. 6 (December 1964), pp. 537–562.

1. The Morgan Chair Company manufactures rocking chairs and sells them under conditions of monopolistic competition. The owner of the company has estimated its demand function as $P = 1625 - 6Q$, where P is in dollars and Q is in dozens of chairs sold per month. The company believes its monthly expenses vary with output according to the equation $TC = 25{,}000 + 25Q - 6Q^2 + \frac{1}{3}Q^3$.
   (a) Determine the firm's short-run profit-maximizing price and output rate.
   (b) How much profit will the firm earn at this price and output rate?
   (c) Suppose the Morgan Chair Company's total fixed costs rise by 10%. Calculate the impact upon the firm's price, output, and profits. How do you account for these results?

2. Using the unit cost and unit revenue curves, graphically illustrate the short-run profit-maximizing price and output for a monopolistically competitive firm which has a production function that exhibits constant returns to variable input over its entire range of output capability. (*Hint:* First determine the shape of the ATC and MC curves which correspond to a production function characterized by constant returns to variable input; then find the price and output at which $MR = MC$.) Indicate on your graph the area which represents the firm's total profits.

3. Using TR-TC analysis, graphically illustrate the short-run profit-maximizing output for a monopolistically competitive firm which is faced with a linear, downsloping demand curve and which has a production function displaying decreasing returns to variable input over its entire range of output capability. Then derive the corresponding total profit function for the firm.

4. Suppose that a firm operating under conditions of monopolistic competition is faced with a linear, downward-sloping demand curve and that its production function is of cubic form $(a + bX + cX^2 - dX^3)$. Using the unit cost and revenue curves $(AR, MR, ATC, AVC,$ and $MC)$, graphically illustrate the price and output at which short-run profit will be maximized. Indicate on your graph the area which represents the firm's total profits.

5. In Chapter 5 it was shown that a linear, downsloping demand curve is half elastic and half inelastic; that is, the coefficient of price elasticity is greater than one along the top half of the demand curve and less than one along the bottom half. Is it possible for a monopolistically competitive firm which is confronted with a linear, downsloping demand curve to maximize short-run profits at a price and output corresponding to the inelastic portion of the demand curve? Why or why not?

6. Graphically illustrate a situation where the use of sales promotion activity by a monopolistically competitive firm results in a higher price and higher profits. The purpose of sales promotion expenditures is to shift the firm's demand-AR function to the right and, at the same time, to make it more steeply sloped (less elastic over the relevant price range). Assuming that a firm achieves this purpose, graphically illustrate the effect this has upon the shape and position of the firm's total revenue function.

TWELVE HOW MARKETS FUNCTION: THE MANY MODELS OF OLIGOPOLY

In this chapter we shift the spotlight from "competition among the many" to "competition among the few." Far and away the most prominent and economically important examples of competition among the few are found in the corporate sector. The list of markets where a *few* very large corporate enterprises supply most of the industry output is a veritable *Who's Who* of American manufacturing. It includes the markets for such goods as aircraft, aluminum, automobiles, alcoholic beverages, appliances, cigarettes, computers, copying machines, copper, farm equipment, flat glass, certain food products, gasoline, locomotives and railroad cars, metal cans, network television, sewing machines, sheetrock, steam engines and turbines, steel, synthetic fibers, telephone equipment, tires, and typewriters. Several geographic areas in the mining, construction, banking, insurance, retailing, and service industries also have just a few firms competing on the supply side of the market. The distinctive feature of *oligopoly* is that a few highly visible and well-known firms supply the lion's share of total output in a given market.

Oligopoly conditions often characterize the markets where big corporations operate—the environment described in Chapter 2 as *corporate capitalism*. However, competition among the few is not limited to the corporate sector. It also arises in markets too small for more than a few firms to exist.

For example, the small town with its two or three banks, auto repair shops, dry cleaners, building contractors, doctors, lawyers, accountants, and so on illustrates this situation. In manufacturing, a number of highly specialized parts, components, gadgets, tools, and speciality products have a total market demand (even nationwide) so limited that a few small firms can easily supply the entire output. Hence, conditions of competition among the few can arise where small firms are involved as well as where large corporations are involved. The zone of demarcation between competition among the many and competition among the few, therefore, does not correspond exactly with the zone between big firms and little firms.

Nonetheless, because the U.S. economy is becoming more and more characterized by corporate capitalism (as opposed to market capitalism), the presentation of oligopoly will be oriented to capture the specific facets of competition among large corporations. Small firm-dominated markets exhibiting the characteristics of competition among the few will be given less attention, but it should be emphasized that many of the conclusions we draw about competition among large firms will apply to competition among a few small firms.[1]

We begin our examination of the principles of competition among the few with a survey of contemporary models of oligopoly behavior. The assumption that the firm's overriding goal is to maximize profits will be continued; however, we shall relax this assumption in Chapter 15 and examine there the effect of alternative goals upon a firm's behavior.

THE DISTINGUISHING CHARACTERISTICS OF OLIGOPOLY

Oligopoly is synonymous with competition among the few. Markets are said to be oligopolistic whenever a small number of firms supply the dominant share of an industry's total output. In oligopoly, firms are *large* relative to the size of the total market they serve, and in the case of giant corporations they

---

[1]Recasting the traditional theory of oligopoly to focus on corporate capitalism has much to recommend it. Generalizing oligopoly theory to the point where it applies to both small, single-product firms and large, multiproduct enterprises forces one to exclude the rich institutional detail which supplies powerful understanding of the behavior of large corporations under conditions of corporate capitalism. Such an exclusion is a serious disadvantage when one is trying to explain the functioning of an economic system dominated by the presence of large corporations. It is very difficult to construct satisfactory models of business behavior which describe equally well the behavior of entrepreneurial firms and the behavior of large managerial firms. After all, the behavior of a hardware store functioning as an oligopolistic firm in a small community differs in several important respects from IBM's behavior in the oligopolistic computer market. Thus, while orienting the presentation of oligopoly theory to capture specific facets of corporate behavior may suffer slightly from a lack of generality, this weakness is more than offset by the extra insight into the economics of corporate capitalism. The approach here is also strong pedagogically because it allows for a strong focus on the *application* of oligopoly theory to readily visible firms and industries.

are large not just relatively but absolutely as well. The principal effect of fewness of firms is to give each firm such a prominent market position that its decisions and actions have significant repercussions on rival firms. What one firm does affects the others. If one firm announces a price change, its competitors take quick notice. If one firm brings out a new product or changes product design or steps up its advertising, other firms must take note and consider whether and how to respond. As a result, competition becomes highly personalized, with each firm recognizing that its own best course of action depends on the strategies its rivals elect. The interdependence among oligopolists extends to all facets of competition: price, output, promotional strategies, innovation, customer service policies, acquisitions and mergers, or whatever. Since rival firms may have numerous alternative courses of action, anticipating their actions and reactions introduces a new and exceedingly complex dimension to the firm's decision process. But trying to anticipate the competitive response of rival firms is an exercise no oligopolist can afford to neglect, for the probability is high that a change in a firm's competitive tactics will elicit prompt and pointed reactions from rival firms. The great uncertainty is *how* one's rivals will react. As we shall see shortly, the interdependence and competitive interaction among firms is *the key feature* of oligopoly.

An oligopolistic market structure has several other characteristics. To begin with, rivalry among the few may involve either standardized or differentiated products. If the firms in an industry produce a standardized product, the industry is called a *pure oligopoly*. The most common examples of virtually uniform products marketed under conditions of oligopoly include steel, aluminum, lead, copper, cement, rayon, fuel oil, sheetrock, tin cans, newsprint, explosives, and industrial alcohol. If a few firms dominate the market for a differentiated product, the industry is called a *differentiated oligopoly*. The most visible differentiated oligopolies involve the production of automobiles, toothpaste, cereal, cigarettes, TV sets, electric razors, computers, farm implements, refrigerators, air conditioners, soft drinks, soap, and gasoline.

Entry into an oligopolistic industry is typically formidable, though by no means impossible. The most pervasive barrier to entry is the presence of substantial economies of scale. In industries where technology is complex, large machine units are used, and sales promotion requirements are substantial, the optimum scale of operation is large. Minimum average costs occur at output rates so large that a firm has to be big to be competitive; firms of lesser size incur unit costs so much higher that the entry of small-scale firms is generally not profitable. Moreover, the fact that existing firms produce well-known, highly advertised products and sell them through established marketing outlets works against the successful entrance of new firms. It is a hazardous undertaking for a relatively new or unknown firm to introduce a new product to compete directly against the brands of firms whose names are known to everyone. Often, entering such an industry entails so sizable a commitment of venture capital that small organizations are effectively foreclosed. The most likely candidates for entry into established oligopolies are other giant enterprises which do have the financial and organizational resources that it takes. This is not, however, an especially common occurrence in mature industries because the added production of another large-scale firm tends to increase supply to the point of driving price below average cost for all firms, thereby making the profit prospects for new entrants, large or small, rather dim. But in young or rapidly growing oligopolies the entry of new firms is not unusual.

Like firms in monopolistic competition, oligopolistic firms, and especially those producing differentiated products, rely upon differences in price, quality, reliability, service, design, rapid product development, promotional outlays, and product images to promote their sales and increase their profits. They attempt to create a very strong awareness among consumers of brands and product reputation. Everything that was said in Chapter 11 about the role of product variations and promotional outlays applies on an even grander scale among corporate oligopolists. The dimensions of competition under oligopoly are limited only by the imagination of the firms themselves.

THE MANY MODELS OF OLIGOPOLY BEHAVIOR

In an oligopolistic market structure, there is no nice, neat clear-cut equilibrium position toward which all firms tend to move—such as we found in perfect competition and monopolistic competition. Two reasons account for this. One, in oligopoly a wide variety of materially different competitive circumstances can and do exist, no one of which is demonstrably more typical than others. Two, even in a given competitive situation, several different and entirely reasonable courses of action may be open to firms in selecting a competitive strategy. Just what firms will decide to do and how their rivals will react is often open-ended. A number of outcomes is possible, and the end result may vary from case to case. No single pattern of behavior stands out from the rest or is dominant.

As a consequence, oligopoly theory consists of dozens of models, each depicting certain facets of oligopolistic conduct and performance but none telling a complete story of competition among the few. The range of oligopolistic behavior is simply too diverse and too complex for one model to cover all the bases at once. Accordingly, our survey of oligopoly will consist of a series of models, each portraying a different set of behavior patterns, traits of firms, and competitive conditions. Taken together, they offer a reasonably accurate survey of the varieties of oligopolistic competition among large corporations. The models in this chapter focus on profit-maximizing aspects of oligopolistic behavior. In Chapter 15 we complete the picture of competition in a corporate economy by presenting models where the goals of an enterprise deviate from simple profit maximization.

The Kinked Demand Curve Model

One of the key questions which an oligopolistic firm must consider is "How will rival firms respond if we decide to alter our selling price?" One answer to this question is contained in the *kinked demand curve model* of oligopoly behavior.[2]

Suppose that three large firms, A, B, and C, are selling their own versions of an essentially identical product, with each firm having about one-third of the total market. Suppose, too, that the firms are selling at a common price of P_1 dollars and that at this price Corporation A's sales volume is Q_1 units, as shown in Fig. 12-1. What will happen now if A independently lowers its selling price to P_2 dollars? One possibility is for B and C to ignore A's lower price, in which case A can expect sharply increasing sales, say to Q_2 units, because by underselling firms B and C it will attract many customers away from its higher-priced rivals. A second possibility is for the two rival firms to match A's price cut to prevent A from gaining sales, market share, and profits at their expense. Such a retaliatory move will tend to have the effect of limiting A's gain in sales to its customary share of the increased

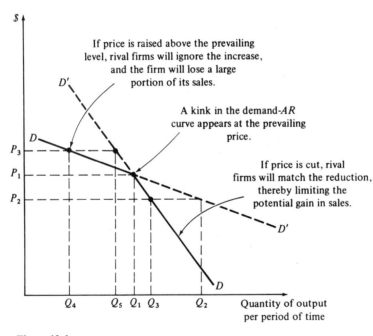

If price is raised above the prevailing level, rival firms will ignore the increase, and the firm will lose a large portion of its sales.

A kink in the demand-AR curve appears at the prevailing price.

If price is cut, rival firms will match the reduction, thereby limiting the potential gain in sales.

Figure 12-1
The kinked demand curve

[2] The kinked demand curve model was first advanced by Paul Sweezy in 1939. For a more extensive discussion of this model, see his article "Demand Under Conditions of Oligopoly," *Journal of Political Economy*, Vol. 47 (August 1939), pp. 568–738. For an evaluation of the model, see George J. Stigler, "The Kinky Oligopoly Demand Curve and Rigid Prices," *Journal of Political Economy*, Vol. 55 (October 1947), pp. 432–449.

business which all three firms will tend to realize because of selling at a lower

price. In terms of Fig. 12-1, matching price cuts by B and C will hold A's sales down to Q_2 units instead of Q_2 units. Thus, A's demand-AR curve for lower prices assumes a position along the path of the solid line extending down from point $P_1 Q_1$ when rivals match the price cut but is positioned along the path of the dashed line when rivals ignore the price cut.

Now, what if A should decide to raise its selling price above P_1 dollars, say to P_3 dollars? Assuming B and C again elect to ignore A's price change, then A would find itself in the lonely position of being the high-priced seller. Firm A might well price itself out of the market and lose so many of its customers to B and C that its resulting sales would be only Q_4 units; the higher price would not cause A to lose all its customers because some buyers may have strong enough preferences for A's brand that they are willing to pay the higher price. Since B and C stand to gain sales and profits at A's expense, there is a strong chance that they will not follow A's price increase to P_3 dollars. But if they should decide to exactly match A's price increase, perhaps because rising costs or other factors motivate them to do so, A's sales will fall less drastically. Why? Firm A will be at no competitive disadvantage with respect to price, and its sales loss is restricted to its share of the decline in marketwide sales which all three firms will incur from selling at a higher price. Referring again to Fig. 12-1, matching price increases by B and C will result in a loss of sales for A from Q_1 to Q_5 units instead of from Q_1 to Q_4 units. Thus, A's expected sales volumes for prices above P_1 will tend to follow the path of the solid line extending up from $P_1 Q_1$ when rivals ignore price increases and will tend to follow the dashed line when rivals follow price increases.

Unless the three firms have specific knowledge to the contrary, they can each expect that *price cuts will be matched* as rivals react to prevent the price-cutter from gaining customers at their expense but that *price increases will be ignored*, because rivals of the price-raising firm will gain the business lost by the price booster. This means that each firm will have a kinked demand curve for its product like the solid line (DD) in Fig. 12-1, with the kink occurring at the prevailing price. The competitive situation among the firms is therefore such that an *independent* price increase will cause a drastic decline in a firm's sales volume, while a price cut will result in only modest sales gains. In more technical language, the demand curve for each oligopolist tends to be highly elastic above the ruling price and much less elastic or even inelastic below the going price.

When the firm's demand-AR curve is kinked, its corresponding marginal revenue curve consists of two disjointed segments (see Fig. 12-2). The upper segment corresponds to the more elastic portion of the demand-AR curve, whereas the lower segment corresponds to the less elastic portion of the demand-AR curve. The vertical discontinuity in the MR curve is at the prevailing price and output rate.

To see how a kinked demand curve can affect a firm's price and output decision, suppose we look further at Fig. 12-2. Assume that a firm's marginal

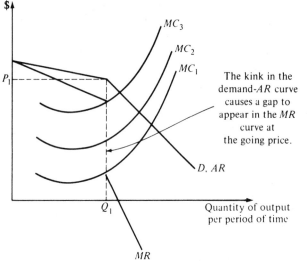

MC_3

MC_2

MC_1

P_1

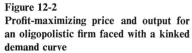

The kink in the
demand-AR curve
causes a gap to
appear in the MR
curve at
the going price.

D, AR

Q_1

Quantity of output
per period of time

MR

Figure 12-2
**Profit-maximizing price and output for
an oligopolistic firm faced with a kinked
demand curve**

cost curve is MC_1. From previous chapters we know that profits are maximized where $MR = MC$. Thus, in Fig. 12-2 the short-run profit-maximizing output rate is Q_1 units, since at outputs less than Q_1 units $MR > MC$ and at outputs more than Q_1 units $MC > MR$. In the event that rising input prices (such as wage increases or increases in raw material prices) push the firm's marginal cost function up to MC_2, a selling price of P_1 dollars and an output of Q_1 units is still the most profitable price-output combination. In fact, the firm's marginal cost function must rise above MC_3 before it would be advantageous to change either price or output. As long as the MC function intersects the discontinuous portion of the MR function, the firm's profit-maximizing point is fixed at the kink in the demand-AR curve.

The same rigidity of prices but not of outputs may occur even though the demand for an oligopolist's product intensifies. In Fig. 12-3, for instance, the firm's demand-AR curve shifts rightward from D_1-AR_1 to D_2-AR_2, generating a new MR function (MR_2). However, the MC function intersects both the old and the new MR functions in the discontinuous segment. Hence, there is no incentive to change price from P_1 dollars, although the profit-maximizing output rate does rise from Q_1 to Q_2 units. So long as the shift in demand is not so large as to result in MC intersecting the new MR curve outside the discontinuous segment, no change in the firm's selling price is called for.

Several important predictions about the price and output policies of oligopolists can be made when competing firms believe they are confronted with a kinked demand curve:

1. Oligopolistic firms will refrain from *independently* raising price above the going rate for fear that charging a price higher than rivals will cause a substantial decline in sales, profits, and market share.

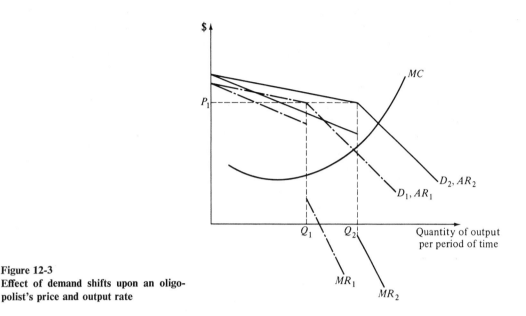

Figure 12-3
**Effect of demand shifts upon an oligo-
polist's price and output rate**

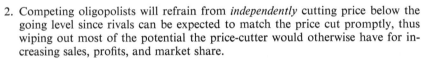

2. Competing oligopolists will refrain from *independently* cutting price below the going level since rivals can be expected to match the price cut promptly, thus wiping out most of the potential the price-cutter would otherwise have for increasing sales, profits, and market share.

3. Competition forces rival oligopolists to charge the same or nearly the same prices for their products since the ease with which consumers can switch from one brand to another results in patronage flocking to the low-priced sellers. Firms simply cannot expect to survive by selling essentially the same product at significantly higher prices than rivals. The chief exception to this fundamental principle of competition is where firms have been so successful in differentiating their products and creating strong brand loyalties that their customers are willing to pay higher prices to obtain a "quality" product.

4. The price and output rate of an oligopolistic firm *will not necessarily* change even though its costs change.

5. An oligopolist's price will tend to be sticky, but its output rate will tend to be responsive to moderate shifts in demand.

All five predictions are consistent with observed corporate behavior in both pure and differentiated oligopolies. Prices in corporate oligopolies appear to be generally more stable as compared to prices in perfectly and monopolistically competitive industries. Experience further indicates the prices charged by rival corporations tend to be *identical* where the products are standardized or else weakly differentiated—as in steel, aluminum, cement, newsprint, explosives, cast iron pipe, sheetrock, bread, and cigarettes. Where their products are strongly differentiated, oligopolists tend to charge prices which are *comparable* (tires, automobiles, household appliances, computers, TV sets). Moreover, executives have been found to evidence a strong conviction that price cuts *will* be matched.[3] During periods of economic decline and falling product demand, corporate-dominated industries have typically been characterized by relatively small price declines and relatively large output declines.[4] Thus, the kinked demand curve model does help account for some significant facets of pricing and competitive behavior in the corporate sector.

Nevertheless, the model is not without serious faults. In the first place, alternative explanations for price rigidity can be found. For instance, firms may hesitate to change prices frequently or independently so as not to disrupt customer relations by introducing an element of uncertainty as to future prices. Some firms profess that from the standpoint of buyer psychology it is better to raise prices in large doses and to do so infrequently than to raise prices frequently but by small amounts. Firms selling at "nationally advertised prices" face practical limitations upon the frequency with which prices can be altered. Obviously, recurrent price cuts run the danger that a price war will be triggered since rival firms may elect to teach the price-cutter a lesson by slashing their prices even lower, and all firms end up as losers.[5] In sum, oligopoly prices may be "sticky" because firms are cautious about making price changes *until cost or demand conditions have plainly changed in well-defined ways.*

A second important limitation of the kinked demand curve model is its inability to explain how oligopolists initially arrive at the prevailing prices. The model is much better at explaining why price persists at the kink than how it reached that level or why and how it might change. In other words, the kink is an *ex post* rationalization of price stability rather than an explanation of price determination.

Finally, the assumptions that price cuts will be matched and price increases ignored do not always hold. When a firm lowers its price, competitors need not interpret this to mean that the price-cutter is trying to steal the market. Rivals may take a price reduction to mean that the item has some fault and is not selling well, the item is about to be superceded by a later model, the company is in financial trouble and is trying to improve its

---

[3]Actual examples may be found in Harold M. Fleming, *Gasoline Prices and Competition* (New York: Appleton-Century-Crofts, 1966), Chapter 5; R. B. Tennant, "The Cigarette Industry," in *The Structure of American Industry*, 3rd ed., Walter Adams, ed. (New York: The Macmillan Company, 1961), pp. 370–372; the records of the Salk vaccine case (*U.S. v. Eli Lilly et al.*) and the tetracycline case (*F.T.C. v. American Cyanamid et al.*); and A. D. H. Kaplan, J. B. Dirlam, and R. F. Lanzilotti, *Pricing in Big Business* (Washington, D.C.: The Brookings Institution, 1958), p. 174.

[4]Gardiner C. Means, *Industrial Prices and Their Flexibility* (Washington, D.C.: U.S. Government Printing Office, 1935), p. 8: also, Gardiner C. Means, "The Administered Price Thesis Confirmed," *American Economic Review*, Vol. 62, No. 3 (June 1972), pp. 292–306. In contrast, in industries where firms were more numerous and the characteristics of competition among the many prevailed, price declines were relatively large, and production fell by relatively small amounts.

[5]The likelihood of a price war and the extent of damage it may do to the firms concerned tend to be greater (1) the more standardized are their products, (2) the more inelastic is the market demand for their output, and (3) the lower are the marginal costs of production. Industries such as petroleum, tires, and steel have a "high-risk" rating on all three counts.

sales, or that the company is hoping the whole industry will reduce its prices in the interests of stimulating total demand. Competitors may react differently depending on whether they view the price change as temporary or permanent. Each rival firm's reaction will be based upon what it *thinks* is motivating the company's price cut, and there is ample room for different firms to react differently.

Insofar as price increases are concerned, when rival firms experience similar shifts in cost or demand conditions, the incentive to change price may be generally recognized and mutually advantageous to all concerned. For example, industrywide price adjustments frequently follow wage and tax increases imposed uniformly upon the firms by collective bargaining and government, respectively. Knowing that its rivals are confronted with comparable cost increases, a firm can boost price in confidence that rivals will follow suit.[6] It is more than coincidental when U.S. Steel announces a price hike following a new settlement with the steelworkers' union that other steel firms also announce higher prices. Indeed, when the incentives for a price change appear generally throughout the industry, the main problem becomes who will be bold enough to raise price first and wise enough to figure out what size price increase will be competitively acceptable. The tendency to ignore price increases also falls by the wayside in an inflationary economy when, after prices have been rising along a wide front for some time, consumers become resigned (however, grudgingly) to higher prices, and firms, both independently and as a group, find it easier to raise prices.

Market Share Models

Another approach to price-output determination in oligopoly is based upon the competitive patterns emerging from variations in the market shares and costs of rival firms. Suppose that we start with a fairly simple competitive situation and then gradually introduce more variables.

Equal Market Shares and Equal Costs. Consider an industry comprised of only two firms A and B, selling identical products, having exactly the same production costs, and dividing the market on a 50–50 basis. These conditions mean that the two firms will have identical demand-AR, MR, ATC, and MC curves, as shown in Fig. 12-4. With each firm having one-half the industry demand, the demand-AR curves of the two firms are located on top of one another, halfway between the vertical axis and the industrywide demand curve at each price. Since profits are maximum at the price and output rate where $MR = MC$, both A and B will be motivated to charge the

---

[6]Linking price increases to wage or tax hikes has the added benefit of making it appear that the blame rests with greedy unions or a revenue-hungry government; such maneuvers help the firm to escape public criticism and charges of profiteering. However, in periods of rapidly inflating costs and prices, more than a few firms appear (to buyers, at least) to have engaged in price pyramiding—raising prices by more than the cost increases incurred in an effort to widen profit margins. Such practices have prompted government price-watchers to jawbone firms into cost-justifying their higher prices.

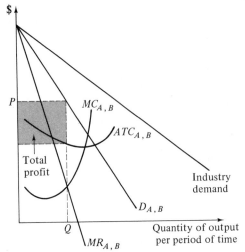

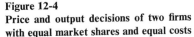

Figure 12-4
Price and output decisions of two firms with equal market shares and equal costs

same price ($P_{A,B}$) and to produce at the same output rate ($Q_{A,B}$). Each firm will earn a short-run economic profit equal to the shaded area in Fig. 12-4. The significant point here is that no pricing conflict exists between the two firms because they maximize profits at the same price.

Each firm can be confident that its preferred price-output strategy will be "satisfactory" to its rival rather than provoking some sort of aggressive competitive activity. Why? Because if one firm initiates a price cut to try to gain increased sales, profits, and market share at the expense of the other, then it is merely inviting a costly price war. The other firm will have little option but to retaliate with price cuts of its own to keep from losing customers and absorbing the high costs of idle production capacity. Price cutting will mean both firms receive less for their product. And, if industry demand is price inelastic, then lower prices mean lower revenues will accompany the increased sales, and, clearly, the profits of both firms will drop. This accounts for why oligopolistic firms selling identical or weakly differentiated products are not usually excited by the prospect of price competition and, indeed, shy away from using price cuts as a competitive weapon.

Equal Market Shares and Different Costs. Suppose, however, that we introduce a cost differential between the two firms, other factors remaining unchanged. Specifically, suppose firm B has a higher *MC* curve, as indicated in Fig. 12-5. Firm B's higher costs might reflect older, technologically inferior production facilities, higher raw material costs, higher labor costs, higher shipping costs due to an unfavorable geographic location, or managerial inefficiency. Examination of Fig. 12-5 indicates that firm A's profit-maximizing price and output are P_A and Q_A, whereas firm B will prefer P_B and Q_B.

A pricing conflict is immediately apparent. Each firm is worse off, profit-wise, at its rival's favored price than at its own, and therefore each will

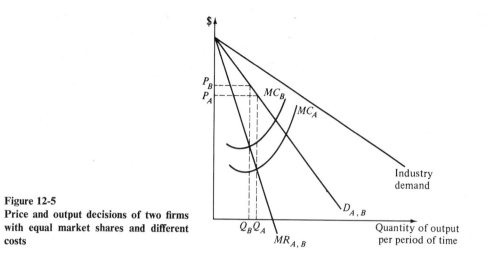

Figure 12-5
Price and output decisions of two firms
with equal market shares and different
costs

prefer to see its own profit-maximizing price established on an industrywide basis. As long as the two firms continue to sell identical products, buyers are not likely to be as willing to buy from B, the higher-priced firm; patronage will flow quickly to the lower-priced seller. Competitive forces thus will soon drive the two firms to sell at the same price. But what price?

One obvious method by which the two firms may resolve their pricing difference is collusion. But collusion carries severe risk. Aside from the fact that price fixing via formal collusion or gentlemen's agreements is illegal under the antitrust laws, collusion can prove to be a fragile means of reaching a long-lasting solution.[7] Collusive arrangements of any variety are fragile because they give some firms an incentive to cheat on the other firms. A collusive price is certain to be a compromise price and is certain to be higher than would prevail in the absence of collusion (it is most unlikely that the purpose of collusion is to lower the going price). The chances are good, therefore, that one or more firms will be sorely tempted to pick up a lot of profitable new business by discreetly negotiating secret price concessions with individual customers. Experience has shown that this temptation reaches monumental proportions when business slackens and the economy turns sour, although it is better contained when business is good enough to provide the colluding firms with at least a satisfactory sales volume and level of profitability. If and when one or more firms yield to the temptation to cheat, collusion quickly disintegrates. Mutual trust and faithful adherence to the bargain (as well as avoiding detection by the legal authorities) are essential for suc-

[7]In fairness, it must be acknowledged that some people do not agree with the contention that collusion is either fragile or the exception rather than the rule. There is a body of doctrine which contends that whenever rival firms are few in number, an almost inherent attraction to collusion and monopolistic arrangements exists. The strong propensity to collude was noted almost 200 years ago by Adam Smith: "People of the same trade seldom meet together, even for merriment and diversion, but the conversation ends in a conspiracy against the public, or in some contrivance to raise prices."

cessful collusion—these are not easy to come by when cheating is lucrative and when more than four or five firms are involved.

A second alternative is for firm A, which prefers the lowest price, to try to force its preferred price upon firm B. Firm A is in a strong position to impose its price preference on B because of its cost advantage and because buyers flock to the low-priced seller. However, firm B is not entirely power-less. Should B's profits be unacceptable if it is forced to sell at A's lower price, then B may seek to intimidate A into a more "reasonable" price by slashing price below P_A and deliberately provoking a mutually unprofitable price war. This may indeed be a very viable option if firm B is a large diversi-fied corporation, since any losses sustained by B from temporarily selling this product at a low price can be offset by profits from the sale of its other products. On the other hand, if firm A is also large or diversified or has ample financial resources, then it may be in as good or better position to weather out a price war. So we cannot say for sure whether firm B will be able to "persuade" A to charge a price closer to P_B, whether the reverse will be true, or whether firm B will be forced to meet A's preferred price.

Only one thing is certain: *Whenever rival firms are selling essentially identical products, competitive forces will sooner or later drive them to sell at the same price.* Until this occurs, even a temporary "price equilibrium" cannot exist, simply because firms attempting to sell at prices above their rivals will face erosion of their sales, profits, and market shares and, conceivably, will be driven out of the market entirely over the long term. In general, then, a high-cost firm has the following options for bringing about a price accom-modation: (1) initiating some form of collusive action to raise price to an "acceptable" level, (2) threatening or actually initiating a price war so as to coerce lower-priced firms into adopting a compromise price somewhere in between the high and low end of the range, (3) revamping its production techniques to bring costs into line with (or even lower than) those of rival firms, (4) shifting into the production of other commodities where expected profits are higher, and (5) doing the best it can at the price chosen by the low-cost firms.[8] Very likely options (3) and (5) will prove to be the most viable, short of shifting into some other business.

Analogous pricing conflicts arise where firms selling differentiated prod-ucts have cost differences and thus different profit-maximizing prices. How-ever, *the competitive imperative to sell at the same price is not so intense if the products are sufficiently differentiated that buyers can be persuaded to accept modest price differences.* Higher-cost firms preferring to sell at higher prices may be able to compete by successfully using the "ours is better than theirs"

---

[8]Going out of business and dissolving the firm, while possible, is not a probable alternative—unless it is driven into bankruptcy by its inability to compete. The closing down of a large corporation is a rare event—much more so than in the case of small owner-man-aged companies. A large corporation normally responds to market adversity and unprofit-able products by either withdrawing from the unprofitable market and redeploying its energies and resources into endeavors with higher expected profits or else undertaking a major overhaul of its production and marketing organization, which it believes will increase efficiency, reduce costs, and improve its long-term ability to compete successfully.

theme in promoting their products or by designing more "quality" into their products. To the extent such efforts win over enough buyers, firms are not so strongly compelled by competition to charge a uniform price and may be able to sell at their respective profit-maximizing prices. But if product differentiation results in sizable cost differences between firms and thereby drives a large wedge between their profit-maximizing prices, then a pricing conflict emerges, and competition will prod firms into reaching a more uniform price structure.

Different Market Shares and Equal Costs. Next, consider the case where firms have identical costs but different market shares. All three panels of Fig. 12-6 illustrate demand situations where firm A has 60% of the total market at each price and firm B has the remaining 40% of the market. Here, the nature of the pricing conflict varies with the shape of the marginal cost function confronting the two firms. In Fig. 12-6(a) the products of the firms are produced under conditions of identically rising marginal costs. Firm A maximizes its profits by producing where $MC_{A,B} = MR_A$; accordingly, A's preferred price is P_A, and its preferred output rate is Q_A units. Firm B's profit-maximizing price and output are P_B and Q_B, respectively. A clash of pricing preferences is apparent, with the firm with the *larger* market share preferring the *higher* price. Other things being equal, this result holds not just for a 60–40 market split but also for any uneven market share split—60–40, 80–20, 55–45, or whatever. It turns out that the more divergent the market shares of the two firms, the greater is the gap between their respective profit-maximizing prices. In this situation, whether the large-share firm will accede to the price preference of the small-share firm, whether the reverse will be true, or whether some compromise price will evolve is open to question. It all depends. The firm with the larger market share may try to intimidate the firm with the smaller share and coerce it into accepting a price close to

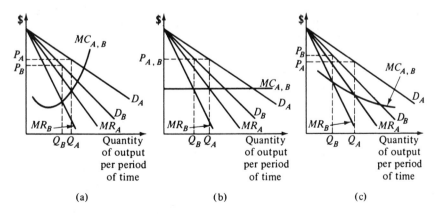

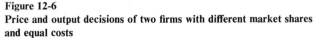

Figure 12-6
Price and output decisions of two firms with different market shares and equal costs

the higher of the profit-maximizing prices. On the other hand, if the small-share firm is in a position to withstand pressure from the large-share firm, then it holds the upper hand, and price equilibrium is likely to be attained near the lower of the two profit-maximizing prices.

In Fig. 12-6(b) both firms produce under conditions of identical and constant marginal costs over the relevant output range. In this instance, firm A will maximize profits by producing Q_A units, and firm B will maximize profits by producing Q_B units. However, the profit-maximizing prices of the firms coincide at $P_{A,B}$. Such a result is not circumstantial but rather is an inherent geometrical trait of linear demand curves with a common vertical intercept. And it holds for a market share split of any combination. Therefore, when oligopolists have identical and constant marginal costs, no conflict over price arises, irrespective of the firms' market shares. Given that (1) cost studies of manufacturing enterprises have shown a fairly widespread tendency for MC to be constant up to 85 to 90% of capacity [refer back to Fig. 8-5(b)], (2) constant returns to scale may prevail as output expands over the long run [see Fig. 8-8(c)], and (3) competition forces rival firms to remain cost-competitive, the lack of a sizable differential among the respective profit-maximizing prices of rival firms as shown in Fig. 12-6(b) may not be uncommon.

Figure 12-6(c) shows declining marginal cost prevailing for both firms over the relevant output range. Here, firm A prefers a lower price (P_A) than firm B prefers (P_B). The firm with the larger market share prefers the lower price because of the lower marginal costs associated with higher outputs. The production economies stemming from larger outputs will likely make firm A less willing to compromise its lower price preference with firm B's preference for a higher price. However, both firms have an incentive to capture larger market shares in order to take advantage of declining costs. This is likely to result in persistent downward pressure on price, and the firm with the largest market share has the advantage of being in the best position to lower prices because of its lower marginal costs. While the antitrust laws will undoubtedly serve to restrain firm A from being so aggressive that antitrust action is invoked, the situation is ripe for one firm to grow larger at the expense of its rivals by initiating bold price cuts. Confronted with this threat, underdog firms may opt to defend or improve their position by making major product improvements (quality, service, convenience, etc.) in an attempt to divert buyers' attention away from price. Their major hope lies not in imitation but in achieving a differential advantage based upon a better product (Zenith's "the quality goes in before the name goes on"), or unconventional distribution outlets (Timex), or stronger appeal to special classes of buyers (Volkswagen), or a superior promotional campaign (Avis's "We're No. 2, We Try Harder"), or personal selling (Avon), or the like.

Different Market Shares and Different Costs. Normally, product differentiation and varying degrees of product acceptance combine to give firms different market shares. At the same time, production technologies of differing vintage and efficiency and slight variations in wage rates, transportation costs, and raw material prices owing to geographic factors make it likely that corporate rivals will not have *identical* cost structures—though competition will force costs to be *comparable* from firm to firm. When both market shares and unit production costs are variable among rival firms, a wide range of outcomes exist. The small-share firms may have a lower profit-maximizing price, or it may be the large-share firms that have the lower profit-maximizing price. The variation in the preferred prices of rival firms may be wide or narrow. Conceivably, differences in market shares and costs will cancel out, and no material pricing conflict will emerge.

Yet, if price preferences do differ, some means will have to be found to decide what the going price (or band of prices) will be.[9] The ease with which buyers can switch to the lower-priced brands guarantees that this will be so. The existence of a pricing conflict occasionally surfaces in the form of short-term price wars, the uncovering of price-fixing arrangements, and competitive behavior with a cutthroat or predatory intent. More usually, pricing conflicts remain latent and are gradually resolved via intermediate- and long-term adjustments on the part of firms, including cost reduction schemes, plant relocations, technological innovation, product diversifications, improved product design and performance, aggressive advertising and sales promotion tactics, and other forms of nonprice competition. Experience has shown that such adjustments are safer and more reliable forms of conflict resolution than mutually unprofitable price wars and collusive arrangements. In the meantime, firms that are at a competitive price disadvantage will suffer lower profits or even incur losses.

The major conclusion to be drawn from the market share models is that, despite the difficulties involved, some attempt at reaching a mutually acceptable price structure *must* and *will* be made by firms in oligopolistic competition. In either the short or the long run, *oligopolists have no realistic alternative to charging identical or comparable prices for their products, irrespective of market share and cost differences. Mutual interdependence and personalized rivalry quickly teach oligopolists that no firm can price blindly without regard for the prices charged by its rivals.* Thus, while corporate rivals may well decide to experiment with charging different prices, the responses of buyers to the prevailing price pattern will exert a natural and powerful force for a uniform price structure to emerge. Daily experience in the marketplace gives each firm a "feel" for what price it can charge and still compete, thereby making either formal or tacit agreements among firms quite superfluous as a mechanism for reaching an accommodation on the going price structure. Consequently, it is hard to tell from simple observation whether

---

[9]An experiment conducted by J. W. Friedman revealed a tendency for price equilibrium to be reached more than 75% of the time. Despite the opportunity to cheat once equilibrium agreements were reached, the agreed-to price was honored in nine out of ten cases. However, Friedman found that a price equilibrium was reached somewhat less often under conditions of different market shares and production costs as opposed to equal market shares and costs. For further details, see "An Experimental Study of Cooperative Duopoly," *Econometrica*, Vol. 35, No. 3–4 (July–October 1967), pp. 379–397.

uniform pricing among rival corporations is indicative of competition or conspiracy.

Attempts at resolving differences in the preferred prices of corporate rivals can entail any of several forms and results.[10] From an industrywide standpoint, the most attractive price compromise is *joint profit maximization* whereby firms cooperate (explicitly or implicitly) to arrive at a price (or range of prices) which is perceived to yield the largest possible *collective* profit. But while joint profit maximization may mean that all firms as a group are better off, some firms may feel they are giving up more than they are gaining; in fact, some firms may not fare well at all at the joint profit-maximizing price (because of cost or market share differences). In this case, attempts at joint profit maximization tend to break down because disadvantaged firms have a strong incentive to act independently on their own behalf.

Another basic approach is *independent profit maximization* where one firm (or a small group of firms) is sufficiently powerful and influential to impose its own profit-maximizing price upon rival firms. There are, of course, any number of forms of intermediate or *hybrid profit maximization* wherein via the market process a trial-and-error compromise is reached between pricing together for maximum joint profits and pricing independently for maximum individual profits. Although more disorganized and less purposeful than the previous two forms of price coordination, hybrid profit maximization may nonetheless entail *conscious parallelism* where competing firms, without any communication back and forth whatsoever, come to the realization that aggressive actions (such as price cutting) invite retaliation and, in the end, leave all firms worse off; thus, they adopt common prices and policies implicitly and in concert, with the conviction that their mutual interdependence makes it beneficial for like businesses to be run in like fashion.

Finally, price coordination efforts may lead to *formula pricing* whereby firms, by custom or agreement, adhere to the same rule-of-thumb procedure of adding a "fair" profit margin to "normal" average total costs to reach a common price. All these price-coordinating procedures are observable in actual situations, but none seems to stand out as *the* predominant form of reconciling price differences among competing oligopolists.

However, perhaps the most significant issue in oligopoly pricing is not so much *how* pricing conflicts are resolved as whether the price equilibrium that is established is higher or lower than could reasonably be expected to prevail with some other form of competitive market structure. Or, to put it another way, is oligopoly as "competitive" as perfect or monopolistic competition? Although we shall postpone a final judgment on these issues until Chapter 16 when more evidence has been accumulated, some preliminary

---

[10]For one fascinating version of how uniform prices can be attained without collusion or communication between the firms, see Thomas C. Schelling, *The Strategy of Conflict* (Cambridge, Mass.: Harvard University Press, 1960), Chapters 2 and 3. Schelling develops a theory of focal points in which it is contended that a tendency exists for choices among alternatives to converge on some prominent value intuitively perceived by those concerned. The focal point owes its prominence to precedent, analogy, an obvious split-the-difference situation, habit, institutional idiosyncracies, educated guess, or the like.

generalizations are possible now. If collusive actions on the part of rival oligopolists are feasible and maintainable, prices are sure to rise above "competitive" levels. However, in the absence of collusion and coercion, the price equilibrium is more likely to approach competitive levels and the lower end of the conflict range due to the upper hand which firms preferring a lower price have over those preferring a higher price.

Price Leadership Models

Competitive pressures notwithstanding, one obvious way for corporate rivals to arrive at a common price is for one firm to seize the initiative and act as price leader for the industry. In such instances, it is customary for the price leader to announce a price change, with the remaining firms accepting the leader's judgment and promptly following suit. Two major forms of price leadership stand out: *dominant firm leadership* and *barometric firm leadership*.

Dominant Firm Price Leadership. Dominant firm price leadership arises when one firm accounts for a much larger market share than any of its rivals. Typically, the dominant firm is a large, vertically integrated corporation whose only rivals consist of numerous "competitive fringe" firms, none of which is able to exert a material influence on the market through its own price-output decisions. On rarer occasions, dominant firm industries are composed of one large firm, several medium-sized firms, and a host of small firms that operate on the competitive fringe of the market.

The assumption underlying the dominant-firm model is that the dominant firm establishes its own preferred price as the going market price and allows the competitive fringe firms to sell all they wish at that price; the dominant firm then produces an amount sufficient to meet the remaining demand at the chosen price. In essence, the competitive fringe firms behave just like perfectly competitive firms. They can sell all they want at the price set by the dominant firm and therefore face a horizontal demand curve at the established price Each of the fringe firms pegs its output at the rate where $MC = MR$; MR is equal to the price set by the dominant firm since the latter lets the fringe firms sell all they please.

The determination of the dominant firm's optimum price is illustrated in Fig. 12-7. Suppose that the dominant firm believes the total market demand curve to be D_m. Suppose further that it estimates the amount of output which will be supplied by the competitive fringe firms at various alternative prices to be S_{cf}—found by summing together the portions of the marginal cost curves lying above average variable cost for each fringe producer. Once the dominant firm estimates how much of the total market demand will be served by the competitive fringe, it can calculate how much will be left over for itself. For example, at prices of P_1 and higher, the competitive fringe is willing to supply all the output the market will absorb, leaving no sales potential for the dominant firm. At price P_2 total market demand is P_2C units; of this, the fringe producers would produce P_2B units, leaving BC units

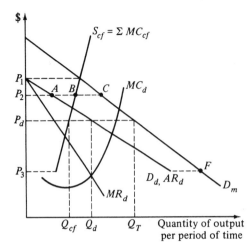

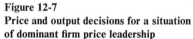

Figure 12-7
Price and output decisions for a situation
of dominant firm price leadership

for the dominant firm. To locate the dominant firm's demand curve at price P_2 we set point A such that BC units equals P_2A units of output. This procedure can be repeated for other assumed prices. In each case the dominant firm's demand is found by subtracting the fringe firms' output at a given price from the total industry demand at that price. The result is a series of points which, when connected, gives the curve D_d, AR_d. Observe that at prices below P_3 the dominant firm has the entire market to itself; no output will be supplied by the fringe firms when price is less than the minimum average variable cost of every fringe firm. Thus, the dominant firm's demand curve below price P_3 coincides with the segment of the industry demand curve labeled FD_m. The dominant firm's entire demand curve is D_d, AR_d plus the segment FD_m.

The dominant firm determines its profit-maximizing price and output in the customary fashion of equating marginal revenue and marginal cost. The marginal revenue curve corresponding to D_d, AR_d is MR_d, and the dominant firm's marginal cost curve is shown as MC_d. Its profit-maximizing output rate is therefore Q_d units, and its profit-maximizing price is P_d dollars. Total market demand at price P_d is Q_T units. Of this, the dominant firm supplies Q_d units, and the competitive fringe firms supply the remainder ($Q_T - Q_d$), which equals Q_{cf} units in Fig. 12-7.

One of the better current examples of dominant firm price leadership arises in retailing where a nationally known seller (such as K Mart, A&P, or Sears) dominates a local market for the commodities it carries. The numerous small, locally owned retail firms carrying comparable products constitute the competitive fringe. The local firms must at least meet the prices of the dominant marketer or risk loss of a major portion of their customers. And they must be wary of trying to undercut the dominant firm's prices because if they get far out of line and begin to cut heavily into the leader's business, they can be certain of retaliatory action. The leader may well decide to discipline fringe firms by discretely cutting its prices in those areas where small firms are strongest. A large firm serving many geographically distinct markets can afford to cut prices to the bone in one or a few areas and still make out with the profits it earns elsewhere.[11] The local firm has no such option. Here, the followership of small firms stems from implicit coercion and potential punishment from the dominant firm and not from genuine popularity of the leader's price.

However, it need not at all be the case that the dominant firm prefers a price higher than its smaller rivals and must throw its weight around to keep potential price-cutters in line. The price leader may well have secured its dominant position because of cost economies derived from large-scale production and because its cost advantage produces a profit-maximizing price *below* that of its smaller rivals. In other words, the dominant firm's market position may be due to its greater ability to attract customers by underselling everybody else. In this case, minor firms must match the leader's price or face the prospects of an even smaller market share.

In times past, dominant firm price leaders have included International Harvester in farm implements, U.S. Steel in steel, Firestone in tires, Exxon (Standard Oil) in petroleum, Alcoa in aluminum, General Motors in autos, Birdseye in frozen goods, R. J. Reynolds in cigarettes, IBM in computers, Coca-Cola in soft drinks, American Can in tin cans, and International Paper in paper products. However, with the exception of IBM and General Motors, the position of these dominant firms has gradually been eroded by growth and expansion of once-lesser rivals.

The frequency with which dominant firms have lost their dominance suggests that a dominant firm market structure may be short-lived and will eventually disintegrate into highly competitive oligopoly. The reasons are straightforward. When the dominant firm's price allows fringe firms to realize positive economic profits, then, over time, they are encouraged to take advantage of scale economies and expand their outputs.[12] Since the dominant firm is a "quantity-follower" and in effect makes room for fringe firm expansion by curbing its own output, the most aggressive smaller firms, via steady expansion, will begin to increase their market shares at the expense of the dominant firm. Sooner or later, the dominant firm will find itself confronted with several emerging rivals of growing influence and power, and its dominant position will be effectively undermined.

The major point here is that the dominant firm, if it wishes to retain its position of advantage in the market, must deviate from the pattern of letting smaller firms produce as much as they please. It is "suicide" for it to buy price leadership at the cost of quantity followership. Instead, to preserve its

---

[11]This is not to say, however, that large firms will readily resort to local price warfare. The profit sacrifices of the dominant firm are likely to be quite large relative to the harm it inflicts upon small rivals. Price wars to discipline minor firms and to teach them the value of cooperation are worthwhile only if the aftermath produces an environment much more conducive to the earning of profits. Otherwise, it may take an inordinately long time to recoup the sacrifices of profit which a price war entails.

[12]The steel industry provides a classic example. In 1901 U.S. Steel controlled 65% of the industry's ingot capacity. As the dominant firm and price leader, it established a high price policy which stimulated the entry and expansion of smaller steel firms. By 1915 U.S. Steel's share of ingot capacity was down to 52%; its share has since eroded to 28% in 1960 and 21% in 1968.

position the dominant firm must abandon the short-run profit-maximizing behavior portrayed in the dominant firm model in favor of long-run profit maximization. Among other things, this means adjusting its short-run profit-maximizing price downward so as to deter small-firm expansion and the entry of new rivals. The dominant firm must be wary of creating short-run market conditions conductive to the growth of the competitive fringe. Of course, it may be that it has no choice in this regard. The antitrust laws and the shape of the long-run average cost curve may preclude the establishment of a price that will perpetuate the dominant firm's position.[13] But even should this happen (as obviously it has), all is not lost. The dominant firm can continue to outperform its lesser rivals by being the source of new product ideas, cost-saving discoveries, customer service improvements, and new distribution techniques. By maintaining a leadership posture on nonprice variables as well as price, it may succeed in discouraging upstart competitors. The principle that the best defense is a good offense applies well in this situation.

Another technique the dominant firm can use is the multibrand strategy whereby it introduces a number of new product variations with different brand names. Although its own brands may be similar and compete with one another, the effect may still be to lock out room for other firms to bring out their brands. Procter & Gamble has used this technique to good advantage. It has several major brands of soaps (Ivory, Zest, Safeguard, Camay, and Lava) and household cleaners (Top Job, Mr. Clean, Comet, and Spic'n Span); this gives P&G a sizable overall market share and reduces the amount of shelf space available to competitors.

Occasionally, when a dominant firm has grown sluggish, inefficient, and complacent and then is challenged by smaller upstarts, it will try to protect its position by throwing its weight around with suppliers, distributors, or legislators and by initiating manuevers to discipline firms which have "gotten out of line." For instance, it may threaten major suppliers with backward integration unless they give it more favorable prices than smaller competitors; it may pressure distributors to give less attention to competitor's products; its salesmen may gossip with buyers about how the fringe firms' products are "really inferior"; it may lobby with legislators for the passage of bills that will make it harder for small firms to compete. Alternatively, it may give special under-the-table price discounts to competitors' best customers or launch a massive promotional campaign which small firms cannot hope to match.

Thus, a dominant firm has several options for maintaining its dominance: (1) keeping the industry price low enough to deter entry and to make expansion of fringe firms unattractive, (2) an innovational offensive on nonprice competitive variables, and (3) a defensive strategy involving confrontation, disciplinary action, and persecution of maverick aggressors.

The smaller "underdog" firms' best hope in successfully competing with a dominant firm usually lies not in mounting a head-on attack but rather in

---

[13]A penetrating analysis of dominant firm pricing is found in Dean A. Worcester, "Why 'Dominant Firms' Decline," *Journal of Political Economy*, Vol. 65, No. 4 (August 1957), pp. 338–347.

striking suddenly and with a concentrated effort to catch the dominant firm by surprise. Innovation and product differentiation are the underdogs' best strategies. The innovation may involve developing a superior product, cutting costs, finding new ways to distribute goods that offer substantial economies or reaches particular buyer segments more effectively, or instituting unique customer services. When one or several of these are coupled with clever advertising, the result will usually suffice to give underdog firms a viable and perhaps increasing market share.

Barometric Price Leadership. Barometric price leadership exists when there are *several* principal firms (surrounded or not, as the case may be, by a competitive fringe of small firms) and when one of the large firms is not powerful enough to impose its will upon the other consistently. Sometimes one, sometimes another of the principal firms will take the lead in initiating price changes. For instance, in rayon yarn, American Viscose (the largest seller) and DuPont (the second largest seller) have in recent years shared the role of leader. In copper, price leadership has been exercised by all of the Big Three—Anaconda, Kennecott, and Phelps Dodge. R. J. Reynolds and American Tobacco share the lead in cigarettes. U.S. Steel, Bethlehem, and occasionally a lesser firm bear the burden of price leadership in steel.

By and large, the barometric price leader appears to do little more than become the first firm to announce new prices consistent with current market conditions. Seldom does the barometric firm possess power to coerce the rest of the industry into accepting its lead, despite the fact that it may aspire to wield such control. In the usual case, the barometric firm acquires its status as leader because of its experience and respect throughout the industry, because other firms may be unable or unwilling to accept the responsibility of continuously appraising industry demand and supply conditions, or because other firms are hesitant to stick their necks out and formally recognize what is already being acknowledged in private. Thus, the barometric firm commands adherence of rivals to its price announcements only to the extent that it has accurately perceived the winds of change in industry demand and supply conditions. But even then, industrywide assent to the price change may not be forthcoming immediately; rival firms often temporize with a wait-and-see strategy for a period of several days or weeks.

The Significance of Price Leadership. Successful price leadership has the important effect of eliminating any perceived kink in the demand curves of oligopolists. The firm whose leadership role is widely and consistently accepted can count upon rivals to follow price increases as well as price cuts. However, for barometric firms whose lead is sometimes undermined by failure to follow, the inhibitions of a perceived kink still lurk close by.

The evidence is not clear whether price leadership results in the establishment of a price structure higher than it would otherwise be. On some occasions, price leadership undoubtedly facilitates the raising of prices. Yet, when the price leader is the lowest-cost producer, it may hold price below levels preferred by rival firms. Then, too, price leaders may sometimes be "statesmanlike" and postpone price increases during inflationary periods so as to cooperate with (or not antagonize) inflation-fighting policy-makers and consumer advocates.

Game Theory Models

It should by now be evident that the mutual interdependence which characterizes oligopoly behooves each firm to consider most carefully the strategies and counterstrategies that rival firms may adopt. With only a few firms in the market, competition pits each firm head-on against rivals whose interests are in direct conflict with its own (much as occurs in chess or poker). In such a situation, *game theory* becomes a useful analytical device for determining a firm's own "best" course of action, the "best" course of action of rival firms, and thereby the optimal solution to the competitive conflict existing between the firms concerned.

Game theory utilizes a convenient device known as a *payoff matrix* to tabulate the alternative strategies being considered by rival firms and the estimated outcomes associated with each possible strategy combination. Use of a payoff matrix has two valuable benefits. First, it forces a firm to give systematic consideration to its own strategic alternatives. Second, it forces a firm to assess how each competitor perceives its own self-interest. From the standpoint of predicting how a rival will react, the latter exercise is most important; it means researching the rival's current financial status, sales trends, the basis of its product's appeal to buyers, its corporate strategy, and so on to try to anticipate what the rival firm's options are and how its management thinks. Does the rival have a set competitive-reaction policy? Can its behavior be predicted accurately on the basis of past actions? Or does the competitor appear to decide afresh on each occasion what sort of competitive response would be in its best interest?

Suppose that two firms, A and B, are faced with a pricing conflict such that firm A's profit-maximizing price is $100 and firm B's profit-maximizing price is $90. For the moment, assume these are the only two alternative prices under consideration by the two firms. The payoff matrices below summarize the annual expected profit payoffs (in millions of dollars) for each firm:

Firm A's Payoff Matrix

		Firm B's Price Strategies	
		$90	$100
Firm A's Price	$ 90	$25 m.	$45 m.
Strategies	$100	$10 m.	$70 m.

Firm B's Payoff Matrix

		Firm B's Price Strategies	
		$90	$100
Firm A's Price	$ 90	$50 m.	$10 m.
Strategies	$100	$75 m.	$20 m.

Looking first at firm B's payoff matrix, we see that B's expected profits are

higher at its preferred price of $90 irrespective of whether A chooses a $90 price or a $100 price. This means that firm B will almost certainly choose a price of $90. Looking next at A's payoff matrix we see that if firm B picks the $90 price, firm A is forced to do likewise because A's profits are $25 million at a $90 price and only $10 million at a $100 price. However, firm A will probably find this price combination unacceptable, since its profits are far below what could be earned if B chose the $100 price. In trying to decide how to "persuade" B to deviate from a $90 price, suppose firm A considers two additional prices: a "compromise price" of $95 and a "war price" of $70 with payoffs as shown below:

Firm A's Payoff Matrix

		Firm B's Price Strategies			
		$70	$90	$95	$100
Firm A's	$ 70	−$ 7 m.	−$ 4 m.	$ 0	$ 2 m.
Price	$ 90	−$10 m.	$25 m.	$40 m.	$45 m.
Strategies	$ 95	−$25 m.	$20 m.	$50 m.	$65 m.
	$100	−$40 m.	$10 m.	$45 m.	$70 m.

Firm B's Payoff Matrix

		Firm B's Price Strategies			
		$70	$90	$95	$100
Firm A's	$ 70	−$5 m.	−$15 m.	−$25 m.	−$50 m.
Price	$ 90	−$1 m.	$50 m.	$30 m.	$10 m.
Strategies	$ 95	$0	$65 m.	$35 m.	$15 m.
	$100	$2 m.	$75 m.	$40 m.	$20 m.

Inspection of the expanded payoff matrices reveals that by selecting a $70 price firm A can "punish" firm B for choosing a $90 price, though not without inflicting losses upon itself as well. Yet if firm A becomes desperate or if it is better able financially to sustain temporary losses than is firm B, then provoking a price war is firm A's best response to B's choice of a $90 price. Faced with the prospect of a price war if it pursues its own self-interest at the expense of firm A, firm B may be persuaded to adopt the compromise price of $95.[14] Although both firms earn less-than-maximum profits at $95, the compromise

[14]J. L. Murphy reported a finding of higher prices and higher profits when rivals faced a threat of flagrant price cutting than when they did not. See his article, "Effects of the Threat of Losses on Duopoly Bargaining," *Quarterly Journal of Economics*, Vol. 80, No. 2 (May 1966), pp. 296–313.

price in this instance yields profits which both firms may view as more palatable than warfare.

Consider another situation where two firms, A and B, are forced to choose between prices of $10 and $15. The annual expected profits (in millions of dollars) for each firm appear in matrix form as follows:

Firm A's Payoff Matrix

		Firm B's Price Strategies	
		$10	$15
Firm A's Price Strategies	$10	$100 m.	$180 m.
	$15	$ 50 m.	$150 m.

Firm B's Payoff Matrix

		Firm B's Price Strategies	
		$10	$15
Firm A's Price Strategies	$10	$ 80 m.	$ 30 m.
	$15	$170 m.	$120 m.

Examination of firm A's payoff matrix indicates that firm A will prefer the $10 price strategy to the $15 price strategy. And if firm A selects the $10 price, firm B's best act is to choose the $10 price also. However, the apparent rationality of such a mental process is misleading; both firms will end up with lower profits by selling at a price of $10 than they could earn by selling at a price of $15. This apparent paradox is known in game theory as "the prisoner's dilemma."[15]

The solution to such a dilemma rests with information and experience. Provided market conditions are reasonably stable, the dynamics of continuous rivalry among oligopolists afford ample opportunity for firms to study one another's behavior and to begin to anticipate one another's moves. It cannot be too long before one or both of the firms recognize the value of information sharing and communication.[16] When this happens, a cooperative pricing strategy may emerge, and competition becomes more a function of nonprice factors.

[15]The prisoner's dilemma gets its name from a situation where two suspects are taken into custody and interrogated separately. Owing to weaknesses in the evidence against them, each believes they may both go free or at worst receive a light sentence on reduced charges if neither prisoner talks. However, they are both informed by the district attorney that if one confesses and the other does not, the one who fails to confess will receive a particularly stiff penalty and the confessor will receive lenient treatment for turning state's evidence. Hence the dilemma: Should each place confidence in the other's strength of character to not confess, or should each prisoner, not having any assurance about what the other will do, protect only himself and confess?

[16]Several controlled experiments have been conducted which tend to confirm the ability of players to "solve" the prisoners dilemma type of game as they acquire experience and information. See Lester B. Lave, "An Empirical Approach to the Prisoners' Dilemma Game," *Quarterly Journal of Economics*, Vol. 76, No. 3 (August 1962), pp. 424–436; L. E. Fouraker and Sidney Siegel, *Bargaining Behavior* (New York: McGraw-Hill Book Company, 1963), pp. 50–51, 165–166, 199.

APPLICATIONS CAPSULE

403
*The Many
Models of
Oligopoly
Behavior*

OLIGOPOLISTIC COMPETITION
AND MILITARY STRATEGY

It is not uncommon for oligopolistic firms to describe their competitive environment in military terms. The analogies are, in fact, very close. In both oligopoly and war there are two or more "sides." Each side seeks to increase its welfare, almost always at the expense of the other. Each side can employ various strategies and tactics to expose or injure the other. Each side has an incentive to resort to decoys, surprises, traps, and other maneuvers to gain an advantage.

Military terms are a standard part of competitive rhetoric. Executives speak of "invading" markets, of competitive "attacks," of developing new sales "weapons," of marketing research as "intelligence," of salesmen as "troops in the field," and of using "secret code names" for special projects. Price "wars" break out in a number of industries from time to time; firms have been known to engage in industrial "espionage" and "spying" with respect to one another's plant facilities, trade secrets, patents, and R&D efforts; advertising is referred to as a "propaganda campaign." Business magazines have talked about "border clashes" and "skirmishes" among computer manufacturers, the "escalating arms budgets" of soap and detergent companies, "guerilla warfare" by Purex against the soap firms, the "battle" over market share in countless industries, and of "takeovers" by acquisition-minded enterprises.

Often lying behind this talk is a conscious application of military principles to gain a competitive edge. Six well-known military maxims have particular relevance:

1. *Principle of the objective*. Every military operation must be directed toward a clearly defined, decisive, and attainable objective.
2. *Principle of mass*. Superior combat power must be concentrated at the critical time and place for a decisive purpose.
3. *Principle of flexibility of maneuver*. Flexibility must be a major consideration in the selection of plans, although the costs and dangers of flexibility must be weighed against its advantages.
4. *Principle of security*. Security is essential and is achieved by measures taken to prevent surprise, preserve freedom of action, and deny the enemy information.
5. *Principle of the offensive*. The commander must exercise initiative, set the pace, and exploit enemy weaknesses.
6. *Principle of surprise*. Surprise results from striking an enemy at a time, place, and in a manner for which he is not prepared.

Out of these principles emerge a number of strategic and competitive considerations. Should a firm concentrate its competitive resources on rivals' weaknesses or their strengths? Is it more strategically advantageous to defend a position of market strength or to attack a position of market weakness? Does a narrow, concentrated approach offer a better chance of success than a broad "hit 'em on all fronts" approach? Does success breed success with respect to winning future competitive struggles? How rapidly should a "victory" be followed up on and the gains consolidated?

However, two major differences between military strategy and business competition should be noted. Whereas wars are fought for "total victory" in which the enemy is either to surrender or be destroyed, competition among firms must be conducted so that no one firm emerges a winner. Winning in oligopolistic competition means becoming a monopolist, and that is a violation of the antitrust laws. In fact, the antitrust apparatus is aimed at *preserving* competition, the philosophy being that competition is properly vigorous and spirited but no one firm is supposed to be so good at competing that it wins the struggle or gains a clear upper hand. Second, whereas "all is fair in love and war," in business competition there are important constraints on the weapon or tactics a firm can use. The antitrust statutes proscribe the rules of "fair competition" and specifically prohibit attempts to monopolize or to lessen competition, discriminatory pricing, restraints of trade, predatory tactics to drive another firm out of business, exclusive or tying arrangements, reciprocal dealing, misrepresentations, fraud, deception, and so on.

Sources: Taken in part from Robert H. Caplan, "Appendix B: Relationships Between Principles of Military Strategy and Principles of Business Planning," in *Planning and Control: A Framework for Analysis*, Robert N. Anthony, ed. (Boston: Division of Research, Graduate School of Business Administration, Harvard University, 1965), pp. 148–156, and Philip Kotler, *Marketing Management: Analysis, Planning and Control*, 2nd ed. (Englewood Cliffs, N.J.: Prentice-Hall, Inc., 1972), pp. 250–254.

Using Public Announcements to Accomplish Price Coordination

A firm's public announcements of its future pricing intentions can be a very effective way of communicating indirectly with rival firms and thereby achieving a coordinated pricing move. For example, firm A, believing that a price increase is warranted, may decide to issue a press release announcing a 10% price increase to take effect in 60 days. By timing its announcement well in advance of when it will take effect and by making its announcement public (so that it will likely be reported in the *Wall Street Journal*, leading trade publications, and similar media), a firm is able to test the sentiments of competitors. If other firms respond favorably to this new pricing development by shortly announcing an equal price increase, A can follow through with the price change as planned and be reasonably confident that its competitors will do the same. However, if rival firms send signals of disagreement by making no announcement or by announcing a lesser increase, A can opt to withdraw its announced price rise or revise it downward to match those of its competitors. Whichever the case, using the media to communicate pricing desires and decisions can be a useful tactic for learning to what extent a price increase will be matched or ignored by firms in the industry.

An alternative way of signaling pleasure or displeasure with an initiating firm's price announcement is by offering one's opinion of the move in interviews with reporters, speeches to securities analysts, and the like. When B disagrees with A's price announcement, it can use speeches and interviews to offer reasons and views about market conditions aimed at persuading A to alter its decision ("if firm A's objective is to make higher profits, its scheduled pricing move is ill-conceived and ill-timed because . . ."). If B's arguments are unsuccessful and if B thinks it is better to go along with A rather than provoke conflict, B can in the due course of events announce it will follow A's lead on price. Using speeches and interviews to communicate reactions and opinions have the advantage of being a less binding commitment to a given course of action because they do not involve making a formal public announcement to actually change or not change one's own price. Doing something later that is inconsistent with opinions expressed earlier does not entail the same loss of credibility that goes with reneging on a prior price commitment.

Publicly announced price changes can also serve as threats. Suppose that firm A announces intentions to lower its prices on certain selected items in its product line. Firm B might elect to retaliate by announcing it is considering lowering its prices significantly below A's. This may suffice to deter A from going through with its intended price cuts because A now has ample indication that B is displeased with the price cuts and is willing to enter into a price war if need be.

On the other hand, a firm can employ public announcements in an effort to minimize the provocation that a price change can have. For instance, firm A may believe that the industry needs to adjust price levels downward. By announcing its intentions ahead of time and taking care to explain its move in terms of evolving market and cost conditions, it can avoid having other firms interpret the price-cutting move as an aggressive bid for increased market share. At the same time, these explanations serve as an attempt to get rival firms to see the logic and benefits of a lower price structure and to follow the move downward.

Quite often, firms comment publicly on their perceptions of current market conditions, what they believe the trend of demand and prices will be in the months and years ahead, how changes in raw material prices and wage rates will affect costs, and so on. Such commentaries can act as a coordi-

**SHOULD PUBLIC ANNOUNCEMENTS OF PRICE CHANGES
BE MADE ILLEGAL?**

In 1979 the Federal Trade Commission charged the four major
companies selling lead additives for gasoline with using the media to
fix prices. The FTC complaint alleged that by publicly announcing their
prices and pricing policies the four companies—Ethyl Corporation,
DuPont, PPG Industries, and Nalco Chemical—were guilty of "price
signaling." The idea behind the FTC complaint was that oligopolistic
firms desirous of coordinating any price adjustments do not have to
meet secretly in obscure locations to negotiate a common course of
action; rather, all one firm has to do is just tell the whole market—
buyers and sellers alike—what it plans to do; other sellers will get the
message and via a series of press releases back and forth—all duly
reported in one place or another—eventually coordinate their actions
with just as effective an outcome as if they had formally met face to
face and hammered out a collusive scheme.

In addition, the FTC complaint against the four producers alleged
other related anticompetitive activities—namely that they sell their
additives only at a transportation-cost-included price; that some of the
four promise their customers as low a price as anyone gets; that all
four use a 30-day-advance-notice-of-price-change clause in their
contracts with customers; and that they often tell the press and *potential*
customers of coming price changes. According to the director of the
FTC's Bureau of Competition, "the practices amount, under the circumstances in this industry, to a modern form of price-fixing. . . .
Sophisticated price signaling usually coupled with other practices,
achieves similar results while avoiding traditional agreements." In
support of its case, the FTC claims that there were 18 lockstep price
increases in the industry in 4 years (DuPont claims that this is untrue,
saying that there were 18 price changes, including 6 price cuts, and that
9 changes were connected to changes in the price of lead).

The FTC's proposed remedies for the allegedly illegal and collusive price signaling were (1) to forbid firms from making advance
announcements on price available to anyone but customers, (2) to
forbid the four firms from selling at delivered prices, and (3) to forbid
them from promising any customer as low a price as they give to any
other customer. In 1978 an assistant attorney general for antitrust in
the Justice Department indicated support for the conspiracy theory of
price signaling, suggesting that it would be sufficient for a firm to just
report its pricing plans to the government; *Forbes* quoted the official

as saying "As to whether it's [a public price announcement] a fit subject for general public consideration, I'm not sure."

The FTC case against the sellers of lead additives is not the first of its kind; in 1972 the Justice Department brought a Sherman antitrust case against General Motors and Ford Motor Company for their "coordinated" action to eliminate price discounts on fleet sales of cars; the alleged mechanism for the price-fixing scheme, according to the Justice Department complaint, was that the two companies signaled each other about their positions and coming actions through speeches and press reports. However, both the criminal and civil cases against these two companies were later dismissed by the federal judge and jury because the government failed to prove any conspiracy. Under FTC rules, though, no proof of conspiracy is necessary; it need only be shown that the practice is sufficiently anticompetitive that it is in the public interest to ban sellers from making announcements of pending price changes public.

Questions for Discussion

1. Should firms be allowed to inform their present customers about pending price changes? What about *potential* customers? If firms are restrained from using the media to announce future price adjustments to *potential* customers, then what avenues should they be able to use?
2. Do you see a potential conflict between the FTC's proposed ban on public price announcements and the freedom of speech guarantees provided by the First Amendment to the Constitution?
3. If the FTC wins its case and implements a ban on advance announcements of price increases, then do you think the effect will be procompetitive or anticompetitive? How important is knowledge about firms' prices and pricing policies to an efficient functioning of the market—especially from the standpoint of buyers and from the standpoint of sellers being alert to a need to match the price cuts of rival firms?
4. Suppose that the FTC is able to ban public announcements but permits sellers to inform their customers (by letter or personal contact with salespersons) and then certain customers turn around and "leak" notice of the pending changes either to the press or to rival sellers or to both. What then? Should such leaks also be banned?

Source: Adapted from information reported in "No Body Language, Please," *Forbes*, June 25, 1979, p. 37.

nating tactic because they reveal a firm's assumptions and beliefs about key market factors. As other competitors speak out and make their views known, it can be determined whether firms in the industry are operating under common assumptions and market perceptions. By trading views and opinions back and forth by means of the media and the customer-distributor grape-vine, a consensus can be developed about what actions and changes are appropriate.

Conclusions about Oligopolistic Price Coordination

The foregoing discussion of oligopoly pricing suggests that the selling prices of corporate rivals will gravitate toward a uniform level. No firm can price its product blindly without regard for what competitors are charging. Although competing firms may well have different profit-maximizing prices (owing to variations in demand or costs), they still have no realistic alternative to selling their products at equivalent prices in the case of identical products or at comparable prices in the case of differentiated products. Only when a firm is successful in differentiating its product to a point where its customers are willing to pay a higher price is it feasible for differences in selling price to persist. Otherwise, patronage flocks to the low-priced sellers—an outcome which prompts either the establishment of a more uniform price structure or efforts to achieve more successful product differentiation.

Competitive pressures not withstanding, collusion is obviously one avenue for deciding upon a "mutually acceptable" price structure. Price leadership is another. Conscious parallelism is still another. And price signaling through media channels is yet another. Of these, collusion is the riskiest and most fragile because it is outlawed by the antitrust statutes and because of the temptations to cheat.[17] In addition, the presence of "maverick" firms, periodic adoptions of new corporate strategies (such as a move to accelerate growth of sales or to assume a leadership position in product innovation), the entry or potential entry of strong competition, and frequently changing demand-supply conditions all tend to make successful price collusion tenuous and often unworkable.

In general, price leadership, conscious parallelism, and collusive arrangements are more likely to be found in *mature oligopolies* where estab-

---

[17]Although both formal and informal collusion (spontaneous meetings in smoke-filled backrooms, secret agreements, publicized pricing formulas, predetermined splitting of the market, prearranged output quotas, cooperation through an exclusive selling agency, and so on) is illegal in the United States, in Japan and in many European countries collusive arrangements are permitted and sometimes even encouraged.

The most spectacular contemporary example of outright price fixing among American firms occurred in the electrical equipment industry, where General Electric, Westinghouse, and a number of other firms were convicted in 1960 of fixing prices and dividing up the market for circuit breakers, switchgears, and related products. Other examples of price fixing have been uncovered in enameled cast iron and vitreous china bathroom and plumbing fixtures, sheetrock, bread, cast iron water and gas pipe, cigarettes, cement, steel conduit, and polio vaccine. Companies that in recent years have pleaded "no contest" and declined to fight price-fixing charges include DuPont, Armco Steel. International Paper, Diamond International, PepsiCo, Pet, Sunshine Biscuits, Ciba-Geigy, H. K. Porter, American Cyanamid, Genesco, and Combustion Engineering.

From an international standpoint, the most prominent conspiracy to fix prices has occurred not among business firms but among the governments of the oil-producing exporting countries (OPEC) in fixing the world market price of crude oil.

409
*Special
Features of
Corporate
Price
and Output
Decisions*

lished corporations sell similar or identical products under *stable* market conditions. In an *immature oligopoly* where firms are new and inexperienced and/or where oligopolists sell differentiated or rapidly changing products under conditions of variable demand, price competition is more active. This generalization has empirical validity. Despite a long record of price uniformity among standard brands of cigarettes, the introduction of new filter-tip and king-sized cigarettes by the major firms during the 1950s was accompanied by several years of frequent price adjusting before the firms again settled upon a uniform price structure.[18] The tire industry, where eight firms account for almost 90% of total output, is noted for its unstable price structure; not only is pricing complicated by a maze of grades, qualities, and innovations, but retail tire outlets also feature a procession of sales, special discounts, and guarantees on name-brand and private-label tires.[19] Pricing in the steel industry, though generally stable, typically breaks down when vigorous competition from foreign imports or depressed business conditions appear.[20] Other examples pertaining to electrical equipment, railroading, rayon, copper, glassmaking, and petroleum could be cited.[21]

At the same time, a number of factors act to impede price coordination among corporate rivals: (1) the entry into the industry of new firms which ignore current customs and practices or which otherwise disturb established buyer-seller relationships, (2) volatile industry demand conditions, (3) the frequency with which producers' cost functions are modified by technological change and the extent to which these changes make for unequal costs among firms in the industry, (4) different market shares among the firms, (5) extreme product differentiation, (6) frequent product variations, and (7) the emergence of a new industry in which firms have not had time to size up rivals' behavior. Even so, given that one or more of these price-destabilizing factors appear often in almost every oligopolistic market, the fact that corporate rivals still price uniformly is powerful testimony to the imperatives of pricing together—whether for reasons of competition or mutual "cooperation."

SPECIAL FEATURES OF CORPORATE PRICE AND OUTPUT DECISIONS

The preceding models of oligopoly have focused upon the knotty problem of price conflict resolution and the strategies for reaching price equilibrium

[18]Tennant, "The Cigarette Industry," pp. 376–377.

[19]Kaplan, Dirlam, and Lanzilotti, *Pricing in Big Business*, p. 203.

[20]*Ibid.*, pp. 19–24.

[21]See Harold C. Passer, *The Electrical Manufacturers: 1875–1900* (Cambridge, Mass.: Harvard University Press, 1953), pp. 62, 161–162, 263–264, 352–353: Jesse W. Markham, *Competition in the Rayon Industry* (Cambridge, Mass.: Harvard University Press, 1952), pp. 103, 130, 127–136, 150–153; J. L. McCarthy, "The American Copper Industry: 1947–1955," *Yale Economic Essays* (Spring 1964), pp. 64–130; G. W. Stocking and M. W. Watkins, *Monopoly and Free Enterprise* (New York: Twentieth Century Fund, 1951), pp. 121–126; and E. P. Learned and Catherine C. Ellsworth, *Gasoline Pricing in Ohio* (Boston: Harvard Business School, 1959), pp. 108, 131–135, 147–149, 237–252.

under conditions of competition among the few. We turn now to matters of internal operations within large corporations and their effects upon price and output decisions. Previously, we have indicated that large corporate enterprises operate many plants, sell in many different markets, and produce many products; in addition, they deal with market uncertainty and changing demand conditions in ways fundamentally different from small firms competing under conditions of market capitalism. The time has come to bring these facets into our analysis of corporate capitalism.

Multiplant Operations

The market demand for such commodities as tin cans, storage batteries, biscuits and crackers, cement, building materials, dairy products, tires, apparel, computers, floor coverings, and steel, among others, is far larger than the existing number of firms can accommodate by operating one plant.[22] As a result, firms operate several plants to manufacture the same product. American Can and Continental Can, for instance, manufacture containers in over 100 domestic locations, often at sites very close to major customers. Boise Cascade in a recent year operated 14 pulp and paper mills, 20 lumber mills, 24 plywood plants, 20 composite can plants, 6 envelope plants, 20 corrugated container plants, 2 particle board plants, 6 kitchen cabinet plants, 2 door plants, and 13 manufactured-housing plants. One decision peculiar to the multiplant firm concerns how to allocate the optimum total output of a product among its several plants in order to minimize costs and maximize profits.

The chances are that the various plants of a particular firm are not only located in different regions but also incorporate different technologies, obtain raw materials and labor inputs at varying prices, and therefore have different cost structures. An illustrative case is indicated in Table 12-1. The firm operates two plants with marginal costs as shown in columns (2) and (3). Inspection of the marginal cost functions of the two plants shows that if the firm wishes to produce three or less units of output it should use plant 1 exclusively, since it has the lowest marginal cost ($3, $5, and $7 compared to $8 for plant 2). However, the fourth through ninth units should definitely be produced in plant 2. Continuing in this fashion, the combined marginal cost curve for the firm can be derived [column (4)]. As usual, profit maximization requires that the firm select the output rate at which the marginal revenue from the last unit sold equals the marginal cost of the last unit produced. This occurs at an output of 11 units and a price of $19; here, the marginal cost of the eleventh unit is $9, and the marginal revenue from selling the eleventh unit is $9.

[22]In contrast, in producing typewriters, soup, sewing machines, photographic equipment, steam turbines, transformers, and locomotives, plants are quite large relative to the size of the total market, and multiplant operations are much less in evidence.

411
Special
Features of
Corporate
Price
and Output
Decisions

Table 12-1 Allocation of Output among Plants

(1) Total Output of the Firm	(2) Marginal Cost, Plant 1	(3) Marginal Cost, Plant 2	(4) Marginal Cost for the Firm	(5) Price	(6) Total Revenue	(7) Marginal Revenue
0	$ 3	$8	3	$30	$ 0	
						$29
1	5	8	5	29	29	
						27
2	7	8	7	28	56	
						25
3	9	8	8	27	81	
						23
4	10	8	8	26	104	
						21
5	11	8	8	25	125	
						19
6	12	9	8	24	144	
						17
7	Capacity	Capacity	8	23	161	
						15
8			8	22	176	
						13
9			9	21	189	
						11
10			9	20	200	
						9
11			10	19	209	
						7
12			11	18	216	
						5
13			12	17	221	
						3
14				16	224	

Given that the optimum total output of the firm is 11 units, how should production of the 11 units be divided between the two plants? The answer is as follows: produce 4 units at plant 1 and 7 units at plant 2. *Production must be allocated among the various plants such that the marginal costs of the last units produced at each plant are equal both to each other and to the value at which the firm's overall marginal cost equals the marginal revenue of the last unit sold.* Unless the marginal costs of the last units produced at each plant are equal, the firm can lower its total production costs for a given output by shifting units of production from the plant where marginal cost is higher to the plant where marginal cost is lower.

In general, then, whenever a firm operates a number of plants to produce a given commodity, proper application of the profit-maximizing rule involves three sequential steps. Step 1 is to determine the firm's overall marginal cost curve from the marginal cost curves of the various plants. Step 2 is to pinpoint the firm's most profitable output by finding the output rate where overall marginal cost equals marginal revenue. Step 3 is to allocate the profit-maximizing output among the various plants so that the marginal costs of the last units produced at each plant are equal. In mathematical terms, the firm should arrange its production activities so that

$$MR = MC = MC_{P_1} = MC_{P_2} = \cdots = MC_{P_n},$$

where MR is marginal revenue from all sales of the commodity, MC is the combined marginal cost, and $MC_{P_1}, MC_{P_2}, \ldots, MC_{P_n}$ are the marginal costs of the respective plants which the firm has for producing the commodity.

The effect of this rule in actual practice is that production activity is concentrated in the most efficient plants and that older, technologically inferior production facilities are used as sparingly as conditions will permit. The newest, most modern plants employing the latest technologies are nearly always operated at or near capacity levels, while older, less efficient plants are relied upon primarily to fill out the balance of the firm's total output and to help fill the firm's need for production capacity in periods of peak demand. In fact, it is partially because a firm's less efficient production facilities are used more intensively at higher output rates that marginal and average costs tend to rise at combined outputs beyond 90% of *total* capacity.

Multimarket Operations

Up until now we have implicitly assumed that a firm sells a given product at a uniform price to all buyers. This is a tolerable first approximation, but many exceptions exist, especially in the corporate sector. Big corporations sell their products in a variety of geographically separate markets (local, regional, national, and international), and they sell to diverse classes of customers (industrial users, commercial users, household users, large-quantity buyers, small-quantity buyers, regular customers, occasional customers, one-time customers, and so on). Firms sometimes find it more profitable to sell the same item to different customers at different prices depending on the market they are in and/or to sell to a single customer at different prices depending on the quantity he purchases. They may also sell products with different costs at the same price (i.e., airlines serve full-course dinners on some flights but only snacks on others, yet ticket prices are the same; some manufacturers may charge all customers the same delivered price even though the freight costs are less for nearby customers than for distant customers).[23]

These types of pricing practices are labeled by economists as *price discrimination*. Price discrimination may be said to occur whenever a particular product is sold at two or more prices; it can take several forms, depending on whether the basis for the different price is the class of customer, the place where it is sold, or the time at which it is sold.

For a firm to employ price discrimination tactics in a profitable fashion, three conditions must be satisfied. First, the firm must face a downsloping demand curve and thus have some discretion in the price or prices it charges buyers of the product. With a horizontal demand curve, the firm has no motive for selling at different prices; in fact, selling at less than the full market price involves a sacrifice of profits. Second, the firm must have easily identifiable groups of customers with different types of demand for the product in question. Put another way, the shape of the demand curve for one class of

---

[23]Such practices are not restricted to business enterprises. Universities, for example, charge the same tuition for a large freshman class taught by a graduate teaching assistant as they do for a small senior seminar taught by a premier professor.

customers must differ from the shape of the demand curve for another class of customers. Third, the firm must be able to segregate its sales to each group of customers in such a way that customers paying the lower price cannot resell the item to customers paying a higher price; the different groups of customers must, in other words, be sealed off from one another so that resale of the product by one group to another is severely constrained or unprofitable.

413
*Special
Features of
Corporate
Price
and Output
Decisions*

Two distinct types of price discrimination serve to highlight the attractiveness of charging different prices for the same product. Consider first the case where the price the customer pays depends on the quantity he purchases (most prominently illustrated by the sales of gas and electricity). Suppose that the individual customer has a demand curve DD', shown in Fig. 12-8. The firm charges a price of P_1 dollars per unit if the customer buys Q_1 or fewer units per period. The firm reduces its price to P_2 dollars per unit on those units purchased in excess of Q_1 but no greater than Q_2 units. For all units purchased in excess of Q_2, the firm charges a price of P_3 dollars. If a customer elects to purchase a total of Q_3 units in a given time period, the firm's total revenue (the customer's bill) is calculated as follows:

$$TR = P_1(Q_1) + P_2(Q_2 - Q_1) + P_3(Q_3 - Q_2).$$

This amount is equivalent to the shaded area in Fig. 12-8. The benefits to the firm of systematically reducing price as purchases increase should now be apparent. Under a single-price policy, sales of Q_3 units would call for charging a maximum of P_3 dollars per unit. Total revenue would amount to only $(P_3 \cdot Q_3)$ dollars, a figure P_1ABCDP_3 dollars less then obtained with a multiple-price policy.

Fig. 12-9 illustrates a situation where a firm charges different prices to customers in two different markets, A and B. The respective demand and marginal revenue curves of the two classes of buyers are given in panels (a)

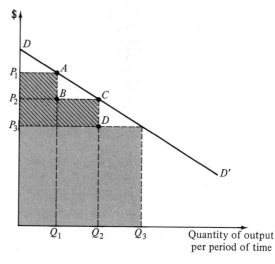

Figure 12-8
Revenue effect of pricing according to volume purchased

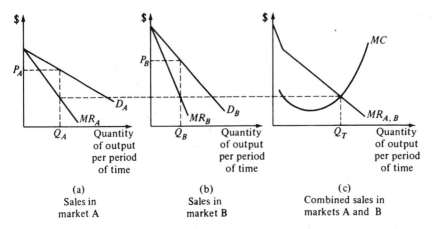

Figure 12-9
Two-market price discrimination

and (b).[24] The firm must decide upon its most profitable combined sales volume, how much should be sold to buyers in each of the two markets, and the price to charge in each market. As usual, the most profitable output rate is where MR equals MC—however, the appropriate marginal revenue concept in this instance is not MR in *each* market *separately* but rather MR in both markets *combined*. The marginal revenue curves in markets A and B are summed *horizontally* to obtain combined MR, shown as $MR_{A,B}$ in Fig. 12-9(c). The intersection of $MR_{A,B}$ with MC in panel (c) defines the most profitable output rate (Q_T) for the firm. Next, a decision must be made as to how much of the total output of Q_T units to sell in market A and how much to sell in market B. The rule for profit maximization in such situations calls for allocating total sales between the markets in such a way that marginal cost at the optimal output equals marginal revenue *in each market*. In terms of our example, the rule requires that

$$MC = MR_{A,B} = MR_A = MR_B.$$

To locate the equalizing value of marginal revenue in the two markets at the profit-maximizing output, a horizontal line is projected from the point in panel (c) where $MC = MR_{A,B}$ to panels (a) and (b) to find where $MC = MR_{A,B} = MR_A = MR_B$. This gives an optimal sales level of Q_A units in market A and Q_B units in market B ($Q_A + Q_B = Q_T$). The profit-maximizing prices, P_A and P_B, are found from the respective demand curves in each market. The firm will necessarily earn higher total profits by engaging in price discrimination than it could earn by following a single-price policy of

[24]Two-market price discrimination is quite common. Many corporations sell their products at one price in international markets and at another price (sometimes higher, sometimes lower) in domestic markets. In the case of products sold nationwide, prices are often higher west than east of the Rocky Mountains.

charging the same price to all buyers. Furthermore, it can be proven mathematically (see Mathematical Capsule 12) that the firm's selling price is always higher in the market where demand is less elastic.

The case of two-market price discrimination is easily expanded to allow for any number of markets. Whenever the firm sells a product in a variety of markets for which demand is different, four steps are required for determining the profit-maximizing prices and outputs in each market. Step 1 is to ascertain the firm's combined marginal revenue curve by horizontally adding together the separate marginal revenue curves in each market. Step 2 is to pinpoint the firm's most profitable combined output rate for all markets by locating the output rate where marginal cost equals combined marginal revenue. Step 3 is to allocate the profit-maximizing output among the various markets in such a way that marginal cost at the optimal output rate is equal to the marginal revenues from the last units sold in each market. In mathematical terms, this means the firm must divide its output such that

$$MC = MR = MR_1 = MR_2 = \cdots = MR_n,$$

where MC is marginal cost, MR is the combined marginal revenue, and MR_1, $MR_2, \ldots, MR_n$ are the marginal revenues for the respective markets in which the commodity is sold. Step 4 is to determine the prices in each market from the respective market demand curves.

A tremendous variety of price discrimination practices can be found in the real world. Table 12-2 summarizes the principal types, along with examples of each. The information contained in this table provides a useful portrayal of pricing tactics often used by business firms.

Whether price discrimination is good or bad hinges upon subjective evaluations over which reasonable people may disagree. Value judgments inevitably creep into the picture. Most academic economists are suspicious of some forms of price discrimination because, if systematically practiced, they can facilitate adherence to a collusive price structure. In addition, since firms choose freely whether to use a single- or a multiple-price policy, the implication is clear that profits are higher with discrimination than without, thereby causing a redistribution of income from customers to the firm. On the positive side, charging different prices in different markets affects the total output of the product little if at all.[25] And since customers with more elastic demands (and for whom price is lower) are likely to have incomes lower than the customers comprising the less elastic markets, price discrimination may work to the advantage of the economically weak and therefore produce "socially beneficial" effects. Moreover, situations may exist in which the costs of production cannot be covered unless revenues are enhanced by multiple pricing. Hence, where profits can be increased with multiple pricing, the added profits may be the margin between supplying a good or service and

[25]For a treatment of the output effects of price discrimination, see E. O. Edwards, "The Analysis of Output Under Discrimination," *Econometrica*, Vol. 18, No. 2 (April 1950), pp. 163–172, and Joan Robinson, *The Economics of Competition* (London: The Macmillan Company, 1933), pp. 188–195.

Table 12-2   Types of Price Discrimination

Individual Customer Discrimination

1. *Bargain-every-time.* Each sale is an individually negotiated deal. The classic case is the purchase of new and used cars; other examples include made-to-order sales and objects of art.
2. *Size-up-his-income.* Wealthier customers are charged more than less affluent customers; price is partially a function of income. Standard examples are the pricing of medical, legal, accounting, and management consulting services.
3. *Cut-price-if-you-must.* Departures from list price are made when buyers shop diligently for the best price; sellers grants secret concessions as a last resort. Examples include the transactions between steel firms and auto makers for hot and cold rolled sheet steel and virtually any industrial product sold to skilled purchasing agents who are always on the lookout for a lower price.
4. *Count-the-use.* Price is based upon the level of use, even though unit costs do not vary appreciably with volume. For example, the rental fees on Xerox copying machines are based upon the number of copies made.

Group Discrimination

1. *Promote-new-customers.* New customers are offered "special introductory prices" lower than those paid by established customers in the hopes of enlarging the firm's regular clientele. Record and book clubs and magazine publishers are avid practitioners of this pricing policy.
2. *Forget-the-freight.* All customers are charged the same delivered price, even though transportation costs vary from customer to customer according to the distance located from the production site. Nearby customers are discriminated against in favor of far-away customers. Examples include cement and steel pricing and, additionally, any commodity which is sold at "nationally advertised prices" irrespective of transportation cost differentials.
3. *Get-the-most-from-each-market.* Prices are persistently held higher in markets where competition is weak than where it is strong. Import quotas and tariff barriers allow some firms to charge higher prices in domestic markets than in international markets (sugar, oil, and domestic wool).
4. *Favor-the-big-buyer.* Large purchasers of a commodity are given price cuts perhaps geared to the cost savings derived from large-scale transactions. The large chain discount retailers buy many of their goods at prices below those of the small retailer; firms which purchase in "carload lots" obtain discounts not allowed to purchasers of just a few units.
5. *Skim-the-market.* A product is introduced at a high price within reach mainly of only high-income buyers. Periodically, price is then reduced step by step (and in conjunction with the availability of new production capacity) to allow steady, but gradual, penetration of broader markets. The pricing of TV sets and Polaroid cameras has followed this pattern.

Product Discrimination

1. *Make-them-pay-for-the-label.* Manufacturers sell a relatively homogeneous commodity under different brand names, charging higher prices for the better-known, more prestigious brand names. Automobile tires, paints, articles of clothing, and food products are examples.
2. *Appeal-to-quality.* Products are offered in packages ranging from the budget variety to the super deluxe. Differences in price are *more* than proportional to the differences in cost. Household appliances are an obvious example. Traveling first class as compared to tourist class is another example.
3. *Get-rid-of-the-dogs.* Price concessions in the form of "special" sales are made periodically, or continuously in the bargain department of the retail store, in order to reduce stocks of poorly selling items and to make room for new merchandise. The seemingly

Table 12-2 (Cont.)

417

*Special
Features of
Corporate
Price
and Output
Decisions*

perpetual end-of-the-model sales, close-out specials, anniversary sales, and inventory reduction sales serve as good examples.

4. *Switch-them-to-off-peak-periods.* Lower prices are charged for services identical except for time of consumption in order to encourage fuller and more balanced use of capacity. Off-season rates at resorts and the lower rates for long-distance calls made at night and on Sundays are examples.

Sources: This table is a composite of the observations of several writers, including Fritz Machlup, "Characteristics and Types of Price Discrimination," contained in the National Bureau of Economic Research conference report, *Business Concentration and Price Policy* (Princeton, N.J.: Princeton University Press, 1955), pp. 397–435; Joel Dean, *Managerial Economics* (Englewood Cliffs, N.J.: Prentice-Hall, Inc., 1951), pp. 419–424, 503–548; and Ralph Cassady, Jr., "Techniques and Purposes of Price Discrimination," *Journal of Marketing*, Vol. 11, No. 2 (October 1946), pp. 135–150.

not doing so.[26] Finally, price discrimination can enhance competition by encouraging more price experimentation. Whereas producers are reluctant to engage in across-the-board price changes, they may be much more willing to test the consequences of a price change in one market or for one class of customers. On balance, the complex crosscurrents at work make it prudent to judge each particular instance of price discrimination on its merits.

Multiproduct Pricing

In the corporate sector almost every firm sells a variety of products. Even so-called single-product firms may have multiple models, sizes, and styles each of which, for pricing purposes, merits treatment as a separate product. In such cases, the single-product models examined to this point are not always adequate for assessing corporate pricing policies and corporate behavior.

Demand Interrelationships. Often, multiproduct enterprises find that the demands for their products are interrelated. They may be substitutes, as with General Motors' Buicks and Oldsmobiles, or they may be complements, as with Betty Crocker cake mixes and cake frostings. These demand interrelationships need to be taken into account in the firm's pricing decision since a change in the price of one has a bearing on the sales of the other. Determining the optimal prices of complementary and substitute products entails a careful assessment of the cross elasticity relationships and how various price combinations affect the combined revenues and profitability of the products in question.

Production Interrelationships. A firm's products can also be interrelated from a production standpoint. For instance, products may be jointly produced in a *fixed ratio* (as with leather hides and beef in a slaughterhouse

---

[26]George J. Stigler, *The Theory of Price*, 3rd ed. (New York: The Macmillan Company, 1966), pp. 213–214.

THE MATHEMATICS OF PRICE DISCRIMINATION

When a firm sells its product in markets that are economically isolated and when the respective market demand curves confronting the firm are different, the firm maximizes total profit by charging different prices in each market. The conditions for maximizing profits may be derived very simply. For illustrative convenience we shall restrict the analysis to a two-market situation.

Suppose that the firm's total revenue from sales of output in market A is represented as

$$TR_A = f(Q_A),$$

the firm's total revenue from sales of output in market B is represented as

$$TR_B = g(Q_B),$$

and the firm's total costs from combined sales in both markets is represented by

$$TC = h(Q_A + Q_B) = h(Q),$$

where Q is total output no matter in which market specific units are sold. In other words, TC depends on the output rate and not on where the output is sold.

As usual, total profit (π) is equal to total revenue minus total cost:

$$\pi = TR - TC.$$

Substituting into this expression gives

$$\pi = TR_A + TR_B - TC,$$

which can be rewritten as

$$\pi = f(Q_A) + g(Q_B) - h(Q).$$

The profit-maximizing conditions are

$$\frac{\partial \pi}{\partial Q_A} = \frac{\partial f}{\partial Q_A} - \frac{\partial h}{\partial Q} = \frac{df}{dQ_A} - \frac{dh}{dQ} = 0,$$

$$\frac{\partial \pi}{\partial Q_B} = \frac{\partial g}{\partial Q_B} - \frac{\partial h}{\partial Q} = \frac{dg}{dQ_B} - \frac{dh}{dQ} = 0.$$

419

*Special
Features of
Corporate
Price
and Output
Decisions*

But, by definition, $df/dQ_A = MR_A$, $dg/dQ_B = MR_B$, and $dh/dQ = MC$. Thus, profit maximization requires that

$$MR_A - MC = 0 \quad \text{and} \quad MR_B - MC = 0,$$

which in turn is equivalent to

$$MR_A = MR_B = MC.$$

Now let us prove that the higher of the two profit-maximizing prices is found in the market with the less elastic demand. Let $P = f(Q)$ represent any demand curve, where P is price and Q is the quantity demanded. The total revenue is

$$TR = PQ,$$

and marginal revenue, according to the rule of differential calculus for the derivative of a product of two variables, is

$$MR = \frac{dTR}{dQ} = P + Q\frac{dP}{dQ}.$$

Multiplying the last term of the expression by P/P gives

$$MR = P\left(1 + \frac{Q}{P} \cdot \frac{dP}{dQ}\right).$$

Recalling from our definition of point elasticity that $\epsilon_p = (dQ/dP) \cdot (P/Q)$ and substituting this into the expression, we get

$$MR = P\left(1 + \frac{1}{\epsilon_p}\right).$$

The latter expression can now be used to demonstrate our proof that price is higher in the market where demand is less elastic. From the expression above, it follows that

$$MR_A = P_A\left(1 + \frac{1}{\epsilon_A}\right)$$

$$MR_B = P_B\left(1 + \frac{1}{\epsilon_B}\right).$$

Since at the optimal output $MR_A = MR_B$, then

$$P_A\left(1 + \frac{1}{\epsilon_A}\right) = P_B\left(1 + \frac{1}{\epsilon_B}\right),$$

which can be rewritten as

$$\frac{P_A}{P_B} = \frac{1 + (1/\epsilon_B)}{1 + (1/\epsilon_A)}.$$

Suppose that $\epsilon_A = -4$ and $\epsilon_B = -2$ at the respective profit-maximizing prices of P_A and P_B; then demand is more elastic in market A than in market B. By substituting these values into the last expression, it is clear that $P_A/P_B < 1$ and that $P_B > P_A$. This result is obtained for any values of ϵ_A and ϵ_B such that $|\epsilon_A| > |\epsilon_B|$. Accordingly, two-market price discrimination always leads to a higher price in the market where demand is less elastic with regard to price.

operation) or in a *variable ratio* (as with gasoline and fuel oil in a crude oil refinery). Products may compete with one another in the sense of being alternatives—a butcher shop has to decide whether to cut beef quarters into roasts or grind it for hamburger; a paper producer must allocate paper pulp between making paperboard boxes and brown paper bags. Still another type of inter-relationship arises when products are complementary in production, as when one product incorporates wastes generated by the production of another (using wood chips left over from lumber production to make particle board).

The Pricing of Joint Products (Fixed Proportions). The simplest case of multiproduct pricing concerns that of joint products produced in fixed proportions. Since joint products are produced as a package, their costs can likewise be considered as a package, and one set of cost curves suffices for both—in fact, it may not even be feasible to separate out their individual costs. Figure 12-10 illustrates the demand, marginal revenue, and marginal cost functions for two joint products, X and Y. Not surprisingly, the key to optimal pricing of joint products is still the *MR-MC* relationship. The *MC* curve in Fig. 12-10 represents the marginal cost of a 1-unit change in the joint output package of X and Y; MR_x and MR_y have the usual meaning. However, a *vertical summation* of the two *MR* curves is required in order to determine the combined marginal revenue change associated with output changes; the combined-*MR* curve appears as the dashed line MR_{x+y} for outputs up to Q_1 and coincides with MR_y for outputs greater than Q_1, since $MR_x < 0$. The intersection of *MC* and MR_{x+y} defines the short-run profit-maximizing joint output of X and Y; P_x and P_y are the respective profit-maximizing prices and are derived from the respective demand curves for X and Y.

But what if *MC* should happen to intersect MR_{x+y} at a joint output past Q_1 where MR_x is negative? This possibility is shown in Fig. 12-11. When *MC* intersects the combined *MR* at a joint output where the marginal revenue of one of the products (X in this case) is negative, profit maximization requires that the firm still produce where *MC* equals combined-*MR*—at Q_2 in Fig. 12-11. But, whereas the price for Y should be set to correspond with the

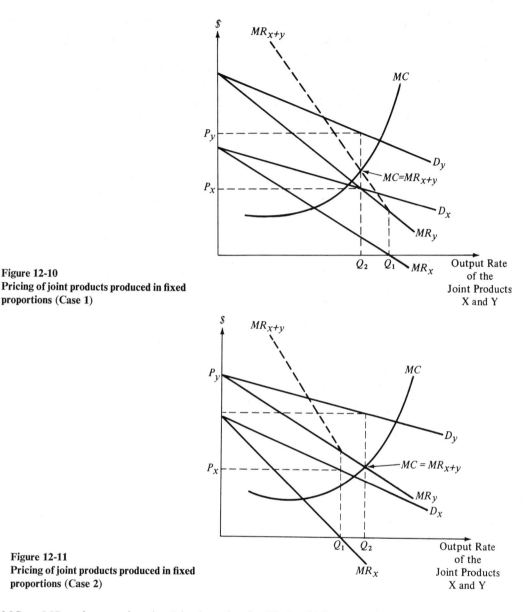

Figure 12-10
Pricing of joint products produced in fixed proportions (Case 1)

Figure 12-11
Pricing of joint products produced in fixed proportions (Case 2)

$MC = MR_{x+y}$ intersection (at P_y), the price for X should be pegged at the demand where $MR_x = 0$, at P_x. Why? Because this is where TR_x is maximum; there is no point in setting a price below P_x in Fig. 12-11 so as to boost sales to Q_2 because TR_x is lower at Q_2 than at Q_1. In other words, to maximize the excess of joint revenues over joint costs, the firm should offer Q_2 units of Y for sale but should restrict sales of product X to Q_1 so as not to drive MR_x into the negative range. This will, of course, mean that the firm will have an excess of X on its hands, $Q_2 - Q_1$ units to be specific. Naturally, some kind of revenue-producing outlet for the excess amount of X should be sought rather than having the surplus of X go to waste. The criterion here

421

should be to dispose of the excess in ways which will not detract from the firm's primary market objective of selling Q_1 units of X at price P_x. However, in the long run, the firm might react to the excess supply of X by (1) advertising or otherwise promoting increased sales of X so as to shift D_x to the right or (2) seeking out technical means of altering the proportions of joint output in ways to increase Y and decrease X—for example, redesign papermaking processes to permit reductions in the output of cheaper grades of paper and increases in the output of finer grades.

The Pricing of Joint Products (Variable Proportions). Generally, multiproduct firms are not hemmed in by the constraints imposed by joint products produced under conditions of rigidly fixed proportions. Some flexibility in proportions is usually possible. When the firm can vary the proportions in which the joint output is produced, optimal pricing quickly becomes complex because of the number of alternative combinations which must be examined. Conceptually, what is required is the construction of a series of *isocost curves* showing the locus of all production combinations which can be produced for a given total cost outlay. Such a series of isocost curves is depicted in Fig. 12-12 as IC_1, IC_2, and IC_3, with total cost outlays of $400, $550, and $800, respectively. The isocost curves are drawn concave to the origin because of the reasonable assumption that it is increasingly difficult to produce successively more units of one product and fewer units of the other, given the inherent limitations on varying the proportions. Next, a set of *isorevenue curves* ($IR_1 = 600, $IR_2 = 800, and $IR_3 = 1000) must be derived to show all combinations of the two products which, when sold, result in equivalent total revenues. The isorevenue lines are shown as being convex to the origin, reflecting the typical short-run market necessity of lowering price to sell a larger quantity.

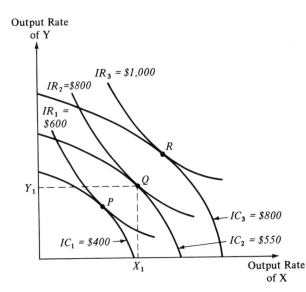

Output Rate
of Y

$IR_3 = $1,000$

$IR_2 = 800

$IR_1 = 600

R

Y_1

Q

P

$IC_3 = 800

$IC_1 = 400

$IC_2 = 550

X_1

Output Rate
of X

Figure 12-12
Price-output determination for joint products produced in variable proportions

Putting the isocost and isorevenue curves on the same graph defines a set of tangency points (each isocost curve will necessarily be tangent to some isorevenue curve). The tangency points (points P, Q, and R in Fig. 12-12) identify the relevant revenue-cost-output combinations since each point represents the lowest cost of reaching the associated total revenue combination. Which of the tangency points represents profit maximization is determined from a comparison of the revenue-cost-profit results at each point. In Fig. 12-12 profit maximization is at point Q, where total revenue from the sales of X and Y exceeds joint total cost by the greatest amount ($\$800 - \$550 = \$250$); the profit-maximizing outputs of X and Y are X_1 units and Y_1 units. It can be shown that at point Q the marginal cost of producing each product equals the marginal revenue it generates.

Multiproduct Output with Resource Constraints

The multiproduct firm is certain to sell its products in markets of varying competitive intensity. It is sure to have stronger positions of market advantage for some of its products than for others and to enjoy larger profit margins on some of its products than on others. However, since the firm's production capacity is limited in the short run and since from time to time demand may exceed supply capability, the question arises as to how a firm should best allocate scarce organizational resources so to maximize the combined profits from all its products. Consider first the simplified case of a two-product firm operating at capacity and unable to increase the output of both items to their respective profit-maximizing rates.

For a two-product firm to maximize total profits from both products, it must divide its limited resource inputs between them in such a way that it receives an equivalent amount of extra profit from the last unit of input allocated to the production of each one. If the condition is violated, the firm can increase total profits by shifting units of input out of the production of the commodity where profit is less and into the production of the commodity where profit is greater. As a numerical illustration, consider a firm which has a total of 300 hours of skilled labor available for producing products A and B. The estimated profits from alternative uses of this labor are as indicated below:

Product A

Hours of Skilled Labor	Total Profit from A	Added Profit
0	0	
100	$ 500	$500
200	$1100	$600
300	$1500	$400

Product B

Hours of Skilled Labor	Total Profit from B	Added Profit
0	0	
100	$ 600	$600
200	$1100	$500
300	$1500	$400

Suppose that the firm is now using 100 hours of labor to produce A and 200 hours of labor to produce B, with resulting joint profits of $1600 ($500 from A and $1100 from B). Is the firm obtaining maximum total profit from both products? The answer is no. Combined profits can be increased by shifting 100 hours of skilled labor time out of producing B and into producing A. In doing so, the firm gives up $500 of profit from the production and sale of B but gains $600 profit from A—for a net gain of $100 and a joint profit total of $1700. By using 200 of the 300 hours of skilled labor to produce A and only 100 hours to produce B, the firm receives $600 profit from the last hundred units of skilled labor used to produce A and also $600 profit from the last hundred units of skilled labor used to produce B. It has equalized the added profit yields of the last batch of input allocated to each product.

The two-commodity situation is easily expanded to n number of commodities and restated as follows: Limited resource inputs should be allocated among the production of commodities $C_1, C_2, C_3, \ldots, C_n$ in such a way as to yield an equivalent amount of profit from the last unit of input allocated to the production of each commodity. The significance of the profit-maximizing rule for multiproduct enterprises is that the limited availability of resource inputs often makes it more profitable to diversify into new products and to move into new markets *before* attempting to squeeze the last dollar's worth of profit from existing products and product markets. The most efficient and most profitable use of the firm's limited productive capabilities requires that the available resources be channeled into the production of commodities with high incremental profit prospects and out of commodities where incremental profits are low. Thus, short-run profit maximization for a multiproduct enterprise does not require that marginal revenue be equated to marginal cost for each and every product the firm produces *unless* the firm has adequate resources and sufficient production capacity in the short run to carry the production of *every* current and potential product to the rate where $MR = MC$. From a total organization viewpoint, price and output decisions require a careful balancing of adjustments among specific product markets to obtain the optimal divisional and companywide profits.[27]

The Role of Inventories and Order Backlogs

The economic environment in which oligopolists operate is typically characterized by ongoing changes in consumer tastes, incomes, technology,

[27] A study of the pricing of steel products by U.S. provides a good illustration. In the production of steel rails and steel cables, where demand was less elastic and also where competition was less intense, U.S. Steel charged proportionately higher prices and maintained wider profit margins. In the markets for stainless steel, galvanized sheets, and tin plate, where U.S. Steel was in strenuous direct and potential competition with aluminum and lumber as well as other steel producers, prices were more than proportionately lower and profit margins were much narrower. Thus, product market elasticities and profit margin differences were major decision variables in U.S. Steel's divisional price and output strategies. For greater detail, see Kaplan, Dirlam, and Lanzilotti, *Pricing in Big Business*, pp. 172–173.

and resource prices. One effect of this is to make it hard for oligopolists to maintain precise equality in MR and MC, owing to the inhibitions against frequent price changes. At the same time, large corporate enterprises are likely to find current sales and current production at least slightly out of balance because it is not always practical to continually fine-tune production rates to meet transitory demand conditions. Where technology is complex, with the various stages of the production process systematically connected and carefully harmonized, it takes time to readjust process flows, reschedule production, and realign workloads. More importantly, frequent production rate changes impair mass production efficiencies and cause unit costs to creep upward. As a result, a large firm has reason to wait for well-defined demand changes before altering production rates. Instead, it is less disruptive, as well as cheaper, to respond to minor market fluctuations by adjusting inventory levels and/or unfilled order backlogs (promised delivery dates).[28]

425

*Special
Features of
Corporate
Price
and Output
Decisions*

This *modus operandi* is of special significance in oligopoly for it provides firms with a practical and readily invoked alternative to price and output changes as a temporary means of balancing sales with production in any given period.[29] Although firms may base their output decision for the next period upon an attempt to bring projected MR into equality with expected MC, miscalculations will inevitably be made. If too much is produced relative to current sales at the prevailing price, inventory levels can be increased or unfilled order backlogs reduced. If production falls short of sales, inventories can be drawn down or delivery times extended. By keeping close tabs upon changes in new order flows, order backlogs, finished-goods inventory levels, and outgoing shipments, the firm can estimate the current position of its demand curve, the direction in which it is shifting, and expected future demand levels. The role of inventories and unfilled order backlogs is therefore twofold. They serve as *buffers* to compensate for fleeting production-sales imbalances, thereby avoiding zigzag production or price adjustments. And they serve as *feedback signals* to facilitate the coordination of future production with future demand. If and when the signals of changed demand conditions come through loud and clear, then substantive changes in production rates or prices are, of course, seriously entertained.

[28] In perfect competition where the demand curve is horizontal, a firm can be confident of selling its entire output. To a lesser degree, monopolistically competitive firms can also anticipate selling their outputs, though perhaps after some price adjustment. Small firms with little or no market power generally carry relatively small inventories. In contrast, oligopolists with their downsloping demand-AR curves are less certain how much they can sell at a given price. The higher a firm's selling price relative to marginal cost, the more profitable it becomes for firms to carry sizable inventories to minimize the risk of losing sales in periods of peak demand. This is especially true for firms with high fixed costs and low variable costs; they clearly prefer building up inventories to shutting plants down. See Edwin S. Mills, *Price, Output, and Inventory Policy* (New York: John Wiley & Sons, Inc., 1962), pp. 82–83, 96, 116–117, and Merton J. Peck, *Competition in the Aluminum Industry* (Cambridge, Mass.: Harvard University Press, 1961), pp. 88, 92.

[29] The material that follows draws heavily from the analysis of F. M. Scherer, *Industrial Market Structure and Economic Performance* (Chicago: Rand McNally & Company, 1970), pp. 149–157.

Inventory and order backlog adjustments thus introduce another element into accounting for price rigidity in oligopoly. Slight demand changes and market fluctuations can be accommodated via changes in inventories and backlogs—an alternative that is easier and more attractive than spending countless hours trying to make price-output changes that will keep MR equal to MC. In this sense, short-run profit maximization is abandoned in favor of long-run profit maximization (or some other goal), and price-output revisions are undertaken only in response to clear-cut changes in long-run demand and cost conditions.

Although evidence is limited, it does tend to confirm that oligopolistic corporations rely more heavily upon inventory and order backlog variations in adjusting to demand fluctuations than upon price variations. Professor Markham's study of the rayon industry revealed that only when sales declines persisted for several months was production trimmed back; price changes were resisted even longer.[30] The three major copper producers, Anaconda, Kennecott, and Phelps Dodge, have repeatedly maintained copper prices by building up their inventories in periods of slack demand.[31] In the durable consumer goods and capital goods industries where large corporations predominate, unfilled order backlogs may run in the hundreds of millions or even billions of dollars and inventory-sales ratios fluctuate over a relatively wide range. In contrast, in nondurable goods industries where small entrepreneurial firms are more numerous, order backlogs are virtually nonexistent; inventory levels are kept to a minimum to reduce the risk of perishability and style obsolescence. Additionally, price cuts in response to short-run demand conditions are discernably more numerous and inventory-sales ratios are lower and less variable.[32]

Other Dimensions of Corporate Strategy in Oligopolistic Markets

Although in market capitalism much of the competitive focus is on *price*, in corporate capitalism (and in oligopoly generally) the main force of competition relates to *nonprice* variables. Rival oligopolists are not prone to build their competitive strategy around successfully undercutting the prices of competitors so as to gain a market advantage. Why? For two reasons. One, a firm which uses price cuts to attract business away from rival firms accomplishes little more than to compel competitors in self-defense to match the lower price—a move which neutralizes the price cut, creates lower prices for all firms in the industry, and limits each firm's sales gain to its customary share of the increased business which flows from a lower industrywide price. Two, a price-cutting strategy is quickly and easily imitiated by other firms; as a consequence, it is extremely hard for a firm to gain more than a fleeting competitive edge via price cutting. Mostly, what happens when firms try to

---

[30]Markham, *Competition in the Rayon Industry*, Chapter 7.
[31]Kaplan, Dirlam, and Lanzilotti, *Pricing in Big Business*, pp. 176–181.
[32]Scherer, *Industrial Market Structure*, p. 155.

use price as a primary competitive weapon is that they expose profit margins and total profits to a good possibility of sharp erosion. Consider a simple example which illustrates why this is so. Suppose a firm is selling an item for $1.00 and that ATC is 90 cents. If the firm tries to gain more business by cutting price, say to 95 cents, then its profit margin ($P - ATC$) is only 5 cents compared to 10 cents before the price cut. For the firm to make as much profit at the 95-cent price as at the $1 price, it will have to sell *twice* as many units as before. In other words it will have to *double* sales just to recoup the loss of profit associated with earning only 5 cents per unit sold instead of 10 cents. True, unit costs are sometimes lowered by the increase in volume, but even if rising volume lowers units costs to, say, 87 cents, the firm will still have to sell 20% *more* than before in order to earn as much as it was earning at the $1 price. Very likely demand will not be this price elastic (ϵ_p = % change in unit sales volume $\div$ % change in price = 20% $\div$ -5% = -4)—especially since rival firms will be sorely tempted to match the price cut in order to avoid losing market share to the price-cutter.

Consequently, unless a firm uses cost-saving technological innovations as the basis for its price-cutting strategy (so as not to impair profit margins with its price cuts) or unless it can realize major cost reductions from an increase in sales volume, using lower prices as a major competitive weapon tends to be an unprofitable strategy. The most attractive strategies for gaining sales, profits, and market share are thus grounded in market variables other than price. Successful nonprice strategies are harder to duplicate and tend to have a longer-lasting effect on strengthening a firm's market position. Hence, there exists a rational tendency among rival corporate oligopolists to channel the main thrust of their head-to-head competitive efforts into forms of product differentiation: product innovation, customer service, quality, performance, convenience of use, terms of credit, styling and design, durability, advertising, and sales promotion. Indeed, billions of dollars are spent each year in efforts to maintain, strengthen, and promote product differentiation.

At the same time, in some industries firms attempt to insulate themselves from aggressive competition from rivals and from adverse cost changes by integrating vertically. Aside from converting a cost center into a profit center, backward vertical integration spares a firm the uncertainty of being dependent on suppliers for crucial inputs, as well as the uncertainty of what prices must be paid for the inputs. By bringing the production of raw materials and critical component goods under its ownership and control, a vertically integrated firm obtains *reliable* sources of supply at *reliable* prices. Such a move may be eminently desirable for defensive reasons if there is a good chance that corporate rivals will do the same or if favorable input prices are essential to preserving the firm's profit margins. Moreover, backward integration *internalizes* such problems as labor disputes, rising production costs, production breakdowns, and delays in scheduled deliveries. A firm is better able to control daily operating problems when they fall within the purview of its own management as opposed to when they are the problems of other managements. Integrating backward has the further advantage of allowing a

VERTICAL INTEGRATION IN THE OIL INDUSTRY

Vertical integration became a way of life among the large, successful oil companies as far back as the early 1900s. The breakup of the Standard Oil trust in 1911 added impetus to vertical integration because many of the 33 newly created firms had major gaps in their business operations. During the following 10 to 15 years, with the demand for petroleum products increasing, with sales of automobiles beginning to mushroom, and with alternating periods of crude-oil shortage and oversupply, nearly all of the major companies found it less risky (and sometimes essential for competitive survival) to integrate both vertically and geographically. In the case of a refiner-marketer, there was always the threat that the feast of new crude oil discoveries would be followed by famine if and when the fields ran dry or demand increased faster than supply. So, both to preserve their profitability in the case of mushrooming supplies and to guard against possible shortages, it was desirable to integrate backward, part or all the way. This meant cultivating the goodwill of producers and drillers and making continued exploratory efforts attractive by constructing gathering lines and storage facilities as rapidly as possible and in sufficient volume to handle whatever was offered. It also meant going into production whenever and wherever necessary.

Crude-oil producers, in turn, could escape their feast-or-famine dilemma only by developing their own marketing outlets, integrating forward into both refining and retail distribution. Without assured markets, producers were necessarily subject to the randomness of crude-oil discovery and the ease of competitive entry in drilling and exploration. In both situations vertical integration contributed to the stability of the integrating company, first by providing some security against market fluctuation and instability and, second, through greater certainty of profit margins associated with a continuous utilization of producing capacity, pipelines, refinery facilities, and marketing outlets. In general, the oil companies that chose to integrate appeared to be seeking a degree of balance in their operations so as to protect them against what they perceived as an uncertain profit and competitive position associated with heavy fixed costs and with being heavily dependent on uncontrolled intermediate markets. By maintaining a balance in each of the stages in which they did business, the operations at each stage tended to become mutually reinforcing and thus a contributor to greater operating efficiency and stability.

According to the classic study of integration and competition in the petroleum industry by Melvin de Chazeau and Alfred Kahn in

429

*Special
Features of
Corporate
Price
and Output
Decisions*

1959, the following composite paraphrase represents a rough consensus of how the executives of almost all the leading oil companies viewed the importance of vertical integration:

> We certainly try, in general, to keep a balanced operation. We will not ordinarily make major investments in one level without seeing that we are pretty well covered at other levels. So we do not expect to make the same return from our investments in production, refining and marketing. As a general rule we will not demand as high a return from prospective investments that put us in balance as from those that put us out of balance. We have a going organization, with substantial commitments at all levels: we cannot shift from one to the other with each short-term fluctuation of returns: we have to protect the positions we already have.*

Currently, about 50 petroleum companies in the United States can be classified as vertically integrated in that they operate in at least three stages—production, refining, and marketing. However, since even the largest oil companies are not so integrated as to be self-sufficient in all stages of operation, significant markets for crude and for refined products exist. Almost every oil company to one extent or another buys or sells crude and refined products to balance out its operations: this results in oil companies engaging in numerous transactions with one another.

These transactions (called exchange agreements) occur for several reasons:

1. To help lower transportation costs.
2. To give refiners greater flexibility in securing appropriate quality crude.
3. To help reduce inventory and operation costs and supply interruptions caused by temporary surplus/shortage situations at refineries or terminals.

For example, when a company's crude is of the desired type and is geographically close to its refinery, the company will arrange transportation from the oil field to the refinery. If the company owns more crude than it needs in its refinery, it will sell the volumes least attractive to it. If its crude is not the proper type or is remote from its refinery, the company can arrange to exchange with another refiner who can run this crude economically. Through exchanges and purchases and sales, companies are able to minimize transportation and refining costs, thus providing lower-cost products to the consumer.

As another example, short-term disruptions may create a need for spot or emergency exchanges. Pipelines or refineries may be shut down for several days due to fires, mechanical failure, process upsets,

---

*Melvin G. de Chazeau and Alfred E. Kahn, *Integration and Competition in the Petroleum Industry* (New Haven, Conn.: Yale University Press, 1959), p. 114.

and so on; tankers or barges may be delayed due to weather conditions, strikes, or operating problems. The short-term disruption can be solved if another company makes a spot or emergency exchange. For instance, company A might lend 5000 barrels of product to company B, whose shipments have been delayed. Then a few days later when its shipment arrives, company B can return the barrels. An exchange of this nature may save many miles of costly trucking from a distant terminal and allow uninterrupted service to consumers.

Many oil industry critics, however, see vertical integration as a monopolistic element. To the extent that firms are integrated, they are insulated in part from demand-supply changes at each of the processing stages; this, in turn, results in prices that may not be completely responsive to market conditions. Critics also allege that vertically integrated firms are able to put a squeeze on independents by shifting profits to their production operations, thereby keeping marketing and refining profits artificially low so as to discourage entry and further expansion of nonintegrated independent refiners and marketers. Allegedly, integrated majors can raise the crude price without raising refined product prices and make their profit primarily in production.

Insofar as exchange agreements are concerned, critics see these as being, on some occasions, a way to exchange information and promote relaxed competition and, on the other occasions, as being a vehicle for squeezing or punishing maverick firms—especially independents.

firm to better coordinate and systematize the many facets of its overall production process, thus deriving efficiency and cost benefits. Holiday Inns, in rapidly expanding its number of inns, diversified into carpeting, candies, furniture items, food-stuffs, and a school of motel management—all of which complemented its main product and serve to supply its 1000-plus inns with basic support services. In general, the reductions of market uncertainty accompanying backward integration are valuable contributors to coordinating and routinizing production cycles, thereby allowing firms (1) to escape the disruptive influence of unreliable suppliers and supply prices, (2) to realize the potential of mass production efficiencies, and (3) to insulate themselves from the repercussions of tactical maneuvers of rival firms.

Also, for reasons of security and uncertainty reduction, firms with mass production capability may be motivated to integrate forward and develop their own distribution outlets. Access to product markets must be dependable. Where ownership of distribution channels is impractical, the large corporation may employ such strategic devices as franchise systems, leasing provisions, and exclusive-dealing arrangements to give it a stronger foothold in dealing with wholesale and retail outlets. For instance, while most gasoline service stations are independently operated, the facilities may be leased to the operator by the brand-name refiner under terms which permit the refiner to maintain a watchful eye over operating procedures and merchandising policies. In a similar vein, a large manufacturer often grants a wholesaler or a retailer an exclusive franchise to handle its product in a specified geographic area; in return, the franchisee agrees to conform to certain prices, terms of credit, customer service policies, and product guarantees and warranties. Exclusive dealerships are commonly found in tires, automobiles, fast-food firms, articles of clothing, sporting goods, appliances, and paints.

Finally, large firms may diversify their product offerings in order to (1) round out their product line, (2) keep from tying the fortunes of the firm to a single product, or (3) exploit the image and success earned in other product lines. For instance, Procter & Gamble took its successful Ivory Soap brand and followed it with Ivory Flakes and Ivory Snow. General Mills spent millions of dollars promoting Betty Crocker cake mixes and then used this brand identification to introduce Betty Crocker pie crusts, rolls, and dehydrated potatoes. The mounting of a competitively strong marketing effort frequently requires each producer to have a full line of products and thereby offer the customer a "total package." Specializing in the production of only one or two items can entail serious market disadvantages, as well as less than full utilization of organizational resources and expertise. Several major oil companies, for example, are diversifying into coal and other fuels in an effort to become total energy firms. Soft-drink firms are moving into the production of related and complementary types of food products. The major cigarette producers are attempting to ward off stagnation and decline by diversification into other totally different product lines—namely foods and consumer goods. As a specific example, Philip Morris over a period of a few years acquired Burma Shave, American Safety Razor, Clark Chewing Gum Company, Miller Brewing Co., and Seven-Up Company.

Table 12-3 summarizes these and other strategies whereby a firm can grow, compete, or shore up its market position. It is significant to note that multiproduct, multimarket enterprises often have both the opportunity and the resources to undertake several of these competitive strategies simultaneously, perhaps gaining a decided edge in competing with smaller firms. Although entrepreneurial enterprises can sometimes equal the production efficiency of big firms (where technology is not especially complex or large-scale and where the marginal costs of production are constant over a wide output range), they are still often hardpressed to match large, diversified firms in terms of overall organization capability, especially with regard to total marketing effort, long-range technological accomplishments, and managerial technology. Yet, these frequently are crucial to successfully competing over the long run—especially in a technologically advanced, affluent economy where, increasingly, business success is predicated on finding needs and filling them rather than just producing products and selling them.

Table 12-3 Major Corporate and Competitive Strategies

I. Strategies for strengthening market share and competitive position
   A. Try to increase market penetration by increasing the use of present products in present markets.
      1. Increase current clientele's usage of the product:
         (a) Sell more units to existing customers.
         (b) Shorten the time it takes for a product to become obsolete.
         (c) Create and advertise new uses for the product.
         (d) Give price incentives for increased use.
      2. Attract buyers away from rival firms:
         (a) Increase promotional and sales efforts.
         (b) Establish sharper product (brand) differentiation.
         (c) Initiate price cuts.
      3. Attract nonusers to buy the product:
         (a) Induce trial use through free samples, cents-off coupons, and low introductory price offers to first-time buyers.
         (b) Create and advertise new uses.
   B. Move to open up new markets for existing products.
      1. Expand regionally, nationally, or internationally into new geographic areas.
      2. Broaden the product's appeal to new market segments:
         (a) Introduce new versions of the product to appeal to new classes of buyers.
         (b) Advertise in other types of media.
         (c) Distribute the product through other channels.
   C. Develop new products for present markets.
      1. Develop new features for existing products:
         (a) Modify (based upon color, motion, sound, odor, form, or shape).
         (b) Magnify (based upon stronger, thicker, longer, or extra value).
         (c) Minify (based upon shorter, smaller, or lighter).
         (d) Substitute ingredients or performance combinations.
         (e) Rearrange designs, components, or standard-extra options.
      2. Develop quality variations.
      3. Add new models and sizes.
II. Integration strategies
   A. Vertical integration.
      1. Integrate backward and get into the businesses of suppliers (convert cost centers into profit centers).
      2. Integrate forward into the next manufacturing stage or into distribution so as to ensure stable, reliable market access.
   B. Horizontal integration.
      1. Move into new geographic areas, add new products, or acquire new businesses so as to capitalize upon
         (a) Company know-how or technology.
         (b) The gains of increased plant utilization.
         (c) Company image and goodwill established in other product lines.
         (d) The market opportunities for related products.
         (e) The existence of "extra space" in the company's channel pipelines or sales force capability.
   C. Concentric diversification.
      1. Enter into new businesses that are related to the firm's present business in terms of customer base, technology, or channels of distribution.
III. Conglomerate diversification strategies
   A. Enter into businesses unrelated to present markets, technology, customer clientele, or channels of distribution.

Table 12-3 (Cont.)

433

Summary and
Conclusions

1. Acquire any firm in any business as long as the projected profit opportunities equal or exceed the company's minimum standard.
2. Seek out a merger of an opportunity-poor, cash-rich firm with an opportunity-rich, cash-poor company.
3. Seek out a marriage of an opportunity-poor, skill-rich firm with an opportunity-rich, skill-poor company.
4. Find profitable companies with a counterseasonal or countercyclical sales pattern so as to smooth out sales and profit fluctuations.

Sources: Prepared by the author from Philip Kotler, *Marketing Management: Analysis, Planning, and Control,* 2nd ed. (Englewood Cliffs, N.J.: Prentice-Hall, Inc., 1972), pp. 237–240; H. Igor Ansoff, "Strategies for Diversification," *Harvard Business Review,* Vol. 35, No. 5 (September–October 1957), pp. 113–214; and David J. Luck and A. E. Prell, *Market Strategy* (New York: Appleton-Century-Crofts, 1968), pp. 175–183.

SUMMARY AND CONCLUSIONS

It should be apparent at this juncture that competition among the few has marked differences from competition among the many. Pricing and competition in oligopolistic markets proceed along lines dissimilar to atomistically structured markets. The fundamental economic reason for this is the high degree of mutual interdependence among competing oligopolists. In oligopoly each firm must try to anticipate the actions and reactions of rival firms in formulating and implementing its own corporate strategy. Nowhere is the effect of oligopolistic interdependence more apparent than in pricing. If corporate oligopolists produce standardized products, a uniform price is imperative, since firms which attempt to charge higher prices will be squeezed out of the market. Where rival oligopolists produce either weakly or strongly differentiated products, prices must be comparable, though not necessarily identical, since customers will tolerate price differentials they believe are justified.

Moreover, differences among rival firms regarding market shares and production costs give rise to divergent price preferences which somehow must be resolved. Whether firms with higher price preferences will win out over firms with lower price preferences or whether the reverse will occur varies with competitive and market circumstances. Collusion to maximize industry profits certainly is one possibility; however, collusive arrangements are fragile and run the risk of discovery and antitrust action. Price leadership is another possibility if follower firms are prone to cooperate with the leader's price judgment. Conscious parallelism, independent profit maximization, and formula pricing are still other possibilities. The ability of corporate oligopolists to cooperate in the establishment of a monopolistic price structure is less likely to be successful the more firms there are in the industry, the larger is the output of competitive fringe firms, the more strongly differentiated and rapidly changing are the products of the firms, the more opportunities there are for secret price concessions, the more unstable are industrywide demand conditions, the more rapid is the rate of technical progress, and the greater is the degree of suspicion and mistrust among company executives. More importantly, the firms which perceive their profits to be greater at lower prices than at higher prices are frequently in a much stronger position to impose their preferences than are the firms which prefer higher prices. Long-run product substitution and the threat of entry by new firms also place a ceiling—and sometimes a low one—upon the ability of oligopolistic producers to peg price at a monopolistic level.

The extremely strong pricing interdependence among corporate oligopolists is further demonstrated by the infrequency with which they change price individually; instead, prices are changed more or less simultaneously. The belief that competitors will ignore price increases and match price cuts and the practice of using inventory and order backlog changes to buffer minor demand fluctuations may combine to produce somewhat more stable prices in the corporate sector than where conditions of market capitalism prevail.

Because of the imperative to charge comparable prices for their products, oligopolists have little incentive to use price as a strategic device for enhancing their market position in the short run. Rather, the competitive emphasis among oligopolists is aimed at product quality and performance, product innovation, design and styling, customer service, advertising, and the like. Often, the thrust of competition is on new product ideas and fresh marketing strategies. In addition, corporations may be induced to integrate vertically, or to employ concentric or conglomerate diversification strategies, as a means of strengthening their market and competitive position.

SUGGESTED READINGS

BAIN, J. S., "Price Leaders, Barometers, and Kinks," *The Journal of Business*, Vol. 33, No. 3 (July 1960), pp. 193–203.

BISHOP, R. L., "Duopoly: Collusion or Warfare?" *American Economic Review*, Vol. 50, No. 5 (December 1960), pp. 933–961.

BOULDING, K. E., *Economic Analysis*, Vol. I, 4th ed. (New York: Harper & Row, Publishers, 1966), Chapter 22.

COX, E. P., "A Case for Price Discrimination," *Business Topics*, Vol. 23, No. 3 (Summer 1975), pp. 39–46.

DEWEY, D., *The Theory of Imperfect Competition: A Radical Reconstruction* (New York: Columbia University Press, 1969).

KAPLAN, A. D. H., J. B. DIRLAM, AND R. F. LANZILOTTI, *Pricing in Big Business* (Washington, D.C.: The Brookings Institution, 1958), Chapters 1, 4.

LEIBENSTEIN, H., "Aspects of the X-Efficiency Theory of the Firm," *Bell Journal of Economics*, Vol. 6, No. 2 (Autumn 1975), pp. 580–606.

SCHERER, F. M., *Industrial Market Structure and Economic Performance* (Chicago: Rand McNally & Company, 1970), Chapters 5–8.

SMITH, R. A., "The Incredible Electrical Conspiracy," *Fortune*, Vol. 63 (April and May 1961), pp. 132ff. (April) and pp. 161ff. (May).

STIGLER, G. J., "The Economics of Information," *Journal of Political Economy*, Vol. 69. No. 3 (June 1961), pp. 213–225.

———, "A Theory of Oligopoly," *Journal of Political Economy*, Vol. 72, No. 1 (February 1964), pp. 44–61.

WESTON, J. F., "Pricing Behavior of Large Firms," *Western Economic Journal*, Vol. 10, No. 1 (March 1972), pp. 1–18.

WORCESTER, D. A., "Why 'Dominant Firms' Decline," *Journal of Political Economy*, Vol. 65, No. 4 (August 1957), pp. 338–347.

PROBLEMS AND QUESTIONS FOR DISCUSSION

1. (a) Graphically illustrate the profit-maximizing price and output for an oligopolistic firm confronted with a kinked demand curve and whose production function reflects constant returns to variable input throughout the firm's range of output capability. Indicate on your graph the area which represents total profit.

    (b) Illustrate the effect upon the firm's optimum price and output of a decrease in the demand for its product.

2. Is it possible for an oligopolistic firm confronted with a kinked demand curve situation to increase its short-run profits by increasing its short-run expenditures on sales promotion? Justify your answer by means of a graph.

3. Titanic Corporation and Mammoth Enterprises are the only two firms selling robots to perform selected domestic services. The Titanic Corporation believes that the annual demand for its particular style of robot is given by the equation $P_T = 2400 - 0.1Q_T$. Mammoth Enterprises estimates that the annual demand for its robots is given by $P_M = 2400 - 0.1Q_M$. Because their robots have different performance features, the cost of producing Titanic's robot differs from the cost of producing Mammoth's. The estimated total cost function for Titanic's robots is $TC_T = 400,000 + 600Q_T + 0.1Q_T^2$, where TC is in dollars per year and Q_T is Titanic's annual output of robots. The estimated total cost function for Mammoth's robots is $TC_M = 600,000 + 300Q_M + 0.2Q_M^2$, where TC is in dollars per year and Q_M is Mammoth's annual output of robots.

    (a) Determine the profit-maximizing price and output for both Titanic Corporation and Mammoth Enterprises.

    (b) Does a pricing conflict exist between the two firms?

    (c) If you were the president of Titanic Corporation, what price would you pick? Why?

    (d) If you were the president of Mammoth Enterprises, what price would you pick? Why?

    (e) Would a collusive arrangement between the firms be advantageous? Why or why not?

4. Reston Enterprises and Super-Technical Corporation are the only two firms producing pollution-free turbine engines for use in automobiles. Reston engines account for one-third of the total turbine engine sales, while Super-Technical engines account for two-thirds. Except for several minor features, both engines compare favorably in terms of quality, performance, and economy of operation.

    (a) Suppose both firms produce their engines under conditions of identically rising marginal costs. Will there arise a conflict of price preferences between the two firms, assuming a goal of profit maximization? Illustrate graphically. Venture a judgment as to how the pricing conflict might be resolved in this particular situation. Is some form of collusion a distinct possibility here? Why or why not? Justify your reasoning.

(b) Suppose both firms produce their engines under conditions of identical and constant marginal costs. Will there then be a divergence of pricing preferences? Is it unreasonable to expect marginal costs to be constant?

(c) Suppose both firms produce their engines under conditions of identically declining marginal costs. Describe and graphically illustrate the nature of the pricing conflict, if any. If you were the president of Super-Technical Corporation, would you be willing to compromise your firm's preferred price with that of Reston Enterprises? Explain. Is some form of collusive arrangement likely to be reached under these circumstances? Why or why not?

5. The American Cracker Corporation has three plants for producing soda crackers. The marginal cost functions of the three plants and the firm's estimated demand-AR schedule are as follows:

Daily Output in Cartons	Marginal Cost of Plant 1	Marginal Cost of Plant 2	Marginal Cost of Plant 3	Price of Cartons of Soda Crackers
0	$0.14	$0.13	$0.10	$0.50
1	0.16	0.14	0.13	0.48
2	0.18	0.15	0.16	0.46
3	0.20	0.16	0.16	0.44
4				0.42
5	Capacity	Capacity	Capacity	0.40
6				0.38
7				0.36
8				0.34
9				0.32
10				0.30
11				0.28
12				0.26

Determine the most profitable price and output for the American Cracker Corporation. Then determine the optimal allocation of output among the firm's three plants.

6. Waxy Products, Inc., has discovered a new way to produce a "plastic wax" which, when once applied to hardwood floors, creates a permanent, waterproof, scuffproof, shiny surface absolutely guaranteed under any conditions to last for 12 months. Waxy Products, realizing the vast market potential for its plastic wax, has employed a market research team to estimate the demand function for plastic wax in both national and international markets. The market research team reports that its estimate of plastic wax demand in the domestic market is $P_D = 100 - 5Q_D$ and that its estimate of demand in the international market is $P_F = 60 - 5Q_F$, where P is in dollars and Q is daily sales in cases. Waxy Products estimates that the short-run production function for plastic wax is $Q = 10X$, where $X =$ units of variable input; units of variable input cost $220 each. The president of Waxy Products, not knowing very much about price policy, asks you to assist him in *maximizing* his firm's profits. Calculate for him the *specific* price and output levels that will maximize profits from the sale of plastic wax.

7. (a) Do you think competition among oligopolists is more strenuous, less strenuous, or about equally strenuous as compared to competition among perfectly competitive firms? Explain your reasoning.

   (b) Do you think competition among oligopolists is more strenuous or less strenuous as compared to competition among monopolistically competitive firms? Explain your reasoning.

8. Barrett Industries is considering reducing the price of its best-selling grease remover from $20 per gallon to $17. Barrett estimates its production costs of grease remover are $14 per gallon; the per-gallon cost is not thought to vary appreciably with volume, owing to constant returns. Currently, sales are running at an average of 20,000 gallons per month, and Barrett's volume, as well as the industry's as a whole, has remained stable for the past two years. Barrett has two major competitors in the grease remover market: Acme Chemical, which has an estimated market share of 40%, and Montana Products, which has approximately 25% of the market. Barrett's market share is thought to be 30%, and the remaining firms have about 5%. The going market price for grease remover is now $19 to $21 per gallon.

   (a) If Barrett cuts the price to $17, how many more gallons will it have to sell to earn just as much total profit after the price cut as before the price cut? What percentage gain in sales volume does this represent?

   (b) What would the value of the short-run price elasticity of demand have to be for the proposed price cut to be profitable for Barrett?

   (c) Would you recommend that Barrett go ahead with the proposed price cut? Why or why not?

   (d) Would your answer be different if the market for grease remover were expanding rapidly? If demand were viewed as being highly elastic and major cost reductions could be achieved if volume could be increased? Explain.

THIRTEEN HOW MARKETS FUNCTION: THE CASE OF MONOPOLY

On rare occasions one firm is the sole supplier of a product in a given market area. Such a market situation is called *pure monopoly*. Strictly speaking, pure monopoly can exit only when there are no *close* substitutes for the product of the single seller. Not only can there be no rival firms producing the same product, but there can be no firms producing products varying in only minor ways. The pure monopolist's product must be clearly and substantially different. Thus, the monopolistic firm faces no direct competition from rival firms and, as a consequence, has significant market power. In terms of market structure, monopoly is the extreme opposite of perfect competition.

Real-world examples of pure monopoly are few and far between. Firms in the business of providing electricity, natural gas, telephone communications, cable TV service, and certain transportation services approach the position of pure monopoly. In years past, conditions approximating pure monopoly have prevailed in the production of aluminum, nickel, magnesium, molybdenum, shoe machinery, and Pullman cars.

The chief reason for the occurrence of pure monopoly is the presence of pronounced economies of scale. The lowest unit costs and therefore the lowest consumer prices are achievable only when one firm supplies the entire market demand for the product. Substantially higher unit costs at small- or medium-scale outputs effectively bar the entry of new firms, and indeed, consumers are likely to be better off with just one producer from which to buy the product. Thus, although it may be technologically feasible to have two, three, or more firms, it is nevertheless economically inefficient to have more than one. Industries in which this occurs are called *natural monopolies*. In the normal case, natural monopolies are granted exclusive rights by government to serve a particular market or geographical area; in return the firm agrees to submit to government regulation as a measure for preventing abuses of its monopoly power. Public utility firms typify the natural monopoly type of enterprise.

Monopoly can also arise from situations where a firm has a patent on a product or on a low-cost technological process. Such monopolies are perfectly legal and give the inventor/innovator exclusive rights (for a period of 17 years in the United States). Patents can be very important in preventing the entry of competitors, although it is often possible to "invent around" a patent by developing a closely related product or process (as Kodak finally managed to do in coming up with an instant-developing camera film capable of competing head-on with Polaroid's instant film).

Three other sources of monopoly can be noted. One is where a firm obtains a franchise or license to be the exclusive producer/seller for a given geographical area. A second is the rare instance where a firm owns or controls the supply of a key raw material (the most oft-cited instance of this is the pre-World War II control that Aluminum Company of America had over bauxite—a key input in aluminum production). The third is where a firm becomes a monopolist by offering a superior product and outcompeting its rivals.

Despite the fact that pure monopoly is a limited market phenomenon, it is useful to examine the price and output decisions of a pure monopolist. Doing so illuminates the patterns of monopolistic business behavior, irrespective of whether a firm is a pure monopolist.

THE PRICE AND OUTPUT DECISIONS OF A MONOPOLISTIC FIRM

We shall assume for the time being that the pure monopolist's market price and output decisions are unconstrained by government regulation. We shall also continue to assume that the principal objective of the firm is to maximize profits.

The key difference between the market situation confronting a pure monopolist and that confronting other enterprises is that the firm's demand-AR curve coincides with the industry demand curve. The firm is the industry. Being the only seller of an item for which there is no close substitute allows a monopoly firm great discretion in setting its prices. It is in a better position to be a *price-maker* than any other firm. However, the demand the product of a monopolist is still subject to the law of demand—more units can be sold at lower prices than at higher prices, so the monopolist's demand-AR curve is downsloping, as shown in Fig. 13-1. Unless there is a shift in demand, the monopolist cannot raise price without losing sales, and it cannot gain sales without reducing its price.

Suppose that the cost structure of the monopolist is given by the *ATC* and *MC* curves in Fig. 13-1(a) and by the corresponding *TC* curve in Fig. 13-1(b). What, then, are the monopolist's optimal price and output levels?

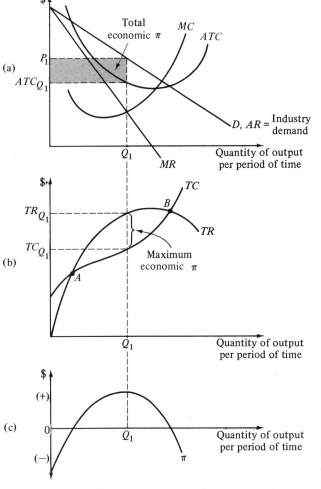

**Figure 13-1
Profit-maximizing price and output of a pure monopolist**

Profit Maximization: The Total Cost–Total Revenue Approach

A monopolist, like any other firm, maximizes short-run profits at the output where total revenue exceeds total cost by the greatest amount. Given the *TR* and *TC* functions in Fig. 13-1(b), the firm will be able to earn an economic profit at any output rate between points *A* and *B*; but short-run profits will be maximum at an output of Q_1 units, where the vertical distance between TR and TC is the greatest. Geometrically, TR exceeds TC by the greatest amount at the output rate where a tangent to the TC curve has the same slope and is parallel to a tangent to the TR function. The total profit function in Fig. 13-1(c) is derived by subtracting TC from TR at each output rate. Logic dictates that the peak of the total profit function correspond to an output rate of Q_1 where TR exceeds TC by the largest amount.

APPLICATIONS CAPSULE

THE MONOPOLY POWER OF BRAND NAMES AND TRADEMARKS: THE CASE OF THE PHARMACEUTICAL INDUSTRY

The pharmaceutical industry offers a dramatic example of how firms can exploit brand names and trademarks to their fullest. Even though patented drugs occupy center stage in the prescription drug industry (in 1974 no more than 15 to 20 of the 200 most frequently prescribed drugs were available from more than one supplier), trademarks and brand names are very valuable to manufacturers who market a drug that either cannot be patented or, if patented, has been so freely licensed as to allow considerable penetration of the competitive barrier of the patent itself.

Just how valuable brand names and trademarks can be is suggested by the findings of a governmental task force on prescription drugs. The task force reported that Squibb's Noctec brand of chloral hydrate (an unpatentable drug because it has been used medicinally as a sedative for a century) had better than a 50% market share even though the wholesale price of Noctec ran 3 to 4 times the prices of the same generic product offered by reliable small firms. The market for meprobamate (a freely licensed patented drug) is dominated by American Home Products' Equanil brand and Carter-Wallace's Miltown and Meprospan brands; the three brands account for nearly 80% of sales at prices to druggists that were more than double the prices charged by generic suppliers. Ciba's brand of reserpine (Serpasil) outsold generic reserpine by a wide margin, at wholesale prices up to 30 times greater than those charged by some of its competitors.

These are impressive price differentials considering that branded and generic versions of the same drug are nearly always chemically and biologically equivalent—in other words, the only real difference between branded and generic versions is that the former is sold under a registered trademark or brand name, whereas the generic version is sold by chemical name derived from the ingredients it contains. There is no other industry in which sellers gain such a wide market advantage from trademarks. Exxon, for example, despite being the largest corporation in the world and enjoying worldwide brand recognition of its products for years, is rarely able to command more than a 1- to 3-cent-per-gallon premium over the price of unbranded or off-brand gasoline. Procter & Gamble prices its best-selling Crest toothpaste at a level very comparable to other brands of toothpaste. Miller, Schlitz, and Budweiser beers all sell at "popular prices."

One major explanation for the monopoly power of brands and trademarks in the prescription drug industry is that the physician makes the buying decision for the patient when the prescription is written. As the late Senator Estes Kefauver observed: "He who orders does not buy; he who buys does not order." Most physicians have little knowledge of the prices of different drugs (although almost all are aware that the branded version will cost the patient more than the generic version). This stems from what probably is a distortion of an excellent medical principle: prescribe whatever drug is deemed to be the best therapy for the patient. Given that the major drug companies flood doctors with advertising and promotional literature touting their brands of drugs (and seldom is price a featured item in such literature), it is somewhat understandable that doctors are prone to prescribe according to how familiar and knowledgeable they are about particular brand names. The pharmacist is usually obligated to fill the prescription exactly as it is written—thus, if the doctor specifies Achromycin on the prescription, the druggist must supply American Cyanimid's brand of tetracycline and not the chemically identical products of Pfizer, Bristol, Squibb, or Upjohn. When getting a prescription filled, the average patient may not even know what he or she has purchased apart from the fact that it is a small bottle of yellow capsules; moreover, comparatively few people shop around for the lowest price—even though the most prevalent retail markup on prescriptions is 40% of the retail price (a 67% margin above the wholesale cost to the druggist).

All this combines to give the prescription drug firms an excellent position to reap good profits from trademarks and brand names. Interestingly enough, the basis of the value of trademarks and brand names derives more from the marketing aspects than from the manufacturing aspects. From a manufacturing standpoint, entry into the pharmaceutical industry is not overly difficult. The technical expertise and ability to maintain the high quality requisite for drug manufacturing are well within the reach of small firms. Nor are capital requirements a significant entry barrier (in 1968, 95% of the firms in the drug industry reported assets under $5 million). The key to business success lies not, therefore, in becoming an able producer but rather in achieving a high degree of marketing skill, most notably in the form of making physicians

443

*The Price
and Output
Decisions of
a Monopolistic
Firm*

sufficiently aware of and knowledgeable about your products that they will confidently prescribe your particular brand for their patients when the need arises.

Source: Based on information in Walter S. Measday, "The Pharmaceutical Industry," in *The Structure of American Industry*, 5th ed. Walter Adams, ed. (New York: Macmillan Publishing Co., Inc., 1977), pp. 250–284.

Profit Maximization: The Unit Cost–Unit Revenue Approach

On a unit cost and unit revenue basis, short-run profits are maximized at the output rate where $MC = MR$ and where marginal profit ($M\pi$) equals zero. The reasoning is precisely the same as in the case of firms operating in other types of markets. As long as an additional unit of output adds more to the firm's revenues than it does to the firm's costs, profit on that unit will be positive and total profits will be increased (or losses decreased) by producing and selling the unit. Alternatively, when MR exceeds MC and $M\pi$ is positive, total profits can be increased (or losses decreased) by increasing output. In Fig. 13-1(a) short-run profits are maximum at an output of Q_1 units— where the marginal cost curve intersects the marginal revenue curve. Observe that this output rate coincides with the value of Q_1 in Fig. 13-1(b). At Q_1, the tangents to TR and TC have identical slopes. Since the slope of TC equals MC and the slope of TR equals MR, MR must equal MC at exactly the output where TR exceeds TC by the greatest amount.

The highest price that the monopolist can charge and still sell Q_1 units is P_1 dollars. The profit-maximizing price corresponds to the point on the demand-AR curve associated with the output at which $MC = MR$ and short-run total profit equals $(P_1 - ATC_{Q_1})Q_1$, or the shaded area in Fig. 13-1(a). At outputs smaller than Q_1 units, MR exceeds MC and larger outputs up to Q_1 will add more to total revenue than to total costs; accordingly, total profit will rise. At an output rate beyond Q_1, MC exceeds MR and additional sales cause total costs to rise faster than total revenue, thereby decreasing total profit.

Calculating the Profit-Maximizing Output

The mathematics of determining the profit-maximizing price and output for a monopolist is analogous to the calculations for firms in competitive markets. Suppose that the monopolist's demand function is described by the equation $P = 5000 - 17Q$ and its total cost function by the equation $TC = 75,000 + 200Q - 17Q^2 + Q^3$. From the preceding discussion we know that profit is maximized at the output where $MR = MC$; both MR and MC can be obtained from the information given. If the demand function is

$P = 5000 - 17Q$, then

$$TR = P \cdot Q = (5000 - 17Q)Q = 5000Q - 17Q^2$$

and

$$MR = \frac{dTR}{dQ} = 5000 - 34Q.$$

The MC function, being the first derivative of the TC function, is

$$MC = \frac{dTC}{dQ} = 200 - 34Q + 3Q^2$$

Equating MR with MC gives

$$5000 - 34Q = 200 - 34Q + 3Q^2,$$

which reduces to

$$3Q^2 = 4800.$$

Solving for Q yields the two roots $Q = -40$ and $Q = 40$. Since output can never be negative, the profit-maximizing rate of output is 40 units. (As indicated earlier, it can be proved that the larger of the two roots is always the profit-maximizing or loss-minimizing output rate.)

The profit-maximizing price is found by substituting the profit-maximizing output rate into the demand function and solving for P. In terms of our example, the profit-maximizing price is

$$P = 5000 - 17Q$$
$$P = 5000 - 17(40)$$
$$P = 5000 - 680$$
$$P = \$4320.$$

Total profit at this price and output can be calculated by subtracting TC at 40 units of output from TR at 40 units of output; this gives \$52,000 per period of time.

LONG-RUN ADJUSTMENTS

In the long run a monopoly firm will tend to alter its scale of operations and the characteristics of its product in whatever ways it perceives will enhance profitability. Increases in demand for the monopolist's product will tend to prompt increases in production capacity—as long as there is a good prospect of larger profits. On the other hand, weak or declining market demand may warrant reductions in plant size and/or closing down inefficient production facilities. In general, the relation between the monopolist's market demand and its long-run average cost curve determines whether and to what extent it should alter plant scale and total production capacity. This same relationship also determines whether a monopolistic seller will find it most profitable to build and operate its production facilities just short of, at, or beyond the minimum point on its *LRAC* curve.

POPULAR MYTHS ABOUT MONOPOLY BEHAVIOR

Thoughtful scrutiny of Fig. 13-1 explodes a number of popular fallacies concerning the price and output behavior of monopolistic firms. A monopolist *does not* "charge the highest price it can get." There are many prices above P_1 in Fig. 13-1(a), but the seller has no incentive to pick them because of the lower profits which they entail.

Second, the demand curve for the monopolistic firm's product is not "inelastic." As discussed in Chapter 5, most demand curves are elastic at the upper end of the price range and inelastic at the lower end; linear demand curves are half elastic and half inelastic. The output that maximizes a monopolistic firm's profits will *always* fall within the elastic range of the demand curve—not the inelastic range. This proposition is quickly demonstrated. Since marginal cost is positive at all outputs, the output at which $MC = MR$ must necessarily correspond to outputs where MR is also positive and marginal revenue is positive only at output rates where the price elasticity of demand is greater than 1.[1]

A third common misconception about monopolistic firms is that they reap exorbitant profits. Weak demand and high costs are no less injurious to the profitability of a monopolist than they are to firms that face the rigors of direct competition. True, a monopolistic firm may be strategically positioned to earn sizable economic profits, but there is no guarantee that this will prove to be the case. It is quite possible for the monopolist's product to have such a weak demand that revenues are not high enough to cover operating costs (as illustrated in Fig. 11-4); alternatively, market demand may be just sufficient to allow only a normal profit (as illustrated in Fig. 11-5).

CONSTRAINTS UPON THE MARKET POWER OF A MONOPOLISTIC FIRM

Although being the sole producer of a good or service for which there is no close substitute confers a great deal of economic power upon a firm, certain market restraints are nevertheless imposed upon an unregulated monopolist's behavior. Three such restraints deserve comment.

First, blatant, self-serving exercise of monopoly power is restrained by a fear of government intervention and regulation. A monopolistic firm

[1]The relationship between price elasticity, total revenue, and marginal revenue is described in the section "Elasticity and Total Revenue" in Chapter 5.

producing what consumers view as a "necessity" will undoubtedly draw bitter outcries from consumers if it fully exploits its short-run profit opportunities. Widespread and persistent public criticism increases the risk of some form of government intervention—whether it be antitrust action, government support of new competitors, or direct regulation (as in the case of natural monopolies). Thus, a monopolist may hold back from charging the full amount of "what the traffic will bear" and curtail its pursuit of short-run profits in order to escape consumer resentment and the likelihood of onerous government regulation—and thereby, perhaps, come closer to long-run profit maximization.

Second, a monopolist may deliberately limit its profits so as not to encourage direct competition. When a monopolistic firm exploits its market power fully and earns large economic profits in the short run, it risks attracting the attention of firms having the financial, technological, and organizational resources to crack the monopolist's entry barriers. The monopolist may also trigger efforts on the part of its customers or on the part of other firms to develop acceptable substitutes. In other words, high monopoly profits activate the forces of *potential competition* from both new firms and new products. This threat is very real. The business landscape is littered with ex-monopolists which have been the victims of emerging competition—Alcoa, American Can, Standard Oil, DuPont, United Shoe Machinery, Ford, International Nickel, Dow Chemical, and Gillette, not to mention the railroads, whose one-time monopoly profits have been reduced by competition from truck carriers and the airlines. Therefore, rather than set price at the level that maximizes short-run profits but invites competition (or regulation), the monopolistic firm may decide to lower price to a level that deters the threat of potential competition and wards off government regulation and antitrust action. Such a pricing practice is called *limit pricing*. The exact level of the limit price depends upon how effectively entry is blocked, the probability of government regulation, and the degree of technological difficulty in developing substitute products. The obvious purpose of limit pricing is to forego short-run profit maximization in favor of enhancing the firm's profits over the long term.

The third restraint upon the exercise of monopoly power is the systematic propensity for *countervailing power* to develop on the buying side of the market.[2] Large customers usually waste little time in attempting to negate the monopoly power of sellers with whom they must deal. Major food packers, for example, have repeatedly threatened to enter into tin-can manufacturing; to avoid the loss of these customers the two major tin can manufacturers have been forced to exercise price restraint. Electric utility firms have from time to time threatened to build nuclear-powered generating facilities to pressure railroad firms into reducing the freight rates on coal

[2]The theory of countervailing power and its application to the corporate sector was originated and developed by John Kenneth Galbraith in his book *American Capitalism: The Theory of Countervailing Power* (Boston: Houghton Mifflin Company, 1952), especially Chapter 9.

shipments to their coal-fired steam-generating facilities. In certain circumstances, therefore, "across-the market" competition may be successful in checking the power of a monopolistic firm and in reducing its price to levels more consistent with competition. Once price is lowered, the monopolistic firm has an incentive to increase output and make its product available to a broader segment of the market.

Taken together, these three restraints lessen the effective market power of monopolists to levels lower than they might otherwise obtain in the short run. True, at a given moment a monopolist may possess substantial power to raise price above competitive levels; they may also earn sizable economic profits. But the situation can be short-lived. Monopolists that produce "necessities" and other essential goods—public utility firms, for example—quickly find their rates regulated and their profits reduced to socially acceptable levels. Over time, technological change regularly undermines the market power of the unregulated monopolists. And large buyers forced to do business with monopolistic sellers attempt to neutralize their market power through bargaining and threats of vertical integration.

BILATERAL MONOPOLY

In bilateral monopoly, a single seller is confronted with a single buyer. The seller has no other outlet for his product and the buyer has no other source. Such conditions are approximated when a particular defense contractor is the only firm in the United States with the technical capability of producing an advanced weapons system for the U.S. government. The question becomes one of analyzing the economics of what happens when monopoly power on the selling side of the market clashes against monopoly power on the buying side of the market.

Suppose that the buyer's demand is described by line D in Fig. 13-2; this demand is the same as the demand for the seller's product, given that a single buyer and a single seller constitute the market. Also suppose that the selling firm's marginal revenue curve is MR_S and its marginal cost curve is MC_S. Assuming that the monopolistic seller could exert its will and preference on the buyer, we could logically predict that the seller would produce Q_S units and charge a price of P_S, since these correspond to the profit-maximizing condition of $MR_S = MC_S$.

However, if the buying firm is able to exert its buying power to maximum advantage, the outcome will be different. Ideally, a monopsonistic buyer would like to view the seller's marginal cost curve (MC_S) as a supply curve—the logic being that if the single buyer can control the market completely, the monopolistic seller can be forced into the position of a perfectly competitive industry; in this situation the marginal cost curve of the industry is also the industry supply curve (as was described and explained in Fig. 10-5). From the buyer's standpoint, the consequence of viewing MC_S as a supply curve is that it indicates the average cost (AC) to the buyer of pur-

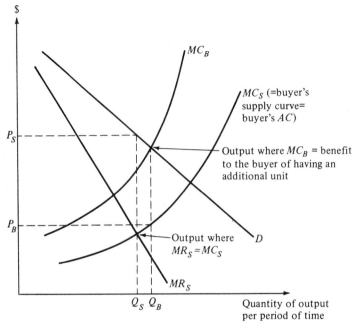

Figure 13-2
The economics of bilateral monopoly

chasing various amounts of output. However, when a buyer is confronted with a rising supply curve, the curve marginal to MC, labeled as MC_B, represents the marginal cost of *buying* an additional unit.

Optimally, the single buyer would purchase additional units as long as the benefit of doing so (given by the buyer's demand curve) exceeds the marginal cost of purchasing the unit. The buyer would like, therefore, to set the purchase level at Q_B—the output at which MC_B intersects the demand curve; the buyer's preferred purchase price would be P_B, which is the lowest price the seller would be willing to accept for Q_B units.

The problem is that the single buyer can no more control the market completely by forcing the seller into the position of a perfectly competitive industry than the single seller can successfully impose its profit-maximizing price and output preference on a single buyer. What, then, is the outcome? Economic analysis provides no definite answer. It is not possible to predict by logical deduction just what terms the buyer and seller will finally agree to in a bilateral monopoly situation. We can say, though, that the range should be between P_B and P_S and between Q_B and Q_S, since neither party has an incentive to settle outside these limits. To a large extent the outcome is a function of (1) which party has the greatest bargaining strength and negotiating skill, (2) how well informed the buyer and seller are about each other, and (3) who aspires most—for whatever reason—to drive a hard bargain. Generally speaking, it is easier for the buyer and seller to agree on quantity than on price.

In situations where pure monopoly and high degrees of monopoly power exist, government frequently elects to undertake some form of regulation so as to "protect the public interest" from undue economic abuse. Of the various alternatives to regulatory control, two approaches will be discussed here: (1) direct regulation of prices, services rendered, and profitability; and (2) indirect regulation through an " excess profits" tax.

Direct Regulation

The first serious attempts at regulating monopolies in the United States involved the attempts of city councils to specify the rates and services of electric, gas, and trolley companies. The political nature and makeup of

APPLICATIONS CAPSULE

GOVERNMENT REGULATION: THE VIEW
OF THE PRESIDENT'S COUNCIL OF ECONOMIC ADVISORS

In January 1977, President Ford's Council of Economic Advisors offered the following summary view about government regulation in the U.S. economy (Paul MacAvoy, a distinguished economist and expert in the economic aspects of regulation, was the Council member in charge of regulatory issues during most of the year covered by this report):

The Government regulates a substantial part of the economy in an effort to improve economic performance and promote individual welfare. Such regulation has created costs as well as benefits, and some anticipated benefits of regulation have never been realized. Regulation has also been difficult to reform or abandon, even when recognized as counterproductive, because elements of regulation frequently tend to satisfy certain special interests. Historically, some business enterprises have sought to avoid competition, and have sometimes been aided in doing so by regulation; other rules and procedures create vested interests and capital values which reform would endanger.

The motives behind efforts to regulate economic activity have generally been commendable, and the net effect of some Government regulatory activity has been positive. Unfortunately it often turns out that regulatory processes are not capable of achieving their intended goals or have generated greater costs than would result from the original problem. In some instances the problem prompting the adoption of regulation has passed but the regulations remain. In other cases the regulatory process has proved too inflexible to accommodate changes in the economy, and a previously beneficial regulatory activity may become ineffectual or harmful. In each of these instances reform of the regulations would lower the nonproductive use of Government resources and would free private resources for productive tasks. More important, some regulation is harmful as well as wasteful since it distorts the allocation of resources and thus lowers the potential output of the economy. The reform of such regulations would increase efficiency, thus making the economy better able to provide current consumers with goods and services and to ensure growth in output for the future.

A major purpose of regulation is to control prices charged and services rendered in industries considered to be natural monopolies, especially those in the transportation and public utility sectors, in order to prevent firms in these industries from exercising market power. The economic characteristics of these industries are such that it is more efficient for a single firm to supply the entire market. Price regulation is therefore usually accompanied by entry restrictions. Price and entry regulations have been extended, however, beyond the select cases where control of monopoly power justifies their implementation. They have been applied to many industries which seem capable of vigorous and healthy competition under less restrictive regulations: for example, trucking and airlines. In these cases it is appropriate to compare the results of price and entry regulation with the level of price and output that would be realized in a freely operating market.

If a regulated price exceeds the market-determined price, consumers will purchase less and output will be reduced. If a regulated price is below the competitive level, firms will provide less output than they would if they were not regulated. In both cases price and entry controls reduce the production of goods and services in the regulated markets. Resources are then reallocated to alternative uses which are less valuable to consumers. The result, coupled with the administrative costs of imposing and enforcing regulations, is to reduce efficiency and production.

Most regulatory legislation since the mid-1960s affects business activity in much more direct ways and in much greater detail than is true of simple price controls. The Federal Government has intervened in such matters as product quality, producer liability, conditions affecting the health and safety of employees, waste disposal, and equal employment opportunity. Much of this legislation is an attempt to deal with the problem of externalities—real costs or benefits that affect individuals other than those directly involved in a transaction. Economic efficiency requires that prices appropriately reflect the full cost to society of producing each good or service. External costs or benefits must be incorporated into each transaction, or internalized, for efficiency to be achieved. The internalization should be accomplished in the least costly manner. Unfortunately some of the regulations concerning health, safety, and the environment appear to be ineffective, and we bear their costs without enjoying much, if any, corresponding benefit. In other cases the benefits might have been achieved at a smaller sacrifice of other goods and services.

There are costs of extending regulation in a free-market economy that go beyond the direct impact on supply. First, the regulatory process itself uses public and private resources which could be used to produce other, more valuable, goods or services. Second, some regulatory procedures reduce the ability of industry to respond to changing supply and demand conditions and so create bottlenecks in regulated sectors of the economy. For example, the lag in implementing price adjustments to reflect the changing supply or demand conditions confronting public utilities can influence the timing of their investment decisions, causing shortages or excess capacity. Third, regulations which protect existing firms from potential competitors may reduce incentives for technological improvement and innovation. Fourth, the uncertainty introduced by the regulatory process itself will cause resources to be used in unproductive ways. Finally, if price controls lower the expected returns to new capital investment, capital formation will be retarded and the economy will grow more slowly.

Source: Reprinted from *The Economic Report of the President*, January 1977, pp. 146–148.

city councils often resulted in franchise awards and terms of services becoming immersed in politics—which made the regulatory process a fertile area for corruption and economic mismanagement. Now, most direct regulation is undertaken by regulatory commissions with civil service staffs to investigate and audit the activities of the regulated firms. Every state has a public service commission, elected in some states and appointed in others, which supervises electric power, natural gas, telephone, and public transportation companies. There is, similarly, another set of regulatory commissions at the federal level to oversee interstate industries where monopoly power may exist— railroads, motor carriers, airlines, water carriers, oil pipelines, interstate telephone service, radio and TV broadcasting, communications satellites, interstate transmission of electricity and natural gas, and public utility holding companies are all subject to direct federal regulations.

The typical bread-and-butter issue in direct regulation is "rate-making" —establishing the prices that regulated firms can charge for their products or services. The traditional standard is that regulators should allow firms to charge rates that will cover all allowable operating expenses and yield the firm a "fair return on the fair value" of the capital investment made by the firm's owners.

In theory, rate regulation is supposed to result in lower prices and greater output than would be the case without regulation. The diagrammatics are shown in Fig. 13-3. An unregulated monopolist would prefer a price of P_1 dollars and an output of Q_1 units, thereby maximizing profits where $MR = MC$. However, with regulation, rates are often targeted toward a level such that price equals ATC, where ATC is defined to include a profit equal to a fair return on the company's capital investment; thus, in Fig. 13-3 regulators would aim at establishing a maximum price of P_2, in which case the company's customers would be inclined to purchase Q_2 units.

In applying the "fair return on fair value" concept, the regulatory focus is on (1) the *rate base,* which is defined to reflect the fair value of the

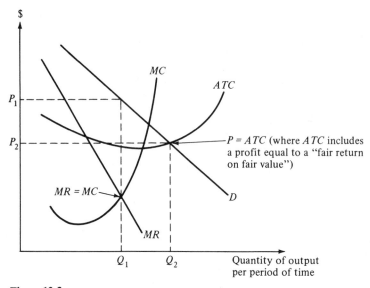

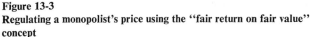

Figure 13-3
Regulating a monopolist's price using the "fair return on fair value"
concept

capital invested by the company in conducting its business, and (2) the *allowed rate of return* on the rate base. Needless to say, controversy swirls around the definition of both what should be included in the rate base and what a "fair return" is. The search for an appropriate definition of the rate base has narrowed to essentially two measures: (1) the actual historical cost, adjusted for depreciation, of assets in use in the business; and (2) the reproduction value of assets employed (i.e., what it would cost the company to replace its capital assets at current price levels). Each has its pros and cons. Until the 1930s, the reproduction value approach predominated, but since then the original cost (or current depreciated book value) approach has the greatest following.[3] Even so, there still remains much debate over how to calculate the current book value of assets employed (there are no hard and fast rules governing what the "correct" depreciation method is); likewise, there is ample room to argue over what a company should be allowed to count as "legitimate" and "necessary" operating expenses (charitable contributions, advertising, and executives' salaries and expense accounts, for example, tend to provoke heated discussions). Quite often, public utility rate-making becomes mired down in nit-picking, emotionalism, and headline politics, even though the concept of regulation is a simple one of setting reasonable prices and profits.

[3]One of the current major issues in how the rate base should be defined concerns whether and how the value of construction work in progress should be treated. Some commissions allow construction work in progress to be included in the rate base, whereas others do not.

What frequently gets lost in the debate is a clear concept of the functions a "fair profit" is intended to perform in a regulated environment. Three functions stand out. First and foremost, profit for a regulated company must be viewed as a payment to investors both for the use of their capital and for assuming the risk that attaches to this use. A regulated firm's profitability must be great enough over the long run that it can attract sufficient new capital to finance whatever new facilities are needed to serve its customers efficiently and reliably. A corollary consideration is that a regulated firm is entitled to a degree of profit that will maintain its financial integrity. By this is meant that the profit a firm is allowed to earn should be sufficient to avoid both an erosion of its stock price and a downgrading of its bond and preferred stock ratings. Second, profit performs the incentive function of rewarding excellent service to customers and punishing the opposite; in this sense a regulated firm's profit should not be viewed as a "guaranteed" rate of return but rather as an allowed rate of return under honest, economical, and efficient management. Third, profit serves to redistribute income from the firm's customers to its owners. Here is where standards of fairness enter the picture. How much profit is needed to ensure "fair" compensation of stockholders? How is this counterbalanced by the desirability of ensuring that the rates charged by the regulated firm do not place an "unfair" burden on the ratepayers—particularly when the good or service being supplied is a "necessity" such as electric power, natural gas, or telephone service? Financial theorists take the position that a "fair" rate of return to stockholders is governed by the prevailing rates of return in investments of comparable risk—an amount currently pegged at 12 to 14% after taxes. However, there are no consensus guidelines regarding what is a "fair" profit from the consumers' standpoint; economic analysis is not very helpful in this regard.

Controlling Monopoly through Taxation

The other general approach to the social control of monopoly power is indirectly through taxation. Although there are several types of monopoly taxation, the one we shall present and discuss here is a profits tax.[4] The logic and rationale underlying a profits tax is very straightforward: allow the monopolist to set whatever price and output it choses, then tax away whatever resulting amount of profit is deemed "excessive." This could be done in principle by increasing the percentage of profits paid in taxes from, say, 50% to 75%. The objective would be to set a tax rate on a firm's reported before-tax profit (as measured in accounting terms) that would tax away all (or most) of the monopolist's economic profits and leave only a normal profit.

The effects of an "excess profits" tax on a monopolist's price and output are shown in Fig. 13-4. In panel 13-4(a), the profit-maximizing price and

[4]For a very readable discussion of other types of monopoly taxation, see David R. Kamerschen and Lloyd M. Valentine, *Intermediate Microeconomic Theory* (Cincinnati, Ohio: South-Western Publishing Company, 1977), pp. 371–374.

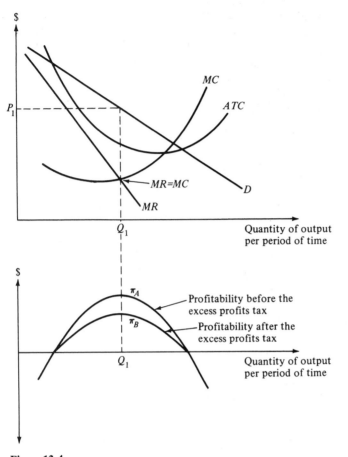

Figure 13-4
Regulating monopoly profits through an "excess profits" tax

output values are P_1 and Q_1. The monopolist's total profit function is shown as π_A in panel (b) and is derived from calculating the profits at each price and output combination shown in panel (a). Suppose that the maximum profit at P_1 and Q_1 is viewed as "excessive" and that Congress passes legislation authorizing an excess profits tax on the monopolist's profits, with the form of the tax being one where the marginal *tax rate* on profits is increased sufficiently to bring the firm's after-tax profitability down close to a normal profit. Such a tax has the effect of lowering the firm's total after-tax profit from π_A to π_B.

Observe in this case that the monopolist's profit is still maximized at the same price and output after the excess profits tax is levied as before the tax. This is because a tax based on a certain fixed percentage of profits does not change the output at which $MR = MC$; therefore, it has no effect on the terms of exchange between buyers and sellers. Observe, further, that since the profit-maximizing price does not change, the seller absorbs the full

THE TRUCKING INDUSTRY: WHERE REGULATION HAS LED TO HIGHER PRICES

In a number of instances, government regulation has resulted in the establishment of prices that are *higher* than would prevail under free-market competition. Just how and why this is so has been reported on by the Council of Economic Advisors:

> Trucking provides a good example of the economic costs of regulations that hold prices above the free-market level. In interstate trucking an antitrust exemption permits motor carriers to agree upon rates through rate bureaus, which are groups of truckers that function like private cartels. Rates tend to be set high enough to cover the costs of less efficient carriers. The result is higher prices to consumers. The Interstate Commerce Commission (ICC) regulates both the entry of new carriers and the expansion of route authority by existing carriers. These restrictions frequently require some trucks to drive extra miles on circuitous routes, prohibit access to intermediate points on routes, limit the commodities that can be handled by some carriers, and prohibit certain kinds of freight on the return trip. The result is excessive truck miles and unproductive consumption of motor fuel, labor time, and other resources.
>
> Where more than one carrier gains a certificate to provide service, competition tends to occur on the basis of service quality—frequency of departure, faster delivery, and so on—rather than through prices. As a consequence trucks are often dispatched with smaller loads than they might otherwise haul. Equipment and labor costs are thus spread over fewer ton-miles and costs and prices are higher than necessary. The regulation of rates precludes price competition, and consequently the range of price-service options available to shippers is restricted. Those shippers who would have chosen less frequent service if it were offered at a lower price pay more for services they do not want. In markets where only one trucker has route authority, this process of rate setting may permit lower costs since the trucker, exercising his monopoly control, may reduce the frequency of scheduling, with the result that a higher proportion of trucks is dispatched fully loaded. However, because such a trucker has no competitors, he is unlikely to lower prices to fully reflect the lower-quality service.
>
> A comparison of the transportation of small parcels with large or bulky shipments illustrates the advantages of multiple price-service options. Shippers of small parcels have several options. The scheduled airlines carry small packages as baggage at substantial prices but with a guarantee of delivery the same day. Some air freight firms collect packages at various cities, fly them first to a central sorting location, then on to their final destination each evening, and provide overnight service at slightly lower prices than those charged by the scheduled airlines. Intercity bus lines and special firms that deliver small packages use surface transportation to furnish delivery service at even cheaper rates. Finally, the U.S. Postal Service offers slower but widely available

parcel delivery. The advantage of having multiple options is that shippers of small parcels may choose between various degrees of service at different prices. Although shippers of large or bulky freight have some flexibility, many are chiefly limited to motor carriers, where the range of price-service options is much more limited because of regulation.

The problems of excess capacity, higher prices, and too few price-service options would be reduced if entry into the trucking industry were not restricted. Unlike public utilities, trucking does not exhibit scale economies. Thus price competition is not likely to result in a single survivor—a monopolist. In trucking, fixed costs are low and except for Government restrictions entry is relatively easy. Competition, not monopoly, would be the natural condition in the trucking industry if it were not for Government regulation.

Recent research has demonstrated that common carrier truck regulations cause large losses in production and efficiency. Freight rates in countries that do not regulate motor carriers are significantly lower than rates in countries like West Germany and the United States where regulation is strict. Excessively high motor carrier rates cause some shippers to substitute alternative modes of transportation, or to provide their own transportation services. These responses to regulation reduce economic efficiency.

Source: Taken from the 1977 Annual Report of the Council of Economic Advisors, as published in *The Economic Report of the President*, January 1977, pp. 148–150.

brunt of the tax. None of the tax is passed on to buyers in the form of higher prices. This feature makes it particularly attractive as a policy alternative.[5]

SUMMARY AND CONCLUSIONS

The major implications and predictions that flow from the market model of pure monopoly are:

1. A monopolistic firm will use its economic power to charge a higher price than would tend to prevail under competition.
2. Because a monopolist tends to charge a higher price, output will be less than in a competitive market; this is because customers will buy less of the product at

[5]Such a result is not obtained when a per-unit-sold tax is levied on the monopolist's product. A per-unit tax is a variable cost to the monopolist because the amount of tax paid is a function of the number of units sold. Consequently, a per-unit tax raises both the monopolist's MC and ATC curves by the amount of the per-unit tax and results in a new intersection of MR and MC—at a higher price and a lower output. (Examples of per-unit taxes are cigarette, liquor, and gasoline taxes; however, the purpose of these taxes is not to control monopoly.) Because consumers bear part of the burden of a per-unit tax, it is generally not viewed as being appropriate for monopoly control.

the monopolist's higher price than they would be willing and able to buy at the lower prices that can be expected with competition.

3. An exception to the higher price/lower output predictions of the monopoly model is the case of *natural monopoly*, where economies of scale are so great that monopoly results in a lower price and a greater output than could be expected under competition. In such cases, there is clear conflict between promoting competition, on the one hand, and seeing that the marketplace provides consumers with the greatest possible output at the lowest feasible price, on the other hand.

Generally speaking, any form of unregulated monopoly and/or the exercise of monopoly power works against the best interests of consumers. Only in the case of natural monopoly is a monopolistic market preferable to a competitive market, and then only with some form of effective economic regulation.

The economic case against monopolistic markets and the unregulated exercise of monopoly power is exceedingly strong:

1. Monopoly tends to produce higher prices and restricted outputs as compared to competition.
2. Monopoly has the capability of producing "excessive" economic profits—an outcome that results in income and purchasing power being redistributed from the buying public to the monopolistic seller.
3. Monopoly can prevent an optimal allocation of economic resources in the sense that monopolistic firms do not necessarily produce at the output rates where unit costs are lowest (the minimum point on the $LRAC$ curve), as is the case in perfect competition.
4. Such monopolistic practices as price-fixing, suppression of technological improvements, erecting artificial barriers to entry, tying contracts, exerting reciprocal purchasing leverage, refusing to sell, and attempting to drive rival firms out of business through predatory tactics are all without economic justification.

A monopolist obviously has a great deal of economic power, which it almost always will use to its own advantage. This can scarcely be condoned. However, the market power of a monopolist is seldom absolute. It can be weakened and even overcome completely by slack demand conditions, by actual or threatened government intervention and regulation, by potential competition from new firms and new products, and by the exercise of countervailing power on the part of buyers.

SUGGESTED READINGS

FELTON, J. R., "The Costs and Benefits of Motor Truck Regulation," *Quarterly Review of Economics and Business*, Vol. 18, No. 2 (Summer 1978), pp. 7–20.

GALBRAITH, J. K., *American Capitalism: The Theory of Countervailing Power* (Boston: Houghton Mifflin Company, 1951), Chapter 9.

HARBERGER, A. C., "Monopoly and Resource Allocation," *American Economic Review*, Vol. 44, No. 2 (May 1954), pp. 77–87.

458

How Markets Function: The Case of Monopoly

LERNER, A. P., "The Concept of Monopoly and the Measurement of Monopoly Power," *Review of Economic Studies* (June 1943), pp. 157–175.

SCHERER, F. M., *Industrial Market Structure and Economic Performance* (Chicago: Rand McNally & Company, 1970), Chapters 2, 18, 22.

STIGLER, G. J., AND C. FRIEDLAND, "What Can Regulators Regulate? The Case of Electricity," *Journal of Law and Economics*, Vol. 5, No. 2 (October 1962), pp. 1–16.

PROBLEMS AND QUESTIONS FOR DISCUSSION

1. Suppose that a pure monopolist's demand schedule and total cost function are as follows:

Selling Price	Quantity Demanded	Total Costs
$20	9,000	$160,000
19	10,000	165,000
18	11,000	171,000
17	12,000	178,000
16	13,000	186,000
15	14,000	195,000

What price should the monopolist charge in order to maximize profits?

2. The XQT Concessions Company paid $35,000 for exclusive rights to sell beer at the seven home games of the local pro football team. Attendance generally averages 60,000 persons per game. The variable costs of obtaining and selling a 12-ounce cup of draft beer are estimated to be 22 cents. The manager of the XQT company has estimated demand for beer at each home game to be the following:

Selling Price	Quantity Demanded (cups)
$0.75	36,000
1.00	32,000
1.25	26,000
1.50	18,000

What price should be selected in order to maximize XQT's profits?

3. Is it possible for a pure monopolist to benefit from sales promotion and advertising, given that there are no close substitutes for the monopolist's product? Explain and justify your answer graphically.

4. How can a firm have monopoly power without being a pure monopolist? How could one measure the strength of a firm's monopolistic position?

5. Why might a monopolist charge a price below what would maximize short-run profits? In practice how important are these considerations likely to be?

6. "The more profitable a firm, the greater its monopoly power." True or false? Explain.

7. What reasons can you give for why a monopolisitc firm's price might be higher under regulation than if it were not unregulated? How often and where do you think this might occur?

8. Does a profit-maximizing monopolist typically produce at an output rate which is optimal from a standpoint of cost and efficiency? Why or why not? Illustrate graphically.

9. Does a monopolistic firm have less incentive to be efficient than a firm confronted with vigorous price competition? Why or why not?

10. Does monopoly always result in higher prices and lower outputs than a competitively structured industry? Illustrate graphically. (*Hint:* Consider the result that might occur if the monopolist has access to economies of scale that are not available if there is competitive rivalry among many small firms.)

FOURTEEN ANALYZING THE STRENGTH OF COMPETITION

Judging from the market models presented in the last four chapters, one would deduce that the nature of the competitive process is governed mainly by the number of sellers comprising the supply side of the market. Indeed, a principal conclusion of the theory of how markets function is that the strength and effectiveness of competitive forces increases directly with the number of firms. But this conclusion is only part of the story. There is more to competitive interplay than just how the supply side of the market is structured.

The task of this chapter is to complete the picture of the competitive mechanism. The primary emphasis will be on the strategic aspects of competitive rivalry, how competition in a particular market is keyed to the economics of the industry, and how competition is shaped by forces other than the firms that already operate in the market.

THE STRATEGIC ASPECTS OF COMPETITION[1]

In observing competitive behavior in the marketplace, one almost has to be struck by how the strategic moves and countermoves of rival firms are

[1]This section is drawn largely from Arthur A. Thompson, "Competition as a Strategic Process," *Antitrust Bulletin*, (forthcoming).

such a basic part of the competitive process. To a large extent, the jockeying of sellers for a stronger position and increased buyer patronage constitutes the most fundamental and direct measure of the pulse of competition.[2] More specifically:

461

The Strategic Aspects of Competition

1. Competition is primarily centered around the activities of sellers.

2. Competition arises out of the conscious attempts of each seller to devise an overall product offering which buyers will perceive as more attractive than those of its rivals, thereby allowing the selling firm to improve and strengthen its position in the marketplace.

3. Competition is manifested by an independent striving for patronage, whereby firms (offering a product that may range from essentially identical to highly differentiated) employ various strategies and counterstrategies aimed at outmaneuvering one another, gaining a stronger foothold in the market, and achieving (or maintaining) a more profitable volume of business.

4. The strategies that rival firms may devise and the dimensions along which they may find openings to compete are limited only by their imaginations and the constraints imposed by buyers (or by government).

5. Fresh competitive pressures are activated when one or more rival firms is induced to make either "aggressive" strategic moves to increase sales, market share, and profits or "defensive" moves to protect its established position.

6. As the competitive process unfolds over the long term, active rivalry will result in firms both *creating* and *responding* to new market forces, market trends, and customer tastes and preferences.

7. Competitive behavior will entail both strategic successes and strategic failures; the strategic successes may, if they are sufficiently dramatic, guide, influence, and/or even "control" the direction of market forces and competitive pressures. Strategic failures, on the other hand, are evidence of a strategy that was insufficient to overcome those of rival firms on account of either poor formulation or poor execution. The point here is that the strategies of firms in most markets are in some degree both controlling and controlled by the unfolding sequence of strategic moves and countermoves and the competitive pressures that these create.

The thrust of these statements can be woven into the following conceptual framework. Any time two or more sellers are market rivals, they are confronted with the strategic issue of how to compete in their approach to the market and prospective buyers. Should their respective strategies of how to compete be identical or different? If the latter, then in what specific respects should a firm attempt to differentiate its strategy from those of its competitors? Imitative or "me, too" competitive strategies can prove to be the most

[2]Elements of the strategic aspects of competition go as far back in the economics literature as Adam Smith's *The Wealth of Nations*, published in 1776. Cournot, Bertrand, and Edgeworth, also well-known classical economists, incorporated strategic aspects in their writings, but their models incorporated assumptions so foreign to actual strategic behavior as to render them void of real explanatory power. More modern treatments can be found in Edward H. Chamberlin, *The Theory of Monopolistic Competition* (Cambridge, Mass.: Harvard University Press, 1933), p. 6; Fritz Machlup, *The Economics of Sellers' Competition* (Baltimore: The Johns Hopkins Press, 1952); J. A. Schumpeter, *Capitalism, Socialism, and Democracy*, 3rd ed. (New York: Harper & Brothers, 1950); and J. M. Clark, *Competition as a Dynamic Process* (Washington, D.C.: The Brookings Institution, 1961), especially pp. 471–476. Numerous other writers have recognized the strategic rivalry aspects of competition in the form of game theory models of oligopoly.

profitable and workable plan in some cases, but many markets tend to be large and diverse enough to warrant firms pursuing distinguishably different competitive strategies. Some firms may choose to emphasize a lower price, others a higher quality; some may elect to integrate vertically, others may concentrate within a single stage; some may strive to become "full-line" producers whereas others deliberately limit themselves to a narrower product line; some may concentrate R&D expenditures on cost-saving process innovations whereas others search harder for new and better products. For obvious reasons, every firm has motivations to formulate a strategy or plan for competing in the market that aims at outdoing its rivals so as to gain a stronger foothold with buyers and reap the rewards of greater market success.[3] In essence, a firm's competitive strategy can be viewed as its action plan for building a comparative advantage over its market rivals.

Out of this motivation of rival firms to secure a competitive advantage, together with an awareness of the interactions of their approaches to the market, emerges a strategic process that, in turn, activates and produces competitive pressures of varying types and degrees. This process consists of an ongoing series of competitive strategies and counterstrategies, some offensive and some defensive, on the part of each seller in the market.[4] Each firm's moves and countermoves are an integral part of its overall corporate strategy for developing a viable business organization and for achieving a degree of success sufficient to sustain operations over the long run. A firm's corporate strategy has both short-run and long-run objectives; likewise, its strategies for competing in the marketplace have short- and long-run features. At any point in time, a firm's overall competitive strategy can be expected to incorporate price and nonprice factors, with the exact mix being a function of management perceptions as to what combination will have the most desirable market impact, given the prevailing strategies (and anticipated counterstrategies) of rival firms. With the passage of time, a firm's overall corporate strategy and its market-specific competitive strategies will tend either to be fine-tuned or to undergo major overhaul, according to the firm's market successes (or failures) and the durability of its chosen strategies in withstanding strategic challenges from rival firms.

---

[3]Lest any confusion arise, suffice it to say that every firm has a competitive strategy—however imperfect or unconscious it may be. A firm's strategy may be explicit or it may have to be deduced from its behavior and policies. The strategy may be carefully calculated and regularly assessed from every angle or it may have emerged haphazardly and be mainly a product of chance and circumstance. Or, it may have evolved gradually over time, standing as a result of trial and error and market feedback relative to what worked and what did not. For a more complete survey of these elements of corporate strategy, see Arthur A. Thompson and A. J. Strickland, *Strategy Formulation and Implementation: Tasks of the General Manager* (Dallas: Business Publications, Inc., 1980), Chapters 1, 2.

[4]Classical treatments of competitive strategy simplified the crucial matter of rivals' responses to a new strategic move to two extreme cases: the firm acting as if rivals will not respond or as if they will respond so promptly as to neutralize any gain the initiating firm might make. Such oversimplification misses the really characteristic cases, which lie between the extremes and need more to explain them than can be represented by a curve on a diagram. See Clark, *Competition as a Dynamic Process*, p. 472.

When a firm makes a successful strategic move, it can expect increased rewards, largely at the expense of rivals' market shares and rates of sales growth. The speed and extent of the strategic encroachment varies with (1) whether the product is standardized or differentiated, (2) the initiator's competence and resources to capitalize on any advantage the strategy has produced, (3) how costly and difficult it is for sellers to shift buyer loyalties, and (4) the ease with which the successful features of a strategy can be copied. The pressures on rivals to respond are, in addition, a function of whether the initiator is (1) a major firm with considerable market visibility, (2) a fringe firm whose efforts can be ignored for some time, or (3) a firm in financial distress and thus whose strategy is predicated on desperation. If a firm's strategic offensive is keyed to a low price aimed at quick penetration but with a substantial risk that full costs will not be recovered, rivals may judge that the strategy will be short-lived; they may choose to respond or not, depending on their estimates of whether it will be better to meet the low price on a temporary basis or to ride out whatever buyer resistance may be encountered. If the initiating firm finds its move neutralized by rivals' counter-moves, it is challenged to seek out a better strategy not as easily defeated or else remain content with the stalemate it has encountered.

The ease with which a firm's strategic thrusts can be neutralized is a major criterion of strategy selection; firms will gravitate strongly toward strategies that can be neither easily initiated nor easily defeated in the market-place. Such considerations suggest that a well-managed firm will try to develop a *distinctive competence* whereby it can differentiate its product in ways not susceptible to successful initiation. By developing a reputation and image on some key facet or facets of its product offering, a firm may be able to set its product above and apart from those of rival firms—thereby acquiring a position of some market advantage and market power which, subsequently, can be converted into added profitability.

It may be that just a few firms (large or small) will tend to initiate fresh strategic moves and, then, only periodically. But to the extent that these few set the pace for the industry, the give and take of strategic move and strategic response is ongoing.[5] An initiatory move may come from a firm with ambitious growth objectives, from a firm with excess capacity, or from a firm under pressure to gain added business. More generally, though, the classic offensive strategies will be made by firms that see what they think are market opportunities and a chance to improve their standing. Such firms, whether they be actual leaders, would-be leaders, or mavericks, will likely be aware of the risks of undertaking a bold strategic move but they also are likely to have confidence (1) that they are shrewd enough to keep ahead of the game and (2) that they will be better off making a bold move than they would be by holding back and letting others take the lead.[6] Often, new marketing strategies are launched by sales-force organizations under pressure

[5] Clark, *Competition as a Dynamic Process*, p. 473.
[6] *Ibid.*, p. 474.

from top management to improve sales-profit-growth performance or otherwise stave off slack sales. Ideally, the more aggressive firms will be able to *create* competitive pressures that are sufficiently strong to *compel* vigorous responses from other firms, yet are not so devastating as to destroy any but the inefficient and ineffective firms (i.e., those which have been unable to build an organization with the competence to attract buyers and carve out a market niche for their product).[7]

A variety of competitive patterns and pressures may flow from the competitive strategies and marketing tactics of the participant firms. The strategies adopted may cause competition to focus on price, new and improved products, the adoption of new cost-saving technologies, service, promotion, guarantees, styling, function, economy of use, convenience, and so on—either singly or in various combinations. The behavioral outcome may range from a cooperative, live-and-let-live atmosphere to highly combative rivalry. Furthermore, the strategic patterns that give rise to competition which eliminates excess profits will tend to be different from those that drive firms to be more efficient. Strategic behavior which has the effect of weeding out ineffective or poorly performing firms will have a character that is discernible from the strategic competition which leads firms to increase sales so as to capture scale economies. At the same time, because what is the best strategy for firm A may depend partly on firm B's choice, and because B, in turn, may elect to fine-tune its strategy in light of A's strategic behavior and options, the optimal strategy for a given firm at a given time is not necessarily clear-cut and readily perceived. And except in the case of distressed firms in dire straits, no strategic choice is ever final. The sequence of move and countermove is never-ending, thus emphasizing the dynamic process aspects of competition.

Any stalemates or market equilibria, if they exist at all, are temporary, owing to the continuous stream of strategic opportunities and threats that emerge from the possibilities for product variation, cost-related technological changes, new buyer tastes and preferences, changing demographics and lifestyles, shifts in buying power, new product availability, and on and on. Apart from these market-related variables, periodic strategic changes can be expected in the host of complex institutional factors that mold a firm's strategy choices from the outside and the intrafirm considerations which shape corporate and competitive strategy from the inside.

All of these aspects, together with the time sequence of strategic moves and the information base underlying them, act to shape the specific features of the competitive behavior and the competitive pressures that develop in a particular market or industry. Initiatory moves can be expected from a variety of firms and for a variety of reasons. Very likely, some firms will be bolder and more aggressive than others.[8] The main thing is that from time to time there will be fresh strategic moves which so stir competitive forces

[7] *Ibid.*, p. 475.
[8] *Ibid.*, p. 474.

A CLASSIC CASE OF COMPETITIVE STRATEGY:
COCA-COLA VERSUS PEPSI-COLA

Historically, Coca-Cola has dominated the American soft-drink industry. Sales and profits have grown rapidly ever since Coke was first introduced. Until the 1950s there was really no second-place firm worth mentioning. Pepsi-Cola, Coca-Cola's nearest competior, was a relatively new drink that cost less to manufacture, but its taste was generally thought to be less unique and satisfying than Coke's. Pepsi's major selling point was that it offered more cola for the same price; Pepsi came in a 12-ounce bottle that sold for approximately the same price as Coke's famous $6\frac{1}{2}$-ounce bottle. Pepsi exploited this difference by advertising "twice as much for a nickle, too." Nonetheless, with its plain bottle and paper label (that often got dirty in transit), Pepsi was generally looked upon as second-class. To many it was "the poor man's drink."

When Alfred N. Steele came to the presidency of Pepsi-Cola, he recognized that the company's main hope for competitive vitality lay in transforming Pepsi into a first-class soft drink and in not being a cheap imitator of Coke. Steele assembled a two-phase grand offensive Coke. In the first phase, which lasted from 1950 to 1955, a determined effort was made to improve Pepsi's taste. The formula was desweetened. Greater quality control was established over local bottlers, who previously added varying amounts of carbonation to the syrup, with the result that Pepsi's taste varied from locale to locale. Pepsi's bottle and other corporate symbols were redesigned and unified. Following up on the product improvements, Pepsi launched an advertising campaign aimed at upgrading Pepsi's image. The ads featured attractive, well-dressed women and debonair men drinking Pepsi, against a background of high-income surroundings. Along with this went the advertising theme "the light refreshment," suggesting indirectly that Coke was "heavy." At the same time, Pepsi made the decision to take dead aim on the "take-home" segment of the soft-drink market in the first phase of its grand offensive. Coca-Cola was particularly strong in the "on-premise" segment (soda fountain sales, vending machines, and refrigerated sales). Pepsi felt that the rifle-shot approach, aimed where Coca-Cola was weakest, gave it the best chance for success. Thus, Pepsi massed its efforts at penetrating the market for grocery retail sales of soft drinks—where it already had a small foothold. The final aspect of Pepsi's phase-one offensive involved singling out 25 cities for special promotional efforts. In these "push" markets Pepsi added company funds to those of the local bottlers for advertising and promotion. The concentrated effort to win market share in these 25 cities was successful in increasing Pepsi's market share.

By 1955, Pepsi's phase-one programs had made enough headway to warrant beginning phase two of the grand offensive. It consisted of attempts to increase Pepsi's share of the "on-premise" market where Coke was so solidly entrenched. However, Pepsi limited its efforts to the vending machine and cold-bottle sales segments because the soda fountain segment showed signs of maturity and perhaps even decline. Pepsi introduced some new bottle sizes to go along with its standard 12-ounce bottle in an attempt to offer more convenience to customers in the take-home and cold-bottle market segments. Additionally, Pepsi offered financing to those bottlers who were willing to buy and install Pepsi vending machines and to begin to push this part of their business.

As Pepsi's phase two began to strike chords of success, Coke decided it was time to initiate some kind of response. Until the latter stages of Pepsi's grand offensive, Coke's attitude had been mostly "ho-hum." For the most part, Coke refused to acknowledge that Pepsi was a threat. Many of Coke's local bottlers had become well-to-do and complacent, owing to Coke's previous success, and were not accustomed to tough competition. Initially, Coke's response consisted of launching new advertising campaigns, using such themes as "the really refreshed" and "no wonder Coke refreshes best." Coke also introduced new bottle sizes. Both steps perked up Coke's sales.

In the early 1960s, Pepsi's rate of growth slowed, and Pepsi responded with two new advertising campaigns—"be sociable" and "think young." The latter was quite successful in tying Pepsi to the youth market, a segment which accounted for the highest per capita consumption of soft drinks. But the youth theme, by implication, also tended to mark Coke as an old-fashioned drink. Coke responded with its new advertising theme of "things go better with Coke."

Then competition, which in the past had revolved largely around taste, bottling, and advertising, moved to new arenas. The first concerned the no-deposit bottle and the use of aluminum and steel cans. Both companies found that it was critical to design their containers carefully and time their introduction astutely. For instance, it was discovered that the metal can affected the taste; it was also discovered by one soft-drink company that the aluminum can it was about to introduce was eaten through by its product within a few days.

The second competitive development concerned product innovation. Using the principle of surprise, Royal Crown Cola introduced what proved to be a major new product—the diet soft-drink. RC's Diet Cola was formulated without real sugar and was intended to appeal to the calorie-conscious segment of the market. Originally, this class of buyers was thought to constitute a small part of the soft-drink market, but it turned out that diet drinks had very broad appeal. Royal Crown's major success quickly forced both Coke and Pepsi to formulate their own dietetic soft drinks.

The third new competitive arena emerged when the soft-drink companies realized that a whole set of other good-tasting drinks could be formulated besides colas. Seven-Up's "un-cola" theme was so successful that Coke brought out its version of the un-cola—Sprite. Attempting to capitalize upon this development, Dr. Pepper sharply increased its advertising budget and market penetration efforts.

Although Coke has continued to retain its number one position in the industry, Pepsi has emerged with a much stronger second-place market share and the smaller firms—Royal Crown, Seven-Up, and Dr. Pepper—also have made inroads, all at Coke's expense.

Sources: Alvin Toffler, "The Competition that Refreshes," *Fortune*, (May 1961); "Things Go Better With Coke," *Sales Management* (March 5, 1965), pp. 28ff.; and Philip Kotler, *Marketing Management: Analysis, Planning, and Control*, 2nd ed. (Englewood Cliffs, N.J.: Prentice-Hall, Inc., 1972), pp. 254–257.

as to demand reactions and responses from other firms in the market; the source of these fresh moves is not overly crucial to the effectiveness of rivalrous competition (although it may well be important to the well-being and performance of specific firms). The defensive responses that follow aggressive moves will not only vary as to time lag, but their character will also tend to differ according to what firm has undertaken the new offensive and whether it consists of a new promotional campaign, introduction of a new product or product variation, a new channel of distribution, or an expansive move toward a new form of horizontal or vertical integration. However, the strategic process will not generally be so active that the market becomes unstable and chaotic—nor should it be.[9] Short intervals of stabilized product offerings may surface so as to permit firms to better gauge trends and opportunities. In fact, a rapid-fire pattern of fresh moves may serve more to defeat effective competition than it does to promote it because of the confusion and uncertainty which it generates among both buyers and sellers.

A Formal Model of Competition as a Strategic Process?

If one accepts the characterization of competition as a strategic process, it follows quickly from the foregoing discussion that there can be no neat, determinate model to predict how the process of rivalrous competition does or will unfold in a given market. Any static equilibrium results of specific

[9] *Ibid.*, p. 475. See also Schumpeter, *Capitalism, Socialism, and Democracy*, pp. 92–96.

strategy sets are just snapshots of an ongoing process whereby markets and competition affect firms' strategies and firms' strategies affect markets and competition. New competitive pressures will regularly be created by the dynamics of change on the demand side of the market and by strategic moves and countermoves on the supply side. Disequilibrium conditions thus are the norm, not the exception—an outcome that justifies why competition should be viewed as a strategic *process* and why the time frame for evaluating strategic behavior and the strength of competitive pressures needs to be lengthy enough to allow an assessment of the strategic conduct of firms and the resulting impacts on price and profitability trends, product performance, quality improvements, new product innovation, and technological change.

OTHER MAJOR COMPETITIVE FORCES

While the competitive strategies of rival firms tend to be the dominant consideration in determining how intense competition is in a particular product market, other major competitive forces can also be at work. These include (1) whether the participant firms are confronted with competitive threats from closely related substitute products of firms in other industries, (2) the likelihood of entry of new competitors, (3) the economic power of suppliers, and (4) the economic power of customers.[10]

The Competitive Force of Substitute Products

All firms selling a particular product are, in a broad sense, in competition with firms producing related substitutes. Steel producers are in competition with aluminum producers—in the case of some customers and end uses. The producers of fiberglass insulation are in competition with the producers of styrofoam, rock wool, and cellulose insulation. Sugar producers are in competition with firms that have commenced large-scale commercialization of high-fructose corn syrup.

The competitive force of closely related substitute products affects sellers in several ways. First, the price and availability of acceptable substitutes for good X places a ceiling on the prices that producers of good X can charge; at the same time, the ceiling price places a limit on the profit potential for good X.[11] Second, unless the sellers of good X can upgrade quality, reduce prices through cost reduction, or otherwise differentiate their product from its substitutes, they risk a low growth rate in sales and profits, owing to the inroads that substitutes may make. The strength of the competition provided by substitutes is suggested by the cross elasticity of demand between the unit sales of good X and the selling prices of the substitute products.

---

[10]Michael E. Porter, "How Competitive Forces Shape Strategy," *Harvard Business Review*, Vol. 57, No. 2 (March–April 1979), p. 141.

[11]*Ibid.*, p. 142.

The more sensitive the sales of X are to changes in the prices of substitutes, the stronger is the competitive influence of the substitutes.

As a rule, the lower the price and the higher the quality and performance of substitutes, the more intense are the competitive pressures posed by substitute products. One very telling indicator of the strength of competition emanating from the producers of substitutes is their growth rate in sales; other indicators are their plans for expansion of capacity and the profits they are earning.

The Potential for New Entry

New entrants to a market bring new production capacity, the desire to establish a market niche and a viable market share, and often substantial resources with which to compete.[12] The entry of strong firms can cause a major market shake-up, particularly in the case of companies that diversify through acquisition into new products and markets (Philip Morris's acquisition of Miller beer and Seven-Up).

Just how serious the competitive threat of entry is into a particular market depends on two classes of factors: *barriers to entry* and the *expected reaction of existing firms to new entry*. A barrier to entry exists whenever the nature of the market for the product and/or the economics of the business puts a potential entrant at a price/cost disadvantage relative to its competitors. There are several major sources of entry barriers:

1. *Economies of scale*. The presence of important scale economies deters entry because it forces the potential entrant to commit to entering on a large-scale basis (a costly and perhaps risky move) or else to accept a cost disadvantage (and consequently, lower profitability). Large-scale entry could result in chronic overcapacity in the industry and/or it could so threaten the market shares of existing firms that they are pushed into aggressive competitive retaliation (in the form of price cuts, increased advertising and sales promotion, and similar steps) so as to maintain their position; either way, the entrant's outlook is for lower profits. Scale economies may be encountered not just in production, but in research, advertising, selling, financing, in-house servicing of products, and distribution as well.

2. *Brand preferences and customer loyalty*. When the products of rival sellers are differentiated, buyers usually have some degree of preference and loyalties to existing brands. This means that a potential entrant must be prepared to spend enough money on advertising and sales promotion to overcome customer loyalties and build its own clientele. Substantial time, as well as money, can be involved. Not only may a new entrant have to budget more funds for marketing than will existing firms (which gives existing firms a cost advantage), but also the capital invested in establishing a new brand (unlike the capital invested in facilities and equipment) has no resale or recoverable value, which makes such expenditures a riskier "investment." In addition, product differentiation can entail costs to buyers of switching brands, in which case the new entrant must persuade buyers that the changeover or switching costs are worth incurring; this may require lower prices or better quality-service-performance—again leading to lower profit expectations.

[12]*Ibid.*, p. 138.

3. *Capital requirements.* The larger the total dollar investment needed to enter the market successfully, the more limited is the pool of potential entrants. The most obvious capital requirements are associated with manufacturing plant and equipment, working capital to finance inventories, offering credit to customers, establishing a clientele, and bearing startup losses.

4. *Cost disadvantages independent of size.* Existing firms may have cost advantages not available to potential entrants, regardless of the entrant's size. These advantages relate to access to the best and cheapest raw materials, possession of patents and unique technological know-how, the effects of the learning curve and the experience curve, having purchased fixed assets at preinflation prices, favorable locations, and availability of financial capital at lower costs.

5. *Access to distribution channels.* Where a product is distributed through established market channels, a potential entrant may face the barrier of gaining adequate distribution access. Some distributors may be reluctant to take on a product that lacks buyer recognition. The more limited the number of wholesale and retail outlets and the more that existing producers have these tied up, the tougher entry will be. Potential entrants, to overcome this barrier, may have to lure distribution access by offering better margins to dealers and distributors or by giving advertising allowances and other promotional incentives, with the result that the potential entrant's profits may be squeezed unless and until its product gains market acceptance.

6. *Government actions and policies.* Government agencies can limit or even bar entry by instituting controls over licenses and permits. Regulated industries such as trucking, radio and television stations, liquor retailing, and railroads all feature government-controlled entry. Entry can also be restricted, and certainly made more expensive, by government safety regulations and environmental pollution standards.

Even if a potential entrant is willing to tackle the problems of entry barriers, it may be dissuaded by its expectations about how existing firms will react to new entry.[13] Will incumbent firms "move over" grudgingly and let a new entrant take a viable share of the market, or will they launch a vigorous, "survival of the fittest" competitive battle for market position—including price cuts, increased advertising, product improvements, and whatever else is calculated to give a new entrant (as well as other rivals) a hard time? A firm is likely to have second thoughts about entry:

1. When incumbent firms have previously been aggressive in defending their market positions against entry.

2. When incumbent firms possess substantial financial resources with which to defend against new entry.

3. When incumbent firms are in a position to use leverage with distributors and customers to keep their business.

4. When incumbent firms are able and willing to cut prices to preserve their market shares.

5. When product demand is expanding slowly, thus limiting the market's ability to absorb and accommodate the new entrant without adversely affecting the profit performance of all the participant firms.

6. When it is more costly for existing firms to leave the market than to fight to the death (because the costs of exit are very high, owing to heavy investment in

[13]*Ibid.*, p. 140.

specialized technology and equipment, union agreements which contain high severance costs, or important shared relationships with other products).

Naturally, a potential entrant can only guess about how incumbent firms will react to entry. Reactions to past entry are one obvious indication; so is how existing firms behave competitively toward each other. Sometimes the "personality" of rival firms can provide clues to their probable reaction to entry; relevant personality indicators include (1) the propensity a firm may exhibit to be aggressive or conservative, a leader or a follower; (2) the backgrounds and experiences of their executives; (3) the priority which rival firms have historically given to research and development, advertising, technology, and similar key competitive variables; and (4) the assumptions and perceptions which the managements of rival firms seem to have about themselves and their business, as revealed by speeches and interviews, the kinds of people they recruit, and how they tend to reward their executives.

One additional point needs to be made about the threat of entry as a competitive force: the threat of entry changes as economic and market conditions change. For example, the expiration of a key patent can greatly increase the threat of entry. Technological discovery can create such a scale economy as to virtually bar new entry. The decisions of incumbent firms to increase advertising or strengthen distributor-dealer relations or step up R&D or improve product quality can result in the erection of higher roadblocks to entry. Dramatic price increases which also produce sharply higher profits can enhance the attractiveness and probability or new entry.

The Economic Power of Suppliers

The competitive impact which suppliers can have upon an industry is chiefly a function of how significant the input they supply is to the buyer.[14] When the input of a particular group of suppliers makes up a sizable proportion of total costs, is crucial to the buyer's production process, or significantly affects the quality of the industry's product, the greater is the suppliers' *potential* bargaining power and influence over firms in the buying industry. The extent to which this potential impact is realized depends upon a number of factors; in general, a group of supplier firms is more powerful:

1. When the input is, in one way or another, important to the buyer.
2. When the supplier group is dominated by a few large firms that are not confronted with intensely competitive conditions.
3. When suppliers' respective products are differentiated to such an extent that it is difficult or costly for buyers to switch from one supplier to another.
4. When the buying firms are *not* important customers of the suppliers. In such instances, suppliers are not constrained by the fact that their own well-being is tied to the industry they are supplying; hence, they have no big incentive to protect the customer industry via reasonable prices, improved quality, or new products which might well enhance the buying industry's sales and profits.

[14]*Ibid.*, p. 140.

5. When the suppliers of an input do *not* have to compete with the substitute inputs of suppliers in other industries. (For instance, the power of the suppliers of glass bottles to the soft-drink bottlers is checked by the ability of the soft-drink firms to use aluminum cans and plastic bottles.)

6. When one or more suppliers pose a credible threat of forward integration into the business of the buyer industry (attracted, perhaps, by the prospect of higher profits than it can earn in its own market).

7. When the buying firms display no inclination toward backward integration into the suppliers' business.

The power of suppliers can be an important economic factor in the marketplace because of the impact they can have on customer profits. Powerful suppliers can squeeze the profits of a customer industry through price increases which the latter is unable to pass on fully to its own customers. They can also jeopardize a buyer's profits through reductions in the quality of the inputs—reductions that enhance their own profits at the expense of the buyer's profits.

The Economic Power of Customers

Just as powerful suppliers can exert a competitive influence over an industry, so can powerful customers.[15] The relative power of customers tends to be greater:

1. When buyers are large and few in number and when they purchase in large quantities. Often large customers are successful in using their volume-buying leverage to obtain important price concessions and other favorable terms and conditions of sale.

2. When buyers' purchases are a sizable percentage of the selling industry's total sales.

3. When the supplying industry is comprised of large numbers of relatively small sellers.

4. When the item being purchased is sufficiently standardized among sellers that not only can buyers find alternative sellers but also they can switch suppliers at virtually zero cost.

5. When buyers pose a credible threat of backward integration, being attracted by the prospects of earning greater profits or by the benefits of reliable prices and reliable delivery.

6. When sellers pose little threat of forward integration into the product market of buyers.

7. When the item being bought is *not* an important input.

8. When it is economically feasible for buyers to follow the practice of purchasing the input from several suppliers rather than one.

9. When the product/service being bought does not save the buyer money.

A firm can enhance its profitability and market standing by seeking out suppliers and customers who are in a comparatively weak position to exercise

[15]*Ibid.*, pp. 140–141.

adverse power. Especially is this feasible in the case of selecting the customer segments to target one's marketing efforts.[16] Rarely do all buyer segments enjoy equal bargaining power, and some may be more price- or quality- or service-sensitive than others. An example is the automobile tire industry, where the major tire manufacturers confront, on the one hand, very significant customer power in selling original equipment tires to the automobile manufacturers and, on the other hand, find themselves in position to exercise the upper hand when selling replacement tires to individual car owners through their own networks of retail stores. Also, Crown Cork and Seal Co. has been very successful in concentrating its efforts on producing cans for two types of buyers—those who use aerosol cans and those who require cans for products with unique characteristics.

A COLLECTIVE PICTURE OF COMPETITIVE FORCES

The discussion to this point has identified five major determinants of the strength of competitive forces in the marketplace: (1) the strategic rivalry among firms producing a particular item, (2) the ease with which buyers can switch to closely related substitute items having much the same functional character, (3) threats of entry of new competitors, (4) the economic power exercisable by suppliers, and (5) the economic power that customers can apply. Figure 14-1 offers a visual portrayal of these five determinants.

The collective impact of these forces determines the intensity of competition in a given market and, ultimately, the profits that the participating firms will be able to earn. As a rule, the more intense is competition, the lower the collective profitability of participant firms. From a profit standpoint, the sternest and most vigorous sort of competition is where the long-term prospects are for no more than a normal profit—the same result as obtained under perfect competition. On the other hand, when a market offers the prospect of superior profit performance, the inference is that competitive forces are not as strong, for whatever reason.

One way for a firm to assess what sort of competitive strategy it ought to employ in a given market is to try to position itself (1) to defend and insulate itself as much as possible from the forces of competition and (2) to influence the direction of competition in its favor by choosing a trend-setting and pace-setting strategy. Doing this requires insightful understanding of what the competitive pressures are and where they are coming from. It also requires careful evaluation of a firm's competitive strengths and weaknesses, market opportunities and threats, and areas where a creative strategy can produce a superior payoff.[17] Very likely, different firms will arrive at different evaluations as to what the "best" competitive strategy is—even though they may be in substantial agreement on what the relevant competi-

[16]*Ibid.*, p. 141.
[17]*Ibid.*, p. 138.

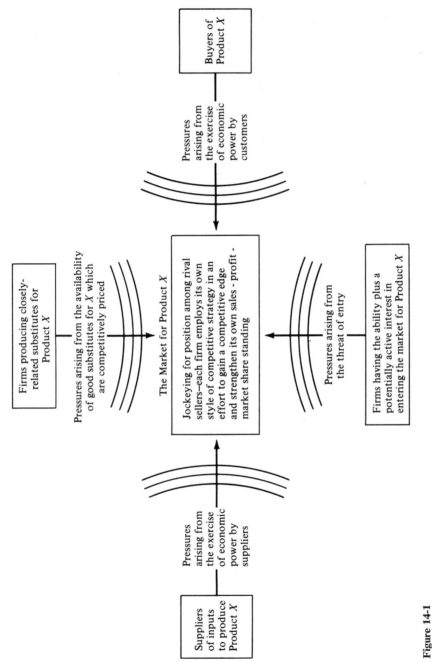

Figure 14-1
How the forces of competition join together and interact

tive forces are. This accounts partly why firms in a given market generally do not follow the same strategy and thus do not have the same market position.

FACTORS AFFECTING THE INTENSITY OF COMPETITION

Having identified the major competitive forces, we are in position to pinpoint what specific features relative to these forces cause competition to be more or less intense.[18] In general, any market characteristic that affects strategic rivalry, barriers to entry or exit, the economic power of buyers or sellers, and the price and availability of closely related substitutes affects the vigor of competition. But while there can be a wide range of specific characteristics directly influencing how strong competition will be, certain ones seem to crop up again and again. These are worth enumerating.

Competition tends to increase as the number of rival firms increases and as these firms become more equal in size and capability. The number of firms is important because, up to some point, more firms increase the probability for fresh, creative strategic initiatives and because greater numbers reduce the effects of any one firm's actions upon the others, thereby reducing somewhat the probability of direct retaliation. Also, economists have a strong bias toward more firms because this gives buyers more choice among sellers and thus reduces the likelihood of any one firm being able to rig the market to its own advantage. When rival firms are more equal in size and capability, the chances are better that the firms can compete on a fairly even footing, a feature that makes it harder for one or two firms to "win" the competitive battle and emerge as dominant firms in a position to exercise leadership and some degree of market control.

Market rivalry is usually stronger when demand for the product is growing slowly. In a rapidly expanding market, rivalry is weakened by the fact that there is enough business for everybody. Indeed, it may take all of a firm's financial and managerial resources just to keep abreast of market growth, much less devoting efforts to steal away the customers of its rivals. But when growth slows, expansion-minded firms tend to ignite a battle for market share that often results in a shakeout of the weak and less efficient firms. Market share competition can be counted upon to product fresh strategic moves and countermoves directly aimed at taking customers away from rival firms.[19]

[18]This section draws upon Porter, "How Competitive Forces Shape Strategy," pp. 142–143.

[19]In average growth markets, aggressive firms may move to build new plant capacity *ahead* of the time it will be needed so as to discourage others from expansion and thereby capture a greater market share. Should rivals catch on to this tactic and decide to retaliate with capacity additions of their own, the outcome can be a vigorous competitive struggle in which overall industry profitability is reduced. Such situations usually occur in oligopolistic markets where increased market share is a key to increased profits.

*Competition is more intense when rival firms are tempted to use price
cuts or other marketing tactics to boost unit volume.* Whenever fixed costs are
high and marginal costs are low, firms are under strong economic pressure
to produce at or very near full capacity. Hence, if market demand weakens
and capacity utilization begins to fall off, rival firms frequently resort to
secret price concessions, special discounts, rebates, and other sales-increasing
tactics. A similar situation arises when a product is perishable or seasonal
or is costly or difficult to store or hold in inventory. It can also occur if an
industry is characterized by long lead times in constructing new plant capacity
or by scale economies which dictate that additions to capacity be made in
large increments or by persistent ups and downs in market demand that
periodically give rise to excess capacity throughout the industry.

*Competition is stronger when the products/services of rival firms are not
so strongly differentiated that buyers become locked in by the high costs of
switching from one brand to another.* Product differentiation per se is not a
deterrent to competition; indeed, it has the capacity for enlivening rivalry
by forcing firms to seek creative new ways of improving their price-quality-
service-performance offering. The strategic moves of one firm to differentiate
its product may well require important countermoves from rival firms. However, when the nature of product differentiation begins to result in layers of
insulation from rivalry—as occurs when switching becomes costly or difficult,
then a firm may gain protection from raids on its customers by its rivals.
Should this occur, competitive intensity is obviously lessened.

*Market rivalry increases in proportion to the size of the payoff from
a successful strategic move.* The essential idea here is that the greater the
potential reward, the more likely some firm will give in to the temptation
of a particular strategic move. How big the strategic payoff is varies partly
with the speed of retaliation. When competitors can be expected to respond
slowly (or maybe even not at all), the initiator of a fresh competitive strategy
can reap the benefits in the intervening period and perhaps gain a lead-time
advantage that is not easily surmounted; the greater the chance this will
occur, the greater will the potential benefits justify the risk of eventual retaliation. Firms which have shrewdly assessed the "personality" of each rival
firm and which also understand the economics of their rivals' business are
in the best position to correctly predict how and when rivals may respond to
a given strategic move; such knowledge is advantageous in assessing the
potential payoffs of strategic alternatives.[20]

*Market rivalry tends to be more vigorous when it costs more to get out
of a business than to stay in and compete.* The higher are exit barriers (and
thus the more costly it is to abandon a market), the stronger the incentive

[20]It is worth noting here that it is important for a firm to understand the reasons
underlying any shifts in the competitive strategies of rival firms. Unless a firm correctly
perceives what the intentions of its competitors are, it is less able to develop appropriate
moves and countermoves of its own. When rival firms change their competitive strategy,
management is thus obliged to ask: What are they up to, why are they doing this, and what
do they expect to accomplish? Is this an aggressive move or is it something we should all
be doing? The answers are almost certain to be relevant in figuring out the firm's own
strategic response.

for firms to remain and compete as best they can, even though they may be earning low profits or even incurring a loss. The point here is that the strength and character of competition is affected by factors that determine how the short-run costs of exit stack up against the long-term costs of staying in and trying to become a more successful competitor.

Competition becomes more volatile and unpredictable the more diverse that rival firms are in terms of their strategies, their personalities, their corporate priorities, their resources, and their countries of origin. When rival firms differ on how to compete (whether this be due to different perceptions about the market or different corporate objectives and personalities), their strategies are likely to produce a head-on clash in the marketplace. Moreover, a diverse range of views and approaches enhances the probability that one or more firms will behave as "mavericks" and employ strategies that produce more market flux and uncertainty than would otherwise occur. In such an environment, it is difficult for firms to predict rivals' behavior accurately; the effects of signaling are uncertain; and the comfortable atmosphere of a "fraternity of insiders" does not prevail. Indeed, the mere presence of "outsiders" or mavericks—particularly foreign firms or new entrants—who either do not understand or else deliberately ignore conventional methods of competing has considerable potential for creating "a whole new ballgame."

At the same time, firms tend to gear their competitive strategies and counterstrategies in part to their own specific internal priorities, strengths, weaknesses, and financial capabilities; the more these factors are divergent from rival to rival, the more likely that the "right" strategy for one firm is the "wrong" strategy for another. Such diversity is consistent with active competition because it stimulates fine-tuning and countermoves as buyer response to one firm's strategy is more favorable than to another's. The only exception arises when rival firms pursue individual strategies which are aimed at catering to different types of buyers; then each firm moves deliberately to carve out its own market niche and build up its own customer following in ways that do not directly threaten or overlap with the market segments of its rival. To the extent that rival firms pursue market segmentation strategies and to the extent each firm limits its competitive energies to only one or a few of these segments, competition in any one market segment may well be weaker than is suggested by the total number of firms in the overall market.

SUMMARY AND CONCLUSIONS

One of the most useful insights into the real world of competition is that the competitive mechanism is fundamentally a strategic process. At the center of the market struggle among rival firms is an ongoing and somewhat unpredictable sequence of strategic moves and countermoves. From a firm's standpoint, the name of the game is to outmaneuver rival firms and capture a market position that not only is profitable but is also relatively well insulated from counterattack.

However, the jockeying for position that goes on among rival firms is just one indicator of the nature and strength of competition, albeit the most important one. Other major competitive forces include (1) threats of entry of new competitors, (2) pressures created by the availability of closely related substitutes which are attractively priced, and (3) the economic power that can be wielded by both suppliers and customers.

More specific variables which affect the intensity of competition in a given market include (1) how many firms compete against one another and whether they compete on a fairly equal footing relative to size, costs, and resources; (2) the rate of growth in market demand; (3) how strongly firms are tempted to use price cuts or other marketing tactics to try to boost unit volume; (4) whether the products of rival sellers are so differentiated that buyers become locked in by the costs of switching from one brand to another; (5) how much a firm stands to gain (relative to the risk involved) if it attempts a new strategic move; (6) whether it costs more to get out of a market than to remain and compete; and (7) how diverse rival firms are in terms of their strategies, personalities, priorities, resource capabilities, and countries of origin.

SUGGESTED READINGS

CASE, J. H., *Economics and the Competitive Process* (New York: New York University Press, 1979).

CAVES, R. E., "Industrial Organization, Corporate Strategy and Structure," *Journal of Economic Literature*, Vol. 18, No. 1 (March 1980), pp. 64–92.

CLARK, J. M., *Competition as a Dynamic Process* (Washington, D.C.: The Brookings Institution, 1961).

COMANOR, W. S., AND T. A. WILSON, "The Effect of Advertising on Competition: A Survey," *The Journal of Economic Literature*, Vol. 17, No. 2 (June 1979), pp. 453–477.

GALBRAITH, J. K., *American Capitalism: The Theory of Countervailing Power* (Boston: Houghton Mifflin Company, 1951), Chapter 9.

MACHLUP, F., *The Economics of Sellers' Competition* (Baltimore: The Johns Hopkins Press, 1952).

NEEDHAM, D., *The Economics of Industrial Structure: Conduct and Performance* (New York: St. Martin's Press, 1978).

PORTER, M. E., "How Competitive Forces Shape Strategy," *Harvard Business Review*, Vol. 57, No. 2 (March–April 1979), pp. 137–145.

THOMPSON, A. A., "Competition as a Strategic Process." *Antitrust Bulletin*, (forthcoming).

QUESTIONS FOR DISCUSSION

1. In which type of market structure would you expect competition to be more vigorous—monopolistic competition or oligopoly? Why?

2. Is the most important determinant of the strength of competition the number of rival firms in the market? Why or why not?
3. Why is it appropriate to view competition as a strategic process?
4. Draw up a list of all those factors and characteristics which promote intense competition.
5. What is the logic underlying the statement that "whenever fixed costs are high and marginal costs are low, firms are under strong economic pressure to produce at or very near full capacity?"

FIFTEEN BUSINESS PRICING PRACTICES AND MULTIPLE-GOAL MODELS

The managers of business enterprises, although very profit-conscious, are not always inclined to base their decisions solely upon profit criteria. As we saw in Chapter 9, other goals tend to creep into business decision-making, especially when profits reach acceptable levels and a firm's long-term profitability does not appear to be in jeopardy. And even where profit is a prime consideration, it does not appear that corporate prices are keyed to the output where $MC = MR$; other factors enter into play. In this chapter we shall look briefly at pricing techniques and pricing objectives where short-run profit maximization is not the overriding criterion. Then we shall explore some of the more prominent multiple-goal models of contemporary business behavior. In all these models, business decisions and strategies are predicated upon a hierarchy of goals. Particular attention will be given to longer-run sales and growth goals and how these are conditioned by new product development, technological change, and competitive pressures.

BUSINESS PRICING PRACTICES

Although economists traditionally view price as *the* dominant competitive variable, in practice it is not clear that pricing receives the greatest amount of attention. Pricing is a major problem in essentially only four types of situations: (1) when a firm must set a price for the first time, as occurs when it introduces a new product, moves into a new market, or regularly enters competitive sealed bids on contract work; (2) when market or competitive circumstances prompt a firm to consider initiating a price change; (3) when one or more rival firms initiate a price change and some response is required; and (4) when the firm produces two or more products having interrelated demands and/or costs, thus posing problems of optimal price coordination. These situations are, of course, not rare, but neither are they so pervasive as to take up the bulk of management's time.

Firms have developed a wide variety of approaches and techniques for solving pricing problems. Interestingly enough, while profit is unquestionably a major concern in the pricing decision, the evidence is not strong that managerial estimates of the relationship between *MR* and *MC* actually form the basis for price selection.[1]

Pricing to Earn a Target Rate of Return

Studies of business pricing practices indicate a widespread use of target return pricing methods. A *target return price* is a price designed to yield the firm a predetermined profit from the sale of specific products or product groups. The desired profit is typically based upon dollar sales (total revenue) or upon some measure of invested capital and may be expressed either as a percentage rate or as a dollar amount. For example, the desired profit target may be stated as a profit on sales of 5%, a profit return equal to 10% of total assets, a profit return equal to 15% of net worth (stockholders' equity), a profit equal to *X* dollars per share of common stock, or as simply a specific dollar figure. The size of the profit target tends to hinge upon such considerations as (1) industry custom, (2) competitive pressures, (3) what managers believe to be a "fair" or "reasonable" return given the associated business risk, (4) a desire to equal or better the firm's recent profit performance, (5) a desire to stabilize industry prices, (6) whether the firm's product is new or a unique specialty item, and (7) the firm's related goals of sales, market share, and growth. Specific profit targets tend to differ among industries and firms, reflecting differing degrees of competition and differing priorities among alternative goals. Normally, however, *after-tax* profit targets tend to fall within a range of 5 to 10% of sales and 10 to 20% of invested capital.

The mechanics of target return pricing may be set forth briefly in terms of two examples—the first illustrating pricing to achieve a target return on investment and the second illustrating what is commonly referred to as cost-plus pricing.

[1]The literature on the subject is immense. Among the more definitive studies are R. L. Hall and Charles J. Hitch, "Price Theory and Business Behavior," *Oxford Economic Papers*, Vol. 2. (May 1939), pp. 12–45; A. D. H. Kaplan, J. B. Dirlam, and R. F. Lanzilotti, *Pricing in Big Business* (Washington, D.C.: The Brookings Institution, 1958), Chapter 2; Burnard H. Sord and Glenn A. Welsch, *Business Budgeting* (New York: Controllership Foundation, 1958), pp. 88–89 and 148; James H. Miller, "A Glimpse at Practice in Calculating and Using Return on Investment," *N.A.A. Bulletin* (June 1969), p. 73; W. W. Haynes, "Pricing Practices in Small Firms," *Southern Economic Journal*, Vol. 30, No. 4 (April 1964), pp. 315–324.

482

*Business
Pricing
Practices and
Multiple-Goal
Models*

1. Assume that a firm has $100 million invested in the production of a particular product and desires to earn a long-run average annual return of 20% before taxes on its investment. This, of course, translates into an annual profit target of $20 million. The initial step is to determine average total cost at some "normal" output rate (often referred to as the standard volume). Usually, the normal output rate is arbitrarily pegged somewhere between two-thirds and four-fifths of the capacity rate, instead of being related to the firm's actual operating rate. Many firms base their normal output rate upon what they believe to be their long-run rate of plant utilization. Suppose *ATC* is estimated to be $50 at the normal output rate of 2 million units. Since the firm wishes a total profit of $20 million on sales of 2 million units, profit per unit must average $10. The target price is then calculated by adding the necessary profit margin of $10 to the projected average total cost of $50 at the normal output rate, giving a price of $60. The target price serves as the initial basis for the firm's price decision; it may be adjusted upward or downward according to prevailing business conditions, actual or potential competition, long-run strategic objectives, and other relevant factors of the moment. Once the target price is chosen, the firm sells whatever amount is then demanded at the target price.

2. *Cost-plus pricing* is a widely used procedure whereby price is calculated by adding a predetermined percentage markup to the estimated unit cost of the product. To determine unit cost, the firm first computes the costs of labor, raw materials, and other variable inputs to get an estimate of *AVC*; to this is added the projected *AFC* at the "normal" operating rate (or standard volume). To illustrate, suppose that the firm is producing a product under conditions of constant returns to variable input such that $MC = AVC = \$30$. Further suppose that 75% of capacity is viewed as the normal operating rate, and at this output rate *AFC* is estimated to be $15. Average total cost is therefore $45 at the normal output rate. To this figure is added a markup of 5, 10, 20, 50, or whatever percent is required to achieve the firm's target profit. The size of the markup frequently reflects what managers believe is an "equitable relation to cost." If the firm desires a 10% return on sales, it should add a margin of $5 to its unit cost estimate of $45 to give a selling price of $50, which in percentage terms is equivalent to a markup slightly in excess of 11% over cost. If the firm desires a 25% return on sales, it should add a margin of $15 to its $45 unit cost to give a price of $60— a percentage markup of $33\frac{1}{3}$% over cost. As with pricing to achieve a target return on investment, cost-plus prices are subject to modification by competitive conditions and other pertinent considerations.

There are numerous variations of these two approaches to pricing. Cost estimates may be based upon "normal" operating rates, forecasted costs, or costs for the most recent accounting period. The amount of the "plus" or the target profit may be based upon either short-run or long-run considerations; it may be fixed for all products of the firm or variable among products; it may be computed as a percentage of costs, invested capital, or sales. Normally, the specific "formula" is keyed to long-standing industry practices, competitive conditions, price-cost-volume relationships, capital investment requirements, and the like. It is not uncommon for multiproduct firms to have different profit targets and to use different pricing formulas for different products, depending on price elasticity considerations, competitive pressures, whether the item carries a name brand or a private label, the intricacy and originality of the product and its design, and the estimate of the product's economic worth and utility to the customer. For example, in the retail goods industry where *variable markup pricing* (a cost-plus hybrid) is common, the markups *over cost* have been reported as 67% for cosmetics, 30 to 35% for household appliances, 38% for cameras, 50% for books (though the markup is usually 25% for college textbooks), 85% for costume jewelry, 25% for tobacco products, 80 to 125% for furniture, from 15 to 87% for frozen foods, and 100% for light fixtures and cabinet hardware.[2]

Another common use of target return pricing is found in corporate strategies for new product development and product innovation.[3] In contemplating the introduction of a new product or the revamping of an existing product, a typical procedure is for the firm first to identify a target selling price using such criteria as the prices of similar products, competitor's prices, and the estimated performance value to the customer. Product design and planning then proceeds toward producing at a cost that fits within the target market price and at the same time allows a margin of profit sufficient to yield the firm's target rate of return. Engineering and production personnel are assigned the task of designing a product which will conform as closely as possible to the targeted unit cost, price, and profit margin. Hence, the firm, in developing and pricing new products, starts from established or preconceived prices and works backward to see whether it can profitably offer the product at or below competitive prices. Failing this, the firm may pursue the question of whether higher costs can be justified by a product that on comparative performance can command a somewhat higher price than the ruling price average and still yield the desired target return. The attempt to design a product within the target cost-price-profit figures is sometimes successful and sometimes unsuccessful. In the unsuccessful instances whether the go-ahead is given depends on management's estimate of the nature of the product in its overall product line. If the product is one which strongly complements or creates a substantial demand for other of the firm's products, the firm may well decide to produce the item regardless of the estimated profits.

Attributes of Target Return Pricing. In practice, both pricing to achieve a target return on investment and cost-plus pricing offer relatively simple and expedient methods of price determination as well as a demonstrated ability to yield "adequate," "fair," or "reasonable" profits. The profitability of the two methods is evidenced by the avowed use of some sort of target return pricing by such "blue-chip" firms as Alcoa, DuPont, Exxon, General Electric, General Foods, General Motors, International Harvester, Johns-Manville, Union Carbide, and U.S. Steel.[4]

Once the target price is chosen, the usual procedure is for the firm to stick by its price (barring major changes in market conditions) and sell whatever amounts of output that customers are willing to buy at the target price.

[2]See, for instance, Lee E. Preston, *Profits, Competition and Rules of Thumb in Retail Food Pricing* (Berkeley: University of California Institute of Business and Economic Research, 1963), p. 31, and *Departmental Merchandising and Operating Results of 1966* (New York: National Retail Merchants Association, 1963), pp. 16, 28.

[3]An excellently documented example of International Harvester's use of this strategy is found in Kaplan, Dirlam, and Lanzilotti, *Pricing in Big Business*, pp. 69–79.

[4]R. F. Lanzilotti, "Pricing Objectives in Large Companies," *American Economic Review*, Vol. 48, No. 5 (December 1958), pp. 921–940.

484

*Business
Pricing
Practices and
Multiple-Goal
Models*

The target return price is therefore a fairly stable price—an attribute that highly recommends itself to oligopoly situations where infrequent price changes are a standard feature. This may partly explain the popularity of target return pricing among corporate oligopolists. However, target return pricing does have the effect of causing wide swings in profits when economic conditions turn up or down; on a year-to-year basis, actual profits may thus turn out to be either higher or lower than the target profit rate. Suppose, for example, that a firm has a short-run average total cost curve as illustrated in Fig. 15-1; the target price is P dollars, the "normal" operating rate is 70% of capacity, the target profit margin is $P - ATC_{70\%}$, and the target amount of total profit is equal to the shaded area. If in a particular year demand is especially strong and actual output corresponds to 90% of capacity, then total profits will be pushed up well above the targeted level. Two reasons can account for this. First, the firm's actual sales of output will exceed the rate required to achieve the profit target. Second, unit costs at 90% of capacity may be lower than at 70% of capacity because of the lower average fixed costs associated with higher production rates. The realized profit margin on each unit sold of $P - ATC_{90\%}$ may therefore be larger than the margin of $P - ATC_{70\%}$ needed to reach the target. The combined effect of wider profit margins and above-normal sales is a realized profit which may be considerably in excess of the target rate of return, as shown in Fig. 15-1. On the other hand, if demand for the firm's product is weak and actual sales of output amount to only 50% of capacity instead of the "normal" 70%, then the profit target will

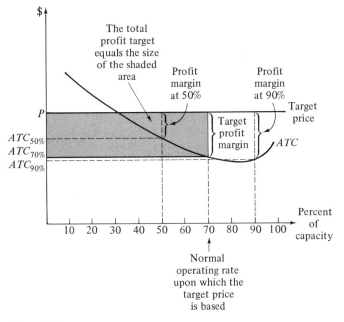

Figure 15-1
Effects of demand fluctuations upon achieving the target rate of return

in all probability not be achieved. At production rates below the normal 70% figure, average fixed costs are sure to be higher, and average variable costs may be higher if the production process cannot be operated efficiently at less than normal rates. With average total cost at 50% of capacity exceeding that at 70%, the realized profit margin of $P - ATC_{50\%}$ will be narrower than the targeted margin of $P - ATC_{70\%}$. This, together with lower sales, produces total profits well below the target rate of return (see Fig. 15-1).

A firm using target pricing is well aware that profits in any given year may not correspond to the profit target because actual sales will almost certainly deviate to some extent from the output rate on which the target price is based. The target profit rate is something the firm hopes to achieve as a long-run average rather than in any particular year. This is apparent from the fact that the target price is predicated upon a normal rate of production instead of the forecasted sales volume for the upcoming period.

It follows from the above discussion that target return pricing is not a strategy for maximizing profits.[5] This is easily demonstrated. Since the target return price is keyed to the firm's normal operating rate (or standard volume), the target return price and the profit-maximizing price will coincide if and only if the normal operating rate just happens to correspond to the output rate where marginal cost equals marginal revenue. Certainly, there is no reason to expect this to occur—except by mere circumstance and coincidence.

Actually, the concept of target return pricing exemplifies a behavior pattern closely approximating satisficing. The target rate of return, according to the evidence available, tends to be based upon managerial concepts of what is an "equitable" or "reasonable" or "satisfactory" rate of return, given the degrees of risk and uncertainty involved. Few managers believe or, more accurately perhaps, admit that their profit targets are indicative of the "maximum" obtainable rate of return. Managers exhibit a propensity to use target return pricing techniques because information is often too sketchy or too expensive to obtain for a full analysis of the relevant factors to be conducted. In essence, target return pricing is an imperfect expedient designed to facilitate, in a rough but ready manner, the handling of a thorny decision prob-

[5]Some economists have argued that if the firm's target rate of return is based upon some concept of the *largest* rate of return the firm perceives it can get, then the firm's behavior reflects a goal of profit maximization. This is misleading if not erroneous. To illustrate why, suppose a firm believes the maximum rate of return market conditions will allow is 20%. The critical question now becomes whether the perceived maximum rate of 20% can be obtained just as well via target return pricing as by marginal cost-marginal revenue pricing. The answer is only by rare circumstance. If 20% is truly the maximum profit rate, then the only way it can be attained is for the firm to elect the price and output corresponding to the intersection of *MC* and *MR*. Since the target return price is based upon the "normal" operating rate (or standard volume), the target return price and the profit-maximizing price will coincide only if the normal operating rate just happens to be the output rate where $MR = MC$. This is a little too much to expect. Thus, while a firm's managers may believe the target return price will yield the maximum rate of profit, the facts of the matter are to the contary. In a sense, the fallacy in their thinking is akin to the fallacy that maximum profit is achieved at the output where profit per unit $(P - ATC)$ is greatest. As was demonstrated in Chapter 10, the output rate at which price exceeds *ATC* by the greatest amount *does not* correspond to the output rate where $MR = MC$.

486

*Business
Pricing
Practices and
Multiple-Goal
Models*

lem under conditions of uncertainty. Parenthetically, it should be added that executives use similar "rules of thumb" in other decision situations. Advertising expenditures are frequently determined by setting aside some fixed percentage of total revenue; inventory levels may be pegged to some preset turnover norm. By translating complicated problems into simple routines, rule-of-thumb procedures economize on executive time and may even contribute to overall operating efficiency. In any event, they serve as classic examples of precisely what is meant by satisficing—the seeking of satisfactory workable solutions to complex decision problems.

Alternative Pricing Objectives

In addition to pricing to maximize profits and pricing to earn a target return, firms have been found to pursue still other pricing objectives.

Penetration Pricing. In introducing new products and/or in moving into new geographical markets, firms sometimes deliberately set a relatively low price in order to develop the market for the item and to capture a large market share. Any of several conditions favor the use of penetration pricing: (1) when demand is very price elastic and many new customers can be attracted by a lower price (and then later induced to pay higher prices), (2) when major economies of scale exist and large sales volumes are needed to achieve maximum efficiency-minimum unit cost, (3) when a low price will discourage the actual or potential entry of new firms as well as the development of substitute products, (4) when it is important for competitive and psychological reasons to get a lead on rival firms and capture as large a market share as quickly as possible, and (5) when a firm is trying to enter an industry and needs to have some basis for attracting buyers' attention and building up a clientele for its product.

Once the firm's market penetration objective is achieved, it can then turn attention to ways to increase profitability, including a planned gradual raising of price over a period of time. A penetration price thus deliberately sacrifices short-run profitability for long-run objectives (long-run profitability, growth in sales, market share, etc.).

Price Skimming. On occasions, firms try to take advantage of the fact that some buyers are always willing and able to pay a premium price because the product, for any of several reasons, has a high immediate value to them. The objective of price skimming is initially to charge as much as these buyers will pay and then gradually to reduce price to gain access to lower-price market segments. In essence, price skimming is a form of price discrimination *over time*; starting with the price-inelastic buyer segments, the firm proceeds over time to draw in the more price-elastic market segments with progressively lower prices (often, the lower prices are keyed to the introduction of lower quality models so as not to interfere with continuing to realize substantially higher margins on top-of-the-line models).

GENERAL MOTORS' PRICING STRATEGY

General Motors has for many years used target return pricing, attempting to achieve a long-run average rate of return of 20% on investment (after taxes). In figuring what price to announce for forthcoming models, GM typically considers production trends for its models, cost changes which it expects to experience, competitors' prices (including imports), the expected industrywide demand for autos, and general economic conditions.

With car prices having been boosted by unprecedented amounts during 1973–1975 and with auto sales slumping so badly in 1974 and 1975 (partly due to the sharp run-up in gasoline prices and partly due to the recession which began in late 1974), GM was particularly concerned about how to price its 1976 models. Being the trend setter in pricing in the auto industry, GM publicly expressed concern over having to announce sharp price increases for the third year in a row. Buyer resistance to the higher 1975 car prices (over $400 per car) was still much in evidence, and GM did not want to risk undermining the modest resurgence in car sales which appeared during mid-1975.

Although observers speculated that GM and the other auto manufacturers would announce increases of 6 to 7% on base sticker prices for their 1976 models, GM surprised the industry by trimming the discounts off sticker price to dealers and by removing various pieces of equipment as standard. The discount cut (estimated by GM to be equivalent to about one percentage point on a sales-weighted basis), together with the shift of some standard equipment to optional extras, still resulted in average base sticker price increases on 1976 cars of 4.4% (sales-weighted). But if GM had not made these moves, it was estimated that the price increases would have averaged about $275 per car instead of $206. In an attempt to pacify dealers over a reduction in their base sticker margins, GM raised the prices of optional equipment by 5% at wholesale and 6% at retail.

Small cars were the principal targets of GM's 1976 equipment deletions. Steel-belted radials were removed as standard from all of GM's six-cylinder compact models; power brakes were removed from Chevrolet Monza-type cars; and a number of deletions were applied to the Monza Towne Coupe. However, maintenance-free batteries were added as standard on Vegas, Astres, Monzas, Skylarks, Starfires, Corvettes, and all Cadillacs. GM's sticker price revisions ranged from a $211 cut on the Monza Towne Coupe to an increase of $808 on Corvettes.

In announcing the 1976 prices, GM Chairman Thomas Murphy

488

*Business
Pricing
Practices and
Multiple-Goal
Models*

indicated that during the past year GM had experienced or was committed to cost increases of about $375 per car. However, according to Murphy, "to increase prices to our customers by the full amount of these increases would, in our judgment, tend to dampen the returning demand in the market."

The table below shows GM's dealer discount structure on its various models:

GM's Dealer Discount Structure
(all figures represent dealer discounts from sticker prices)

Model Names	*Historical*	*1975 Models*[a]	*1976 Models*
Vega, Astre	17	15.5	15
Monza type	17	16.6	15
Compacts (Nova, Omega)	17	15.9	15
Camaro, Firebird	17	16.3	15
Intermediates (Cutlass, Century)	21	20.1	19
Monte Carlo	21	19.9	19
Chevrolet, Pontiac, Olds Delta, Buick LeSabre	25	24.1	22
Olds 98, Buick Electra	25	24.1	24
Toronado, Riviera, Corvette	25	23.8	24
Cadillac Seville	25	25	25
Other Cadillac	26	25.1	25

[a]The "historical" dealer discount was reduced by government-ordered pass-through of price increases for federally mandated equipment for safety and emission control. This occurred during the price-control period of 1971–1974.

Questions for Discussion

1. What effect would you predict that GM's price strategy might have on dealer pricing?
2. What benefit, if any, did such a price revision offer to GM? To dealers? To GM car buyers?

Sources: A. D. H. Kaplan, J. B. Dirlam, and R. F. Lanzilotti, *Pricing in Big Business* (Washington, D.C.: The Brookings Institution, 1958), pp. 48–55, 131–135; and *Automotive News* (August 18, 1975), pp. 1, 7.

Price skimming makes good economic and business sense (from the standpoint of sellers) whenever (1) different classes of buyers have materially different price elasticities of demand and the firm has ample time to "ride" down the demand curve, charging each buyer segment as much as the traffic will bear; (2) the innovating firm has a lead time long enough that the initial high price will neither stimulate entry of rival firms nor the development of substitute products; (3) the diseconomies of producing at smaller volumes do not cancel out the advantage of premium prices; (4) high initial prices support the impression that the product is superior and of exceptional quality; and (5) there is substantial risk to setting an initial price that is too low (because demand is uncertain and may not materialize or because unit costs may exceed expectations). In addition, a high initial price leaves room for reducing price if things do not go as expected; usually, price cuts are easier to implement than price increases.[6]

Loss-Leader Pricing.   Some firms, particularly food retailers and discount stores, price one or a few items at bargain levels (even below wholesale cost) in order to (1) increases future sales of the item or (2) attract customers to their stores and boost sales on other items. The objective, of course, is not to produce losses but rather to increase total profits. A successful loss-leader therefore is really a profit-leader. Loss-leader pricing can be defined as pricing an item at a level which generates a subpar or even negative unit contribution profit (i.e., $P - AVC$ will be less than the customary margin) but which is nonetheless expected to result in higher total profits through either increased future sales of the item or greater sales on the firm's entire line of items. Loss-leader pricing works well in situations where (1) it is desirable for buyers to become familiar with the product (or with the store), (2) it is apparent to buyers that the price represents a good value, (3) the price cut is sizable enough to cause buyers to respond, and (4) the lower price does not signify a reduction in quality.

Pricing for Early Recovery of Investment Costs.   Some firms aim for a price that offers the quickest recovery of sunk investment costs. This could mean pricing either "high" or "low," depending on such factors as buyer's sensitivity to price, whether the market is developed, the competitive threat from substitute products, barriers to entry, and so on. Firms may lean toward such a pricing objective if they are cash-poor or if market change is too rapid to justify patiently cultivating demand.

Going-Rate Pricing.   Competitive fringe firms, as well as larger firms which do not have a leadership position, may have a pricing policy that consists of no more than simply charging the going price. This is referred to as going-rate pricing, imitative pricing, or price followership. In oligopolistic markets such a pricing policy has obvious appeal for firms not in a position to exert price leadership of for firms whose products are not differentiated strongly enough to give them some price freedom. But the policy is also used by firms unaffected by oligopolistic interdependence. Why? Because it is

[6]However, Kotler cites the case of a home permanent kit which did not sell well when priced at 39 cents and marketed through dimestores but which caught on when repriced at $1.98 and sold through drugstores. See Philip Kotler, *Marketing Management: Analysis, Planning, and Control,* 2nd ed. (Englewood Cliffs, N.J.: Prentice-Hall, Inc., 1972), p. 520 footnote.

490

Business
Pricing
Practices and
Multiple-Goal
Models

easy. The price imitator can sit back and let other firms worry about demand elasticities, changing market conditions, and what to do next; managers then have more time to devote to other decisions. This is a tenable position as long as acceptable profits can be earned being a price follower.

Sealed-Bid Pricing. In construction, defense contract work, and capital goods manufacture, firms compete for jobs on the basis of bid prices. Here, pricing strategy is necessarily keyed to expectations of how competitors will price. While overall market conditions and costs are relevant in deciding how hard to try to get a particular job, the firm's success is predicated upon being low bidder on a sufficient number of jobs to build a viable business. The firm thus confronts something of a dilemma: The higher its bid price is above variable costs, the higher are potential profits but the lower is the chance of getting the contract. On the other hand, if the firm consistently bids too close to variable costs, it may not earn enough contribution profit to cover total fixed costs.

Other Price Considerations. Some sellers believe that odd-number prices are more attractive to buyers than round-number prices. A $5.99 price may, for psychological or subconscious reasons, be more stimulating to sales than a $6.00 price. A 33-cent price may have more buyer appeal than a 32-cent or even a 30-cent price. Items may sell more rapidly at 3 for 88 cents than for 29 cents each. The problem here is to determine which numbers, if any, have more appeal and whether this appeal applies only to certain items or extends more broadly.

Still other pricing problems arise in special situations. For instance, food products firms which periodically offer buyers "cents-off" coupons and in-store "cents-off" specials face the problems of deciding upon seasonal timing, magnitude of the price discount, and competitive effect. Clothing stores regularly mark down the prices of fashion goods as the season progresses, giving rise to decisions about the appropriate size and timing of the markdowns. Pricing tactics also come under serious scrutiny during periods of industrywide overcapacity, recession, and inflation. During the era of price controls in the early 1970s, a number of firms—even those with sagging sales—refrained from lowering prices for fear that price controls might suddenly be reimposed, thereby imperiling profit margins if costs should go up; in fact, the mere threat of price controls induced many companies to announce precautionary price increases, thus ironically fueling the inflationary spiral.

Conclusions. The economist's marginal cost-marginal revenue models offer firms guidance in finding the short-run profit-maximizing price when estimates of demand and cost are available. Such models do not, however, allow for explicit consideration of long-run profit objectives, goals other than profit, nonprice competitive variables, and uncertainties as to demand and/or cost. In practice, quite a large number of enterprises orient their pricing toward cost (as in target return and cost-plus pricing) or toward demand (as in price skimming) or toward market share and sales growth (as in penetration pricing) or toward competition (as in going-rate pricing and sealed bids). Although marginal cost-marginal revenue considerations enter to some extent into these alternatives, they are not decisive in choosing the actual price.

MULTIPLE-GOAL MODELS OF CORPORATE BEHAVIOR

Revenue Maximization with a Profit Constraint

One of the best known of the multiple-goal models of corporate behavior is the model of sales revenue maximization with a profit constraint.[7] This model, first proposed by William Baumol, is founded upon the premise that once profits reach acceptable levels, the firm's profit goal becomes subordinate to its goal of increasing its sales revenue (the rationale underlying this goal hierarchy was presented in Chapter 9). According to Baumol, the drive to increase sales revenues assumes such strong proportions that the firm's managers are willing to forego higher profits to obtain greater sales revenues.

Figure 15-2 illustrates the revenue maximization model. The firm's TR, TC, and π curves are shown in their conventional shapes. Total profit is maximum at an output rate of Q_1 units, and TR is maximum at an output rate of Q_3 units. Thus, it is evident that the firm cannot simultaneously maximize short-run profits *and* sales revenue. Profit is always maximum where $MR = MC$, whereas TR (or sales revenue) is maximum where $MR = 0$. The price and the output rate which maximize profits definitely do not correspond to the price and the output rate which maximize sales revenue. Suppose the firm has a profit target of π_1 dollars [Fig. 15-2(b)]. If profits of π_1 dollars are required before other objectives such as sales revenue maximization are pursued, then the firm is in no position to increase the sales of output beyond Q_1 units, since even at the profit-maximizing output the profit target is still out of reach. The firm must produce at Q_1 units just to come as close as possible to satisfying its profit constraint. However, if profits of π_2 dollars will fulfill its profit requirements, the firm is in a position to pursue a sales revenue goal as well as a profit goal. By a lowering of its price, the output rate can be expanded to Q_2 units and sales revenues pushed up to TR_{Q_2} dollars. Profits will still be the desired amount of π_2 dollars, though they will be below their potential maximum. Nonetheless, the firm is able to meet its profit objective, and it enjoys a higher level of sales revenues than it would at the profit-maximizing output of Q_1 units. This is what is meant by

[7]Baumol's model, with all of its price-output and policy ramifications is presented in his book *Business Behavior, Value and Growth*, rev. ed. (New York: Harcourt Brace Jovanovich, Inc., 1967), Chapters 6–8.

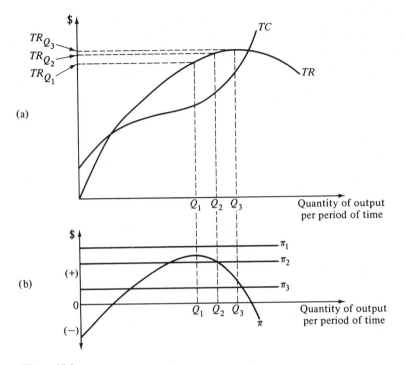

(a)

(b)

Figure 15-2
Revenue maximization model

sales revenue maximization with a profit constraint. Finally, suppose the profit constraint is only π_3 dollars. Then price can be lowered yet further, the sales of output pushed to Q_3 units, and revenue pushed to the maximum value of TR_{Q_3} dollars. The firm has no motive to expand its output rate past Q_3, even though its profit goal of π_3 dollars is overfulfilled. The reason? Additional output can be absorbed in the market only at prices reduced so much that total revenue will fall. Hence, revenues are smaller at output rates greater than Q_3 than they are at Q_3, effectively undermining the firm's revenue incentive to push sales past Q_3 units.

Observe that at outputs below Q_1, a strategy of lowering price and increasing output enhances both profits and sales revenues. Up to an output of Q_1 units, the two goals are complementary in the sense that success in achieving higher sales is concomitant with success in achieving higher profits. On the other hand, between outputs of Q_1 and Q_3 units, lower prices and greater outputs cause profits to fall but sales revenues to rise. Therefore, between Q_1 and Q_3, greater sales revenues are achieved at the expense of profits—the two goals compete with one another. Beyond an output of Q_3 units, a lower price and consequently larger sales of output result in lower profits and in lower sales revenues.

APPLICATIONS CAPSULE

493

*Multiple-Goal
Models of
Corporate
Behavior*

THE EXPERIENCE CURVE: PATHWAY TO HIGHER
SALES, PROFITS, AND MARKET SHARE?

The Boston Consulting Group (BCG) has in recent years gotten the attention of a number of businessmen with a concept it calls "the experience curve." The experience curve derives from the well-known learning curve (a phenomenon discovered by an Air Force officer in the 1920s) which holds that the time needed to perform a task decreases by a constant percentage the more often it is done. The power of the learning curve is such that in some firms unit labor costs have declined 10 to 15% each time output is doubled.

In the late 1960s, Bruce D. Henderson, founder and president of Boston Consulting Group, observed that the learning curve principle seemed to apply to the *overall* unit costs of making a product as well as to just unit *labor* costs. On the basis of BCG's experiences with client firms, Henderson claimed that each time the number of units produced doubled there was a tendency for unit costs to also decline by a fixed percentage—usually in the 20 to 30% range. He attributed this decline in cost with each doubling of experience to the combined effect of learning, specialization, increased scale of operation, and increased intensity of capital investment. The relationships were deemed predictable enough that the declines in unit cost, relative to volume, could be accurately plotted—BCG labeled the resulting graphical relationship "the experience curve."

In BCG's view, the experience curve can be a "powerful and universal tool for strategic planning," as well as a simple means of predicting and controlling a firm's costs. The rationale is as follows: The firm which produces the most units will probably have the lowest average costs. If that firm also has the largest market share, then it should earn the greatest profits. Therefore, a firm should strive to gain a dominant market share in as many products as possible, even if that means temporarily lower profit margins. The value of the experience curve is that it permits the profitability of an increase in market share for a particular product to be calculated with more precision than otherwise. The experience curve shows the decline in costs that can be anticipated with increases in volume and market share. And, as volume grows, prices can be reduced because of lower realized unit costs. Then it is merely a matter of weighing the worth of the increased market share against the investment it takes to achieve it and the probable reaction of competitors. The implication of this, according to BCG, is that a company should strive to dominate a market for its products, either by

494

*Business
Pricing
Practices and
Multiple-Goal
Models*

introducing product variations, segmenting the market, or discouraging competitors by keeping prices low.

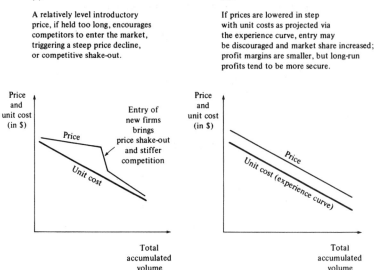

(a)

A relatively level introductory price, if held too long, encourages competitors to enter the market, triggering a steep price decline, or competitive shake-out.

(b)

If prices are lowered in step with unit costs as projected via the experience curve, entry may be discouraged and market share increased; profit margins are smaller, but long-run profits tend to be more secure.

BCG has found that some companies ignore these principles, even though they seem elementary. This particularly applies to a firm which finds itself with early leadership in market share of a product but then tries to translate lower costs into higher profit margins instead of lower prices; in BCG's view it is better to increase profits through greater volume rather than wider profit margins—as depicted in the accompanying graph. When price does not follow cost down, the door is open for rival firms to begin to gain on the market leader.

One of BCG's first efforts at applying experience curve theory was with Norton Company of Worcester, Massachusetts. Norton was having trouble profitably penetrating the market for pressure-sensitive tape—a market dominated by 3M Company. Norton had successfully cut production costs and lowered prices but still was unable to make a dent in increasing its market share. BCG's experience curve analysis showed that Norton, in effect, was chasing 3M Company down the cost curve, and that as long as 3M followed pricing and growth strategies to maximize market share, it was a fruitless struggle for Norton. Subsequently, Norton concluded that it could not compete successfully against 3M by trying to produce a broad range of products sold in a large number of markets; rather, the company decided it was better off concentrating in selected areas. BCG claims that the Norton situation illustrates an important experience curve commandment: If you cannot get enough market share to be cost-competitive, then get out of the business. Another instance where the same lesson applied was the effort of Allis-Chalmers Company to compete against General Electric and Westinghouse in steam turbine engines. Between 1946 and 1963 Allis-Chalmers' market share was too small to give it a chance to be competitive on cost and therefore on price with larger-volume manufacturers; thus, A-C's best decision was to withdraw from the industry.

Black & Decker, Texas Instruments, and Weyerhaeuser are among former Boston Consulting Group clients which seem to have adopted the experience curve philosophy. For example, Texas Instruments sums up its strategy for expanding market share this way: "Follow an aggressive pricing policy, focus on continuing cost reduction and productivity improvement, build on shared experience gained in making related products, and keep capacity growing ahead of demand."

More recently, BCG has applied the experience curve concept to conglomerate enterprises. In BCG's view, conglomerates should pursue different strategies for different product lines, depending on growth rates and market shares in each. For example, BCG has advocated that a multiproduct enterprise use the excess cash flow from slow-growth, high-market share products to support more rapid expansion of sales of products having a high (or potentially high) market share in fast-growing markets and which may need big infusions of cash to support such expansion.

Henderson claims that the experience curve contradicts some widely held beliefs about free enterprise and competition. "It simply is not true," he says, "that economies of scale are eventually exhausted"; in his view, as long as production of an item keeps doubling, the cost per unit will decline (although, as a practical matter, it is not possible for firms to continue to double output indefinitely because of market saturation problems). In turn, the prevalence of continued economies of scale make it false to base antitrust legislation on the assumption that market prices tend to be lowest where a large number of relatively small firms compete against one another. Instead, Henderson argues, it is better to allow (and even encourage) only a few firms to dominate the market for a product whenever firms have to be big to take full advantage of the experience curve. Henderson concludes that competition among the few can lead to lower prices, a better deal for consumers, higher profits for firms, and increased ability of U.S. firms to compete in world markets. In this regard, Henderson claims that we could learn a lot from the Japanese experience (where, incidentally, government treats business as a partner rather than an adversary). Of the Japanese, Henderson says, "I don't know whether they follow the experience curve intuitively or deliberately, but whatever they do, it's in accord with the curve and it works."

496

*Business
Pricing
Practices and
Multiple-Goal
Models*

Questions for Discussion

1. What, if anything, is "new" or "unique" about the experience curve? Is it any different from the concept of economies of scale?

2. Does pricing a product based upon BCG's experience curve concept [as indicated in panel (b) of the diagram] go against the $MC = MR$ profit-maximizing rule? Why or why not?

3. Evaluate the concept of "experience curve pricing." Will lower prices based upon the experience curve likely lead to higher profits as is claimed? In what kinds of situations?

Source: "Selling Business a Theory of Economics," *Business Week* (September 8, 1973), pp. 85–90.

A chief conclusion to be derived from the sales revenue maximization model is this: *If a firm has a goal of maximizing its sales revenue subject to a profit constraint and if the firm's profit constraint (or profit target) is below the maximum attainable profit, then the firm will charge lower prices for its products and will produce greater outputs than it would with a goal of profit maximization.*

Advertising Expenditures and the Goals of the Firm. The decision as to how much to spend on advertising and sales promotion is also influenced by the firm's choice of goals. A revenue-maximizer tends to spend more money promoting its products than does a profit-maximizer. This proposition is illustrated in Fig. 15-3. The horizontal axis in panels (a) and (b) represents the dollar magnitude of advertising outlays; the vertical axis measures dollar costs, revenues, and profits. For simplicity, total cost is shown to increase linearly with advertising expenditures, starting from a value of TC_0 dollars where advertising is zero. The TC curve includes all production and selling costs, including advertising outlays. The total revenue curve is drawn on the reasonable assumption that increased advertising tends to increase sales of output and revenue, but by progressively lesser amounts. In other words, diminishing returns to promotion exist, and additional advertising expenditures result in ever more slowly increasing revenues. The total profit (π) curve in panel (b) is found by subtracting total costs from total revenues at each level of advertising outlay; it indicates the profitability of various-sized advertising outlays.

Figure 15-3 indicates that the profit-maximizing amount of advertising outlay is A_1 dollars. In contrast, a revenue-maximizing firm with a profit constraint of π_1 dollars has an optimal advertising outlay of A_2 dollars. The additional advertising pushes sales revenues from TR_{A1} dollars to TR_{A2} dollars without causing total profits to fall below the targeted level of π_1 dollars. As long as the revenue-maximizer's profit target is *less* than the maximum profit level, the revenue-maximizer will find it advantageous to spend more heavily on advertising than will a profit-maximizer. The revenue-maximizer's output

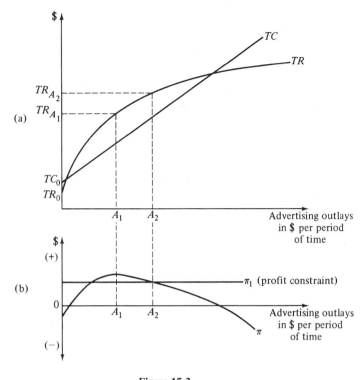

Figure 15-3
Advertising expenditures and the goals of the firm

rate will, accordingly, be greater than the profit-maximizer's output rate. However, the revenue-maximizing firm's selling price may be higher, lower, or equal to the profit-maximizing firm's, depending on the effect advertising has upon unit costs and upon customer demand for the firm's products (see Fig. 11-7). On occasions, the extra advertising undertaken by the sales-maximizer may shift the firm's demand-AR curve so as to make it advantageous to charge a price slightly above that of rival firms. On other occasions, the additional advertising may simply result in selling more units at the prevailing price level. And on still other occasions, the extra advertising may entail a lower price as well as expanded sales.

The Effect of Fixed Cost Changes. One of the most surprising and interesting aspects of the economics of the firm is the effect of fixed cost changes upon price and output decisions. Consider Fig. 15-4, where the firm's initial cost-revenue-profit functions are given by TFC_1, TC_1, TR_1, and π_1. Note that if the firm's primary goal is profit maximization, then its optimum output rate is Q_1 units, but if its primary goal is sales revenue maximization with a profit constraint of π dollars, then its optimum output is Q_2 units. Now suppose the firm experiences a rise in the prices of its fixed inputs such that total fixed costs rise to a level indicated by TFC_2. This will cause the firm's

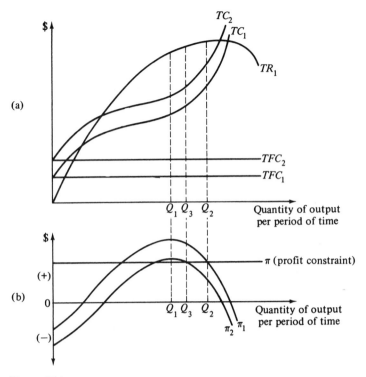

Figure 15-4
Effect of fixed cost changes upon the firm's optimum price and output

total cost function to shift upward by the amount of the rise in fixed costs to TC_2. The rise in fixed costs will further cause the firm's profit function to shift downward from π_1 to π_2, with the amount of the downward shift being equal to the increase in fixed costs.

What effect does this sort of cost increase have upon the firm's optimum price and output rate if the firm's principal goal is profit maximization? The answer, surprisingly enough, is *none*. The rise in fixed costs *lowers* the peak of the total profit curve, but it moves the peak neither to the right nor to the left. Moreover, changes in fixed costs have no effect whatsoever upon *MC* or upon *MR*, thus leaving the point at which $MC = MR$ completely undisturbed. Hence, total profit is maximized at precisely the same price and output as before the rise in total fixed costs. And we have the inescapable conclusion that changes in fixed costs do not influence the short-run price and output decisions of profit-maximizing firms so long as it is possible to earn positive contribution profits.

But what of the effect upon a revenue-maximizing firm? From Fig. 15-4 it is apparent that given the downward shift in the total profit curve an output of Q_2 units will result in profits below the minimum acceptable level. The revenue-maximizing firm will therefore be compelled to reduce output to

Q_3 units to meet its profit constraint; concomitantly, it will raise price as the vehicle for effecting the reduction in unit sales. Thus, the goal of the firm is the pivotal factor in analyzing its response to a rise in fixed costs. Firms which seek to maximize profits will leave their price and output rates unchanged when fixed costs change, whereas firms which seek to maximize sales revenue subject to a profit constraint will tend to reduce their outputs and raise their selling prices in response to an increase in fixed costs.

Insofar as actual business practice is concerned, there is little question which of the two responses to fixed cost increases is the more commonly observed. An increase in fixed costs is usually an occasion for serious consideration of a price increase.

The Effect of Tax Changes. Whether a firm is a profit-maximizer or a revenue-maximizer has significant public policy implications. An outstanding illustration concerns the use of federal taxation policies to control inflationary tendencies. Increases in corporate tax rates have on occasions been used to help contain inflationary forces and to promote price stability and full employment. The logic seems plain enough: With steeper corporate profits taxes, the business sector has fewer after-tax dollars to spend for new capital investment and less of a profit incentive to invest these dollars, so that investment spending is curtailed and the investment component of aggregate demand is reduced. In turn, the pressure of aggregate demand upon production capacity is relieved somewhat, and the motive of business enterprises to raise product prices is dampened.

However, the successful use of increases in corporate profits taxes as a weapon for fighting inflation depends implicitly on the principal goal of business enterprises. This can be seen from the cost-revenue-profit curves shown in Fig. 15-5. Given a total revenue curve of TR, a total cost curve of TC, a net-profit-after-taxes curve of π_1, and a profit target of OA dollars, the profit-maximizing and revenue-maximizing outputs are Q_1 units and Q_2 units, respectively. Now suppose an additional tax of 10% of all profits is imposed upon the firm. The effect of the tax is to shift the firm's after-tax profit curve downward at each level of *profitable output* by the amount of the additional tax, as shown by π_2. Observe that the peak of π_2 corresponds to the same output as does the peak of π_1. Hence, we may correctly conclude that the profit-maximizing output rate is the same after the additional tax is paid as it was before. The profit-maximizing firm therefore has no incentive to change either its output rate or its price. But the same cannot be said if the firm's goal is to maximize sales revenue subject to a profit constraint. Imposing additional corporate profits taxes upon a revenue-maximizing firm induces the firm to restrict its sales of output to Q_3 units and to raise its price as the means of reducing sales of output from Q_2 to Q_3 units. Raising price and restricting output allows the firm to cover the costs of higher taxes and still meet its after-tax profit constraint.

The preceding analysis highlights the effects of different goals upon the

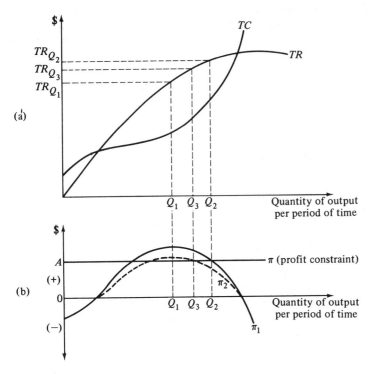

Figure 15-5
Effect of tax changes upon the firm's optimum price and output

optimal price and output decisions of the firm. It indicates how seriously wrong predictions of business price and output behavior can be unless care is exercised first in determining the actual goals of business enterprises.

The Extent of Revenue-Maximizing Behavior. The evidence is inconclusive whether or not a significant number of business firms actually base their price and output decisions upon a goal of maximizing sales revenue subject to a profit constraint. The major obstacle is that the decision process of large corporations is exceedingly complex. Many factors influence and constrain corporate pricing decisions; it is quite difficult to know just what set of motivations and priorities are reflected in managerial decisions. In addition, the behavioral differences between profit maximization and revenue maximization are difficult to detect with the available empirical data because so many economic forces must be untangled. The few available studies of business behavior, the public pronouncements of business executives, and the consulting experiences which several academicians have had with major firms do, however, combine to give credence to the revenue maximization model.[8]

[8]See, for example, the instances cited by Baumol, *Business Behavior, Value and Growth*, Chapter 6; Marshall Hall, "Sales Revenue Maximization: An Empirical Examination," *Journal of Industrial Economics*, Vol. 15 (April 1967), pp. 143–154; J. W. McGuire,

The numerous examples of target return pricing are also quite consistent with a revenue-maximizing goal. Nevertheless, the final verdict is still out on the extent of revenue-maximizing behavior among business enterprises.

The Related Goals of Sales, Profit, and Growth: An Integrative Model

All the preceding models of corporate behavior have been largely *static* in their approach. They have concentrated upon pinpointing the firm's optimal price and output decisions at a particular moment, given some specified set of cost and revenue conditions. The result has been an illuminating snapshot description of firms and markets in motion. But a complete picture of business behavior and market performance requires that the time frame of our analysis be lengthened to include the long-run goals of business enterprise and the dynamic influences of such powerful forces as technological progress, shifts in consumer buying patterns, and long-run competitive pressures. Progress in raising the quality of economic life is best gauged by *trends* in prices, in product quality, in rates of growth in output, and in the pace of innovation, rather by their respective values at some moment of time. Even more important, the growth of the economy as a whole presumably does not proceed in some mysterious fashion that is independent of the growth of its constituent parts.

As emphasized in Chapter 9, large corporate enterprises may exhibit interest in such goals as profits, sales revenues, market share, long-run survival, security, managerial autonomy, technological virtuosity, and rising dividend rates, as well as fulfillment of the personal objectives of top management. The surest strategy for achievement of these goals over the long term is maintaining the growth and expansion of the firm itself. Searching for some optimum short-run equilibrium condition and then seeking ways to maintain it is a strategy totally abhorrent and foreign to most corporate executives. Instead, their energies are almost always focused on how the corporation can escape the throes of a static state and the stagnation and decline which it soon entails. Every management is acutely aware that the activities upon which the firm presently relies will over time lose their sustaining power through changes in consumer tastes, the appearance of superior commodities, increased competition from foreign and domestic rivals, and growth in the market power of suppliers and customers. Change is certain, thereby making it imperative for firms to stay abreast of any new opportunities and expansion possibilities that change brings. Specifically, this means blueprinting the growth of the firm and deciding in what markets, with what products, at what speed, and with

J. S. Y. Chiu, and A. D. Elbins, "Executive Income, Sales, and Profits," *American Economic Review*, Vol. 52, No. 4 (September 1962), pp. 753–761; B. D. Mabry and D. L. Siders, "An Empirical Test of the Sales Maximization Hypothesis," *Southern Economic Journal*, Vol. 33, No. 3 (January 1967), pp. 267–277; and Y. Amihud and J. Kamin, "Revenue vs. Profit Maximization: Differences in Behavior by the Type of Control and by Market Power," *Southern Economic Journal*, Vol. 45, No. 3 (January 1979), pp. 838–846.

502

*Business
Pricing
Practices and
Multiple-Goal
Models*

what competitive strategies growth should best be pursued. Expanding sales revenues and expanding profits—the two most focused upon measures of business growth—thus tend to be foremost in the typical corporation's goal hierarchy.

The concern with growth has very important implications for corporate behavior in the marketplace. In all probability, a growth-conscious management will avoid employing any sort of short-run strategy which interferes with the attainment of long-run goals. For example, firms commonly elect to deviate from their short-run profit-maximizing prices and output rates in order to better achieve long-run profit maximization. This was indicated in Chapters 12 and 13, where dominant firms and near monopolists were seen to have strong incentives for choosing actual selling prices below those at which $MC = MR$ and for increasing short-run output rates past the $MC = MR$ intersection. Via this short-run price-output strategy, these firms (1) discourage the entry and expansion of rival firms, (2) reduce the chances of government intervention, and (3) contain the motives for countervailing power. The intent of such a strategy is, of course, to forsake short-run for long-run profit maximization. In the same vein, firms may price new products below short-run profit-maximizing levels in order to open up more uses for the product, attract more new customers, and thereby enhance their long-term profits, sales, and market shares. Some firms may invest heavily in technologies which they know have little or no short-run payoff but which offer substantial long-run benefits in terms of costs and efficiency, given expected changes in input prices. Target return pricing, which makes use of long-run "normal" operating rates as the basis for price determination, is another situation where long-run considerations dominate those of the short run.

Growth Equilibrium. Given that growth and expansion comprise the major strategy for long-run goal achievement, it is imperative that growth considerations be incorporated into our analysis of business behavior. Specifically, we shall concentrate upon the criteria for determining how rapidly the firm should expand its production activities in pursuit of its goals. The analysis follows closely the lines proposed by Professor Baumol in his "growth-equilibrium" model.[9]

Consider first the effects of growth and expansion upon a firm's total costs. Two types of cost arising from the growth process are of particular interest: (1) *output cost*—ordinary fixed and variable costs stemming from the operation of production processes with greater output potential and (2) *expansion costs*—costs associated exclusively with the expansion process. Output costs can reasonably be expected to increase linearly as a firm's annual rate of growth in output rises—in other words, constant returns to scale may be said to characterize the expansion of production capacity. Once the optimum scale of plant for a productive activity is identified, a firm can build as many such plants as may be required to satisfy output needs. Techni-

[9] Baumol, *Business Behavior, Value and Growth*, Chapter 10.

cal progress also helps to ward off more-than-proportional increases in output costs as production rates are expanded or as the scope of a firm's activity is widened.

In contrast, the faster a firm seeks to grow, the faster *expansion costs* can be counted upon to rise. The reasons for this deserve brief mention. First, to shorten the time required to build a new plant facility or to build more plants of the same sort at a given time is likely to strain the abilities of construction firms and add substantially to the prices at which they will agree to build such facilities. Second, ever more rapid expansion requires ever more money to finance it. Beyond some point, firms generally find that the more money they must raise for investment, the higher is the cost of obtaining it. The amount of growth which can be funded by retained earnings is limited. Issuing large amounts of new stock or selling bonds drives their prices down and so raises the cost of obtaining capital. Negotiating loans also tends to become more expensive, since lenders may well insist upon higher interest rates for larger and more leveraged loans. Third, growth of a firm entails the recruitment of more executives, middle- and lower-echelon managers, technical staff, and production workers. It takes time for them to be trained and to gain experience in their assignments. The more rapidly a firm tries to assimilate new personnel into the organization, the more opportunity there is for inefficiency and rising costs to accompany growth.

Consequently, as a firm seeks to accelerate the rate of expansion in its long-run production capabilities, it typically finds it difficult to accommodate faster growth without encountering severe "growing pains" and a concomitant rise in inefficiency. Construction costs, capital costs, and organizational staffing costs all increase disproportionately, causing the firm's total cost function to rise more and more sharply. Thus, while ordinary output costs tend to increase linearly in view of the prevalence of constant returns to scale, expansion costs can be counted upon to transform an otherwise linear total cost curve into one which increases at an increasing rate as a firm's annual growth rate of output becomes progressively larger. This is illustrated in Fig. 15-6.

Now, what about the effect of growth upon a firm's total revenues? Barring totally unfavorable market conditions, a firm's total revenues can be expected to rise as the rate of growth in output rises above zero. However, market conditions will seldom permit a firm to expand without limit and still realize increases in total revenue. True, a firm is usually capable of fostering greater sales via some combination of lower prices, advertising, innovation, and diversification, but the ability to generate greater revenues over the near term is not boundless. Internally generated strategies to spur sales are likely to encounter diminishing success even in a favorable market environment. Hence, the firm's total revenue curve tends to increase at a decreasing rate, as shown in Fig. 15-6.

It is obvious from Fig. 15-6 that different rates of growth in output result in different degrees of profitability. The gap between *TR* and *TC* widens, then narrows, as the annual rate of growth in output increases. A firm will

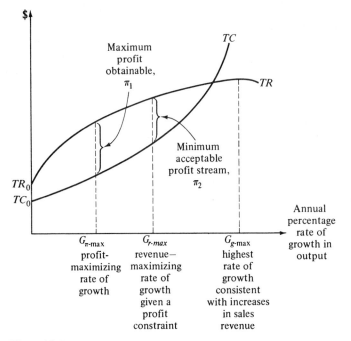

Figure 15-6
Growth equilibrium for the firm

therefore find it unprofitable to expand either too slowly or too rapidly, and there is some rate of output expansion that will maximize long-run profits. The profit-maximizing growth rate, shown as $G_{\pi\text{-max}}$, results in a maximum profit stream of π_1 dollars. It follows from this analysis that a firm grows partly because growth makes the firm more profitable.[10]

However, as we have emphasized on numerous occasions, corporations may have objectives other than profit. One very plausible alternative to long-run profit maximization is maximization of the *rate of growth* of sales revenue subject to a profit constraint. Given that corporations stress the *percentage* by which sales and profits have grown rather than the *amount* of sales and profits, *growth rates* may more accurately describe corporate goals than absolute dollar values.

Referring again to Fig. 15-6, suppose a profit stream of π_2 dollars will suffice to meet the firm's capital needs as well as to satisfy stockholders' expectations. Then the firm can push its rate of growth past $G_{\pi\text{-max}}$ to $G_{r\text{-max}}$—$G_{r\text{-max}}$ may be delineated as the maximum rate of expansion consistent with maximizing sales revenues *and* attaining the desired profit. Hence, a firm with an objective of maximizing its rate of growth of sales revenue will tend to

[10]The motives for profitable growth are, of course, not the exclusive province of large corporations; small firms have growth ambitions too. Over the years a number of small firms have been so successful in executing a growth strategy that they now rank as large corporations—Control Data, Holiday Inns, TRW, Textron, and Xerox are good examples.

expand faster than a profit-maximizing firm. It is apparent that past a growth rate of $G_{\pi\text{-max}}$, profits and sales *compete*—higher revenues can be achieved only by sacrificing some profits. Yet, if growth is carried too far, the profit stream will be too small to generate the needed investment capital. This explains why the firm stops short of a growth rate corresponding to the peak of the *TR* curve (shown as $G_{g\text{-max}}$ in Fig. 15-6).

Two very important conclusions are implied by this analysis. First, the corporation's behavior over the long term (as well as over the short term) varies according to its goals. The price and output decisions of profit-maximizers differ from those of revenue-maximizers; the decisions of growth-maximizers will result in yet a third set of prices and outputs. The implication is strong that the pursuit of other goals will entail still different price-output decisions and growth strategy sets. In other words, price-output combinations, growth rates, and growth strategies all vary according to the priorities which a corporation may assign to its goal hierarchy.

Second, an enterprise has a very powerful motive to expand production over time. Irrespective of whether the firm's ultimate goal is long-run profit maximization or maximizing future sales revenues or something else, increased volumes of output are to be expected. This is not to say that the output rate for each and every product will be increased, for obviously shifts in consumer demand may dictate otherwise, but it does say that the combined output of the firm's products will tend to rise over time. A positive rate of output growth—and maybe a substantial rate—is a virtual prerequisite to achievement of multiple-goal hierarchies.

Aspects of Corporate Growth. In corporate capitalism the motives of rival firms for growth are highly contagious. One firm hell-bent on growth can so jeopardize the market position of other firms in the industry that they must follow suit or face the unpleasant consequence of being squeezed into relative obscurity. Few firms opt for the latter; hence, the growth of one or a few firms catalyzes the growth of other firms and causes a strong growth psychology to pervade the entire industry. In addition, once growth competition appears, the posture of firms toward growth tends to become aggressive. Managers understand thoroughly the tactical advantage a firm gains from staying in the ranks of the growth-leaders. It is much more satisfactory to seize the initiative in pursuing growth because this permits the firm to pick the specific strategy and timing that seem most propitious.

However, from management's standpoint, expansion should be steady and planned; bursts of innovation and expansion are undesirable. Erratic growth is a destabilizing influence as regards staffing, financial planning, and capital investment. In addition, extraordinary sales and profit gains create stockholder expectations of repeat performances when, in fact, they may not be repeatable. A record of vigorous, uninterrupted progress is the most enviable. This has led to attempts to fund research and development programs in ways calculated to generate a dependable flow of new but pretested ideas. these ideas can then be implemented at a tempo sufficient to yield the firm's target growth rate, provided adequate financing is available and provided the

506

*Business
Pricing
Practices and
Multiple-Goal
Models*

economic environment is not hostile to expansion. At the same time, managers may try to reduce wide fluctuations in the firm's investment spending and put capital outlays expenditures on a more regular, programmed schedule. On balance, the effect of a stable corporate growth strategy upon the economy can be quite favorable. Not only does national economic growth tend to be stimulated by expansion-minded firms, but business investment is made less volatile and full employment is made somewhat easier to achieve.

Growth Equilibrium for the Firm and for the Economy. Although the drive for growth permeates the corporate sector, a critical issue yet remains. How can the firm, year after year, find customers for its ever-growing flow of output? One answer is that if there is simultaneous growth in the production activity of a large segment of the economy, many new job opportunities will be created, and wage and salary incomes will expand. At the same time, investment spending for new production capacity and purchases of more inputs will cause the incomes of resource suppliers to rise. Then, in due course, the ripples of corporate expansion spill over into other economic sectors. The rise in incomes triggered by corporate expansion has the effect of generating increases in the total demand for goods and services throughout the economy and thereby expanding the markets in which the increased production can be sold. The process of output growth thus begets the increases in demand needed to ratify and sustain the firm's expansion. Provided growth in production occurs neither too slowly nor too rapidly among firms and among industries, the entire economy can be kept on a path of reasonably balanced growth and full employment equilibrium. Such is the skeleton of the economic links between growth equilibrium for the economy. We defer a more thoroughgoing treatment of these links to Chapter 18.

SUMMARY AND CONCLUSIONS

We have seen that the firm's goals have a definite effect upon its price and output decisions. A profit goal in terms of target rates of return will not lead to the same price and output decisions as will one based upon marginal revenue and marginal cost concepts. A firm whose primary goal is revenue maximization subject to a profit constraint tends to produce at a greater output rate and to sell at a lower price than does a firm whose goal is profit maximization—other things being equal. Whereas a profit-maximizing firm has no incentive to alter its price and output in the face of increases in either fixed costs or taxes, a revenue-maximizing firm tends to respond by curtailing output and raising selling prices. A revenue maximizer also tends to spend greater amounts on advertising and sales promotion, which, if effective, will tend to push its output rate beyond that of a comparable profit-maximizing firm.

Unless confronted with an unfavorable economic environment, corporations will exhibit a strong propensity to grow. This holds whether their

principal goal is long-run profit maximization or some combination of higher
profit, greater sales revenues, and stronger market position. A powerful
growth psychology tends to develop among corporate enterprises. Over the
long term, corporate growth strategy tends to emerge as a major dimension
of corporate capitalism. The effect is to thrust the business sector into the
role of being the driving force behind overall expansion of the economy. In
a very real sense, business enterprises are the engine of economic growth
and economic progress.

SUGGESTED READINGS

BAUMOL, W. J., *Business Behavior, Value and Growth*, rev. ed. (New York: Harcourt
Brace Jovanovich, Inc., 1967), Chapters 6–10.

KAMERSCHEN, D. R., "The Return of Target Pricing?" *Journal of Business*, Vol. 48,
No. 2 (April 1975), pp. 242–252.

KAPLAN, A. D. H., J. B. DIRLAM, AND R. F. LANZILOTTI, *Pricing in Big Business*
(Washington, D.C.: The Brookings Institution, 1958), Chapter 2.

MARRIS, R., "A Model of the 'Managerial' Enterprise," *Quarterly Journal of Economics*, Vol. 77, No. 2 (May 1963), pp. 185–209.

MARRIS, R., *The Economic Theory of 'Managerial' Capitalism* (New York: The Free
Press, 1964).

MONROE, K. B., *Pricing: Making Profitable Decisions* (New York: McGraw-Hill
Book Company, 1979).

PENROSE, E., *The Theory of the Growth of the Firm* (New York: John Wiley & Sons,
Inc., 1959).

SHEPHERD, W. G., "On Sales-Maximizing and Oligopoly Behavior," *Economica*,
Vol. 29, No. 116 (November 1962), pp. 420–424.

WESTON, J. F., "Pricing Behavior of Large Firms," *Western Economic Journal*, Vol.
10, No. 1 (March 1972), pp. 1–18.

WILDSMITH, J. R., *Managerial Theories of the Firm* (New York: The Dunellen
Company, 1973).

WILLIAMSON, J., "Profit, Growth and Sales Maximization," *Economica*, Vol. 33,
No. 129 (February 1966), pp. 1–16.

WILLIAMSON, O. E., "A Model of Rational Managerial Behavior," which appears as
Chapter 9 of *A Behavioral Theory of the Firm*, R. M. Cyert and J. G. March,
eds. (Englewood Cliffs, N.J.: Prentice-Hall, Inc., 1963), pp. 237–252.

WILLIAMSON, O. E., *The Economics of Discretionary Behavior: Managerial Objectives
in a Theory of the Firm* (Englewood Cliffs, N.J.: Prentice-Hall, Inc., 1964).

WILLIAMSON, O. E., *Corporate Control and Business Behavior* (Englewood Cliffs,
N.J.: Prentice-Hall, Inc. 1970).

PROBLEMS AND QUESTIONS FOR DISCUSSION

1. If a firm selects its selling price via some sort of "cost-plus" technique, is it possible for the firm to ever lose money? Why or why not?
2. Minnick Corporation has invested $50 million in facilities and equipment to

508

*Business
Pricing
Practices and
Multiple-Goal
Models*

produce miniature portable color TV sets with a 4-inch screen. Minnick's annual production capacity is 2 million sets. Over the last five years, Minnick's sales of these miniature TV sets have averaged 1.6 million per year. The company's fixed costs have remained relatively stable at $10 million per year. The firm estimates its annual total variable cost function to be $TVC = 120Q + 10Q^2$, where Q is *millions* of units of TV sets sold per year.

(a) If Minnick desires to earn a target rate of return on its investment of 30% (before taxes), what target return price should Minnick select?

(b) If Minnick's pricing policy is to add 15% to its normal production costs to determine selling price, what price should it charge, based upon the above information?

3. In the college textbook business, it is standard practice for the author's royalty to be some percentage of the total revenue which the publisher receives from sales of the book. The publisher, of course, incurs all costs of manufacturing, promoting, and distributing the book. Would the price and the sales volume (the number of books sold) which maximize the publisher's profits on the book also maximize the author's royalty payments? Why or why not? Demonstrate your answer graphically.

4. Suppose that in the short run a firm produces under conditions of constant returns to variable input over the entire output range for which it has production capability. Suppose further that the firm selects its selling price in order to earn a target rate of return on its investment and follows the practice of selling at the target return price no matter what short-run demand conditions happen to be.

(a) Graphically illustrate the firm's short-run AVC, MC, and ATC curves.

(b) On the same graph, illustrate a target return price.

(c) Under these circumstances what is the value of MR?

(d) At what output rate would the firm maximize short-run profits?

(e) At what output rate would the firm maximize sales revenues?

5. Suppose that a firm's short-run production function is characterized by constant returns to variable input. Suppose further that the firm faces a linear, downsloping demand curve for its product.

(a) Graphically illustrate the firm's TR, TC, and π functions.

(b) Indicate on your graph the profit-maximizing output.

(c) Indicate on your graph a profit constraint which is smaller than the maximum amount of profit.

(d) Indicate the revenue-maximizing output, given the profit constraint.

6. The Harco Instrument Corporation has estimated its monthly demand function to be $P = 416 - 7Q$ and its monthly total cost function to be $TC = 1700 + 16Q + Q^2$.

(a) If Harco's goal is to maximize sales revenue subject to the constraint that profits equal no less than $3200 per month, what is Harco's optimum price and output rate? (*Hint:* Recalling that $\pi = TR - TC$, substitute the appropriate expressions into this equation and solve for Q.)

(b) If Harco's goal is to maximize profits, then what is its optimum price and output rate? How does the profit-maximizing price and output compare with the revenue-maximizing price and output?

(c) Suppose Harco's total fixed costs rise from $1700 to $1750. Determine the impact upon Harco's profit-maximizing price and output rate.

(d) Determine the impact of the increase in total fixed costs from $1700 to $1750 upon Harco's revenue-maximizing price and output rate, given the profit constraint of $3200.

SIXTEEN ▼ EVALUATING COMPETITION AND MARKET PERFORMANCE

The preceding six chapters have emphasized how markets function and how firms compete, with only modest attention devoted to evaluating how these processes impact society. However, it is now time to stand back and appraise competition and market structure from the standpoint of "the public interest." Which, if any, of the four types of market structures is the "best" one from society's standpoint? Does a perfectly competitive type of market structure give rise to a lower price and greater output than an oligopolistic type of market structure? How much and what kinds of competition are socially and economically desirable? In the long run is competition among the few more or less socially beneficial than competition among the many? Are giant corporations in a position to take advantage of consumers? Is big business monopolistic? How large is the economic impact upon society of collusion, monopolistic practices, the exercise of market power, and weak competitive pressures? How can these impacts best be reduced or contained?

Make no mistake about it, these are very tough questions. They involve some very thorny issues which bear directly upon the overall economic welfare of society. Unfortunately, not many categorical answers can be given; in most cases "it all depends." This is partly because actual business behavior and market conditions do not neatly correspond to the theoretical models of perfect competition, monopolistic competition, oligopoly, or pure monopoly.

There are numerous intermediate and borderline situations; in some industries the size distribution of firms produces characteristics that partly fit one model and partly another.

More important, most formal models of business behavior are *static* in their analytical approach; that is, they portray how firms and markets will behave under a particular set of circumstances. The models are presented as operating toward an equilibrium, the essence of which varies with the original set of market circumstances. The character of the equilibrium position is what commands the center of attention, with only incidental concern for the time and the path for reaching equilibrium. This sort of analytical procedure is called *comparative statics*, since it ultimately involves comparing results at some equilibrium point with those obtained at another equilibrium point.

The fact is, however, that the static equilibrium results of particular competitive patterns are just snapshots of an ongoing process. Market conditions and competitive pressures are always in a state of flux. New equilibrium positions are constantly in the process of being created. Disequilibrium conditions are thus the norm, not the exception, as markets respond and react. In short, as indicated in Chapter 14, *competition is a dynamic process, not an equilibrium outcome.* Consequently, the effectiveness of competition is not readily discerned from statically oriented models of business behavior. Furthermore, an economically advantageous equilibrium outcome in the short run may prove to be unfavorable in the long run, or vice versa. This means that rendering a true and objective judgment about the effects of competition on society's economic welfare requires extending the time frame of the evaluation period and examining business performance as it unfolds over a period of years. Price *trends* and output *trends*, taken in conjunction with quality improvements, new product innovation, technological change, and the *patterns* of market change, give a more complete and valid evaluation of the competitive process and its impact on society.

For these reasons, caution is warranted in using the conclusions of the many static models of business behavior to project the ultimate impact on society's economic welfare over the long term. While static theoretical models do yield valuable insights into competitive processes (and for that alone they are worthwhile), they are far from being the last word in microeconomic theory. There is much more to learn about the mechanics and processes of disequilibrium adjustment and the long-run competitive effects of technological change, innovation, shifts in firms' competitive strategies, and market growth.

All this amounts to saying that the state of microeconomic theory is too underdeveloped and too untested to permit *unequivocal* answers to the questions posed above. Besides, as we shall see shortly, numerous subtle value judgments quickly creep into any discussion of what is and what is not in the best interest of society. However, we shall not use these circumstances as an excuse to dodge the issues. Having come this far, we shall proceed to try to tie things together—if only provisionally—and to arrive at some conclusions—even if they are tentative and weighted by value judgments. Nonetheless, you are dutifully forewarned that what follows is neither totally accepted nor thoroughly tested economic doctrine. Our dicussion will be laced with generalizations and tendencies, and ample room will exist for exceptions. No economist pretends that this is a satisfactory state of affairs, but it is about the best that can be done, given what we now know about the economics of the firm and competitive processes.

THE CRITERIA FOR EVALUATING BUSINESS BEHAVIOR

The first step in launching an evaluation of a competitive private enterprise system is to decide upon the standards for judging business conduct and market performance. This, in itself, is a controversial task because it necessarily entails subjective judgments as to what is important and what is not. Reasonable people can disagree over both the criteria and the priorities. Nonetheless, some common ground does exist.

We begin with the fundamental assertion that the business sector of the economy performs well when it provides consumers with whatever goods and services they want to buy at prices no higher than required to make production feasible and sustainable. From this statement follow several explicit criteria or standards for judging business behavior, not necessarily listed in order of their priority or social importance:

1. The production decisions of business firms regarding output rates and the range of quality must be responsive to consumer demand.
2. Production activity should be undertaken according to the most efficient technological and organizational means.
3. The operations of business firms should be progressive in the sense that new technological achievements both for increasing output per unit of input and for producing new and superior products are encouraged and exploited.
4. The constraints upon discretionary business decisions should be severe enough to preclude firms from securing profits much in excess of those needed to sustain the desired amount of production.
5. The operations of business firms should be compatible with the achievement of such national economic goals as full employment, price stability, economic growth, a rising standard of living, an increasing quality of life, economic freedom, an equitable distribution of income, and so on.

Unfortunately, these criteria are not always completely consistent. For example, letting companies like Chrysler or Penn Central go bankrupt may not be compatible with achieving full employment. Being technologically progressive and substituting capital for labor may mean laying off workers and creating unemployment. Reducing automobile pollution may mean increasing fuel costs and more consumption of gasoline at a time of growing scarcity of oil resources. Trade-offs and compromises are inevitable. Moreover, different individuals and groups are certain to place different priorities upon the various criteria. Value judgments as to which should take precedence will creep in. Still, good industrial performance implies that all five standards be satisfied to the greatest extent feasible.

THE MANY DIMENSIONS OF COMPETITION

In a capitalistically oriented economy, competition is *the chief vehicle* for promoting good industrial performance. The essence of competition is an *independent striving for patronage* by firms selling competing products. Except for the unique circumstances of natural monopoly, there can really be no argument as to the desirability of having vigorous competition in each and every market. Indeed, the presence of a number of rival firms, each independently and aggressively striving for patronage, diffuses economic power and control over a product. The more firms there are, the more diffused market power becomes and the more difficult it becomes for any one firm to "rig the market" to its own advantage. As long as consumers can freely choose to purchase from any one of several competing firms, it is hard for any one firm to exercise control over market price and consumers acquire a measure of protection from excessively high prices. Furthermore, it is competition, in conjunction with profit incentives, which induces firms both to synchronize their production decisions with consumer demand and to employ efficient production and managerial technologies. Consequently, by limiting the bounds of discretionary, and perhaps arbitrary, business decisions, competition serves to monitor business behavior in ways that protect consumers from being exploited and that limit the potential abuse of economic power. The extent to which competitive forces are actually strong enough to yield the foregoing results determines just how good the performance of firms and markets will be.

However, competition assumes many forms and comes in many different shades of intensity. Competition can and does proceed simultaneously along several routes. There is price competition, technological and innovational competition, quality competition, growth competition, and potential competition. In addition, business firms strive for greater patronage and increased market shares through advertising and sales strategy campaigns, thereby giving rise to what might be termed promotional competition. Still other dimensions of the competitive process relate to such matters as location, convenience, terms of credit, delivery, design and styling, customer service, product guarantees, packaging, ego-satisfaction, status, and prestige.

As might be suspected, society derives considerably more benefit from some of these dimensions of competition than from others. This proposition can be dramatically illustrated by comparing the results of "competition among the many" with those of "competition among the few."

CONTRASTS IN COMPETITIVE BEHAVIOR:
MANY-FIRM COMPETITION VERSUS
FEW-FIRM COMPETITION

513

*Contrasts in
Competitive
Behavior*

There are some significant differences in the style and vigor of competition in markets where there are many sellers (perfect competition and monopolistic competition) as compared to markets where there are only a few sellers (oligopoly and monopoly). These contrasts in competitive styles and intensities are important because they provide the touchstones for weighing the merits of various market structures and for evaluating the performance of giant corporations relative to small entrepreneurial firms.

Price Competition

Traditionally, economists have used two criteria to assess the degree and effectiveness of price competition in the marketplace. One relates to the extent to which prices are responsive to changing market demand–market supply conditions. The other relates to the propensity of firms to seek out new business by cutting price below rival sellers. The conventional wisdom is that competition is ineffective and competitive forces not powerful enough (1) unless the going market price is at or moving toward a level that balances demand and supply and (2) firms are aggressive in trying to undersell rivals. Price competition is, almost without exception, viewed as superior to any form of nonprice competition.

In general, competition among the many scores very highly in terms of the vigor of price competition. To begin with, the more sellers there are in the marketplace, the more each one is forced to be a price-taker. The presence of so many sellers, each with small to negligible market shares, means that any one firm's influence over market price is minimal to nonexistent. Thus, each individual firm is straitjacketed by demand-supply factors beyond its control—except when its product has been differentiated sufficiently to give it some discretion over the price it charges.

Price competition in many-firm market structures, consequently, takes the form of firms struggling to produce profitably at the price established by supply and demand. This is particularly true where the products of firms are essentially homogeneous and each firm's demand-AR-MR curve is horizontal at the prevailing market price. Perfectly competitive firms have no real incentive to *independently* lower price in an effort to increase sales because, with perfectly elastic demand, there is no profit in a firm's deciding to sell below the going price. Hence, in perfectly competitive markets where firms are price-takers, any change in market price mirrors a change in market demand–market supply conditions.

However, in monopolistically competitive markets, price competition can be more than just a reflection of market change; it can take the form of firms trying to attract more buyers by means of a lower price. Product differentiation, when made effective in the minds of buyers, gives firms a modest influence over their selling prices and allows some to rely upon lower prices as a major tactic for increasing patronage of their products. But even here, different selling prices among firms may be more a reflection of real (or imagined) quality differences or a lack of accurate price information on the part of buyers than it is a measure of producers' attempts to attract more patronage by selling at a price lower than rivals.

On the other hand, oligopoly is seldom viewed as conducive to active price competition, at least in theory. Oligopolistic firms, because of their high visibility and market share, are often able to frame their own pricing policy. In other words, they are price-makers. Although by no stretch of the imagination are they able to charge whatever they please for their products, oligopolists do have a degree of price-making influence which in general exceeds that in markets where firms are more numerous. This is illustrated by the propensity of oligopolists (especially large corporations) to use target return pricing and price leadership as a means of price determination. Nonetheless, the close personal rivalry among oligopolists, the rapid shift of patronage to a lower-priced seller, and strong mutual interdependence regarding price combine to create an overwhelming need for oligopolists to be competitive on price.

However, it is true, for reasons explored in Chapter 12, that oligopolists are not prone to use price cutting *regularly* as a *standard* competitive weapon. Many economists point to the lack of aggressive price cutting as evidence of weak competitive pressures. According to their view, competition is deficient whenever firms can avoid a struggle whereby the "high" profits of firms are eventually competed away by successive rounds of price reductions. This, however, presumes both that prevailing prices are "above competitive levels" and that oligopolists never learn that price cuts will be matched and that the profits of all firms, including the price-cutter, will tend to vanish should price cutting become a common way of life. For firms not to realize, sooner or later, that it will not pay to reduce profit margins any further via price cuts suggests a most inept and naive form of business judgment. No firm can long fail to recognize the folly of initiating round after round of lower prices, watching the price cuts matched by rivals, and observing that the resulting increases in sales fail to make up for the lower price. The futility of this sort of "price competition" is likely, therefore, to be quickly appreciated by competing firms.

Generally, what seems to happen in oligopolistic markets is that firms, one way or another, arrive at an industrywide price structure high enough to allow most firms to earn at least "satisfactory" profits but not so high as to induce some firms to engage in price cutting and cause continual downward pressure on price or to induce entry. In industries where oligopolists sell essentially identical products, uniform prices are imperative because higher-priced firms will tend to be squeezed out of the market. In industries where oligopolists sell differentiated products, the prices of rivals will be comparable, although not necessarily identical, since some buyers can be persuaded to tolerate price differentials based upon either real or imagined product differences. Consequently, as long as buyers are well informed about the selling prices of rival oligopolists, competitive pressures can be reliably counted upon to create a narrow price band, if not a single price. The ease with which patronage flocks to lower-priced sellers demands such an outcome.

This brings us to a key question: Are prices more "competitive" under competition among the many or under competition among the few? There is no satisfactory research evidence to answer this question. About the most that economists can say at this point is that price competition is *likely* to be more vigorous the more firms there are in the marketplace. In other words, "many" firms is a preferable condition to "few" firms. But this reflects more a belief that oligopoly carries a greater *risk* of lax price competition than it does any strong empirical evidence which shows price competition to be more prevalent in many-firm markets than it is in few-firm markets.

Technological and Innovational Competition

Among the most powerful and socially beneficial forms of competition is that associated with the emergence of the new product, the new technology, the new source of supply, and the new type of business enterprise.[1] The competitive impact of new things has, as a matter of historical fact, regularly undermined the established positions of market advantage possessed by monopolistic or oligopolistic corporations. Victims of technological and innovational competition include the steel firms, which now face strong competition from plastics, aluminum, and other metal alloys; the railroads firms, whose share of freight traffic has been substantially eroded by trucking firms and the airlines; and the motion picture industry, which has been plagued by the advent of television. Gillette's monopoly position in the safety razor market was irreparably weakened by the emergence of electric razors and by the development of long-lasting blades by other firms. As almost any downtown retailer will quickly point out, the new competition that has really mattered has arisen not from additional downtown retail outlets of the same type, but from innovative retailing organizations—the chain store, the mail-order house, the shopping mall, the discount store, the supermarket, the self-service department store, and the convenience store.

In a technologically dynamic environment new products are constantly replacing old products; new technologies are rendering older methods obsolete; some types of enterprises are prospering while others are dying out. The faster the procession of new innovations, the shorter becomes the life cycle of more products, technologies, and industries. Technological and innovational competition produces a "perennial gale of creative destruction"

---

[1]Joseph A. Schumpeter, *Capitalism, Socialism and Democracy*, 3rd ed. (New York: Harper & Brothers, 1950), p. 84; John Kenneth Galbraith, *American Capitalism: The Concept of Countervailing Power* (Boston: Houghton Mifflin Company, 1952), Chapter 7.

and few firms and industries are sheltered from its winds. Thus, like it or not, firms are drawn into competing on grounds of technological superiority and product innovation.

Over the long run, whether a firm is technologically progressive is much more crucial to society than whether it is operating at the lowest possible unit cost at some moment of time. Long-run performance is ultimately what counts most because it is principally from technological change and innovation that society realizes gains in productivity (output per unit of input), gains in the quantity and quality of output, and gains in the level of per capita income. Hence, the truly effective enterprise must do enough research and development that it will be in a timely position to (1) improve its product or service, (2) install more efficient production processes, (3) adopt better methods of transportation, (4) move into new markets, and/or (5) take advantage of new sources of supply of raw materials and component parts. Simply trying to operate its *present* facilities most efficiently—at the minimum point of its short-run and long-run average total cost curve—is not enough.

This leads to the crucial question of this section. Is a market environment which tends to squeeze profit margins and force price close to minimum average total cost in the short run compatible with the achievement of a high rate of technological progress and innovation? Based upon real-world industrial performance, the answer to this question is "often not." While the competitive style of many-firm markets is powerful in pushing individual firm output rates toward the least-cost point, technological and innovational competition reaches its most dramatic heights in oligopolistic markets populated by large corporations. The large corporation—not the small firm—is often in the best position to spearhead innovation and technological achievement.

Technological and Innovational Competition in the Corporate Sector. A number of interrelated reasons account for a relatively stronger focus on technological and innovational competition in the largely oligopolistic corporate sector as compared to small-firm markets. First, corporate oligopolists find price competition an unrewarding strategy for enhancing their sales-profit-market share positions since a price-cutting strategy is easily copied. Competing on the basis of new product variations, innovation, and production superiority is far more fruitful—especially over the long run, because the innovator can get a jump on rivals of several months to several years and acquire a reputation for leadership as well. The profit successes of IBM, Xerox, Polaroid, Eastman Kodak, DuPont, and other high-technology firms vividly illustrate the value of a competitive strategy based on technological and innovational leadership. But, at the same time, an innovator can scarce afford to rest on past laurels. A decided advantage currently will gradually be dissipated as rivals successfully imitate or even better the original innovation. It thus behooves a firm to press forward to develop still better products and production processes just to maintain its sales-profit position, much less improve it.

Second, many large firms are always on the lookout for new businesses to enter (either via acquisition or internal startup); this puts all firms under the gun to remain efficient and technologically progressive. Failure to do so merely gives rivals or new entrants the opportunity to attract customers away from the laggard firm with increasing ease. The terrific pressure that technological competition brings to bear upon the highly personalized competitive environment of corporate oligopoly is illustrated every time a firm introduces a new product and rival firms scramble to bring out their versions. The same applies to technological breakthroughs which produce dramatic cost savings.

Third, as a firm becomes larger, it becomes more able to undertake innovations and to compete on the basis of technology. Technological progress may be viewed as occurring in four steps: invention, development, implementation, and diffusion. *Invention* is the act of conceiving a new product or process and working out the details in its essential but rudimentary form. *Development* is the lengthy sequence of trial-and-error testing through which the invention is modified, perfected, and worked out in finest detail to make it technically ready for practical application. *Innovation* involves implementing the finalized version of the invention and putting it into practice for the first time. *Diffusion* relates to the rate and speed at which the innovation comes into widespread use as other enterprises follow the lead of the innovator. The available evidence indicates that steps 1 and 2 (invention and development) are often relatively inexpensive and can be undertaken on a small scale.[2] They are thus within the reach of both small and large firms. The third step, however, can be a costly, time-consuming process. The product may have to be test-marketed, unforeseen technical bugs eliminated, new productive facilities built or expanded, marketing channels organized, promotional campaigns designed and instituted, and competition from other products surmounted—a process that can take several years and require major organizational and financial commitments before a profit payoff is realized. Past experience shows that it is difficult for groups of small firms locked in a struggle for short-term survival to find the resources to support such efforts.

The financial and organizational limitations of small entrepreneurial firms explain why many inventions which originated in small companies have ended up as major products of large corporations. Well-known examples include air conditioning, the jet engine, cellophane, the cotton picker, the helicopter, power steering, and the cracking of petroleum.[3] This also explains why big companies may end up producing products discovered by academicians, independent inventors, and specialized R&D firms. Examples include the development of titanium metals, Eastman Kodak's Kodachrome color camera film, the development of Dacron fibers by DuPont, and Xerox's

[2]For an excellent discussion of this and related points, see F. M. Scherer, *Industrial Market Structure and Economic Performance* (Chicago: Rand McNally & Company, 1970), Chapter 15, especially pp. 350–352.

[3]John Jewkes, David Sawers, and Richard Stillerman, *The Sources of Invention* (New York: St. Martin's Press, 1958), pp. 71–85.

development of quick copiers. A number of other innovations have required such large-scale funding that only large firms could undertake them. The design and development costs of civilian jet airliners soared past the $100 million mark. Polaroid, over an 8-year period, invested $500 million to bring the SX-70 camera and film onto the market—a bold technical achievement that represents one of the biggest gambles ever on a consumer product. RCA sunk $65 million into R&D on color television before achieving a product with mass market potential. IBM staked its future and $5 billion over a 5-year period in designing, developing, and marketing its System/360 line of computers. Many millions were also spent by Alcoa in aircraft metals fabrication, by General Electric in refining X-ray equipment, by Westinghouse in designing nuclear-powered generating equipment, by steel firms in developing continuous casting of steel, and by General Motors in its development of diesel locomotives, automatic transmissions, liquid-cooled aircraft engines, and catalytic converters.

Technological and Innovational Competition in Small-Firm Markets.
Even so, there are numerous instances of innovation in small firm markets. By no means do all or even most innovations entail so much time, money, and risk that they can be undertaken only by giant firms. A census of the innovations in any one year would unquestionably reveal that the number of less-costly, minor innovations is far greater than the number of very expensive, more spectacular innovations. Thus, there are many technical challenges which can be successfully met by small entrepreneurial firms willing to bear the risks. Examples where small firms have been active in innovation include specialized applications of computer technology, semiconductors and electronic circuitry technology, numeric process control equipment, the use of bank credit cards, and retailing. Innovational opportunities for small firms also arise when the managers of large corporate enterprises are skeptical of the possibilities of proposed new products or new processes and when entrepreneur-minded scientists and researchers leave the employ of large firms to create their own enterprises.[4] For these reasons, small enterprises cannot be relegated to an insignificant role in advancing the cause of technological progress. While a small firm is sometimes at a clear disadvantage in the process of technological and innovational competition, at other times and in other industries it is capable of competing on an almost equal footing.

The Empirical Evidence. It is indisputable that large-scale enterprises have made bigger financial and organizational commitment to technology than have small-scale firms. Statistics compiled by the National Science Foundation consistently show that the biggest firms undertake the lion's

[4]Within the last 25 years, hundreds of research enterprises have been founded by entrepreneur-minded scientists and researchers who became disenchanted with the highly-structured, results-oriented R&D programs of high-technology corporations. See E. B. Roberts, "Entrepreneurship and Technology," *Research Management*, Vol. 11, No. 4 (July 1968), pp. 249–266, and A. H. Rubinstein, "Problems of Financing New Research-based Enterprises in New England," *New England Business Review* (July and August 1958).

share of all formal industrial R&D activity. For many years firms having 5000 or more employees have accounted for 85 to 90% of industrial R&D spending; firms with fewer than 1000 employees account for only 5%.[5] Over 85% of the companies with 5000 or more employees have R&D budgets of at least $1,000,000, and over 200 of these companies spend more than $10 million for R&D activities. Moreover, in 1976 over 80% of the scientists and engineers engaged in R&D were employed in firms with 5000 or more employees. Fewer than 4% of these scientists and engineers were employed in R&D labs with budgets of less than $250,000. Very little formal scientific and engineering effort is in evidence in industries where the four largest firms have a combined market share below 15%.[6]

R&D outlays, of course, are only an input measure; they do not reflect innovational success or significance. Yet, it seems unlikely that innovation will occur as regularly where R&D is haphazard and casual as it will where it is organized and results-oriented. That this is so is suggested by the infrequency with which entrepreneurial firms operating in atomistically structured markets produce the *showcase* results of U.S. technological superiority and economic achievement; most of the time they are built by large-scale enterprise.

However, it is true that once a firm passes some threshold size there is room to question just how supportive bigness is of technical progress. Instances have occurred where companies dominating their markets have been slow to lead and quick to follow innovation. Sometimes progressiveness is as much the result of technological opportunity and profit potential as it is bigness, while on other occasions the largest firms' share of significant innovations has been found to be inversely correlated with high market shares.[7] Furthermore, where large firms are solidly entrenched, there is always the chance that technical progress will be retarded by a restricted number of independent sources of initiative and by a dampened incentive to gain an ever-stronger market position through accelerated R&D.

But these illustrations of monopolistic suppression of technological advance in no way undermine the fact that large corporations—from the standpoints of capacity to absorb risk, organizational knowhow, and financial capability—are better-positioned than small companies to serve as *potential* pace-setters for implementing profitable technological discoveries and

[5]National Science Foundation, *Research and Development in Industry 1975* (Washington, D.C.: U.S. Government Printing Office, 1975).

[6]Jewkes, Sawers, and Stillerman, *The Sources of Invention*, p. 117; F. M. Scherer, "Market Structure and the Employment of Scientists and Engineers," *American Economic Review*, Vol. 57, No. 3 (June 1967), pp. 529–530.

[7]See, for instance, Scherer, *Industrial Market Structure and Economic Performance*, pp. 371–376; Oliver E. Williamson, "Innovation and Market Structure," *Journal of Political Economy* (February 1965), pp. 67–73; W. S. Comanor, "Market Structure, Product Differentiation, and Industrial Research," *Quarterly Journal of Economics*, Vol. 81, No. 4 (November 1967), pp. 639–657; Almarin Phillips, "Patents, Potential Competition, and Technical Progress," *American Economic Review*, Vol. 56, No. 2 (May 1966), pp. 301–310; and Morton I. Kamien and Nancy L. Schwartz, "Market Structure and Innovation: A Survey," *Journal of Economic Literature*, Vol. 13, No. 1 (March 1975), pp. 22–26.

new product improvements. What they do say very clearly is that the large corporation's potential for innovation must be kept activated by competitive pressures if faster technological progress is to result from bigness and oligopoly.

In general, it can be said that technological progress is potentially enhanced more by large corporations than by small enterprises. Big firms are fully capable of engaging in technological and innovational competition of the highest order of magnitude; little companies are not. The corporation's larger profits and cash flow, its ability to absorb the losses from research which proves unfruitful, its superior access to money capital for financing new investments, and its greater organizational capacity in terms of scientific, engineering, and managerial know-how necessarily place it ahead of the typical entrepreneurial firm as the potential pacesetter for pushing back the barriers to technological progress. When the corporation's *capacity for innovation* is combined with its motives for competing on the basis of technological superiority, the result is an organizational vehicle of significant social importance for advancing the cause of technological progress. The rise of the large corporate enterprise and its attendant scientific and managerial establishment underlies much of the increase in the rate of technological advance which characterize the modern industrial economies of the twentieth century.

The Key Issue. The reason it is important to determine whether corporate capitalism is, on balance, more progressive than atomistic competition is simply this: *An industry composed of many small firms whose rate of technological progress is "slow" will in the long run prove to be less efficient and will make less of a contribution to society's economic well-being than will a competitive industry composed of firms large enough to achieve a higher rate of technological achievement.* This result holds even though the technologically slow firms start from a position of lower costs and lower prices. Consider the following situation, which illustrates this point.

Assume that an industry is composed of 100 small companies, each producing 10 units of output and operating its facilities at peak efficiency and minimum ATC. Total industry output would therefore be 1000 units, which, let us say, could currently be sold at a price of $6 a unit. Suppose further that (1) the introduction of new technological innovations raises efficiency and permits the firms to increase production by 3% each year using the same amounts of resource inputs, and (2) competition causes any cost savings (exclusive of inflationary effects) to be passed on to consumers through price reductions of 1% annually. At the end of 5 years, then, industry output will have risen to 1159 units and the market price will have fallen to $5.71.

Now let us assume that this same industry is, instead, composed of three large corporations each producing 300 units of output but operating just short of minimum ATC at 333 units of output. Total industry output initially would total 900 units or 10% less than the output under a 100-firm market structure. The lesser initial output of the three large corporations, assuming identical market demand conditions, will allow them to obtain a higher price, say $6.30. But suppose that the large firms invest more heavily in R&D and, because of resulting efficiencies, are able to expand output by 5% per year using the same amount of resource inputs (but still producing short of ATC). Suppose also that competitive pressures are strong enough to force them to pass part of the cost-savings along to consumers in the form of price reductions of 2% per year.[8] At the end of 5 years the total output of the three large corporations will be 1149 units and price will have fallen to $5.70— results that are comparable to the small-firm market structure even though the three corporations started out with a lower total output and higher prices.

Moreover, every year thereafter the three-firm oligopolistic market will *outperform* the small-firm market on both *price* and *output* by an increasing amount. Prices in the oligopolistic market will fall by 2% compared to only 1% in the small-firm market; output in the oligopolistic market will expand by 5% compared to only 3% in the small-firm market. These results will occur without any economies-of-scale advantage and despite the fact that the three oligopolists may earn greater profits per unit of output and may not produce at minimum *ATC*.

This example, although oversimplified, illustrates the importance of long-run performance in evaluating corporate capitalism. The rate of technical progress, not prices, profits, or efficiency at some moment of time, ultimately determines the quality and quantity of a product and the impact on the consumer's pocketbook. For this reason alone, it follows that *the socially optimum type of market structure is the one most conducive to achieving technological advance and innovation yet competitive enough to protect consumers against abuses of market power.* In some situations, oligopoly can be closer to this optimum than either perfectly or monopolistically competitive small-firm markets; in other situations, the reverse may be true. Ideally, a market structure of large or medium-sized corporations operating under conditions close to monopolistic competition might function best if market demand for the product is sizable enough to support a *large* number of *large* firms. Unfortunately, national and international markets for specific products often have too limited a total demand to permit the supply side of the market to be comprised of large numbers of large firms.

Quality Competition

By *quality competition* is meant an independent striving among firms for increased patronage based upon differences in durability, value, functional

---

[8]In many instances, of course, the fruits of technological progress are passed along to consumers in the form of increased quality rather than lower prices. (Color TV serves as a good example.) This alters the form but not the substance of the outcome insofar as the benefits to consumers are concerned. It could also be argued that none of the cost savings will be passed on to consumers, owing to the market power of large firms and the lack of price competition, which allows them to keep prices up and thereby earn greater economic profits. However, trends in the profit margins of large U.S. corporations do not indicate that such has historically been the case.

performance, styling, reliability, economy of use, service, delivery, the degree of completeness with which consumer needs are met, or whatever else in the value-quality-service spectrum fulfills buyer preferences. Quality competition thus emphasizes the competitive aspect of something *better*, whereas technological and innovational competition emphasizes the aspect of something *new*.

Competition among firms on matters of quality appears both in small-firm markets and in corporate-dominated industries and, typically, reaches its most intense proportions where the products of rival firms are differentiated. Where firms produce homogeneous products, quality competition is a short-lived phenomenon; firms may strive to improve their products but the improvements are quickly adopted by rival firms, thereby wiping out quality differentials. Obviously, were this not to happen the firms would soon be producing differentiated products.

Quality competition interacts with the processes of technological change and innovation on a broad front. Product improvements are a result of research and development efforts aimed specifically at developing superior products. On the other hand, using a marketing strategy predicated upon offering consumers a high-quality product acts as a spur to product research and product innovation over a period of time.

On the whole, oligopolistic markets are characterized by vigorous quality competition. Obtaining a decisive quality advantage over rival firms' products is a forceful way in which to strengthen one's own market position, particularly when the higher-quality product can be sold at a price equal to or not much above the prices of lesser-quality products. Having a reputation for quality can give a firm a significant and perhaps long-lasting marketing edge that extends not only to the markets in which it currently competes but to the future product markets that it may seek to enter as well. Thus, oligopolistic rivals are very conscious of quality differentials and are attentive to developing product features that will give them a quality advantage.[9] It does not take long to learn that sustained success in the marketplace depends on consumers remaining satisfied with the quality of the item; it is repeat business and not one-time business that generates long-term economic profits. At the same time, intense quality competition among oligopolists develops because market pressures make it essential to charge the same price as do competitors offering identical or closely substitutable products.

Atomistically competitive markets with their characteristically smaller activity in new product research and development are, generally speaking, not as likely to be characterized by spirited battles over quality. The technological, pioneering type of entrepreneurial firm is, of course, an exception, but markets comprised of such firms are not relatively numerous. Quality competition in the small-firm sector often takes the form of specializing in the production of handcrafted or custom-made products for a very limited group

[9]During an inflationary spiral, however, when consumers become more price-conscious, firms may elect to reduce product quality as a means of holding down costs and reducing the need for even larger price increases.

of customers who want and can afford "the very best." Examples include furniture, articles of apparel, decorative items, and jewelry. Since economies of scale are negligible in producing these types of products and since the markets for such goods are typically limited, small firms tend to dominate the production of them. This type of quality competition is important to only a small elite group of consumers and cannot be said to stand at a rank equal in overall social importance to that found in mass-consumption industries.

Major benefit can accrue to consumers from quality competition. This is because all consumers do not share the same tastes and preferences for each product. When firms compete on the basis of quality-value-services differences, consumers end up with a wider range of choice, balanced between economy and luxury models; firms have an incentive to cater to the specific interests of small groups of consumers with specialized tastes as well as to the preferences of the great mass of consumers. Such a widening of consumer choice, provided that it is not carried to such an extreme as to create buyer confusion, allows buyers to select the specific variation best suiting their tastes, needs, and pocketbook. For example, General Motors has numerous styles and models of automobiles, each with a big array of accessory options. Each of the several producers of kitchen appliances, TV sets, stereos, radios, sewing machines, or typewriters offers the consumer a choice of the regular model, the deluxe model, or the superdeluxe model, and each model comes in a variety of colors and designs.

This is not to say, however, that some aspects of quality and service competition could not be better directed. There is more than an element of truth to the claim that some firms resort to "planned obsolescence" as a means of getting consumers to replace products more frequently. Products are sometimes deliberately engineered to have a short life. A few so-called new or improved products (cologne-scented shaving cream) have doubtful social value. Firms may fail to incorporate certain feasible improvements because the resulting increase in durability may greatly reduce replacement sales and total profits over time—the longer-lasting light bulb serves as a good example. Firms may also focus strongly on the aspects of quality that are most visible and profitable and neglect other features such as product safety. These practices can in no way be condoned and, as some disgruntled consumers apparently believe, the quality of many products could stand further improvement—the prevalence of such consumer attitudes at least partially underlies "consumerism."

Growth Competition

The character of competition is sometimes dependent on the priorities and goals of the firms themselves. For instance, the predominance of market demand–market supply conditions and the style of "competition among the many" often results in small entrepreneurial firms concentrating on how best to adjust to unfolding market conditions; decisions tend to be made with an eye toward their impact on short-run profitability. The preoccupation with short-run problems, coupled with the fact that if the owner-manager dies, retires, or sells out, the enterprise may come to an end, gives small entrepreneurial firms less of a long-range-growth orientation than professionally managed corporations. At the same time, the owner-managed firm's limited product line, limited resources for expansion, and short-term planning horizon, together with the ease of entry into small-firm dominated markets, leaves it with less growth opportunity. Once scale economies are exhausted (and this occurs at a relatively low output in atomistically structured markets), increased production is achieved not so much by expansion of existing firms as by the entry of new enterprises into the industry. In other words, market growth results in an increased number of firms in the industry, or, if profit opportunities are especially attractive, in large-scale corporate entry into the market.

In contrast, the goals of large corporations are typically more diverse and distantly focused; long-term survival is usually more certain and more top management attention is given to where the firm will be 5 to 20 years later. There is strong importance attached to growth strategies that will strengthen the firm's overall business interests not just with respect to a given product or market but with respect to the whole mix of products and markets in which the firm participates. Furthermore, relative to small entrepreneurial firms, the large corporation tends to place more emphasis on long-run performance than on short-run performance. Corporate behavior seems to be more nearly approximated by long-run profit maximization or revenue maximization or satisficing than by short-run profit maximization.[10] The importance that large corporate enterprises attach to long-term growth is so pervasive and so strong that new competition is created by the diversification and expansion attempts of large firms to grab a share of emerging market opportunities—a phenomenon we shall refer to as *growth competition.*

If demand for a particular product is expanding so fast that there is plenty of business for all sellers, it is possible for rival corporations to keep out of one another's way.[11] Serious head-on competition for new customers is unnecessary. But such relaxed competitive pressures are subject to quick reversal. As production capability catches up with demand, growth-minded managements find it harder to achieve their target rates of expansion. Respect for rivals' market positions and product emphasis succumbs to more aggressive actions. At this point competitive forces begin to stiffen by impressive proportions and a battle for market position arises. Thus, the process of growth competition within a particular market tends to be catalyzed by managerial pressures for increased sales volume and profits.

[10]Actual evidence to this effect was reported by Bjarke Fog in a study of international price-fixing agreements. In the industries he studied, Fog found that small firms preferred a price which was most advantageous in the short term, while large enterprises were in favor of a longer-range pricing policy. For further details, see Bjarke Fog, "How Are Cartel Prices Determined?" *Journal of Industrial Economics*, Vol. 4 (November 1956), pp. 16–23.

[11]G. C. Allen, "Economic Fact and Fantasy," Occasional Paper 14, The Institute of Economic Affairs, London, 1967, p. 20.

Once growth-oriented corporations find that they are approaching the limits of expansion for their existing products, either because of market saturation or because of possible allegations of monopoly power from the Antitrust Division of the Justice Department, they begin to cast about for new outlets for their investment capital. Diversification into new product lines, both related and unrelated to existing products, will be contemplated, as will expansion into international markets. Even product markets in other industries that have been long dominated by "name" firms are liable to invasion, unless, of course, entry is blocked or profit opportunities are especially dim. Expansion-minded firms are likely to be particularly attracted by the prospects of invading fast-growing markets comprised mainly of small companies and by the opportunities for launching into the production of new products where competition is currently minimal to nonexistent.

The ability of large corporations to move into new industries, new markets, and new product lines is relatively strong and their growth strategies can trigger a formidable set of competitive pressures. Well-entrenched corporations can seldom block the invasion of another large corporation when the latter is seriously bent on entering.[12] It is at this juncture that the path of expansion pursued by one corporation begins to intrude upon the territories of corporations in other industries. As a general rule, growth competition is most prevalent in markets where the demand outlook is highly favorable and/or where there is ample room for new firms to maneuver. In markets where demand gathers more slowly and can easily be absorbed by those companies already in operation, entry is less attractive and growth competition is much less of an effective force.

[12]A good example of how big corporations can invade the markets of other big corporations and thereby touch off a major competitive struggle is provided by Procter & Gamble's invasion of the market for household paper products. Twenty years ago, Scott Paper Co. was the undisputed leader in the household paper products field (toilet tissue, paper towels, and disposable diapers). But in 1957 P&G elected to enter the paper products market. Using its potent marketing muscle, which included heavy advertising (P&G is the nations' biggest advertiser), head-on invasions of new territories, the introducing of colors, scents, and designs, and a dazzling array of discounts, coupons, and special promotion deals, P&G steadily upped its share of the market to 25%. Scott Paper's overall market share in household paper products fell below 40%. According to Nielsen figures reported in *The Wall Street Journal*, P&G as of 1971 held 16.2% of the singleply toilet tissue market, which gave it a slim edge over Scott; it held 13.6% of the paper towel market, compared to Scott's 27.7%; and its Pamper diapers had grabbed off almost 100% of the disposable diaper market, forcing Scott to discontinue its disposable diaper line at a loss of $12.8 million. (The remainder of the household paper-products market is divided up primarily among American Can, Kimberly-Clark, Georgia Pacific, and Crown Zellerbach.)

Kotler has characterized Procter & Gamble's strategy of entering new markets as follows: "It [P&G] prefers to enter markets where there is only one major competitor. It positions its first brand not in the major competitor's segment but in a neglected segment. Then it creates additional brands for other neglected segments. Each entry creates its own loyal following and takes some business away from the major competitor. Soon the major competitor is surrounded, his revenue is weakened, and he is in no position to launch a counteroffensive of new brands in outlying segments. P&G, in a moment of final truiumph, then launches a brand against the major segment." See Philip Kotler, *Marketing Management: Analysis, Planning, and Control*, 3rd ed. (Englewood Cliffs, N.J.: Prentice-Hall, Inc., 1976), p. 169.

Examples of growth competition include the invasion of the U.S. steel market by Japanese steel firms, the battle by both domestic and foreign airlines for increased passenger traffic, the rise of the small foreign-made car in the United States, the decision of IBM to invade the field for copying equipment long dominated by Xerox, the hundreds of small-company acquisitions made by large corporations to gain immediate footholds in emerging markets and industries, and the formation of the giant conglomerate enterprises with their special emphasis upon diversified growth by merger.

Promotional Competition

It goes without saying that business enterprises seek to gain a strategic advantage over rival firms by the many various means of product promotion which are at their disposal. This process may be thought of as *promotional competition*.

Depending upon the circumstances, product promotion may enhance competitive forces in ways that are socially beneficial or it may serve to diminish competition and, consequently, diminish overall economic welfare. Promotional activity that is aimed at identifying sellers, giving instructions for use, describing performance features, and giving terms of sale facilitates competition by making buyers more fully informed about the products that are available. Advertising is the medium through which new firms, new products, improvements in existing products, and prices are made known. Advertising enables innovative firms to reach larger numbers of potential buyers rapidly and efficiently, enhancing the profits from innovation, and strengthening the incentive for investing in innovative endeavors.[13] It also permits the realization of production scale economies which might otherwise be unattainable. Additionally, advertising *may* signal a certain level of quality; products that are advertised and have been produced by well-known manufacturers are more likely to prove satisfactory than are nonadvertised products about which consumers know little or nothing (see the Applications Capsule on p. 528). Brands and trademarks help consumers select products of high quality and reliability and they assist buyers to reward through repeat purchases those firms whose products they find especially appealing. Hence, the practice of using brands and trademarks as an aspect of product differentiation motivates firms to maintain adequate quality standards. Multiproduct firms are particularly aware that one poor product, through the adverse reputation it creates, can impair the sales of other of its products.

On the other hand, it is doubtful whether consumers benefit from the more persuasive aspects of advertising and the exaggerated claims of "ours is better than theirs." The notorious soap, beer, toiletries, and soft-drink commercials are of dubious social benefit, except insofar as they serve to finance the entertainment supplied by the radio and television programs which they sponsor. The reason is that such advertising tends to be "self-

---

[13]Jules Backman, *Advertising and Competition* (New York: New York University Press, 1967), pp. 23–27.

canceling." The million-dollar advertising campaign of one brewery is quickly

countered by expensive advertising campaigns waged by the other breweries to protect their market position. Few additional people will drink beer because of the beer ads; about all that happens is that the firms fight over whose brands will be favored by those who will drink beer anyway. The extra advertising thus drives up the costs of the brewers and results in higher prices than might otherwise prevail. It raises the financial barriers to the entry of new firms by increasing the costs which they must incur to penetrate the market. And one can argue that it wastes economic resources that might be put to better social use in other endeavors.

There is some theoretical reason to expect promotional competition to be stiffer in oligopolistic markets than in atomistically competitive markets. Where consumers regard the products of rival firms as very close substitutes and individual firms are small relative to the market, then a product may tend to be less intensively advertised, because one firm's advertising expenditures will promote the product almost as much as it promotes the particular *brand* of the product of the advertisor.[14] The advantage of advertising is thereby greatly diluted. However, if individual firms are large relative to the market, advertising is more likely to pay off even if buyers view rival brands as close substitutes. In the latter case, the market share of the advertising firm is large enough relative to the total market so that its sales gains justify the advertising expense despite the fact that its advertising may spill over and benefit rival firms by persuading consumers to buy more of the product as well as more of its own brand. Moreover, because the competition among oligopolists is so personal and because they are so sensitive to each other's marketing strategy, they are often forced to advertise heavily not merely as a strategy for expanding their market share but as a means of defending their existing position from the promotional tactics of rival firms.[15]

It is readily observable that advertised brands are generally more expensive than nonadvertised brands. Whether this reflects the powers of persuasive advertising or the existence of quality differences between the two classes of products is unclear, but it is clear that large numbers of consumers often consider highly advertised brands as superior to less-advertised brands. We have only to observe the sometimes striking price differentials among compet-

[14]Lester G. Telser, "Advertising and Competition," *Journal of Political Economy*, Vol. 72, No. 6 (December 1964), pp. 540–541.

[15]Among the more recent and definitive studies of the competitive effects of advertising are Telser, "Advertising and Competition," pp. 537–562; Comanor and Wilson, "Advertising, Market Structure, and Performance," *Review of Economics and Statistics*, No. 3 (August 1969), pp. 423–440; H. Michael Mann, J. A. Henning, and J. W. Meehan, Jr., "Advertising and Concentration: An Empirical Investigation," *Journal of Industrial Economics*, Vol. 15 (November 1967), pp. 34–45; Richard A. Miller, "Market Structure and Industrial Performance: Relation of Profit Rates to Concentration, Advertising Intensity, and Diversity," *Journal of Industrial Economics*, Vol. 17 (April 1969), pp. 104–118; Leonard W. Weiss, "Advertising, Profits, and Corporate Taxes," *Review of Economics and Statistics*, Vol. 51, No. 4 (November 1969), pp. 421–430; W. S. Comanor and Thomas A. Wilson, *Advertising and Market Power* (Cambridge, Mass.: Harvard University Press, 1974); and Philip J. Nelson, "The Economic Consequences of Advertising," *Journal of Business*, Vol. 48, No. 2 (April 1975), pp. 213–241.

ADVERTISING: ITS IMPACT AND ECONOMIC SIGNIFICANCE

A theoretical revolution going by the name of "the economics of information" has begun to affect economists' view of the impact and significance of advertising. The conventional economic wisdom is that advertising tends to act as the handmaiden of market power, of downside price rigidity, and of long-term price inflation. Whereas businessmen judge advertising primarily in terms of its power to increase sales and attract customers from other firms, economists judge advertising on how it affects the overall performance of markets and the economy at large. The criteria economists generally use to evaluate advertising are its effects on price competition, product prices, the achievement of large-scale economies, and the extent to which it promotes full employment and maximum production efficiency.

By and large, economists view anything but price advertising with hostility, arguing that nonprice advertising is generally aimed at convincing consumers that a firm's products are somehow different from those of rivals. This creates brand loyalty, making the buying public much less sensitive to price and thereby giving the advertiser some degree of price influence. Beyond that, economists maintain that heavy advertising erects financial barriers to the entry of new firms because, to break into a market, companies must be willing and able to spend large sums on advertising to attract buyers' attention. To the extent that advertising barriers keep out new competitors, the market power of those firms already in the industry is enhanced, with the result that prices are higher and output is smaller than would be the case if markets were more oriented toward price competition. This view is supported by statistical studies showing a correlation between the amount an industry spends on advertising and both its profitability and degree of sales concentrated in a few firms.

However, the revolution going on with respect to the economics of information holds that advertising may contain virtue as well as vice. The new view addresses the question of how advertising affects the consumer and, particularly, the kind and scope of information it provides for consumer decision-making. Starting with the premise that advertising provides at least some information to consumers that they would not otherwise get, the argument is that information about a variety of products is far more likely to decrease monopoly power than to increase it.

George Stigler, of the University of Chicago, triggered the economics of information revolution in 1961, castigating economists for analyzing the prices in different markets in great depth, while relegating the analysis of consumer information about prices to "a slum dwelling in the town of economics." Whereas the customary economic view of advertising maintained that price differences for the same *type* of product were due to the ability of firms to differentiate their products and were taken as evidence that advertising gave firms too much price-making power, Stigler argued that a good part of the variability of prices, even among homogeneous products, existed because consumers did not know the prices being charged by various firms. It followed, then, that increased information about prices would enable buyers to bargain more effectively with sellers. As a consequence, reasoned Stigler, price advertising that makes search less expensive will reduce the average price consumers pay for a product.

However, in a recent study Phillip Nelson has carried Stigler's argument a step forward. Nelson claims that getting information on price is relatively easy; the difficult task for the consumer is getting a handle on quality. Nelson's study endeavors to explain how consumers get information about the quality of products from mass-media advertising, given that the information provided is likely to be self-serving and may actually be little more than image-building or boastful puffery. Nelson found that the informational content of advertising differs drastically, depending on the type of product being advertised. For what he called "search goods" (those products whose qualities can be more easily checked before purchase, such as a suit or a dress), the advertising content often consists of direct information on the quality and characteristics of the products; usually, this information is accurate since for advertisers to give misleading information invites legal action.

On the other hand, for "experience goods" (such as soft drinks, soaps, and deodorants, where ascertaining quality requires purchasing the item), advertising generally provides little or no direct quality information. For example, Nelson observes there is no direct information to "join the Pepsi generation." But even here, according to Nelson, the advertiser is saying to the consumer that the believes his product to be of high quality and well worth the consumer's dollar. And to the extent that highly advertised brands have a larger market share than less-advertised brands, there is a strong implication that the heavily advertised brand does have higher quality or yield more value to the consumer.

In support of this proposition, Nelson argues that companies will advertise their winners, not their losers, because heavy advertising of an inferior-quality product risks creating a bad image in the mind of the consumer not only of the brand but of the company as well. In the case of "experience goods" it is especially true that companies live or die from repeat purchases, so it stands to reason that over the long run the higher-quality products will win out over the lower-quality products. This leads Nelson to conclude that *on the average the best buy is the heavily advertised brand*—a proposition which traditionalists find somewhat appalling.

In addition, Nelson maintains that because advertising provides information on many similar products, consumer demand will become more responsive to price for any given product, rather than less responsive, as argued by anti-advertising critics. In other words, advertising increases information about the availability of substitutes, thereby undermining the monopoly power of any one brand—however highly advertised it may be.

Nelson's rule for buying the most advertised brand rests on two key assumptions. One, that sufficient numbers of consumers can judge quality differences between brands after they have used them. Two, that quality differences between brands would exist without advertising, given cost-efficiency differences between companies and given that companies have different opinions as to what product features consumers are looking for.

With respect to the overall market efficiency of advertising, Nelson argues that advertising permits the more efficient companies to increase their sales faster and that less efficient companies are weeded out more quickly than if there were no advertising. This yields a net economic benefit to society compared to a situation where companies do not advertise and where marginal firms may be able to hang on for longer periods of time.

The notion that advertising may be more good than bad has come under sharp attack. Perhaps the most fundamental weakness in this approach is the assumption that consumers can validate advertising claims easily and cheaply. If consumers are able to learn from experiences quickly, then it is more likely to be true that the advertised brand is the best buy—for many goods. But there are many products which require extensive testing by consumers, and other products, such as consumer durables, are purchased infrequently; in such cases, the experience information which consumers have may be too outdated to be of value. Another view is that advertising shapes and molds consumer tastes and works to the advantage of advertisers, thereby allowing firms to manage demand and to undermine consumer sovereignty. Then, too, there are studies which show that in heavily advertised consumer goods industries (such as nonprescription drugs, soaps, breakfast cereals, razors, and soft drinks) firms consistently are able to earn above-average profits. This finding has been held to confirm the existence of barriers to entry, because otherwise, it is argued, firms would be induced to enter such industries to take advantage of the above-average profit opportunities. To the extent that a new company will have to spend more than a dollar on advertising its product to counteract one dollar's worth of advertising by an entrenched firm, then the new company is at a disadvantage, and a barrier to entry exists. Moreover, it has been observed that investing in advertising is not the same as investing in tangible capital assets because if a firm fails in an industry in which it has invested heavily in capital goods, then those capital goods have a liquidation value. However, if a firm fails in an industry where it has invested heavily in advertising, its investment is water down the drain.

Questions for Discussion

1. In your opinion, how able are consumers to validate the quality of what Nelson calls experience goods? Search goods?
2. Do you agree with Nelson that for most items, the most highly advertised brand is the best buy? Cite examples to support your answer.
3. Can you cite cases where advertising has probably tended to increase the market power of established firms? In what industries is it likely that advertising has reduced market power by facilitating the entry of new firms?

Sources: George J. Stigler, "The Economics of Information," *Journal of Political Economy*, Vol. 69, No. 3 (June 1961), pp. 213–225; Phillip J. Nelson, "Advertising As Information," *Journal of Political Economy*, Vol. 82, No. 4 (July–August 1974), pp. 729–754; William S. Comanor and Thomas A. Wilson, *Advertising and Market Power* (Cambridge, Mass.: Harvard University Press, 1974); "A New View of Advertising's Economic Impact," *Business Week* (December 22, 1975), pp. 49ff.; Phillip J. Nelson, "Information and Consumer Behavior," *Journal of Political Economy*, Vol. 78, No. 2 (March–April 1970), pp. 311–329; and Phillip J. Nelson, "The Economic Consequences of Advertising," *Journal of Business*, Vol. 48, No. 2 (April 1975), pp. 213–241.

ing brands of aspirin, toiletries and cosmetics, soap, alcoholic beverages, and canned goods to recognize the extent to which consumers (rightly or wrongly) associate quality with price. One study of advertising and competition found that the introduction of new and "improved" products is more frequent in some of the most heavily advertised groups (particularly cigarettes and health and beauty aids).[16] This implies a high degree of new product entry and new product competition within these product groups, since advertising is the major means of introducing new and improved goods to the consumer. Particular brands within these product categories were also found to be unable to maintain consumer acceptance for as long a time as branded products in other categories. Therefore, heavy advertising may be indicative of the relative ease with which new products can squeeze out old products; in such cases

[16]Telser, "Advertising and Competition," pp. 549–551, 556–557.

competitive pressures would appear to be strong even though the number of firms remains the same.[17]

Nevertheless, advertising and sales promotion can be carried well past the point where it is informative, serving merely to barrage consumers with jingles, catchy phrases, sex images, and mutually canceling persuasion. The most visible offenders seem to be firms selling consumer products rather than industrial products, particularly firms producing soaps and detergents, beer, soft drinks, headache pills, toothpaste, mouthwash, cereal, tires, and automobiles.[18]

Contributions to National Economic Goals

Earlier it was indicated that one of the criteria for judging business behavior and market performance is the extent to which the operations of business firms facilitate, or at least do not hinder, the pursuit of national economic goals. The issue upon which we shall focus attention in this section is the relative contribution of small-scale and large-scale enterprises toward achieving national economic objectives. Although empirical evidence on the issue is less than definitive, there are a number of points on which some judgment can be rendered.

The Goal of Price Stability. On an economy-wide basis, the term "price stability" refers to a general economic condition in which prices *on the average* are neither rising (inflation) nor falling (deflation). In other words, price stability requires an inflation/deflation rate of no more than 1 to 2% per year.

During the inflationary 1970s, the issue repeatedly arose whether the market power of oligopolistic firms helped fuel the fires of inflation. Usually, the issue took the more precise form: Is big business a major cause of inflation? The politically popular answer to this question is often an emphatic "yes," the fundamental *economic* reason being that bigness begets power in the marketplace and that this power is likely to be used by big firms to raise their selling prices proportionately more than costs are increasing, and thereby reap greater profits. However, several important economic factors weigh against this conclusion:

1. Large corporations often gear prices changes more toward responding to changes in fundamental long-run market conditions rather than to transient short-run conditions. This is borne out by the short-run kink in the demand curves of cor-

---

[17]In many cases, much of the most formidable new-firm competition comes in the form of existing firms diversifying into new products or expanding into new markets, rather than from the entry of newly organized firms.

[18]In the case of industrial products, the information that the buyer has about the seller's product is often more factually complete. Purchasing agents usually endeavor to develop a sharp eye for differences in quality and performance and are less likely to be swayed by "puffery." Persuasive types of advertising and sales promotion tactics for industrial products are therefore less effective in creating preferences for branded products which do not serve the industrial buyer's requirements at least as well as competing brands.

porate oligopolists, by their propensity to rely upon price leadership and target return pricing methods, and by their use of changes in inventory levels and order backlogs to smooth out temporary demand fluctuations.

2. Large firms may very well have greater organizational capacity for dealing with inflationary forces than do lesser-sized firms. This applies both to *demand-pull* and *cosh-push* types of inflation.[19] Insofar as demand-pull inflation is concerned, corporate ambitions for growth, plus their greater attention to long-range planning and to anticipating long-run shifts in demand, reduce the probability of their being caught short of having whatever production capacity is required for meeting consumer demand. This implies that under normal circumstances demand-pull inflationary conditions are less prone to inhabit corporate-dominated markets than atomistic small-firm markets. In addition, expanding industry output via the entry of new firms (as represented by the transition from short-run to long-run equilibrium in the perfectly and monopolistically competitive market models) may prove to be a more time-consuming process than output expansion of a growth-minded corporation, especially when the latter devotes much top management attention to the process of planning for and anticipating expansion in the first place.

With respect to cost-push inflation, large firms are masters at using managerial technology, automation, vertical integration, and technological innovation to suppress rising costs. The large corporation's breadth and depth of managerial talent, its financial resources for attacking the problems creating rising production costs, and its propensity to invest in research and development combine to give large-scale firms a potential advantage over small-scale firms in holding the line on price during periods of rising input prices.[20]

The Goals of Higher Incomes and Living Standards. We have already seen that business firms contribute to higher living standards and material well-being through new product innovations and the implementation of new technologies. But there is more to the story of economic progress than just more and better products being produced in more efficient ways. The decisive factor underlying higher incomes and living standards is increases in *productivity*. Productivity, in its simplest form, can be thought of as the volume of output produced per hour of labor input.

To illustrate the importance of productivity in the economic process, consider the situation where the average worker in a particular firm earns $5.00 per hour and, utilizing the various equipment provided, is able to

[19] *Demand-pull inflation* refers to a market situation where consumers are anxious to buy a larger volume of goods and services than producers are presently capable of supplying. Hence, a current demand level in excess of productive capacity tends to *pull* prices upward as sellers find they can sell all that they can currently produce at prices higher than the prevailing level. Prices are then raised as a means of rationing the available supplies among those buyers who are most willing and able to pay for them. *Cost-push inflation* is said to represent situations where rising raw material prices and rising wage rates *push* prices upward; firms are "forced" to raise prices in response to rising production costs in order to preserve a margin between prices and average total costs that is consistent with target rates of return and "fair" profits.

[20] According to the president of one large electric utility firm: "We were for many years able to avoid seeking rate increases, even though our expenses were going up. So long as our costs were increasing at a fairly moderate and stable pace, the Company managed to offset the increases by installing improved and more efficient generating units, by providing line crews with improved tools and equipment, by using computers for many functions, and by taking other measures to hold down expenses."

produce an average of 100 units of output in 1 hour of work time. The firm's labor costs will then average 5 cents per unit produced. However, in the normal course of events, the efficiency of the average worker can be expected to rise. An added year's experience, coupled with formal education and employee training programs, will tend to increase employee skill levels and the ability to produce. Likewise, productivity may be expected to increase through a combination of more and better equipment, gradual elimination of "bugs" in the technical process, and the "learning curve" effect that comes from becoming familiar with a production process and identifying means of refining it. It would not be at all unusual for production-worker efficiency to rise by an average of 4% per year, especially in a technologically progressive firm. In such a case the average output per labor-hour would rise to 104 units and the firm could "afford" to pay its workers $5.20 per hour (a 4% wage increase) without encountering any increase in unit labor costs. Moreover, the firm would have no cause to raise prices to cover the wage increase, since labor costs would remain at 5 cents per unit of output.

Herein, then, lies the key to firms paying higher wages without having the resulting income gains eaten up entirely by inflation. When a firm realizes an increase in productivity of some percentage, it can increase wages and salaries by an equal percentage without incurring higher unit costs and without being confronted with the necessity of raising its selling prices to protect profit margins. On the other hand, if a firm realizes a 4% annual gain in productivity and is "forced" (perhaps by union pressures) to increase wages by *more* than 4%, its labor costs per unit of output will rise and a price increase may be necessary to preserve the firm's profitability. And, just as plainly, the larger a firm's average annual gain in productivity, the more able it is to pay higher wages and salaries to its employees, thereby laying the foundation for higher incomes and living standards.

It is no secret that large corporations often have "above-average" productivity gains. Indeed, productivity gains in a number of highly visible, big-firm-dominated industries have consistently been above the total private-sector average of 2.7% during the period 1950–1975.[21] For example, during the 1950–1975 period the rates of gain in output per labor-hour (all employees) averaged 5.4% in petroleum refining, 3.9% in tires and inner tubes, 4.2% in primary aluminum, 5.0% in major household appliances (1958–1975), 3.6% in motor vehicles and equipment (1957–1975), 4.2% in radio and television sets (1958–1975), 6.8% in air transportation, 3.9% in pulp and paper, and 6.2% in gas and electric utilities.[22] On the small-scale-firm side of the ledger, the average annual gain in output per labor-hour (all employees) was 2.8% in canning and preserving (1950–1974), 2.5% in bakery products, 1.0% in footwear, −0.7% in hospital and clinics (1967–1973), 1.9% in ready-mixed concrete (1968–1974), 2.2% in gray iron foundries (1954–

---

[21] *Handbook of Labor Statistics 1977*, U.S. Department of Labor, p. 145.

[22] *Ibid.*, pp. 145–154. The productivity changes cited represent the average annual percent change based on the linear least-squares trend of the logarithms of the index numbers.

1975), 6.1% in hosiery (1950–1975), 2.4% in retail food stores (1958–1975), 2.5% in franchised new car dealerships (1958–1975), and 2.4% in hotels, motels, and tourist courts (1958–1975).

The above-average productivity gains in the corporate sector go far toward explaining why large firms are often wage and salary leaders. One is hard-pressed to find employees of IBM, General Motors, or Exxon who are flirting with poverty and welfare and whose wages are close to the legal minimum wage. Not many, if any, large corporations attempt to compete on the basis of substandard wages and working conditions. Rather, it is where small firms predominate, as in agriculture, apparel, textiles, lumber, furniture, leather products, and the service industries, that subpar productivity gains are largely responsible for employees earning close to the minimum wage.

THE CONSEQUENCES OF MONOPOLY POWER

Anticompetitive Practices in Small-Firm and Large-Firm Markets

It has been astutely observed on numerous occasions that businesspeople think competition is a good thing—unless and until they become its victims. Thus, both large and small firms have been ingenious in devising ways to escape the discipline of competition. Scores of anticompetitive practices, some outlawed and some still legal, have been instituted to keep prices at higher levels than might otherwise prevail and to restrict output so as not to cause prices and profits to tumble downward. Despite the illegality of nearly every form of collusive agreement, formal or informal, to fix prices, restrict output, restrain trade, or lessen competition, antitrust violations are uncovered each year and unknown numbers of schemes go undetected.

Collusive arrangements may pertain to base or list prices, shipping allowances, charges for extra features, guarantees, warranties, service policies, output quotas, market shares, or the specific geographic areas or product lines that are to be regarded as each firm's exclusive sphere of interest. In addition, firms may reach understandings regarding product standards, specifications, and the frequency with which products will be restyled and redesigned. Industry trade associations may be formed to promote information sharing among the member firms (these are popular in the lumber and wood products, electrical products, textile, aerospace, alcoholic beverage, utility, transportation, and insurance industries). Among steel, copper, oil, and chemical firms, joint ventures are a popular means of instituting interfirm cooperation and, at times, may have facilitated anticompetitive practices. Some firms have knowingly and willingly, although not necessarily collusively, acceded to price leadership in order to avoid price competition. Other firms have utilized conscious parallelism to sidestep strong rivalries.

Some firms have abused the patent laws by aggressively buying up patents, licenses, and copyrights so as to preclude the emergence of competition from rival products.[23] Firms in such fields as plastics, cellophane, shoe machinery, photo supplies, electric lights, copying equipment, computers, telephone equipment, television, and synthetic rubber have attempted to insulate themselves from competition by systematically building up an impregnable portfolio of patents. On other occasions, firms patent inventions which they have no real intention of using directly but which they do not want others to have.

A restrictive approach that is often used because of its effectiveness and compatibility with antitrust and patent laws is for firms holding a monopolistic patent position to insert competition-reducing provisions into the patent licenses which it may grant (willingly or unwillingly) to potential rival firms.[24] These provisions take several forms. First, firms to which licenses are granted may be constricted to sell only in a specified geographic area. Second, the price of the licensed product may be stipulated as one of the terms of the license. Third, direct or indirect output limitations may be incorporated into the licensing agreements. As a case in point, General Electric in the 1930s granted a license to Westinghouse to produce improved light bulbs that called for a royalty rate of 1 to 2% on the sales made by Westinghouse up to 25.4421% of the two firms' combined sales but a royalty rate of 30% for sales exceeding this quota.[25] Also, Westinghouse had to sell the bulbs at prices and terms set by General Electric.

To the extent that anticompetitive practices exist, they tend to be more prevalent in oligopolistic markets than in atomistic markets. Oligopolistic markets are inherently well suited to some sort of collusive agreement, since fewness of firms is a necessary prerequisite for reaching viable arrangements. Restrictive practices are virtually impossible to institute where markets are comprised of large numbers of firms, despite the fact that business executives in atomistically competitive markets may be equally desirous of escaping the control of market forces. For a large number of firms to reach an acceptable and enforceable agreement is exceedingly difficult—so difficult, in fact, that illegal collusion is almost totally absent in atomistic market structures. Such is one of the built-in social benefits of competition among the many. This is not to say, however, that small companies do not engage in monopolistic practices. At the local and regional level small firms may compete in small enough numbers that oligopoly prevails, and thus they may well be in a position to exercise monopoly control.

Nevertheless, restrictive practices are likely to be the exception rather than the rule—even in an environment of corporate oligopoly. The frailty of collusive agreements, the ambitions for growth and expansion, the general existence of spirited nonprice competition, the more rapid pace of technological change and innovation, the fear of potential competition, plus the antitrust laws all combine to make collusive arrangements among giant cor-

---

[23]Scherer, *Industrial Market Structure and Economic Performance*, pp. 390–392.
[24]*Ibid.*, p. 162.
[25]George W. Stocking and Myron W. Watkins, *Cartels in Action* (New York: Twentieth Century Fund, 1947), p. 309.

porations more an illustration of deviant behavior than normal behavior. The antitrust laws, if vigorously enforced, can obviously be an effective deterrent to anticompetitive behavior because of the potential punishment, embarrassment, and loss of public image accompanying discovery of illegal practices. Indeed, the mere likelihood that antitrust officials will be diligent in prosecuting the parties to restrictive agreements, punishing abuses of monopoly power, opposing acquisitions and mergers that tend to consolidate market power and lessen competition, and blocking avenues for creating new kinds of monopolistic arrangements undeniably improves the functioning of markets in constructive ways.

The Welfare Loss From Anticompetitive Practices and Abuses of Market Power

Several statistical studies have been made of the short-run economic impact of monopolistic practices, business inefficiency, and resource misallocation arising from competitive deficiencies and market imperfections.[26] These studies have found monopolistic price-output distortions giving rise to welfare losses ranging from less than 1% to perhaps as much as 12% of the gross national product; however, most of these studies place the losses at less than 6% and probably less than 3% of GNP.

Scherer's study has produced the most explicit sources of output loss associated with the exercise of market power; his estimates are summarized in Table 16-1. Although Scherer admits that each of his individual category estimates is subject to a wide margin of error, he concludes that if the "true" output loss could be ascertained, it would probably fall within the range 3 to 12%. This is higher than the estimates of other experts, who have concluded that the static annual monopoly loss is "small" and perhaps even "trivial" and "inconsequential."

The wide disparity in the estimates of the economic welfare loss from monopoly power correctly suggests that there are major statistical problems in determining the size of the monopolistic sector, the extent to which monopolistic prices exceed competitive levels, and the size of the relevant firm and industry demand elasticities—all of which are pertinent to the estimating procedure. Nonetheless, the weight of evidence is heavily on the side of

[26]Arnold Harberger, "Monopoly and Resource Allocation," *American Economic Review*, Vol. 44, No. 2 (May 1954), pp. 77–87; David Schwartzman, "The Burden of Monopoly," *Journal of Political Economy*, Vol. 68, No. 6 (December 1960), pp. 627–630; David R. Kamerschen, "An Estimation of the 'Welfare Losses' from Monopoly in the American Economy," *Western Economic Journal*, Vol. 4, No. 3 (Summer 1966), pp. 221–236; William G. Shepherd, *Market Power and Economic Welfare* (New York: Random House, Inc., 1970), pp. 195–198; Scherer, *Industrial Market Structure and Economic Performance*, pp. 400–409; John J. Siegfried and T. K. Tiemann, "The Welfare Cost of Monopoly: An Interindustry Analysis," *Economic Inquiry*, Vol. 12, No. 2 (June 1974), pp. 190–202; Dean A. Worcester, Jr., "On Monopoly Welfare Losses: Comment," *American Economic Review*, Vol. 65, No. 5 (December 1975), pp. 1015–1023; R. A. Posner, "The Social Costs of Monopoly and Regulation," *Journal of Political Economy*, Vol. 83, No. 4 (August 1975), pp. 807–827.

Table 16-1 Best-Guess Estimates of the Output Losses Attributable to Collusion, the Exercise of Market Power, and Related Breakdowns in the Competitive Process, Expressed as a Percentage of 1966 GNP

Causes of Output Losses	*Estimated Percentage Reduction in 1966 GNP*
Output losses due to monopolistic resource allocation in the unregulated sectors of the U.S. economy	0.9
Output losses due to pricing distortions in the regulated sector of the U.S. economy	0.6
Inefficiencies in production and higher costs associated with enterprises insulated from competition and therefore not compelled to use the lowest-cost production technology	2.0
Inefficiencies due to deficient cost control by defense and space contractors	0.6
Wasteful advertising and sales promotion efforts	1.0
Producing at less than optimal scale for reasons other than product differentiation	0.3
Extra transportation costs stemming from inefficient plant locations	0.2
Idle and inefficient production capacity due to monopolistic practices and collusion	0.6
Total losses	6.2

Source: F.M. Scherer, *Industrial Market Structure and Economic Performance* (Chicago: Rand McNally & Company, 1970), p. 408.

studies indicating that the *static* effects of slack competitive pressures probably do not place an undue burden on the economy, especially considering that dynamic performance is the truly significant determinant of society's overall economic welfare. As it turns out, the static deadweight welfare loss from monopoly power and resource misallocation is overcome by technologically induced growth in the GNP in a surprisingly short time. The annual average economic welfare gain from innovation and technical change has been estimated to be in the range 1.2 to 1.5% as a minimum.[27] Accepting even the high figure of 12% welfare loss from monopoly power, the "worst-case" length of time required for innovation-related growth to surmount the adverse effects of monopoly power is about 9 years, with a more probable time being 1 to 4 years.

The conclusion to be drawn here is straightforward: if a large portion of technological progress is, in fact, attributable to the activities of giant corporations, the static monopoly welfare loss would have to be much larger than is presently indicated before society could be made better off by breaking

[27]Jesse Markham, "Market Concentration and Innovation," in *Industrial Concentration: The New Learning* (New York: Columbia University Press, 1974).

large firms up into many small companies in an effort to create allegedly more competitive market conditions.

The Social Control of Corporate Power

The antitrust laws, as written and applied, offer a reasonably sufficient body of rules for eliminating and preventing anticompetitive practices. But barring new interpretations, they leave almost untouched the troublesome issue of the kinds of corporate power that attaches to merely being big. As yet, existing antitrust legislation has not been deemed applicable to the power that accrues to large *absolute* firm size. Historically, antitrust has aimed almost exclusively at combating the kinds of power that attach to restraints of trade and monopolizing the market for a particular product—problems of large *relative* firm size. Only recently has large size per se become a point of public concern. The antibigness critics argue that:

1. Giant corporations have grown to a point where they are too large and too powerful. Horizontal and vertical integration, diversification, and conglomerate merger have been carried beyond the bounds justified by efficiency considerations.
2. The size and power of giant firms puts them in a position to manipulate markets rather than respond to them; this is evidenced by administered pricing, output restrictions, anticompetitive trade practices, tacit collusion, and conscious parallelism—each of which is the antithesis of free market economics.
3. Competitive forces are no longer strong enough or reliable enough to protect consumers from inflated prices, excessive profits, and self-serving corporate policies.
4. The oligopolistic structure of corporate-dominated markets diverts competitive rivalry away from price competition (the most desirable competitive form) into nonprice areas—a much less desirable competitive style that encourages overemphasis on persuasive advertising, product proliferation, planned product obsolescence, and cosmetic production improvements.
5. Because of the political leverage which goes with bigness and which big firms deliberately cultivate, corporate enterprises are able to gain undue access to government in achieving private economic goals.
6. The motives and pressures for improved corporate performance (growth in sales, profits, etc.) have led to questionable mergers and acquisitions, manipulative accounting practices, and financial machinations that have doubtful social or economic value.
7. Reforms both from within and without are needed to curb corporate power, enliven competition, and make large firms more responsible and responsive to the general economic welfare of society.

Out of these concerns have emerged several proposals for the social control of corporate power for reducing the adverse consequences of the power accompanying the rise of large corporate enterprise; these may be grouped into four basic approaches: (1) the social responsibility model, (2) the regulatory model, (3) the public ownership model, and (4) the workable competition model.

The *social responsibility* approach to corporate power involves leaving power in the hands of corporate executives but persuading and teaching them to use this power in "socially responsible" ways. Much has been written and said about the need for corporations to assess the social impact of corporate activities and to formulate policies that are in accord with the goals and concerns of society at large. Some degree of corporate response to the call for social responsibility is visible, although it is debatable whether the response is enlightened and committed or whether it is the result of a fear of increased government regulation. More boards of directors are being constituted from a broader segment of society. A number of large firms have created new departments to analyze the social consequences of alternative corporate policies. Some corporations have deliberately located plants in urban ghettos; and many have instituted programs to increase corporation participation in community improvements. Irrespective of whether the actions are sincere or cosmetic, it is clear that corporations are increasingly inquiring into conflicts between corporate policy and the "general social welfare." Still, corporate social responsibility is inherently voluntary and can only be a partial answer to containing corporate power.

The *regulatory* approach to controlling both corporate power and anticompetitive practices essentially involves direct government approval of key corporate decisions. The use of formal wage and price controls in the early 1970s, along with legislation establishing federal controls over oil and natural gas prices and production rates, put the regulatory model back in the public spotlight. A few proposals advocate the two most extreme forms of regulation—rationing and government fixing of prices and wages—as being attractive and permanent weapons of corporate control. However, the majority of economists do not view regulation, rationing, or permanent wage-price controls as viable policies for remedying the deficiencies of corporate capitalism. The reason lies basically in a strong conviction that bureaucratic fiat is a poor and often woefully ineffective substitute for a competitive price system. The freedom of buyers and sellers to exercise their own choices in a competitive marketplace *generally* has the remarkable and durable property of yielding social results that are hard to improve on by public action.

This is not to say that the functioning of either oligopolistic or atomistic markets is without defect, for clearly both have shortcomings requiring public action. But most economists are skeptical of the ability of government regulators to superimpose their judgments upon those of business managers and consumers and produce a result that is superior to the marketplace. To begin with, government regulation concentrates power in the hands of a few persons to an even greater extent than exists in oligopolistic markets. While the power of government regulators theoretically is deployed to serve "the public interest," there is ample room for disagreement and confusion as to what "the public interest" actually is.

More important, history repeatedly shows that government policymakers are every bit as prone to use power to serve their own purposes or those of special interests as they are to serve the larger "public purpose."

This is confirmed by the frequency with which special interest groups have successfully lobbied for favored treatment and by the ambitions of government officials to enhance their own images and to expand the role and scope of their departments. More important, though, is that the checks and balances on the actions of government regulators operate only in election years or when public opinion is strongly aroused. In contrast, the checks and balances imposed by vigorous competitive pressures operate daily and have the further advantage of keeping economic power diffused. Even though government regulators usually have good intentions, there still are few instances where it can be shown that making private decisions subordinate to government decree has yielded superior and less costly social results. In sum, the consensus view of economists is that the regulatory process is never likely to function so efficiently that government regulators understand and influence marketplace conditions better than buyers and sellers who are on the scene.

The *public ownership* model, although once popular among a modest number of economists, has fallen from favor. Nationalizing giant corporations and bringing their activities under the management and scrutiny of Congress and the president has little economic appeal or purpose. The British experience with nationalization of key industries has, to put it mildly, been ineffective in promoting the economic welfare of any but unionized employees of the nationalized firms; in Britain it is the politics of nationalization, not the economic advantages, that perpetuate public ownership. The chief trouble with public ownership is the lack of incentives to ensure efficient performance and prompt response to changes in consumer preferences and market conditions.

This leaves the fourth category—the model of *workable competition*—as being the approach with the greatest following. This model has as its goal making the structure of industry and the conduct of individual firms such that market performance over both the short run and the long run is as good as can be expected. As indicated earlier, the criteria for measuring market performance include whether output rates and the range of product qualities are in harmony with consumer demand, whether production activities are efficient and technologically progressive, whether competitive pressures are strong enough to keep profits down to a reasonable and fair minimum, whether the exercise of market power is adequately contained, and whether private business activities are in accord with the broad public interest and national economic objectives.

These criteria are, for the most part, quite unobjectionable. Yet, problems exist. Value judgments can hardly fail to enter into drawing a line between too little and enough competition. In deciding whether a firm's production operations are efficient, one needs a yardstick indicating the highest achievable efficiency when, quite clearly, the boundaries of what is possible may never have been revealed in actual practice (this difficulty, however, can be skirted if comparisons with other national, international, and publicly owned enterprises are available). Most important, there is difficulty in assessing the workability of competition when some but not all of the criteria are satisfied. This has led to the suggestion that competitive forces be judged workable and effective if and when no clearly indicated public policy measure could be implemented to produce superior competitive performance.[28] While this suggestion also runs afoul of the same value judgment and measurement difficulties, it does have the merit of focusing attention on the prescribing of constructive remedial actions.

However, we are still left with what sort of new public policy measures can be devised within the framework of the model of workable competition to counter the exercise of corporate power and to improve the effectiveness of competitive pressures. One proposal has been to break up large enterprises into smaller units so as to diffuse corporate power and create larger numbers of rival firms. The thrust of this proposal, as well as much antitrust legislation, is to force corporate capitalism into an economic model of many small companies in a free-market environment. To many, unless markets are such that small companies can compete effectively against big companies, the power and influence of the large-share firms is too big.

A second allegedly competition-enhancing proposal involves enacting stringent restrictions on corporate merger and acquisition, with the burden for approval being placed upon large corporations to show that the merger would not lessen competition and that net social advantages would derive from combination.[29] Such restrictions would reverse the current procedure whereby the burden is placed upon Justice Department officials to show cause (a substantial lessening of actual or potential competition) why corporate acquisitions should not be allowed.

A third proposal aims at providing consumers with more and better product information and creating a federally sponsored bureau of consumer affairs to protect consumers from market abuses. Specific consumer-oriented programs might include developing uniform grading and rating systems for major purchase items, conducting and publishing government test reports on product durability and performance, regulating product safety, increasing government assistance to independent consumer research organizations, and more financial support for consumer education.

SUMMARY AND CONCLUSIONS

Despite the hazards of generalizations, it is worthwhile to attempt to draw some conclusions about the relative merits of competition among the many

---

[28] For a more complete discussion of this concept, see Jesse W. Markham, "An Alternative Approach to the Concept of Workable Competition," *American Economic Review*, Vol. 40, No. 3 (June, 1950), pp. 349–361.

[29] The determination would be materially aided by requiring all multiproduct enterprises to disclose the annual operating results (sales, costs, output, profits, assets, employment, productivity, etc.) for each separate product line or product grouping. Current regulations allow firms to file consolidated reports that preclude external analysis of efficiency and performance on a product-by-product basis.

and competition among the few and to indicate the character of socially optimum market structures. However, the reader is again forewarned that this is inherently a subjective task because it requires judgments as to the best mix of trade-offs and compromises among competitive alternatives and performance criteria. The following conclusions are therefore judgmental and subject to alternative interpretation.

1. Competition among the many (as epitomized by perfect and monopolistic competition) is likely to produce relatively lower prices and relatively narrower profit margins *in the short run* as compared to competition among the few. Herein lies the fundamental social benefit of atomistic competition. When this is coupled with the general inability of atomistic firms to exercise market power or otherwise exploit consumers, the static short-run results of competition among large numbers of relatively small enterprises tend to be more advantageous to consumers than is oligopolistic competition—*provided that economies of scale are not such as to make oligopoly more cost efficient.*

2. In the long run, however, corporate oligopoly may tend to outperform atomistic competition. As the late Harvard professor, Joseph Schumpeter, observed over 30 years ago, inquiry into the origins of high living standards "leads not to the doors of those firms that work under conditions of comparatively free competition, but precisely to the doors of the large concerns . . . and a shocking suspicion dawns upon us that big business may have had more to do with creating that standard of life than with keeping it down."[30] Despite an initial handicap imposed by the exercise of market power, collusive and other monopolistic practices, and various breakdowns in competition, corporate performance is stimulated over the long run by the desire for growth and expansion and by market mandates for technological virtuosity. The large firm's cash flow and access to financial capital, its ability to withstand short-term setbacks, and its scientific, engineering, and managerial know-how render it better suited to engage in quality competition and technological and innovational competition than is the representative small owner-managed business.

Corporations also evidence greater organizational ability to suppress rising cost pressures for much the same reasons. Corporate contributions to the process of national economic growth often outweigh those of small businesses. In some cases, corporate prices evidence a tendency to rise more slowly than in atomistically structured markets. Large enterprises are well positioned to act as pacesetters in implementing new product innovations and in pushing back the barriers to technological progress; they tend to achieve above-average gains in output per unit of input; and they have been in the forefront of enterprises that have raised wages faster than prices. It is precisely on such performance features that the principal foundations of economic progress and rising standards of living rest. Hence, the dynamic patterns of corporate capitalism can have socially beneficial results that may offset the superior short-run performance of atomistic competition.

[30]Schumpeter, *Capitalism, Socialism and Democracy*, p. 82.

Yet, some qualification is clearly needed. Although competitive forces in the corporate sector do, in general, have a restraining effect upon arbitrary corporate policies and upon the self-serving exercise of corporate power, the strengths of competitive forces nonetheless operate unevenly in corporate-dominated markets. Some giant corporations are able to exercise a considerable degree of market power while others exercise little or none. Some large corporations have maneuvered themselves into a strong market position and are able to earn substantial profits while others possess no particular unique advantage and earn average or subpar profits. The winds of technological and innovational competition blow strongly in some corporate oligopolies but only occasionally in others. Cross currents such as these mean that long-run performance in the corporate sector varies from "not so good" to "fair" to "very good" to, occasionally, "excellent."

3. Ideally, the socially optimum form of competition and market structure would combine the short-term results of competition among large numbers of small firms with the long-term performance of competition among giant corporations. The benefits to consumers are greatest when there are enough firms producing competing products so that short-run competitive forces are strong enough (a) to prevent abuses of market power, (b) to prevent collusion, (c) to keep price close to average cost and not allow firms to earn "excessive" profits, and (d) to force firms to operate at maximum efficiency and minimum costs. However, firms should be allowed to become large enough and diverse enough to acquire those organizational traits of giant corporations that are responsible for superior long-run market performance. Improving the economic well-being of consumers ultimately depends upon a style of competition that promotes optimum dynamic performance, and it cannot be denied that large corporate enterprises possess several inherently strong features which are crucial to effective business performance over the long run.

4. The most important shortcomings of competition among the few revolve around the excessive accumulation of power by large corporations and the existence of various anticompetitive practices. To remedy these, efforts need to be made to strengthen the forces of the short-run competition among giant corporations with the specific objective of (a) curtailing wasteful promotional activities which raise costs and prices, (b) minimizing the ability of firms to use their size and power to serve corporate purposes not compatible with the public interest, (c) causing firms to operate at or near full production capacity before they raise prices, and (d) encouraging the entry of rival firms into those markets where corporate profits appear unduly "excessive" or "monopolistic." Generally speaking, the thrust of antitrust policy should be geared toward (a) enforcing as much competition as is consistent with achieving realizable economies of scale, (b) enough product differentiation to satisfy consumers, and (c) rates of technological progress, innovation, and economic growth that are consistent with the national interest. Whenever conflicts appear between policies that stiffen short-run competitive pressures

and policies that stiffen long-run competitive forces, the long-run oriented policy should normally take precedence, since sacrifices in short-run performance are sooner or later overwhelmed by improvements in long-run performance.

5. Without question, any sort of anticompetitive practice among sellers to fix prices, restrict production, divide markets, suppress innovation, or foreclose the entry of new firms should be prohibited and any violation vigorously prosecuted. Aggressive enforcement of antitrust laws can go far toward discouraging business firms from restraining competition or attempting to monopolize a product. However, it is doubtful whether the national interest is served by specifying any particular limits to the size of firms or to the market shares which they are allowed to achieve. Mergers of a horizontal, vertical, or conglomerate nature may well enhance the organizational capabilities of firms in efficiency-increasing ways. Thus, larger firm sizes can be consistent with the public interest, unless, of course, they involve a manifest attempt to subvert competitive forces. The optimum number of firms in an industry is different, depending on technological considerations, the importance of research and innovation, the size of the relevant market, the strengths of competition from foreign firms, and various other factors.

6. Finally, it should be recognized that competition can be "too strong" —especially with respect to its long-term impacts and consequences. A year-in, year-out competitive struggle where firms are locked in a perpetual battle for market survival and walk the tightrope of narrow and uncertain profit margins can be financially and organizationally debilitating. It is questionable whether consumers benefit from this more than from a workably competitive style that allows firms to provide steady jobs at good pay, earn profits commensurate with risk and capital investment, foster technological progress, and spur economic growth in directions consistent with social priorities. It is precisely with regard to the latter traits and results that corporate capitalism has the potential to excel.

SUGGESTED READINGS

BERRY, C. H., *Corporate Growth and Diversification* (Princeton, N.J.: Princeton University Press, 1974).

BORK, R. H., *The Antitrust Paradox: A Policy at War with Itself* (New York: Basic Books, Inc., 1978).

CLARK, J. M., *Competition as a Dynamic Process* (Washington, D.C.: The Brookings Institution, 1961), Chapters 4, 8, 10, 19.

COMANOR, W. S., AND T. A. WILSON, "Advertising and Competition: A Survey," *Journal of Economic Literature*, Vol. 17, No. 2 (June 1979), pp. 453–476.

HAY, D. A., AND D. J. MORRIS, *Industrial Economics: Theory and Evidence* (New York: Oxford University Press, 1979).

MARRIS, R., "Is the Corporate Economy a Corporate State," *American Economic Review*, Vol. 62, No. 2 (May 1972), pp. 103–111.

MARRIS, R. AND D. C. MUELLER, "The Corporation, Competition, and the Invisible Hand," *Journal of Economic Literature*, Vol. 18, No. 1 (March 1980), pp. 32–63.

NEEDHAM, D., *The Economics of Industrial Structure: Conduct and Performance* (New York: St. Martin's Press, 1978).

REEKIE, W. D., "Price and Quality Competition in the United States Drug Industry," *Journal of Industrial Economics*, Vol. 26, No. 1 (March 1978), pp. 223–237.

SCHERER, F. M., *Industrial Market Structure and Economic Performance* (Chicago: Rand McNally & Company, 1970), Chapters 2, 15, 17.

SCHUMPETER, J. A., *Capitalism, Socialism and Democracy*, 3rd ed. (New York: Harper & Brothers, 1950), Chapters 7, 8.

SILBERSTON, A., "Price Behavior of Firms," *Economic Journal*, Vol. 80, No. 319 (September 1970), pp. 511–575.

SOSNICK, S., "A Critique of Concepts of Workable Competition," *Quarterly Journal of Economics*, Vol. 72, No. 3 (August 1958), pp. 380–423.

TELSER, L. G., "Advertising and Competition," *Journal of Political Economy*, Vol. 72, No. 6 (December 1964), pp. 537–562.

TEMIN, P., "Technology, Regulation, and Market Structure in the Modern Pharmaceutical Industry," *Bell Journal of Economics*, Vol. 10, No. 2 (Autumn 1979), pp. 429–446.

THOMPSON, A. A., "Absolute Firm Size, Administered Prices, and Inflation," *Economic Inquiry*, Vol. 12, No. 2 (June 1974), pp. 240–254.

THOMPSON, A. A., "Corporate Bigness—For Better or for Worse?" *Sloan Management Review*, Vol. 17, No. 1 (Fall 1975), pp. 37–62.

TUERCK, D. G., ED., *Issues in Advertising: The Economics of Persuasion* (Washington, D.C.: American Enterprise Institute, 1978).

WORCHESTER, D. A., JR., "On Monopoly Welfare Losses: Comment," *American Economic Review*, Vol. 65, No. 5 (December 1975), pp. 1015–1023.

QUESTIONS FOR DISCUSSION

1. Would it be fair to say that while corporate oligopolists do not compete on the basis of price in the short run (since they all charge identical or comparable prices), they nevertheless compete strenuously on the basis of price over the long run via new product variations, quality differences, and innovation? Explain and evaluate.

2. Do you think that large corporate enterprises are in a position to exploit consumers in terms of the prices they charge for their product? in terms of the quality of the products they offer consumers?

3. Explain why the *incentive* for undertaking technological advance may be weak in industries where firms are small and the market is atomistically structured.

4. Is the number of firms an important determinant of the degree of competition that will tend to exist in the market for a product? Is the size of the firms comprising an industry an important determinant of the degree of competition?

5. Should business enterprises undertake to solve social and economic problems? Is it socially desirable for business firms to direct a portion of their energies toward solving such problems as urban congestion, poverty, slum housing, and racial discrimination? What would you expect to be the impact of such behavior

upon the prices and output levels of the products of firms which undertake to solve such problems?

6. Do you think it is possible for competition to be "too strong"? What are the social and economic consequences of an "overly" competitive environment if there is such a thing? Do you think these consequences are better or worse than those which arise when competition is "too weak"? Explain.

7. Some of the critics of corporate capitalism, most notably John Kenneth Galbraith, Ralph Nader, and consumer advocate groups, contend that the persuasive powers of advertising and sales promotion tactics unduly manipulate consumers. They argue that the barrage of advertising messages extolling the virtues of white teeth, clean shirt collars, sporty automobiles, soft drinks, headache remedies, and the conveniences of microwave ovens, no-wax floors, and aerosol sprays act to mold the life-styles and tastes of some consumers—ultimately perhaps inducing them to spend more than they can really afford or to purchase frivolous items.

   (a) Do you agree? Do you feel that you personally are influenced or "manipulated" by advertising?

   (b) How likely is it that the powers of advertising can induce consumers to buy repeatedly an item which they find unsatisfactory or lacking?

   (c) How strong are consumer brand loyalties for highly advertised items? Do such loyalties reflect consumer satisfaction with the product or the persuasive powers of advertising or both?

   (d) How would one attempt to measure the persuasive powers of advertising on a firm's sales—as distinct from the effect of consumer satisfaction?

SEVENTEEN THE PRICING AND EMPLOYMENT OF RESOURCE INPUTS

In this chapter we shift attention from product markets to resource markets. The involvement of business enterprises in the functioning of the markets for resource inputs is evident. Engaging in productive activity of any short requires that firms purchase resource inputs. Moreover, any change in output dictates a change in resource usage. Business behavior in product markets thus quickly reverberates into resource markets, affecting both resource prices and resource employment.

The analysis of this chapter is aimed first at the firm's input decision, with the specific goal of identifying what determines the amount of a resource input a firm is willing to purchase at various input prices. The input decisions of business enterprises are then used as the takeoff point for examining on a broader front the employment rates of resources, the prices of resource inputs, and ultimately the incomes that accrue to resource owners.

To bring out the principles governing the operation of resource markets, it will be necessary to examine the resource input decisions of business firms in three contexts: (1) when the firm sells its output in a perfectly competitive product market and buys its input in a perfectly competitive resource market, (2) when the firm sells its output in an imperfectly competitive market and buys its input in a perfectly competitive resource market, and (3) when the firm is confronted by imperfectly competitive conditions in both its product and resource markets. These are the three situations most frequently approximated in practice.

Some Preliminary Considerations

Before we embark on the analysis of resource markets, three points warrant mention. First, the concepts of demand, supply, revenue, production, and costs apply to input decisions as well as to price and output decisions. The prices of resource inputs, for example, are in large measure determined by the interaction of demand and supply. However, as regards input markets, the roles of the firm and the consumer are reversed. Resource inputs are demanded by firms, not consumers, and some important inputs, such as labor and managerial talents, are supplied by consumers, not firms.

Second, while a firm's inputs may be broadly classified as consisting of land, labor, capital, and managerial ability, the fact remains that each of these classifications contains an enormous variety of particular inputs. The range of labor inputs for a firm extends from the unskilled to the highly skilled, with each job class having its own wage rate. Thus, even within the same plant the types of labor services employed by the firm may include such diverse sorts as those provided by an aerospace engineer, a secretary, a machinist, a maintenance man, a computer programmer, a drill press operator, and a shipping clerk. Since each type of labor service is characterized by its own unique wage rate and demand and supply conditions, it is not really very meaningful to speak of *the* demand for labor or *the* price of labor. The models of input markets will therefore be presented in terms of an unspecified input. Because the principles underlying input decisions and the operation of input markets are essentially the same, the models presented will have general applicability to almost every resource market—irrespective of whether the input is some type of land, labor, capital, or managerial talent.

Third, although firms may have a variety of goals, the principles of resource pricing and employment are indicated most easily by assuming that the only goal of the firm is to maximize profits. Accordingly, throughout this chapter, we shall assume a goal of profit maximization. This assumption in no way disturbs the thrust of the analysis and the resulting conclusions.[1]

---

[1] For an illustration of the effect which a goal of sales revenue maximization has upon the firm's input decision, see William J. Baumol, *Economic Theory and Operations Analysis*, 3rd ed. (Englewood Cliffs, N.J.: Prentice-Hall, Inc., 1972), pp. 328–330. Baumol demonstrates that a minor adjustment in the profit-maximizing input rules will give the revenue-maximizing input conditions.

550
*The Pricing
and
Employment
of Resource
Inputs*

THE RESOURCE INPUT DECISIONS OF A FIRM OPERATING UNDER CONDITIONS OF PERFECT COMPETITION IN ITS PRODUCT AND RESOURCE MARKETS

The simplest case of resource pricing and employment arises in an environment where firms sell their products in a perfectly competitive market and buy their inputs under perfectly competitive conditions. For our purposes the most important aspect of a perfectly competitive *product* market is that the firm can sell additional units of output at the going price; consequently, the firm's demand-*AR* curve is horizontal, and product price equals marginal revenue. In perfectly competitive *resource* markets the essential feature is that the firm can purchase as many units of an input as it may wish without affecting its price. In other words, the supply curve for an input which confronts the firm is horizontal at the prevailing input supply price.

The Perfectly Competitive Firm's Input Decision: The One-Variable Input Case

To identify the key factors underlying the perfectly competitive firm's input decision, suppose we consider first the situation where the firm has only one variable input, all the other resource inputs being fixed. The profit-conscious firm in a perfectly competitive environment will evaluate the outcomes of employing different quantities of its single variable resource— suppose we call it resource X—by their comparative effect upon total revenue and total cost. If using more units of resource X per period of time will add more to the firm's revenues than to its costs, then the extra input unit will increase the firm's total profits (or decrease its losses). On the other hand, if employing more units of resource X per period of time causes costs to rise by more than revenues, then using these input units will result in lower total profits (or larger losses). Hence, *to maximize profits a firm should purchase additional units of a resource input until the added costs associated with employing one more unit are equal to the added revenues it contributes.* This is the basic principle underlying the optimum input decision of a profit-maximizing firm; in fact, it is the $MC = MR$ rule applied to the firm's input decision.

The Revenue Gain from a Unit of Variable Input. When a firm employs another unit of variable input per period of time, its output rate rises by an amount equal to the marginal product of the variable input (MP_X). But the prime motivation of the firm for employing more of an input is not the output gain so much as the subsequent revenue gain. If the firm sells under conditions of a horizontal demand-*AR* curve, then each additional unit of output —suppose we call it product A—can be sold at the prevailing market price (P_A), which in turn equals marginal revenue (MR_A). The perfectly competitive firm's revenue gain from using one more unit of variable input may thus be calculated by multiplying the marginal product of the additional unit of input (MP_X) by the amount of revenue which the firm receives from selling another unit of the product (MR_A). For instance, if adding one more machine operator to the firm's production line causes the output rate to increase by 10 units per day and if each of these units can be sold for $5 each, then the firm's revenue gain is $50.

551

The Resource Input Decisions of a Firm Operating Under Conditions of Perfect Competition in Its Product and Resource Markets

The change in total revenue associated with using one more unit of variable input (X) is called the *marginal revenue product* of the input (MRP_X), and it may be calculated according to the expression

$$MRP_X = MP_X \cdot MR_A.$$

Alternatively, marginal revenue product may be conceived as the change in total revenue resulting from a change in the use of variable input X, which in discrete mathematical terms is equivalent to the expression

$$MRP_X = \frac{\Delta TR}{\Delta X}.$$

As usual, MRP_X may be more rigorously defined as the rate of change in total revenue as the rate of usage of variable input X changes, or

$$MRP_X = \frac{dTR}{dX}.$$

Note carefully that the concept of MRP differs from that of MR. Whereas MRP refers to revenue changes which result from changes in the usage of *variable input*, MR refers to revenue changes associated with changes in the rate of *output*.

A second and more restricted concept of the revenue change from using more or less of variable input X may be referred to as the *sales value of the marginal product* of the input ($SVMP_X$). $SVMP$ is just what its name implies —the dollar value of the increased output associated with using another unit of variable input. Put another way, $SVMP_X$ is the amount of extra output (MP_X) multiplied by the average price per unit at which it can be sold (P_A), or

$$SVMP_X = MP_X \cdot P_A.$$

Inasmuch as the perfectly competitive firm's selling price equals its marginal revenue ($P_A = MR_A$), it follows that $SVMP_X = MRP_X$. However, the equality between $SVMP$ and MRP holds true only for a perfectly competitive firm. If the firm must reduce product price to sell the extra output (as is the case in all market situations other than perfect competition where firms face down-sloping demand-AR curves), then product price is always greater than marginal revenue, and the values of $SVMP_X$ will exceed the values for MRP_X at a given input rate. Thus, in reality, the concept of $SVMP$ is only a special case of MRP: the case where price equals MR—a situation unique to a perfectly competitive product market

Although in a perfectly competitive market structure $SVMP$ equals MRP, we shall nevertheless use the concept of MRP to refer to the change in total revenue resulting from a change in input usage. The concept of $SVMP$ will be reserved to apply only to the gross market value (in dollars) of the marginal product of a unit of input.

The Profit-Maximizing Rate of Input Usage. To illustrate how a firm can ascertain the profit-maximizing rate of usage of variable input X, consider the hypothetical production, cost, and revenue data in Table 17-1. The first three columns of the table show how the output of product A (Q_A) and the marginal product of variable input X (MP_X) change as successively larger doses of variable input X are combined with the available fixed inputs.[2] The price of product A (P_A) is constant at $20 [column (4)] because of the perfectly competitive product market, and the corresponding total revenue from the sale of product A (TR_A) is shown in column (5). The values for marginal revenue product (MRP_X) are shown in column (6) and are found by either (1) multiplying the gain in output from using another unit of X (MP_X) by the extra revenue the firm receives from the sale of a unit of output (MR_A) or (2) subtracting the successive values of TR_A in column (5) to find the change in total revenue per unit change in variable input. Column (7) indicates the price at which units of variable input can be purchased; the constant price of $180 correctly implies that the firm can buy as many units of variable input as it wants at the given price without inducing a change in the input price. Hence, the marginal cost of an additional unit of variable input is the same as its price. We shall find it convenient to refer to the amount which each additional unit of variable input adds to the firm's costs as the *marginal resource cost* (MRC).[3] Since the supply price of X is fixed, $P_X = MRC_X$, and the supply function for X coincides precisely with the MRC function for X. Column (8) lists total variable costs (units of variable input X multiplied by its price per unit). The last column in the table shows the amounts of total contribution profit ($TR - TVC$) at each input rate; total contribution profit reflects total profit inasmuch as the former differs from the latter only by the amount of total fixed costs.

---

[2]Hypothetical amounts of fixed inputs, the prices of the fixed inputs, and the resulting amount of total fixed costs are not included in the table, since they do not really enter into the determination of the profit-maximizing rate of variable input.

[3]As with all other marginal concepts, marginal resource cost may be defined mathematically as the rate of change in the firm's costs as the rate of usage of variable input changes; in symbols this becomes

$$MRC_X = \frac{dTC}{dX} = \frac{dTVC}{dX},$$

where X refers to the units of variable input. Marginal resource cost differs from marginal cost in that the former refers to the changes in costs associated with a change in *input*, whereas the latter refers to a change in costs stemming from a change in *output*.

Table 17-1 Profit-Maximizing Rate of Resource Input Usage for a Firm Operating in Perfectly Competitive Product and Resource Markets[a]

(1) Units of Variable Input (X)	(2) Units of Output (Q_A)	(3) Marginal Product (MP_X)	(4) Price of Product A ($P_A = MR_A$)	(5) Total Revenue from the Sales of Product A ($TR_A = P_A \cdot Q_A$)	(6) Marginal Revenue Product ($MRP_X = MP_X \cdot MR_A = \Delta TR_A/\Delta X$)	(7) Supply Price of the Variable Input ($P_X = ARC_X = MRC_X$)	(8) Total Variable Cost ($TVC = P_X \cdot X$)	(9) Total Contribution Profit ($TCP = TR - TVC$)
0	0		$20	$ 0		$180	$ 0	$ 0
1	14	14	20	280	$280	180	180	100
2	40	26	20	800	520	180	360	440
3	60	20	20	1200	400	180	540	660
4	78	18	20	1560	360	180	720	840
5	94	16	20	1880	320	180	900	980
6	108	14	20	2160	280	180	1080	1080
7	120	12	20	2400	240	180	1260	1140
8	130	10	20	2600	200	180	1440	1160
9	138	8	20	2760	160	180	1620	1140
10	144	6	20	2880	120	180	1800	1080

[a]Observe that total contribution profit is maximized at an input of 8 units of resource X, which means that total profit is maximum (or losses minimum, depending on the amount of total fixed costs) at this input rate. By interpolation, it is seen that $MRP_X = MRC_X$ at 8 units of variable input.

553

554

*The Pricing
and
Employment
of Resource
Inputs*

As stated above, profit maximization requires that the firm purchase additional units of input until the added cost of one more unit just equals the added revenue it contributes. Given that the price of variable input remains unchanged irrespective of how many units the firm purchases, the cost of an additional unit of variable input is a constant equal to $180 [column (7)]. The revenue contribution of a unit of variable input is given by the *MRP* figures [column (6)]. A comparison of columns (6) and (7) in Table 17-1 indicates that it will pay the firm to employ 8 units of variable input. Increasing the usage of variable input from 7 to 8 units adds $200 to the firm's revenues but only $180 to costs. Should the firm employ the ninth unit of variable input, revenues will rise by $160 but costs will rise by $180; thus, the employment of 9 units of variable input is clearly a less profitable act. By interpolation, it is evident that at 8 units $MRP_X = MRC_X$, which satisfies the profit-maximizing condition and, in fact, is the rule by which the firm identifies its profit-maximizing rate of input usage. Inspection of the total contribution profit figures in column (9) confirms that 8 units is the optimum amount of variable input. Total contribution profit is greatest when 8 units of variable input are used. Since total profit is maximum where total contribution profit is maximum, the profit-maximizing rate of variable input usage is 8 units per period of time.

The determination of the profit-maximizing rate of variable input can be illustrated graphically. We have just seen that a firm's input decision is based upon a comparison of how much an input is worth relative to what it costs. How much an input is worth in essence determines the firm's demand for the input, whereas what an input costs is a function of the available supplies of the input and the demand for it in the total market. The firm's input decision can therefore be approached by an analysis of the firm's demand and supply curves for the input.

The demand and supply approach to the firm's input decision is shown in Fig. 17-1(a), using the same data as in Table 17-1. The firm's demand curve for a variable input is obtained by plotting the *MRP* figures in column (6) of the table. The *MRP* curve is synonymous with the demand curve for resource X if X is the only variable resource employed. The reason? A firm's demand for a resource input is necessarily predicated on what the resource is worth to the firm in terms of the revenue contribution it can make; this is precisely what is meant by *MRP*. The *MRP* curve rises briefly and then falls because the marginal product of the variable input first increases (due to increasing returns to variable input) and then decreases (due to the inevitable occurrence of diminishing marginal returns to variable input). The relevant portion of the *MRP* curve is the downsloping segment where MP_X is declining but positive.[4] The firm's supply curve for the input is determined by the entries

[4]For reasons explored in Chapter 7 (pp. 217–220), the firm will find it profitable to use enough variable input to get beyond the point of diminishing marginal returns unless product demand is very weak or the cost of variable input so high as to make production unprofitable. Hence, the truly relevant portion of the *MRP* curve is the downsloping segment.

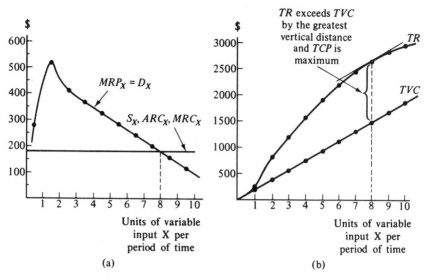

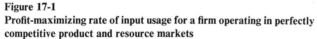

Figure 17-1
Profit-maximizing rate of input usage for a firm operating in perfectly competitive product and resource markets

in column (7) of Table 17-1. It is a horizontal line at the level of $180—the prevailing market price of the input. Since the input supply price is a constant, the input's price is exactly equal to both the *average resource cost (ARC)* and the marginal resource cost (*MRC*) of adding more variable input. Or, to put it another way, when perfectly competitive conditions prevail for input X, it follows that $P_X = ARC_X = MRC_X$ and that the supply curve for X coincides with the ARC curve for X and the MRC curve for X. These relationships are so indicated in Fig. 17-1(a).

The firm's demand and supply curves [Fig. 17-1(a)] intersect at a point corresponding to 8 units of variable input. This intersection identifies the profit-maximizing amount of variable input. At inputs of fewer than 8 units per period of time an additional unit of variable input adds more to total revenue than it adds to total cost, thereby giving the firm a clear incentive to increase its variable input usage. This is the same as saying *MRP* exceeds *MRC* at inputs below 8 units. However, to go beyond 8 units per period of time will result in total costs rising faster than total revenues, and the additional variable input will fail to "pay its own way." Hence, the firm will reduce its total profits (or increase losses) by purchasing more than 8 units of variable input. Therefore, it can be concluded from the demand and supply analysis that *a perfectly competitive firm will maximize profits by employing additional units of variable input until the point is reached where the input's marginal revenue equals its marginal resource cost.* The rationale underlying the *MRP = MRC* rule is analogous to the *MR = MC* rule. The only real difference is that the former refers to the profit-maximizing rate of

DETERMINING THE PROFIT-MAXIMIZING INPUT RATE UNDER CONDITIONS OF PERFECT COMPETITION IN THE PRODUCT AND RESOURCE MARKETS

The proposition that a perfectly competitive firm will maximize profits by purchasing units of a variable input until the point is reached where *MRP* equals *MRC* is easily demonstrated in mathematical terms.

Let the firm's production function for producing product A be

$$Q_A = f(X),$$

where Q_A = units of output of product A and X = units of any variable resource input. Then the marginal product function for input X may be written as

$$MP_X = \frac{dQ_A}{dX} = f'(X).$$

The firm's profit function may be expressed as

$$\pi = TR - TC.$$

But by definition

$$TR = P_A Q_A$$

and

$$TC = TFC + TVC.$$

Since $TVC = P_X X$, we can rewrite the expression for TC as

$$TC = TFC + P_X X.$$

Substituting into the profit function gives

$$\pi = P_A Q_A - (TFC + P_X X).$$

However, since $Q_A = f(X)$, the expression for TR_A becomes $P_A \cdot f(X)$, which when substituted into the profit function gives

$$\pi = P_A \cdot f(X) - TFC - P_X X.$$

In mathematical terms, profit maximization requires that

$$\frac{d\pi}{dX} = 0,$$

557

*The Resource
Input Decisions
of a Firm
Operating
Under
Conditions
of Perfect
Competition
in Its Product
and Resource
Markets*

which, translated into words, means variable input must be added to the point where profits cease to increase.

Taking the derivative of the profit function with respect to X gives

$$\frac{d\pi}{dX} = P_A \cdot f'(X) - P_X.$$

Setting this expression equal to zero to satisfy the profit-maximizing condition gives

$$P_A \cdot f'(X) - P_X = 0.$$

For this condition to be met, it is apparent that the first term of the above expression must equal the second term or that

$$P_A \cdot f'(X) = P_X.$$

But $f'(X)$ is, by definition, the same as MP_X, which gives

$$P_A \cdot MP_X = P_X.$$

The term $P_A \cdot MP_X$ is precisely equal to MRP_X, because in perfect competition $P_A = MR_A$. and $P_X = MRC_X$, because the input supply price in a perfectly competitive resource market is a constant value. So the condition for obtaining the profit-maximizing input rate becomes

$$MRP_X = MRC_X,$$

which is what we set out to establish.

input usage and the latter to the profit-maximizing rate of output. The two rules give the same operating results in terms of price, output, and profit, but they approach the determination of the profit-maximizing conditions via a different route.

Plotting the total revenue and total variable cost data in columns (8) and (9) of the table verifies the $MRP = MRC$ rule from another vantage point [see Fig. 17-1(b)]. Note that in Fig. 17-1(b) the horizontal axis has been drawn to represent units of variable input rather than units of output, thereby relating TR and TVC to the usage of variable input rather than to output. The maximum vertical distance between TR and TVC occurs when their slopes are equal. The slope of the TR curve when variable input (X) is plotted on the horizontal axis is dTR/dX, which, by definition, is MRP_X. Similarly, the slope of the TVC curve in these circumstances is $dTVC/dX$, which corresponds precisely to the meaning of MRC_X. Hence, the profit-maximizing rate of variable input usage is reached when the revenue gain from using more

558

*The Pricing
and
Employment
of Resource
Inputs*

variable input (MRP_x) equals the added cost of purchasing the variable input (MRC_x). Can you explain the economics of the shapes of the TR and TVC curves in Fig. 17-1(b)? Why is the TVC curve linear? Why does TR increase at a decreasing rate? (*Hint:* Your answers should concern the fact that the graph shows TR and TVC to be a function of the usage of variable input rather than the quantity of output.)

The Perfectly Competitive Firm's Input Decision: The Two-Variable Input Case

When the firm's production process utilizes two or more variable inputs, its input decisions become considerably more complex. The reason rests with the interdependence which exists among the variable inputs. A change in the price of one variable input not only affects the amount it will pay the firm to use of that input but also alters the optimum amounts of the other variable inputs. Moreover, these alterations in the usage of the other variable inputs will trigger changes in the marginal product of the variable input whose price changed, thereby resulting in still further input adjustments.

To illustrate the nature of the firm's input decision when several resource inputs can be varied, consider the simplest case where the firm has only two variable inputs—X and Y. To keep things manageable, we shall restrict discussion to determining just the firm's optimum input rate for X. Suppose the price of input X is initially fixed at P_{X_1} and the amount of input X which will maximize the firm's profits is X_1, as shown in Fig. 17-2. When the amount of resource Y is held constant, the marginal revenue product curve for X is MRP_1. Now suppose a shift in the supply conditions for input X causes the price of X to fall from P_{X_1} to P_{X_2}. The change in the

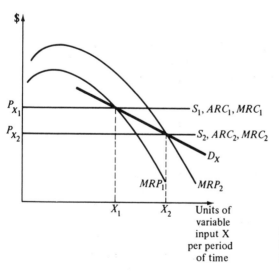

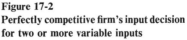

Figure 17-2
Perfectly competitive firm's input decision for two or more variable inputs

supply price of X has three effects which are pertinent to determining the new profit-maximizing input rate of X: the *substitution effect*, the *output effect*, and the *marginal cost effect*.

559

The Resource Input Decisions of a Firm Operating Under Conditions of Perfect Competition in Its Product and Resource Markets

As explained in Chapter 7, when the price of one input falls, the firm will be induced to use more of it and less of other variable inputs.[5] Let the initial prices of inputs X and Y be P_{X_1} and P_{Y_1}, the initial output be on isoquant Q_1, and the equilibrium input rates be X_1 and Y_1 at point A, as shown in Fig. 17-3. If the price of X falls from P_{X_1} to P_{X_2}, the isocost line rotates to the right, allowing the firm to produce Q_2 units of output with the same total cost outlay, using X_2 units of variable input X and Y_2 units of variable input Y (point B).

The movement from A to B can be broken down into the substitution effect and the output effect. The substitution effect shows the change in the optimum input combination that would result if the firm decided to continue to produce Q_1 units of output; it is indicated graphically by the movement from point A to point C on isoquant Q_1 in Fig. 17-3. Point C is found by drawing a third isocost line tangent to isoquant Q_1 but parallel to the isocost line with extreme points TC_1/P_{Y_1} and TC_1/P_{X_2}. The isocost line tangent to Q_1 at point C has a slope equal to the new price ratio of inputs X and Y (P_{X_2}/P_{Y_1}) and serves to identify the optimum input combination for producing Q_1

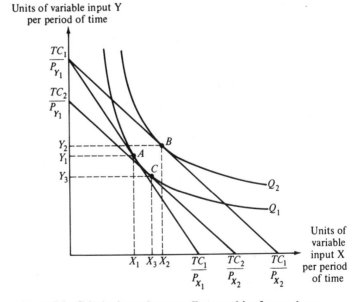

Figure 17-3   Substitution and output effects resulting from a change in an input's supply price

[5] For a review of the pertinent material, see the section in Chapter 7 on "The Impact of Changes in Resource Prices," pp. 213–16.

560

*The Pricing
and
Employment
of Resource
Inputs*

units of output, given input prices of P_{X_2} and P_{Y_1}. The difference in the input combinations at A and C indicates the extent to which the firm is induced to use *more* of input X and *less* of input Y when the price of X falls from P_{X_1} to P_{X_2}, the price of Y remains fixed, and the firm decides to produce the *same* amount of output after the reduction in the price of X as before the price change. The relevance of the substitution effect to the firm's input decision is that substitution of input X for input Y will cause the marginal product curve for input X to shift downward, thereby making the values of MP_X smaller at each input rate of X than before. The lower marginal productivity of X arises from the fact that having fewer units of input Y to work with makes input X less productive.[6]

The output effect is represented by the movement from point C to point B in Fig. 17-3. It reflects the change in optimum input combination which is associated solely with a change in the firm's output rate, the ratio of input price being held constant. The output effect can be counted upon to result in an increase in the usage of both inputs X and Y.[7] Taken by itself, the output effect will shift the marginal product curve for input X upward because the presence of more of input Y will make X more productive. In other words, having more of input Y to work with will cause the values of MP_X to be higher at each input of X than they otherwise would be. (Note that the impact of the output effect upon MP_X is in the opposite direction as the impact of the substitution effect.)

The marginal cost effect stems from the lower price of input X. When the supply price of resource X falls from P_{X_1} to P_{X_2}, the marginal cost of producing each unit of output is reduced, because it costs less than before to obtain the variable input needed to produce more output. Thus, the marginal cost curve shifts downward, with the result that the firm's marginal cost curve will intersect the firm's marginal revenue curve at a *larger* output than before (the reader should verify this statement by drawing a graph). Accordingly, the profit-maximizing rate of input for the firm is increased. The marginal cost effect thus leads to an expansion of output; in turn, more of both inputs X and Y will be required, and the marginal product curve for input X will shift upward.

To recapitulate, when the price of variable input X falls (the prices of all other variables inputs remaining constant), the substitution effect (by itself) tends to shift the marginal product curve for input X *downward*. In

---

[6]The logical basis for this statement may be more apparent if one recalls that in situations where one input is variable and the remaining inputs are fixed, a reduction in the amount of fixed inputs causes the production function to shift downward, reflecting lower marginal productivity for the variable input. Consequently, it follows that reductions in the use of input Y will make input X less efficient because the units of X have fewer units of complementary input with which to produce the product.

[7]Only in rare and relatively unimportant cases will the output effect fail to affect both variable inputs in the same manner. Increases in the output rate normally require increased usage of all variable inputs. Similarly, decreases in output usually are accompanied by reductions in the use of each variable input.

contrast, the output and marginal cost effects precipitate an *upward* shift of the MP_X curve. The net result will be a shift of MP_X upward (and quite possibly a change in its slope at each point as well).[8]

561

The Resource Input Decisions of a Firm Operating Under Conditions of Perfect Competition in Its Product and Resource Markets

The consequently larger values of MP_X at each level of input, when multiplied by the firm's marginal revenue from additional sales, will cause the firm's MRP curve for input X to shift upward and to the right. Now, turning back to Fig. 17-2, suppose that the input adjustment and the subsequent changes in MP_X combine to shift the firm's marginal revenue product curve from MRP_1 to MRP_2. The new MRP curve, coupled with the new supply price of P_{X_2}, will generate a new profit-maximizing equilibrium input rate at X_2 units. By changing the price of X again, tracing through the substitution, output, and marginal cost effects upon MP_X, and then finding the new MRP curve for input X, other profit-maximizing input rates for X can be generated. The resulting equilibrium supply prices and input rates, when connected, form the firm's input demand curve for X, shown as line D_X in Fig. 17-2. The points along D_X show the quantities of input X which will maximize the firm's profits when the prices of other variable inputs are held constant and the usages of all other variable inputs are appropriately adjusted for changes in the supply price of X.

The Factors Influencing a Firm's Input Demand

We are now in a position to indicate explicitly the factors which ultimately determine a firm's demand for a resource input.[9] These factors may be grouped into two classes: (1) those which influence the *location* of the firm's input demand curve and which cause it to *shift* and (2) those which determine the sensitivity or elasticity of the firm's input demand to input price changes.

Changes in the Firm's Input Demand. As the previous discussion suggests, the determinants of a firm's input demand relate to the input's productivity and to the revenue contribution it makes to the firm's activities. However, we can be much more specific than this.

First, it is obvious that a firm's input demand is derived from the demand of consumers for the firm's products. The more intense is consumer demand for its products, the greater will be the firm's need for resource inputs to produce them. If improvements in a product or reductions in its

---

[8]Unfortunately a proof of this statement involves an onerous mathematical exercise. The reader is thus asked to accept the statement on faith. Those who desire to pursue the point should consult Charles E. Ferguson, "Production, Price, and the Theory of Jointly Derived Input Demand Functions," *Economica*, Vol. 33, No. 132 (November 1966), pp. 454–461, and Charles E. Ferguson, " 'Inferior Factors' and the Theories of Production and Input Demand," *Economica*, Vol. 35 No. 138 (May 1968), pp. 140–150. An additional treatment may be found in Charles E. Ferguson, *The Neoclassical Theory of Production and Distribution* (New York: Cambridge University Press, 1969), Chapters 6 and 9.

[9]This discussion is equally applicable to firms operating in either perfectly or imperfectly competitive product markets.

562

*The Pricing
and
Employment
of Resource
Inputs*

price stimulate consumer demand, then the firm's input demand will also increase. A resource input that is very proficient in helping to produce a good in strong demand by consumers will itself have a strong demand. On the other hand, a firm's demand for an input will be slight if product demand is small, irrespective of the input's own productivity. There will be no demand for an input which is extraordinarily efficient at producing something no one wants to buy; thus high efficiency of an input, by itself, is insufficient to create a demand for that input.

Second, a firm's input demand is dependent on known technology and the directions of technological change. The technological character of a firm's production process is a fundamental factor in determining the marginal product function for each and every input. And, clearly enough, technological change alters the marginal productivity of a firm's resource inputs. Thus, technological progress that makes an input more productive also increases the demand for that input. Technological progress which makes an input less productive relative to other inputs ultimately reduces the demand for the input and may even eliminate demand for it entirely.

Third, the price of an input relative to other inputs influences input demand. As isoquant-isocost analysis demonstrates, the relative prices among substitutable inputs determine a firm's choice of production technologies from the array of known production recipes. If an input becomes cheaper relative to other inputs, the demand for it will gradually increase as producers alter their production techniques so as to substitute the lower-priced resource inputs for the relatively higher-priced ones.

Fourth, the demand for an input will be greater the higher is the marginal revenue which the firm receives from additional sales of output. Whatever the marginal product of an input is, the higher the value of MR, the larger will be the input's marginal revenue product. Since an input's MR values are of paramount importance in determining the profit-maximizing input rate, it necessarily must be true that anything which increases MRP will also increase the firm's input demand—other things being equal.

And last, the greater the quantity of cooperating inputs employed, the greater the demand for a given input. This proposition follows from the fact that giving an input more of other inputs with which to work and produce allows the input in question to be more productive and thereby have a higher marginal product at each input rate than otherwise. For example, providing automobile workers with more high-speed metal-stamping machines and automated assembly equipment will result in their being more productive and more capable of achieving a greater output per labor-hour worked—which clearly means a higher marginal product of labor and, in turn, a higher marginal revenue product for labor.

The Firm's Elasticity of Demand for a Resource Input. Four important factors influence the degree to which a firm's input demand will respond to changes in the price of an input. As is customary in economics, we shall refer to this responsiveness or sensitivity as a firm's elasticity of demand for a resource input.[10]

563

The Resource Input Decisions of a Firm Operating Under Conditions of Perfect Competition in Its Product and Resource Markets

First, the rate at which the marginal product of an input changes as the firm increases or decreases its usage has a bearing upon the degree to which a firm will alter its input rate as a consequence of a change in the input's supply price. This follows from the fact that the marginal revenue product of an input is equal to $MP \cdot MR$. Whatever the value of MR, the faster the value of MP declines, the more rapid will be the decline in MRP and the less elastic will be the firm's demand for the input. If, for example, the technological character of a firm's production function is such that the marginal product of variable input X declines slowly as larger doses of X are combined with the fixed inputs, then the effect will be to cause the MRP values for X to decline more slowly than otherwise. This will enhance the elasticity of the firm's demand for the input. On the other hand, if the marginal product of X falls off sharply as more of X is used, then the effect is to cause the MRP curve for X to decline more swiftly, thereby reducing the elasticity of the firm's input demand.

Second, the derived nature of resource demand necessarily makes the elasticity of a firm's input demand dependent on the elasticity of demand for the firm's product. A decline in the price of a product having an elastic demand will give rise to a sharper increase in output and therefore a stronger increase in the amounts of the variable inputs used to produce it than will a comparable decline in the price of a product having an inelastic demand.

Third, the degree to which resources can be substituted for one another determines an input's demand elasticity. The larger the number of substitutes for an input and the greater the ease with which substitution can be initiated and accomplished, the greater will be the elasticity of demand for that input. If a book publisher finds that some six or seven grades of paper are equally satisfactory in manufacturing college texbooks, then a rise in the price of any one grade of paper can be counted upon to cause a very sharp drop in its demand as other grades of paper are readily substituted. At the other extreme, where an input has few if any good substitutes, the demand for it tends to be highly inelastic. For instance, the lack of good substitutes for sheet steel in manufacturing automobile bodies, for electricians in performing electric wiring functions for new construction projects, or for crude oil in the refining of motor fuels explains why their demands are relatively unresponsive in the short run to increases in their supply prices.

Finally, the elasticity of demand for a resource input is determined in part by the fraction of total production costs accounted for by the input. The construction industry offers a good illustration of this proposition. In con-

---

[10]It will be recalled from earlier discussion (Chapter 5) that the concept of elasticity is nothing more than a ratio of percentage changes. The elasticity of demand for a resource input X (ϵ_X) may be thought of as

$$\epsilon_X = \frac{\% \text{ change in the input rate of X}}{\% \text{ change in the supply price of input X}}.$$

struction, labor costs are approximately 50% of total costs. If the wage rates of all the many types of construction labor rise by 10%, then total construction costs will rise by 5%. Rising construction costs will push the prices of new construction upward and reduce new construction activity. In turn, the demand of construction firms for construction labor will be weakened. However, suppose only the wage rates of bricklayers rise by 10%, the wage rates of other types of construction labor remaining fixed. Further suppose that the total wages paid to bricklayers amount to only 2% of total costs. Then a 10% rise in bricklayers' wages will cause total costs to rise by only 0.2%—an amount not likely to affect the demand for new construction to any important degree nor therefore the demand for bricklayers and other construction labor. Hence, as a general rule, the smaller the fraction of total costs accounted for by an input, the more inelastic will be a firm's demand for the input.[11]

Industry Demand for a Resource Input

The total industry demand for a resource input is found by combining the amounts of input that all firms in the industry will employ at a given price. This is slightly different from horizontally summing the individual firm demand curves for the input, because in perfect competition, when all firms change their output rates simultaneously, the market price of the product will also change. The resulting change in marginal revenue will trigger a shift in each firm's MRP curve for the input. Despite these complexities the industry demand curve for the input can be determined; the procedure is illustrated in Fig. 17-4.

The profit-maximizing input rates for a representative firm in a perfectly competitive industry are shown in panel (a). Given some market price for the firm's product, the firm's demand for input X is represented by the curve labeled D_1, derived according to the method described in Fig. 17-2. If the supply price of the input is P_1 dollars, the firm's equilibrium input is X_1 units. Adding together the optimum input usages of all the firms in the industry gives a total demand of X_{T_1} units at input price P_1, shown as point A in Fig. 17-4(b).

Now suppose the price of input X falls to P_2, perhaps because of greater available supplies of the input. This shifts the firm's marginal cost curve downward at each output rate and causes MC to intersect MR at a greater output rate. Assuming nothing else changes, the representative firm will expand its output rate by moving along D_1 in panel (a) and increasing its usage of X to X_3 units per period. However, we cannot assume that nothing else changes; what the representative firm does, the other firms will find it

[11]It is, incidentally, the small portion of total costs coupled with a lack of good substitutes which explains why craft unions having more or less monopoly control over the supply of a specific type of labor have been consistently able to negotiate substantial wage rate increases for their members.

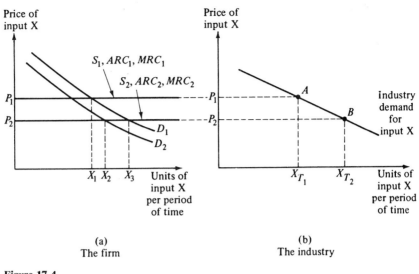

Figure 17-4
**Deriving the industry demand for a resource input in a perfectly
competitive environment**

advantageous to do as well. The lower price of X affects the MC curves of all
the firms. Hence, when the price of input X falls, *all* firms will be induced to
expand their output rates and thereby use more of input X. The industrywide
expansion of output will shift the industry supply curve for the product to
the right, causing the market price of the product to fall. In turn, the lower
product price means a lower marginal revenue and thus a lower marginal
revenue product for X at each input rate. The effect is to shift the firm's input
demand curve for X down and to the left, say from D_1 to D_2. The new profit-
maximizing input rate for the representative firm at input price P_2 therefore
is X_2 units and not X_3 units. Aggregating for all firms in the industry gives a
total industry demand of X_{T_2} units at input price P_2, shown as point B in
Fig. 17-4(b). Points in addition to A and B can be determined by considering
still other input prices. Connecting these points by a line gives the industry
demand curve for input X.

Industry Supply of a Resource Input

The supply of a resource input to an industry refers to the various input
quantities which owners of the input are willing and able to make available
to firms in the industry at various prices. Since in a free economy resource
owners have a choice of supplying their resources to one line of production
or another, it is reasonable to presume that they will direct them to the use
and to the industry which offers the greatest prospect of reward—and not
necessarily just the greatest monetary reward, because the reward package
often includes nonmonetary as well as monetary elements.

Insofar as capital and land inputs of various types are concerned, the expected monetary reward is generally the predominant consideration. However, the case of labor inputs is more complicated. Wage rates and salaries are certainly important, but so are such features as the time and expense in learning a job or entering a profession, the opportunity for obtaining personal satisfactions from the job, the prospects for promotion and advancement, the regularity of employment, the environmental conditions under which the work is performed, the specific community and geographical area in which the job is located, and the social status of the occupation. Each job type offers a package of monetary and nonmonetary considerations that each potential worker may evaluate differently in the light of his own preferences. Given a choice of occupation and jobs, each member of the labor force can reasonably be expected to choose the one perceived as offering the best total package relative to one's interests, skills, and capabilities. Nonetheless, the supply of labor inputs may be expressed as a function of monetary rewards in the short run. Experience indicates that the nonmonetary elements affecting resource allocation change rather slowly and can therefore be treated as a constant for purposes of short-run analysis.

Logic dictates that a positive relation between input prices and input supplies will exist for most all types of land, natural resources, manpower, and capital goods inputs. As the amount of monetary reward accruing to an input rises, resource owners will ordinarily be induced to supply the input in larger quantities per period of time. For instance, higher prices for minerals and natural resources intensify efforts to discover and tap more sources of supply. As wage rates in one occupation rise relative to wage rates in other occupations, the number of people seeking employment in that occupation will tend to rise. The greater the wage differential between firms, the more will workers gravitate from low-paying to high-paying firms; similarly, the greater the wage differentials between industries and between geographical regions, the more mobile will workers become.[12] Accordingly, input supply curves are upward sloping, owing to the tendency of inputs to be drawn to employments where the rewards are highest.

How responsive input supplies will be to changes in input prices depends on several factors:

1. *The size of the economic unit under consideration—the total economy, a locality, an industry, or a single firm.* The supply of an input to the economy as a whole may be fixed in the short run, while at the same time the supply to a particular locality, industry, or firm may be highly elastic or even perfectly elastic. Although at any given time there is just so much land, labor, or capital input in the entire

---

[12]Sometimes substantial wage differentials exist and are maintained for long periods, but beyond some point a wage differential can become too great for a firm, or an industry, or a locality, or a region to maintain without affecting labor supply conditions. The wages workers expect from one firm bear some relationship to the wages similar workers elsewhere receive, and if workers' expectations are grossly unrealized, the supply of labor is bound to be affected. The supply of job applicants for firms paying subpar wages may not totally dry up, but the quality may deteriorate. Moreover, their labor turnover is likely to be above average as workers' dissatisfaction with their wages pushes them to look for alternative employment.

economy (or in a more restricted geographical area), one firm or industry may be able to obtain as much of the available supply of an input as it may need without changing its offer prices because, by itself, it may require only a negligible fraction of the available input supply.

2. *The period of time considered.* The response of input supplies to input price changes is greater over the long run than over the short run, primarily because the degree of resource mobility increases with time. It takes time to discover and develop new mineral deposits, to shift capital investment out of less profitable endeavors into more profitable endeavors, to convert land from one use to another, to retrain workers or induce them to move into areas where job opportunities are expanding, and to inform people preparing to enter the labor force of the changing prospects of economic reward in the various professions. Hence, the elasticity of supply of an input becomes greater with the expansion of the time frame under consideration.

3. *Whether the input is unique to a particular industry or whether it is widely used.* The supply of an input used only by a single industry tends to be less elastic than inputs which are used by a number of different industries. The more versatile and mobile an input is, the more elastic will be its supply to a particular industry.

The size of the coefficient of the elasticity of supply, however, is not of paramount importance for our purposes. The basic analysis will be the same whatever the shape and degree of elasticity of the industry supply curve—even if it is vertical or backward rising.[13]

The Pricing and Employment of a Resource Input

The industry demand and supply curves for an input determine the equilibrium price which firms in the industry pay for the input and the equilibrium amount of the input employed in the industry. Figure 17-5 shows the industry demand and supply curves for input X and the resulting equilibrium input price of P_1 dollars and employment rate of X_{T_1} units per period of time. If the prevailing price exceeds P_1 dollars, the available supply of the input will exceed the quantity which firms are willing to employ. Some units of the input will be either idle altogether or else used only part of the time. The excess supply of the input will generate a downward pressure on its price. On the other hand, if the actual price of X falls below P_1, the quantity demanded by firms in the industry will exceed the quantity supplied to the industry, and upward price pressures are automatically activated.

Thus, market forces push resource prices and employment rates toward levels that will clear the market. Multiplying the equilibrium input price by the equilibrium employment rate of X gives the amount of money income which the owners of input X will receive from the firms in the industry. Aggregating the income of input X over all industries which use input X

567

The Resource Input Decisions of a Firm Operating Under Conditions of Perfect Competition in Its Product and Resource Markets

[13] A backward-bending supply curve for an input may arise from the fact that above certain input price levels, resource owners prefer to withdraw some units of input from the market to meet leisure-time or other personal preferences, since those units still being supplied will provide an income which is regarded as adequate. Hence, above some input price level, the higher the price, the smaller the quantity of the input supplied by resource owners. The effect is to cause the supply curve for the input to bend backward and upward—or to be backward rising. Generally, the concept of a backward rising supply curve is most applicable to the case of labor input.

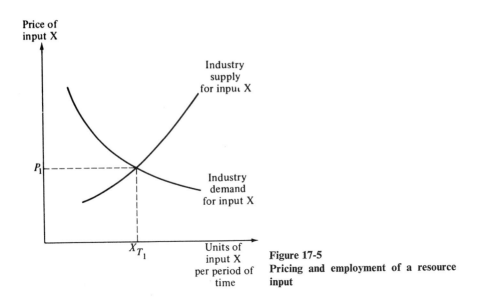

Figure 17-5
Pricing and employment of a resource input

gives the total money income received by the owners of X and the share of the economy's output they will earn from having supplied X. This explanation of how the income accruing to resource owners is determined is called the *marginal productivity theory of income distribution*. It derives this name from the fact that particular input prices and employment rates are a function of the input's marginal productivity.

However, it must be recognized that if the input is widely used in many industries and if its supply to a particular industry is very sensitive to input price changes, it is misleading, if not wholly inaccurate, to examine input equilibrium in terms of one industry alone. The reason is that what firms in one industry pay for an input and the amounts they use of this input necessarily are related to the prices that firms in other industries pay and the amounts of that input they employ. In fact, input prices and employment rates among the various industries using that input are interconnected; price or employment adjustments in one industry transmit pressures and influences to other industries, though with "impulses" of varying degrees of intensity. The linkages between industries are usually sufficiently strong to cause an input's price to *tend* toward the same level in all industries. Different input prices for the same quality input can prevail without stimulating the movement of input supplies among firms and industries, but at some point the tolerance of resource owners for differentials becomes stretched so thin that firms and industries, in order to keep the inputs they need, will be forced to lessen the gap. Consequently, where an input is employed in several industries, the appropriate focal point for analyzing input prices is at the level of the total market for the input rather than at the level of the firm or industry.

The total market demand for an input on an economywide basis may be thought of as the sum of all the various industry demand curves, where the industries may be structured along any sort of lines and may contain any number of firms of various types and sizes. Similarly, the total market supply of an input is the result of combining the industry supply curves. Again, the intersection of market demand and market supply determines the input's economywide equilibrium price and rate of usage per period of time. The resulting price and employment rate form the basis for ascertaining the total amount of income which owners of the input in question will receive per period of time.

569

The Resource Input Decisions of a Firm Operating Under Conditions of Imperfect Competition in Its Product Market and Perfect Competition in Its Resource Market

While it is generally agreed among economists that resource prices and employment rates are outcomes of supply and demand forces, in particular situations the operation of supply and demand forces may be suspended or modified. The presence of labor unions, the imposing of minimum wage requirements, a wage-price freeze, plus a host of other institutional considerations combine to cause input prices and employment rates to deviate from the free market results. We shall discuss some of the ramifications of these market aberrations in the concluding section of this chapter.

The Applicability of the Perfectly Competitive Resource Input Model

It goes almost without saying that the model of the firm's input decision under conditions of perfect competition in both the product and resource markets applies only to those few markets where the products of the firms are homogeneous and where the number of firms comprising the product market is quite large. Only under these conditions is perfect competition in the product market even approximated. Thus, strictly speaking, the preceding model of resource pricing and resource employment provides a theoretical description of but a small segment of the economy. Nevertheless, many of the principles governing business behavior in perfectly competitive product and resource markets are much the same as in other types of market structures. In this sense, the perfectly competitive input model is valuable for its introduction to more widely applicable models of resource pricing and employment.

THE RESOURCE INPUT DECISIONS OF A FIRM OPERATING UNDER CONDITIONS OF IMPERFECT COMPETITION IN ITS PRODUCT MARKET AND PERFECT COMPETITION IN ITS RESOURCE MARKET

A somewhat more prevalent model of the functioning and behavior or resource input markets concerns the situation where the firm sells its product under conditions of imperfect competition (i.e., monopolistic competition, oligopoly, or monopoly) yet buys its inputs in a perfectly competitive resource market. This model characterizes many resource markets in the small business sector of the economy and some in the corporate sector.

570

*The Pricing
and
Employment
of Resource
Inputs*

The Imperfectly Competitive Firm's Input Decision: The One-Variable Input Case

When the firm sells its product in an imperfectly competitive market structure, its input decision is determined in a manner analogous to the perfectly competitive case, but with a slightly modified calculation procedure. In monopolistic competition, oligopoly, or pure monopoly the firm's product demand curve is downsloping, and the firm must lower price in order to increase its sales volume. This has a very important consequence. Whereas the MRP curve of an input used by a perfectly competitive firm falls solely because the marginal product of the input declines, the MRP curve of an input used by an imperfectly competitive firm declines for two reasons: a declining marginal product and a lower marginal revenue from the sale of additional output. The perfectly competitive enterprise can sell additional output at a constant price and obtain a constant MR, so that its MRP curve falls at the same rate as does the MP curve of the variable input. But when an imperfectly competitive firm adds one more unit of variable input and output rises by the amount of its marginal product, it is forced to lower selling price to sell the increased output. Barring the opportunity for price discrimination, the price decrease applies not just to the marginal product of the last unit of variable input but also to the units of output previously produced.[14] Hence, the marginal revenue received from additional sales is a decreasing function, and the firm's MRP curve for variable input falls faster than it otherwise would if the firm sold its output under conditions of perfect competition. However, in either case, MRP still equals the net addition to total revenue associated with a change in the variable input rate.

The Profit-Maximizing Rate of Input Usage. To illustrate how a firm confronted with a downsloping demand-AR curve can ascertain the profit-maximizing rate of usage of a single variable input (X), consider the hypothetical production, cost, and revenue data in Table 17-2. Column (4) shows the extent to which the firm must lower price in order to sell the extra output of each successive unit of X, while columns (5) and (6) concern the corresponding TR and MR values. Column (7) contains the $SVMP_X$ figures, obtained by multiplying MP_X by the price at which the added output can be sold. Observe carefully that, unlike the perfectly competitive case, the figures for $SVMP_X$ in column (7) do *not* coincide with MRP_X values in column (8). The figures for the sales value of the marginal product represent the gross addition to total revenue attributable to an additional unit of X. However, the firm's total revenue does not rise by the amount of $SVMP$, because to sell the added output the firm must reduce its price on the preceding units of output, thereby causing the *net* addition to TR to be less than the gross addition. To illustrate: The eighth unit of X has a marginal product of 10

---

[14]We shall assume throughout the following discussion that the firm employs a single price policy and does not therefore engage in any of the several forms of price discrimination.

Table 17-2 Profit-Maximizing Rate of Resource Input Usage for a Firm Operating in an Imperfectly Competitive Product Market and a Perfectly Competitive Resource Market

(1) Units of Variable Input (X)	(2) Units of Output (Q_A)	(3) Marginal Product (MP_X)	(4) Price of Product A (P_A)	(5) Total Revenue from Sales of Product A $(TR_A = P_A \cdot Q_A)$	(6) "Average" Marginal Revenue[a] (MR_A)	(7) Sales Value of Marginal Product $(SVMP_X = MP_X \cdot P_A)$	(8) Marginal Revenue Product $(MRP_X = MP_X \cdot MR_A = \Delta TR_A/\Delta X)$	(9) Supply Price of Variable Input $(P_X = ARC_X = MRC_X)$	(10) Total Variable Cost (TVC)	(11) Total Contribution Profit $(TCP = TR - TVC)$
0	0		$25	$ 0				$140	$ 0	$ 0
1	14	14	24	336	$24.00	$336	$336	140	140	196
2	40	26	23	920	22.46	598	584	140	280	640
3	60	20	22	1320	20.00	440	400	140	420	900
4	78	18	21	1638	17.67	378	318	140	560	1078
5	94	16	20	1880	15.12	320	242	140	700	1180
6	108	14	19	2052	12.29	266	172	140	840	1212
7	120	12	18	2160	9.00	216	108	140	980	1180
8	130	10	17	2210	5.00	170	50	140	1120	1090
9	138	8	16	2208	-0.25	128	-2	140	1260	948
10	144	6	15	2160	-8.00	90	-48	140	1400	760

[a]The term "average" marginal revenue is used here because, strictly speaking, the concept of MR refers to the extra revenue associated with a single-unit change in output; since the output changes in the table are multi-unit, the only MR values which can be computed from the information in the table are the average MR values for the multiunit output increment in question.

572

*The Pricing
and
Employment
of Resource
Inputs*

units of output; these can be sold for $17 apiece for a total of $170—the figure for *SVMP*. But this is not the *MRP* value for the eighth unit of X because, to sell these 10 units of output, the firm must accept a $1 price reduction on the 120 units of output produced by the preceding 7 units of X. Hence, the *MRP* of the eighth unit of X is [$170 − 120($1)] or $50, as shown in column (8). The other values in column (8) can be determined in like fashion. The figures in columns (9), (10), and (11) of the table are obtained in the usual way.

The principle upon which the imperfectly competitive firm's input decision is based is precisely the same as that of the perfectly competitive firm: *The firm should purchase additional units of a variable input up to the point where the added cost of more input equals the added revenue it contributes.* In short, the usage of variable input must be carried to the rate where *MRP = MRC*. A comparison of columns (8) and (9) in Table 17-2 indicates that the profit-maximizing input rate is 6 units of X. For the firm to go beyond this point and employ the seventh unit of X will result in revenues increasing by $108 but costs rising by $140—plainly an unprofitable act. For the firm to stop short of using 6 units of X will result in smaller total contribution profits [see column (11)] and hence smaller total profits (or greater losses).

The profit-maximizing input decision can be approached graphically in a somewhat more general fashion. Figure 17-6 shows an imperfectly competitive firm's *MRP* curve for a variable input. Suppose the input supply curve is S_1, with a resulting input price of P_1 dollars. The profit-maximizing input rate is X_1 units, where $MRP_X = MRC_X$. Should the input supply price fall to P_2 dollars, giving a new input supply curve at S_2, the firm's profit-maximizing input rate would expand to X_2 units per period of time. And should the input supply curve shift downward to S_3, the new equilibrium

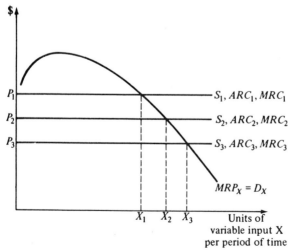

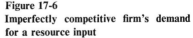

Figure 17-6
Imperfectly competitive firm's demand for a resource input

input rate would become X_3 units. Consequently, the profit-maximizing input rate of X is found along the input's MRP curve, which makes the MRP_X curve the firm's demand curve for input X, provided only one variable input is used in the firm's production process.

The Imperfectly Competitive Firm's Input Decision: The Two-Variable Input Case

The analysis for an imperfectly competitive firm using two or more variable inputs parallels that for the perfectly competitive firm. As portayed in Fig. 17-7, suppose that the supply price of input X is temporarily fixed at P_1 and that the input's marginal revenue product curve is MRP_1. The profit-maximizing rate of input is therefore X_1 units per period of time.

Now let the supply price of X fall to P_2. This change triggers four effects at the level of the firm; the substitution effect, the output effect, the marginal cost effect, and the marginal revenue effect. The substitution, output, and marginal cost effects operate in exactly the same way for firms in monopolistic competition, oligopoly, or pure monopoly as they do for firms in perfect competition.

However, the *marginal revenue effect* is unique to imperfectly competitive product markets and arises from the fact that the firm's marginal revenue will change as a consequence of the output changes induced by the shift in the price of input X. The decline in the price of X lowers the firm's marginal cost curve, causing a new intersection of MC and MR at a *larger* output, a *lower* price, and a *lower MR* value. (The reader should verify this statement by drawing a graph.) Since $MRP_X = MP_X \cdot MR$, a decline in MR necessarily acts to reduce MRP_X.

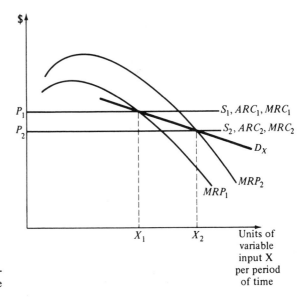

Figure 17-7
Imperfectly competitive firm's input decision when two or more inputs are variable

574

The Pricing
and
Employment
of Resource
Inputs

On balance, the output and marginal cost effects will override the substitution and marginal revenue effects, with the result that a decline in the supply price of X will shift the MRP curve for X upward and to the right, say from MRP_1 to MRP_2.[15] The profit-maximizing input rate for the imperfectly competitive firm thus becomes X_2 units at a supply price of P_2 dollars. Other profit-maximizing input rates for X can be generated by changing the price of X again and again, tracing through the substitution, output, marginal cost, and marginal revenue effects, and finding the new position of the firm's MRP curve. Connecting the points formed by the equilibrium input supply prices and input rates gives the firm's input demand curve for X, labeled as D_X in Fig. 17-7. The points along D_X show the various quantities of input X that maximize the firm's profits when the prices of other variable inputs remain constant and the usages of all other variable inputs are appropriately adjusted for changes in the supply price of input X.

The Input Demand of an Imperfectly Competitive Industry

To derive the industrywide demand for an input when the firms compete under conditions of imperfect competition requires that the demand curves of the individual firms somehow be combined into a single input demand curve for the industry. In an imperfectly competitive market of two or more firms, whatever shade of oligopoly or monopolistic competition may exist, the demand curves of the firms cannot simply be summed horizontally to give the industry demand curve.[16] This is invalid for the same reason it does not work for perfect competition. To begin with, a change in the input's supply price affects the optimum output rate of each firm in the industry. A change in the firm's output rate leads then to a price change. The price and output adjustments made by the firm will combine to shift the MRP curve of the input via the substitution, output, marginal cost, and marginal revenue effects. In turn, the shift in MRP alters the firm's optimum input demand at the new input supply price. In such situations, the industrywide input demand curve is derived by first finding the profit-maximizing input rate for each firm at each possbile input price after allowing for shifts in the MRP curve and then by summing these optimum input amounts over all firms in the industry. The rationale and the graphical analysis are identical to that described in Fig. 17-4 and need not be reiterated here.

Once the industry demand for the input is determined, the industrywide equilibrium price and input rates are found at the intersection of the industry demand and supply curves for the input. The nature of the input's industry supply curve, discussed in an earlier section of this chapter, is unaffected by the existence of imperfect competition in the product market. Again, however,

---

[15]For a formal proof of this claim the reader may consult the references in footnote 8.

[16]Obviously, if the industry is one of pure monopoly, no combining is necessary, because the firm's input demand and the industry input demand are one and the same.

the equilibrium price of an input on an industrywide basis is bound to be affected by the price of the input in other industries. When resource inputs are versatile enough to be used by several industries and when they are relatively mobile from industry to industry, the equilibrium price and employment rates of an input are best analyzed on a marketwide or economywide basis rather than on an industrywide basis. Barring the existence of resource immobility or other powerful institutional determinants of an input price, the tie between a resource input's price in one industry and its price in other industries is usually strong enough to cause the overall price of the input to *tend* toward the same level in all industries using that input. A valid explanation of how input prices are determined must therefore hinge upon overall market demand and supply conditions rather upon demand and supply in any one industry.

575

The Resource Input Decisions of a Firm Operating Under Conditions of Imperfect Competition in Its Product and Resource Markets

THE RESOURCE INPUT DECISIONS OF A FIRM OPERATING UNDER CONDITIONS OF IMPERFECT COMPETITION IN ITS PRODUCT AND RESOURCE MARKETS

In numerous geographical areas the supply of an input *in the short run* is relatively limited. Enterprises with large plants in the area may utilize such a sizable fraction of the local input supply that their decisions to employ more or less of the input have a discernible impact on the input's short-run local supply price. The effect is to make the firm's input supply curve upward sloping. The more of an input the firm wishes to obtain, the higher the price it must offer to bid supplies of the input away from alternative users.[17] The less of an input the firm needs, the smaller the price it can get by with paying, since it does not have to bid so high to attract the desired supply away from other firms.

Several types of input supply situations other than perfect competition may be delineated. A resource input market in which only *one* firm uses the input is referred to as *monopsony*.[18] If only a *few* firms are the predominant purchasers of the input, the resource market is designated as *oligopsony*.

[17]As regards labor inputs, it should be recognized that a large firm may be able to expand the size of its labor force without raising the going wage rate by increasing recruiting efforts and/or by lowering its standards for hiring new employees. Either of these strategies, however, really means that the effective price of a given quantity and quality of labor is rising, even though the nominal wage scale remains the same.

[18]The term monopsony is on occasions also used to refer to product market situations where there is only a single buyer of a product. Hence, strictly speaking, monopsony refers to a single buyer—it matters not whether the buyer purchases an input or a final good or service. Likewise, pure monopoly refers to a single seller—whether the seller is selling a product or an input again really makes no difference. For example, the craft union which is able to unionize all persons having a particular skill is just as much a monopolist in "selling" the skill it controls as is the local telephone company in rendering telephone service. Analogous meanings and interpretations can be attached to the terms oligopoly, oligopsony, and so on.

576

*The Pricing
and
Employment
of Resource
Inputs*

Where *many* firms are using an input but their numbers are still small enough to allow each firm a small influence over the input's supply price, the resource market may be characterized as *monopsonistic competition*. A particular firm can sell its output under conditions of oligopoly yet buy its inputs under conditions of monopsonistic competition. Likewise, it is possible for a firm to sell its product under conditions of monopolistic competition and to obtain its inputs under conditions of monopsony; this could occur if the numerous small producers were geographically dispersed but still large enough to dominate the market for labor in a local area. Plainly, a variety of product and resource market combinations can result: monopoly-monopsony, oligopoly-monopsony, oligopoly-monopsonistic competition, perfect competition-oligopsony, and so on. However, in any short of imperfectly competitive input market, whether it be one of monopsony, oligopsony, or monopsonistic competition, the analytical considerations governing the supply aspects of the firm's input decision are the same. Thus, it is sufficient merely to examine imperfect competition in the input market to learn about the firm's input decision in other than a perfectly competitive resource market.

The Marginal Resource Cost Curve and a Rising Input Supply Curve

The key feature of an imperfectly competitive input market is an upward-rising input supply curve. With a rising supply curve the firm is forced to pay a higher price if it wishes to secure more of the input, and the firm can get by with paying a lower price for the input should it choose to use less of the input. Since the supply curve for an input represents the firm's average cost for obtaining the input, the firm's ARC curve is also upward sloping and coincides with the supply curve. This has a most important consequence insofar as the firm's marginal resource cost is concerned.

Under imperfectly competitive input supply conditions, the MRC curve does not correspond to the input supply and average resource cost curve. Consider the hypothetical data in Table 17-3. Columns (1) and (2) show how much the firm must increase its offer price in order to obtain additional units of X; these two columns represent the firm's input supply and ARC schedules. Column (3) presents the total cost of input X associated with each of the various input rates of X. Column (4) shows the marginal resource cost of each additional unit of X and can be calculated by successive subtraction of the TC_X figures; that is, $MRC_X = \Delta TC_X / \Delta X$.

When the firm must pay a higher price to obtain larger amounts of input X, the marginal resource cost of each extra unit will be higher than the input's supply price and average resource cost. As shown in Table 17-3, suppose the firm increases its usage rate of X from 7 to 8 units per period. The price of the eighth unit is $8.50. But this value is not the marginal resource cost of the eighth unit. To obtain the use of 8 units of X, the firm

577
The Resource
Input Decisions
of a Firm
Operating
Under
Conditions
of Imperfect
Competition
in Its Product
and Resource
Markets

Table 17-3 **Marginal Resource Cost for a Firm Operating under Conditions of Imperfect Competition in the Resource Input Market**

(1) Units of Variable Input (X)	(2) Supply Price of Variable Input ($P_X = ARC_X$)	(3) Total Cost of Variable Input (TC_X)	(4) Marginal Resource Cost (MRC_X)
1	$5.00	$ 5.00	
2	5.50	11.00	$ 6.00
3	6.00	18.00	7.00
4	6.50	26.00	8.00
5	7.00	35.00	9.00
6	7.50	45.00	10.00
7	8.00	56.00	11.00
8	8.50	68.00	12.00
9	9.00	81.00	13.00
10	9.50	95.00	14.00

must pay $8.50 for *each* one.[19] Hence, the firm's cost of obtaining each of the previous 7 units of X rises from $8.00 to $8.50 for an added cost of $3.50 (7 × $0.50). Adding this to the $8.50 cost of the eighth unit gives a total increase of $12.00 in the firm's cost of upping the input rate of X from 7 to 8 units. Thus, the marginal resource cost of the eighth unit is $12.00. The MRC of the other units can be derived in the same fashion.

A graphical portrayal of the relationships among the firm's input supply curve (S_X), the average resource cost curve (ARC_X), and the marginal resource cost curve (MRC_X) is depicted in Fig. 17-8. The MRC_X curve lies above the input supply and average resource cost curve at each and every input rate. The rationale is the same as for the relationship between ATC and MC; in fact, the ARC_X-MRC_X relation parallels that of ATC and MC. As is the usual case with marginal and average concepts, if the average cost (or supply price) of input X is rising, then the marginal cost of input X (MRC_X) must be greater than ARC_X and the MRC curve for X must lie above the input supply and average resource cost curve.

The mathematics of the relationship between S_X and MRC_X is easily indicated. Assume, for convenience of illustration, that the input supply curve for X is linear and upward sloping. Then the general equation for the supply

---

[19]This is not only required by the supply conditions, but it is also equitable. Since we assume each unit of X is just alike, there is no cause for the firm to reward 1 unit of X any differently from the others. If, for example, the firm has 8 identical units of input X, then the second unit (assuming it can be picked out from the rest) is no more "valuable" than the fifth or the eighth unit. The *order* in which the units of X are hired has no real bearing on their worth to the firm. Nor is it usually feasible for the firm to pay different units of the same input a different price. Consequently, the price which it takes to get the *total* amount of X that is desired is what determines the price *each unit* must be paid.

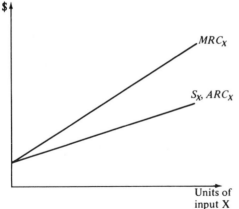

Figure 17-8
Relationships among the input supply
curve, the average resource cost curve,
and the marginal resource cost curve in
an imperfectly competitive input market

curve is

$$P_X = ARC_X = a + bX.$$

The total cost of the input at any input rate is

$$TC_X = P_X \cdot X = ARC_X \cdot X = (a + bX)X = aX + bX^2.$$

Marginal resource cost is, by definition, the rate of change in the total cost of the input as the input rate changes, which in terms of calculus is the first derivative of the input's total cost function. The equation for MRC_X thus becomes

$$MRC_X = \frac{dTC_X}{dX} = a + 2bX.$$

A comparison of the equation for the input supply-average resource cost curve and the equation for the MRC curve indicates that the MRC_X curve will rise twice as fast as S_X-ARC_X when S_X-ARC_X is linear and upward sloping. The marginal resource cost curve can be determined in like fashion for other types of input supply-average resource cost functions.

The Imperfectly Competitive Firm's Input Decision in an Imperfectly Competitive Resource Market: The One-Variable Input Case

Determining the firm's profit-maximizing input rate with respect to resource X follows the same principle when imperfect competition exists in the input market as it does when there is perfect competition. As we have just seen, the distinctive feature of an imperfectly competitive resource market is an upward-rising input supply curve and an even more rapidly rising marginal resource cost curve. Nonetheless, the firm will still find it advantageous to increase the usage rate of X as long as additional units of X add more to revenues than to total costs. As before, the firm's net revenue gains from using additional units of an input are given by the input's *MRP* function, whereas the extra costs incurred are indicated by the input's *MRC* function as derived from the input's supply and *ARC* functions.

579

The Resource Input Decisions of a Firm Operating Under Conditions of Imperfect Competition in Its Product and Resource Markets

The relevant curves are shown in Fig. 17-9. The firm's profits will be maximum at an input rate of X_1 units, where $MRP_X = MRC_X$. To use more than X_1 units per period of time would add more to the firm's total costs than to its total revenues. To stop short of using X_1 units would mean a sacrifice of some profits, because the marginal revenue products of all units below X_1 exceeds their respective marginal resource costs. Clearly, then, X_1 is the profit-maximizing input rate. But now the question becomes: What price must the firm pay to obtain X_1 units per period of time? Although the marginal revenue product at X_1 is MRP_{X_1}, this is not the price which the firm need pay to get X_1 units. The input supply curve (S_X) shows the price which the firm must pay for various quantities of the input. From S_X it is apparent that to obtain X_1 units of resource X, the firm will find it necessary to pay a price of P_1 dollars—this, then, is the firm's equilibrium input price.

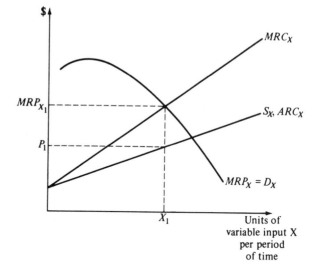

Figure 17-9
Profit-maximizing input rate for a firm operating in imperfectly competitive product and resource markets

The Imperfectly Competitive Firm's Input Decision in an Imperfectly Competitive Resource Market when Several Variable Inputs Are Used

Ordinarily, a firm's production technology will call for the use of several inputs—some fixed in the short run, others variable, but all subject to change in the long run. Consequently, it is important to consider how the

580

*The Pricing
and
Employment
of Resource
Inputs*

firm's profit-maximizing input combination is determined when several inputs are variable.

In Chapter 7 it was shown that to minimize its total costs for a given output the firm must adjust its input mix so as to obtain an equivalent amount of output per dollar spent on the last unit of each input used. In more formal terms this requires the firm to combine its various inputs $(X_a, X_b, X_c, \ldots, X_n)$ such that

$$\frac{MP_{X_a}}{P_{X_a}} = \frac{MP_{X_b}}{P_{X_b}} = \frac{MP_{X_c}}{P_{X_c}} = \cdots = \frac{MP_{X_n}}{P_{X_n}}.$$

If the least-cost input combination rule is violated, the firm can either obtain more output for the same total cost or else get the same output for less total cost. Suppose, for instance, a dollar's worth of input X_a contributes more to output than a dollar's worth of input X_b. Then the firm would find it advantageous to shift its expenditures on inputs; more dollars should be allocated to the purchase of X_a and fewer to the purchase of X_b—the firm should substitute input X_a for input X_b. As the substitution is made, the marginal product of X_a declines and the marginal product of X_a rises; the substitution process ceases when

$$\frac{MP_{X_a}}{P_{X_a}} = \frac{MP_{X_b}}{P_{X_b}}.$$

However, this proposition holds if and only if the inputs are purchased in perfectly competitive resource markets. If the firm's input supply curves are all upward sloping such that input prices vary with the quantity used, then a substitution of one input for another entails input price changes as well as marginal product changes. The firm must therefore consider an input's marginal resource cost (MRC) rather than its supply price when making its input decision. The rule for minimizing the cost of a given output under imperfectly competitive input conditions thus becomes

$$\frac{MP_{X_a}}{MRC_{X_a}} = \frac{MP_{X_b}}{MRC_{X_b}} = \frac{MP_{X_c}}{MRC_{X_c}} = \cdots = \frac{MP_{X_n}}{MRC_{X_n}}.$$

To see the rationale underlying this proposition consider the two-input case where inputs X_a and X_b are being used in such proportions that

$$\frac{MP_{X_a}}{MRC_{X_a}} > \frac{MP_{X_b}}{MRC_{X_b}}.$$

This inequality says that at the existing input combination the firm can realize a greater increase in output per additional dollar outlay on input X_a than on input X_b. Consequently, by substituting X_a for X_b the firm can realize more output for the same cost or else it can get the same output for less cost. As substitution is initiated, the marginal product of X_a declines and the

MRC_{X_a} increases, whereas the marginal product of X_b increases and the MRC_{X_b} declines. Sooner or later the substitution of X_a for X_b will result in equality in the ratios of MP and MRC. At the point of equality, no further change in the firm's input mix will prove beneficial from the standpoint of costs or output.

581

The Resource Input Decisions of a Firm Operating Under Conditions of Imperfect Competition in Its Product and Resource Markets

The preceding discussion shows, albeit in a nonrigorous fashion, that if a firm *buying its inputs* under conditions of imperfect competition is to achieve the lowest possible total cost for a given output, then it should adjust its input combination to the point where the ratio of marginal product to marginal resource cost is the same for all inputs used. An interesting question now arises: What adjustments in the rule, if any, are necessary to identify *the profit-maximizing resource input combination*? Is the rule for attaining the least-cost resource combination for a given output also adequate for ascertaining the profit-maximizing input mix? The answer to the latter question is *no*, though the reason may not be apparent at first glance.

The rule for determining the least-cost resource combination for a *given output* reveals only the correct *proportions* in which to employ variable inputs. It says nothing about which output rate maximizes profits, and therefore it leaves unanswered the question as to the correct *absolute amounts* of each variable input. To illustrate the significance of this point, consider the following numerical example. Suppose that a firm is using 10 units of input X_a and 15 units of input X_b to produce 3500 units of a particular product per week. Suppose further that at this input combination the specific values of marginal product and marginal resource cost for X_a and X_b are $MP_{X_a} = 40$ units of output, $MRC_{X_a} = \$10$, $MP_{X_b} = 60$ units of output, and $MRC_{X_b} = \$15$. The least-cost rule that

$$\frac{MP_{X_a}}{MRC_{X_a}} = \frac{MP_{X_b}}{MRC_{X_b}}$$

is satisfied, as we can see by substituting the MP and MRC values into the above expression:

$$\frac{MP_{X_a}}{MRC_{X_a}} = \frac{40 \text{ units of output}}{\$10} = 4 \text{ units of output/\$},$$

$$\frac{MRC_{X_b}}{MP_{X_b}} = \frac{60 \text{ units of output}}{\$15} = 4 \text{ units of output/\$}.$$

At the current input combination, the firm obtains 4 units of output per dollar spent on each input, which says that there is no advantage to be gained from shifting the input mix insofar as cost or output is concerned. However, how do we know whether or not it would be more *profitable* to use more (or less) of both inputs X_a and X_b? There is no way to tell from the information given. Thus, while it is clear that the firm is using its inputs to the best advantage to produce the current output of 3500 units, we do not know from the information given whether 3500 units is the profit-maximizing output rate

582

*The Pricing
and
Employment
of Resource
Inputs*

and therefore whether 10 units of X_a and 15 units of X_b constitute the profit-maximizing input combination.

This shortcoming in the least-cost rule is easily disposed of by bringing the marginal revenue products of the two inputs into consideration. Suppose the marginal product of the tenth unit of input X_a (40 units of output) adds $20 to the firm's total revenue and the marginal product of the fifteenth unit of X_b (60 units of output) adds $30. Then, clearly, the MRP of both inputs exceeds their respective marginal resource costs of $10 and $15, and the firm will find it profitable to increase its usage of both X_a and X_b. As demonstrated previously, the firm should increase an input's usage to the point where $MRP = MRC$. This rationale applies to any and all resources. Thus, *in general it can be said that a firm attains the profit-maximizing input rate when each and every variable input is employed to the point where its marginal revenue product equals its marginal resource cost.* In algebraic terms this becomes

$$\frac{MRP_{X_a}}{MRC_{X_a}} = \frac{MRP_{X_b}}{MRC_{X_b}} = \frac{MRP_{X_c}}{MRC_{X_c}} = \cdots = \frac{MRP_{X_n}}{MRC_{X_n}}.$$

Hence, converting the numerator of each term of the least-cost rule from a measure of marginal product to a measure of marginal revenue product gives the expression for the profit-maximizing input combination. The latter expression satisfies the need for determining both the absolute quantities and the proportions of the various inputs that will maximize total profits, since it incorporates measures of each input's productivity (marginal product), revenue contribution, and cost—all of which are essential for input optimization. However, since each input must be used at a rate such that its $MRP = MRC$, then it follows that the input ratios must not only be equal to each other but they must also be equal to 1. In other words, to use each variable input in the profit-maximizing *proportions* and in the profit-maximizing *absolute amounts*, the firm must adjust its input mix to the point where

$$\frac{MRP_{X_a}}{MRC_{X_a}} = \frac{MRP_{X_b}}{MRC_{X_b}} = \frac{MRP_{X_c}}{MRC_{X_c}} = \cdots = \frac{MRP_{X_n}}{MRC_{X_n}} = 1.$$

It should be recognized that (1) changes in an input's marginal productivity, (2) changes in the marginal revenue received from the sale of output, or (3) changes in an input's marginal resource cost will tend to change both the proportions and the absolute amounts of the inputs which a firm will find it most profitable to use.

The profit-maximizing rule derived above is applicable to firms operating under any and every type of product and resource market combination. This is necessarily so because, as we have seen, every firm—no matter what sort of market circumstances it faces—finds it advantageous to adjust its input rate of a variable resource to the point at which the input's marginal revenue product equals its marginal resource cost.

583

*The Impact
of Minimum
Wage Laws
upon Labor
Markets*

AN EVALUATION OF THE MARGINAL PRODUCTIVITY APPROACH TO INPUT PRICING AND EMPLOYMENT

The discussion in this chapter has so far been chiefly theoretical with little emphasis on actual practice. The principal reason is that something of an abnormal gap exists between theoretical models of the functioning of input markets on the one hand and what goes on in the real world on the other hand. This gap has left the economic theories of input pricing, input employment, and income distribution in a very unsettled state, with a host of honest differences prevailing among various authorities.

The problem lies partly with the almost countless number of institutional interferences, market imperfections, and artificially imposed restraints that have gradually become an integral feature of input markets. A representative sample of some of the most important of these interferences and imperfections includes (1) the enactment of minimum wage laws; (2) the exercise of whatever monopoly power unions have to obtain wage increases in excess of productivity gains; (3) the imposing of wage-price controls; (4) restrictive union work rules and featherbedding practices; (5) the long-standing traditions regarding the size of wage differentials between certain types of occupations; (6) job discrimination and wage discrimination based upon race or sex; (7) the educational, apprenticeship, and license-to-practice requirements for entering an occupation; (8) the regulation of rates of return to monopolistic enterprise; (9) the effects of monetary policy upon interest rates; (10) zoning regulations which preclude the use of land for certain types of activities; and (11) the relative immobility of resource inputs among firms, industries, and geographical areas—at least in the short run.

The effects which such factors have upon input prices and employment are well worth illustrating. Two examples will be given, both taken from the labor input sector because of their widespread applicability to real-world events.

THE IMPACT OF MINIMUM WAGE LAWS UPON LABOR MARKETS

Minimum wage legislation is generally aimed at accomplishing three things: (1) reducing the poverty associated with wage payments which do not afford workers a "decent" standard of living; (2) curtailing the practice whereby marginal firms pay substandard wages to a relatively immobile work force, thus keeping production costs low enough to enable them to compete with other enterprises (this practice is sometimes labeled as "unfair competition"); and (3) increasing the purchasing power of low-income families. By and large, the firms affected by minimum wage laws are small companies operating on

584

*The Pricing
and
Employment
of Resource
Inputs*

slim profit margins and stressing short-run profits, their work force is non-union, and they have a relatively low capital investment per worker.

The higher wages and higher labor costs which minimum wage laws impose upon the affected firms put them under severe pressure to correct their already precarious cost-price-profit position. When higher minimum wages are legislated, there is likely to arise a sort of "shock effect" which forces the affected firms to upgrade management practices, implement new production technologies, and increase labor performance and efficiency if they are to survive. Several specific responses present themselves, and each has, in fact, been observed to occur in practice. Management can improve plant layout and the quality of supervision; labor-saving equipment can be installed; inefficient employees can be weeded out; new employee selection standards can be raised; working conditions can be improved so as to reduce labor turnover and to increase the general efficiency and morale of the firm's labor force; the amount of overtime work offered employees can be cut back; jobs which no longer pay their way can be eliminated entirely; and selling prices can be raised to cover the increased labor costs.

But whatever response set each affected firm elects, one important outcome is almost certain to emerge: the opportunities for employment in the affected occupations will be less than otherwise. The minimum wage law will peg the supply price for such labor above the level which would be determined by the forces of market demand and supply for such labor—otherwise the minimum wage has no *raison d'être*. The outcome of a higher-than-equilibrium input supply price is a reduced optimum employment rate, as depicted in Fig. 17-10.[20] If the minimum wage is set at W_2 dollars, given the market demand and supply curves for labor of a particular type, then firms will adjust their employment rate downward from L_1 to L_2 units per period of time, and L_2L_3 units of labor will be involuntarily unemployed. The reduction in employment takes the form of dismissal of the least efficient employees, the closing down of marginal firms, cutbacks in the average number of hours worked per employee, or reductions in the number of new job opportunities in the affected occupations. Studies indicate that the groups hit hardest by the lower employment rates tend to be teenagers, blacks, and persons lacking in skills and training.

[20]Empirical studies of this phenomenon are numerous. See, for instance, *Studies of the Economic Effects of the $1 Minimum Wage: Effects in Selected Low Wage Industries and Localities*, Wage and Hour and Public Contracts Divisions, U.S. Department of Labor, January 1959; H. M. Douty, "Some Effects of the $1.00 Minimum Wage in the United States," *Economica*, Vol. 27, No. 106 (May 1960), pp. 137–147; N. Arnold Tolles, "American Minimum Wage Laws: Their Purposes and Results," *Proceedings of the Twelfth Annual Meeting of the Industrial Relations Research Association* (Madison, Wis.: Industrial Relations Research Association, 1960), pp. 116–133; Neil W. Chamberlain, *The Labor Sector* (New York: McGraw-Hill Book Company, 1965), pp. 529–533; Finis Welch and Marvin Kosters, "The Effects of Minimum Wages on the Distribution of Changes in Aggregate Employment," *American Economic Review*, Vol. 62, No. 3 (June 1972), pp. 323–332; and Finis Welch, "Minimum Wage Legislation in the United States," *Economic Inquiry*, Vol. 12, No. 3 (September 1974), pp. 285–318.

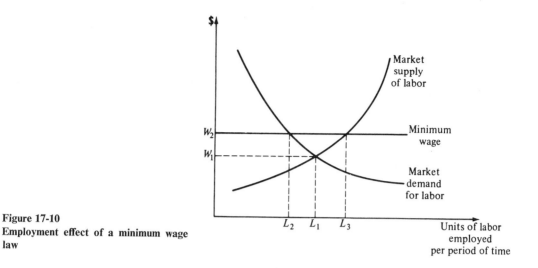

Figure 17-10
Employment effect of a minimum wage law

Hence, the economic effect of minimum wage laws upon resource pricing and employment is (1) to push wage rates for the lowest-paid occupations up above the equilibrium rates that would prevail in their absence and (2) to suppress employment rates in the affected occupations. On the other hand, many workers can benefit from a higher minimum wage, owing to the progress made in achieving the three aforementioned objectives of such legislation.[21] Inefficient firms are also forced to bring their operations up to par or else face the penalty of lower profits or even losses. For our purposes, the major point to be noted about minimum wage legislation is that it *artificially* causes the supply prices of low-skill, low-productivity types of labor to be higher than they would be if the forces of market demand and market supply were allowed to function freely. In this sense, governmental policy toward minimum wage rates, as well as labor's marginal productivity, are major factors in determining wages, employment, and income in the affected occupational categories.

It is also worth nothing that minimum wage laws can affect wage rates in occupations which carry higher than the minimum wage. A higher minimum wage allows unions to press for further wage increases through collective bargaining. The unions' philosophy is that while they will use their bargaining power to become wage leaders, upward adjustments in the federal minimum rates provide them with a new platform from which they can launch demands for still higher union wages on the grounds of maintaining historical wage differentials.

[21]When the demand for labor is *inelastic*, a rise in the minimum wage may lessen employment opportunities, but the total income of those who remain employed will definitely be greater than before. However, when the demand for labor is *elastic*, increases in the minimum wage will reduce both employment and the total income accruing to those who remain employed. Hence, only when labor demand is relatively inelastic do increases in the minimum wage have their most beneficial impact.

HOW THE MINIMUM WAGE DESTROYS JOBS
Fortune's **Interview with J. Willard Marriott, Jr.**

Over the last forty years, six different Administrations have tried to improve the lot of the workingman by raising the minimum wage. The most ambitious of these efforts was a bill signed by President Carter in 1977 that advances the minimum, through annual stepups, to a level of $3.35 by January, 1981—an increase totaling nearly 46 percent. Recently, however, the Administration has been paying some attention to the majority view among economists, which is that the minimum wage worsens inflation and destroys jobs. Carter may ask Congress to delay the 1980 increase and establish a lower minimum for teenagers.

With this issue back on the public agenda, FORTUNE'S Aimêe Morner paid a call recently on J. Willard Marriott Jr. As president and chief executive of a hotel and restaurant chain that pays the minimum wage to some 20,000 employees, he has learned a lot about the effects of this well-meaning social legislation on the real world of jobs and prices.

Q. With two successive jumps in the minimum wage, from $2.30 an hour in 1977 to $2.90 last January 1, what's happened at Marriott?

A. Several months before Congress passed the legislation, we felt it was imminent, so we got ready to combat the effect it would have on our costs. We first set up what I would call productivity specialists, who analyzed primarily how managers in each Marriott unit were utilizing and scheduling labor. Then we organized teams to find ways to reduce the number of man-hours, and the amount of work being done, in order to become more productive—to serve the same number of customers in fewer labor hours, and in some cases with fewer people.

Unlike many other restaurant chains, we did not open our restaurants later, or close them earlier. However, in some cases we closed parts of a restaurant, opening one dining room instead of two. For years we have been shifting to self-service salad bars in our Dinner Houses and other restaurants to cut down the number of waitress hours, and we accelerated that shift.

We achieved what I think are good, though not dramatic, results. Overall, we eliminated more than two million manhours, or about 5 percent of the total. It's very difficult for me to be too precise, because of the growth in our business, and the change in its mix. But we stopped hiring at many locations, and so cut our work force by 2 to 3 percent.

Q. So the increase in the minimum wage wiped out perhaps 1,500 jobs at Marriott?

587

*The Impact
of Minimum
Wage Laws
Upon Labor
Markets*

A. Yes. And though we got a slight increase in productivity, it was not enough to make up for our higher costs. Wages rose by 15 percent in 1978 for employees at the minimum level, and our food costs went up, too. We estimate that we got back less than half of these added costs from gains in productivity, so we had to increase prices in some restaurants by as much as 10 percent.

Unfortunately, as we raise prices, we often lose customers; it's axiomatic. Throughout the restaurant industry, customer counts have not been as strong during the last twelve months as before, and in many of our restaurants customer counts have been down slightly. And as we serve fewer customers, we lay off more people; it becomes cyclical. The National Restaurant Association recently surveyed 2,000 of its members and found that after the minimum wage was increased on January 1, 1978, 95 percent of them raised prices, 78 percent reduced man-hours, 63 percent laid off people, and more than half bought equipment that would help them reduce their labor force. But it's hard to automate restaurants and hotels—they haven't invented a machine yet that makes beds.

Q. Who gets hit the hardest when the minimum goes up?

A. What's happening as it keeps rising is that more people such as wives are coming into the work force, replacing teenagers. Restaurant owners screen people better, and by and large hire more mature, more productive people at the higher rates.

Q. Of course, that is to your advantage.

A. True, but as we pay those higher rates, we in turn have to raise our prices, and nobody wants to do that. Given the option, I would prefer to hire people at a more reasonable wage and train them.

Q. Economists now agree that increases in the minimum wage reduce employment, mostly among minorities and teenagers, and yet they have little empirical evidence to prove their theory. Do you have any definitive proof that the phenomenon occurs?

A. I can give you a concrete example. We used to have about twenty restaurants in the District of Columbia, which has traditionally had one of the highest minimum-wage levels in the U.S.—until recently even higher than the federal minimum. The cost of wages is our highest cost of doing business. And during the last three or four years, as the minimum wage increased in Washington, our wage situation became so acute that we had to close fourteen restaurants and terminate 1,300 people, about a third of whom were minority youths.

When we close restaurants located in a center city, the minorities who lose their jobs often are unable to find other work nearby, or in the suburbs. The few jobs that are available in the suburbs go to the

588

*The Pricing
and
Employment
of Resource
Inputs*

most productive workers, and in most cases these minority youths are just not as experienced as other workers. It's a terrible social problem.

What happens if 37 percent of the minority youths in this country reach age twenty and have never worked and are on the government dole? There is already a tremendous number of these people enrolled in government make-work programs. In fact, it's estimated that the government's bill for programs like CETA—the Comprehensive Employment and Training Act—will increase by $135 million this year because the minimum wage rose to $2.90. The government doesn't want to be in the business of hiring people and training people—it wants business to do that. But it's not economic for business to do that as long as the minimum wage keeps going up.

Q. The minimum wage for employees who work for tips stood at $1.33 last year, and rose to $1.60 on January 1. How will that increase of 20 percent affect operations at Marriott?

A. The tip credit, as it is called, is a serious concern of ours. This year it is being reduced for the first time, from 50 percent of the minimum wage, to 45 percent. That is, employees who get tips must be paid 55 percent of the regular minimum wage. Most tipped employees earn between three and five times their base wage as tips. So a 20 percent increase in their hourly base pay, or $2.16 a day, is peanuts compared with their earnings from tips, which can run more than $50 a day. But an increase of 27 cents an hour in the base wage is very costly to the employer. It's going to change the way the restaurant business is run, and eliminate many minimum-wage jobs.

There will be less specialization. In the past, a waitress only waited on tables. Today she makes fountain items, cuts pie, and clears tables. That reduces the need for fountain boys and busboys. As the minimum wage continues to rise, there will be more self-service, which will cut down the number of waitresses needed, too. We have to continue to improve efficiency, but I don't know how much more creative we can be without hurting the service.

Q. Does a higher minimum kick up wages all along the line at Marriott?

A. Yes. On January 1, 1978, the minimum wage rose by 15.2 percent, to $2.65. At Marriott, many workers at the next higher level got an automatic 10 percent increase, and at the next higher level, an 8 percent increase. A person in our Houston hotel earning $3, for example, got a raise to $3.25; a person making $2.60 got a raise to $2.85. The reason is very simple: if you've had a person working for you for a year or so, doing a good job, and making $2.75 an hour in 1978, and you hire a youngster off the street at $2.65 an hour, you've

589

*The Impact
of Minimum
Wage Laws
Upon Labor
Markets*

got an inequitable situation. That longer-term employee will come to you and say he's worth more than that kid is, and wants an increase in pay. We tell him we can't give him 15.2 percent, but we recognize the inequitable situation, and so we'll give him 10 percent. And, of course, our costs for Social Security and benefits rise because of the higher wages paid.

Q. Union leaders, notably George Meany, argue that as the minimum wage is increased the lowest-paid workers will have more money to spend, and so the entire economy benefits. Do you agree?

A. That's just a superficial argument. The labor unions want the minimum wage to increase because that gives them a better floor from which to bargain for higher wages for their members. Most of our workers are not unionized, but we know that the higher the minimum wage is, the greater the ripple effect—and the same thing occurs among unionized workers.

You must consider the fact that people who earn the minimum wage do not take home as much money after each increase, because they work fewer hours. Very few of our employees are putting in forty hours a week, though they may have done so two years ago; most of them work about thirty hours a week. We now schedule our workers so that we don't pay overtime, and neither do most companies in our industry.

Q. Then who benefits from an increase in the minimum wage?

A. I think everybody loses. Employees lose because their hours are shortened, so they take home fewer dollars. And at the same time, the minimum wage is inflationary, and inflation hits each worker in the pocketbook. People coming into the labor force lose because there is a strong tendency on the part of employers to hire more productive workers instead. And in a downturn in the economy, the less productive workers are the first to be put out of their jobs and onto welfare. In the end, the minimum wage practically wrecks the people it is supposed to help.

Q. So you would agree with Finis Welch, an economist at U.C.L.A., that the time for a mandated minimum wage has passed?

A. I think there needs to be a maintenance-level minimum wage to protect people from unscrupulous employers, of which there are probably some throughout the country. But a federal minimum wage at any level fails to take into account the characteristics of different regions. In many southern cities, we could probably hire quite a few people for $2.30 an hour, but we have to pay $2.90 an hour because somebody in Washington tells us to, and so we hire fewer workers.

I think a minimum-wage level should be set by each state, instead

590

*The Pricing
and
Employment
of Resource
Inputs*

of by the federal government, and it should be based on a fair wage for each geographical area. Some forty-one states have a minimum wage, but in most cases it applies only if it is higher than the federal level. Only Alaska and Connecticut now have a higher minimum than the federal minimum. So, let each state determine its own minimum wage—or roll back the federal minimum to a level, say $2.30, that would not prevent people from coming into the work force.

Q. Because of concerns about inflation, there have been various proposals to reopen this question. President Carter is now considering whether to ask Congress to defer the jump scheduled for next January. Do you support that proposal?

A. Yes. There have been several estimates made recently of the impact of the minimum wage on inflation. Barry Bosworth, director of the Council on Wage and Price Stability, has said that the increases in the minimum wage and in the Social Security tax were among the biggest contributors to inflation in 1978. I agree absolutely. The Federal Reserve Board has estimated that if there had been a one-year postponement in the increase in the minimum wage, inflation would rise by 0.4 percent less in 1979. The U.S. Chamber of Commerce estimates that the inflation in consumer prices would be reduced by about 0.8 percent under the same circumstances, and that there would be about 524,000 additional jobs available. We would contribute to that. We would be able to keep our wages at a more reasonable level, and hold our prices down. In many cases we could build up our business, hire more people, and the people we already employ could work for longer hours and earn more. That would make our company and the economy much stronger, and provide better opportunities for employees.

Q. Carter is also considering a two-tier minimum wage, with a lower level for teenagers. Is that a good idea?

A. Yes, a wage differential would help give young people a chance to get a job.

But even better than a two-tier minimum wage would be some sort of tax rebate—like the investment tax credit—for every teenager hired.

Q. Would Congress go along with such a proposal?

A. I think that Congress is listening to the drumbeat of the unions.

Q. How do you assess the likelihood of future increases in the minimum wage being delayed by congressional action?

A. I'm skeptical. I don't think the Administration will support such a proposal. In 1977, I went to the White House and begged a member of the President's staff not to increase the minimum wage.

He listened, was friendly, but finally said that President Carter was committed to raising the minimum wage. Some members of the Administration now say they wish he hadn't pushed for the increase. Now he's in a bind. He has to be reelected, and he's worried about his labor constituency. He has had enough problems with labor, and I guess he doesn't want any more.

Source: Reprinted from the January 29, 1979 issue of *Fortune* magazine by special permission; © Time, Inc.

SOME ECONOMIC EFFECTS OF UNIONS

In modern industrial economies trade unions are an integral and accepted part of the functioning of labor markets, especially in the manufacturing sector. In the United States, nearly 85% of the workers in plants employing 100 workers or more are unionized; union membership totals approximately 18 million persons; and the pattern-setting wage settlements reached in certain key industries are quickly transmitted to other sectors of the economy. Thus, unions have a major impact upon national labor markets; their presence does make a difference. The added power workers gain by union organization creates a very strong presumption that the resulting wage and employment rates will be different from what they would have been had workers remained unorganized. Consequently, any analysis of wage rates and employment which ignores the impact of collective bargaining is suspect in its ability to explain and to predict the behavior of real-world labor markets.

Incorporating union behavior into the analysis of labor markets first requires some notion of the economic goals of unions. Casual observation suggests that unions pursue some satisfactory, and perhaps quite complex, balance of increased wages and incomes, increased leisure, and an adequate number of job opportunities for current and potential union members. However, depending on their own unique circumstances, different unions may place differing emphases and priorities on these goals; collective bargaining is by no means a uniform process whereby each union consistently pursues the same objectives with the same intensity.

The Wage-Employment Preference Path

A union's preferred trade-off between wages and employment can be viewed graphically. Suppose collective negotiations between a firm and a union result in the establishment of an average wage of W_1 dollars and an equilibrium employment rate of L_1 units of labor per period of time, as shown in Fig. 17-11(a). Now consider the combination of wage and employment rates which the union would prefer and which it will attempt to attain in

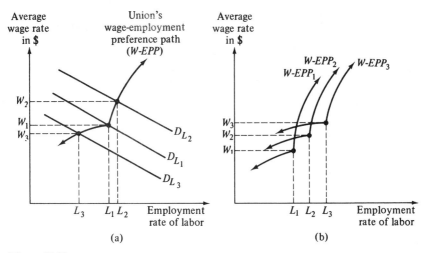

Figure 17-11
Wage-employment preference path of a typical union

its negotiations with the firm. If the firm's product demand should shift in such a manner that its demand for labor input shifts from D_{L_1} to D_{L_2}, the union's preference is generally for substantial wage increases, say from W_1 to W_2 (which may, incidentally, be in the form of overtime wages), and modest increases in the number of persons employed, say from L_1 to L_2. This reflects the usual union attitude that its first responsibility is to the existing membership and that it is obliged to win them higher wages whenever the opportunity presents. Hence, the union's preference path is a steeply rising curve above the initial wage-employment combination.[22] However, the stronger the rise in the firm's demand for labor, the more the union is ordinarily willing to temper its wage demands in return for increases in employment (and gains in union membership). For this reason the portion of the union's preferred wage-employment path above the prevailing wage-employment combination is shown as rising at a decreasing rate.

If economic conditions should shift the firm's demand for labor input downward, say from D_{L_1} to D_{L_3}, the union usually exhibits a strong preference for larger cutbacks in employment (say from L_1 to L_3) relative to wages (which might be reduced from W_1 to W_3). The reasoning behind such a preference is that wage reductions weaken the ability of the union to win wage gains in future bargaining sessions, whereas employment cutbacks are self-correcting as soon as business conditions pick up again.[23] Hence, the lower section of the wage-employment preference path falls slowly and at a rate

[22]An exception to this general case arises in instances where large numbers of union members are unemployed at the prevailing wage-employment combination. Here the union will probably pursue a policy of getting the unemployed members back to work before seeking major wage advances.

[23]An excellent discussion of the tactical advantages which the union receives from following such a policy is found in Allan M. Cartter and F. Ray Marshall, *Labor Economics: Wages, Employment, and Trade Unionism*, rev. ed. (Homewood, Ill.: Richard D. Irwin, Inc., 1972), pp. 245–246.

commensurate with employment reductions that are more than proportional to the wage reductions.[24] The union's wage-employment preferences therefore tend to produce a curvilinear pattern, kinked at the current wage-employment position. As new wage negotiations are consummated, the curve shifts to a new position, and a kink appears at the newly instituted wage-employment combination, as depicted in Fig. 17-11(b).

In viewing the union's wage-employment preferences, care must be taken not to view employment as referring solely to the number of workers employed. A firm's employment *rate* (L) is composed of n number of workers working h number of hours per period of time. Thus, a reduction in the union's preferred employment rate may reflect preferences for cutbacks in the number of workers *or* in the number of hours worked by each worker *or* both. Similarly, increases in the union's preferred employment rate may mean more workers *or* more hours worked by each worker *or* both. By observing the composition of the employment rate the union bargains for over a period of time, it is possible to infer what the union's preference is toward greater membership versus more leisure time for the rank and file. Therefore, the union's wage-employment preference curve is indicative not only of the union's wage (and income) goal and its employment (and membership) goal but also of its leisure-time goal.[25]

To the extent that unions are successful in imposing their wage-employment preferences upon firms we have at least a partial explanation of why wages rise at above-average rates in periods of strong business expansion, yet employment gains are modest, and why wages fail to fall and labor employment cutbacks are comparatively severe in times when business conditions are slack. Such wage-employment behavior is particularly prevalent in the corporate sector where most firms have unionized labor forces.

The Effects of Unions on the Firm's Labor Input Decision

From a supply standpoint the effect of union-negotiated wage rates is to make the firm's supply curve for union labor horizontal (or perfectly elastic) at the agreed-to wage scale, at least until the supply of labor runs out at

[24]Again, the preferred wage-employment path may assume a different shape if significant employment cutbacks have been recently imposed and many union members are already laid off. In such instances the union may be more amenable to cutting wages and maintaining employment, in which case the lower section of the curve may reflect a preference for relatively larger wage cuts and relatively smaller employment cuts.

[25]Unions historically have shown a keen interest in shortening the standard workday and workweek. During periods of depressed business conditions, shorter working hours are a means of sharing the available work among greater numbers of people. During periods of prosperity, the shorter workweek is a means of raising wage rates by instituting time-and-a-half overtime rates after fewer hours worked. On occasions, unions may find it easier to persuade firms to pay workers the same total income but allow them to work fewer hours to earn it (which is equivalent to raising the average wage rate) than to persuade them to pay workers a higher wage rate for working the same number of hours as before. The former does not raise the firm's total labor costs provided the same amount of work can be accomplished in the fewer working hours, whereas the latter is sure to increase the firm's total wage bill.

594

*The Pricing
and
Employment
of Resource
Inputs*

these wage rates. This is illustrated in Fig. 17-12, where the firm's supply curve for labor in a nonunion (though still imperfectly competitive) labor market is S_L, the corresponding marginal resource cost curve for labor is MRC_L, and the firm's demand for labor is D_L, the last reflecting the firm's marginal revenue product of labor in an imperfectly competitive product market. The intersection of MRC_L and MRP_L determines the equilibrium wage and employment rates for the firm—W_1 and L_1, respectively.

But if a union organizes the firm's employees and uses its bargaining power to push the effective average wage rate to W_2, the firm's supply curve for labor becomes the kinked line W_2CAS_L, which is horizontal over the range W_2CA. Observe the effect this has upon the unionized firm's optimum employment rate. Since the unionized firm's labor supply curve is the line W_2CAS_L, the firm's marginal resource cost curve for labor becomes $W_2CABMRC_L$. A new intersection of MRC_L and MRP_L occurs at point C, giving an equilibrium employment rate of L_2 units. Thus, not only can the union benefit its members by increasing wages, but it can also increase employment rates because of the effect which contract wage rates have upon the shape of the firm's labor supply curve. Actually, the union can push the average wage rate all the way up to W_3 before the firm find it advantageous to reduce its labor employment rate below the preunionization rate of L_1 units. Thus, we have the rather surprising conclusion that a union *may* initially have the effect of increasing both a firm's average wage rate and its employment rate, provided it does not insist upon pushing the wage rate up too far. This indeed constitutes a powerful argument in favor of unions—at least from the standpoint of union members.

Referring again to Fig. 17-12, suppose that the union bargains for and gets wage increases that push the average wage above W_3, thereby making it advantageous for the firm to cut its employment rate below L_1. Further

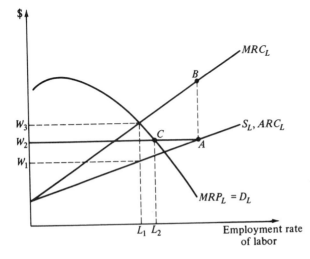

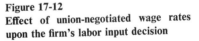

Figure 17-12
**Effect of union-negotiated wage rates
upon the firm's labor input decision**

DO UNEMPLOYMENT COMPENSATION BENEFITS REDUCE THE SUPPLY OF LABOR?

A 1979 report by the General Accounting Office indicated that a substantial number of able-bodied people may prefer to remain unemployed and collect unemployment compensation benefits rather than seek new employment or go back to work. According to the GAO study, about half of the people collecting unemployment compensation realized an after-tax income equal to at least 60% of what they had earned while working at their previous job; one-fourth of UC recipients realized at least 75% of their regular working wages; and roughly 7% received total unemployment payments *greater* than their working wages. Furthermore, people who elect to stay at home and draw unemployment avoid work-related expenses—estimated by the GAO to average $17 per week (not counting child care); this makes unemployment compensation payments even more of an effective replacement for employment income.

More important, though, the GAO report suggested that the level of UC payments was so generous as to provide an incentive *not* to work; according to GAO findings:

1. The higher the proportion of after-tax income being replaced by UC benefits, the longer it took recipients to get back to work. Recipients whose UC benefits represented 30% or less of normal income remained jobless for an average of 16.5 weeks. But recipients whose benefits were more than 90% of job income remained jobless for over 22 weeks, on average; moreover, such recipients were much more likely to remain out of work until their UC benefits expired (normally, after 26 weeks).
2. About 65% of the UC recipients receiving the highest UC benefits (relative to normal income) were in occupations that appeared to coincide with job openings listed by their state employment service and advertised in the help-wanted ads of area newspapers.
3. Individuals who lost little after-tax income by being unemployed were more likely to have quit their last jobs than were those individuals receiving smaller UC benefits.

Based on its findings, the GAO report recommended (1) that Congress consider making UC benefits subject to income taxation and (2) that UC benefits be reduced by the amount of any retirement income that recipients are also receiving.

Source: Adapted from information reported in *Fortune*, September 24, 1979, pp. 33–34.

596

*The Pricing
and
Employment
of Resource
Inputs*

suppose that the union views this cutback as undesirable. The union can then use its bargaining power to preclude the firm from so reducing labor employment. A major aspect of collective negotiations between unions and managements concerns working conditions and, in particular, such matters as the content of jobs, how certain operations are to be performed, the size of work crews, the quantity of work which can be expected, safety rules, the length of paid vacations, the number of paid holidays, seniority provisions, guaranteed annual wages, and supplemental unemployment benefits. In other words, there is a *work and effort bargain* in the contract, just as there is a wage bargain. A principal effect of the provisions relating to the work and effort bargain is to give unions a measure of influence over the firm's employment rate, either directly or indirectly—at least in the short run.

Experience clearly indicates that unions use these provisions to "make work" and to keep the number of persons employed in specific jobs, firms, and industries higher than managements might otherwise maintain. The notorious instances of featherbedding in the railroad industry and the output quotas in the construction industry are classic cases in point. Consequently, in a unionized firm the mere fact that labor's MRC exceeds its MRP is no guarantee that the firm will adjust its input of labor downward. The discretionary action of the firm's managers in regard to the labor input decision is heavily constrained by the provisions of its collective bargaining contract. Because of this, managers of unionized firms find strict adherence to the $MRC = MRP$ rule a practical impossibility; work schedules, job assignments, and work loads can be altered only within limits. To some extent, therefore, the marginal productivity approach to input pricing and input employment is impeded, if not replaced, by the institutional mechanism of collective bargaining insofar as unionized firms are concerned. However, since most managements retain almost complete authority over the capital-labor input mix in building new production facilities, the power of unions to influence employment rates in the long run is somewhat less; managers are undoubtedly guided in their selection of the capital-labor input mix for new facilities by their perceptions of the expected relative contributions and costs of capital and labor.

The Effects of Unions on Economywide Wage Rates and Employment Rates

Few economists would deny that unions in certain firms and industries have won highly favorable wage increases for their members. But whether unions have pushed wages up faster than they would have risen anyway is a much trickier (and hotly contested) issue.[26] And, significantly, the issue defies

[26]The literature on this issue is large and contains a number of studies with conflicting findings. The interested reader should consult, *inter alia*, Arthur Ross and William Goldner, "Forces Affecting the Interindustry Wage Structure," *Quarterly Journal of Economics*, Vol. 64, No. 2 (May 1950), pp. 254–281; Harry Douty, "Union and Nonunion Wages," in *Employment and Wages in the United States*, W. S. Woytinsky and Associates,

precise resolution, since it involves a comparison of what has actually happened with what might have happened under another set of circumstances. There simply is no way of knowing for sure what the relative wages of various industries would be if all industries were nonunion; any estimates to this effect are little better than educated conjectures.[27] Even so, it seems fair to say that unions are in a good position to win "above-average" wage gains on a consistent basis when (1) the percentage of unionized firms in the industry is high and it is difficult for nonunion firms to enter; (2) bargaining is on an industrywide basis so that all firms in the industry are equally affected; (3) industry and firm profits are high enough that the firms can "afford" substantial wage increases without endangering their competitive position; (4) the industry is a strategic one such that work stoppages have serious economy-wide implications; and (5) the union controls entry to the trade via apprenticeship and other regulations.

On the whole, it is significant to note that in most occupational categories, wage rates in unionized firms exceed those in nonunion enterprises —even after allowing for differences in regional location, size of firm, size of community, and type of pay system (incentive wages or hourly wages).[28] Moreover, it is in the corporate sector where unions are strongest and where newly negotiated collective bargaining pacts set the pattern of wage changes throughout the economy. In manufacturing, large-scale firms have proven easier to organize than small companies mainly because some of the above conditions appear more frequently in the corporate sector than in small-firm-dominated industries. Particularly does the greater ability of corporate oligopolists to pass along higher wage costs in the form of higher prices offer unions an attractive target.

The wage-raising effects of collective bargaining, to whatever extent they exist, therefore fall first and most heavily upon corporate oligopolists. As a consequence, the supply price of blue-collar labor services to large corporations tends to be higher than for small entrepreneurial firms—a trait which partially accounts for the propensity of large-scale firms to substitute capital for production labor.

---

eds. (New York: Twentieth Century Fund, 1953), pp. 493–501; Frank C. Pierson, "The Economic Influence of Big Unions," in *Labor Relations in an Expanding Economy*, Annals of the American Academy of Political and Social Science (January 1961), pp. 96–107; Martin Segal, "Unionism and Wage Movements," *Southern Economic Journal*, Vol. 28, No. 2 (October 1961), pp. 174–181; Albert Rees, *The Economics of Trade Unions* (Chicago: University of Chicago Press, 1962), Chapter 4; Gregg Lewis, *Unionism and Relative Wages in the United States* (Chicago: University of Chicago Press, 1963); and Vernon T. Clover, "Compensation in Union and Nonunion Plants 1960–1965," *Industrial and Labor Relations Review*, Vol. 21, No. 2 (January 1968), pp. 226–233.

[27]Comparisons of wage movements between union and nonunion firms and industries are not really very satisfactory because of the differences which exist in geographical location, sizes and types of firms, competitive pressures, technological processes, the proportion of labor costs to total costs, productivity changes, and so on. These factors, as well as the presence or absence of a union, affect wage movements and parceling out their separate effects presents almost insurmountable statistical difficulties.

[28]Douty, "Union and Nonunion Wages," *op. cit.*, pp. 496–497.

598

*The Pricing
and
Employment
of Resource
Inputs*

SUMMARY AND CONCLUSIONS

The marginal productivity approach to input pricing and input employment is a systematic attempt to analyze the principles governing a firm's input decision and to explain the functioning of the markets for resource inputs. Three basic models of input pricing and employment stand out: (1) the model of perfect competition in both product and resource markets, (2) the model of imperfect competition in the product market and perfect competition in the resource market, and (3) the model of imperfect competition in both product and resource markets. In all three models, one theme underlies the firm's input decision: To maximize profits the firm should adjust the usage of each input to the point where the added revenue the firm receives from using the last unit of the input equals the added costs associated with employing the input. A firm's usage of an input depends on what the input is worth to the firm relative to the costs of using it. This principle holds irrespective of the type of market circumstance in which the firm's product is sold or in which the input is purchased. It is from the $MRP = MRC$ rule that input prices and input employment rates are ultimately determined and the incomes accruing to resource owners are ultimately derived.

As a first approximation to the functioning of input markets, the demand and supply analyses of the three marginal productivity models is relatively sound. However, there exist numerous imperfections in and barriers to the free interplay of market forces. Collective bargaining, minimum wage laws, wage-price controls, and resource immobility, to mention only the more important, impede the attainment of free market equilibrium and cause outcomes which may deviate far and long from the equilibrium position suggested by marginal productivity analysis.

SUGGESTED READINGS

BAUMOL, W. J., *Economic Theory and Operations Analysis*, 3rd ed. (Englewood Cliffs, N.J.: Prentice-Hall, Inc., 1972), Chapters 16, 17.

BISHOP, R. L., "A Firm's Short-Run and Long-Run Demands for a Factor," *Western Economic Journal*, Vol. 5, No. 1 (March 1967), pp. 122–140.

CARTTER, A. M., AND F. R. MARSHALL, *Labor Economics: Wages, Employment and Trade Unionism*, rev. ed. (Homewood, Ill.: Richard D. Irwin, Inc., 1972), Chapters 8–11, 13.

CHAMBERLAIN, N. W., *The Labor Sector* (New York: McGraw-Hill Book Company, 1965), Chapters 17–19.

DYE, H. S., "A Bargaining Theory of Residual Income Distribution," *Industrial and Labor Relations Review*, Vol. 21, No. 1 (October 1967), pp. 40–54.

FERGUSON, C. E., *The Neoclassical Theory of Production and Distribution* (New York: Cambridge University Press, 1969), Chapters 6, 7, 9, 11, 12.

PERLMAN, R., *Labor Theory* (New York: John Wiley & Sons, Inc., 1969), Chapters 1, 2, 5, 10.

PIERSON, F. C., "An Evaluation of Wage Theory," *New Concepts in Wage Determination*, G. W. Taylor and C. Pierson, eds. (New York: McGraw-Hill Book Company, 1957), pp. 3–31.

REDER, M., "The Theory of Union Wage Policy," *Review of Economics and Statistics*, Vol. 34, No. 1 (February 1952), pp. 34–55.

REES, A., "The Effects of Unions on Resource Allocation," *Journal of Law and Economics*, Vol. 6 (October 1963), pp. 69–78.

REES, A., *The Economics of Work and Pay* (New York: Harper & Row, Publishers, 1973).

RUSSELL, R. R., "A Graphical Proof of the Impossibility of a Positively Inclined Demand Curve for a Factor of Production," *American Economic Review*, Vol. 54, No. 5 (September 1964), pp. 726–732, and the critique of this proof by D. M. Winch, "The Demand Curve for a Factor of Production: Comment," *American Economic Review*, Vol. 55, No. 4 (September 1965), pp. 856–861.

WELCH, F., "Minimum Wage Legislation in the United States," *Economic Inquiry*, Vol. 12, No. 3 (September 1974), pp. 285–318.

PROBLEMS AND QUESTIONS FOR DISCUSSION

1. (a) Explain the difference between marginal revenue and marginal revenue product.
   (b) Explain the difference between marginal cost and marginal resource cost.
   (c) What is the relationship between an input's $SVMP$ and its MRP when the output is sold under conditions of perfect competition? Under conditions of imperfect competition?

2. Complete the following table:

Units of Variable Input X	Quantity of Output	MP_X	Product Price	TR	MRP_X	Supply Price of X	MRC_X
0	0	——	$5	——	——	$50	——
1	20	——	5	——	——	50	——
2	44	——	5	——	——	50	——
3	64	——	5	——	——	50	——
4	80	——	5	——	——	50	——
5	92	——	5	——	——	50	——
6	100	——	5	——	——	50	——
7	104	——	5	——	——	50	

(a) Do the figures in the table suggest a perfectly or imperfectly competitive product market? Why? Do the figures indicate a perfectly or imperfectly competitive input market? Why?
   (b) What is the profit-maximizing input of X?

3. Suppose a firm employs only one variable input (X) and that the equation expressing the firm's marginal revenue product function for X is $MRP_X = 60 + 4X - X^2$. Suppose the firm's supply price for input X is fixed at $28 per unit. What is the firm's profit-maximizing input rate of X?

600

*The Pricing
and
Employment
of Resource
Inputs*

4. Complete the following table showing production, cost, and revenue data for a firm having only one variable input:

Units of Variable Input X	Quantity of Output	MP_X	Product Price	TR	"Average" MR	MRP_X	Supply Price of X	TVC	MRC_X
0	0	—	$25	—	—	—	$400	—	—
1	50	—	24	—	—	—	420	—	—
2	110	—	23	—	—	—	440	—	—
3	160	—	22	—	—	—	460	—	—
4	200	—	21	—	—	—	480	—	—
5	230	—	20	—	—	—	500	—	—
6	250	—	19	—	—	—	520	—	—
7	260	—	18	—	—	—	540	—	—

(a) What type of product and resource markets are indicated by the figures in the table?

(b) What is the profit-maximizing input rate of X?

5. The Alpha-Omega Corporation uses only one variable input in its production process—input X. Studies of the firm's revenue data indicate the following relationship between TR and the input rate of X: $TR = 144 + 70X - X^2$. Studies also indicate that the input supply curve for X which confronts Alpha-Omega may be expressed by the equation $P_X = 13 + 0.5X$. Determine the profit-maximizing input rate for X.

6. Given the following data for labor input, product prices, and wage rates:

Number of Workers of a Given Skill and Training	"Average" MP_L	Product Price	Daily Wage $(P_L = ARC_L)$
0	—	$2	—
10	18	2	$12
20	17	2	14
30	16	2	16
40	15	2	18
50	14	2	20
60	13	2	22
70	12	2	24
80	11	2	26

(a) Determine the profit-maximizing employment rate of labor and the equilibrium daily wage for a firm faced with the above schedules.

(b) Suppose a minimum daily wage of $24 is imposed upon the firm. Determine the profit-maximizing employment rate of labor.

(c) How do you reconcile the differences, if any, in your answers to parts (a) and (b)? Explain fully.

7. Consider the following two statements:

"An increase in the demand for an input raises its price."
"An increase in an input's price reduces demand for the input."

How can this pair of statements be reconciled? Does it make any difference in your answer whether perfect or imperfect competition characterizes the input market? The product market?

8. It has sometimes been advocated that firms should reward inputs according to their respective marginal products. That is, if the last unit of an input has a marginal product of 10 units and if these 10 units have a market value of $50, then the input is entitled to a monetary reward of $50. Any payment less than $50 entails "exploitation" of the input. What validity, if any, do you see in this position?

9. Suppose input X is the only variable input which a firm uses to produce product A. The firm sells product A under conditions of imperfect competition and buys input X under conditions of imperfect competition. What effect would you expect each of the following to have upon the firm's usage of input X? Be sure to distinguish between a movement along the firm's demand curve for X and a shift in the location of the demand curve. If any uncertainty exists as to the impact upon the usage of X, then specify the causes of the uncertainty.
   (a) An increase in the demand for product A.
   (b) The appearance of a new and very good substitute for product A.
   (c) A technological improvement in the capital equipment which input X works with in producing product A.
   (d) An increase in the supply of input X.

10. It is well known that average wage rates in the United States are higher than in most foreign countries. Business firms often lament that this puts them at a severe cost disadvantage in competing with foreign firms. Unions reply that U.S. workers are generally healthier and better trained than workers in foreign nations and, further, that U.S. workers generally have more and better capital equipment with which to work. These factors, the unions claim, offset the wage rate differential.
   (a) Explain the rationale of the union argument in terms of marginal productivity analysis.
   (b) In recent years, Japan and several Western European nations have greatly closed the gap in worker productivity by raising the living standards of their population and by adopting the very latest production technologies. What implications does this have for the ability of U.S. firms to continue to pay higher wages and still compete in world markets?

EIGHTEEN ▼EQUILIBRIUM: THE CONSUMER, THE FIRM, THE ECONOMY

Preceding chapters have emphasized the decisions of consumers, firms, and resource owners and the functioning of both product and resource markets. The decisions of individual economic units and the workings of individual markets have been viewed separately and in isolation from one another—mainly because one cannot undertake a detailed analysis of everything at once and not because it actually works this way in the real world. In fact, of course, the decisions and behavior of consumers interact with and affect the decisions and behavior of firms; the decisions and behavior of firms interact with and affect the functioning of product and resource markets; and the operations of product and resource markets interact with and affect economic activity as a whole. Indeed, whatever goes on in one part of the economy is related either directly or indirectly to what goes on in another part, though sometimes the relationship is negligible or imperceptible. The point is that individual economic units and markets, taken together, make up an economy. Microeconomics is ultimately very concerned about how these units and markets fit together and how well the resulting *economic system* functions.

This chapter explores the branch of microeconomics that deals with the interactions and interrelationships among the various decision-making units

and the various markets. Attention is first directed toward the conditions
requisite for establishing static general equilibrium throughout the economy.
Next, the analysis shifts to the problem of maintaining general equilibrium
over time, with emphasis on dynamic growth equilibrium at the levels of the
firm and the economy.

603
*Static
Equilibrium
on an
Economywide
Basis*

STATIC EQUILIBRIUM ON AN ECONOMYWIDE BASIS

In broad terms, general equilibrium for an entire economy exists when all
economic units simultaneously achieve equilibrium positions, when the quantity demanded equals the quantity supplied in each and every product and
resource market, and when the major economic sectors are in balance. Suppose we examine these conditions in a bit more detail.

The Conditions of General Equilibrium

Given the limitations of his income and the prices he must pay for the
available goods and services, a consumer is in equilibrium when his expendi-
ture-saving mix yields maximum satisfaction. This requires not only that he
make full utilization of his income but that he arrange his purchases so the
marginal utility per dollar spent on the last unit of each item is equal for all
goods and services actually purchased. For general equilibrium to prevail, all
consumers must be at their perceived utility-maximizing equilibrium positions. However, this is not to say that consumers are guaranteed satisfaction
or happiness in this mechanism. All that is implied is that they realize the
most advantageous combination of satisfactions, given the prevailing set of
circumstances.

A business firm is in equilibrium when its product prices, output rates,
and input rates have been adjusted to the point where the firm attains its set
of goals (profit, sales, market share, and so on) to the fullest extent that
demand and cost conditions will permit. As a point of clarification, it is long-
run, not short-run, equilibrium that is the pertinent equilibrium state for the
firm, because short-run equilibrium positions are temporary and market
forces are working to move the firm to the long-run equilibrium position.
Firms cannot really be said to be in a state of rest with no incentive or opportunity to make adjustments unless the markets in which they operate are in
long-run equilibrium.

A resource owner is in equilibrium when the resource inputs he owns
or controls are employed to their maximum advantage, balancing the consideration of monetary reward with his nonmonetary preferences. More specifically, workers are supplying labor at equilibrium rates when they have
attained the most advantageous combination of work, leisure, and income,
subject to the constraints imposed by their skills and abilities and the realiz-

able opportunities for employment. The owners of property resources, being less affected by nonmonetary elements in deploying such resources, may be viewed as supplying property resources at equilibrium rates when the latter are allocated to the uses yielding the highest long-run monetary income and taking into consideration the attitudes of resource owners towards risk.

For the equilibrium conditions of consumers, business firms, and resource owners to be met simultaneously, a number of other less apparent conditions must be present. First, general equilibrium requires the price and output rate for each separate product to be pegged at levels consistent with demand and supply. Neither surplus nor shortage conditions for a good or service can exist, since the presence of either will elicit price and/or output rate adjustments by the firms concerned.

Second, the equilibrium which emerges in each product market must be based not only upon the particular demand and supply conditions for that product in isolation but also upon demand and supply conditions for complementary and substitute products. That is, the various prices and output rates for all items must be mutually consistent. The flows of goods and services through the economy must not result in the accumulation of surpluses in one sector and the appearance of shortages in another. This requirement is in recognition of the interdependencies among commodities and sectors. (We shall elaborate upon the specifics of this requirement later in the chapter.)

Third, the same equilibrium characteristics of product markets must be present in resource input markets. Input prices and employment rates must be at positions which allow for a mutually consistent equilibrium *among* input markets as well as for equilibrium in a particular input market. The average price of each input must call forth an overall supply of that input which, when allocated among the alternative uses of the input, results both in equilibrium employment rates in each of the alternative firms and industries and in an equilibrum demand-supply combination for the input on an economywide basis. Given the prevailing patterns of input prices, firms must have no motive for changing their input mix.

Although the market mechanisms of changing prices, output rates, and input rates are most prominent in the process of reaching equilibrium, other factors are present. Underneath the surface are the guiding forces of consumer tastes and preferences, production and managerial technologies, limitations of resource supplies, business goals, and national priorities. In a static analysis, these forces are generally assumed to be constant. Provided that they remain fixed long enough, it is conceivable that the entire pattern of economic activity could adjust to them. Then each product and resource market would reach its own unique equilibrium, the equilibrium results in all markets would be consistent, and no forces would be acting to cause further adjustments. The economic system would settle into a fixed pattern whereby the same amount of the same good/service would be produced via the same technology-input mix by the same firms and would be bought by the same consumers with the same-sized incomes. The overall rate of economic activity would neither rise nor fall. This state of affairs is what is meant by *static general equilibrium*.[1]

The Interrelationships of Industries and Markets

The complexities of static general equilibrium are worth further exploration, especially as concerns the interrelatedness of product and resource markets. Suppose initially that a state of static general equilibrium exists and there then occurs an increase in the demand of consumers for mobile homes. Let us trace through some of the chief effects of this "disturbance" upon the system of markets.

The first response to the demand increase will be a shift in the optimum price of mobile homes. Most likely, the retail prices of mobile homes will stiffen (the discounts from list prices will be smaller) as retailers discover the greater willingness of consumers to pay a higher net price. The brisk sales stemming from the rise in demand will prompt the sellers of mobile homes to increase the orders they place with manufacturers. The mobile home manufacturers can be counted upon to react to the influx of new orders by stepping up production rates and perhaps by raising wholesale prices,

[1]Economic theorists have spent a great deal of time and energy formulating mathematical models and deriving sets of equations in an effort to determine whether general equilibrium is possible. Most of the modern work has concerned general equilibrium in a *perfectly competitive environment*, primarily because of the mathematical simplicity and neatness of the perfectly competitive model. The results of these efforts do indicate that in a perfectly competitive economy it is possible to achieve general equilibrium without imposing unacceptable constraints upon the values of the relevant economic variables. However, no set of reasonably realistic, sufficient conditions for a stable equilibrium has yet been presented. For a simplified mathematical treatment of the theory of general equilibrium in a perfectly competitive economy, the reader is referred to K. J. Cohen and R. M. Cyert, *Theory of the Firm: Resource Allocation in a Market Economy* 2nd ed. (Englewood Cliffs, N.J.: Prentice-Hall, Inc., 1975), Chapter 11. For more advanced discussions, see J. Quirk and R. Saposnik, *Introduction to General Equilibrium Theory and Welfare Economics* (New York: McGraw-Hill Book Company, 1968); R. E. Kuenne, *The Theory of General Economic Equilibrium* (Princeton, N.J.: Princeton University Press, 1963); Kenneth J. Arrow and Gerard Debreu, "Existence of an Equilibrium for a Competitive Economy," *Econometrica*, Vol. 22, No. 3 (July 1954), pp. 265–289; and Lionel McKenzie, "On the Existence of General Equilibrium for a Competitive Market," *Econometrica*, Vol. 27, No. 1 (January 1959), pp. 54–71.

But while it is valuable to be able to demonstrate that general equilibrium can exist in a perfectly competitive economy, the fact remains that real-world economies are far removed from being perfectly competitive and are becoming even further removed as the trend toward a corporate economy proceeds to run its course. Thus, the more relevant theoretical question revolves around the possibilities of an internally consistent general equilibrium in an *imperfectly competitive environment*. This problem so far has not been satisfactorily resolved by economic theorists, although in recent years it has received increasing attention. See Wassily Leontief, *The Structure of the American Economy* (New York Oxford University Press, 1951), and the articles by Kenneth Arrow, John Lintner, and Robert Solow in *The Corporate Economy: Growth, Competition, and Innovative Potential*, Robin Marris and Adrian Wood, eds. (Cambridge, Mass.: Harvard University Press, 1971).

Since the mathematics of general equilibrium in an imperfectly competitive environment entails a degree of sophistication well beyond the scope of this book, we shall confine our discussion to presenting a conceptual framework for economywide equilibrium in a corporate economy, sidestepping the issue of whether the conditions required are in fact wholly compatible with each other.

depending on how hard pressed they are to fill the additional orders from retailers and depending on their relative preferences for more profits, faster growth, a larger market share, and so on. The rise in the output of mobile homes will affect the demand of those firms manufacturing the resource inputs used in the production of mobile homes—sheet aluminum, window glass, axles, tires, sinks, shower stalls, carpeting, electric wiring supplies, and light fixtures, as well as the labor services of the various semiskilled and skilled construction workers needed for the mobile home assembling process. Since these resource inputs will have to be bid away from other uses, their prices will tend to be pulled upward. The mobile home manufacturers, by intensifying the competition for the needed resource inputs, will be forced to increase their offer prices for inputs. As this occurs, the firms losing the inputs may find it necessary to increase their offer prices in order to counteract the shift of needed inputs to the mobile home industry. The higher input prices imply rising costs and narrowing profit margins in the affected firms and industries.

Furthermore, should the induced shift of labor to the mobile home industry entail either a geographic relocation of workers and their families or the construction of new mobile home production facilities in areas where the needed supply of labor is available, the construction firms and the suppliers of building materials will experience an increase in the demand for their products (either from the demand for new housing or from the demand for new production facilities). This will further enlarge the affected product and resource markets, requiring additional price, output, and input adjustments.

However, the effects of the increase in the demand for mobile homes do not just reverberate back through the shifts in the input demands of the mobile home manufacturers. The higher demand for mobile homes will increase the demand for mobile home spaces in trailer parks, for compactly styled furniture, for equipment and accessories to transport mobile homes, and for portable power equipment. In addition, increases in mobile home ownership will elicit changes in the demand for other types of living accommodations—apartments, rental dwellings, and family-owned residences—thereby causing further adjustments in the residential construction and building materials industry. All the businesses catering to consumer loans, home mortgages, and real estate financing (banks, savings and loan associations, and finance companies) will feel the effects of the resulting rise in the demand for credit to finance the purchase of mobile homes and the diminished demand for credit to finance other dwellings. Insurance companies will need to respond to the shift in the demand for various types of homeowner's policies regarding fire, theft, property liability, and damage from acts of nature, perhaps by changing policy coverages and premium rates to cover the special risks of mobile home ownership. The higher demand for mobile homes also implies a shift in life styles and consumption habits which may have ramifications in such markets as those for household appliances, lawn and garden accessories, recreation goods, automobiles, camping equipment, tourism, and local convenience services. The resulting market demand changes not only will entail additional price and output rate adjustments by the affected firms but also will be transmitted back into the resource input markets relevant to all these products.

This is still not all: An increase in the number of mobile home owners has important consequences for the supplies of labor and land. Greater use of mobile homes should make workers more mobile, thus rendering the supplies of some labor services more elastic over time. More land will be needed for mobile home parks, mobile home communities, mobile home campsites, and sales display facilities; less land will be needed for permanently located single-and multiple-family residences. In the public sector, the changing makeup of housing and living patterns will alter the nature of the demand for local government services and the structure of property taxation, the latter having implications for shifting the relative profitabilities of various types of housing investments and causing a realignment in real estate investment patterns. Finally, the whole array of price-output-input adjustments will affect wages, salaries, profits, rents, and interest rates in the affected firms and industries, causing some redistribution of personal income. These income changes will prompt yet another series of price-output-input reactions as the affected consumers revise their expenditure patterns and saving rates to conform to the new income constraints.

If one had the tenacity and the inclination, the entire sequence of equilibrium adjustments and market linkages could be pursued to its ultimate conclusion and the entire set of market interrelationships pinned down. But the major point is already apparent. Product and resource markets are linked together directly and indirectly to form a *market network*. Given a state of static general equilibrium, any initial disturbance, whether it be a change in product demand, a change in resource supply conditions, an increase in population, a breakthrough in production technology, or a new product innovation, will trigger a complex chain reaction through the network of product and resource markets. The initial disturbance creates effects which spill over into adjacent markets and causes them to move toward new equilibrium positions. These secondary effects in turn generate new waves and ripples, which are carried by the various market linkages into a third set of product and resource markets. The third-order changes may extend back into the primary market where the initial disturbance occurred or back into the secondary markets and may also generate still higher-order effects transcending yet more distant markets. Barring further disturbances, the effects of the initial disturbance will eventually dissipate, new equilibrium positions will be reached, and a state of general equilibrium will be restored.

The Interrelationships of Economic Sectors

The foregoing paragraphs explain how markets are linked together. We now turn to the linkages between economic sectors. The term *economic sector* refers simply to a grouping of closely related markets.

Figure 18-1 provides a convenient graphical summary and synthesis of the flow of dollars and products through the economy, showing how the major economic sectors are related. Starting at the box on the left, we see that the process of producing goods and services gives rise to an aggregate amount of income equal to the market value of what has been produced. This simple, but crucial, proposition follows from the fact that the monetary value of a product is determined by the market value of the economic resources required to produce it.[2] Four basic things can be done with the income which economic units (firms and households) receive from the production process: (1) a portion is paid to government in the form of taxes (T); (2) a portion is saved (S) and, temporarily at least, deposited in various financial institutions; (3) a portion may be used to pay for goods imported from foreign countries (M); and (4) far and away the major portion goes to purchase consumer goods and services (C).

Obviously enough, governmental units use the tax revenues they receive to pay for the goods and services required for carrying out governmental functions and for various income redistribution programs. Foreign countries use the dollars they receive from the sale of goods to U.S. citizens to purchase goods which they desire to buy from us; hence, the leakage of income out of the economy via imports tends to be counterbalanced by an inflow of money back into the economy from export sales. The flow of savings into financial institutions comes out in the form of funds for consumer credit and for private investment spending; the latter includes financing the replacement of worn-out production facilities, the expansion of production capacity, and new housing (considered as investment spending by national income accountants). The demand side of the economic picture therefore consists of four major components: (1) personal consumption expenditures (C), (2) government spending for goods and services (G), (3) private investment spending (I), and (4) sales of goods to foreign countries or exports (X). Figure 18-1 thus presents a model of the linkages between the major economic sectors, emphasizing the flows of dollars and products and the relationships between total supply and total demand.[3]

For analytical convenience suppose we refer to the tax, savings, and import flows as "leakages" and the government spending, investment, and export flows as "injections." The rectangular boxes across the diagram may be viewed as the main income-spending stream. It is evident that the balance between the leakages and the injections provides the key to overall economic stability and to the direction of change in the rate of economic actitity. If during some period of time (a month, a quarter, a year, or whatever) the

---

[2]This is a fundamental proposition of macroeconomics, usually explained in detail in principles of economics texts. See, among others, Campbell R. McConnell, *Economics*, 7th ed. (New York: McGraw-Hill Book Company 1978), Chapter 9, and G. L. Bach, *Economics*, 10th ed. (Englewood Cliffs, N.J.: Prentice-Hall, Inc., 1980), Chapters 7–9.

[3]This model can easily be expanded to portray in more detail the ties between various subsectors of the economy. However, for our purposes the simplified model of Fig. 15-1 will suffice.

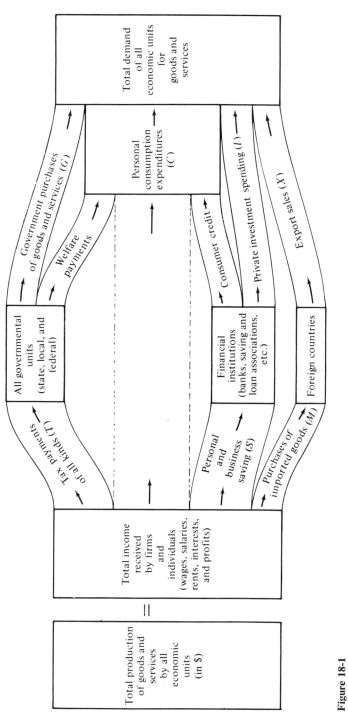

Figure 18-1
Simplified model of the operation of a market economy

dollar sum of the leakages $(T + S + M)$ is just equal to the dollar sum of the injections $(G + I + X)$, then the total dollar value of the goods and services produced will be equal to the dollar value of total spending on goods and services. To put it differently, when the leakages equal the injections, then the income generated from the current rate of production is, after being allocated to the various spending components, converted into a volume of expenditures just sufficient to provide a matching total demand; the total demand for goods and services is exactly equal to the total supply of goods and services. Assuming, not unrealistically, that the composition of these goods and services is in accord with buyer preferences, all markets will be cleared of their output, and the economy may be said to be in equilibrium—no forces will operate to cause the overall rate of economy activity to either increase or decrease. Such is the nature of general equilibrium at the level of the whole economy.

On the other hand, whenever the leakages and the injections do not balance, a state of disequilibrium exists, and forces immediately and automatically spring into action to rectify the situation. Suppose, for instance, that a portion of the dollars flowing into government, or foreign countries, or financial institutions somehow get trapped and are not spent. Then the size of the leakage flow will exceed the size of the injection flow. This has the effect of causing the prevailing production rates to exceed the rates at which goods are being purchased. Total supply will exceed total demand. As business firms see sales slipping and inventories of unsold goods piling up, they will respond by cutting prices and/or curtailing production rates. Typically, the prices of perishable, seasonal, and faddish items, as well as those which are expensive to store, will be reduced in an effort to stimulate buying and eliminate unwanted surpluses. But, in the cases of durable and easily stockpiled items, firms may find it more profitable to maintain prices and cut back on production rates until demand conditions become more favorable. The combination of falling prices and lower production rates will reduce incomes—wages and salary incomes will be lower because of the lessened need for labor inputs, and profits will be lower because of lower sales volumes and slimmer profit margins. The decline in incomes and profits will cause tax revenues to fall and will also cause business firms to review the profitability of new investment spending, probably revising investment spending plans downward unless the downturn in economic actitvity is viewed as clearly a short-term disturbance. In general, then, when the leakages exceed the injections, the rate of economic activity will fall. The economic decline will continue until production rates and spending rates are brought into line and supply-demand equilibrium is restored in the various product markets.

At the other extreme, it is quite conceivable that the sum of the injections $(G + I + X)$ will exceed the sum of the leakages $(S + T + M)$. There are several ways in which this can occur. Governments, of course, can spend more than they collect in tax revenues by borrowing the difference; this practice, known as deficit spending, is commonly engaged in at all levels of government. Scarcely any unit of government has not at one time or another issued bonds to finance some project and then paid off the bonds over time with new tax revenues. Financial institutions can also provide new funds for investment and consumer credit in amounts which exceed current saving rates; banks, in fact, create new money whenever they exchange IOUs for demand deposits.[4] Thus, both the government sector and the investment spending sector are fully capable of causing the injections flow to exceed the leakage flow at some moment of time. When and if such circumstances occur, current output rates will be inadequate to meet the total demand for goods and services; total demand will, in other words, exceed total supply. Producers who find the demand for their products outstripping current production rates have three alternative responses, which they can employ singly or in combination: (1) they can draw down inventories to help meet the excess demand; (2) they can increase production rates, provided they have unused production capacity and provided they can obtain the necessary labor and raw material inputs; and (3) they can raise prices to ration the available supplies among those buyers most anxious to obtain their products. Whatever response set producers elect—and most likely it will be some combination of all three—incomes will tend to rise, thereby stimulating further spending and expansion of economic activity. The general rise in incomes and in the overall pace of economic activity will cause tax revenues to rise, saving rates to increase, and investment in new production capacity to increase. Whether government spending will rise, fall, or remain unchanged is, of course, more a political than an economic question. The major point is that when the injections exceed the leakages, economic activity in the various economic sectors tends to be stimulated. The rise in economic activity will lose its steam when production catches up with demand and producers are just able to meet the demands for their products.

This thumbnail sketch of the interrelationships of the major economic sectors is sufficient to indicate why static general equilibrium requires not just equilibrium in each market and each related market but also balance between and among the major economic sectors. Spending patterns must be consistent with income patterns; production flows must in the aggregate match the rates at which outputs are purchased; the siphoning off of dollars in leakages must somehow be offset by the pumping of an equivalent amount of dollars back into the income-expenditure stream.

General Equilibrium and the Overall Rate of Economic Activity

From the standpoint of society's overall economic welfare, the level of economic activity at which general equilibrium occurs makes a great deal of difference. For instance, national goals and priorities call for the achievement of full employment. Full employment requires two things: (1) that an

---

[4]The money-creating activity of commercial banks is explained in all basic economics books. See, for example, McConnell, *Economics*, Chapter 15; Bach, *Economics*, Chapter 16.

adequate number of jobs be available for those persons who are willing and able to work and (2) that the available human and property resources be deployed among alternative uses in an efficient manner. The question becomes: If general equilibrium is attained, then must it or does it occur at a level of activity consistent with full employment?

The answer to this question is "not necessarily." Certainly there is neither an economic "law" nor a compelling economic force operating to peg the level of economic activity at the full employment position. As we have seen earlier, static general equilibrium requires that the total supply of goods and services be equal to the total demand for goods and services; or, putting it another way, the leakages must equal the injections. This condition guarantees that the flow of products through the major economic sectors will be mutually consistent; no forces will be operating to cause the overall rate of economic activity to rise or fall. Moreover, the composition of total output must be such that the demand and supply conditions for each separate commodity are consistent with equilibrium. This condition has several dimensions. Business firms must have no motives for altering prices or output rates, given the existing demand conditions. Consumers must be allocating their incomes in the optimum fashion, given the existing price and income constraints. Resource owners must be deploying their resources in the optimum pattern, given the existing demand for resource inputs and prevailing resource prices.

However, the static equilibrium position reached under these conditions may or may not represent a full employment equilibrium. Too low a level of total spending will call forth an equilibrium production rate requiring less than a full employment rate of input usage; unemployment rates for labor will rise above the tolerable and expected 3 or 4% target rate, and the related static equilibrium will be below the full employment level of economic activity. Too high a level of total spending will strain resource supplies and production rates to the point where higher product prices and input prices will be necessary to curb total demand and artificially bring it into line with total supply.

Nevertheless, the insatiability of consumer wants tends to generate a consistently "high" rate of economic activity; this tendency is further reinforced by the drive of business firms for growth and expansion and by the want-creating effects of new product innovation and sales promotion. But whether total spending will automatically be high enough to generate full employment is another matter. For this reason it is deemed desirable for the federal government to take an active role in using monetary and fiscal policy to promote full employment.

Statics versus Dynamics

The concept of static general equilibrium has practical importance because it is a useful tool of economic analysis. It would be a mistake, however, to conceive of static general equilibrium as either achievable or desirable.

It is impossible in a complex industrial economy for the underlying economic conditions ever to remain fixed long enough for the forces of change to adjust to a point where they are in balance. Indeed, change is a product of the normal operation of a modern economy, and this change in turn affects the operation of the economy. The milieu of change transcends population size, consumer tastes and preferences, incomes, costs, product prices, output rates, business strategies, national economic priorities, the pattern of international competition, and so on. New technological processes and product innovations are constantly injecting new disturbances into the economic picture. Population growth, education, and training programs produce persistent rises in the quantity and quality of labor services available to producers. The net effect of these wide-ranging and perpetually emerging tendencies for economic change is to prevent a static equilibrium from ever being achieved. Instead, new economic developments and new patterns of economic activity are constantly appearing in response to changing demand and supply conditions; in turn, product and resource markets are forever pursuing newly created general equilibrium positions.

As indicated previously, the direction and the pace of economic change determine the gains in society's economic welfare. In a static stationary economy, the standard of living is fixed, and society as a whole is doomed to exist at the prevailing output, income, and employment rates. Progress is nonexistent. But in modern industrial economies things are quite different. Change is commonplace and all-pervasive; technological advance and corporate growth strategies tilt the forces of change toward economic expansion —rising outputs, rising incomes, rising living standards, and a higher quality of life. Insofar, then, as economywide equilibrium in a progressive environment is concerned, the focus is not upon static general equilibrium but upon *dynamic growth equilibrium*.

DYNAMIC GROWTH EQUILIBRIUM

The study of dynamic equilibrium growth paths for an economy and the associated equilibrium growth patterns for firms constitutes one of the newest and least explored areas of economics. Moreover, because of the vast array of variables that must be taken into account, the theoretical models dealing with these topics are especially complex. For this reason, the body of theory which does exist is highly mathematical, involving a degree of sophistication well beyond the scope of this book.[5] We shall therefore restrict our considera-

[5]A representative sample of the literature of microeconomic and macroeconomic growth models includes W. J. Baumol, *Economic Dynamics*, 3rd ed. (New York: The Macmillan Company, 1970); Bent Hansen, *A Survey of General Equilibrium Systems* (New York: McGraw-Hill Book Company, 1970); Robert Dorfman, Paul A. Samuelson, and Robert Solow, *Linear Programming and Economic Analysis* (New York: McGraw-Hill Book Company, 1958), Chapter 11; Edith Penrose, *The Theory of the Growth of the Firm* (New York: John Wiley & Sons, Inc., 1959); Joan Robinson, *Essays in the Theory of Economic Growth* (New York: St. Martin's Press, 1964); and Edwin Burmeister and Rodney Dobell,

tion of dynamic growth models and of the links between growth equilibrium for the firm and for the economy to a presentation of basic concepts, indicating in nonrigorous terms some of the basic relationships and some of the tentative conclusions which have been reached. Again, the reader is forewarned that what follows is in the formulative stages; by no means has it survived sufficient empirical testing to warrant great confidence.

Growth Equilibrium for the Economy

In an industrialized economy the quality of economic performance is judged by how well the economy adheres to a path of stable growth and noninflationary full employment. The less frequent the deviations from a path of orderly economic expansion and the smaller such deviations from the full employment level of economic activity, the better an economy's performance is judged to be. As long as the pace of economic activity is proceeding at a rate commensurate with a stable growth path, the economy may be said to be in *growth equilibrium*.

The character of growth equilibrium on an economywide basis has a number of fundamental features. Ideally, the total output of goods and services must expand fast enough to provide employment opportunities for all persons seeking jobs but not so fast as to strain resource supplies to the point of unleashing wage-price-cost spirals and the knotty inflationary problems which such conditions present. Given an economy's resource capabilities, the optimum growth rate of total output is one that is consistent with the limits of technological progress and with the simultaneous achievement of price stability and full employment. Joan Robinson has called such a smooth, steady expansion "a golden age" of growth.[6]

For the optimum growth rate to be realized, the leakages $(S + T + M)$ and injections $(G + I + X)$ must be kept in balance, growing in step with each other as expansion occurs. The total demand for goods and services must grow at the same pace as does the overall output rate of producers; otherwise, the size of the market for the new output will be deficient. Ordinarily, the process of growth is capable of generating the increases in income and spending needed to sustain the growth of output over time, because

---

Mathematical Theories of Economic Growth (New York: The Macmillan Company, 1970). More specific studies and also more advanced mathematical discussions of economic growth paths include J. A. Mirrlees, "Optimum Growth When Technology Is Changing," *Review of Economic Studies*, Vol. 34, No. 97 (January 1967), pp. 95–124; T. C. Koopmans, "Objectives, Constraints, and Outcomes in Optimal Growth Models," *Econometrica*, Vol. 35, No. 1 (January 1967), pp. 1–15; T. C. Koopmans, "On the Concept of Optimal Economic Growth," in *The Econometric Approach to Development Planning* (Chicago: Rand McNally & Company and North-Holland Publishing Co., 1966); Robert Solow and Paul A. Samuelson, "Balanced Growth Under Constant Returns to Scale," *Econometrica*, Vol. 21, No. 3 (July 1953), pp. 412–424; and the Symposium on the Theory of Economic Growth, *Journal of Political Economy*, Vol. 77, No. 4, Part II (July–August 1969).

[6]Mrs. Robinson has attached corresponding nicknames to other possible phases of growth: a limping golden age, a leaden age, a restrained golden age, a galloping platinum age, a creeping platinum age, a bastard golden age, and a bastard platinum age. See her *Essays in the Theory of Economic Growth*, pp. 51–59.

economic expansion generates new investment spending and creates new employment opportunities in amounts sufficient to provide the income requisite for purchasing the additional goods and services produced. A steady state of expansion then rolls smoothly along, with technological progress and productivity gains paving the way for increases in real incomes. New production technologies are implemented as firms build new production capacity. Profits are sufficiently high to continue to attract and provide the money capital requisite for expansion. Firms may be said to be in growth equilibrium because their realized expansion rates are, on the average, compatible with what is possible.

One may further characterize an economy in growth equilibrium by supposing that technological advances, combined with gains in the quantity and quality of resource inputs, allow for a 5% annual increase in the total output of goods and services when production rates are maintained at the full employment rate of input usage. Investment spending for the new production capacity needed to increase output rates and an increased demand for raw material inputs will serve to push the incomes of suppliers upward. Similarly, the new production activity will give rise to new job opportunities for blue-and white-collar workers and for managers, thus increasing wage and salary incomes. Suppose the 5% increase in production yields a 5% gain in total income. If the leakages are in balance with the injections, then the 5% rise in total income will in turn produce a 5% increase in total spending, thereby providing ample market potential for selling the additional production. Repeating this process year after year would put the economy on a steady growth path of 5% which, if attained, would constitute a stable "golden age" growth equilibrium for the economy.

Growth Equilibrium for the Firm

Although growth equilibrium entails even and steady expansion of total output for the economy as a whole, it would be erroneous to view the output rates of each and every product as expanding at the economywide equilibrium growth rate. The very process of economic growth will give birth to changes in consumer tastes and preferences and to variations in the intensity of competitive pressures. Some products will die out, and others will rise to prominence via the perennial gale of creative destruction. The discovery and implementation of new production techniques will alter optimum input mixes and economies of scale. These changes will provoke a variety of responses in the business sector, and all of them will play a role in determining the growth equilibrium for particular firms.

Growth equilibrium for a firm may be thought of as the path along which the firm must continually adjust its prices, output rates, and input rates so as to optimize the attainment of its complement of goals (profits, sales revenue, market share, growth, technological virtuosity, security, and so on), given the constraints imposed by the economic environment. Whatever the particular goal set of the firm, management's function in attaining growth equilibrium is to search out the particular activity mix which yields the best perceived outcome insofar as the firm's goal set is concerned. Decision-makers must juggle price-output-input combinations so as to obtain the best performance, given the existing uncertainties. This is not to say that once the optimum price-output-input combination has been identified, it should be maintained into the indefinite future. Realistically, new developments arising from further economic growth of the economy will cause the optimum combination to change; thus, decision-markers will continually be forced to modify the firm's strategy set, revising prices and output rates, adding new products and dropping old ones, implementing new technologies, shifting the organization's resources into new activities, and revamping the organization's structure and orientation to meet new priorities.

Where the demand for a product is increasing faster than average, firms will be motivated to respond with above-average increases in production rates. Where the demand for a product is increasing at below-average rates, production rates can be expected to rise more slowly than the average. Where demand is shrinking or on the verge of disappearing entirely, firms will be forced to cut back production and perhaps to go out of business or shift into the production of items with more attractive profit and sales opportunities. The variability in the growth rates of the demand for various goods and services will change the composition of the economy's total output. In turn, firms will have to realign the usage of the various resource inputs in accord with demand changes and technological developments. The chief requirement which economywide growth equilibrium imposes upon producers is that the required output and input adjustments for specific products be orderly. When slack appears in one firm or industry or economic sector, it must be absorbed by expansion elsewhere in the economy; otherwise the achievement of full employment is jeopardized. Individual product prices and input prices can be raised or lowered, but on the average product prices cannot rise or fall by more than 1 or 2% and input prices must be kept in line with productivity changes, lest inflationary or deflationary pressures interfere with attainment of price stability.

The growth equilibrium position of particular firms will vary according to two factors: (1) the quantity and quality of the opportunities for expansion offered by the overall economic environment and (2) the respective organizational capabilities of firms regarding the quality of management, the financial resources they can marshal, and their propensities for undertaking new activities. These relationships warrant further attention, because they comprise the link between growth equilibrium for the firm and growth equilibrium for the economy.[7]

Insofar as any one product is concerned, the firm's optimum growth rate is clearly a function of the market potential of that product—the rate at which demand is rising (or falling), the profit opportunities, the strength of

---

[7]However, to the extent that the operations of firms take on an international character, rather than being constrained by the boundaries of a single national economy, the link between growth equilibrium for the firm and growth equilibrium for the economy is supplemented by a link between growth equilibrium for the firm and growth equilibrium of the international economy in which the firm operates.

competitive pressures in that product market, and the like. But firms are not restricted to producing a single product; they may widen the range of their activities to include any number of related or unrelated products and they may extend their activities to include producing and selling in international markets rather than just national markets. This is why the growth equilibrium of a particular firm is a function of the *entire* set of economywide expansion opportunities which are open to it and not just growth in the demand for the commodities it currently produces. It is clear that the size of the set of opportunities for expansion is very much dependent on the growth equilibrium path of the economy as a whole. An economywide growth of 5% per year will necessarily offer firms greater expansion potential than a growth rate of only 2%. One may think of the economy's equilibrium growth path as opening up a certain amount of new expansion potential for firms each period which, if taken advantage of, will result in achievement of the equilibrium growth rate.

Given the full range of opportunities for expansion offered by growth equilibrium on an economywide basis, firms may be viewed as competing for the available new market potential, with each firm's own growth equilibrium being a function of (1) its perceived role in the economic setting, (2) the strategic position it has for meeting the new commodity demands generated by growth, and (3) its aggressiveness in committing resources to the available expansion opportunities. Some firms are content to continue to operate within the bounds of their current activities; thus, their growth rates are pegged directly to the expansion of the product markets in which they operate—the steel and railroad firms serve as examples. Other firms take a broader view of their capacities and branch out into new products and new markets as they approach the limits of expansion in their present products—the popularity of this strategy is reflected by the pronounced trend toward diversification by merger and acquisition evidenced by U.S. firms during the late 1960s. Firms confronted by shrinking markets and declining profit opportunities are faced with the choice of accepting a negative growth equilibrium path or else breaking out of their traditional molds and launching into new activities and new markets. In some cases, firms are in position to initiate and shape the course of economic expansion by means of new product innovations and new managerial technologies; other firms will be growth followers. Some firms are able to achieve high growth rates not so much because of careful planning and foresight but because they just happen, fortuitously, to be engaged in activities for which demand vigorously increases. Some firms may lack the financial resources to exploit fully the new opportunities which present themselves, while others will expand cautiously, engaging only in those activities which are viewed as low-risk. Thus, there is a variety of growth equilibrium patterns for firms.

National Economic Policy and Growth Equilibrium

It goes without saying that the achievement of a stable growth equilibrium on an economywide basis is an enormously complex task. Not only must the process of economic change be kept orderly and tidy and the proper degree of flexibility in the production mechanism be maintained, but the economic environment must also be kept conducive to just the right rate of business expansion. None of these is likely to be accomplished without design and carefully executed strategy, despite the tendency for the economy to move toward growth equilibrium. The only institution capable of promoting and coordinating growth equilibrium on an economywide front is the federal government.

In general terms, the aim of national economic policy is to see to it that the target rates of national economic growth and the associated growth equilibrium become a reality. When stimulation of investment or consumption spending is needed to provide a boost to the economy, it is the responsibility of the monetary and fiscal authorities to design an appropriate strategy and to implement it at the proper time. Such a strategy may include tax cuts, increases in government spending, increases in the money supply, and lower interest rates in whatever combination is deemed most appropriate for the particular situation. On the other hand, when growth proceeds so fast that inflation is a by-product, then the economic pulse must be slowed by means of some combination of tax increases, restraints upon government spending, a tightening up of the money supply, higher interest rates, and wage-price controls. In other words, the federal government has the responsibility of orchestrating national economic policy such that the economic throttle is kept turned to the right speed; otherwise, the possibility of attaining a stable growth equilibrium is remote.

Actually of course, keeping a trillion-dollar economy directly on the path of a stable growth equilibrium over the long term is really too much to expect of policy-makers, given the uncertainties of economic change, the lack of well-defined and coordinated policies for maintaining economic stability, and the political constraints which are inevitably present. Steering a course of noninflationary full employment and at the same time keeping the rate of increase in economic activity steady is much like trying to guide a raft through swirling rapids on an unknown river—the course ahead is uncharted, the going is tricky, and the margin for error to either side is razor thin. Thus, a more realistic interpretation of the role and function of public policy is for it to attempt to minimize the size and the frequency of deviations from the target growth path. But even this objective is likely to prove elusive—as is amply testified to by the recurrent ups and downs in the pace of economic activity and by the frequently unrealized predictions of governmental policy-makers. Nevertheless, attempting to keep the economy as close to the target equilibrium growth path as is possible is a very reasonable way of conceiving the goal of national economic policy.

Needless to say, the growth equilibrium path ought to be consistent with consumer preferences, social goals, human values, national priorities, and preservation of the environment. In the United States, at least, living standards are approaching the point where economic growth just for the sake of growth is an untenable policy. It is becoming increasingly possible to stress the quality of goods and services as well as the quantity and it is certainly imperative that society's technological apparatus be pointed in the direction of solving the problems of environmental pollution that are a byproduct of industrialization and economic growth. Moreover, the problems of poverty, discrimination, and urban decay must be factored into the growth matrix.

However, while there is general accord on the nature of a socially desirable type of growth equilibrium, there exists a wide diversity of opinion as to the specific policies which ought to be deployed to support its achievement. Furthermore, differences exist as to priorities. Plainly enough, there is room for reasonable people to disagree as to whether clamping down very hard on industrial pollution is more important than keeping plants open and avoiding widespread unemployment or whether fighting inflation is more important than fighting recession or whether the federal government should finance research and development activities in developing new energy technology but not in computer technology. For this reason, even if it could be assumed that policy-makers are wise enough to know just what sort of policy mix is called for in specific situations, it would not be possible to prescribe an "optimal" growth equilibrium strategy. Thus, economic policy issues will necessarily remain in the realm of conflict, despite the powers of economic analysis to explain and to predict economic phenomena.

SUMMARY AND CONCLUSIONS

The part of economic theory that concerns the interdependencies and linkages among prices, output rates, and input rates in all of the various markets and economic sectors is called general equilibirum analysis. The purpose of such analysis is to determine what the equilibrium configuration of prices, output rates, and input rates will be for each firm and in each market, given the guiding forces of consumer tastes and preferences, production technologies, available resource supplies, business goals, and national priorities.

In a state of static general equilibrium there are no forces operating to cause the pace of economic activity to rise or fall. The leakages equal the injections, and the total supply of goods and services equals the total demand for goods and services. At a lower level, each product market is in equilibrium; so is each input market. Consumers, business firms, and resource owners have no motives for changing what they are doing, given the prevailing economic circumstances. In theory, general equilibrium can occur at, above, or below full employment, depending on the level of total spending.

In practice, however, static general equilibrium is never attained because the underlying forces are never constant long enough for all product and resource markets to reach their respective equilibrium positions. The real world is very much dynamic, with changes occurring constantly in such basic economic forces as consumer tastes and preferences, the range of possible products and production technologies, the quantity and quality of available resource inputs, the distribution of income, the styles of managerial technologies, and so on. Over the long term in a progressive society, the most appropriate concept of general equilibrium is growth equilibrium—a state of stable growth and noninflationary full employment, the optimal growth rate being a function of technological progress, the availability of new resource supplies, and societal preferences.

Insofar as firms are concerned, the character of economywide growth equilibrium is important because it determines the extent of expansion opportunities open to enterprises and ultimately their own individual growth equilibrium positions. The individual firm's own growth equilibrium path depends on the strategic position it has for meeting the new commodity demands generated by growth and the aggressiveness with which managers commit organizational resources to the available expansion opportunities. Growth equilibrium for the firm thus may be thought of as the path along which the firm continually adjusts its prices, output rates, and input rates so as to optimize the attainment of its complement of goals.

Even though there are strong tendencies for the economy to move in the direction of the growth equilibrium path, deviations and lags in adjustment are inevitable. Change is too frequent, resource mobility too imperfect, and the adjustment mechanism too slow in responding to change for the economy to remain fixed on a steady, even growth path. For this reason, it is appropriate for the federal government to play an active role in promoting economywide growth equilibrium and in facilitating the process of adjustment to economic change.

SUGGESTED READINGS

BAUMOL, W. J., *Economic Dynamics*, 3rd ed. (New York: The Macmillan Company, 1970), Chapters 17, 18.

CODDINGTON, A., "The Rationale of General Equilibrium Theory," *Economic Inquiry*, Vol. 13, No. 4 (December 1975), pp. 539–558.

COHEN, K. J., AND R. M. CYERT, *Theory of the Firm: Resource Allocation in a Market Economy*, 2nd ed. (Englewood Cliffs, N.J.: Prentice-Hall, Inc. 1975), Chapter 11.

CORNWALL, J., *Modern Capitalism, Its Growth and Transformation* (New York: St. Martin's Press, 1978).

HAHN, F. H., AND R. C. O. MATTHEWS, "The Theory of Economic Growth: A Survey," *Economic Journal*, Vol. 74, No. 296 (December 1964), pp. 779–902; reprinted in *Survey of Economic Theory*, Vol. II (New York: St. Martin's Press, 1965).

HANSEN, B., *A Survey of General Equilibrium Systems* (New York: McGraw-Hill Book Company, 1970).

KOOPMANS, T. C., "Is the Theory of Competitive Equilibrium with It? *American Economic Review*, Vol. 64, No. 2 (May 1974), pp. 325–329.

SCHUMPETER, J. A., *The Theory of Economic Development* (New York: Oxford University Press, 1961), Chapters 2, 4, 6.

1. Trace through the chain of economic effects triggered by
   (a) An innovation which allows waste paper to be recycled and made reusable.
   (b) A permanent increase in the demand for sports entertainment.
   (c) A sharp decline in the number of women seeking employment.
   (d) A precipitous decline in natural gas reserves.

2. Distinguish between static general equilibrium and dynamic growth equilibrium for an economy.

3. (a) Do you think that some deviations from economywide growth equilibrium are inevitable? Why or why not?
   (b) Would it be fair to state that the economywide pace of economic activity *tends* toward the growth equilibrium path?
   (c) Is it likely that the nature of an economy's growth equilibrium path can be (and is) altered by basic changes in the economic environment? If so, what sorts of basic changes can cause the growth equilibrium path to shift?

4. Explain the relationships and the linkages between growth equilibrium for the economy and growth equilibrium for the firm.

5. Do you think managers of firms are able to keep their respective firms steered on a course of steady growth? Why or why not? Do they try to do so even though they may not succeed? Why or why not?

6. What, if any, guarantee does society have that growth of the economy and of firms will proceed in directions consistent with societal preferences and priorities?

7. It has been observed that business enterprises thrive on "problems," that these problems typically precipitate a search for technological solutions, that the resulting technological discoveries point the way to new investment opportunities, and that the resulting new investment spending is the cornerstone of economic growth. Critically evaluate this sequence of events as an "explanation" or "cause" of economic growth and expansion.

INDEX

624

variable, 239–45, 247, 248–49, 251, 253, 255, 256, 260, 265, 328–30, 357, 553, 557–58
Total cost-total revenue approach to profit maximization, 324, 354, 440–41
Total profit or loss, 327, 356–59
Total returns, diminishing, 185–86
Total revenue, 113–21, 128–31
  growth and, 503–5
  in monopolistic competition, 353–58
  in monopoly, 440–41, 443
  in oligopoly, 413
  in perfect competition, 322–26, 553, 557–58, 570–71
Total utility, 44–55
  defined, 44
  functions, 44–46
  marginal utility and, 45, 47–52
  for related products, 54–55
Total utility surface, 54
Traditional economic system, 20–21
Trucking industry, 455–56
Trusts, 25
TRW, 504n

Unemployment compensation benefits, 595
Union Carbide Corporation, 314, 483
Unions, economic effects of, 591–97
  on economywide wage rates and unemployment rates, 596–97
  on firm's labor input decision, 593–94, 596
  wage-employment preference path, 591–93
Unique-product production, 156–57
Unitary elasticity, 125
Unit contribution profit, 328
Unit costs, 240–43, 443
Unit cost-unit revenue approach to profit maximization, 324–26, 354–56, 443
United Shoe Machinery Company, 24, 446

U.S. Postal Service, 455–56
U.S. Steel Corporation, 24, 25, 397, 399, 424n, 483, 526
Unit revenue, 443
Utility:
  cardinal, *see* Cardinal utility
  concept of, 43–44
  ordinal, *see* Ordinal utility

Valentine, Lloyd M., 453n
Vanderbilt, William, 23
Variable costs:
  average, 240–41, 245–46, 247, 250, 251, 253–56, 258, 260, 263, 265, 328, 330–31, 333–34, 356–58
  total, 239–45, 247, 248–49, 251, 253, 255, 256, 260, 265, 328–30, 357, 553, 557–58
Variable inputs, 177–94
  average product of, 180, 181, 183, 185–88
  constant returns to, 188–90, 193–94, 247–51
  cost behavior and, 243–60
  decreasing returns to, 184–85, 190–94, 251–60
  defined, 178
  diminishing average returns to, 187
  diminishing marginal returns to, 183, 184
  diminishing total returns to, 185–86
  in imperfect competition, 570–74, 576–82
  increasing returns to, 184, 192, 193–94, 243–47, 256–60
  marginal product of, 180–83, 185–88, 550–53, 561, 580–81
  in perfect competition, 550–61, 570–74, 578–82
  profit-maximizing rate of, 552–58
  revenue gain from, 550–52
  stages of production and, 194–97
Variable markup pricing, 482–83
Vertical integration, 427–30, 432
Vogel, Ronald J., 224n
Volkswagen of America, 392

Wages:
  effects of unions on economywide rates of, 596–97
  employment preference path, 591–93
  minimum, 583–91
Walters, A. A., 263n, 279
Watkins, Myron W., 409n, 536n
Weber, Max, 7n, 274
Wein, 263
Weiss, Leonard W., 527n
Welch, Finis, 589
Welsh, Glenn A., 304n, 481n
Westinghouse, George, 23
Westinghouse Corporation, 408n, 536
Weyerhaeuser Company, 495
Whitcomb, D., 217n, 223
Williamson, Olvier E., 220n, 273n, 294n, 301n, 519n
Wilson, Thomas A., 272n, 527n, 531
Wood, Adrian, 605n
Worcester, Dean A., 398n, 537n
Workable competition model, 541–42
Work and effort bargain, 596
Woytinsky, W. S., 596n
Wylie, 263

Xerox Corporation, 222, 291, 504n, 516, 517–18

Yntema, 263

Zenith Corporation, 392